LIGHT BLUE DOWN UNDER

THE HISTORY OF
GEELONG
GRAMMAR SCHOOL

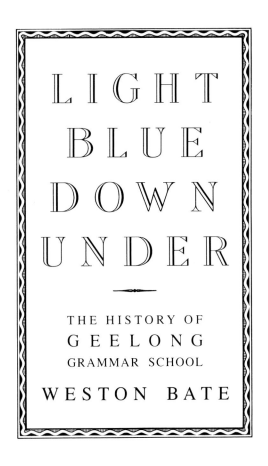

LIGHT BLUE DOWN UNDER

THE HISTORY OF
GEELONG
GRAMMAR SCHOOL

WESTON BATE

OXFORD

UNIVERSITY PRESS

MELBOURNE OXFORD AUCKLAND NEW YORK

OXFORD UNIVERSITY PRESS AUSTRALIA

Oxford   New York   Toronto
Delhi   Bombay   Calcutta   Madras   Karachi
Petaling Jaya   Singapore   Hong Kong   Tokyo
Nairobi   Dar es Salaam   Cape Town
Melbourne   Auckland
and associated companies in
Berlin   Ibadan

OXFORD is a trade mark of Oxford University Press

National Library of Australia
Cataloguing-in-Publication data:

Bate, Weston, 1924–
   Light blue down under: the history of Geelong Grammar
   School.

   Includes index.
   ISBN 0 19 553106 X.

   1. Geelong Church of England Grammar School — History.
   2. Church schools — Victoria — Geelong — History. I.
   Title.

373.9452

Edited by Heather Kelly
Designed by Derrick I. Stone Design
Typeset by Setrite Typesetters, Hong Kong
Printed by Kyodo in Singapore
Published by Oxford University Press,
253 Normanby Road, South Melbourne, Australia

Contents

Introductory note

In 1969 the Council of Geelong Grammar School commissioned Professor Weston Bate to write a history of the School. The decision was founded not on any improper pride but on the expectation that such a record would be of particular interest to those familiar, for whatever cause, with the School. It was also hoped that the work would have a more general interest: the School is almost as old as the State of Victoria and its story must to a degree reflect, or even illuminate, the history of education in Victoria—the concepts and the standards, and the teaching profession itself.

The task proved to be of greater magnitude than had at first been supposed, but such delays as have arisen between the making of the original agreement and publication have resulted in the emergence of a much more significant book. It has now been possible for Professor Bate to cover in full the period of Mr T.R. Garnett's headmastership and to deal also with the introduction of co-education, begun tentatively at the beginning of the 1970s, and given decisive impetus by the amalgamation between Geelong Grammar, Clyde School and The Hermitage under The Hon. C. D. Fisher.

The Council welcomes the publication of *Light Blue Down Under*. It has sought to sustain Professor Bate in his task and to facilitate his research. That he had previously had no formal connexion with Geelong Grammar was seen as an advantage. It is a work of independent scholarship and the approach, the selection and the analysis made, as well as the views expressed and conveyed, are Professor Bate's and his alone.

Richard Searby, Chairman
1 September 1989

*In memory of
Philip St John Wilson of Brighton Grammar School,
Brian Hone of Melbourne Grammar School,
and John Moulsdale and Tony Chenevix-Trench
of Bradfield College, Berkshire,
from whom I gained strength and inspiration
while learning what schools are all about.*

*As a tribute, also, to the achievements of
John Bracebridge Wilson and James Ralph Darling,
whose lives and work at Geelong Grammar School
have confirmed, delighted and challenged me.*

Preface

A school can have as many histories as a cat has lives, and all of them different—administrative, social, general or highly detailed, inward or outward looking, boy-centred, staff-centred and so on. There can be a pictorial treatment, an emphasis on buildings, a narrative of events and activities, a parade of people, a register of pupils and staff.

What does this one do? In some ways it treads uneasily on all the tails of the cat in attempting a conspectus; but its central preoccupation is with the meaning given to and found in the school by successive generations of staff and pupils. Each generation has made its own contribution, yet worked within an accumulating tradition to produce an accretion of ideas, ideals, procedures, understandings and attitudes that is the school as we know it today.

I make no apology for providing a chronological framework through head-masterships. Change has usually come that way. For instance, in the twentieth century there have been dramatic differences of approach between the regimes of F. E. Brown, J. R. Darling and T. R. Garnett and a sea-change because of co-education in C. D. Fisher's day.

I hope that those who know the school will be happy to place their own experience within that framework, and that those who do not will be pleased with the broad sweep—rather than, as sometimes happens, a muster of names known to few but the actors themselves, forty, fifty and sixty years on.

Much social life, many personalities and special events are, however, subsumed within that chronological treatment. As well, in separate chapters at the end of parts I and II, an attempt is made to recreate coherently the everyday world of the school and those who shaped or responded to it.

So many cannot be named of the thousands who have passed through GGS that it will seem almost impertinent on my part to have included some and not others. May I plead that those chosen are representatives—that I have tried to find in people and events essences that reveal the character of the place. I hope that the record is a useful one, for I am conscious that it cannot be *true*. Often I have had to work from sources tangential to the action. I also plead guilty to selecting material to flesh out personal views of GGS that I have developed during the many years that this study has taken. I think that mature judgements of that kind are an essential part of history.

There are multitudes of people to thank. I have been sustained not only by those whose names appear in these pages but also by thousands left out who have helped to define the shape of the book and many of its flavours. Intimations were gained, for instance, from Course 37 of the RAAF where aircraftsman Bate, W. found himself on the roll of recruits with an identifiably GGS group—aircraftsmen Balloch, J., Dalziel, R., Dunstan, K., Hancock, A., Stott, D. and Tolhurst, N. Why they, of all school groups, were distinctive is a question I have carried forward into this history.

Secondly, there is the congregation of those in the foreground of the study on whom I have drawn for help and inspiration, thoughtfully and unsparingly given. I cannot name them all. Many of the staff, at various times, have contributed directly; others, by making me welcome, have smoothed the path. The talk at Morris Room breakfasts and dinners is especially memorable. I treasure the hospitality and frankness of Sir James and Margaret Darling and Tommy and Penelope Garnett, the generous help of Bob Southey, John Béchervaise, Rolf Baldwin, 'Nogger' Newman, Philip Brown, Don Marles, Alby Twigg, Bill Hayward, Dick Johnson, 'Boz' Parsons, Bill Lester, Bill Panckridge, Peter Desborough, Jim Winchester, John Dahlsen, Andrew Lemon, Alan Patterson, Frank Covill, Peter Jardine, John Bedggood, Claire and Mike Hanley, Gem Reid, John Herbert, Richard Maddever, Sam McCulloch, Michael Charlesworth, Keith Dunstan and Ivan Sutherland. I regret that Stephen Murray-Smith, Kay Masterman, Peter Westcott and 'Bully' Taylor have not lived to see the fruit they helped to set. I have benefited greatly from the writings of Philip Brown, Russel Ward, Tom Judd, Rod Andrew, and Keith Dunstan, and the art of Bill Beasley, Michael Lodge and Rix Wright.

For comradeship and special insights I owe debts to J. R. Darling's biographer Peter Gronn and two former MA students, Jane Carolan and Fay Marles, who worked under my supervision on the F. E. Brown and J. B. Wilson periods respectively, and who helped closely with further research. In addition, Fay wrote an undergraduate thesis on L. H. Lindon and Jane's husband, Kevin, during his architecture course, explored the school's built environment. Robin Bedggood and Margaret Tucker, resourceful Corio wives, assisted with a study of the school's clientele. I thank them all.

Deakin University has been supportive in the allocation of scarce research funds and a period of study leave which I spent with old friends in the Department of History at the University of Melbourne. My colleagues at Deakin, especially in Australian Studies, have stimulated and encouraged the writing, which has emerged from my scrawl through many drafts thanks to the skill and patience of Judy Barber and Beverley Bartlett.

The present headmaster, John Lewis, at whose advent this history closes, has given me great encouragement. His secretary Christel O'Neill provided active support and a dozen or more of the Corio office staff, who are faces rather than names to me, have guided and assisted the wandering historian.

John Lewis, Fay and Don Marles, John Béchervaise, Rolf Baldwin and the late Peter Westcott made helpful comments on the draft. So, too, with generosity and detachment, did Sir James Darling and Tommy Garnett. To have been close to them and their work has been a privilege.

Michael Persse, who complicated the editing by converting Collins from a Christian to a surname half-way through his career, has been ubiquitous. Without his efforts and those of his helpers at the school archives and *The Corian*, the pictures and reminiscences which have enlivened the book might have been skimpy and hard to find. Without his passion for GGS my insights would have been weaker. Without his meticulous comments on the manuscript many infelicities, rash judgements and careless errors might not have been corrected.

I thank the school council for giving me the task and not threatening the freedom that keeps institutional histories from being just public relations exercises. I hope they will be pleased that I have not pulled any punches.

The book should bring to the growing list of Australian school histories the unusual flavour of a specialist boarding school. In the search for a title, I found that *Light Blue Down Under* summed up for me the process of cultural transmission by which traditions akin to those of Eton (the original light blue) were transplanted under matching skies and the southern cross to become a strong and peculiarly Australian hybrid.

PART I

Home from home for the sons of pastoralists

The school gathered in 1869
across Maude Street to the
south-west of the building.

The market square, Geelong,
1857.

1

An ambitious foundation

When Geelong Grammar School was founded in 1855* the community at Geelong was twenty years old. A confident frontier town of about 20 000 inhabitants, bustling with the energy of great pastoral and mining hinterlands, became the setting for ancient English educational activity. This was not, however, a simple transplanting of ideas and institutional forms from the old world to the new, but an interaction, at that unusual time, of strong elements of tradition with powerful, free-wheeling and distinctive social forces, from which sprang a mixed day and boarding school of a type unknown in England. From 1858 the school was situated in handsome new buildings on a ridge to the south of the town, between a busy harbour and a quiet river. It was planned, like an English grammar school, to provide an academic education for local boys, but at the same time to offer boarding accommodation for the sons of pioneer pastoralists, who hoped for status similar to that conferred by foundations like Winchester and Eton.

Pastoralists had always been important to Geelong, which in the first phase of its history was the depot for the pastoral exploitation of the rich volcanic plains of western Victoria. Although major transactions with banks and government officials had to be made at the capital, Melbourne, 70 kilometres further north at the head of Port Phillip Bay, Geelong supplied most of the needs of the few hundred Western District sheepowners, each of whom, for a nominal sum, occupied many thousands of hectares of Crown land to the west and north-west. Most had come from Van Diemen's Land (later Tasmania), where a boom in the British demand for fine wool had stimulated a system of granting land and the use of convict labour to people with money or good connections. A community of capitalist sheep farmers developed. But, as Tasmania is small and

---

* Although the official date was long considered to be 1857, the case for 1855, argued later, is now generally accepted.

mountainous, its useful soil was soon taken up and new opportunities were sought across Bass Strait in the occupation of unexplored country.

Some of the adventurers who came chasing capital gains were from established families, others were newcomers for whom prospects in Van Diemen's Land were limited. Many were Scots, the younger sons of Lowland farmers, drawn to the colonies by hopes of bettering themselves. There was also a sprinkling of young bloods, gentlemen listed by Burke or even true-blue according to Debrett. Their inclination to chase kangaroos rather than supervise their shepherds impeded money-making and their antics in Melbourne and Geelong scandalized the townsmen, who nevertheless milked them whenever possible. One excuse for their behaviour and for the roughness of life on the runs during the 1830s and 1840s was the shortage of females, especially ladies. The presence of teacups and a piano astonished a young man in 1843 as he stood on the threshold of the Manifold brothers' Purrumbete, from which emerged one of the most important of Geelong Grammar families.* Thomas's wife, Jane, was the softener.

The pace of urban life during the pastoral era was faster than that of the groaning bullock wagons which took stores from Geelong to distant squatting stations and returned precariously, piled high with the valuable clip. But it was leisurely in comparison with the energy generated by the discovery of gold at Ballarat in August 1851. Ballarat, 86 kilometres inland, was best approached through Geelong, whose citizens regarded it as their goldfield. Even professional men, washing for gold with gloves on their hands, had joined the first rush. Geelong was deserted, and from time to time over the next few years many townspeople were drawn to the fields and hundreds of new migrants returned from digging to take up urban occupations. When Ballarat's miners struck alluvial treasure worth over £10 million between 1853 and 1856, busy paddle-steamers connected the port of Geelong with Melbourne, where overseas shipping tied up. Geelong's population grew beyond 20 000 by 1854 and was 23 338 in 1857. Businesspeople protested that it would have been much larger if Melbourne interests had not dominated government spending: no funds were made available to remove a sand-bar across Corio Bay that prevented large ships from docking at the town's wharves. The issue was not Geelong's first taste of the bitterness of its provincial status, but it was the worst example up to that time of treatment that led to permanent envy and suspicion. Geelong has always been too close to Melbourne and too similar, economically and socially, to its much larger rival** to stand firmly apart, too far away to be

---

* There were three Manifold brothers in that partnership—Peter, Thomas and John. The last fathered William who, as chairman of the GGS Council, inspired the move to Corio in 1914. His son John was chairman during a period of great expansion in the 1930s.

** In 1857 Melbourne's population was 95 502, over four times that of Geelong. Since the 1880s, when Melbourne increased its dominance extraordinarily, the metropolis has been up to twenty times the size of its early competitor.

effectively absorbed. Geelong's schools as well as its businesses have been affected.

Nevertheless, the town's growth in the 1850s led to diversification and the speed of growth to splendid opportunities. Town boosters called Geelong 'The Pivot', as if the economy of Victoria centred upon it. The presence of about 30 000 people in Geelong's pastoral and goldfields hinterlands, in addition to 20 000 in the town itself, stimulated intense commercial, industrial and service activity. Fifty-three different occupations were indicated in the Geelong directory for 1854, seventy-nine in 1856 and ninety-four in 1858. Thousands of houses were needed on land that had to be surveyed, subdivided, sold and conveyed. Thousands of tents were required to shelter nomadic hordes and hundreds of coaches and wagons for the Ballarat road.

Gold-saving cradles, picks, shovels, cans, barrels, lamps, clothing, footwear, food and all kinds of necessities and luxuries were in great demand on the goldfields. Although imports dominated the market, small-scale local manufacturing was stimulated by special needs, by sudden shortages and by urgent repairs. Carpenters, blacksmiths, saddlers, wheelwrights, wagon-builders and many other skilled tradesmen were in clover. Geelong's brewers, distillers, flour-millers, importers, wholesalers, dealers and publicans had a bonanza, while at the apex of society lawyers, bankers and doctors were lifted to unexpected levels of affluence by the general prosperity. At the 1857 census Geelong appeared to be quite mature economically; it was larger and more vigorous than many county towns in Britain and seemed to have a future just as secure. On the other hand it was still a frontier settlement—masculine, crude and brash, lacking the influence of settled family life and cultural institutions.

This economic growth and social flux were expressions of a materialistic, democratic ethos, the fruit of a special stage of British expansion that swelled and ripened with a distinctive flavour in Victoria. As a major participant in both the pastoral and gold booms, Geelong was a perfect expression of the free-enterprise forces that had suddenly formed the colony of Victoria, in contrast to a slower, more structured development in the penal colonies of New South Wales and Van Diemen's Land and a more idealistically planned community in South Australia. There was a stronger sense of destiny, a wider range of possibilities than in the other colonies, although, superficially, because derivative British institutions were adopted everywhere, the forms of economic, social and constitutional experience were similar. In the Victorian parliament, from 1856 the pioneer merchants and pastoralists were entrenched in the upper house, the Legislative Council, where they were able to defend their interests against the demands of the more cosmopolitan, more radical members of the Legislative Assembly, the majority of whom were gold migrants. Everyone was agreed about development and about the primary role of government in financing infrastructure; what was at issue was who would reap the benefits and whose views about social control

3

were to prevail. The squatters fought to convert their grazing runs into freeholds, with an eye to turning landowner status into traditional English upper-class pre-eminence. The fact that in Geelong's Western District hinterland they were particularly successful with freeholding and tended to assume social leadership had important implications for the grammar school so many of their sons were to attend.

Decisions about education were one aspect of a process by which the community adopted a framework of institutions on which its future would take shape. Just as the Westminster system was accepted as the basis for constitutional arrangements and overseas models were followed in the organization of religious denominations, industrial unions, friendly societies, museums, art galleries and the like, schools were planned on British precedents, but without direct copying. Because local government was weak and there were no county authorities or parish officials with a traditional role, no artisan guilds or other organizations needing to found and finance schools, colonial governments were urged to take responsibility for primary education, which therefore tended to fall under central bureaucratic control. A dual system of State-funded national and denominational primary schools, of which the denominational was by far the stronger, had been inherited from New South Wales. Until the 1850s there was little secondary education. Older children (mainly boys) were sent to Van Diemen's Land or Britain, although some entrepreneur scholars ran private schools, like William Brickwood's, established at St Ninian's, Brighton, in 1842. Colonial schools of this sort, a majority of which seem to have been run by clergymen, offered a general education—as opposed to the classical diet of English public schools—quite openly appealing to 'gentlemen' who wanted their sons polished without reducing their ability to make money. Commercial subjects were an important part of the curriculum. Such schools were transient so their clientele, the colonial elite (mainly Anglican and Presbyterian), decided to build on the success of denominational primary education. A Melbourne Diocesan Grammar School was founded at St Peter's Church of England, Eastern Hill, in 1848, and in 1851 the Free Presbyterians (who until then had used the Anglican school) started the Melbourne Academy, which became Scotch College.

Then came the deluge of the gold rush, during which Melbourne was thought to burgeon into the finest city of the empire. It possessed many amenities and cultural institutions, including parliament, university, public library, observatory, botanic gardens, markets, theatres, railways, banks and schools. The chance was given to those with influence and confidence to shape the future. In education this meant that in 1853 a handful of top government servants, some squatters and a few churchmen, whose opinions had been canvassed already by a select committee of the Legislative Council (which was until 1856 the only, and elitist, house of parliament) were able to achieve public capital for church-run secondary schools. They were

4

anxious, as were the Council, who were discussing a new constitution, to prepare bulwarks against the ungodly goldfields masses.

There was no surplus capital with which to establish schools as joint-stock enterprises like most new English public schools at the time, so the colony went back to the medieval model of church and state foundations. Bishop Perry, the lawyers Redmond Barry and W. F. Stawell, and successive inspectors of denominational schools, H. C. E. Childers and Colin Campbell, all Anglicans, all university graduates, all talented protagonists, were influential in achieving government grants of £20 000 in 1854 and £15 000 in 1856. Because the grants were allocated according to the strength of religious affiliations revealed in the pre-gold census of 1851, the Anglicans received in total an inflated £20 784, the Presbyterians £6445, the Methodists £2769 and the Roman Catholics £2500.* The Legislative Council was generous because it had already decided to establish the University of Melbourne, which would not have been viable without good secondary schools. In pressing that point, Childers, a young Cambridge graduate destined for high office in his homeland and by this time auditor-general, found in education a common ground between the partisans of wool and gold:

There has been a great deal said, as to whether the democratic or the aristocratic principle ought to prevail in the colony. If there is to be an aristocracy, it should be one of intelligence, and not of wealth. Nothing can be more calculated to bring the colony safely through all its dangers and difficulties than the encouragement of education.[1]

It was a rare moment in Australian history. Those with power were vitally interested in education.

The churches had then to decide what to do with the money. In 1854 their thoughts were for schools in Melbourne, where the Melbourne Academy, with new buildings, was renamed Scotch College and the Church of England school on Eastern Hill was closed in favour of Melbourne Grammar School, located on 6 hectares at South Yarra. The whole Church of England grant of 1854, £10 392, and £3392 of the 1856 grant, as well as £3695 in subscriptions, was spent on a handsome bluestone edifice to hold four hundred boys, fifty of them boarders. About £7000 (from the 1856 grant) was left, which, after the people of Belfast (Port Fairy) failed to seek a share, Bishop Perry offered to Geelong, provided that a building costing at least £10 000 was erected.

The challenge was accepted in Geelong (and not Belfast—where there were only 2000 people) because of the strength of the middle class, the energy of the local clergy and the existence of a church school. As in Melbourne, the church could look to men of public-school and university education who were socially prominent and, as

[1] Quoted in P. L. Brown, *Geelong Grammar School, The First Historical Phase*, p. 6. Childers moved for the establishment of the select committee in November, 1852.

---

* The Anglicans would still have done well if the 1854 census had been used because they had so many nominal adherents, but the Methodists in particular would have received more.

in Melbourne, there was already a Church of England secondary school. This had been founded in 1855 and, unlike its Melbourne counterpart, moved holus-bolus into the new building. It had the same name, the same headmaster and mostly the same pupils. The case for 1855 as its foundation date—and not 1857 when the new building was begun—is therefore at least as good as that for the accepted foundation date of 1851 for Scotch College. In the 1860s the school's writing-paper carried an engraving of the building over a bracketed statement: 'Geelong Grammar School—founded 1855'.

The strength of the demand for a secondary school had been tested in August 1855, when the following advertisement appeared in the *Geelong Advertiser*:

The Archdeacon of Geelong will be obliged by communications from parents and guardians willing to support a really good Grammar School in Geelong. The services of a highly accomplished English graduate are now available, and the school might be commenced as soon as a sufficient number of pupils had been secured, leaving the question of the erection of suitable buildings for subsequent consideration. St. Paul's Geelong. August 2nd, 1855.[2]

The archdeacon was the Ven. T. C. B. Stretch,* a graduate in classics of Worcester College, Oxford, who became the second vicar of Christ Church, Geelong, soon after his migration in 1852 at the age of thirty-five. A vigorous man, of average height, with fine well-chiselled features, he rode about his parish with 'the aspect of an officer of dragoons'. He was appointed archdeacon in 1854 and moved to the newly-completed St Paul's. As he had to cover vast distances in his new role, he was given a curate, the colonially-ordained George Oakley Vance, BA. Vance was born in 1828 in London, had won a scholarship to Lincoln College, Oxford, and had worked for eighteen months as a schoolmaster ('a most valuable man') at Exmouth Grammar School before coming out, in 1852, to the diggings. There he met the Dean of Melbourne, who persuaded him to join the ministry. A warm, scholarly man, not really the type for gold-digging, he was ordained on Christmas Day 1853.**

If Vance had intended to use his ordination, as was common among schoolmasters, to open the door to a headmastership, he was fortunate that Stretch had two small sons and that Geelong responded strongly to the archdeacon's advertisement. Stretch had probably had the venture in mind when Vance was suggested as his curate; he was determined to secure a good education for his boys, so that his colonial stay would not disadvantage them. On their part, the bishop

---

* Theodore Carlos Benoni Stretch (1817—99), apparently of Spanish descent, graduated and was ordained in 1841. Vicar of Pottespury, Northants, 1844—51. Later Archdeacon of Sale (1863—6), Ballarat (1866—75) and Melbourne (1887—94).

** A clergyman's son, educated at King's College, London, he had won the top scholarship to Lincoln College in 1846, and was runner-up for the Newdigate Prize for poetry in 1848. In 1850 he graduated with second-class honours in classics. After GGS he went to parishes at Chewton, Kyneton and Kew. He became Dean of Melbourne in 1894 and died in 1910.

[2] *Geelong Advertiser*, 4 Aug. 1855, p. 4.

and the dean were conscious of a general need for sound learning and religious education so that there would be—as Dr Bromby put it in his initial prayer at Melbourne Grammar—'a sufficient supply of persons duly qualified to serve Thee, whether in Church or State'. It was the best way to maintain the Anglican ascendance of the early years.

The Church of England, whose bishop stood next to the governor in colonial society, was already greatly advantaged, as we have seen, by its educated and influential laymen. In Geelong, besides the pastoralists George Armytage and James Austin, whose ecclesiastically-named town houses 'The Hermitage' and 'The Priory' were landmarks, it could call on Charles Sladen, a well-connected forty-year-old lawyer. Educated at Dr Butler's, Shrewsbury, then Cambridge, Sladen had been vigorous in church affairs since his arrival at Geelong in 1842. He also played cricket, sailed and hunted and in the mid-1850s acquired a freehold near Birregurra so that he could taste the life of a country gentleman. At about the same time he stood successfully for the Legislative Council and moved more or less permanently to Melbourne, where he was Geelong's most powerful influence.

The Geelong Grammar School (GGS) venture began about 1 October 1855 with thirteen boys. Stretch's sons, Theodore and Samuel, were joined by Frederic and Henry Pincott, George and Joseph Davies, Charles and Alfred Gates, Thomas and Henry Riddell, Arthur Cresswell, Archibald Gilchrist and P. Champion. By the end of 1856 there were over fifty on the roll, including at least twenty boarders. Vance had to hire an assistant master and move from cramped quarters in two semi-detached brick houses in Villamanta Street to a former hotel, Knowle House, in Skene Street near La Trobe Terrace.* The fees, set at three guineas per quarter for day boys, six guineas for day boarders and twenty for full boarders, when bank clerks earned about £100 a year, ensured that middle-class children predominated. Among the first parents were a doctor, a lawyer, a flour-miller, a tanner, a banker, two merchants and several shopkeepers.

In August 1856 some parents joined Stretch, Vance and George Goodman, vicar of Christ Church, Geelong, on a provisional committee formed to take advantage of Bishop Perry's offer of £7000 from the government grant, if £3000 was raised locally. It was a marvellous case of 'to him who hath shall be given', for the strength and speed of the response to Stretch's initiative clearly depended on the existence of Vance's school, already outgrowing its second home. The committee of fifteen adopted a set of rules and began raising money. Seven canvassers were appointed, who took to the town with lists, signing up friends and acquaintances for contributions. From the beginning, though, the committee thought that the target was

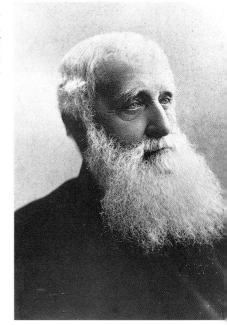

Theodore Carlos Benoni Stretch, Archdeacon of Geelong, founder of GGS, shown here in later life.

George Oakley Vance.

* It had been the Hotel Garni. Knowle House became popularly known as 'Knowledge House'. After GGS it was occupied for a time by Geelong College and later by other schools.

too high: they asked the bishop to consider lowering it to £1500. He replied on 17 November 1856:

I am prepared, in the event of the inhabitants of Belfast not complying with the terms on which a portion of the grant was to be appropriated to them, to propose to my council of advice that the sum of £7000 shall be appropriated to the Grammar School at Geelong upon the understanding that £10 000 at the least shall be expended upon the building and premises. Although the Government does not require the Grant from the Colonial Treasury to be met by any voluntary contributions, I think that the Church is bound to raise a certain proportion of the cost of such a building, especially as those for the benefit of whose families it is particularly designed are the wealthier class of the community.[3]

In contrast to his generosity to Melbourne Grammar, the bishop's target for Geelong's wealthier classes was a tough one. He was expecting as much from them as had been raised in Melbourne, where the grant was twice and the population four times as large. So it is not surprising that in April 1857, when subscriptions had reached only £1000, but the school was bursting with over a hundred pupils, Bishop Perry softened his 'understanding'. He would hand over £7000 with only 'the hope and belief' that at least £10 000 would be spent on the building.

The bishop's hope, coupled no doubt with a continued growth in enrolments and a natural ambition for Geelong, seems to have set the scale of the project. A design by the local architects Backhouse and Reynolds was approved by the school's trustees on 20 April 1857 and by the time the Governor of Victoria, Sir Henry Barkly, laid the foundation stone on 24 June, tenders totalling £10 077 had been let. The site, of about 2 hectares, was a further gift from government. Placed half-way between Corio Bay and the Barwon River, on the south slope of the ridge, it took in the block bounded by Moorabool, McKillop, Yarra and Maude Streets. When completed, the building stood out boldly on open ground, a major landmark. Its general outlook was south to the river but, with unconscious symbolism, the grand entrance faced west, as if beckoning the squatters of the region. The principal schoolroom, at ground level, was on the north side, closest to the town—on which Geelong Grammar School was eventually to turn its back. At the time it was occupied a third of the pupils were boarders, a proportion almost exactly the same as the specification for boarding accommodation for 80 in a roll of 250.

Construction took place between June 1857 and April 1858, to the great excitement of existing pupils, especially the boarders, who walked across on Sundays from their cramped quarters at Knowle House and its outriders. In November, when the structure had become large enough to arouse general curiosity, the *Geelong Advertiser* printed the following description:

The building is quadrangular in form, 147 feet 6 inches long by 118 feet wide. It is designed in the late Gothic style, which is chaste and simple, and combines those two great essentials—adaptability for all purposes required, and economy in cost ... An open quadrangle is in the centre of the range and this can be used as a

[3] Bishop Perry to secretary provisional committee, Geelong Grammar School, 17 Nov. 1856.

8

gymnasium and playground, particularly in rough weather. No windows will look out on this quadrangle except those necessary for light, which are all placed high—all the closets and out-offices being accessible therefrom. The fall of the ground has been made to assist materially in effecting all the arrangements. On the north side (McKillop Street) the first floor is only a few feet above the level of the ground, which falls as much as one in four towards the south side; this gives ample room (without excavating) for a ground story on the lower side. In this story are the kitchen, servants' hall, housekeeper's room, store, pantry, cellars, stable, etc; and to preserve a uniformity in the exterior appearance of the building a terrace-wall will run round from the principal entrance along the south side, and the area thus formed will afford sufficient light to those lower apartments, while at the same time the ground will be shut off from communication therewith.

On the north side is the general entrance; there is a spacious hall, from which ascends the staircase to the visitors' gallery in the principal schoolroom and there are also hat and cloak rooms. The schoolroom is 67 feet. long by 27 feet. wide, and affords room for two hundred boys, allowing eight feet superficial for each; beyond this a corridor runs the whole length of the building, on the inner side, by which access to the classrooms and out-offices can be obtained without causing any interruption in the schoolroom. The writing and drawing room is on the other side of the hall, and is 36 feet 6 inches long by 18 feet 3 inches wide next the French and music classes' room, 14 feet by 18 feet 3 inches; and then the junior classroom, which is somewhat larger than the last-named.

The corridor continues to the grand entrance [on the west side], between which and the junior classroom, the library, 26 feet by 17 feet 3 inches, is situated. There is a flight of steps before the principal entrance, and these terminate on the terrace, from thence the vestibule and hall are entered, and the principal stair case. The porter's room is on the right hand, and a hall leading to the head master's sitting room; the remaining space is occupied by seven small apartments, which are to be set apart as private studies for the more advanced pupils. The dining room is entered next to the sitting room, there being a clear passage by the corridor from the schoolroom, and is 48 feet long by 27 feet wide; it may also be entered from the quadrangle.

Knowle House, occupied by GGS during 1857 and part of 1858.

The trowel used by Sir Henry Barkly, Governor of Victoria, to lay the foundation stone of GGS.

9

The principal's or private entrance is on this [the south] side, and his quarters may be distinguished from any other portion of the building by the wall falling back a few feet. On this side the garden will be laid out, for which there is ample space of land. The principal's study, drawing room, and dining room are on the right of the hall and after them, in the north-east corner, is a room designated as the 'nursery'; there is also a back staircase for the use of the domestics only.

The eastern or back part of the premises will be only one story high, and, being over the cellar story, will comprise a covered yard, lavatories, hay loft, male servants' sleeping room, etc., and, at the upper corner, an entrance wide enough to admit a carriage to the quadrangle. The whole of the upper story will be divided into dormitories; there will be accommodation for eighty boys, with a separate apartment for each exclusive of the masters' and tutors' apartments. As there will be a tower and turret over the principal entrance, by a judicious arrangement the sick room will be in the tower.

For such a purpose this is the quietest and most retired part of the building. The turret would answer admirably as an observatory.

The structure when completed will have a very imposing appearance. It is built of a blue honeycomb stone, which is very hard and durable; the door and window cornices to be of white stone, smoothly cut and rubbed. A half parapet wall, surmounted with iron railings, will enclose the garden and grounds, which it is understood, will be laid out in very ornamental style, and will give a completeness to the whole that cannot fail to be attractive.

The architects, Messrs. Backhouse and Reynolds, contemplate having the school finished within six months, or as they announced when operations were first commenced, in about nine months from the laying of the foundation stone.[4]

Vance moved his school to its new building on 15 April 1858. After two years of makeshift accommodation it seemed an unbelievable opportunity for him; luxurious, too, for C. O. Helm, his senior master, as well as Edmund Sasse and three new resident masters, who with a monitor were responsible for most of the teaching and for boarding care. Staffing was generous: there were ten domestic servants and visiting masters for music, drawing, singing, dancing and drill. The smell of fresh paint, the feel of new woodwork, the discovery of unusual vistas, the exploration of rooms, corridors and a large playground excited the pupils. Then on 24 June, despite the absence through illness of the governor, the official opening went off like a state occasion. The celebrants clapped and cheered numerous optimistic and elevated speeches. Well lubricated with champagne and regaled by a generous colonial lunch, they whirled through a grand ball that night, convinced that they were launching the finest school in the land.

Was it a new school? A later council, in fixing the date for its jubilee as 1907, not 1905, certainly thought so, and seems to have preferred the laying of the foundation stone in 1857 to the completion of the building as the vital moment, thus stealing a year's march on Melbourne Grammar School.* There the foundation stone was laid in 1856, but the foundation date has been accepted as 7 April 1858, when the building was occupied by Dr Bromby, with mostly new

---

* There have been debates at MGS about whether R. H. Budd's Diocesan Grammar School, founded in 1848, had been merely suspended in 1854, when the headmaster left and the school was closed. The same governing body then took up the church grant, but a three-year break and a new headmaster destroyed any strong continuity of pupils and staff.

pupils and staff. That was a week before Vance and his existing Geelong Grammar School took possession of their grand structure. To be consistent, in terms of their buildings, the GGS date should be 1858 or that for MGS 1856. On another tack, if the critical difference between Vance's venture, albeit church-based, and the new Geelong school was that it had become a 'public school' on the English model (which conferred a status dear to the hearts of many of its old boys at the end of the nineteenth century), the critical date would have been 3 December 1856. That was when Bishop Perry formally accepted a set of rules drawn up by the provisional school committee. He also announced the election of seven trustees who, on 10 December 1856, appointed Vance as headmaster and advertised a competition for the design of the building.

The school in 1863, from Moorabool Street, to the west.

But what is a school? A common-sense approach, consistent with the history of dozens of independent schools, which have become public after private beginnings, is that of continuity. Vance's appointment to the headmastership by the GGS trustees in December 1856 (although not effective until the building was completed) ensured that the old school, which had prompted the new, would simply change its venue. All but one of the thirteen original pupils of 1855 made the transition. Public opinion in Geelong and in the Church of England linked the two stages unquestioningly.

The formal constitution did, however, provide a significant

11

THE
GEELONG GRAMMAR SCHOOL.

AT THE MEETING of the Provisional Committee, held August 27th, the following resolutions were adopted ;—

I. That the Rules, as now read, be adopted and printed, together with an Appeal for Contributions.

II. That the following gentlemen be appointed to canvass for Contributions to the Geelong Grammar School:—

    Mr. COTTON, Treasurer.
    Mr. O. NANTES.
    Dr. PINCOTT.
    Mr. ROBERTSON.
    Mr. SANDFORD.
    Dr. F. SHAW.
    Mr. E. WILLIS.

GEELONG GRAMMAR SCHOOL RULES.

1. That the Objects of the School shall be to impart a sound English Education, and to afford such instruction in the various branches of Literature and Science as may fit the Pupil, either for Business, or for Matriculation at the University of Melbourne.

2. *Trustees.*—That when the sum of £500 shall have been contributed, an Election of Trustees shall take place—such Trustees to be Seven in number, and Members of the Church of England,—to whom the administration of the affairs of the School shall be committed.

That the first Trustees shall be elected by the Contributors, as hereinafter mentioned ; and, as vacancies occur, by Contributors of not less than £20, and parents and guardians of pupils, who shall have attended the School for Twelve months previously—such parents and guardians to be entitled to one vote for each pupil.

That any Trustee absent from the Colony for six months and upwards, or ceasing to be a Member of the Church of England, shall be considered to have vacated his office, and a fresh Trustee shall be forthwith elected.

3. *Governors.*—That Contributors of £50 and upwards, shall be styled Governors.

That payment of the sum of £50 shall entitle the Contributor always to have, during his life, one Pupil under education in the School, at half fees ; and that payment of the sum of £100 shall entitle the Contributor always to have, during his life, one Pupil under Education in the School, with entire remission of fees.

That in case of a Governor dying, and leaving issue, the presentation shall remain in the hands of his or her representative, for the benefit of such issue only.

4. *Qualification for Voting.*—That a Contribution of £20 and upwards shall entitle to a vote for life, at the election of Trustees—such Contributions, except in the case of the first election of Trustees, to have been made at least three months prior to the date of voting ; and that a Contribution of £5 and upwards shall entitle to a vote at the first Election of Trustees.

5. *Religious Instruction.*—That the School shall be open to the children of parents of all religious denominations. That a Form of Prayer, selected

difference between the two phases of the school's existence. It set a new framework for management and was to be of great legal importance. There was a provision in Rule II for seven trustees to run the school and take responsibility for any debts, and Rule VI stipulated that the headmaster should be a clergyman of the Church of England as well as a graduate of Oxford, Cambridge, Dublin* or Melbourne. He was to conduct the school at his own expense, paying the trustees a vaguely defined amount for repairs and other outgoings. It was assumed that the capital cost would already have been met. In Rule XIV it was stated that the constitution could only be altered by a two-thirds majority (including all the trustees) at a general meeting of trustees, contributors and parents, to whom three months' notice had been given.

As the building cost £11 892 and furniture and equipment £1557, the bishop's ambition had been achieved—but at great cost. To supplement the initial £7000 only £1896 had been privately subscribed, leaving a debt of £4553, which, in a suddenly depressed economy, was to throw the school into confusion, bringing bitterness and

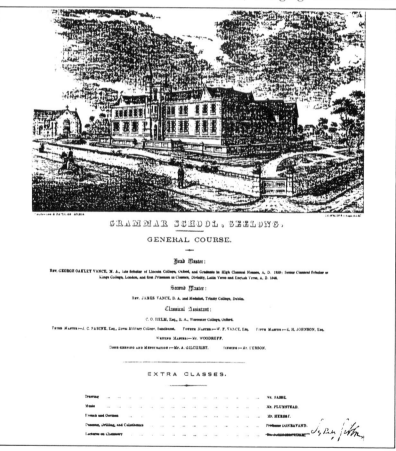

GRAMMAR SCHOOL, GEELONG.

GENERAL COURSE.

Head Master:

Rev. GEORGE OAKLEY VANCE, M. A., late Scholar of Lincoln College, Oxford, and Graduate in High Classical Honors, A. D. 1850 ; Senior Classical Scholar of Kings College, London, and first Prizeman in Classics, Divinity, Latin Verse and English Verse, A. D. 1846.

Second Master:

Rev. JAMES VANCE, B. A. and Medalist, Trinity College, Dublin.

Classical Assistant:

C. O. HELM, Esq., B. A., Worcester College, Oxford.

Third Master:—J. C. SABINE, Esq., Royal Military College, Sandhurst.   Fourth Master:—W. F. VANCE, Esq.   Fifth Master:—E. H. JOHNSON, Esq.

Writing Master:—Mr. WOODRUFF.

Book-keeping and Mensuration:—Mr. A. GILCHRIST.   Singing:—Mr. PERSON.

EXTRA CLASSES.

Drawing .... Mr. SABINE.
Music .... Mr. PLUMSTEAD.
French and German .... Mr. HERBST.
Fencing, Drilling, and Calisthenics .... Professor DONRAVAND.
Lectures on Chemistry ....

---

* The inclusion of Dublin is a measure of the importance in early Victoria of well-educated, Protestant Irishmen who had graduated from Trinity College.

recrimination. Geelong was hit by a general decline in gold yields during 1858, when Ballarat was particularly quiet. Merchants and storekeepers were caught with imported goods ordered perhaps a year before. Thousands of diggers embarked for Queensland on the rumour of good strikes at Port Curtis—a tragic episode, from which they returned starving, unable to pay their debts. The economy was in trouble anyway because of a recession in Britain in 1857, and local farmers were being ruined by cheaper South Australian grain. Many Geelong businesspeople were also caught in an investment in a railway to Melbourne, floated in 1852 and completed in 1857, which not only failed to compete with the bay steamers but actually assisted centralization on Melbourne. The dredging of the port or a line to Ballarat would have made more sense.

The outcome for the reconstituted Geelong Grammar School was disastrous. Launched on the crest of a wave of economic and population growth, it dropped into the trough at the same time as national and denominational schools, with generous recurrent government grants, cut into the market for younger pupils. The Flinders National School, for instance, to accommodate 500 students, was built in 1859. Fees were a trifle.

Thus, while the building stood on rock, the financial foundations of the school lay in shifting sand. To the huge initial debt the first year's operations added a heavy loss, and as there was no prospect of another government grant, like the one that had rescued Melbourne Grammar, and as the church was impecunious, the full burden had to be taken by the trustees. Besides Bishop Perry they were Frederic Champion, Charles Nantes, Dr Forster Shaw, Charles Sladen, Archdeacon Stretch and Edward Willis.* All except Perry came from Geelong, although, to be close to parliament, Sladen spent most of his time in Melbourne and was rarely available for meetings. They were experienced men, so the decision to go into debt was deliberate. Soon after the laying of the foundation stone the bishop pressed the trustees to approach sympathetic individuals for a bridging loan. This was to be serviced by operational profits, though it is hard to see how that could be done for the headmaster was empowered to run the school for his own benefit, paying only a small amount for repairs, etc. Moreover, in August 1857 when no one had been found to lend them a penny, the Geelong-based trustees committed themselves to complete the building as planned and, at Stretch's urging, in October they went even further by authorising Vance to order desks and furniture costing £1557. The stage was set for a debacle as Geelong went into recession. Where was the money to come from?

Possibly in answer to that question, the four Geelong trustees decided in January 1858 to take the management of the school into

from the Liturgy, shall be used at the opening and closing of the school, and that the Holy Scriptures and the Church Catechism shall form a part of religious instruction; but where parents object to the study of the Catechism, such study shall not be enforced.

6. *Head Master.*—That the Head Master shall be a Clergyman of the Church of England, and a Graduate of one of the following Universities, viz.:—Oxford, Cambridge, Dublin, or Melbourne. He shall be appointed by the Trustees, and shall hold office *quamdiu se bene gesserit.* He shall enter into such formal agreement with the Trustees, as shall obviate any difficulty in the event of his resignation, absence, or dismissal. He shall conduct the School at his own expense, and shall have the use of the Buildings, and receive the School Fees, subject to such deductions as shall be rendered needful for the repairs of the building, or otherwise, as shall be specified in the agreement made with him.

7. *Subordinate Masters.*—All the Subordinate Masters shall be appointed by the Head Master, and shall be Members of the Church of England; but in the case of the Second Master, the preference shall be given to a Graduate as above.

8. *Fees.*—That the School Fees shall be £12 12s. per Annum, payable Quarterly in advance, subject to such alterations as the Trustees shall consider desirable.

9. *Age of Pupils.*—That no Pupil shall be admitted into the School, under the age of Seven years, except in special cases to be reported on, and recommended to the Trustees by the Head Master.

10. *Vacations and Holidays.*—That there shall be such Vacations and Holidays as the Trustees and the Head Master shall determine.

11. *Expulsion.*—That the Head Master shall have the power of Expulsion from the School, in any extreme case, but it shall be incumbent upon him to obtain the sanction of the Trustees to such Expulsion.

12. *University.*—That the School shall, as soon as possible, be connected with the University of Melbourne.

13. *Scholarship.*—That any Person founding a Scholarship at the University of Melbourne of the Annual value of £30 and upwards, such Scholarship being for the benefit of Pupils from this School exclusively, shall have a perpetual presentation of One Pupil to this School, with entire remission of Fees, such Presentation to be deemed personal property and transferable.

14. *Alteration of Rules.*—That at any time a General Meeting of Trustees, Contributors, and Parents of Pupils, then under Education, all such being members of the Church of England, shall have power to alter the Constitution contained in the above Rules, provided that such Meeting be convened by the Trustees, who are hereby required to give Three months' previous notice, by advertisement, of such Meeting, and of the substance of the proposed alterations; and that any such proposed alterations shall be carried by a majority of two-thirds of such Meeting, in which majority all the Trustees present shall be included.

A General Meeting for the above, or any other purpose, shall be convened by the Trustees, on the written Requisition of Twelve Contributors, or Parents, or Guardians of Pupils, who shall have attended the School for Twelve months previously.

---

* Champion, a magistrate, had opened Geelong's first store; Nantes was first mayor of Newtown and Chilwell and a director of the Geelong – Melbourne railway; Shaw was coroner; Willis, a former squatter, was farming on the Barwon. In July 1857 Willis was replaced by another absentee, J. G. Ware, a squatter.

their own hands. Apparently the move was suggested by their secretary, Edward Mellish, but one suspects that Archdeacon Stretch, the dominant voice, had decided, from earlier experience of Vance's management, that direct control by the trustees was their only chance to handle the debt. Although the headmaster alone could dismiss staff, they were to be appointed and paid by the trustees. Vance was given the generous salary of £750 per annum in addition to excellent accommodation and maintenance for himself and family. He had married Harriett Cresswell, the daughter of a Melbourne solicitor, in 1855, and was on his way to fathering fifteen children.

The responsibility of the trustees became a burning issue as the financial affairs of the school fell apart. Bishop Perry, who had not attended a meeting since July 1857, refused to accept responsibility for the debt. This was partly because the general meeting of contributors at which, under the rules, the trustees were given control, had not been properly called. Although before the school opened he seemed to have accepted the change of management, Perry wrote months later, in October 1858, that his support depended on the original rule that the headmaster should be 'in every respect the responsible manager'. He regarded the local trustees as confused, unwise and over-ambitious. Not that he had been as wise himself as Charles Sladen, who resigned in March 1858 when, to pay contractors, a loan of £2000 was arranged with the Union Bank. Sladen understood his trusteeship to be 'merely for the purpose of holding the legal estate in the land'. He would have nothing to do with the building debt. Perhaps the bishop saw his own role as a formal ecclesiastical one, or confined to a trusteeship for government funds provided through the church. The first annual report of the school, dated April 1859, seems to accept that neither the bishop nor the archdeacon was legally responsible:

It is to be observed, that whilst the Lord Bishop of Melbourne and the Archdeacon of Geelong, as Trustees, share in the above liability, they feel themselves prevented from giving any legal acknowledgment thereof, which obliges the lay trustees to obtain all monetary accommodation upon their own responsibility.[5]

By that time the legal responsibility was crushing. Money was scarcer than ever; debt-collectors were settling like birds of prey on every financial carcase in Geelong. Because parents were hard-pressed, the grand building failed to attract new pupils, while the numerous staff ate up funds. Vance was so lax that, in addition to irresponsibly wasting food, the boys vandalized the furniture and fittings. Far from being able to pay off £1000 from the capital debt, the trustees recorded an operating loss of £1538. Somehow or other the struggle continued until the end of 1859 when, despite the reversion by a properly-constituted meeting of contributors to the original rule charging the headmaster with financial responsibility, the trustees decided to close the school. They could not face the possibility of a further loan and were at loggerheads with Bishop Perry in a debilitating argument about his moral and legal responsibility, something which

[5] First Annual Report of the Committee of Management of the Geelong Grammar School, 8 April 1859.

even the school's creditors did not press upon him.

Defiantly, Vance opened the school as usual in 1860, and continued, without paying rent, until 19 June, when pressure from his own creditors obliged him to quit. By then the bishop had relented and there was hope that the debt could be handled through the church. The Geelong trustees were willing to accept the operating deficit of £2000 if relieved of the capital amount of £5000. But Vance had gone, and possibly with him the impetus to continue.

What exactly had happened that so much went astray? Maybe the clerics put too much emphasis on an illustrious school, through which the church could maintain its traditional leadership in society. Archdeacon Stretch's original sponsorship and the use of his curate gave the school and probably the education of his own sons a higher priority in Geelong than parish work. His influence on the lay trustees also favoured the most ambitious of building plans. Both he and Bishop Perry seem to have urged expenditures which as religious men they considered to be neither their legal responsibility nor their proper role. They left the task of wrestling with mammon to laymen. Unfortunately the laymen were confused, as if called into battle and then deserted by their leaders.

A greater puzzle is Vance. If he was as bad a manager as his performance in the new school suggests, why had he been appointed headmaster? The answer seems to be that it was through Stretch's influence, for, in the absence of Perry and Sladen, Stretch was the moving spirit at the meeting in December 1856 when Vance successfully threatened to close the existing school if he was not given the new headmastership. At best Stretch made an error of judgement in suggesting the appointment, without advertisement, of a man who had taught for less than three years. Vance had run the school for only a year with a maximum of sixty pupils, a small staff and makeshift buildings. Although the numbers grew dramatically in 1857 it may have been the prospect of the wonderful new building, rather than Vance's skill, that filled Knowle House. His managerial ability was certainly severely in doubt before the move took place.

It is even harder to explain why the trustees held to so great an expenditure. Perhaps they saw the school as a retaining wall against the social avalanche of Victorian democracy, or as a light indicating the channel of middle-class opportunities and responsibilities through which Childers' aristocracy of intelligence would find its way, or as a necessary boost to Geelong and therefore their own fortunes, or all of these. They were not the only ones who saw a great vision in the mid-1850s, not the only ones who dutifully stuck to their commitments and went under.

One of the vanities of the time was a readiness to see Geelong Grammar as an Australian Eton, Rugby or Winchester—a true public school, drawing on upper-class traditions. Perhaps the founders hoped that the entrepreneur graziers of the Western District, because of their landholdings, might supply an aristocratic ethos, ill-prepared though most of their children were to take a traditional classical and

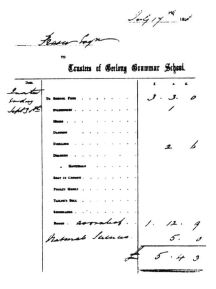

GEELONG GRAMMAR SCHOOL,
June, 22nd, 1857.

FIRST CLASS.

Examiner:—The Archdeacon of Geelong.

LATIN AND GREEK PAPER.

VIRGIL ÆNID, BOOK III.

1 Translate from "Fama Volat" 121 to oris 131.

2. Say what you know of Idomeneus and the Curetes, and give the position of Ortygia, Naxos, and Paros, showing the reason of the name Ortygia, and the appropriateness of the Epithets, "Bacchatam jugis" and "niveam."

3. Point out the names in this passage bearing the Greek form.

4. The difference between "pelagus," 124 and "freta" 127. Give the reference of the word "proavos" in 129.

5. The mood of petamus 129, the rule of Syntax exemplified in 131.

HOMER'S ILIAD BOOK L.

1. Translate from 130 to 139.

2. What are the chief dialects in the Greek language? Give me some characteristics of that dialect in which Homer wrote.

3. Parse the verbs employed in 132 and 134.

4. Give the force of   and say in what respect the use of the subjunctive in Greek differs from the same in Latin.

5. Exemplify the use of the Middle Voice by comparing the middle verb in 137 with the active of the same verb in 139.

mathematical education. That was the rub: the social elite was academically backward, while many bright boys were destined for commerce.

On the strength of existing records, responsibility for the failure of the school cannot be precisely apportioned. At the outset the trustees may have condoned an unrealistic scale of staffing, but they responded quickly to the need for economy by pressing Vance to sack some masters, by cutting his salary to £600, by stopping free beer for resident staff, by enlisting their own wives as a domestic committee and, at Perry's insistence, getting an assurance from Vance that he would take steps to prevent waste. Despite the existence of a house steward (an extravagant appointment for only forty boarders), buttered toast was thrown under the tables and there seemed to be no control of spending on food. Vance promised to be thrifty, but he was an impractical man with little administrative experience. He promised a code of rules, but, just as they had after classes at Knowle House, boys ran wild in the building, causing 'havoc and dilapidation'. Out of school hours they were unsupervised and probably gathered on vacant blocks, as they had in the Knowle House days, 'to play "fly-the-garter" and other unorthodox games, led by burly, bearded young bushmen, one of whom was believed to have spanked a master'. If things were bad in 1858, they were worse in 1859 after Mellish resigned as secretary, to be succeeded by an incompetent who finally absconded with the fees.

Vance was a fine teacher, thorough in exposition, with the charm and enthusiasm to make every task interesting; a scholar whose opinions commanded respect; a sportsman, particularly at cricket, who could join the boys naturally at their games. It was tragic that the responsibilities of such a large undertaking at such a difficult time were beyond him. Some of his old boys felt that he had been too fond of show. It may have been the flaw that brought him into conflict with the trustees when he took over the school buildings one evening to entertain his friends, a proceeding that was thought to have alienated many Geelong citizens.

Vance was no fool: his curriculum was a sensible compromise between English and colonial social goals. In that way, although he was not a practical man (he could 'do nothing with his hands'), he was pragmatic and clear-sighted. His own scholarship did not blind him to the fact that for most of his clients scholarship was a luxury. Getting and spending was the main colonial way. If he had not been able to understand that, he would never have left Britain. Having roughed if for a year or two on the goldfields* and then having the chance to achieve his migrant aim of opening a grammar school, he did not allow high standards or an undue emphasis on classics and mathematics to stunt its growth or his profits. He had to cater for two hemispheres of talent. Above the Equator were the clever sons

---

* Family tradition says that he was a circus hand when Dean Macartney enlisted him.

16

of professional men and some squatters, who wanted to go at least to Melbourne University and for whom Oxford and Cambridge were merely on another meridian. Below the Equator was that colonial stew of sharp materialists, good-humoured bovine creatures, the indifferent, the wayward and the neglected.

How he compromised is revealed in the headmaster's statement printed as part of the *First Annual Report of the Committee of Management of the Geelong Grammar School*:

SCHOLASTIC REPORT

The Educational plan of this establishment, though modeled upon that pursued in similar public schools in England, differs from the latter in some arrangements of importance. The reasons for departing from the model have been chiefly found in the want of preparatory schools in the colony, the shortness of the time which parents as a general rule allow for the education of their sons, and the demand on the part of many for a sound English education to the exclusion of the dead languages and the higher mathematics.

To meet this last demand, without lowering the standard of the classical or mathematical education given in the school, it has been found necessary, after devoting the morning to general study, and the afternoon hours to mathematics and French, to create in the morning school two departments, the former for exclusively commercial training, the latter for imparting a liberal education and especially instruction in the subjects demanded by the University of Melbourne for candidates for matriculation.

As in the lower three forms the classical instruction given is very rudimentary, and occupies but a small portion of the school time, a line is drawn in these classes between the pupils who desire a liberal education and those who are designed for mercantile pursuits, but on leaving this part of the school, which happens to most boys of ordinary opportunities about the age of the twelve years, the scholar may elect to proceed into whichever department his friends prefer. If he should choose the commercial department, he will be at once released from the necessity of learning either Latin or Greek, and will be educated solely in such subjects as are necessary to make the English scholar and well-informed man of business. If, on the other hand, he should elect to proceed with the study of the dead languages, he will not on that account give up the study of commercial subjects, but will still be called upon to attend daily classes in writing, bookkeeping, history, geography, English grammar, and composition; but in addition to these he will be expected to devote about an hour of his time each day to Latin and Greek literature. The study of Greek, indeed, can be entirely dispensed with at the parents' desire, except in the first class.[6]

Comprehensiveness with respect to curriculum was matched by a religious tolerance unusual to the Church of England. It probably stemmed from an interest in the enrolment of Presbyterians, especially the sons of Scottish pastoralists.

PRAYERS

School is opened and closed with prayer conducted by the principal or vice-principal. No scholar is compelled to join in these services, if his parents object to the Church of England forms of worship.

RELIGIOUS INSTRUCTION

Every master conducts the religious instruction of his own class. The lower classes are taught Scripture History from the Bible or works on the subject suited to their capacities. The senior classes are instructed in Biblical literature and the evidences of Christianity. No scholar is compelled to attend these classes, if his

[6] First Annual Report.

parents or friends object: but it is found that, although nearly a third of the scholars are not members of the Church of England, in only two or three cases the wish has been expressed that the pupil should cease to receive religious instruction.[7]

Vance reported that the boys worked hard and that the results were better than for similar English schools. Then as now performance at matriculation was the major test of scholarship. Yet only a handful of boys from an enrolment of 120 aimed that high, getting up for special classes at 7.00 a.m. two mornings a week and staying for another at 7.30 p.m. one evening. Vance expected three or four to sit for entrance to Melbourne University in 1860. If successful, they would join Cresswell, Giblin, and Woolley from 1859 and Gilchrist from 1858. Cresswell and Gilchrist, successive winners of the school's Barkly scholarship to the university, had done extremely well. For the majority of boys, on the commercial side, success was measured by those who left for 'posts of usefulness in this town and elsewhere'. All were kept up to scratch by regular examination. The headmaster's report reveals a regime which, according to one's imagination, can be interpreted either as a recurring horror or as a judicious testing and toughening of the new generation:

EXAMINATION

Once in each month all the classes in the school are examined by the Principal, partly by paper questions on the subjects which they have been learning, partly viva voce. The results of each examination are registered with a view to the award of prizes at the yearly distribution, and also made the subject of monthly reports to the friends of pupils. The yearly distribution of prizes to meritorious scholars takes place at mid-summer, immediately before the Christmas vacation, and is preceded by a rigorous examination of the whole school, occupying several days, conducted by the Principal, assisted by gentlemen unattached to the institution, invited for the purpose by the Trustees. In addition to several gold and silver medals, and the usual list of prizes, a scholarship, value £20 per annum, tenable for two years at the Melbourne University, is competed for on this occasion.[8]

Masters were not exempt from the pressure of examinations. The use of outsiders at the end of the year could expose any professional incompetence.

When the school closed in June 1860 and Vance moved on to be vicar of Chewton, and to start another school in Castlemaine, the trustees were left with a debt of more than £6000. Their creditors were despondent. The speculations of the mid-1850s, during which the school was born, had brought ruin to many, especially those whose assets, like the school's, were in buildings. In few cases, however was the legal situation so complicated or the social strands so crossed. The bishop, in dispute with the school's butcher about overdue accounts, was in no mood to help. The building stood empty.

[7] First Annual Report.
[8] First Annual Report.

2

Revival under
Bracebridge Wilson

The school reopened in the middle of February 1863. For most of
the boys it was a new experience, as exciting as the initial opening
under Vance; but some faces in the playground, some footsteps in
the corridors, had been there before, and the headmaster, John
Bracebridge Wilson, knew the place well. Second master when Vance
gave up, he had kept about sixty day boys together at a private
venture, the Geelong High School, in Pakington Street. More purposeful than Vance, he was a good manager. In his hands the school
was reshaped.

After the trauma of the false start it could not be the same. The
financial mess could only be tackled through an amended constitution,
which Charles Sladen was determined to achieve. He stood outside
the enduring squabble between creditors and trustees and was powerful enough to draw them towards a solution. That was after Bishop
Perry made an ecumenical move. He proposed a joint venture with
the Presbyterians, who, by injecting funds to liquidate the debt,
would share control. Headmasters would be chosen alternately from
adherents of each church, starting with a Presbyterian. There was
logic to it: of all denominations the Anglicans and Presbyterians were
most concerned about secondary education and the suspended school
had had a large contingent of the sons of Caledonian pastoralists; in
Melbourne many Presbyterians had attended the Diocesan Grammar
School before Lawson's Melbourne Academy opened in 1851. Also,
it was probable that without further growth one school the size of the
grammar school was as much as Geelong could support.

Perry moved quickly. Within a month of Vance's departure the
churches were talking and by October 1860 the original subscribers
had approved the new arrangement, which was then expressed in a
formal agreement to be ratified by each side. For the Anglicans the
trustees of Geelong Grammar School were regarded as competent
signatories, but with one complication. On Charles Sladen's advice
Bishop Perry deferred signing until he had referred his special responsibility as trustee to the Church Assembly, which ruled that

19

amalgamation would be a breach of trust. So the scheme went no further. Then, with the birth of The Geelong College in 1861, competition rather than co-operation between the churches began, foreshadowing a sporting and academic rivalry between the schools that was to shape many of the attitudes of Geelong's middle class.

The issue may not have been decided on purely legal grounds. Behind Sladen's advice lay the hope that the Anglican dream might still be realized. He proposed to sort out the trust situation himself, enlist new subscribers to keep the creditors at bay, advertise immediately for a headmaster and, by reopening and running the school efficiently, trade out of difficulty. To set things going he drew up a new constitution and gave himself fully to the task of convincing friends and enemies that this was the best course. At first he failed; only enough money was available to offer the creditors 7/6 in £1, which they refused. The school was therefore in limbo. For a year the trustees and creditors fought over its future. To save several of their number from ruin, the trustees tried to persuade the government to take over the school building, debts and all, while the creditors started legal proceedings against the church, claiming that it was liable for the debt. Because neither side was successful, both were at length convinced that reopening was the only solution. The trustees reached their decision on 16 August 1861, at a meeting which also resolved to ask the contributors to remove the requirement under Rule VI that the headmaster should be a Church of England clergyman.

Such a radical change in the constitution and its subsequent acceptance by Bishop Perry and the contributors was very significant, both at the time and for the future. It would not have been made lightly. Clergymen headmasters were the rule in England, where no layman was headmaster of a public school until after 1900.* It may be that Vance's failure suggested that clergymen were less appropriate in the fluid colonial scene, where the absence of a gentry class and the greater needs of commerce challenged traditional models. In creating a church assembly strong in laymen, Bishop Perry had already institutionalized the colonial social difference, which was also expressed in his willingness to accept a Presbyterian headmaster, if amalgamation had gone ahead. A pragmatic spirit possessed the friends of the school. Bishop, trustees and contributors saw that, above all else, an efficient headmaster was needed. During the previous debacle Perry's insistence that the headmaster must be the responsible manager was indicative, and was matched by Sladen's decision in 1860, when the resuscitation of the school was the prime consideration, to drop the stipulation about the clerical status of the headmaster.

It has been argued that Sladen had a particular layman in mind as headmaster when he began his crusade to save the school, that he was moved by personal motives to clear the way for the appointment of his friend Wilson. Even so, apart from lack of evidence that they

---

* Fletcher, appointed to Marlborough in 1903, was the first important exception.

20

were close friends at that time, the appointment of Wilson was logical. Just as Vance had supplied a ready-made school in 1857, J. B. Wilson could provide sixty pupils, without whom, in the face of competition from Geelong College, there would probably have been no revival. Wilson was also essentially, if not formally, closer to the typical English public school headmaster than Vance was. He belonged to the upper class and was received unquestioningly into Geelong's polite society. That, as well as his efficiency, would have impressed Sladen. Later they were friends, so Sladen may have been attracted to him as early as 1860 and was possibly his sponsor in Anglican circles. Certainly, by 1862 Wilson was well known as an educator, not just for his work at the high school but as president of the Geelong Teachers' Association and as the provider of evening adult-education classes.

The delay of a year between the decision to reopen and the formal settlement of the legal situation in August 1862 was caused by sluggish fund-raising. Geelong was passing from depression into forty or fifty years of commercial hibernation, quite early in which rivals of the boastful 'Pivot' dubbed it 'Sleepy Hollow'. According to censuses the population, which had been 23 338 in 1857, was 22 986 in 1861, 21 459 in 1871, and only 14 363 in 1881, after which it rose very gradually to 23 338 again in 1901. Money came in so slowly in 1861 that Bishop Perry once again provided Archdeadon Stretch with a curate so that he could go about raising money—and encouraged the church to release £1100 from its education funds. Even so, the school was not freed of debt: the settlement (which was largely an indefinitely deferred payment) gave the creditors 10/- in £1 in cash, left the three remaining Geelong trustees carrying £1500 each, and—for the second time in its history—set a large interest and repayment bill against future profits. The debt hung like a black cloud over the school, its colour deriving as much from moral as financial obligations to the church and trustees—especially the trustees, two of whom were almost ruined by the settlement.

The way was cleared for Charles Sladen to bring forward a new constitution for GGS, which the Church of England Assembly adopted in December 1862. Apart from allowing for a lay headmaster, the most important provision separated the role of the trustees, who held the estate, from that of a board of management, which ran the school. The original trust was dissolved and new trustees were elected. Then, on 22 January 1863, a duly constituted meeting of subscribers appointed a board of management whose first task was to find a headmaster. That Wilson, who was appointed soon afterwards, was seen as a silver lining on the cloud hanging over Geelong Grammar seems to go without saying. The board can scarcely have considered an alternative. Geelong College had opened under the robust headmastership of George Morrison, who had come to Geelong in 1859 as founding headmaster of the Flinders National School. It would have been courting disaster to ignore Wilson's presence and

Aug., '43   THE CORIAN   67

THE SCHOOL IN 1863

We are glad to publish in full the following Prospectus of the School and Headmaster's Address, originally produced in 1863, and are sure that it will prove of exceptional interest. The fees were not excessive in those days, even if we allow for four quarters in the year. It is somewhat astonishing to see the comparative size of lettering allotted to the Commercial Master and to the Headmaster, but we feel sure that this state of affairs did not last long. For the rest, the actual address to parents seems to us a peculiarly revealing document, disclosing both the great difficulties of the School in its early days and something of the greatness of character of the great man to whom in the succeeding thirty-six years the School was to owe so much.

CONCORDIA PARVAE RES CRESCVNT

CHURCH OF ENGLAND GRAMMAR SCHOOL
GEELONG

Head Master:

J. BRACEBRIDGE WILSON, B.A.
(St. John's College, Cambridge)

Appointed Headmaster by the New Board of Management, on the 4th February, 1863.

Commercial Master:

THOMAS HUTTON
(Late of King's College School, London)

Assisted by other Resident and Visiting Masters.

School Fees:

Day Scholars	Three Guineas per Quarter
Day Boarders	Seven
Ditto at Luncheon	Four
Boarders	Twenty

Visiting Masters:

Drawing (Mr. Sasse)	One Guinea per Quarter
Singing (Mr. I'Erson)	Five Shillings
Drilling (Sergt. Cripps)	Five
Dancing	
Stationery	Two Shillings and Sixpence per Quarter

The Boarders must be provided with two pairs of sheets, two pillowcases, and six towels.

A quarter's notice is required before the removal of a Boarder.

Trustees:

GEORGE ARMYTAGE
WILLIAM ROWE
JOSEPH MARTYR
COLIN CAMPBELL
CHARLES SLADEN

take the field against two formidable rivals. There is nevertheless strong evidence that Archdeacon Stretch, who was bitterly opposed to a lay headmaster, used his influence as chief fund-raiser and virtual founder to stop Wilson's appointment. Thus Sladen's support may have been very significant. Although Wilson had made his mark in Geelong and was known further afield, Stretch's opposition would have needed a powerful counterforce.

No records of interview or comments justifying Wilson's appointment exist, but much can be adduced from his career in Geelong. He had joined the grammar school as third master in April 1858 and was second master before the end of the year. Also in that year he was elected founding president of the Geelong Teachers' Association, whose general aim was to raise the standard of education. The first trustees had had no doubt about his value. At the same time as their brush with Vance in May 1859 about the 'wanton destruction of all parts of the premises', they intervened to prevent Wilson's resignation:

The Trustees consider that to accept at this time the resignation of the Second Master would be most prejudicial to the school ... and they would hope that Mr. Vance will endeavour to come to an amicable understanding with Mr. Wilson so as to be able to retain his services.[1]

What had happened is not mentioned. Perhaps Wilson criticized Vance's lack of control and Vance responded hotly. The trustees clearly took Wilson's side and rebuked Vance for writing Wilson a letter of 'too menacing a character'.

If the constitution had not precluded his appointment, Wilson might have been asked to succeed Vance in June 1860. The trustees tried in vain for a fortnight to replace Vance with a clergyman and only after their daily advertisements ceased did Wilson's first notice for the Geelong High School appear. Thus he kept the school together and, by adopting the title of rector, seems to have indicated his interest in preserving its links with the Church of England. Similarly the church kept the school in mind. The *Church of England Record* continued to report progress, with encouraging comments on Speech Day 1860 and then, a little later (possibly the pen was Charles Sladen's), with enthusiasm about Wilson's performance:

The vitality of Geelong Grammar School is not extinct. That unfortunate establishment has been exhibited to the world as a defeated army, borne down by heavy brigades of creditors, outflanked by opposition and driven from its battlemented stronghold by the beleaguering foes. But the fugitives have been rallied with marvellous tact and discipline by the late second in command and have been so well organised as to promise future triumphs under his able generalship. In other words Mr. John Bracebridge Wilson the late vice-principal of Geelong Grammar School has succeeded in forming from the old pupils with additions from other sources a school that has surpassed expectation.[2]

Wilson offered continuity. The curriculum of the high school had been a development of Vance's two streams, commercial and classical, together with much the same range of useful and liberal

---

[1] *First Annual Report*, pp. 33–4.
[2] *Church of England Record*, 1 Jan. 1861, p. 4.

subjects. Wilson took French writing and conversation himself and gave lectures and field lessons in his special love, natural history. In addition, as is often the case in the appointment of a new headmaster, he was strong where Vance was weak. Each month a report on the conduct and progress of every boy was sent home, and out of class there was no slackening of care. He was realistic as well as brave in raising his fees by 10 per cent to £3.10.0 at the beginning of 1861 and sustaining them at that level despite Geelong College's £3.3.0. His energy was extraordinary. From July 1860 he conducted classes at the Mechanics' Institute for two hours, three nights a week, to teach adults classics, mathematics and composition—including business letters in French.

The new head was an interesting man. In the prime of life, aged thirty-five, he was tall and strongly built, with a broad forehead, good features, a full beard and piercing large blue eyes. Formal and dignified, but humane, he spoke and acted officially with the courtesy of a cultivated gentleman, but was relaxed and warm, even passionate, in personal affairs, for as part of his genuineness he tended to anger quickly at injustice or irresponsibility and yet to forgive handsomely if he met contrition. This gentle man, who took on the mantle of firmness because it was needed for his task, was to express his personality, social outlook and educational vision through the school for nearly thirty-three years and perhaps to give it a permanent ethos. Whereas the ambition of the trustees and architects had provided the building and Vance a colonial curriculum, Wilson injected great warmth and humanity. He had an aristocrat's tolerance and an emphasis on the two great Christian commandments: to love God and to treat your neighbour as yourself. He seemed a natural schoolmaster, full of progressive ideas, and yet, as his life-story reveals, he had never been to school himself, or taught in a school before he came to Australia. Indeed, but for his Australian career he might have been thought a failure.

John Bracebridge Wilson, born in 1828, was one of the twigs on an aristocratic family tree. His father, Edward, rector of Topcroft on the Norfolk Broads, was a nephew of the ninth (and tenth) Lord Berners, and was a delicate, artistic, erudite and unworldly man, somewhat detached from the rest of the household. Family bonds were sustained by Wilson's mother and four sisters with a frankness and affection he valued greatly and that may account for his striving for a family atmosphere at GGS. Wilson's gentleness and probably his ability and interest in swimming, sailing and natural history may also be explained by the decision to have him taught at home rather than attend one of the generally brutal schools of the period. His tutor, the rector of nearby Ditchingham, was the Reverend W. E. Scudamore, who had taken first class honours in mathematics at Cambridge in 1835. Wilson spent four years at St John's College, Cambridge, between 1848 and 1852 and, although proficient at classics and mathematics, took out a degree, mainly in the sciences.

23

John Bracebridge Wilson in his prime, *c.* 1865.

It was his strongest interest, the beginning of a life-long commitment, but a poor preparation for advancement. At that time science, regarded as an inferior discipline, could not be taken at honours level.

Wilson's character is reflected in that decision: he followed his intellectual interests at the expense of alienating a potential patron, his godfather, C. H. Bracebridge, of Atherstone Hall, Warwickshire, who wanted him to read classics and become a diplomat; and at the expense of an estrangement from his father that diverted the main stream of his life. After graduation he went abroad and wandered for three or four years, filling his days with freelance journalism, drawing, painting, reading and scientific enquiry. At length, in a letter to his mother from Toulouse in France in 1856 (his French, by the way, was excellent), he discussed 'the grand question—*what is to be done?*' Teaching in England did not appeal: he might get a job but remain a junior master for twenty years or more. Sketching abroad, as he had done for the *Illustrated London News*, was also a dead end; so he decided on a longer journey, a greater opportunity. Joined by a Cambridge acquaintance and hoping for a loan from Bracebridge, he intended to start a school at Melbourne, or, if that seemed inappropriate, to make a fortune storekeeping on the Victorian gold diggings. In that mood, like many a hopeful, many a black sheep before him, and just as the colony moved into recession, Wilson stepped off the *Guy Mannering* at Port Melbourne in November 1857 to begin no school, open no store. Instead, early in 1858 he went to Geelong Grammar.

It may be going too far to suggest that Wilson was a black sheep, but no examination of his character, or the motive for his migration, is complete without facing the evidence in his correspondence that he was alienated from his father for about twenty years from the time he left for Cambridge in 1848. From Australia he wrote regularly and affectionately to his mother (and with her his sisters) until she died in 1860, although prevented, presumably because of his father's attitude, from seeing her to say farewell in 1857:

It is painful to leave my country without saying a last adieu to those who are dearest to me in it. But when toil and perseverance have redeemed the errors of my earlier life you will see me with more pleasure and pride. May God spare us all to meet once more in happier times.[3]

How he survived financially from 1848, we do not know. Early letters from Australia indicate that he could not have expected support from his family. Quite the opposite, he felt that he was working for his mother and sisters:

At the end of this time I should be pretty much where I am now—equally unable to provide for the comfort of my sisters and yourself.[4]

[3] J. B. Wilson, letterbook 1, no. 3.
[4] J. B. Wilson, letterbook 1, no. 1.

Perhaps Bracebridge, who wrote to him cordially in 1859, had provided some help; perhaps he had modest private means. Even so, he

was used to battling to an extent that made him contemptuous of Vance's carelessness and a skilful manager himself.

Although an intangible asset, his kinship with Lord Berners was of consequence among transplanted Britons, and Wilson used it. Conscious of the chain of patronage, he was flattered to hear from Bracebridge in 1859 that Lord Berners was gratified by his success. His diary for that year reveals social contact with Bishop Perry, a close friendship with Raymond, the manager of the Union Bank, and visits to other Geelong notables. He told his mother in 1860 that he was 'well situated here for becoming known' and was making valuable friends: 'Mr. Amsinck is in parliament and I shall make use of him if I can'.*

From what has been said about him, it is surprising that Wilson considered schoolmastering as his colonial career and strange that he knew it was viable. What prompted the idea of starting a school in Melbourne, and what explains the excellence of his work in Geelong, has been hidden. It is possible that at Cambridge Wilson was influenced by the pupils of James Prince Lee, headmaster of King Edward's School, Birmingham. Lee had taught under Dr Arnold at Rugby and had sent a new breed of scholars to Cambridge at that time.** The majority went to Trinity College, but some were at St John's, which is next door anyway. The evidence is circumstantial but persuasive. Fay Marles has used it to argue:

It would probably have been in fact, this group of highly talented, well educated and inspired young men who gave Wilson his first real knowledge of the modern public school and made him aware of what he himself had missed.[5]

Thus the spirit of Thomas Arnold, noticed by C. E. W. Bean in Wilson's philosophy, probably came via Cambridge through James Prince Lee rather than via Oxford, where Arnold's former pupils congregated. With it came a general scepticism, redolent of Cambridge science, that made Wilson question accepted religion, producing scruples that prevented his ordination. That he brought to Australia the moral principles of Arnold and humanity of Lee, without accepting their close religious underpinning, matched the secular tone of Australian society. His closer connection with Lee may also have led to a broadening of the curriculum, although we have already seen that Vance and others before him had made that break. Bean cites Wilson's 1863 prospectus as an important retreat from the classics, about which Arnold was firm, whereas Lee, a finer scholar, was less narrow. The latter had a remarkable knowledge of art, science and

[5] Fay Marles, 'The Early Headmastership of J. B. Wilson at Geelong Grammar School, 1863–1875', MA thesis, University of Melbourne, 1974, p. 45.

* Henry Amsinck, a member of the official party at the opening of GGS, was a naval officer who came to Melbourne in 1853. He speculated in mines, was agent for the dock and railway commission and MLA for West Bourke, 1859–61.

** Between 1828 and 1841 Thomas Arnold reformed Rugby School and with it the brutal traditions of English education. He asked senior boys to accept great responsibility and through his fervent preaching and unremitting personal influence placed a sense of fairness and service to others at the centre of the school's ethos.

topography, and treated his pupils as fellow seekers after truth, just as Wilson did.*

What occurred, then, was a creative coincidence of time, place and person. Wilson was a free spirit, tied to no set of educational precepts and serving a community which valued the acquisition of practical skills. If he had had English experience, especially in public schools, he might have been constrained by the classics. As it was, his scientific training and his freedom from set educational and religious experience seem to have inspired him to work from first principles, and he was fortunate that Vance had already established a broad curriculum. Within five years of his arrival in the colony he responded so deeply to its challenges and opportunities that he was able to set down in his first prospectus a notable foundation stone for GGS— not the masonry kind that is so often invested with a special mystique, but one that represented the emotional, intellectual and social substance from which such institutions properly emerge.

Few schools have such a credal statement as Wilson's 1863 prospectus, which Bean, writing about Australian public schools, almost a century later, found remarkably up to date. That was the mark of Wilson's greatness: that he could express a whole way of looking at education that was not only coherent, original and relevant, but also so based on first principles that it withstood a hundred years of social and educational change. Its essence was child-centredness and social relevance. Following Vance, Wilson's first statement was a radical undertaking to prepare boys equally for commerce and the learned professions:

At the desire of parents, the classics may be dispensed with altogether, and the attention of the pupil directed exclusively to subjects bearing upon commercial pursuits.[6]

That being said, the headmaster advised parents to allow their sons to be at least thoroughly grounded in Latin.

He went on to an even more important point, placing the needs of those proceeding to the university no higher than others. The school would look to the requirements of entrance to the University of Melbourne (not Oxford or Cambridge, it should be noted) for those wishing it, and would make sure that they had mastered Latin, Greek, and mathematics, but would take great care 'not to sacrifice the interest of the general body of scholars, to that of a few advanced boys in the upper class'. It was firmly stated that the average boy would become competent enough in English to write a well-expressed letter, would be able to keep ordinary mercantile accounts, would read and write French, would know basic history and geography, and would have a good idea of natural science, especially chemistry.

---

* The disposal of Wilson's library after his death reveals both breadth and depth of reading in history, literature, art, travel and, of course, science. He had about 700 volumes on science, including large runs of scientific journals.

[6] Headmaster's address to parents, included in GGS *Prospectus*, 1863, reprinted *Corian*, Aug. 1943, p. 88.

Above all, though, 'it will be found that his instruction in each of those departments of knowledge has been made subservient to the training of his reasoning faculties.'

Because education, to Wilson, was the getting of wisdom and becoming self-propelled, he added a paragraph about motivation, which emphasized that punishment would be minimal and work regarded as a pleasure for staff and pupils. Boys were to be encouraged to be responsible by taking a genuine personal interest in their own progress. They were also to learn to stand on their own feet. The free-for-all of the playground was seen as both pleasurable, healthy exercise and an important moral training, for Wilson was conscious of the need for freedom as well as supervision:

Great care is taken, while exercising a proper control over the conduct of pupils in play hours, not to injure by a mistaken system of espionage their manly independence and uprightness of character.[7]

Discipline and deportment were to be linked through regular drill with rifles and bayonets, and further physical development was to be achieved in a projected gymnasium. Consistent with Wilson's own experience and Geelong's seaside location, there was an emphasis on sea-bathing. Every day (only during the summer, one assumes) a party of boys would be taken to the beach under the charge of a master and non-swimmers were to receive instruction.

Punishment was to be light:

In conducting the discipline of the school, the Headmaster has ever kept before him the following principles: on the part of the masters strict justice, united to kindliness and forbearance; on the part of the boys, truth and obedience. Untruthfulness in word or act, and wilful disobedience, are the only offences for which corporal punishment is inflicted, and it is rarely found necessary to resort to it.[8]

With these words Wilson jumped several generations and summed up more clearly than anywhere in his prospectus how strongly he was at odds with most English public schools and how confident he was that boys would respond. 'No impositions are ever given', he also stated firmly, for he relied on generating a feeling of trust which he would not put at risk by punishing idleness or poor performance. He bravely expressed the belief that boys were not naturally idle, 'when properly managed and properly taught', and envisaged the backsliders being carried along by group momentum. To emphasize that boys were 'properly managed', he spoke of his 'peculiarly careful and accurate method of recording and reporting the progress of each boy'. Every month he drew up the results himself and forwarded them to parents with general remarks on conduct and progress. In doing so he obviously had a view of the school as a happy community achieving openness and trust between parents, masters and boys. To that end he often exhorted masters to write encouraging reports.

That sense of community, indeed of family, is emphasized in the arrangement not just to accept day boys for meals and prep, for

[7] *Prospectus*, 1863.
[8] *Prospectus*, 1863.

28

four guineas a term, but to set aside for any boys who brought their lunches a separate table 'laid in the same manner as for the boarders and provided with bread and vegetables'. Members of any (Christian) sect were welcome, at least as day boys, although Christ Church, across the road, was de facto the school chapel. During the week religious instruction avoided contentious issues and on Sundays boarders were free to worship at their own churches; but they also had pretty heavy doses of catechism, Greek Testament, scripture study and church history.

The power of that foundation-stone prospectus of Geelong Grammar School will be better understood as the history of the school is told. But while it is fresh in the mind let us emphasize that its coherence, its innovative spirit and its humanity made it more Christian and less elitist than most churchmen of the period could achieve. In seeking the welfare of every boy, Wilson was turning his back on the idea of the privileged, classical sixth form of Arnold or Prince Lee. He would treat everyone equally and expect his masters to do the same.

Wilson had discovered the individual. What he had done in his own classes at the original GGS and had explored further at the high school had become well developed and was adopted for the whole school. He threw out a superficial rank ordering in favour of a comprehensive knowledge of each boy's performance, which was seen as relevant only to his own results. Wilson explained the approach in the following letter, which is quoted extensively as the benchmark of what he was trying to do. The first sentence, in particular, expresses his challenge to existing attitudes:

You cannot fairly judge a boy's progress in education by the mere position he happens to hold in relation to other boys. By my system the results of every day's work are recorded and a numerical value attached to each boy. At the end of each week an average is struck and again at the end of each month and quarter. By having these results always before me and by examinations, I can form a good opinion of a boy's progress, while by my own daily observation and by the opinion of various teachers I can judge with some accuracy how far he is diligent. If a boy is seen to be working honestly and earnestly neither parents nor teacher have a right to censure him because he may not be high in his class. That depends on the ability God has given him and on many other circumstances which he cannot control. The old plan of recording the place of each boy at the end of each lesson is utterly useless as a test of each boy's actual progress and unworthy of any master desiring to be called an educator ... The plan I have for eight years had in operation and which has largely contributed to the success of the school ... I was led to adopt ... from observing the bad effects on the boys produced by the old method and I may add the bad effect on parents also by really misleading them as to the condition of their sons. Of course if a boy relaxes his exertions a corresponding fall in his class is inevitable; but what I wish to impress on you is that a lower position is not necessarily a sign of diminished diligence nor even of diminished progress. In one quarter he may be working at his best and two or three others [may be also]. If his ability is better or previous education sounder or health better or one or other of very many other contingencies, he may be at the top of his class. The next quarter in addition to him some *ten* others may take to working hard. One or two may turn out to have better abilities or better previous opportunities and may stand above him in the next report while neither his exertions have been less nor his progress less satisfactory.[9]

[9] J. B. Wilson, letterbook 1, no. 526

If that approach to reports had been all, it would have been a most remarkable step, but it was a stumble compared to the leap he made in providing an individual study programme for each boy. Included in what Wilson came to identify as 'my system' was a complicated sorting of boys into subject classes according to their progress.* Every new boy was tested by the headmaster and placed separately, and later promoted, according to his performance in each subject. A boy might be low in English, high in mathematics and middling in French or Latin, moving along in each subject according to his ability in that subject. This was an appropriate way to achieve his expressed aim of taking 'the greatest care not to sacrifice the interest of the general body of scholars to that of a few boys in the advanced class'; yet at the same time the bright were not held up for the dull.

What made him adopt this approach is not clear, but, apart from his consistent concern for individuals, it probably emerged as the best answer to the uneven preparation of boys coming to the school from instruction by parents, tutors, the private dame schools and the State-supported common schools of the period. How he managed to implement it is also an enigma. No doubt the flexibility was only achieved by adopting a rigid timetable. The whole school must have been taking the same subject at the same time for boys to be moved, as they were, from one level to another, and to staff the system every master would have had to be flexible. A mathematician would have been able to take only one mathematics class, unless at some time of day there was a separate programme for, say, the upper school. Wilson's mark-books clearly show that the senior classical master taught the lowest mathematics and the senior mathematician taught junior English.

That was the rub. While his system catered for the ordinary boy it wasted the talents of his most academic masters and forced him to employ only versatile men. 'From the experience I have had,' he said, in dismissing a master in 1868, 'I think it unlikely that I shall be able to retain much longer the services of a master whose attainments are almost exclusively classical.' There was also the social problem of having boys with age-ranges of as many as eight years in the same class or coping with the three brothers Henty, aged thirteen, fifteen and seventeen, who were taking elementary arithmetic together in 1868. Perhaps, though, as his great reputation suggests, Wilson carried his system by the strength of his personality and persuaded staff and boys to think nothing of such an age-range.

When tackled about it by a parent, who was concerned that the curriculum was too restricted, Wilson replied:

---

* The evidence for this practice can only be taken back to 1868, to Wilson's mark-books and the first extant admissions book. It was so well developed and so consistent with his headmastership and the system of reports that, as no letters defend its introduction, it seems probable that it was in place from 1863. On the other hand, it is strange that he did not mention so important a scheme in his 1863 prospectus.

We cannot do everything at once and it never answers to divide a boy's attention amongst too many studies at a time. When Victorian parents will send boys to a good upper class school as soon as they can read instead of keeping them, as many do, for years under tutors, or at Common Schools, we shall be able to arrange our course of study more advantageously.

At present both Dr. Bromby* and I find ourselves obliged to provide for the intellectual wants of boys of 14 or 15, who come to us with the mental condition of a well taught boy of seven or eight and who will we know probably leave us again in two or three years. In judging our arrangements you should give this full weight.[10]

There was another weight, the weight of English precedent, that fell suddenly upon Wilson and put his arrangements under stress. In 1864 his friend the Reverend George Goodman, secretary of the board of management, conducted the mid-year examination of the school with particular reference to its aim to educate boys in the classics, mathematics, literature and science 'so as to qualify them for any of the learned professions'. He examined the senior boys in Latin, algebra, arithmetic and English grammar, cast his eye over the rest of their work and observed how neatly the whole school wrote. Then, musing over the experience at his Christ Church vicarage, he wrote a report which challenged Wilson's basic assumption that education should above all be relevant to the colonial situation, calling particularly for more attention to Latin. Worse than that, for Wilson, he wanted the school to pay no attention to the matriculation requirements of the University of Melbourne, which put 'subjects of a more *directly* useful character' like geography, history and English, ahead of classics and mathematics, but to follow 'the more modern schools at home', where Latin, Greek, Euclid and algebra ruled supreme. The board, with an apparent colonial cringe, agreed, resolving that the headmaster should 'obtain the services of a duly qualified graduate of some university as a *Classical* master' and should emphasize the classics. Hitting strongly, they expressed the opinion that 'too early a compliance with the wishes of parents may tend to impair the character of the school'.

This position was so at odds with the statement in Wilson's prospectus that the classics might be dispensed with altogether, that it must be seen as a severe blow to his educational philosophy and a great financial and management problem. He would have to find and pay a senior man in classics who, if the rest of Wilson's system and timetabling continued, could be given little classical work. He would have to be very lucky (and he was not in the first instance) to find a man who was at ease with both senior and junior boys and with subjects other than the classics. The expense of that additional tall poppy was not the only outcome of Goodman's examination. It led also to the resignation of Thomas Hutton, the commercial master, whose name had appeared in larger letters than Wilson's on the 1863 prospectus. Goodman found him responsible for shortcomings in the teaching of arithmetic, and that may have led to his departure to a

---

* The headmaster of Melbourne Grammar School, 1858–74.

[10] J. B. Wilson, letterbook 1, no. 135.

relatively junior position on The Geelong College staff, where commerce was not highly regarded.

Rivalry with Geelong College was probably a hidden element in Goodman's report. His concern for the prestige of the school and the performance of scholars at the top of it (which was woeful in comparison with its Geelong rival) has to be considered in both social and financial terms. From the board's point of view numbers were low. By Wilson's agreement to farm the school, the board received no income to fund maintenance or improvements until the enrolment reached fifty day boys and twenty-one boarders,* a target that looked out of reach in 1864 when the total enrolment was fifty-nine. That was no improvement on the original number; no gain, despite the fine buildings, on the sixty Wilson brought with him from the high school. Overheads could not be met without an increase, so Goodman may have made his peace with Wilson by arguing that the potential for growth was not in Geelong, where the population was stagnant and where Geelong College was so strong a competitor, but in the country, where the status-conscious squatters looked for a gentlemanly, classical education as a preparation first for Oxford and Cambridge and later for the life of a landed proprietor. To them Wilson with his aristocratic background and GGS with its boarding set-up, already had much to offer.

Boarding numbers grew slowly, however, from four in 1863 to fifteen in 1865 and forty-three in 1867, at which level they remained for six years. The dormitories were never more than half-full. In such circumstances Wilson felt keenly the competition of Geelong College, whose founding principal, George Morrison, was wonderfully successful in preparing candidates for matriculation. As the history of Geelong College states, Morrison was a gifted all-rounder. His academic background was far superior to Wilson's.

There was nothing surprising in Dr. George Morrison being a good school master ... His preparation for a university career gave abundant promise of the academic successes that were before him. He won a scholarship which entitled him to four years at Aberdeen University and before he had been there a year he was recognised as the most brilliant student of his time. In every year he carried off the highest honours. The Simpson scholarship for distinction in mathematics and physics—one of the most coveted prizes at the university—fell to him in his first year. Instead of devoting himself to one school of learning George Morrison took up three—classics, mathematics and natural philosophy—and obtained honours in them all.

At the University his debating powers were highly thought of, and among the many men who came under his rule as President of the [Debating] Society was Archibald Forbes, whom all the world learned to know in later years as the famous war correspondent.[11]

In his first year at Geelong College, with forty pupils, two assistant masters and a purely academic curriculum, Morrison secured

---

[11] G. McLeod Redmond, *The Geelong College, History, Records and Register 1911*, Melbourne, 1911, p. 30.

* The minutes indicate some confusion about cut-off points. At first ten shillings was paid on every day boy above fifty (but later the number became sixty) and twenty-five shillings on every boarder above twenty-one. Wilson's original agreement may have been a flat sum for all enrolments over seventy.

three of the eleven matriculation passes awarded by the University of Melbourne. Between 1863 and 1868 his twenty-four matriculation passes contrasted painfully with Wilson's two. As might be expected, boys intended for the university were removed from GGS and sent to the more successful school, further enhancing its reputation. In acknowledging the situation at Speech Day 1867, Wilson asked the public of Geelong to give him a chance and not send all aspiring university students to one school, simply because that school had secured the name, 'a well-earned one he would admit', for preparing boys for the university. He gave himself a chance in 1869 by replacing the original classical master with William Crompton, a young Oxford graduate who had been to school at Winchester and who was, according to Wilson, 'a gentleman and an excellent scholar—and about the most valuable master I ever had'. So valuable was he that Wilson overlooked in him what he could not pardon in others, though it may be that Crompton, who was found drunk in the street by a parent on one occasion and who played up in a Ballarat billiard saloon on another, managed to avoid being tipsy at school. Strongly in his favour was a turn-around in matriculation performance. Against the two of the previous four years, in his four years at GGS twenty-three boys matriculated. This was well behind the thirty-eight from Geelong College in the same period, but it was a respectable number.

On other counts, especially his reputation for pastoral care, Wilson had nothing to fear from Geelong College. His day boy numbers reached a peak of seventy-nine in 1870, and his whole operation was larger and more cost-effective. In 1870 Geelong College had an enrolment of eighty-five and a staff of five, whereas Geelong Grammar used only six masters for 124 boys. What Morrison offered in the upper school may not have been equalled at GGS, but in general care and in the boarding-house Wilson was supreme. Despite the board's interference over classics, he lived up to the aims of his 1863 prospectus, not to sacrifice the general run of boys to the needs of scholars.

He taught many of the lower classes himself, thus getting to know well the whole school rather than a privileged minority. Humble enough to act as dogsbody by filling gaps left by masters whose shortcomings had earned them the sack, he often carried an immense load. He worked from six in the morning, when in summer he usually took the boarders for a swim, until the last boys went to bed at 10 p.m., when he probably found time for correspondence and reading. He was immensely popular. At the prize-giving in 1867 the boys clubbed together to present him with a crystal claret jug, chased with silver, and every time his name was mentioned there were outbursts of applause. The speaker who said that Wilson had gained the love of his pupils was confirmed by the rounds and rounds of cheering that greeted the presentation of the jug and the tremendous applause that followed Canon Goodman's announcement that he would naturally be reappointed for a five-year term.

A group of staff and boys, outside the tower entrance, 1871. E. S. Jackson supplied the following information for the *Quarterly*, Oct. 1904, pp. 19–21.

In the background, with the trencher on, is John Bracebridge Wilson, Head Master. On the left you will recognise William Crompton, a master. At his left hand, just above the pillar of the steps, Frank Edols; next T. G. Clarke, with Albert Austin in front, and Charles Sherrard to the left of him. The master whose head is just in front of Mr. Wilson's left shoulder is Mr. Chater (Richard B.), mathematical master; and on his left, Frederick Jackson, also a master.

Wilson's popularity yet effectiveness vindicated a major premise of his educational philosophy, that boys deserved his trust and would return it. He wanted them to have freedom so that they would learn responsibility. With that in mind, quite early in his headmastership, although the date is uncertain, he gave the boarders the run of the bush in small groups every Saturday from dawn to dark. As will be discussed in chapter 7, within the careful organization of what came to be known as Saturday Parties boys had complete liberty.

As numbers increased Wilson was able to give his senior classics and mathematics masters less junior work, and in 1872 he employed a master solely for a separate junior form. By 1869 his wish that parents would allow their sons to be thoroughly grounded in Latin was reflected in the fact that 86 per cent of boys were taking it. By then, too, the intake was more even. He was having to place fewer boys at different levels for different subjects: between 1868 and 1874 there was a steady trend from a majority of boys at three or more levels to a majority at only one level. He was also able to extend the range of the curriculum. As well as the basic offerings of Greek, Latin, French, English, arithmetic, geometry and algebra, there were classes in writing, spelling, mapping, book-keeping, dictation, scripture, physical and local geography and history. Extra-curricular subjects, for which special fees were paid, included dancing, singing, gymnastics, elocution and drawing. For a short period, while two of Isaac Pitman's grandchildren were at the school, the study of shorthand, then called phonography, was offered.

Little science was taught, although the 1874 prospectus listed a visiting chemistry master. There was no natural history, despite Wilson's proficiency. He established a reputation as a botanist and spent many vacations on his yacht, dredging for marine plants in Port Phillip Bay. The bar was probably the conservatism of the University of Melbourne which, although teaching science itself in the School of Medicine, was not to accept it for matriculation until 1881, when the public-school headmasters at length won their battle for its inclusion. Until then it was not seen as relevant to either the professional or commercial streams in schools, although, with numbers strong in 1879, Wilson considered it viable enough to justify the expense of a separate laboratory.

Before leaving the curriculum and classroom teaching, some discussion of the staff is necessary. They were the headmaster's greatest headache, coming and going with unpleasant frequency. In the nine-year period between 1867 and 1875, for which good records are available, only one man stayed the whole time and only one other for more than four years. On a staff of six teachers until 1872, and then seven, thirty-four men were employed. Of the two-thirds who were dismissed, half went for professional and half for moral and personal reasons. Wilson was often at his wits' end wondering how to find a suitable teacher. In 1867 he fired five, only one of whom was incompetent. Despairingly he wrote to his sister:

I have constant difficulty about masters. When I get quiet, steady men they often turn out noodles and the clever men turn out unsteady... This difficulty is the greatest drawback to the entire success of the school.[12]

Over half his appointments between 1863 and 1875 lasted for only one year.

He had high standards and tried to insist on the principle, expressed in his 1863 prospectus, that boys were to be encouraged to take pleasure in their work by masters who also enjoyed what they were doing. Alas, what was natural to a gentle but commanding person like Wilson, a transparently sincere man who loved boys and even preferred the naughty ones, was beyond the reach of the common herd of colonial schoolmasters. They could not measure up and must have found it impossible to maintain order in a school at which the sanctions of corporal punishment, detentions and impositions were frowned upon and where their example, not just their rhetoric, was regarded as essential. For if there is anything that distinguished this great man it was his adherence, throughout his headmastership, to the fundamental Christian principle of 'love thy neighbour'. Every boy was given dignity. The feeling was just as strong in him thirty years after he took over Geelong Grammar School as it had been at the beginning, and the following letter to

On the left of the last stands Frank McLeod, above the picture's right-hand pillar of the steps. In front of Mr. Chater, with his hand on his hips, stands Bonny Were, with John Rae Menzies Thomson at his elbow. In front of McLeod, with his elbow on the pillar, is my brother, Henry Bowtell Jackson; and immediately in front of him, leaning against the pillar and standing on the steps, Arthur Daly. The fair-haired boy with his hat in his hands, is John Warrington Rogers. Sitting on the steps, with a belltopper alongside of him, Mr. Rowcroft is to be seen. Leaning against the pillar beside Mr. Rowcroft you will see George Fairbairn. Standing on the garden path, with his back against the picture's left-hand pillar, is William Guthrie, a connection of mine, long since dead; while on his left stands Mr. Fitzgerald, then a master, and since, after study in Melbourne and St. Mary's, London, become a member of the noble profession (medicine). Last, on the extreme right of the picture stands Walter Henty, fair-haired Wattie, with his left hand in his coat pocket. At the end of the garden-plot in front of him is a heliotrope plant, from which I am sure I plucked many a blossom.

12 J. B. Wilson, letterbook 1, no. 10.

The building used for the preparatory school across Moorabool Street from the main building. The picture was taken in 1960. As The Source Restaurant the structure is still a Geelong landmark.

staff in 1893 is quoted as the total expression of that enduring concept.

I have a strong feeling that there is a greater tendency than is either wise or right to say harsh things about boys in the talk of the masters' common room. Such and such a boy is put down as a 'cad', another as a hopeless 'duffer', and all that sort of unkindly and harsh judgement. It should never be forgotten that if boys who have been here for a long period are not as bright and as gentlemanly in bearing as they should be, much of the fault must lie on us, ourselves. They are here for us to train as well as to teach. If men want to really improve the lads they should on no account dwell chiefly on their bad points, and set themselves against them by speaking of them unkindly. The good which is in every boy should be sought, and the boy himself *liked* for what he has of good. The evil and the unpleasant should be gently and kindly pointed out and remonstrated with, letting the boy feel that what is good about him is recognised.[13]

Unfortunately he soon found out that few could operate according to his ideals. In dismissing one among many of those whose methods offended him, he wrote:

My principal reason for coming to this decision, is that although very zealous, you do not possess the tact and temper required to work my system successfully.[14]

It was the case of a conscientious man who could not control his temper and who gave no encouragement to good, hard-working boys. Gradually, though, Wilson had to become less demanding and even to use the tawse to support a weak master. He also abandoned his opposition to impositions and made detentions the most common punishment. Perhaps the school had grown too large for the enlightened methods he had been able to operate at the high school. For all that, he was known for his justice and humanity and for a gentleness which contrasted strongly with the 'beat first and ask questions afterwards' approach of many schools in that period.

In their rapid movement through the school few members of staff at this time became identities. William Crompton (1869−73) was remembered not just for his excellent teaching of classics and a rather short temper but for the delight boarders took in his readings from Macaulay's lays on wet afternoons. Dick Chater (1869−78) was a gentle type, and rare in being an old boy. If you were in his good books in maths he would sit beside you, put an arm around your neck and pull your ear, not meaning to hurt, until it was sore. A. G. McCombe (1872−85) was the commercial master. A surly old dog, he was nicknamed 'Giglamps' because of the spread of his ears. Oliver Thomas (1875−80), the senior maths master, was one of a family of nineteen and a miracle at managing boys, according to Steve Fairbairn (who should have known). Steve discovered his mettle the first time Thomas took prep when, making a show to his fellows of reading *Tommyhawk, Rifle and Revolver* under his desk, he was sprung by the vigilant master. Spotting the activity in the reflection of the window, he took the book and burned it. Another boy remembered Thomas's Wellingtonian nose and the great snuffle

[13] J. B. Wilson, folio 2.
[14] J. B. Wilson, letterbook 2, no. 544.

it produced, as well as the peculiar action behind his really good fast bowling. F. Jackson (1868–71) was vividly remembered by his namesake E. S. Jackson after he found him, sleepwalking like a ghost in his white nightshirt, perched on the end of his bed. A. P. Rowcroft (1865–71), the headmaster's brother-in-law, resigned to open the nearby preparatory school, where some boys remembered him for his black moods and great strength.* Another master, who remained nameless, was just called 'The Terror', in condemnation of his arbitrary temper. Wilson probably made sure it was not experienced for long.

To be successful in the nineteenth century a headmaster had not only to contend with inadequate staff and win pupils in the race against competitors, but also to run his school efficiently as a business. Wilson had no bursar or financial adviser, only a board of management whose members might individually prove helpful but whose general priorities in maintaining the buildings and grounds might not always match his own. After the experience of Vance's mismanagement they had adopted the farming system by which Wilson was to run the school at his own risk, paying a capitation fee for every boy over fifty day boys and twenty-one boarders. The margin was small and the income negligible until the late 1860s, when the capitation income would have still been a drop in the bucket of what was needed, considering the vandalism under Vance and during the period of closure. Indeed Wilson had at his own cost, though with the board's approval, paid for urgent repairs and had begun to remodel the dormitories. How he found the money is not clear, but as already stated, he was a skilful manager. Not a skinflint, but careful of every penny, he had the energy to haggle with shopkeepers and double-check their accounts. His letters show him playing off two butchers against each other and bargaining about every cut of meat.

He needed to. During the 1860s he often lived hand to mouth, hoping for an increase in numbers, especially of boarders, that would make him secure. Even that had its problems. Between 1867 and 1868, when boarding numbers rose from twenty-five to forty-two, he had to get in a builder to make alterations and was left carrying the £14 by which the work exceeded the amount approved by the board, who begrudged every penny that could not be put towards the redemption of the school's huge debt. This, at a time when he had extended his overdraft too far and reduced it too slowly to please an unsympathetic bank manager, brought three months of harassment and then legal action from the bank while he, in his turn, pursued recalcitrant parents for fees, raised a loan on his life and approached several well-to-do parents for guarantees. The pressure was particularly strong at that time because the pastoralists, including many with sons among his new boarding intake, were in even greater trouble

---

* The preparatory school was a separate venture to which Wilson contributed capital and which acted as a feeder to GGS. It was located just across Moorabool Street from the main school, in a building that became The Source Restaurant in the 1970s.

than he was with the banks. Low wool prices could not service the huge debts they had contracted in the 1860s to defeat the democratic land selection acts and achieve the freehold of their runs. A sign of the time was the insolvency, early in 1869, of Hugh Glass, the most ambitious and therefore the most vulnerable of Margaret Kiddle's *Men of Yesterday*. A measure of the pastoral downturn was Wilson's inability to raise the number of boarders from a plateau of about forty-four between 1868 and 1873. It even fell below forty in 1871. At the same time, of course, Geelong's failure to grow (see p. 21) limited the day-boy potential.

Boarders were probably the chief hope financially. In the absence of account books it is only possible, using his letter books, enrolment books, mark books and prospectuses, to guess that the profit on the day side of the school would have given Wilson only pin money. He might well have done the following sums himself for 1867:

Income:	84 boys at 12 guineas	£1052
Expenditure:	Senior classical master	£200
	Senior assistant and maths	£150
	Junior assistant, upper school	£100
	Commercial master	£200
	Senior assistant, lower school	£150
	Junior assistant, lower school	£100
		£900
	Capitation to board* 34 × £2	£68
	Cost of cleaning, consumables, etc.	£40
Total costs		£1028
Profit		£24

Apart from tuition, boarders were charged 68 guineas per year, giving an income of about £2500 from thirty-five boarders in 1867. Expenses, assuming his wife's help, would have been the boys' and masters' food, and wages and keep for, say, three maids, a porter-handyman, and a cook.

Income:		£2500
Expenses	Masters' and boys' food (£40 each)	£1640**
	Wages and keep	£300
	Rates	£150
	Lighting, etc.	£24
	Capitation † 14 × £9	£126
		£2220
Profit		£280

---

* Assuming ten shillings per quarter for every boy in excess of fifty.

** This is probably understated. In 1868 he wrote to a friend from whom he sought to borrow money for a farm to provide meat, vegetables and dairy produce that meat cost him £400, milk £60 and butter £80–£100 per annum.

† Assuming twenty-five shillings per quarter for every boy in excess of twenty-one.

Allowing for the fact that many boarders' parents were behind with their fees, perhaps totalling £200, and for the considerable sums he spent on improvements (including beds and other furniture), Wilson's take from the operation was probably less than the £200 he paid to his senior assistants. The board, quite apart from dealing with the debt, had less than £200 in capitation to support improvements and provide maintenance. It was a hand-to-mouth operation, from which Wilson was receiving nowhere near the princely £1000 plus of Irving at Wesley College.

Better times were coming, however. Although boarding numbers remained steady, day boys increased dramatically from forty-five to seventy-nine between 1867 and 1870. The school's reputation had never been better in the town and Wilson must have slept more easily at night. Even when Geelong College moved to a fine new building and spacious grounds at Newtown in 1871 and his day boy numbers fell back to sixty-three in 1872, he had no cause for concern, except for news from the board that his success was putting them under pressure from the creditors of the previous decade. Hearing that things were going well, the local butcher, John Taylor, who had sued Bishop Perry in 1861 to recover monies owed to him by the Reverend George Vance, wrote to the board in 1870, asking a leading question about the income of the school. Carefully they replied that the revised constitution of the school provided for the plough-back of profits through a capitation fee that had yielded nothing for the first four years after reopening and thereafter was just enough to meet urgent needs. They assured the butcher that they would all like to see the creditors reimbursed—the banks £2500, the former trustees £1700 and others like him £800—but there were no immediate prospects of a sufficient surplus.

They were nevertheless vulnerable and in March 1870 deferred a request from Wilson that they pay £30 towards the new gymnasium he had organized. Instead, they opened a reserve fund into which regular payments were made at the expense of repairs, improvements and new works. That was not all. A renewed interest from the Anglican hierarchy in Melbourne, in the person of the dean, H. B. Macartney, who took over the chairmanship of the board on a number of important occasions, seemed to be linked to the reduction of the debt. Behind him, probably, loomed Archdeacon Stretch, under pressure from fellow trustees who were carrying the burden he had escaped (see p. 14), and from the bankers, the cream of that society, to whom the due payment of debts was like one of God's laws.

Under considerable pressure from this phalanx, Wilson was obliged in 1872, when his second five-year term was up, to accept a contract by which he paid the capitation fee on all pupils. Then in 1875, when the reserve fund had crawled up to only £300 in five years, the dean proposed that the school should accept the repayment of the creditors as its first duty. The past was threatening to take over in a way that would be much worse for Wilson than the increased

39

NAME *Robert Barlow. 15.*

Date of admission ... *Jan 28th 1873.*

Previous education *Here some years since called G. S.*

Special arrangements about Fees, &c. } *Son of clergyman.*

Religion ... ... *Ch of E..*

Sicknesses ... ...

WHERE PLACED ON ARRIVAL

Greek ... ... *Cl....* ...... *Mr.................*

Latin *Smith Reader.* *Cl. IV.* .... *Mr.................*

French *Ahn Reader.* *Cl. ...* ...... *Mr.................*

English ... ... *Cl. V.* .... *Mr. McConnel* ...

Euclid *Commenc.* *Cl....* ...... *Mr.................*

Algebra ... ... *Cl....* ...... *Mr.................*

Arithmetic .. .. *Cl. V.* ...... *Mr.................*

EXTRA SUBJECTS.

Music · ... ...

Singing ... ... *original entry Oct 1869*

Elocution ... ...

Drawing ... ...

Dancing ... ...

Gymnastics ... ...

capitation. The debt of £5000 might absorb all the school's resources for ten or even twenty years and would soon leave him with incomplete and deteriorating buildings. He was a man of honour but it was too much to be asked to suffer so heavily for the folly of his predecessor and the extraordinary ambition of the church at that earlier time.

On the other hand, the trustees who had generously put up the funds in 1858 and had been deprived of them for over ten years deserved consideration. The issue split the board and brought the resignation of Mr S. V. Buckland, its most energetic member, who seems to have refused to accept the dilapidation and the threats to health inherent in the policy of putting the debt first. Because he was so influential and the board of management so obviously in crisis his departure triggered the first meeting in eight years of the board of governors. With the significant support of Dr Shaw, the school's largest private creditor, they voted for Buckland's reinstatement. What went on behind the scenes will never be known, but the outcome was clear: Buckland returned to the board and the priority of the debt was lowered. Only the first of four resolutions put on notice by the dean at the crisis meeting was passed:

That with the continued increase in the number of boarders together with the want so strongly felt of bathrooms and rooms for sick pupils it has become imperative to provide additional accommodation.[15]

The other resolutions, limiting expenditure on those improvements to £600 and making them the last building activity until the debt was cleared, were withdrawn. The dean went home defeated and after that no member of the church hierarchy appeared at a board meeting during Wilson's term of office. Mr Buckland was appointed convenor of a sub-committee charged with overseeing the provision of new bedrooms and bathrooms and effecting the repairs for which Wilson had been asking for many months.

Although the formality and sparseness of the minutes obscures the drama, it is obvious that the meeting on 7 June 1875 was a critical one in the school's history. It released the resources to support a new era that began in 1875, with the arrival of an attractive young Englishman, James Lister Cuthbertson, the school's poet, the creator of its sporting traditions and a great purveyor of the mystique of the English public schools. It is not improbable that an exciting new spirit in the school, for which Cuthbertson was responsible, had taken hold of Buckland, whose son joined the school at the beginning of the year.

[15] Minutes, 7 June 1875.

3

J. L. Cuthbertson
and greater confidence

James Lister Cuthbertson brought to Geelong Grammar a great enthusiasm for public-school life. He dared to equate that still strugging colonial foundation, tainted though it was by commerce, with places like Rugby, Winchester, and his own Scots Glenalmond, which were distinguished for their high moral purpose and their emphasis on manly games. He was an enthusiast who found his vocation under Wilson and who treasured it; a rare spirit who discovered his ultimate meaning among boys, and yet, through all his intimacy with them and his transparent human frailty, retained his adult distance and dignity. We know little about his relationship with Wilson, except their mutual admiration and Wilson's remarkable tolerance of Cuthbertson's dependence on alcohol. What must be assumed is respect at first sight and a congruence of aims and beliefs that was stimulating and strengthening to both. There is no other way of explaining Cuthbertson's immediate influence on the school, except, of course, his personal magnetism.

Like Wilson, he was impressive to look at, athletic in build and with a strong, well-proportioned face in which a bold forehead, bushy moustache and prominent, thoughtful eyes were notable features. Everything about him was English and clean, one boy remembered—'just pure unexaggerated Oxford'—but his heavy underlip pouted out when he was displeased. A sensitive person, he was nevertheless keen on sport and dressed with some bravado and appropriately for every occasion. He liked a bright tie, usually yellow and black, and smoked a straight-stemmed pipe. All in all, on top of his great interest in them, he was a boys' man. As Charles Belcher put it, for the late 1880s, 'to that generation of boys Cuth was the model of all we should have liked to be'.

Looking back, those who were there in 1875 were conscious of the dawn of a new era. To E. S. Jackson and Reginald Stephen, who left at the end of that year, Cuthbertson was unforgettable. Jackson, later a renowned physician, wrote:

At the beginning of 1875 there came to Geelong Grammar School, James Lister Cuthbertson, then a young man straight from Oxford, who in the years to come was

J. L. Cuthbertson—'every boy who met him fell under his spell' — showed a close identification with his charges.

41

to wield a great influence on the school. Those who were there in that year will bear witness to his influence from the first. He took the senior class in classics. Never had we had the hitherto dull Latin and Greek authors displayed to us in so attractive a way. There was more to Cuthie than the mere attractiveness of his teaching. Soon we realised that not only was he anxious for our scholarship, but that before all he wanted us to be men and gentlemen. It was not that he was forever telling us to honor what was straight and right. I do not remember any direct talk from him on such subjects though no doubt in his talk with us he used illustrations. For instance, if in our relation to one another, or to other schools, if in sport we were inclined to allow ourselves to be tempted to take advantage of our opponents which he thought savoured of not playing the game, he would tell us so. There are a lot of men, grey beards today, but boys then who still remember the little curl of scorn in his upper lip while in a few words he summed up the situation and gave his opinion, appealing to us generally to uphold the Light Blue Standard. That had to be considered. Whatever the standard set by other men and other schools, the Light Blue must be kept clean. Thus he did much for the spirit de corps of the school, much for the individual character of the boys who became so devoted to him. Never, in all the years have I heard a boy speak, except in loving terms of 'Cuthie' as he soon came to be called. What he said came to be regarded as the last word that could be said about anything.

During 1875 he began the long connection with School rowing which bore fruit in some of the best oars that Australia—aye and even Oxford and Cambridge have known ... Fortunate, indeed, in more ways than one were the boys who got into the School Boat. Necessarily they were brought more closely into touch with their beloved coach. He loved them and their doings for their own sake and for that of the School. I was a boy of 14 when he came to Geelong. I was a year under Cuthie, and left for the University at the end of it. I did not therefore sit under him very long. As the years went by after I left school I gathered an indefinite impression that he had been at the school much longer than that in my time—testimony to the extent to which he loomed large in the affairs of the place.[1]

Bishop Reginald Stephen, who was dux of the 1875 matriculation class, cut through the hero-worship to add the complexity which has to be faced when assessing Cuthbertson's impact:

When we come to masters we are faced with a mixed bag ... The most important was Cuthbertson. The simplest description of him was that he was a drunkard, but that gives an absolutely false impression. He was a good classical scholar with enormous influence and high ideals and it speaks well for J. B. Wilson's wisdom and the insight of the boys that he was retained for many years as a master. Every boy who met him fell under his spell and recognised him for a struggler for the right and was anxious to help him. When the groups were formed for Saturday excursions there was competition for the honour of taking Cuthy as their leader which included the duty of shepherding him from the temptations of the public house door. Strange though it may seem to our total abstinant, enthusiasm at his influence at school or abroad was entirely on the right side. We saw his fault but knew he hated it and we loved him for his efforts to conquer it. Incidentally, he had the power of making a Greek chorus seem attractive and beautiful.[2]

From Stephen's account it will be no surprise that, like Wilson, Cuthbertson had failed in England and had come to Australia almost in desperation. He was born in 1851 at Glasgow, where he lived until about 1861 when his father went to manage a Shanghai bank and sent him to Trinity College, Glenalmond. In 1869 he moved to London to prepare for the Indian Civil Service exam. He was very successful, finishing high on the list, and gained a scholarship to

[1] E. S. Jackson, reminiscence, archives.
[2] R. Stephen, reminiscence, archives.

Merton College, Oxford, in 1872. Here he was required to spend two years completing his probation for the Indian Service, but drinking and frivolity apparently took over and he failed. Possibly because his father was then manager of the Bank of South Australia, he decided to emigrate and reached Melbourne some time in 1874, when Wilson, who had had four senior classical masters in two years, was prepared to take a risk with him.

Behind the appointment of one so young (he was only twenty-three and had never taught) we can imagine a fruitful interview at which the two men found exciting common ground. Each showed daring—Cuthbertson to apply and Wilson to appoint him. But there is more to it than that, for, in reporting the appointment to the board of management, Wilson represented his find as a graduate of the University of Oxford. It seems that Cuthbertson misled him and therefore that his great part in the future of Geelong Grammar School, whose honour he laboured unwaveringly to sustain, rested upon a lie.

In looking back over the year Wilson would have been delighted with 1875. Administratively, his supporters had defeated those on the board who wanted to curtail expenditure, and academically the school's performance at the matriculation and civil service examinations was second to none, earning high praise from the Melbourne press. He had cause to congratulate himself on the appointment of Cuthbertson, who had prepared the boys in Latin, Greek and English. He had also been able to complete the phasing out of his original system of multi-level programming, which had placed so much strain on him; what had been practicable with sixty boys was onerous and problematical with over twice that number.

Wilson had also found the year propitious to introduce prefects, a system of self-government he believed in but had been unwilling to persevere with after an unsuccessful attempt some years before. That Cuthbertson had prompted him, which contemporaries and tradition affirm, goes almost without saying, once Cuthbertson's passion for the English public-school ethos is accepted. The School *Annual*, later the *Quarterly*, which he founded in 1875 and edited until 1896, became the vehicle for its beliefs.

We have given reasons for the want of public school feeling in these colonies, and have also stated what we believe to be the best means of creating such a feeling. As far as this school is concerned, we are on the threshold of a new state of things. We have commenced to give practical effect to the principle of self-government by the election of prefects; and although this may be regarded as now in its infancy, it is slowly but surely making its influence felt, and in years to come we may have at least this one tradition—that we were the first school in the new colony to introduce a system which relies for its efficacy on a trust in the honour of boys.[3]

His claim for an Australian first is confirmed by C. E. W. Bean. Such is the running power of ideas that what Arnold began with his praepostors at Rugby came to Australia by way of Cuthbertson's boyhood at Glenalmond.

[3] *Annual*, 1876, p. 31.

The prefects, 1876.

From left, back row: F. S.
Brush, C. N. Armytage,
D. Mackinnon; centre row:
A. I. Black, S. H. Puckle,
D. S. Walker; front row:
W. J. Austin.

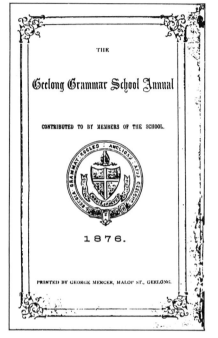

Control of the magazine magnified Cuthbertson's influence. The interest taken in it by other schools gave him a wide audience, particularly in Victoria, where the public schools were strongest and where he operated in person as well as in print. In 1876 the *Annual* carried six pages of news and general comment. Then, and as the *Quarterly* from 1877, it conveyed Cuthbertson's mind on the everyday life of the school, even though he used boys like Steve Fairbairn as co-editors. He attached precepts to the minutiae of behaviour, aired grievances and promoted reforms. As Charles Belcher was to say:

In fact, if there is one thing that one associates more than another with Cuth it is that in all things he was a constant critic whether of dress, speech, rowing, behaviour or what not, and yet one profited by it rather than resented it.[4]

That Cuthbertson identified closely with Wilson and was deferential about his own role is indicated in an article on Public School Feeling in the *Annual* for 1876:

Our Head Master has for years striven to instill into those brought under his influence a true sense of honour and consciousness of trust, and by the introduction of 'prefects' has tried to make boys feel that it rests with them as to whether or not their school becomes essentially a place for the fostering of gentlemanly and straight-forward habits.[5]

Most powerfully, Cuthbertson used the magazine to stimulate interest in competitive sport. To Cuthy (or Cuthie), as he was soon generally known (or *C* as he usually signed his writing), work was a game and games were the essence of life. He put an immense amount into them, finding perhaps, as in alcohol, an essential relief from harsher realities. On his own definition of them, he could never lose at games, for it was the playing, not the winning, that mattered. To such a spirit the virtual absence of competitive sport was a blight upon the school, which he strove single-handed to remove. In December 1875, in what was described as the match of the season, Geelong Grammar played cricket in Melbourne for the first time since 1858, soundly beating Melbourne Grammar, who had until then been undefeated. Cuthbertson, who had been a member of his own school eleven, was coach, and he used the occasion to launch an editorial campaign to get the school to purchase its own cricket ground. Similarly in football, although it seems unlikely that he was coach, the light blue challenged the dark blue and by defeating them in Melbourne claimed the 'Public Schools' football premiership for 1875'. In that age of innocence the public-school spirit was invoked to enshrine premierships, which sixty years later J. R. Darling found antipathetic to the same ideal (see p. 331). It is possible that Cuthbertson, who was one of three masters on the football committee in 1877, played in the twenty. Masters were quite eligible to do so. Verses he wrote in the *Annual* for 1875 contain a reference to the involvement of Melbourne Grammar staff in a football match:

[4] C. Belcher, reminiscence, archives.
[5] *Annual*, 1876, p. 300.

44

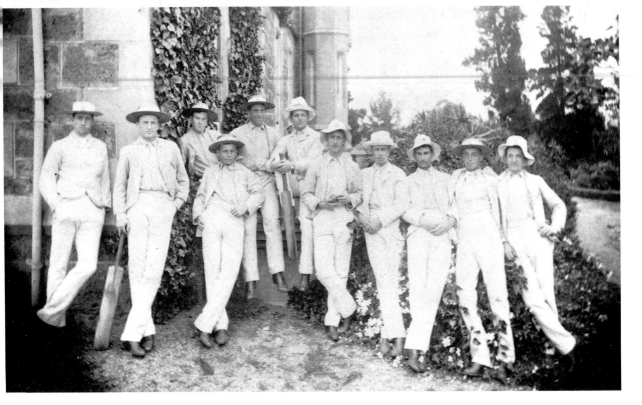

The cricketers of 1886.

The game became faster, their 'junior master'
        Is bowled like a ninepin all over the place,
And white's become darker, and many a marker
        Has signs of a 'purler' or two on his face.[6]

Yet what most stimulated *C*'s poetry and most aroused his sporting passion was rowing, at which he had had some experience at Oxford and from which he gained immense satisfaction. Rowing had been introduced among a small group of boarders the year before he came (see p. 118), but again it was under him in 1875 that a crew began training for the Public Schools' Cup. In this case defeat was a victory for the spirit of competition:

It was said by some that the crew should not have competed at all after losing Cole,* but we are perfectly certain that every Grammar School boy would rather see his School beaten than unrepresented.[7]

That 'we are perfectly certain' was a rhetorical device Cuthbertson often used to commit his readers to the ethos he preached. He offered them no room to doubt that sportsmanship came before victory. It was, importantly, exactly the line Wilson is reported to have constantly urged upon his boys. As *C* wrote of a great football match in 1877:

That match with the College,
        The best one of all
Although we were beaten
        And went to the wall.[8]

---

[6] *Barwon Ballads*, p. 300.
[7] *Annual*, 1875, p. 4.
[8] *Quarterly*, Dec. 1877, p. 18.

* The number three oar, in a crew of four, who contracted measles ten days before the race.

Daring young men in dazzling uniforms: the footballers, 1886.

On the river a special freedom was achieved through discipline, and he took great delight in young men straining to perfect their technique and to cement their fellowship in the rhythm that drove the boat. He wanted them to be alive to every movement they had to make.

> 'Time, now, and listen for the rattle of the row-locks:
>   Into it and out of it together as you go.
>
> Down to your work—press well against the stretcher—
>   Eyes in the boat—and—Are you ready?—
>   Row!'
>
> 'Row!' and the light oars catch the quiet water;
>   'Row!' and the light craft answers to her crew.
>
> 'Now, the beginning, all of you. And Bow, there,
>   Back straight and arms straight; and further forwards, Two.'[9]

'How he hated talking in the boat', said C. F. Belcher, who remembered his rich vocabulary and eagle eye. He worked his crews hard but was so sensitive to their needs that after one lost race in Melbourne he ran away to cry, not because of the loss but for the great chaps who had put in so much effort.

On the river, too, he extended Wilson's invention, the Saturday Party, always looking as though he had just stepped out of a boat on the Isis. 'Not the least like us young bushwhackers', said one observer. He would be out before first light, making for favourite places, using the adventure to open boys' eyes to nature, which he found immensely stimulating and of which he sang without expatriate yearning.

[9] *Barwon Ballads*, p. 165.

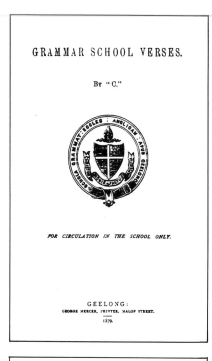

Before the dawn, when all the world was dreaming,
    When clear the white stars shone,
Silent and swift, o'er water darkly gleaming,
    The ebb tide bore us on.

From lake, and creek, and channel, to the ocean
    The weight of water drew,
And like a bird with easy-gliding motion
    Our light craft forward flew.

There was no sound but that sweet magpie chorus
    To greet the coming morn,
But that deep note from seaward pulsing o'er us
    And faintly inland borne.

This is the hour that best we love for rowing,
    In the cool silent night,
Before the cross above the sandhills glowing
    Has paled in morning light.[10]

More will be said in chapter 7 about Cuthbertson's influence on games. At this point what should come through clearly is the range, strength and speed of his impact. It is hard to imagine anyone who was not the headmaster having so great an effect so quickly on a school, and even on the Victorian schools in general, whose rivalry was essential to his purpose. His arrival led to important changes in attitude and organization, beginning in 1875 with the broadening of the competition and the adoption of his suggestion for a new athletics costume. The *Annual* and *Quarterly* carried his ideas to other schools, effectively backing up his face-to-face efforts. In one number of the *Quarterly* in 1877 he argued for a Central Public Schools' Committee to organize sporting fixtures and draw up rules, and in the next he reported its establishment.

At last, it would seem, Wilson had an ally who welcomed responsibility and took initiatives, a master who gave himself fully and effectively to the boys. Whereas Crompton had been scholastically 'about the most valuable master I ever had', Cuthbertson was impressive all round and gained the chief's acquiescence to innovations about which Wilson was hesitant. Almost always they were made in the name of public-school tradition, of which Cuthbertson became the Victorian embodiment. Provincials bowed to his superior insights and within a few years the other schools were upstaged by Geelong Grammar, which combined Wilson's impeccable background, Cuthbertson's true-blue ideals and an upper-crust Western District clientele. Because it was dominated by boarders from 1875, it was able soon to see itself as the only real example of the English public school in Australia. Within a few years that association was cemented by the fame of Old Geelong Grammarian rowers, like Steve Fairbairn, whose success when wearing the original light-blue colours at the great metropolitan university of Cambridge, lent an aura to every light-blue boy who grasped an oar. With Cuthbertson, as it could not have done under Wilson alone, GGS socialized boys into a stimulating though narrow code of values. Because the school was his whole life (and his drinking a substitute for it out of term?), Cuthbertson offered a well-fenced, comforting world of desk, playing-field, camping-ground and river, with boyhood going on for ever.

The force of his opinion had influence even in swimming, where Wilson, very competently, was in charge. After the 1875 *Annual* lamented the virtual absence of the breast-stroke, 'so commended by the Lancet ... and proved to be so effective, at least in long distances, by the remarkable performance of Captain Webb', Cuthbertson's suggestion that a special cup be given for a long-distance breast-stroke event was adopted. The result in 1876, when compared to the Australian crawl, was a very slow time.

Of more substance was his introduction of 'fives', an ancient, aristocratic game, whose 'sole nurseries', according to the *Britannica*, were the universities and the great public schools, some of which had developed their own rules, which were valued as an essential tradition. Eton fives, for instance, was taken to other parts of England by devotees who ordered the construction of facsimiles of the particular buttressed wall at Eton where the little balls had, at first idly, been hit. At Geelong nothing flash like that could be done. Even the modest expenditure Cuthbertson campaigned for in the first *Annual* was held up:

> We believe we are right in saying that we are the first school in Victoria which has made this game one of its regular school amusements. Hitherto we have played on rough ground and against a rough wall, but the new court will be ready for play after Christmas, and we may look for a great improvement in our mode of playing the game. It would be advisable if a keeper of the new court were appointed, and if permission to play were given by him according to priority of application; and a Junior and Senior Fives Cup should be established, and played for before the beginning of the cricket season.[11]

It was not until 1880 that an asphalt surface in the quad gave 'a marvellous impetus to Fives', which were played, we are told, on every available bit of wall and on every available occasion from sunrise to sunset. Cuthbertson must have been delighted. He had been the only master regularly involved and had been one of the team of two who played in the first outside match, against Melbourne University, in 1877. Wilson, on the other hand, might have asked himself whether he had given way too much to Cuthbertson's enthusiasm. The reminiscence of a boy who left in 1875 leaves no doubt about his attitude then.

> We were banished from our study and 'quadded' for a week. It was a nasty blow for us. No cricket, no rowing, no Saturday Excursions during the term of our sentence, so for the next few days in play hours, he and I were seen disconsolately playing a sort of bastard 'fives' with a tennis ball against the wall of the quad. There was nothing on which the Boss had a greater down than the game of 'Fives' as we played it at the school. He had passed through the quad a few times and seen us at it. Perhaps on the second or third day of our exile as he was going out he saw us again at the game. He stopped and said 'What are you fellows doing here, playing that abominable game? Why don't you go out into the field and have a decent game of cricket?'[12]

[11] *Annual*, 1875, p. 7.
[12] E. S. Jackson, reminiscence, archives.

The case being built up for Cuthbertson's astonishing influence, which is based on a penetrating study by Fay Marles, has one further and probably cardinal aspect, the cult of boarder superiority in the school. What we know of Wilson suggests an even-handed treatment of boys, except for a clearly stated preference that he be given them full-time. In a most unusual arrangement he tried (what Darling much later insisted upon) to get day boys to stay for the evening meal and supervised prep, and he felt that weekly boarding was imperfect because it broke the continuity of the school's influence. He probably thought that the experience they gained exploring the bush and fending for themselves on Saturday Parties was an excellent education in independence and that Sundays were profitably spent as a family at church, Bible study and quiet reading. He had also allowed boarders to organize an exclusive boat club. There is therefore a strong indication that day boys were of inferior status before 1875.

But after Cuthbertson came they were much worse off. For more than ten years, when only boarders were made prefects, no day boy could achieve 'the highest and most honourable office a boy could obtain within the school'. Whether or not prefects were most beneficial in the boarding-house, as the *Quarterly* suggested when reviewing the system in 1896, the outcome was discrimination against day boys, which was even more pronounced in sporting teams. If games were the life of the school, as Cuthy often suggested, the absence of day boys from the committees which ran them and the selection of a strong majority of boarders in all teams except swimming, where Wilson was in control, must be a sign of discrimination. Fay Marles compiled the following table for the years 1875—77:

Table of day boy—boarder ratios in all areas of school activity between 1875 and 1877

Activity	1875 D	1875 B	1876 D	1876 B	1877 D	1877 B
Total in 5th and 6th forms	17	18	16	17	14	14
Prefects	0	6	0	9	0	7
Crew	0	4	0	4	0	4
Football	6	14	5	18	6	14
Cricket	2	10	3	8	2	9
Aths	7	25	9	44	18	49
Inter-school aths	0	15	2	16	1	12
Swimming	9	6	9	8	11	5
Matriculated	5	6	4	3	5	2
Academic prizes	31	24	24	29	36	26
Special prizes	1	25	5	24	9	31
Sports committees	0	14	0	14	0	17

Clerical founders:
top left, The Very Reverend
Hussey Burgh Macartney, Dean
of Melbourne.

GEORGE A. J. WEBB

top right, The Venerable
Theodore Carlos Benoni
Stretch, Archdeacon of
Geelong.

DENNIS RAMSAY

lower, The Right Reverend
Charles Perry, Bishop of
Melbourne.

W. B. McINNES

It would be hard to argue that, with equal numbers of day boys and boarders at the top of the school, boarders would have been so much more skilful that they dominated the cricket, football and athletics, especially as we know that in 1873 five of the eight names on trophies won at the United Public Schools' athletic sports were those of day boys.

What the table shows is borne out by reminiscences. Reginald Stephen (1869–77) puts the basic point:

Unfortunately I was not a boarder, and only a boarder can gain full knowledge or gain full benefit from school life. The boarder knows this and feels if not contempt rather pity for his less fortunate brothers ... I have only one regret and that is that I was not a boarder to gain the full school life.[13]

What he accepted with regret, T. J. Allen (1871–75) regarded as a reprehensible persecution:

To the shame of the authorities be it said that though day scholars were admitted, even angled for, they were as a class apart, were not allowed to wear the school badge and were 'not wanted' in cricket and football, though compelled to go down to the ground on half holidays.

I sincerely hope that pernicious feeling has been stamped out.[14]

In the outcome there was a division not so much into first and second as into first and fourth class citizens, which hastened the ultimate domination of the school by boarders. Quite rapidly day boys opted out. Except for a brief period in 1884–85, they became a small minority. During 1875 their numbers shrank from seventy to fifty-five and, despite the rejuvenation of scholarship, they stayed away, frozen out by a combination of Wilson's family emphasis and Cuthbertson's passion for the English boarding model. It appears that Cuthbertson transformed Wilson's underlying, though not active, prejudice against day boys into an exclusion from the centre of school life and feeling. They were outsiders allowed the privilege of participation in certain aspects only of its life.

As a final indignity, day boys were not allowed to wear the school badge, which Cuthbertson introduced in those days before there was a school uniform, as the only possible distinguishing mark. Again he worked on schoolboy opinion through the school magazine:

It is proposed that all boys shall wear round their caps, the school ribbon with a mitre, as a distinguishing badge of the school, sewn on to it. This would look well, particularly with straw hats, and we shall hail with delight the disappearance of the peculiar head-coverings adopted by some of us.[15]

There was no compulsion. Wilson issued no decrees about dress, and as boys were conservative, Cuthbertson had to follow up the original idea by appealing to the trend-setters to start the fashion:

We hope that some decided action will be taken to carry out the project mentioned as regards caps, and would suggest to the prefects the advisability of setting the example of wearing the school ribbon, etc.[16]

Left:
The Reverend George Oakley Vance, Headmaster 1855–60.

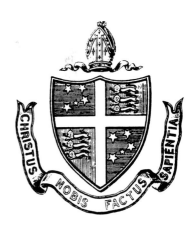

[13] R. Stephen, reminiscence, archives.
[14] T. J. Allen, reminiscence, archives.
[15] *Annual*, 1875, p. 35.
[16] *Quarterly*, Apr. 1877, p. 19.

51

His own absorption with the mystique is indicated by a portrait showing him in cap and badge, a truly cult figure.

That may be the most accurate impression—Cuthbertson as the cult figure alongside Wilson, the 'boss', the 'chief', the manager. Nothing can fully reconstruct their relationship, but it can be inferred that, because of his disability, 'Cuthy' could not have become the legend he did without Wilson's compassion and support. So, in the same breath as it can be argued that Wilson needed Cuthbertson's magic for the full development of the school, there is little doubt that, without Wilson, the younger man would have foundered—which he did, despite his good intentions, when Wilson died in 1895 and the prop on which he depended was removed. He wrote revealingly to Wilson's widow:

No man I think ever had a higher sense of right and wrong and no man ever devoted himself so wholly to his work and stamped his mark so clearly on the characters of those who were under his influence. Though, with some shame I write it, I was often untrue to him, I yet loved him well, yes from the first moment when he took me by the hand and helped me along twenty years ago. I do hope and pray that I may with God's help keep this vow I made by his bedside on the morning of his death and that it may be allowed me to be in some measure what he was to the boys of the school. I cannot be what he was I know very well, but I can and will try to honour him by endeavouring to follow in his footsteps. I know, none knows better, how entirely unworthy I am to be even for a brief space in his position and if it was not for the hope of a better life I could not look the boys in the face.[17]

The suggestion here is that on his death-bed Wilson made Cuthbertson promise that he would give up drink and continue the influence they had shared. It is charged with pathos, for Cuthbertson could not stand alone. Despite his intellect, he completed only a pass degree at Oxford when he took leave from 1882 to 1885 and went back to England to recover his scholastic fortunes and perhaps prepare for a headmastership. Under Wilson's successor, he lasted only a year.

It says much about the school that a man so flawed was allowed to give it so much, and that in a tradition of 'Cuthy duty' senior boys in his later years made sure that he was safely in bed at night. In the same way, according to Stephen, the boys of the 1870s had learned Christian forgiveness and steered him past public houses. 'We saw his fault but knew he hated it and we loved him for his efforts to conquer it.'

Boys, universally, loved 'Cuthy'. When Donald Mackinnon, the leader of his generation and the prime mover for a new leap forward by the school in the 1930s, spoke at the launching of the memorial edition of C's *Barwon Ballads*, published by the old boys in 1910, his mind went back to his own boyhood in the upper fifth of 1875, when Cuthbertson arrived and began traditions that Mackinnon later strove to maintain:

His history for us began on the day he came to this school and it should continue as long as the school does. To us . . . though many years have rolled between, he remains a real living entity and though dead, he is still with us while we cumber this earth. What, let us ask, is the secret of his influence? He loved boys, he loved truth and honour and manliness; he loved our games, he loved the way we played them. His presence was a constant oxygen in our school life. All the things he loved are embalmed in those verses which he wrote for us and which shall be our possession forever. It was this great love which built up what corporate school sentiment we have.[18]

J. L. Cuthbertson, the face of the poet.

Modern medical research suggested to Marles that Cuthbertson, using drink as a way of coping with his sexuality, was an alcoholic. She notes the lack of romantic love in his poetry, cites Lindon's opinion that in the normal sense he was sexless, never really looking at a woman, and believes that the intense emotional relationships he developed with his pupils caused tensions that, within his moral framework, only drinking could relieve.

'I heard some comment on his having favourites, though I saw no instance of it', reported Charles Belcher (1886–93); and no hint of an accusation of anything else than having favourites has come from the multitude who knew him. Through the thicket of legend one sees a romantic individual who was able under Wilson to sublimate his passion and who, during the whole period of his service, though less in the middle of it, went away to desensitize himself with heavy drinking during the emptiness when the boys were on holidays. He wrote nothing to explain himself,* except that everything he wrote about the school shows that, rather than for specific boys, his chief love was for the life of Geelong Grammar School.

Cuthbertson was able, through his association with Wilson, to articulate more clearly than Arnold himself that great headmaster's vision of a school as an ideal society offering its members challenging opportunities for personal growth:

> The True Republic
> Who is our Leader? He who works
> The hardest and who never shirks.
> Who is the freest? He who shows
> That he the worth of freedom knows.
> Whom do we trust in? Those we must
> Confide in who have earned the trust.
> Who holds no place upon our roll?
> The laggard and the sluggard soul.
> Who do the honours most deserve?
> They only who will gladly serve—
> They win the praise and hold the rule
> In the Republic of the School.[19]

The concept of the school as a republic was daring and certainly not Arnoldian. It expresses an Australian attitude and suggests the special experience Australia had offered to the young poet who had given himself to Geelong Grammar and had found himself through it.

---

* In 'Christus Consolator' he expressed the belief that the Son of Man did not come to those who fear no danger and who know no doubt, but to the afflicted—the weak, the sad, the lonely and the sorrow-laden souls.

[18] *Quarterly*, Dec. 1910, p. 18.
[19] *Barwon Ballads*, p. 149.

The old chief

The old chief, *c.* 1890.

Wilson had seven great years from 1875 to 1881. Cuthbertson was at his peak before taking leave of absence in England from 1882 to 1885, and rheumatism had not greatly restricted his own activities. But even at the highest point of Wilson's enrolments, the 150 of May 1879, the school had nowhere near reached its planned capacity of 250. Despite their heavy spending, the founders had given him deficient buildings on a tiny piece of ground and Wilson partly at his own expense, partly by soliciting gifts had to work extremely hard, with very little help from the board, to add a gymnasium, a laboratory, extra classrooms, a cottage hospital and the distant cricket ground, as well as to supply beds, bedding and furniture for the booming boarding-house (see pp. 85–7).

Compared to twentieth-century schools it was a small operation, and was suited to Wilson's family approach. Even so, the boarders overflowed, as the following table shows. In the second half of 1878 they passed eighty for the first time and reached a peak of ninety-four in August 1880, far more than at any other school in Victoria. Failing to get the impecunious board to provide more accomodation, Wilson rented a nearby house, but only briefly because numbers fell below eighty again in June 1881.

Average numbers of boarders, day boys and total enrolments 1875–95*

Year	Boarder	Day	Total	Year	Boarder	Day	Total
1875	68	60	128	1886	65	27	92
1876	70	60	130	1887	59	28	87
1877	69	58	127	1888	48	28	76
1878	80	60	140	1889	58	29	87
1879	90	54	144	1890	73	35	108
1880	90	42	132	1891	72	29	101
1881	78	41	119	1892	68	21	89
1882	74	32	106	1893	60	19	79
1883	78	28	106	1894	45	43	88
1884	76	28	104	1895	47	40	87
1885	68	25	93	Average	68.4	37.5	105.9

* The figures are given quarterly in the minutes of the board of management.

In hindsight, too, the years from 1875 to 1881 were of more than immediate importance; from them came most of an energetic group of old boys who moved the school and reconstituted it in the twentieth century (see chapter 8). They had known Wilson and Cuthbertson at the height of their joint achievement, when Wilson was free of immediate pressure for the reduction of the debt, confident that his methods worked and warmed by the appreciation of his pupils.

What mere numbers do not reveal is the roll-call of the scions of the Western District—the Mackinnons, Fairbairns, Armytages, Manifolds, Chirnsides, Austins, etc.—who brought wealth and social privilege to GGS and received what was not available elsewhere, an aura of gentility. Others might teach, but Wilson and Cuthbertson passed on by precept, example and expectation English gentry values that were successful simply because they were precious to those aspiring squatters who needed social legitimation. If they could not be made into gentlemen scholars, as many could not, at least they would shine in that splendid English tradition of gentlemen sportsmen. In searching for the spirit of the school nothing is so plain as that emphasis. True sportsmen of course, who lost graciously, and men of character who would be ashamed of a mean thought or deed. In that way, although some laughed at its scholastic shortcomings, the school emphasized values in education. As one of Wilson's earliest old boys said:

Sometimes I think he did not make us work hard enough but he certainly made his scholars gentlemen and very few G.G.S. boys have turned out cads, although not all succeeded in life.[1]

What must also be noticed is a great love for the school as a family. Wilson and Cuthbertson spoke man-to-man with boys, treating their concerns and behaviour with a seriousness few schoolmasters achieved and urging them to accept the school as the focus of their lives. Both made boys feel that they were the centre of attention and that reasonableness rather than authority lay behind their decisions. As Canon Goodman perceived it, Wilson knew intuitively how to infuse his own spirit into his staff and prefects so that boys would be able to respond well:

It was not mere imitation, as though he would take Arnold of Rugby as his model, and try to copy his methods. He loved his boys, he instinctively read their minds and characters, and with the most consummate tact knew how to deal with them at all times.[2]

Reminiscences reveal that Wilson sometimes lost his temper and it was well known that Cuthbertson drank, but both won great respect and affection. A generation grew up within their framework of love and a deep concern for truth and honour.

What was characteristic? For the sake of the family, Wilson persuaded some young bloods to dispense with the finery of gold rings, watch chains and tiepins by asking them to think about other

[1] C. Pitman, reminiscence, archives
[2] *Quarterly*, Dec. 1895, p. 14.

boys who might feel downgraded by their presence. For the sake of the family, he delighted in sporting victories and was forthright in praising the whole school when it had pleased him. With individuals he was creative. One boy caught in a lie was sent to Wilson's 'wonderful old booklined study' where, far from the corporal punishment he feared, he felt the headmaster's rheumatic hand on his shoulder and heard a quiet voice explain what he had done wrong and ask him to promise never to lie again. More than that, Mrs Wilson chanced to come in and after asking, 'Oh, Bracebridge, what's the matter with the laddie?', and being told that something had been wrong that was now right, took the boy in her arms, kissed him and said that she was sure it would be.

In the same way as the *Quarterly* assumed a knowledge of *Tom Brown's Schooldays*, Wilson may have been strengthened by the example of Dr Arnold to temper the natural loftiness of his role as 'the boss' or 'the chief' with the closeness of a special father–son relationship. At least within his study and during private encounters he used boys' first names, and he allowed them freedom, physically and morally. He preferred boys without studies to bank their money, as an insurance against theft and false accusations of theft, and as a curb on rash spending; but he did not force his opinion. About half the school made use of their honorary bank manager, accountant, teller and ledger-keeper, who sat at his desk every morning after breakfast, cash-box and ledger in front of him, paying and receiving. He had the knack of finding out, because of his interest in them, what boys were doing. Angus Greenfield gave a good example when he recalled Wilson quizzing him about not playing, as he usually did, for the Geelong football team one Saturday. Wilson insisted that he should always be told of even a minor injury (it had been a sore toe) that kept him out.

He ruled by kindness and by appealing to a boy's better nature, as Steve Fairbairn, a natural rebel who had already been expelled from Wesley, recalled. Talking on one occasion to Steve and his brother Tom, Wilson declared, 'Tom, if all boys were like you, no discipline would be necessary and Steve, if all boys were like you, no discipline would be any use'. Steve's school career was a procession of serious troubles until one night Wilson came to the end of his patience. Not angry, but grieving, he said, 'Stevie, I don't know what to do with you. I love you as a son but I can't keep you. You are destroying the discipline of the school'. The thought of 'the boss' caring for him and despairing because of him was a new one for Steve, who like many a tamed rebel became before long a firm supporter of law and order.

Within the territory of trust all kinds of things could and did happen. Honour was often sorely tried, not just through the pranks of a strong-willed Steve Fairbairn, or the madness of throwing lighted matches to test a gas leak in the ceiling, or stealing the duty master's supper, but by quite open bending of morality. Such a case was the

J. B. Wilson's purse.

cheating that kept a popular sportsman (probably A. M. Greenfield) above the 30 per cent needed to avoid an encounter with 'the boss'. The sportsman was the idol of his peers—tall, well-built, skilful and unselfish, a splendid, happy creature who seemed to be unmoved by study. The boys regarded it as a matter of honour to supply him with answers during exams and masters turned a blind eye, although there was sudden death if anyone else was involved.

Although, as he told them, he was happy to trust them and risk being let down, and although his ideal when he set out in 1863 was to rule by kindness, Wilson did beat boys. A case in the 1870s is mentioned on page 122. Those who lied or cheated were invariably caned. Among snippets of evidence about his practice there is T. Aylesbury Brown's recollection of only once seeing the tawse in the five years he was at school between 1889 and 1893. Even so, it was used with vigour a horrifying twelve times to each hand of a boy who had been impertinent to a master. Wilson, who had limped to the classroom to give the strap, sent the boy to his dormitory, from where, apparently, he packed himself off home.

Like Arnold of Rugby, he used the prefects as his hot-line to the boys, quite separate from the more formal approach through the staff. As one boy remembered of 1889, this was not done without a pragmatic awareness of their shortcomings. He assembled the prefects at his bedside (the poor man's gout had laid him low) and charged them to act as under masters, revealing that he knew quite well that most of them smoked and played up in their studies, because he had heard the boy keeping nit call out, 'Here comes Old Charlie'. With a disarming frankness, he said that he had come to quite like his nickname. They said that they would do their best and often went as a group to see him.

There was in that reliance on prefects (in part what Cuthbertson called in his poem 'the Republic of the School') a soft underbelly to his morality. Or maybe it was the same 'leave it to them' philosophy as he expressed in his 1863 prospectus about there being no demeaning system of espionage in the playground. He trusted the primitive justice of the peer group and in 1893 did not want to know the name of a boy the prefects had been told to catch after the school honour board had been mutilated. With repressive measures, including the gating of the whole school, they found their culprit, took him to the prefects' room, and while two at a time held him down, all seven took it in turns to give him three cuts with a cane.

As Wilson told the school at one of his special heart-to-heart assemblies at the end of first term 1887, boys had two lives, one known to him, the other known only to themselves. He explained that he did not pry and spy because the essence of a public school was that they should be treated as gentlemen and have a large confidence placed in them. It might be thought very easy to put one over him, but that was only if they had no honour.

The honour of the school was regarded as its most precious possession, and the quality of the boys it turned out was seen as its

58

great contribution to the development of the colony of Victoria. 'As I have often said before', Wilson observed in 1891, 'we seek to emulate the public schools of England, and there are some features of public school life in which we are not very far behind'. By that he particularly meant that there were old boys all over the world who looked back with pride to their schooldays, that present boys felt it a 'hateful and vile thing' for a boy to lower the tone and tradition of his school and that generations to come would be influenced by its life. This, as Cuthbertson also recognized, needed neither ancient buildings nor a long history, merely subservience of self to a noble code of honour.

Whether they had achieved it or not was part of a constant soul-searching. Yet how would they know? Expressing a typical colonial cringe with, 'What do they think of us?', Cuthbertson speculated in 1877 about the opinions of those voyaging 'invalids of status' (healthy men of privilege stayed home) who came to the colony and formed judgements about its streets, shops, clubs, parliament, schools and university. While he considered that the university was promising, that the clubs might pass muster and that the lower-house parliamentarians were better not mentioned, he saw the schools, especially those of the Church of England, as exemplary—'of none of our institutions have we more hope than of these schools and none would we more fearlessly submit to the inspection of the cultured traveller'. As long, that is, as the boys did not open their mouths, for we are told elsewhere that a life up-country among shepherds and bushmen had given them loud and harsh voices.

Cuthbertson would have been delighted to show his invalid of status the Saturday Parties going free all day and the noble sportsmen at their honorific games. As Wilson's chief aim had always been character-building, Cuthbertson's special emphasis on games underlined his approach. 'It might be practicable', Wilson said again in 1895, 'for a day school to excel at examination results and leave character-building to parents, but a school like ours must use the playground as well as the schoolroom to develop character'. He was glad that the other headmasters sided with him against Dr Alexander Morrison of Scotch, who wanted to play his rivals once instead of twice a year in each sport. That, thought Wilson, would give too little opportunity to sow acts and reap habits; sow habits and reap character; sow character and reap destiny. Rivalry, to him, was a great stimulus and eight hours' work—the famous Victorian labour movement achievement— was quite enough. More would be bad for health. 'Believe me', he said, 'the fresh open air and the joyous game . . . furnish the only alternative to brain work'.

Former pupils also defended this position. In 1883, during the period of sporting success that followed Cuthbertson's arrival (which was very like Adamson's early years at Wesley), the *Quarterly* quoted an old boy's 'trenchant and true' reply to 'enemies of the school' who tried to 'prejudice parents against us' by saying that 'we turn out athletes and gentlemen but not scholars', and went on to discuss the

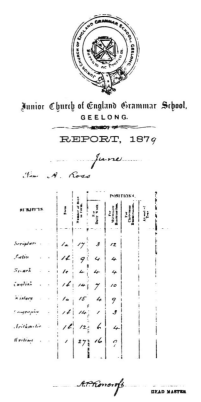

Junior Church of England Grammar School,
GEELONG.

REPORT, 1879

June

Name *A. Ross*

SUBJECTS			POSITIONS	
Scripture	1a	17	3	12
Latin	1c	9	4	4
French	1c	6	4	4
English	1b	14	7	10
History	1a	15	4	9
Composition	1b	14	1	3
Arithmetic	1b	12	6	4
Writing	1	27	16	9

A. P. Kennedy

HEAD MASTER

Church of England Grammar School.

HEAD MASTER'S REPORT,
1878.

Read on the occasion of the Distribution of Prizes, Dec. 19th.

MY LORD, LADIES AND GENTLEMEN,

I suppose you have all had sufficient experience of mountain climbing to know how pleasant it is to reach a level spot, and to rest; then to look downwards at the road you have passed, and upwards and forwards to the onward track.

So is it with us now. Our work is laborious but not unpleasant, the air is bracing and healthy, and we are constantly striving to rise to a higher and yet a higher level. We have now reached a resting-place, and on turning to look back we see much good work done, and many pleasant and gratifying features in the past school year. On looking upwards also and forward, " *Sursum ac prorsum,*" we see much yet to conquer, and a far higher level yet to be attained.

On the whole I have cause to be well satisfied with the working of the school during the year now past, and I thank my Masters, one and all, for their zealous devotion to their duties, and yet more for their unvarying cordiality towards myself.

The Honour List, which I will now read with your permission, records the position and the successes of our former pupils at the various universities :—

The Course of Instruction

Is equally adapted for the learned professions or for commerce. In the higher Forms the subjects taught and the books used are selected with especial reference to the requirements of the Melbourne University.

Boarding Establishment.

The Grammar School Building (one of the finest of its kind in Victoria) offers many advantages to parents who desire for their boys a healthy and quiet residence, in addition to the best teaching. It is situated on elevated ground, and at a convenient distance from the busy part of the town. The class-rooms are numerous, large, and well ventilated; the bed-rooms are airy and comfortable. There is a large bath-room, with every convenience for shower-baths, &c. The School is unsurpassed in the Colony as a healthy residence.

The climate, the position on the borders of Corio Bay, the facilities for travelling by railway and steamer, and the quietness of the town itself, render Geelong particularly well adapted for the site of a public school on the model of the public schools of England.

There is an excellent LABORATORY, with all necessary appliances for the use of the class in Practical Chemistry.

The SURVEYING CLASS takes lessons in the field, in the use of the Theodolite and Level.

A spacious GYMNASIUM, fitted up with the best apparatus is attached to the School, and the Gymnastic Class is under a skilful and experienced instructor.

There is a covered PLAYING SHED, and a COTTAGE HOSPITAL detached entirely from the main building.

There is a PLAYING FIELD of ten acres belonging to the School, in which an excellent cricket pitch has been formed.

The SCHOOL ROWING CLUB affords abundance of healthy exercise for the resident pupils. The Club possesses a boat-shed of its own upon the banks of the Barwon, an eight-oar, and four four-oared racing and practice boats, and two pleasure boats.

One of the large class-rooms is set apart during play hours for the purposes of a READING ROOM; here the Boarders can always retire to read undisturbed; and they have access to a large and well-selected Library.

criticism that the public schools, with the support of the press, pandered to a popular Australian taste for sport. In fact, it was pointed out, school fixtures had decreased from twelve cricket and football matches in 1880 to ten in 1881 and six in 1882 and crews had only raced eight times in three years. This was half the commitment of most English schools and fewer than colonial rivals. The real reason for success at sport was an efficient use of time and the spirit of the boarders. At 4 p.m. they were free to go to flat or river, and on Saturdays and holidays they returned from the bush weary in limb but with reinvigorated brain. No day school could match that dedication or fitness.

Wilson was not aiming to do what other schools did, and he left parents in no doubt about his intentions. He sought a manly independence, the ability to accept challenges and a toughness as well as decorum that suited the unscholarly. Boys like Steve Fairbairn who were bright as well as athletic had no difficulty in completing an Oxford, Cambridge or Melbourne degree. Like the girls at Merton Hall under Dorothy Ross in the 1940s and 1950s, they were flexible and self-propelled. What critics of a relatively low proportion of boys achieving matriculation did not understand was that by and large the future of the clientele of GGS did not depend on their scholarship. Indeed, through Wilson, the gentleman-scholar with a world reputation in botanical research,* the school was free from the materialism of the middle class. The latter dominated the commercial cities of the new world and put such store in examination results that a system devised to select university undergraduates has dominated education in Australia. It was not, however, free from the assumptions of a ruling class. Cuthbertson certainly, and Wilson probably, nodded approval when Charlie Fairbairn, with George and Tom beside him, rode in the vanguard of Queensland pastoralists, organizing scab labour and defying the striking shearers in 1891. At the risk of his life he is said to have saved many others. The capitalist side was the side of Australian history for Geelong Grammar School, preserving ancient English notions of the rights of property and freedom of contract between employer and employee against the more recent rights of labour and the power of a well-organized working class. Charlie Fairbairn, the outstanding prefect of 1875, had been prepared for his later role in the corridors of the old gray school. After he left, whenever anything serious was amiss, masters could be heard saying, 'If only Charlie Fairbairn were here'. To which Wilson is reported to have said, 'Damn Charlie Fairbairn'. He always wanted the present to take care of itself and a new group of boys to face the eternal challenges.

The past did not come up to expectations. After a strong

---

* In 1887, as a result of his long-term interest and his great collection of sponges, Wilson became a foundation member of the Port Phillip Biological Survey Committee. He collaborated with the noted biologist and anthropologist Baldwin Spencer in the discovery of a new family of marine hydroids, which Spencer named after him. (Mulvaney and Calaby, *So Much That Is New*, pp. 98, 151)

statement about the importance of old boys to the school, the *Quarterly* of July 1882 (noting that English schools had old-boy societies) offered a page to publicize their activities and achievements. Claiming them even more strongly, the December 1885 *Quarterly* called for stronger links between present and past and suggested that old boys had a sacred duty to revere their Alma Mater—to see it as a 'throned lady whose bright colours like the knights of old they must wear between their hearts and armour'. It supported that romantic view with reports of their doings at the universities of Melbourne, Oxford and Cambridge and revealed their whereabouts up-country and interstate. Nevertheless, despite having a strong committee of 1860s and 1870s boarders, an Old Geelong Grammarians' society, founded in 1883, was short-lived. It has to be assumed that there was little support for the aims of its prospectus:

The bicycle club, 1881, on the tennis court to the north of the main building, with the gymnasium in the background.

To unite all old boys into one body, interested in the past reputation, present success and future progress of the school; and to preserve in the minds of old boys a memory of school days and school friends and facilitate social meetings at convenient seasons.[3]

61

Officers and NCOs, 1907,
Colonel Garrard in command,
Sgt, Major Webb on the right
flank.

An attempt by a group at Trinity College at the University of
Melbourne in 1897 also failed. Perhaps they were reaping the fruits
of the emphasis on boarders, who were now scattered across vast
distances, making it hard to organize dinners and smoke nights.
Only 18 per cent were living in Melbourne and the 36 per cent in
Geelong were the alienated 'day cads'.

There was clearly a gap, which must be taken seriously, between
rhetoric and performance. The roots of the school family had not
struck deep. Calls for scholarship endowment fell on deaf ears in
1877 and 1882, despite an attempt at the latter date to shame
potential benefactors into action by reporting that MGS and Wesley
had several scholarships and that St Peter's, Adelaide, had as many
as four of £50 each and a total of £300. In 1896 only one scholarship
was in place; the 'Mary Armytage', it supported an old boy for three
years at Trinity College, Melbourne.

Apart from Cuthbertson, the master old boys remembered most
clearly and affectionately was A. F. Garrard, nicknamed 'Boots', a
tall, commanding figure with the resonant voice of a parade-ground
disciplinarian. He joined the staff in 1883 but had always wanted to
be a soldier and found great satisfaction in the militia. As captain,
then major, he commanded the school cadet corps, which he helped
to establish in 1884 and inspired with patriotism and a love of rifle-
shooting and drill competitions (see pp. 125—7). Distinctly
Australian from accent to attitudes, he had been educated at Geelong
College and was one of the few masters who had roamed the bush
from his youth and who shared without reserve the enthusiasm of
Saturday Parties, especially when they went nesting. He was a good
companion, having the knack of taking boys into his confidence and,
like Cuthbertson, talking easily to them at their level. He loved
games; Charles Belcher remembered him about 1892, outswimming
any boy over 180 yards at the Eastern Baths. A good teacher, he had
charge of the lower sixth in Belcher's day.

While that heartiness and charisma were the norm, one master,
at least, proved a contrast. He was little known outside the classroom
and never on a Saturday Party, although sometimes seen on the river
in a scull. This was Arthur 'Jarps' Morris, prudent, precise, solitary
and generally regarded as the best teacher in the school at the end of
Wilson's period. He came as senior English master in 1889. The
embodiment of his own easily-remembered lessons, he was dry, clear
and a mild but effective disciplinarian, and warm within the precincts of
the classroom. His nickname came in a typically schoolboy way from
the resemblance his round face and short brown beard gave him to a
circus clown called Jo Jo. Through the practice of adding 'arp' to
every element of their speech, boys soon turned Jo Jo into Jarpo
Jarpo and eventually—through the habit of adding 's' to everything
and an inevitable shortening—it became Jarps.

Men like W. E. P. Austin, who came in 1886 and stayed
initially for only three years, despite Wilson's attempts to keep him,

Officers and NCOs, 1888.

Assistant masters on the steps of the headmaster's house, 1881.

were greatly valued. The *Quarterly* bade him farewell in 1889 as the best oarsman and rowing coach the school had had. He was an honours graduate of Oxford, captain of the Magdalen Boat Club and reserve for the Oxford crew of 1883. Remembered, too, for his fine singing voice at the Saturday night 'Pastime', especially when he broke into 'Jolly Boating Weather', he came back as head of the junior school in 1890 and was later headmaster of the choir school at St Paul's Cathedral, Melbourne. Another young man, trained for the law, made a great impact during a short stay before he went to Sydney as a solicitor. Through Wilson's influence, one assumes, that close-knit community welcomed suitable newcomers warmly and enabled them to make an immediate contribution.

Turnover of staff outside a core of three or four was always high. Wilson dutifully reported resignations and replacements to the board, sometimes assuring them that he had a man who was in all respects efficient, sometimes revealing that he had a good scholar but no disciplinarian. He was happy to say, following the appointment of Patterson as mathematics master in 1888 and Cuthbertson's return from three months' leave, that classics and mathematics had been raised to their proper level. In 1894 he received the congratulations of the board for excellent reports from the staff, and towards the end of the year he was overjoyed at the state of the school. Not only was the health of the boys excellent but their conduct and the efficiency of their masters was 'good beyond anything he had seen in a long experience of school life'.

The personality of 'Old Charlie', 'the boss', 'the old chief', remained dominant. A tallish figure in cap and gown, hobbling with a stick across the quad from his study to take roll-call in the Big Schoolroom at nine in the morning, his grey beard tossing to the characteristic shake of his head and the flash of his blue eyes when he was annoyed, he was as commanding as ever. His fine face and pleasant, cultured voice still captured them. Despite a growing vagueness about boys' names and less grip on the details of their lives, he was wonderfully responsive to the needs of individuals.

Towards the end of his headmastership, although fighting the board over financial matters, Wilson was relaxed and confident that the school was achieving his objectives. Because of the depression which began to bite in 1892, day-boy numbers were below seventy in 1893 but they rose the following year, compensating for a sharp reduction in boarders, whose numbers dipped for a while to the level of the 1860s. For almost a year day boys outnumbered boarders (an unheard of thing). Fewer boys would have made it easier for a crippled Wilson to keep in touch. In 1891 he read the examination papers of every boy in the school and checked the way they had been marked; that formidable task cannot be associated with a headmaster who was in decline. As he had often done, he also asked E. H. Sugden, the Master of Queen's College in the University of Melbourne, to check the papers and the marking and to assess the performance of

64

Wilson on his velocipede with members of the Bicycle Club, 1883.

the school as a whole. Dr Sugden was satisfied. He thought that the matriculation form was up to standard, especially in English with 'Jarps' Morris, where only one boy among thirty failed.

For a school not aiming to be purely academic this was satisfactory, but there was always tension in boys who sought examination success. While there was nothing in Sugden's report to cause alarm, there was also no commendation of scholarship. Only neatness, hand-writing and map-making were exemplary. For a boy who had to get on through his own ability the atmosphere could be daunting. C. H. Birdsey remembered being regarded with scorn when he came as a new boy in 1890 from the Matthew Flinders School. He wanted to work in his free time but could find nowhere to go, until the sub-prefects offered him the shelter of their room. That was probably the atmosphere throughout Wilson's era. H. Speed, who was at school from 1876 to 1882, thought that the standard of scholarship was appalling. Apart from the inertia of the squatters' sons, Wilson's endeavour to educate for life, rather than cram for exams, seemed useless to a boy who knew he had to make his own way. He asked his father to move him.

Geelong Grammar applauded the broadening of matriculation in 1881. The *Quarterly* had campaigned for it since April 1879, when what was a long-standing desire of colonial headmasters was being raised with the university. With the timelessness of a debate that would underlie changes from VUSEB to VISE to VACE and the further liberalization of the curriculum a hundred years later, the *Quarterly* pointed to the dilemma that the matriculation examination was failing to act as both a test for university entrance and a general certificate of a pupil's readiness to leave school. At that time there

Rowing up the headmaster's steps—the cox in no position to steer—is the 1888 crew with coaches J. L. Cuthbertson (left) and W. E. P. Austin.

was also the confusion of a concurrent exam for entrance to the civil service. Both examinations promoted 'cram' and engendered an unhealthy competition between schools for acknowledgement by the press as leaders in scholarship. What the reforms achieved, when they emerged from the university senate and council, was a broadening of the traditional diet of Greek, Latin, modern languages and maths to include physics and chemistry, physiology and botany, history and geography. At last, the *Quarterly* thought, lower forms would be given time for the new subjects and greater relevance would result. It regretted, nevertheless, that more attention was not paid to biology and geology, through which Saturday Parties would receive extra meaning, by bringing home specimens for examination through the microscope, or searching for new plant-forms, or prospecting for minerals with a geologist's bag and hammer.

In response to the change to pass and honours levels at matriculation, the school remodelled its sixth form so that the scholars would take a limited offering at honours level in the upper sixth and a wider range for pass in the lower sixth. The outcome was greater satisfaction for both groups and popularity for the new subjects. In 1888 boys were staying back voluntarily to put in extra time at chemistry, which was given a new laboratory in 1890. The chemistry master pored over plans for a room with a fume chamber, twelve basins along the walls and a test-tube-cracking Bunsen burner for each of his twenty-four students. Botany became a separate subject in 1893, when boys moved from the collection, drying and mounting of specimens to the study of plant nutrition and reproduction, and from macroscopic to microscopic investigation. Drawing attention to the trend, the *Quarterly* pleaded once more for a new-look Saturday, with boys vying as strongly with each other to discover new plants as they already did in seeking rare birds' eggs and 'decimating the feathered population within twenty miles of Geelong'. But they were not like that, and their Saturdays were bound to be more hedonistic than scientific despite the fact that their headmaster rubbed shoulders with Baron von Mueller and Professor Baldwin Spencer and that his botanical specimens were in the great museums of the world.* For he was clear-headed in separating the adult and the juvenile, never pressing his own specialty but looking to what worked best with boys in that place at that time. His greatest skill had always been discerning what was appropriate.

Appropriately, Wilson died in harness, early on Tuesday morning 22 October 1895, aged sixty-seven. Following many years of suffering, his health had for some months been deteriorating more rapidly, but he kept up his classes and saw masters and boys in his study until a week before his death. Even then they expected him to rally, as from a temporary setback in 1893. Headmaster for thirty-three years and

---

* After his death the British Museum, which acknowledged his previous generosity, purchased his collection of dried algae, 1485 sheets in all.

connected with the school since 1858, he was an epic figure, both lion and lamb, whose strength and compassion were the wonder of his peers. The school council summed up his contribution in the following minute:

With perfect confidence they can testify that as a scholar he had the mastery of all subjects required for the training of boys;—as a man of science he was held in admiration by some of the foremost men of the day;—as a teacher he was lucid, thorough and effective;—as a disciplinarian he was no less kind than strict. Of the parents of the boys he secured the fullest esteem, of his assistant masters their enthusiastic co-operation, of the boys themselves their lasting respect and affection.[4]

Among the boys, T. A. Brown, who had known his compassion a few years before, went to his room and wept when he heard the news.

On Wednesday 23 October Christ Church was crowded with family, friends, masters, boys, the board, old boys and many citizens of Geelong. Those who knew them would also have noticed the headmasters of Scotch College and Melbourne Grammar School and the scientists von Mueller and Baldwin Spencer. Wilson's usual chair was not empty, but swamped with flowers. According to his wishes, the funeral service was simple.

His coffin, covered with wreaths tied by the school colours, was carried by the masters of the school, and in the funeral procession the present members of the School* followed the single mourning coach. Then came the old boys and then the prefects and masters, and after them a large number of friends and parents.[5]

Along the ridge that separated the town from the river, looking out over the peninsula he had encouraged his boys to explore and towards the sea whose botanical secrets he had himself unlocked, he was taken to a plot at the Eastern Cemetery alongside his old friend, Charles Sladen, without whose help he would not have become headmaster.

The following Sunday his other long-time friend and associate, the vicar of Christ Church, George Goodman, used the text, 'As every man has received the gift, even so minister the same one to another as good stewards of the manifold grace of God', to tell his congregation about the manifold gifts and challenging grace of John Bracebridge Wilson. Turning finally to the boys, gathered as usual in the south aisle, he said:

You may remember his cheery voice, his pleasant smile; you can call to mind a hundred little things by which he made you feel that he cared for you, and had every disposition to seek your good. And then you feel how manly was his character, how thoroughly opposed to everything that was mean or sordid or vulgar. If you needed an object-lesson in true dignity of bearing and perfect refinement of manner, you had it in your Head Master.[6]

Over his grave there is a Celtic cross of Sicilian marble on a bluestone base, and the words, 'Blessed are the pure in heart, for they shall see God'.

* Carefully arranged in ascending order of height, according to one of them.

After almost thirty-three years, rheumatic but undaunted, Bracebridge Wilson was firmly in control.

Leonard Harford Lindon, Headmaster 1896–1911.

W. B. McINNES (from photographs)

[3] *Quarterly*, Dec. 1883, p. 45
[4] Minutes, 29 Oct. 1895.
[5] *Quarterly*, Dec. 1895, p. 2.
[6] *Quarterly*, Dec. 1895, p. 16.

67

5

L. H. Lindon—not fully welcome

The Lindons in the headmaster's garden.

The man who succeeded Bracebridge Wilson, Leonard Harford Lindon, aged thirty-seven, had excellent credentials which put him ahead of the forty other applicants, including J. L. Cuthbertson and Dr Crowther of Brighton Grammar School. Well built and of above average height, with a strong nose, balding dome of a forehead, large droopy moustache and slightly hooded eyes, he was a classical scholar of Jesus College, Cambridge, the most popular destination of Old Geelong Grammarians going to an English university, and had been educated at Rossall School.

At Rossall he had been school captain, the leading scholar of his year and for two years captain of cricket, under a dynamic young headmaster, the Reverend H. A. James (later headmaster of Cheltenham and Rugby), who had instituted a house system, built up the numbers, vastly improved the scholarship and preached strong discipline and hard work. James had relied on prefects like Lindon, who would have received many insights into the implementation of a new regime.

A year after graduating from Cambridge Lindon migrated to Sydney, where he worked for eleven years under A. B. Weigall, who was making a great mark, especially academically, at Sydney Grammar School. Lindon, who became housemaster of the only boarding-house, received a glowing testimonial from that demanding man:

1). His teaching is appreciative and absolutely methodical. He has taught English, French, German, Latin, Greek, and Mathematics, and has taught them all thoroughly well. He is not a stagnant teacher, but is always improving his knowledge and methods. 2). His discipline is consistent and systematic. He is so just that he can afford to be strict; he is sympathetic without being sentimental. The boys consider it an object of ambition to get into Mr Lindon's form, and they are the better for being there. 3). In character Mr Lindon has a high sense of duty and of personal honour, is dignified in demeanour, and refined in his tastes. He is well suited to win the confidence of parents, and to become popular in the best sense of the term.[1]

Popular he never became at Geelong Grammar. He was respected, even liked, especially by the boys, but was not accepted into

[1] *Quarterly*, Dec. 1895, p. 23.

L. H. Lindon and staff, 1910. Lindon is flanked by A. F. Garrard and A. Morris. To the right behind him is E. T. Williams.

the Wilson—Cuthbertson tradition. The dice were loaded against him from the start, for Cuthbertson was like an albatross around his neck. In the sad story of the deterioration of the school's cult figure, Lindon was the other principal actor, who could not be forgiven by Wilson's old boys for failing to succour and sustain, as Wilson had, the embodiment of their ideals.

Cuthbertson's tragedy reads like a novel. Feeling that Wilson on his deathbed had charged him to continue their work (although the legend is strong that Wilson's last words were 'not Cuthbertson'*), Cuthbertson acted as headmaster from October to December 1895, keeping the place together in a friendly, bumbling way and hoping for the permanent appointment. To what extent he was drinking we do not know, but it is probable that, grieving for his friend and without Wilson's support, he slid into depression, was drunk more frequently and, although on the short list of four, ruled himself out of final contention. It was not through lack of appreciation of his work over many years as second master, filling in frequently at assemblies, talking long and earnestly with boys about their problems and sustaining, almost as co-headmaster, the image and ideals of the school, but rather that, standing alone, he was a risky, unknown quantity.

---

* This version came via P. L. Brown from Lindon, who had good reason for amplifying it.

Standing instead under Lindon, whose sharper tongue and strong, though carefully applied, reforms seemed often, to his sensitivity, to go against all that he had helped to build up of trust and honour, Cuthbertson crumbled. Although there is no direct evidence of his competence in 1895, the fact that the council* trusted him with the school suggests that he was in much better condition then than in 1896, when at the end of the year Lindon dismissed him. Only forty-five, he was never to work again. After a year in England he spent his days haunting the school, its sports-fields and the river, from his room at the Geelong Club or Mack's Hotel, a focus of attention for old boys, one of whom, at least, organized his honeymoon so that his bride could meet 'Cuth', and swelled with pride during the encounter. Put on the wrong foot, Lindon publicly bemoaned the fact that *he* had no old boys and looked for the day when the school was full of his own recruits. This earned him the contempt of those who had been taught to think of the school as an entity above and beyond particular people. His desire was not, anyway, fulfilled if E. C. H. Taylor's avowed love for Cuthbertson and lukewarm feelings towards Lindon are taken as typical, for Taylor, who came in 1900 and left in 1906, was definitely one of Lindon's boys.

That Cuthbertson did deteriorate rapidly in 1896 seems probable, putting extra pressure on the senior boys whose 'Cuthy duty' saw him safely in bed. To youngsters, with whom he had always had less rapport, he became something of a joke. At the top of his form he would no doubt have had a place in Lindon's plan to run the school academically through senior subject masters; at the bottom of it he was a stumbling-block. Lindon probably applied pressure to get him to perform and was as disappointed in his failure to do so as he was horrified by the laxity he found in the place. It took ten minutes or more for the school to settle down at the beginning of a period and Cuthbertson seemed positively to delight in a mild anarchy. Cribbing** was rife and clearly condoned. Lindon castigated the school and wrote for help to Weigall, who counselled that there was nothing wrong with the boys. All they needed to learn was respect for their own work. This, of course, implied that a great deal was wrong with the staff, and Lindon asked the council for permission to employ an outside examiner to test the whole school and probably to provide him with an excuse to bring in reforms. He had already indicated his earnestness about academic standards by offering, largely at his own expense, two scholarships a year, tenable for four years, for talented day boys—and a residential scholarship for the son of a clergyman. At that stage he was steering the school away from its concentration on squatters' sons and their desire mainly to acquire social polish, to meet the right people and to enjoy themselves. One

---

* In 1896, when Lindon took over, the board is suddenly, and without explanation in the minutes, referred to as the council.

** Using prepared translations to help with the construction of Latin and Greek sentences.

70

of his earliest reforms was to give day boys equal status in terms of possible appointment as prefects, the privilege of wearing the badge and eligibility for colours. He also provided them with a room at the Bracebridge Wilson Hall, erected in 1896 (see pp. 91—2) to honour the memory of the 'old chief'.

These concessions did not endear him to die-hard Western District old boys, the guardians of the 'boarders first' tradition. Neither did the outcome of the examination of every subject at the higher levels of the school, for which he employed Dr Sugden of Queen's College. Sugden had done the same service for Wilson and his report, read out at Speech Day 1896, was published in the *Geelong Advertiser*. On the whole it was satisfactory, but in senior classics and history, which were Cuthbertson's responsibility, there was nothing to praise:

History—Generally history was disappointing.
Latin —The higher forms were disappointing, but from the fourth form down-
             wards, capital work was sent in ... No continuous composition or sight
             translation was presented even in the highest form.
Greek —Division A. Translation was, with one exception, extremely poor. Accidence
             quite uncertain; sentences for re-translation hardly attempted.[2]

These defects were singled out by the headmaster, who spoke after the reading of the examiner's report and whose emphasis was on the crying need for improved scholarship and his determination to achieve it. To a crowded Bracebridge Wilson Hall, in which it was common knowledge that the beloved Cuth was leaving after twenty-two years' association with the school, he said nothing about Cuthbertson's great contribution. He let him go with the egg of that final report on his face.

That this was unforgivable needs no argument. That Lindon was constrained by his own awkwardness over other circumstances surrounding Cuthbertson's dismissal and hoped that the implied condemnation of the report would justify him seems likely. He may also have arranged that Lord Brassey, the guest speaker, would pay a tribute, as he did, to Cuthbertson's twenty years of remarkable service. His mind had probably been made up after Cuthbertson, left in charge of the boarding-house one Friday night when Lindon went to Melbourne, was picked up drunk in the street. It was at least the second time that had happened, 'Cuthy duty' having failed and Cuth himself having gone back on a solemn promise. In other words, without Wilson to help him, sympathetically, to master it, indeed with Lindon's cold eye damning him, Cuthbertson's alcoholism ran out of control. He had to accept that he was finished.

As he promised, Lindon tightened up the work of the school. Using his senior masters as pace-setters to vet the performance of form masters, rather than trying to check all the work himself as Wilson had done, he introduced monthly cumulative exams on the lines followed at Sydney Grammar, thus subjecting boys regularly to tests

[2] *Quarterly*, Apr. 1897, p. 2.

71

The more formal world of L. H. Lindon is summed up in this photograph with his prefects, 1910. It is interesting that he chose a bowler hat not a mortar board.

of what they had learned at any time in the year. This, he believed, increased the interest of boys and enabled their weaknesses and any poor teaching to be identified. It was much the same regime that earned W. S. Littlejohn the title of 'mark fiend' at Scotch a decade or so later; and Lindon kept a similar eagle eye on form averages, challenging his staff, like a sergeant-major with his NCOs, to keep their forms up to scratch.

Like a sergeant-major, too, he had a decisive bark and an epigrammatic turn of speech that tended to cut the ground away from under people's feet. E. A. Austin thought that he was quite unaware of the bitterness of his tongue which, allied to an unfortunate, abrupt manner had the opposite effect to the warm, friendly enthusiasm with which Littlejohn sugared the pill of his demands. Lindon hurt the feelings of staff by talking of a deplorable scholastic level and slack tone in the school when he inherited it and by saying that it would be better when the present boys had left. When challenged by A. F. Garrard about the inaccuracy and tactlessness of those remarks, he was unable to see any wisdom in retracting. Thus, however good his cause, he built up resentments and inspired nothing like the love required by the GGS tradition. It was left to Garrard, E. T. Williams, 'Jarps' Morris and the orbiting Cuthbertson to keep the old warmth alive. When Lindon took his prefects for an outing to Barwon Heads one year, we learn that he and his wife left them and went to play golf, only rejoining them at a café for the evening meal.

Against this, Cuthbertson was still around and, thanks paradoxically to Lindon, was allowed to maintain his close association with the school. He helped to coach the crew, took them on successive visits to Adelaide for the St Peter's race, acted as an official at the swimming and athletic sports, donated numerous sporting trophies and contributed as much verse as ever to the *Quarterly*. The boys were so exposed to him that E. C. H. Taylor could develop the deep attachment already mentioned.

These impressions are important in charting the response of the school to a headmaster whose scholarship and zeal were never in question and most of whose reforms in themselves were accepted as a necessary tightening up. He spoke convincingly on educational matters, across a wide range of topics, blending strong reading with an incisive ability to see to the heart of a question; and he cared about his men. From the outset he improved the living conditions of resident staff, who had previously eaten with the boys without benefit of table napkins, stabbing at their food with nasty, two-pronged iron forks. He put masters on a regular monthly salary, terminating the informality with which Wilson had doled out what he thought he could afford whenever they indicated that they were in need.

After the initial shock of a different style and personality that always visits such schools upon a change of headmaster, and after adjusting to the sterner demands he made upon them, masters and boys settled down to a regime that respected the sporting traditions,

72

the prefect system and the gentlemanly ethos of the school. It was not as exciting or as warm a family, but it prospered. Council was happy. Indeed, the minutes reveal much less friction than Wilson had had over the last ten years of his headmastership. Money was easier. During recovery from the 1890s depression, Lindon had a downhill run financially, building up day-boy numbers at first and then, when the long drought broke in 1904, achieving record enrolments of boarders. A strong sign of prosperity was the reopening in 1899 of the preparatory school (see p. 36) in its former buildings across Moorabool Street. Significantly, this became Lindon's private venture because the council was not prepared to finance the purchase. As Wilson had, Lindon advanced and donated large amounts of money to the school. When the Bracebridge Wilson Hall appeal was stagnant at £869 in 1896, he put in the final £280. Also like his predecessor, in the face of fresh challenges and pressing needs, he won a new classroom to the east of the quadrangle and a further, this time towering, excrescence within it (see p. 86).

After the 1899 interstate contest with St Peter's, the two crews and coaches (Cuthbertson on the right) posed for posterity.

It was clear in 1906, just before the school's jubilee, that there was an accommodation problem. The boarding-house was overflowing for the first time since 1880. While he was wondering what to do, Lindon took the unprecedented step of deferring several enrolments. Ninety-one boys so crowded the dormitories, originally designed for eighty, that Lindon bought a house nearby, sent A. F. Garrard off

The whole school and staff, 1907.

The school cricket ground, half a mile along McKillop Street, as photographed for the 1913 prospectus. There are signs of extensive work undertaken in 1907.

The Old Boys Dinner in the Bracebridge Wilson Hall, 1906.

with half-a-dozen boys to run it on his own account in a typical English manner, and claimed it as the beginning of the 'house system'. The following year the pressure of having ninety-eight boarders was relieved by putting another six with Garrard and by sending several masters to another house he purchased himself. He was moving into a confrontation with the school council. In June 1907 he suggested that they should increase boarding accommodation within the school grounds and in December called for urgent repairs and improvements, but was successful in neither case. He was dealing with a group who had grown old with the school; they had weathered the long era of crippling indebtedness as well as the recent depression. 'Stay small, stay out of trouble' was their philosophy.

Lindon turned to the old boys: not to his own, whose absence he had lamented in his first years and who would not have had the substance to help him, but to Wilson's and Cuthbertson's boys. These were the core of a 400-strong association called the Old Geelong Grammarians (including sixty-nine mainly pastoralist life members), whose formation Lindon had supported late in 1900 by hosting a dinner that followed the first full-scale Old Boys' Day at the school. Before that there had been a few false starts and, from 1897, an Old Boys' Dinner at Show time in Melbourne when country people flocked to the metropolis. Why the new century should have welcomed the society is explained by an event of great social importance, from which otherwise Geelong Grammar would have been the only absent public school. To mark the foundation of the Commonwealth of Australia in 1901, the combined associations of the old boys of Victorian public schools decided to hold a function under vice-regal patronage. No Old Geelong Grammarian, including Donald Mackinnon, MLA, who was on the organizing committee, could have been present if the association had not been formed and formed quickly.

74

Once in existence, the association grew rapidly to 250 members in December 1901 and 350 in 1904. By the jubilee in 1907 there were 435, including 168 from pastoral properties across Australia, whose names were a roll-call of celebrities from the Western District and Riverina—like Affleck, Austin, Bailey, Black, Calvert, Chirnside, de Little, Fairbairn, Falkiner, Hood, Hopkins, Lang, Manifold, Moffatt, Mackinnon, Macpherson, McLaurin, Reid, Robertson, Ross, Russell and Staughton. There was an energetic and confident committee who became deeply involved in fund-raising for the cricket ground in 1907. Their commitment was strengthened by the fact that their sons were entering the school in increasing numbers. Boys who had left in the 1870s, like Donald Mackinnon, who had one son at the school and three more to come, held a vested interest in its future. So it is not surprising that when Lindon became frustrated in 1907 he was not alone. In fact it is hard to separate out responsibility for the initiatives taken during that year. Perhaps Lindon, but more likely Garrard, began the attack.

Garrard, it will be remembered, was Bracebridge Wilson's son-in-law, the outgoing and effective 'Boots', who had been put in charge of the extra boarding-house in 1906 and was ambitious to develop it. In his enthusiasm for the school he was also honorary secretary of the Old Geelong Grammarians, a power-broker in their ranks and for that reason a formidable champion of change. In consultation with Lindon and Donald Mackinnon, president of the old boys, he worked out a scheme and took the initiative of putting it to the school council and *then* to his own committee towards the end of 1908. The idea was to buy from Bracebridge Wilson's estate (of which Garrard was an executor), land the old chief had prudently secured adjacent to the cricket ground (see p. 114) and build on it a group of houses to accommodate a hundred extra boarders, at the same time adding new classrooms, a music room, a laboratory and other facilities at the main site. A chapel was envisaged in the longer term. Donald Mackinnon told the Old Geelong Grammarians that £12 000 would be required and that most of it would have to come from their pockets.

The council agreed to the scheme, but showed deference to the new force in the school's affairs by delegating further consideration and the approval of the necessary fund-raising to a joint committee of the OGGs and the council, chaired by the headmaster. This was a very large straw in the wind. Acknowledging soon afterwards that the decision meant dedication to growth and change, the ageing Geelong-based council accepted a further proposal from the old boys, perhaps inspired by the frustrated Lindon, and certainly in defence of the money they were risking, that the OGG should be given direct representation on council. To that effect they approved a new constitution, which was ratified by the synod of the diocese early in 1909. Not only were three old boys elected under that constitution, but the chairman, T. C. Harwood, and two other members of the old council resigned after a strenuous but fruitless

The Old Geelong Grammarians.

April 15th, 1909.

To all Old Boys and Supporters of the School.

AT a Committee Meeting of the Old Geelong Grammarians, held at the School on the 10th of November, 1908, a scheme which had for its object the development of the School was fully discussed and approved. It was then decided that the scheme should be referred to the Council of the School, and if it met with its approval a Conference should be held. The Council approved of the scheme, and on the 23rd November, 1908, a Conference was held at the School. At this Conference the Council was represented by The Hon. T. C. Harwood (Chairman), Archdeacon Crossley, Messrs. C. M. Poynter, W. F. Volum, E. A. Austin, H. A. Austin, and the Rev. F. W. Newton; the Old Geelong Grammarians by their President The Hon. D. Mackinnon, M.L.A., H. P. Douglass, and the Hon. Secretary; and the School by the Head Master.

On the next page the whole scheme is outlined, but the idea at present is to carry out a part only, namely:—

(a) To complete the purchase of the land (6½ acres in extent) adjoining the School Cricket Ground, and only separated therefrom by Normanby Street, 99 feet wide.

(b) On this land to build one School House which will have accommodation for between thirty and forty boarders, sanitorium, and suitable accommodation for the House Master, etc.

(c) To build two new Class Rooms, one Science Room, two Music Rooms, also Bedrooms for servants, rooms for Housekeeper at the School, to re-build the boys' and masters' bath rooms, and to thoroughly renovate and re-furnish all the school portions of the main building.

attempt to prevent the election of Donald Mackinnon, who was a Presbyterian and who had clearly been throwing his weight around. This hiatus produced virtually a new council.* Eight of the ten appointed members could shake hands as old friends: E. A. Austin, H. A. Austin, J. P. Chirnside, H. P. Douglass, D. Mackinnon, W. T. Manifold, R. Stephen and A. G. White were all old boys. In addition the other laymen, T. E. Bostock and W. F. Volum, were supporters of change. Through its old boys, the school was now shaping its own destiny. The ideals and attitudes of Wilson and Cuthbertson and their own Australian and English experience were to be ploughed back by a council of predominantly Western District men—the Austins, Chirnside, Mackinnon, and Manifold—whose attitudes were shared by the wool merchants Bostock, Douglass and Volum.

No phase in the history of the school since its foundation had been as important as this. For a time the running was being made not by the current headmaster but by memories of what his predecessor and his exciting lieutenant had taught, leavened by a mounting ambition which only the very wealthy could experience, to make Geelong Grammar School, at last, a true boarding-school on the English model. Before long, as we shall see in chapter 8, the success of Garrard's fund-raising made the council aware that it would be possible to move to an entirely new site and begin again, free of the great disadvantage of a main school separated by nearly a kilometre from its playing-fields and projected boarding-houses.

In all of this Lindon, at first the initiator, was more and more the subordinate, responsible not for policy but for implementation. Either he did not take kindly to the change or else they presumed too much, for feelings became strained. Rather than expressing pride, as Mackinnon had in 1906, about the way he was running the school, the council began to doubt his capacity as a financial manager. This suddenly loomed large because, as a corollary to undertaking a huge new investment, and in the manner of English schools, the council decided to terminate Lindon's farming arrangement and put him on a salary. He agreed and may even have suggested the move. If so, it rebounded, bringing nasty disputes about the ownership of furniture and fittings, the proper compensation to be paid if they were Lindon's and the manner in which his account-books should be scrutinized to establish the viability of the business. The council was shocked. For all its growth and apparent prosperity, the school was barely paying its way. Doubts were sown about Lindon's capacity and these were aggravated by confrontations with the formidable Mrs Lindon over the furniture and domestic management. Despite all this, the council informed Lindon early in 1910 that it would delay until the end of

Geelong Grammar School Quarterly.

Vol. XXX.]   APRIL, 1906.   [No. 1.

School Jubilee.

CRICKET GROUND IMPROVEMENT FUND.

THE past and present School may congratulate each other upon the now assured success of their united efforts to celebrate worthily the Jubilee of the School, by improving the School Cricket Ground.

The execution of the work has been entrusted to a Committee, of which the Head Master is the chairman, and of which Messrs. F. Fairbairn, H. A. Austin, and H. P. Douglass, representing the Old Boys, and Mr. M. Conran, representing the School Council, have consented to become members.

The intention of the Committee is to regrade, level and lay down in turf the whole area of ten acres, in order to provide sufficient accommodation for the whole School for

---

* The archbishop (who remained president), the archdeacon of Geelong and the incumbent of Christ Church were members *ex officio*, while six lay communicants were to be appointed by the bishop-in-council and four lay communicants by the school council. Mackinnon's religious status was obviously an issue.

the year its assumption of financial management. At the same time it began seriously to consider whether to reappoint him for a fourth five-year term, giving him fair warning, in June 1910, that it might throw the headmastership open for competition in 1911. Finally, despite Lindon's angry demand that he be told what the council had against him, and his statement that he would not be a candidate for the headmastership in open competition, the position was advertised early in 1911.

There is poetic injustice in all this, Lindon being trapped by what were probably his own initiatives to mobilize the old boys, change the council and abolish the farming system. He had been riding high at the time of the jubilee and Cuthbertson, who had failed to complete the register he had undertaken in 1904, was not in the spotlight. Quite the opposite! Cuthbertson had not been re-elected to the committee of the old boys' association, was not formally missed (as would have been expected) at their annual meeting and wrote very little for the *Quarterly* for several years.

The ebb and flow of council sentiment between Cuthbertson and Lindon is used by Fay Marles as a condition for, or at least as a very significant coincidence in, the new council's coolness towards Lindon in 1909 and his downfall in 1911. For Cuthbertson came back into the picture in 1909, writing vigorously for the *Quarterly* and appearing once more about the school. It could have heartened him that most of the new council had played in teams under him, many during his great days in the 1870s and that several had been clever members of his upper fifth. None was closer to him than Mackinnon, who had paid an unusually warm tribute to Lindon in 1906 but who spearheaded the criticism of him in 1909–10.

Then Cuthbertson died. During bad weather on one of his regular fishing trips to the Glenelg River early in 1910, he decided to visit old boys at Mount Gambier where, probably drinking heavily, he fell ill, became very despondent, took an overdose of Veronal and died. He was fifty-eight. Back at Geelong and right across Australia the feeling of loss among old boys was acute. As one of them put it in the *Quarterly*:

Truly his heart seemed to beat with ours, and his love never wavered to the end. Our hearts would indeed be of stone, did they not respond to so much affection and devotion.[3]

Mackinnon's heart was not stone. In unveiling a memorial tablet to his mentor, he dwelt upon a warmth that Lindon, who accepted it abruptly on behalf of the school, quite painfully lacked. Later, at the official launching by the Old Geelong Grammarians of a commemorative edition of Cuthbertson's poems, entitled *Barwon Ballads and School Verses*, Mackinnon eulogized Cuthbertson's great love of everything that was significant in the school, crediting him with the creation 'of what school sentiment we have'. About the same time, Adamson of Wesley described himself as 'one who loved the man, and honours the poet as the greatest factor in Public School life

[3] *Quarterly*, Apr. 1910, p. 4.

known in Victoria'. It seems possible that the death of Cuthbertson magnified through grief a feeling among the council that, just as Cuthbertson was a lame duck without Wilson, Lindon was too cold a fish, despite his many fine qualities, to be entrusted with such a school in the absence of its poet, the guardian of its true identity.

The school drag, with the headmaster and Mrs Lindon up front, taking guests to the south bank of the Barwon to watch the school row against St Peter's, Adelaide, in 1903.

Do grown men feel like that? We cannot be sure. But the way they acted extended the breach between council and headmaster during the critical months of 1911 when the headmastership was open, yet when Lindon might well have been asked to fill it. If he had wished to; for, apart from the pressure placed on him by the slur on his ability and the negation of his previous success represented by the advertisement for a new headmaster, a provision it contained—that the headmaster's wife should have no part in running the school—must have made him boil. To a proud man who worked as a team with a proud wife, this would have been galling. As well as its being a piece of politicking, that slight may have been behind his statement to the old boys at their smoke concert in June that he was probably addressing them for the last time as headmaster. What made that prediction come true, if it was not already his intention to stand aside, was a nasty contretemps with the council over the visit of the Governor of Victoria to the annual assault-at-arms in July 1911.

The invitation to the governor may have been a desperate indication by Lindon of his status, and was possibly read as such by the council, who said no when he asked them if they wished to make any arrangements for the vice-regal occasion. They may have decided to keep a low profile with the headmastership in the balance, but that did not mean that they were inviting the slight which Lindon delivered by escorting the governor straight past them up the hall, without an

A composite picture celebrating the school's jubilee in 1907.

attempt at introduction. Onlookers gasped and no doubt the governor felt uncomfortable: he knew the MLAs Austin and Mackinnon and the squatters Chirnside and Manifold as more than passing acquaintances. By that action, said E. A. Austin, Lindon virtually abdicated, and he rubbed salt into the wound by suggesting to council an inordinately high rent for the preparatory school if they wanted to use it without reappointing him.

In all of this the sympathies of the records are biased against Lindon, who was rejected in favour of Francis Brown late in 1911. Even the scrupulous E. A. Austin, who was interviewed by Philip Brown in 1931, during research for a history of the school, may have been influenced by the need to justify and explain why Lindon was not reappointed. For Philip Brown, who later in the same year sought out Lindon, the meeting was a shock. Because the school tradition had painted a sour, sarcastic man, scarcely capable of a smile, he was unprepared for the cultivated, charming gentleman who greeted him. In that tweedy, prosperous, mellow, plump, retired-colonel type, with a quick, active brain, there was no hint of the man found wanting at GGS, the man whose major fault, perhaps, was that he lacked the supernatural power to lay the ghosts of Wilson and Cuthbertson.*

* Warden of Christ's College, Hobart, 1912–26 and concurrently headmaster of The Hutchins School 1912–17, Lindon died, aged almost ninety-five, on 12 May 1953.

6

The gray-turreted mother

She knows, the gray-turreted Mother,
Green-crowned on the crest of the hill.[1]

At first the world of the school was neat and contained. English in concept, it was dropped into place all of a piece through the bishop's ambition, the government grant and the willingness of the trustees to take a great financial responsibility (see p. 7). The quadrangle and the Big Schoolroom acted like echo-chambers repeating the notes of each day and each year long into the future. A place speaking of tradition even when first built, it gradually became less formal as it extended into a straggle of outbuildings. Many of its functions can be inferred from boys' reminiscences and reports in the school magazine.

The main focus was the Big School—the large, galleried room which occupied the whole width of the ground floor in the north wing, to the east of the day-boys' entrance (see p. 86). There the school assembled each morning at 9 o'clock. The boys lined the walls, waiting expectantly for the footsteps of the headmaster; alert to the swish of his gown as he passed down the central aisle to the dais at the east end; restrained for roll-call and prayers, then absorbing a homily or cheering the report of victory in games. Each headmaster created his own atmosphere: boys remembered Vance's friendliness, Wilson's warm voice reading from the Bible, Lindon's questioning bark and Brown's measured tones. The family atmosphere of Wilson's time might flower into an unexpected half-holiday to mark some special achievement or to be a release from the heat of an oppressive summer's day.

In class hours, on either side of the central passage the iron-framed benches lost their backs, which folded up to become desk-tops. Big School must then have been like Babel, not so much with the noise of many tongues (though Lindon thought things lax when he arrived) but criss-crossed with a range of lessons. Before the days of placing each class in a separate room, this gave a strong coherence to the school, especially felt at the end of each half-year under Wilson,

[1] 'C', 'For the Jubilee of the Geelong Grammar School, 1907', Prefatory to *History and Register*, 1907.

81

when the whole school was examined for a week, culminating (in the early years) with an oral performance in front of the local clergy and the board of management. After Lindon arrived in 1896 the boys faced exams every month and probably crammed for them in a mood foreign to Wilson. Lindon also tightened up by ending the day with prayers and announcements, when those whose work or behaviour was bad might expect to hear their names on the detention list, ruled over by the master on duty at the west end of Big School. Worse still was the Thursday list, prepared at a weekly staff meeting to reward persistent academic failure with a Saturday morning in the same prison. According to R. E. Higgins, it was like a life sentence: 'Not many boys were ever on the list, fortunately for them, for once a boy's name was placed on the Thursday list, it was most difficult to achieve its removal.' Francis Brown abolished both detentions.

Also in Big School, in the early morning and in the evening, if they were not elevated enough to share one of the nine studies or one of the smaller classrooms, boarders came to do their prep. The busiest part of the school, the most redolent of work, Big School was nevertheless softened by its adaptability to all kinds of gatherings, and was the best place to feel the pulse of the school. One thing that strikes a twentieth-century mind is its inappropriateness to the climate. Having windows unprotected by eaves on its long north side and little chance of a breeze, it must have been oppressive in summer and, possessing only a tiny fireplace in the middle of the north wall, could only have been freezing in winter, except for a few bodies roasting near the hearth.

In Big School too, until 1896 when a separate hall was added, the year ended with prize-giving and speeches in front of a galaxy of visitors, thronging even the gallery. The private world of the school was briefly on show, scrubbed, tidied and decorated with trophies and samples of work. Behind the dais at the 1871 prize-giving the words *Dulce Domum** appeared, in an arrangement of laurel and many coloured flowers, 'surrounded by festoons in equal taste'. On the ceiling in diamond patterns, crowns of laurel and flowers 'acted as centrepieces to festoons of sweet smelling rosemary'. The orchestra was hidden behind ivy, lilies and other flowers. Crayon and pencil drawings ornamented the side walls. Women and girls were also blooming.

At the beginning and end of each of the four terms, the boarding family gathered in a special atmosphere for rituals of welcome and farewell. There might be speeches and presentations, as in 1897 at the end of the first quarter, when Mrs Lindon gave out pewter pots (not gold and silver medals, as before) to crews successful at the school regatta. Popular boys received their tributes. Forth and Maxwell, a winning pair, sweltered in applause intended as a farewell to Forth. T. N. Collins, the captain of boats, though winning no

---

Church of England

GRAMMAR SCHOOL,

GEELONG.

G. Mercer, Printer, 31 & 33, Malop Street.
1872.

EXAMINATION,

SATURDAY, December 7th.

A.M. *Class* III. ... Dictation and Physical
      Geography—Paper.
  ,,   IV. ... Dictation. ·
  ,,   V. ... Dictation.
  ,,   VI. ... Spelling, vivâ voce.
  ,,   VII. ... Spelling, vivâ voce.

P.M. *Class* II. ... Scripture, vivâ voce.
  ,,   III. ... Scripture, vivâ voce.
  ,,   IV. ... Scripture, vivâ voce.
  ,,   V. ... Scripture, vivâ voce.
  ,,   VI. ... Scripture, vivâ voce.

Class I. will be examined in the Classics, Mathematics, English and Logic required during the First Year at the Melbourne University.

Class II. has already been examined at, or in connection with, the late Matriculation Examination in the Classics. Mathematics, French and English subjects required at that Examination.

The Boarders will be examined on Sunday, December 8th, for the purpose of awarding Divinity Prizes.

G. Mercer, Printer, Malop-street.

---

* 'Let us sing sweetly of home.' The phrase came from a Winchester song, traditionally sung to greet the Whitsun holidays. (See Brewer's *Dictionary of Phrase and Fable*.)

pewter was farewelled with an outburst of clapping and three hearty cheers. At such times boys identified their heroes and held them in their consciousness for ever. Fifty years later F. W. A. Godfrey, who joined the school in 1872, remembered the giants of his early days. Jim and Charlie Fairbairn, J. C. F. Ulbrich, the Moffatts, Norman Armytage, 'Kookey' Walker, Ian Black, Selwyn Puckle, Percy Douglass, Reg de Little and Bob Broth retained their boyhood elevation above him, especially Charlie Fairbairn, whose aura captured masters as well as boys (see p. 60). Also incomparable in his generation was Thomas K. Parkin, captain of the school, captain of boats, captain of football in 1889, twice stroke of a winning crew, but approachable, unaffected, sincere, of whom Wilson wrote:

I have never in a very long experience, had a young man under my charge of whose personal character I had a higher opinion.[2]

For Wilson and Lindon, Cuthbertson and Garrard, the procession of boys through the school was a series of vintages, never the static set of peer-group and graded relationships apprehended by a boy.

On a Saturday night, just before the midwinter and summer break-ups, 'a zealous band of boys', keyed up by the knowledge that girls would be coming to admire their handiwork, transformed Big Schoolroom for an entertainment called Pastime, when the extended school family had fun together and raised money for causes like the Boat Club, Cricket Club and Tennis Club. Decked out according to

The interior of the Big Schoolroom, the traditional focus of life in public schools.

THE PRIZES

Will be distributed

On Monday, 9th Dec., at 3 o'clock p.m.

By the Hon. T. T. ÀB*k*CKETT, M.L.C.

———

Parents, Guardians, and Friends of the Boys are invited to attend.

———

The Classes will re-assemble, after the Christmas Vacation, on Monday, January 27th.

———

Parents who do not live in Geelong are requested to forward the money necessary for their sons' travelling expenses.

[2] J. B. Wilson, folio 1.

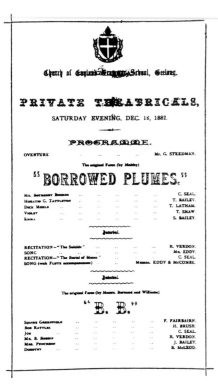

the mood of the occasion with various mixtures of flowers, rifles, bayonets, wreaths, ferns, flags, pictures and shields, it was usually given special effects. When funds were being raised for the Boat Club in 1888, in addition to side walls sprouting flowers, flags, rifles and bayonets, the east wall was draped with the school flag over which were crossed two oars won that year in the St Ignatius race, their blades emblazoned with the school arms, and in the centre the rudder of the *Alice* and the flag from her stem. As expressive of loyalty to the school as a Cuthbertson poem, as elementally trophies of war as Indian scalps, they gleamed like the display of the male bower bird caught up in much the same sexual imperative.

Most Pastime programmes contained piano solos and duets, straight and comic recitations, numerous songs and a one-act comedy. Sometimes a section of the programme took the form of a Christy minstrel show, sometimes there was a sailors' hornpipe or the young cadets doing drill to music. The daughters of the vicarage, the children of the music teacher, a few boys, various masters and Mr and Mrs Lindon, in their day, were the chief performers. Quite often Mr Lupton, the elocution teacher, and his pupils, having rehearsed for months, put on stagey songs and recitations followed by a farce. This was said to be for the amusement of their lady friends, who indeed predominated on such occasions, the school denoting by its absence a certain scorn for elocution. Most of the fare at Pastimes was imported, but occasionally over the years 'The Sick Stockrider' and 'The Geebung Polo Club' thrust themselves in among 'The Charge of the Light Brigade', 'The Revenge' and the like. Gradually too, Cuthbertson's poems were set to music so that as well as Eton's 'Jolly Boating Weather' and the cadets' rendition of 'The Old Brigade', the school's own boating and football songs were heard and probably other Cuthbertson poems set to music. The evening usually concluded with a scratchy attempt at the national anthem and an enthusiastic three cheers for the ladies. In 1890 there was also a splendid supper, which was rapidly mowed down:

'First fighting line retired, bring out the reserves', remarked one youngster, pulling a large box of tarts from under the table.[3]

Occasionally during these entertainments the school joined in a chorus, but, in keeping with their hearty outdoors tradition and in spite of the visiting music and singing masters advertised on the 1878 prospectus, their singing was atrocious. Possibly indicating the level of performance at Pastimes, the author of an article in the *Quarterly* for December 1881 decried the lack of music in the school, referred to an excruciating attempt to sing 'God Save the Queen' at a previous breakup and bemoaned the absence of singers at cricket and football dinners. The glee club and musical society of the English tradition did not easily take root. A family quartet singing a part song in 1888 was a rare event and people talked throughout the clarinet solo of a young master in 1890, although the commentator said it was one of the best things of the evening. Despite the Reverend Sproule's

Sunday evening music class in 1889, the level of appreciation tended to remain that of 'second class nigger melodies'. But there was some progress. At midwinter 1891 a small orchestra played Handel's 'Largo' and 'Liebesliedchen' by Taubert.

Hints of what happened on other Saturday evenings include dancing and 'socials'. We know very little about the dancing except that it was in the headmaster's classroom and that on one celebrated occasion in the middle of a party someone pulled the handle in the masters' common room that turned off all the gas.

> The dance began, a ripple ran
> Of music and of laughter
> When lo! The light evanished quite
> From floor to wreathed rafter[4]

No verse explored the ensuing chaos or the rush to relight gas jets all around the school. In winter, 'when the fellows get in earlier',* there were socials, described in 1887 simply as pleasant, casual meetings. These had been abandoned in 1890 when a correspondent in the *Quarterly* pleaded, 'Could we not have a social on Saturday evenings and could not the fellows who get it up have a lot of songs with a good chorus?' Along the same 'couldn't we' line in the same year was a call to form a chess and draughts club just for something to fill in time—'some fellows do not care to read books night after night'. Some sixth formers that year began filling in winter nights, probably Saturdays, throwing words at each other on topics like the everlasting contemporary issue, 'Free Trade Versus Protection', or 'The Chinese Question', or 'Giffen [South Australia] versus Bruce [Victoria] as cricketers'. This Senior Debating Society, when floundering in 1894, looked nostalgically back to 1892 when a motion to exclude the Chinese had kept them up all night. Like the rest of the nation they voted white.

When a day boy entered the big doors from McKillop Street and turned right, or a boarder came from the quad and turned left, away from Big School, a corridor led west and then south to the grand west entrance, beyond which were studies and, after 1875, the prefects' room. Opening from that main corridor in succession at first were the writing and drawing room, the French and music room, a junior classroom and the library, but by 1882 French and music had given way to the sub-prefects and, because there was a separate junior school, the junior classroom had become a masters' common room. By then, too, the library walls bore handsome landscape photographs and two large frames containing small portraits of old boys, who had been approached through the *Quarterly* to supply their likenesses for that family album.

The functions of such rooms are never hard and fast, but it comes as a surprise that, with numbers never more than 150 in Wilson's day and strongly shackled by debt, a school designed in 1857 for 250 required so many changes. And not just changes. Additional lean-to structures were built in the north-east and south-west corners of the quadrangle, the first as a special classroom for the

---

* From Saturday rambles (see p. 101).

[4] *Quarterly*, July 1882, p. 31.

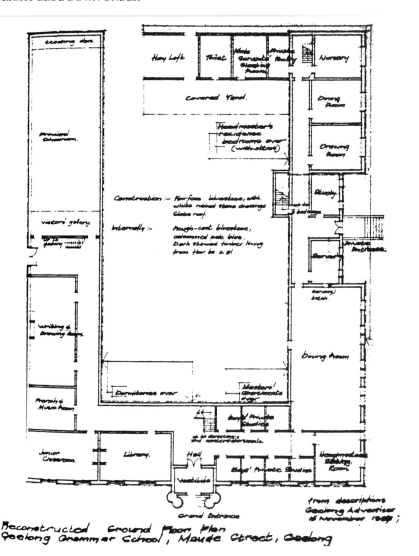

Construction :- Few face limestone, with white ruled stone dressings slate roof.

Internally :- rough-coat limestone, colourwashed pale blue, dark stained timber lining from floor to a sil

from descriptions Geelong Advertiser 15 November 1857;

Sketch by Kevin Carolan

Reconstructed Ground Floor Plan
Geelong Grammar School, Maude Street, Geelong

headmaster (1870) and the second as a chemistry laboratory (1879). This did indicate poverty, however, for it put paid to the possibility, raised by Judge Rogers in 1868, that the quad should be graced by a cloister. Because nothing could be added to Big School or the dining hall, extensions had then to be made as new free-standing buildings to the east beyond the service wing, except, in Lindon's day, for a final indignity to the quad in the form of a new staircase to the south wing, off which there were additional servants' rooms, pantries and linen rooms.

A view of the school from the north-east, probably taken early in the twentieth century, shows what strong outposts had been set up in that direction to join a large shelter-shed, with verandah, which had opened onto the playground from the beginning. These easterly extensions, reached in bad weather by a dash through the service arch, were a detached laundry (1869), gymnasium (1872—

86

Relaxing in a sunny corner of the quad, *c.* 1880.

when the playground was levelled), cottage hospital (circa 1876—enlarged early twentieth century), new chemistry laboratory (1890), the many-faceted Bracebridge Wilson Hall (1896), a new classroom abutting Big School (circa 1904), a miniature rifle range and stabling for fifty bicycles; and that leaves out the splendid new free-standing toilets of 1874. The latter replaced the inefficient water closets (beside the male servants' quarters in the east wing) with a double urinal, draining into a 150-gallon tank, and four dunnies with pans to which the nightman had access from outside.

Those toilets came under sharp scrutiny in 1887 when an outbreak of typhoid fever struck the school and filled the nearby cottage hospital to overflowing. Such an epidemic was the great bogey of boarding-schools; it could be a killer for them even if their pupils survived. So Wilson had prepared carefully for illness by framing up a sickroom at the end of the long dormitory in 1865, and when numbers grew fast in the 1870s he built the cottage hospital to the east. His sensitivity about disease led to heart-searching in 1868, when one of his favourite boys, the captain of football, died of pneumonia after playing when he was not well. He was a day boy at the time, so his death was probably less Wilson's direct fault than that of the games-playing ethos.* What chance did he have when a boy like Steve

---

* The boy's father, Judge Brewer, had died early in the year. Arthur gave up boarding to be with his mother and had been quarantined when his sister caught scarlatina. As Wilson reported the event, he got out of bed to play rather than disappoint the team.

Fairbairn, who was sent to the sanatorium with a headache when scarlet fever was prevalent in 1877, skipped out a window next morning to act as hare in a paper chase and played an important football match in the afternoon.

Whether the matron, who is generally pictured as a clothes-mender, was a trained nurse, and whether she looked after the sick, is not clear. Whoever did had so many measles cases in 1884 that the headmaster and the school doctor called for extra accommodation. The board refused, but did accept Dr Pincott's plea for a hot bath to treat cases of sudden chill and incipient rheumatism—a winter hazard in a school so dedicated to sending boys out into the bush on Saturdays.

Headmaster, matron, doctor, staff and boys were thrown into alarm in second term 1887. On the fourth of May a boarder reported with a raging fever, on the sixth the headmaster's wife succumbed and then, in quick succession between the tenth and nineteenth, sixteen or seventeen more boarders and two domestic servants were stricken. It was the dreaded typhoid, which appeared guardedly in the minutes of a special board meeting on 18 May as 'certain cases of illness among the boys', engendering worried talk about the state of the drains, the likelihood that the Town Council would order the school to close and the wisdom of sending all the boys home immediately on their midwinter holidays. Many were withdrawn anyway and upon recovery the invalids went home for a long convalescence. H. M. R. Rupp did not return until the new year. From sixty-four the number of boarders fell to thirty-six and was only forty-three a year later when the headmaster spoke to the board about prejudice against the school. Some parents seemed to be waiting to see if the anniversary of the outbreak would bring a recurrence.

There were no fatalities, though Rupp believed that several boys had a close call. A quaint case was Tom Parkin who, recovering his appetite in the absence of food and the nurse, ate the poisoned cheese from a rat-trap and had a relapse. Apparently the trick of sending up clandestine tucker on a rope was not working at the time.

The school emerged fairly satisfactorily from an enquiry by Dr Shields of the Central Board of Health, whose examination of the sanitary arrangements encapsulates nineteenth-century notions of hygiene. He checked that the boys' toilets were properly supplied with earth and Hunter's disinfectant for covering faeces and found that the nightmen were lax about changing the pans twice a week as required. The worst situation was in the headmaster's house, where a trendy water closet fed two 5-metre cesspools which, not being ventilated, and rarely emptied, sent nasty gas back into the house every time the toilet was flushed. He recommended the scrapping of those cesspools, the ventilation of the drains carrying urine and waste water into the street channels and the cleaning of tanks holding drinking water collected from the roof. The cause of the outbreak seemed to be the milk supply, some of which came from a dairyman called Stokes who had contracted typhoid before the school was affected. Dr Shields was caught between the miasmic theory of disease transmitted through foul air and the emerging emphasis on contagion and infection. After considering his report, the board decided to ventilate the drains, replace the water closet and accept the suggestion of a number of parents, who were clearly miasmatists, that the ventilation of the dormitories should be improved.

In the fear and confusion the *Quarterly* missed its July issue. Then in October Cuthbertson recovered the experience with two poems. One, plumbing the depths, began:

> Too near, too near, the angel Azrael stayed—
> Almost we heard the rustle of his wings,[5]

A carpentry class shown in the 1913 prospectus. The shop was originally the gymnasium.

The other expressed relief, and the solidarity of those who had come through a testing experience together.

> Gone is the poison of the fever's breath
>   And gone the shadow that upon us fell
>   When the companions whom we loved so well
> Lay in the border land twixt life and death:
> Now once again are mingled in our hall
>   Old friends, old comrades; once again we hear,
>   In bush, on field and river, ringing clear,
> The echoes glad of youth's triumphant call.
> To welcome back each true undoubting son,
>   Unswerving in your steadfast loyalty
>   And confident amid the evil rain:
> With you shall later laurels yet be won,
>   With you shall come a new prosperity
>   And fortune smiling on us once again.[6]

To the gymnasium, which became a carpentry shop with twenty-five benches when the Bracebridge Wilson Hall was built, the (inevitably European) visiting instructor came once a week at dinner time. For most of Wilson's time a German named Reichman challenged his charges with feats of strength and timing on the bars, the ladders and trapeze and built their muscles with a system of weights and ropes. Boxing, incidentally, is not mentioned; nor is it clear how the gym was used for the greater part of the week. The Bracebridge Wilson Hall was not only a new venue, it marked a change of policy. For Lindon introduced a British army instructor who mixed gymnastics with military drill (see p. 124).

Just as the gym became a carpentry shop, the original chemistry laboratory in the quad was converted into a museum in 1890, housing a collection Bracebridge Wilson had begun years before and had stored in a dingy basement. It moved again, in 1896, from what was a crowded and stuffy room to an annexe of the hall which bore his name, the board of management having purchased the collection from his estate. The *Quarterly* in 1890 spoke of it as a collection few schools in the world could rival. In the hope of stimulating the observation and appreciation of nature, Wilson had not only gathered a remarkably strong collection of minerals, but had painstakingly

[5] *Quarterly*, Oct. 1887, p. 6.
[6] *Quarterly*, Oct. 1887, p. 6.

The school's tennis court was one of the first in Geelong.

drawn up illustrated manuals as guides to the shelves. J. R. Godfrey, a future inspector of mines for New South Wales, was only one of a generation of boys to get the message that geological knowledge was a fine key to the future of a country teeming with mineral wealth. It was typical of Wilson that this teaching collection should be devoted to material that would catch the boys' interest, not parade his world-famous research into marine plants. No wonder the school was disappointed that geology was not more prominent in the new science syllabus for matriculation in the 1880s.

When the bell rang for the half-hour morning recess or lunch, or when school ended for the day and the boys poured out onto the playground, it was Wilson's policy to leave it unsupervised, so that (within a general code of gentlemanliness) feuds and bitterness could be purged. Boys were free to use one of the larger classrooms as a reading room, but they were expected to rush for the playground and, according to their age, compete at games like marbles, kick-the-tin and a yard version of cricket. Some boys stayed about the quad, beating balls against the walls in a bastard form of fives, or just talking. A few made for the asphalt tennis court between McKillop Street and the west end of the building.

These were times for teasing and settling old scores, and inevitably for day boy—boarder conflicts. To the standard division of Australian public schools into boarders and their despised lesser brethren, GGS added a special flavour related to the more elevated social class as well as the numerical superiority of boarders. Even before the extra discrimination which Cuthbertson began in 1875, of denying day boys the right to wear the school badge, excluding most of them from teams and locking them out of rowing, their pride was close to flash point; and this led to stand-up fights between champions of the two factions out of sight of their mentors. Less vicious than Tom Brown's encounter with Flashman, the following account has the ring of medieval chivalry, constructed as a clash more of honour than of spite.

In my time there was always a general warlike feeling between boarders and day 'cads' as we were called. Having frequently to run the gauntlet when forgetful in anything up [?] our cricket and football subs. At about that time young Fletcher (the younger) was the ringleader for the boarders, and Ike Hodges the day-cads. However this came to a climax one afternoon when the two leaders were pitted against each other with bare fists. It was behind the gymnasium. The whole school (masters excepted) witnessed the affair. It was do or die for the day-cads, so Ike was backed for all we were worth. Details—both shaped up and each appeared confident of success. First result. Ike was sent head over heels with a fearful blow. Boarders jubilant. Day C. anyhow. However the fight went on for three quarters of an hour, when old Dick Chater appeared walking very slowly from the Quad towards the gymnasium reading (he knew of course what was on and thought time should be up) this stopped the fight and the referee awarded the battle to the man who appeared in class next morning with the least bruises. Ike after applying raw steak to his face all night came to the scratch next morning almost devoid of marks, while his opponent could only just about see his way to the breakfast table. The D. Cs. had won and thereafter our lives were saved from torture. Prefects were formed and all went merry. Hurrah for the old school.[7]

[7] C. M. Garrard, reminiscence, archives.

90

What have we seen? A drama played out before the whole school with a tacitly agreed method of achieving a points decision in the case of a draw, formalizing the in-built animus between boarders and day boys? Probably! But deeper than that there was, as Wilson hoped and preached, a definite code of honour, respected by authority in the gentle signal of the slowly approaching master. The date was probably 1875 when the two Fletchers entered the school, allowing C. M. Garrard, who told the story, a small lapse of memory in his reference to prefects because they were, in fact, introduced in that year.*

Another Garrard, the master A. F., warned Philip Brown in 1931 that the ancient feud between the two factions should not be over-emphasized. Much of it, he thought, sprang from the opposition to 'townies' in English schoolboy novels. He underscored Wilson's preference for boarders because they could be more easily trained, and remembered his elder brothers coming home from Geelong Grammar raging against the boarders, whom they taunted with Higin-botham's famous phrase 'the wealthy lower orders'. This transference of English class attitudes, developed in communities where the young gentlemen were outsiders in the town, to groups within a school, was peculiar to the mixed day and boarding scene in Australia. Another old Geelong College boy wrote of sport there in the 1860s that 'the day boys though able to defeat the boarders, found it more discreet to play a losing game'. At Geelong Grammar in the 1870s, of course, the day boys could no more have beaten the boarders than change their inferior social status. There would have been no point in making up teams of day boys versus boarders as a means of achieving the internal competition which in English schools (and later at GGS) was found in rivalry between boarding-houses.

When J. C. Taylor**constructed the Bracebridge Wilson Hall in 1896 along McKillop Street, across from the north-east corner of the main building, there was a new focus for boys. A tall timber struc-ture, the main hall was 27 metres long (including the stage), the auditorium being 23 metres by 14 metres. Opening off it to the north were the museum and (cadets?) uniform room, a dressing room and a bathroom boasting six 'tank showers' cascading onto a 'modern asphalt floor'. As an expression of Lindon's concern for them, day boys were given a room of their own on the south side and next to that a sitting room opened into the tuckshop, nicknamed the 'Cale' (pronounced Cally), which was managed by a master and an elected committee of boys. It was open at lunchtime and between 5 p.m. and tea and was 'ready to sell whatever boys like in the way of tucker'. This was less of a boon, perhaps, to day boys than to boarders, who, being forbidden the streets at lunchtime, had to

---

* Isaac Hodges entered in 1872 and C. M. Garrard in 1873.

** The Geelong building firm still intact in 1986.

The Bracebridge Wilson Hall, seen from McKillop Street.

plead with 'day cads' to go to the original 'Cale' (the Caledonian Store in Moorabool Street) and fetch them delicacies, especially Canterbury cakes. In the 1860s an ancient pieman, with long hair and earrings, had peddled pies, tarts and those unbeatable Canterbury cakes at the McKillop Street gate.

The Bracebridge Wilson Hall drew off some of the magic of Big School. It was a great place for Pastimes and prize-givings as, apart from its special stage, it had twice the capacity of the older space. A new approach to gymnastics and drill (see p. 124) was made possible and a more relaxed approach to special occasions. One of these left an enduring mark. For years after the hall was moved to Corio the space above the proscenium arch carried the message (in white on a red background) 'Welcome Old Boys', put there for the dinner in 1900 from which sprang the Old Geelong Grammarians. It was the kind of memorial hall not possessed by most public schools until after World War I.

By the turn of the century the school grounds, at least to the west and south, were thick with trees and shrubs and bright with flowers, especially the Lindons' celebrated roses, which were exhibited with great success at local shows. Bracebridge Wilson, botanist, had been responsible for the initial planting, especially below the terraced entrance to his house and had dissected the area fashionably with neatly bordered paths. When the Browns arrived in 1912, Philip found a greenhouse fit for a playroom and a Norfolk Island pine that stood in a circle of buffalo grass at the centre of the garden like the Tree of Life. Along the south and west and around the playground fences, after the manner of his friend von Mueller, Wilson had planted fast-growing wattles and gums but, as early as 1867, a range of exotics was well established. The reporter of the *Geelong Advertiser* who covered the prize-giving that year could not 'refrain from admiration at the perfect transformation under Wilson'. According to his ornamental prose, the grounds teemed with 'horticultural and floricultural gems'.

In the 1880s the boys joined in. By 1883, after two years' work, forty small plots had been allotted to aspiring gardeners, who so pleased the headmaster that he arranged a flower show. Like illustrations from a modern seedsman's catalogue, the plots were ablaze with snapdragons, foxgloves, lupins, larkspurs, cornflowers, penstemons, calceolaria, pelargoniums, roses, phlox, pansies, forget-me-nots, candytuft, primroses, etc. There was even a rare white and black pansy. More significant, however in that transplanted English world, were Australian natives—grevilleas, heaths and deliciously perfumed boronias—as well as exotics from other lands, the daphne and bouvardia. Wilson gave two prizes, the lady judges two and the gardeners themselves another. No reports bridge the years to 1891, when we read that the boys' gardens were neglected except for one hero, who was irrigating from the overflow of a deep hole. Was there a spring in the grounds or had he through some quirk of the school's drainage system discovered a reservoir in the headmaster's old cesspit?

Comparable photographs of the south front of the building early in Wilson's day and late in Lindon's reveal a striking change. Apart from the trees and shrubs, the raw building had become in Cuthbertson's words 'deep-ivied to the topmost tower of all'. Otherwise there was no change. After mounting the steps that led to the terrace beneath the headmaster's entrance and then taking another flight to bridge the moat around the servants' basement, one entered the same distinctly domestic area, gabled rather than parapeted and rising to third-storey attics. To the right of the entrance hall near the main stairs was the headmaster's study, a kind of buffer between the official and private sides of the school. Further east were a drawing room, dining room, nursery, private pantry and the back stairs down which one went to the kitchen, servants' hall, housekeeper's room, store, pantry, cellars and stable. Food and servants came up.

Guests of the Wilsons, perhaps, in Maude Street outside the headmaster's residence, *c*. 1880. One of many fine photographs taken by Mrs Wilson.

Upstairs on the first floor there were three bedrooms, a bathroom and a water closet (until it was converted after the typhoid outbreak of 1887), and on the second floor three smaller attic rooms. A convenient and comfortable home for the Wilsons and their two daughters, it provided space to burn for the childless Lindons, even when Lindon's orphaned nephews Jack and Leonard were staying with them. Only during the Browns' brief stay from 1912 to 1914 was the accommodation stretched. Wilson wrote to his mother enthusiastically about his new home and, as he did with the garden, furnished it with care. He and his wife Oriana seemed to achieve comfort and taste with very little money. They could not be lavish entertainers, merely doing their duty when the bishop or other dignatories visited, or when 'people connected at home' made their appearance.

Public hospitality was offered in the school dining room, which, like Big School diagonally across the quad, occupied the whole width of the building and was entered separately from the headmaster's premises, the study corridor and the quad. Three tables with bench seats ran the length of the room and a maid for each brought the food from a serving hatch. Masters presided over the tables, checking attendance and carving furiously to appease the everlasting hunger of boarders. At the servery the school porter strained on the ropes of a crude lift bringing food from the basement kitchen, exchanging shouts through the shaft with the cook and her helpers working at the big table and huge range down below. For all the thought that was given to improving things about the school, it was not until 1895 that a counterbalanced cupboard, working smoothly in a proper frame, was installed in place of that backbreaking contrivance.

Occasionally the staff lifted their game for an official feast, like the luncheon preceding the 1867 prize-giving. On that occasion Wilson entertained about sixty ladies and gentlemen, including Canon Goodman's house-guest, Lord William Phipps. The board of management treated the lord with the respect given to the great silver sporting trophies which, with the photographs of crews, teams and

1857-1907

Jubilee Dinner.

June 24th, 1907

≋ Menu ≋

Oysters on Shell.

Roast Turkey.   Apple Jelly.

Roast Duck.

Roast Fowl.   York Ham.

Ox Tongue.

Saddle Lamb.   Red Currant Jelly.

Roast Beef.

Sucking Pig.

Lobster Salad.   Plain Salad.

New Potatoes.   Green Peas.

Almond Pudding.   Apple Meringues.

Peach Pies.   Cherry Pies.

Maraschino Jelly.   Orange Jelly.   Wine Jelly.

Charlotte Russe.

Vanilla Cream.   Chocolate Cream.

Raspberry Cream.

Trifle.

Almonds and Raisins.   Fruits in Season.

Strawberries and Cream.

Ice Creams.

Cheese Straws.

prefects, gradually adorned the walls of that boarders' shrine. The board had not been so pleased when Vance threw extravagant private parties in 'their' premises. A day everyone remembered like a trophy was Tuesday 27 June 1893, when the governor, Lord Hopetoun, an Old Etonian, who had come to open a bazaar to raise funds for the projected hall, lunched with local celebrities and let it be clearly known that he wholeheartedly supported the public-school ideal.

The dining room was the setting for cricket, football and probably rowing and other dinners. It had seen the breakdown of discipline and the throwing of food in Vance's time, and the stealing of butter for Saturday loaves, which was connived at by the maids but brought a confrontation between Wilson and his wife. Oriana had tried to save money by trimming the Saturday provisions. Not one for penny-pinching, Wilson was greatly offended in 1883 when all the boarders except the prefects protested about the food. He assembled them in the dining hall and explained that he paid top prices for meat and all other provisions. The meals improved.

Quite often during or after a meal, in the closest thing to a family gathering, Wilson would have a word to his boys. They were also moved spontaneously—at any rate in 1891—after breakfast on the last morning of the year, to give 'three very hearty cheers' for the school servants who had 'shown such a disposition to oblige us in all ways, especially on Friday nights'. Friday night was a time of special activity after supper when the 'Saturday Book' was signed and the designated member of each party brought his bag to the servery in anticipation of a great day in the bush, sustained largely by bread (see p. 102).

Leaving the dining room by its western door, boys spilled out into the corridor that led to the great west entrance, where the main staircase rose to their bedrooms. On the left, after 1875, was the prefects' room, formerly a sitting room where the headmaster probably saw parents and boys. With fireplace and bookshelves, a dado carved with names and rough stone and brick walls sprinkled with pictures and the photos of sporting teams, it was hearty rather than comfortable, being dominated by a large table and seven or eight straight-backed, wooden chairs. Here the author of 'a Ramble through the School Buildings', in the *Quarterly* of October 1882, noted billies and pannikins used for the application of eucalyptus oil—the embrocation of sporting heroes during the football season.

Off that study corridor, from the prefects' room to the entrance hall, nine doors opened into tiny dens, unheated, but prized for their privacy. A table carved deep with the names of successive occupants and the two chairs of the pair who shared it left little room even for the shelves on which were crowded books and paraphernalia—especially bags, billies and frying-pans for Saturday outings. Naked gas jets, for which eye-shields were needed, provided light and acted as boilers for coffee or cocoa, whose aroma filled the study passage at supper time. This passage according to English custom, would have been the scene of most of the fagging in the school, but whether it was a privilege confined to prefects, or extended to all who inhabited studies, is not clear. In fact, the only evidence of fagging comes in the reminiscence of H. R. Gillett, who started in the lowest form in 1883 and says he was Fred Fairbairn's fag for a time.

If not playing organized games, after school the boarders had the run of the place. They could knock a ball around the quad, go down Moorabool Street to the teashops or, once the Bracebridge Wilson Hall was built, wait for the tuckshop to open at 5 p.m., read in the library or quiet room, garden (in the 1880s) or just muck about. Some looked after pets in a space provided at the stables for what at times became quite a menagerie of animals and birds captured in the bush. Possums, koalas, gliders, hawks and rosellas were mentioned. In study or bedroom, where junior boys had lockers, they worked at their wildflower and egg collections until the bell rang and it was time for tea and prep.

Evening prep for the younger boys was probably in Big School, but the library and other classrooms may have been used. In about 1887 some boys not quite at the top of the school were doing their prep with the Boss in his private classroom off the quad when Mrs Wilson came to tell him that the woollen mills near the Barwon breakwater, about 2 kilometres south-east of the school, were on fire. When he left with her, probably to look at the blaze from an upstairs window in his house, they skipped across the road and took a reel and hose to help put out the fire. Returning at 3 a.m., they found Wilson waiting for them with a present of 200 lines of Virgil to translate. Typical of Wilson, he is said to have relented after a few days 'because he knew we took the reel to fires without leave'. Perhaps he appreciated their public spirit.

Where they should have been by 10 p.m.—upstairs asleep— had at first been one vast dormitory running like a warehouse around the first floor of the north, west and south wings as far as the headmaster's house. Where the masters slept then is anyone's guess, though there was one room in the tower above the main entrance. Two years' experience of a handful of boys shivering in that great dormitory was enough for Wilson. In December 1864, when there were thirteen boarders, he did away with some of that wilderness by creating five bedrooms, each holding four or five boys and entered from a passage leading to the main staircase by a new doorway knocked into the wall of his house. A year later he built two more and added a hospital ward at the extreme east end. And so it went on, two rooms, and then another two, as the boarding numbers climbed above forty in 1869.

In the 1890s we know that there were nineteen boys' bedrooms, with masters' rooms interspersed, along bleak passages lit by unguarded batswing burners. That proximity of masters' and boys' rooms provided Ernest Jackson with the shock of his life when a master, sleepwalking in his long white nightshirt, appeared like a ghost at the end of his bed. The boys were allowed an inch of candle per room per night to light them to bed, and apart from primitive

A prefect's study.

The Old Geelong Grammarians.

OLD BOYS' DAY

October 21st, 1910.

DINNER GIVEN BY THE PRESIDENT
:: MR. DONALD MACKINNON ::
IN THE BRACEBRIDGE-WILSON HALL

individual lockers they shared an enamel jug, basin and pot and took a weekly (rostered) communal hot tub. When the cottage hospital was built near the gym in the 1870s the sickroom became a bathroom and a small night lavatory. That coincided with a more liberal approach to water because the town supply was connected on a memorable day in February 1874, ending the reliance on tanks in the ceiling of the north wing. Noel Learmonth even remembered getting pleasure from the primitive cold showers:

The bathroom was a square well about 10ft. x 10ft., with a line of cold showers along one wall. The floor and walls were lead, and one of Saturday night's joys on returning from a day in the bush was to plug the drainage hole with the posterior of a small boy, turn on all showers, and flood the well.[8]

Perhaps the masters had some kind of plug. On one occasion a huge fall of plaster downstairs was blamed on carelessness in the masters' bathroom, which the board thought Wilson should have controlled.

Whether the matron showered or just took a tub in her room is not revealed. For much of the period she was Miss J. Boyd, known universally as Jennie, who soothed aches and scratches, mothered the little ones and kept clothes in repair. According to the 1878 prospectus, boarders were to bring four sheets, three pillow cases, six linen towels, two bath towels, 'the usual underclothing' and the following:

1 Great Coat or Cape	1 Pair Slippers
1 Suit Best Clothes	1 Best Hat
1 Suit Second-best Clothes	1 Hat for Common Wear
1 Suit for Common Wear	Brush and Comb and Bag
1 Pair Best Boots	Nail Brush and Tooth Brush
2 Pairs Common Boots (stout)	Sponge

It is particularly requested that every article belonging to a boy should be marked clearly with his name in full, not initials only; and an accurate list should be placed in his box.[9]

Some of those boxes had come hundreds, even thousands, of kilometres by road, rail and steamer, from the far ends of Victoria and from interstate. Some sense of the boarders' notion of distance, an important element in their world view, is given by E. S. Jackson, whose father, late in January 1868, drove his own two boys and two others in an American wagon from Sandford on the Wannon, beyond Hamilton. The journey of 350 kilometres took five days, with picnic lunches and overnight stops at hotels. The return was worse—by a little steamer, tossing like a wild horse, to Portland, and then by the station wagon. While at sea Ernest felt like Mark Twain, afraid at first that the ship would go down, then afraid that it would not. Later he was allowed to link home and school by the Ballarat train and a Cobb and Co coach. Assuming such travel, the 1878 prospectus concluded that the 'facility for train and steamer', together with the climate and quietness of Geelong, made it an ideal place for a public school on the lines of those at home.

[8] *Corian*, May 1960, p. 13.
[9] *Prospectus*, 1878, archives.

Even after the railways extended far to the west, arrival at school was not necessarily straightforward. Noel Learmonth arrived from Portland late at night on the Saturday after Easter, discovering more about the school than he had bargained for:

I entered the School after Easter, 1895, and probably no boy before or since has done so by the same route, through the kitchen at 10 p.m. In the old rectangular school building there were three main entrances—through a door into the 'quad.', the kitchen on the basement, and the Headmaster's front door, which, of course, no new boy would dare approach. It was the Saturday after Easter, and the School was due to re-open on Monday morning, but there was not a boy in the building and none turning up. The 'quad.' was locked, so the 'cabbie' deposited me with baggage at the kitchen entrance, and departed. After some hesitation I knocked on and opened a door and interrupted a staff party. After due inspection and questioning, one of the maids escorted me upstairs along a passage to the 'Head's' study door, and also departed. Thus I had my first interview with J. B. Wilson. Though school was scheduled to start on Monday, there was not a boy nor master in the building, so Mrs. Wilson provided me with a bed and I had breakfast with the old 'Chief' and his wife, who were tremendously elated with news they had received of the School's rowing victory over St. Peter's College in the first of the many contests between the schools. On Sunday morning a day boy appeared to collect some books, and he took me to his home.

School openings were very casual in those days. On Monday morning a few boys turned up and by next week-end they had all trickled back, the last to arrive being the crew and 'Cuth.' from Adelaide.[10]

There, in a new boy's arrival, the warm, informal character of Wilson's regime is revealed. Of course, once the school settled in, the term was full of significant routines. Each morning John, the porter—handyman, strode along the dormitory passages at 6 o'clock, ringing a large bell. In winter (after 1874 and town water) this began a rush to the cold showers and in summer a hasty grab for trousers and coats to supplement nightshirts, then off at the double for nearly 2 kilometres by short cuts across vacant allotments to Blunt's baths, where the bottom was muddy and the water often murky. Back at school by 7 a.m., for hot coffee and biscuits, boys dressed and did half an hour's prep before breakfast. In Lindon's day reveille was at 7 a.m. and many boys rode bikes to the baths. Instead of prep they assembled for roll-call and prayers before breakfast.

Being held on a tight rein in house and school by Lindon, they relished the opportunity to buck when he was absent:

A great jubilation would circulate on occasion on 'Friday night—"Boss" has gone to Melbourne and C—'s, on duty.' After lights-out there would be a tremendous rumble as the 16lb. shot rolled the whole way from 10 to 19 dormitories, followed closely by the 14-pounder. C—would rush upstairs and be greeted by a Feu-de-Joie, all doors 10−19 being slammed in succession. Being in No. 8 myself, we did not participate, as it was at the head of the stairs. A further refinement of torture was also practised. Dormitories were lit individually by a one-inch piece of candle. The means of ignition of these glims was a batswing gas-burner in the passage, after drawing the nightly issue from Matron's room. Door handles were of brass, and before the feu-de-joie each handle was nicely warmed up. Poor old C—would make several attempts to open a door before finding one cool enough, and then probably would have his glasses removed by a stretched thread, and be greeted by gentle snores.[11]

10 N. Learmonth, reminiscence, *Corian*, May 1960, p. 13.
11 P. N. Dobson, reminiscence, *Corian*, May, 1960, pp. 16−17. Dobson joined the school in 1904.

In contrast to Saturdays (see p. 103), when the boarders were scattered far and wide, Sundays were spent around the school. There was no sea-bathing so they slept in, making a rush for the dining-room door before it shut at 8.30, adjusting final items of clothing, but almost regretting their fragile punctuality when gentle 'Jarps' Morris was on duty. He let latecomers in with the penalty, 'awarded with such kindly grace that the culprit received it almost as a treasured prize', of writing out the passage from Proverbs commencing, 'Go to the ant, thou sluggard'.

After breakfast there was a period of scripture and at 10.30 a.m. Lindon (at least) appeared at the quadrangle door of the dining room, doling out sixpence church money and letting boys know if they had been invited to lunch by a Geelong family. Church was at 11 a.m., the various denominations hiving off to their own churches and the Anglican majority crossing the road to Christ Church, into a low, sloping gallery in the south transept, where the seats were so close together that a normal-sized boy had to sit bolt upright to fit his knees in. Tall boys suffered agony during Canon Goodman's forty-minute sermons. The only time he was known to preach briefly was one Sunday night when number 19 dormitory caught fire and several seniors who put it out came to church half-way through the service, smelling so horribly of burnt feathers and wool that 'Goodie's discourse' was cut to twenty minutes.

Despite the convenience of Christ Church, those long, usually inappropriate sermons, set Cuthbertson's mind running in 1886 along the line of English precedent to bemoan the absence of a chapel with its mellow windows and pews hallowed by the bottoms of generations of schoolboys:

How seldom do the boys of this school receive a word of advice as to the special trials and temptations of Public School life. How often is the language and style of the sermons which they hear above their comprehension. We hold that every boy ought to hear every week, plain words of sympathy, of encouragement, of reproof from his place in the school chapel.[12]

He hoped for the effect Dr Arnold had on Tom Brown. Lindon tried to satisfy that need by conducting a Sunday night service once a fortnight in Big School, and at least one of his boys found his straight talks of much greater moment than any number of Christ Church sermons.

Lindon, like Wilson a warden and vestryman at Christ Church, but unlike him a slightly pompous man, made a show of putting a gold sovereign into the collection each week and took pleasure in counting it when he was on duty. One week it failed to survive the passage of the plate and he created a fuss. That shining coin became a *cause célèbre*, magnified when Garrard teasingly asked Lindon if he had recovered his half-sovereign. 'My sovereign, if you please', was the reply.

Lindon was impeccable in his relationships with the church and in his tightening up of scholarship at the school, the teaching of

[12] *Quarterly*, Dec. 1886, pp. 1–2.

scripture became more systematic and rigorous. As Manning Clark would say, he was a straightener, whereas Wilson was an enlarger of mankind. Wilson had been vulnerable to clerical criticism despite his long friendship with Canon Goodman and the influential layman, Charles Sladen. A major crisis of his headmastership came out of the blue in 1872 when Archdeacon Stretch, one of the founders of the school, who had opposed the appointment of a layman as headmaster, laid the serious charges against him that he had neglected to attend church and had even been yachting on Sundays. Wilson made no denial, but explained to the satisfaction of the board of management that many of his absences from church were caused by serious illness among the boys or other urgent matters. He acknowledged putting a lesser duty before a greater and promised not to offend again. The Sundays on which he appeared in his yacht at Queenscliff would have been during holidays when he had been prevented by rough weather in the notorious Rip at Port Phillip Heads from returning earlier to his moorings.

The boys had their secular moments on Sundays. Skilful Romeos could make romantic contacts at Christ Church, running the gauntlet of prefects by slipping out the side doors and around to the front, but their best bet was the compulsory Sunday-afternoon walk of Lindon's day or the ostensible training run of Wilson's, 'in the course of which we very happily met the girls of our fancy'. Women were drafted into the nooks and crannies of that male world, which they were allowed to foster with the mending of clothes, soothing of sores, making of beds, tidying of rooms, cooking and serving of meals, ordering of provisions and softening of formal occasions. Wilson's and Lindon's wives, partnering their husbands in farming the school, shouldered significant managerial tasks, Oriana Wilson gently in the background, Annie Lindon sometimes fiercely visible.

Oriana Wilson, *c*. 1865.

The Lindons, indeed, were inseparable. Mrs Lindon was as formidable as her husband, whether growing prize-winning roses for the Geelong Horticultural Show, hiking in the New Zealand Alps (where she was the second woman known to ascend Mount Cook) or scoring well at the Geelong Golf Club, of whose associates Mrs Lindon was treasurer. She represented the club on the Victorian Ladies' Golf Union, of which she became the founding president. More forceful than her predecessor around the school, she wrote frequently to the council proposing alterations and expenditures and helped her husband plan special functions. She played the harmonium for the fortnightly Sunday evening services in Big School and the piano at Saturday-night concerts. All in all, she served the school so energetically, so far beyond a woman's role and so interferingly in the eyes of the new council of 1909, that they wrote into the next headmaster's contract a clause forbidding his wife from taking any part in the formal organization of the school. The boys called her 'Ma Tit', presumably relating her size and activity to the behaviour of a small bird of their acquaintance.

The proper place of women in a boys' school was to be useful

The Jubilee Ball, 1907, in the Bracebridge Wilson Hall.

when required, to fill the audiences and receive three cheers at Pastimes, to colour ceremonial occasions, to pander to rather fragile male egos and to be (though not in the language of the day) sex symbols. J. F. Stretch,* Bishop of Newcastle and President of the Old Geelong Grammarians, speaking at the jubilee in 1907 said that the young woman 'always had a place that was simply adorable', but he was a little uncertain whether gaining the vote had affected her position on that pedestal. Emblematic of male—female sentiment was the making of a new school flag by Wilson's daughters in 1887. It was presented by the headmaster on their behalf to the captain of cricket at a school assembly in the quadrangle on a day the eleven were going into battle for the purity and truth represented by its blue and white colours. 'It is not defeat which brings disgrace upon the school colours,' he reminded them, 'but forgetfulness of the path of honour'. The team took the field and won, with three cheers for the flag, three cheers for its donors and three cheers for Mr and Mrs Wilson still ringing in their ears.

---

* A churchman of exceptional charm, Stretch was the prototype for the Reverend Mr Shepherd in Henry Handel Richardson's *The Getting of Wisdom*. (H. H. Richardson, *Myself when Young*, Heinemann, London, 1948 pp. 53—61.) He was one of three future bishops at GGS in 1870.

100

7

Youth's triumphant call

Old friends, old comrades; once again we hear
In bush, on field and river, ringing clear,
The echoes glad of youth's triumphant call.[1]

Most of the myths of Geelong Grammar School in the nineteenth
century were outdoor myths. Its ideals, more moral than scholarly,
were found in the freedom of the bush and in the challenge of the
playing-fields and river. Cuthbertson's poetry shaped the experience,
the rhetoric of the *Quarterly* embalmed it, but coming through the
reminiscences of those who participated is the impression of great
satisfaction and indelible memories not matched at other schools.*
The reality must have been very strong. In addition, it is important
to notice that in the shaping of the school the man-made challenges
of games could not, apparently, compare with the magic of the bush.

The Bush
Every weekend the whole boarding-house went out in 'Saturday
Parties' of at least three members into the surrounding countryside.
They went by boat, cart and on foot (or later by bicycle), making for
regular camping places at which to breakfast and then go further
afield to nest or fish or swim or just ramble about. How these
unusual 'Saturday Camps' began is not recorded, but the fact that
they were deeply ingrained by the time Cuthbertson arrived and
started the magazine in 1875 suggests that they grew out of J. B.
Wilson's love of nature and from his concern for the development of
independence of spirit and comradeship among his boys.** At first
the camps were probably reached on foot or by cart, but it is possible
that quite early boats were borrowed and the Barwon explored

---

* Boarders at Scotch, for instance, had occasional outings, dependent upon the enthusiasm of a
particular master at a particular time. There was no boy-centered routine.

**Wilson wrote to a government official in 1874 to protest about the appropriation for private
purposes of land at Spring Creek (Torquay) 'which has for many years been one of our most
popular spots for picnic and fishing parties'.

[1] *Quarterly*, Oct. 1887, p. 6.

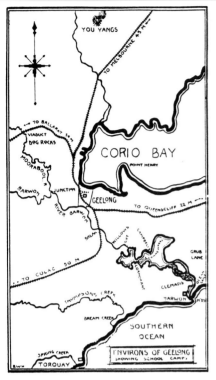

upstream and down. John Tait, a day boy, made several expeditions in the 1850s and in 1862, after he left school, made his own simple outrigger boat which he sailed and rowed to camps at Barwon Heads. The greatest rowing days followed the formation of the boat club in 1874, after which, as the fleet grew, more and more boys took their billies down the river.

By the 1880s the camps were an ancient institution. School was unthinkable without them. In October 1886 'Two Boys and a Master', who wrote up the term's excursions for the *Quarterly*, ended on this philosophical note:

> How good are these long bright days, when we shake off the routine of School life and when boy and master meet on equal terms. We believe that it is to this companionship on the river and in the bush that we owe much of the loyalty which has so long been the distinguishing mark of the boys of this School ... and we are firmly persuaded that the Saturday holiday has the effect of softening the roughness of School life, of making fellows feel their responsibility to the School, and of saturating them, one and all, with that unreasoning and indefinable love for 'the Grammar' which, wherever they may be, will never leave them.[2]

In simple terms, it relaxed them and gave them a powerful common experience, a vital part of which was the trust placed in boys not to take advantage of 'our healthy holiday for base purposes'.

The writers placed the Saturday Parties above even games for sheer enjoyment.

> These days spent in the pure bush air, with jolly comrades, are the happiest which we enjoy. Matches and races, no doubt, are good and exciting, especially when we know our opponents treat us fairly; but they are not to be compared to a good long day at the creeks or the river. Long flourish the School Camps.[3]

Nothing could be a greater disaster to a boy than to miss a Saturday in spring when, as one of them said, 'the wattle was in bloom, the birds singing in the bush, when the billy boils most pleasantly and bird nesting was in full swing'.

That day boys were excluded from this defining experience seems to follow from the fact that the parties set off, officially at least, at 4 a.m., having entered their names and destinations the night before in the 'Saturday Book'. They arrived back well after sunset, dirty, tired and immensely hungry, despite their 'well stuffed and solemn' bread bags and the pancakes, potatoes, meat, fish, mushrooms and other food they cooked. Friday night preparations included pinching butter from the tea table and leaving one food bag per party with the domestic staff, who consulted the Saturday Book and filled the bags before supper with half a loaf of bread for each boy and rations of tea, sugar and salt. Extras like condensed milk, coffee, jam and sardines had already been bought at the local shop, each boy putting in a shilling. These luxuries were stored ready in studies or lockers, alongside tomahawks, billies and frying-pans. Every boy got out his strongest boots and selected clothes of 'almost ragged simplicity'.

[2] *Quarterly*, Oct. 1886, p. 6.
[3] *Quarterly*, Oct. 1886, p. 6.

A Saturday with 'Cuth', 1902. H. M. R. Rupp, destined to be a fine naturalist, is second on the right from Cuthbertson.

Within this tradition the hinterland became so much part of the school that as late as 1929 the *Corian** carried on its back cover a map showing the location of school camps. Boys roamed from the You Yangs to Torquay and off the map towards Anglesea. On the river their favourite breakfast place was The Willows, 8 kilometres downstream past the Barwon Breakwater, called simply 'the Break'. Depending on their mood and strength and on the state of wind, weather and tide, they then decided whether to go on to Cormorant, Campbell's or Clematis, or even to Barwon Heads for a swim in the ocean. Upstream they sought the junction of the Barwon and Moorabool rivers and Buckley's Falls, a relatively easy row, especially pleasant in autumn when grapes could be bought for a shilling a bucket from vineyards on the Barrabool slopes. On land, the carts went to Grub Lane, Spring Creek or the You Yangs, the walkers to the Dog Rocks, Bream Creek and out on the Queenscliff Road, short of Grub Lane. In winter especially, when time was short, they settled for 'Gillies', where the wattles were beautiful in grassy paddocks on the edge of 20 hectares of forest only 8 kilometres south of Geelong.

Gillies may not be marked on the *Corian* map because of clearing and subdivision and because depredation by the boys themselves had reduced its attractiveness.** They attacked the bush in the

---

* The name given to the magazine when the school moved to Corio in 1914.

** It was also absent from a similar but earlier map published in the jubilee *History and Register* in 1907, following an article by Cuthbertson on the camps.

103

same savage spirit as their pioneer ancestors, making life difficult for the birds whose eggs they coveted, joining with shouts of joy in possum hunts, carving their names on trees and hacking and burning the timber. Nothing so excited the large winter contingent at Gillies as a ringtail possum leaping from tree to tree, pelted with rocks, unless it was their almost competitive cooking of pancakes as they rested by their fires after the chase.

This little army of boys fouled their own paradise. By the late 1880s the camps at 'the Bridge', on the Queenscliff Road near the Ocean Grove turnoff, and at Bream Creek gave little joy. C. F. Belcher, writing as an old boy in 1893, mourned the changes at Bream Creek. The black-robin nests, which had been a school tradition, had all gone years before and so had those of duck and teal, which used to be plentiful. Even the bream had vanished. Gone were the days as in the first quarter of 1878, when every Saturday evening boys trudged home with loads of fish. Floods had previously opened the mouth of the creek.

'Lovers of the river have many pet haunts', said the *Quarterly* in October 1886, and there were dozens of these amateurs. Even in 1878 the Boat Club could put all its thirty-one members on the water at the same time, in four fours, an eight and two pleasure-boats. H. M. R. Rupp recalled happy Saturdays crossing the Break at sunrise to laze at the Willows or swing energetically to Campbell's, Cormorant, Clematis or Barwon Heads. Just to row was pleasure, and in spring those who went furthest were rewarded with flowering tea-tree, cascading into glassy, silver strings of clematis. Even so, at that season many oarsmen forsook the river for nesting, despite the presence of eggs in the reeds and good spots inland from their landing places. Rowers usually returned muddier, wetter and more bedraggled than anyone, especially if they had been stuck at low water in the mud flats of the Gut or had trouble at the Break. In capricious conditions of wind and tide, and especially if the river was high, they had a gruelling slog home in the dark.

Feats of endurance were common. In September 1890, when Clematis was at its most beautiful, 'a four of youngsters had a very hard fight home against a strong tide and half a gale of wind'. It took them over six hours. The same day three of the first crew had to abandon a heavy pleasure-boat at Campbell's and walk home because they could make little headway; and the second crew's boat was blown away while they were nesting after breakfast and had to be located by telescope and rescued by a friendly Old Melburnian in a punt. He spent over two hours bringing it back a few kilometres. A day was easy to fill with such adventures and the desire to tell a good story on returning home established a canon of epic journeys. In September 1886 two pairs, one with fixed and the other with sliding seats, got to Barwon Heads and back. In the fixed pair the captain of boats and the captain of cricket rowed for nine and a half hours in a seventeen-hour day (say 4 a.m. to 9 p.m.) and in the sliding pair two masters were out for thirteen hours of which eight hours forty minutes were rowed. They were lucky that the strong tailwind of the morning died for their return. Back at school over supper, when the day's experiences were shared, boys grew wiser in the ways of the river and exulted in their comradeship.

Nesters also talked of the distances they covered and, after their showers and supper, crowded around the lucky parties who had brought home rare eggs. On one Saturday in October 1890 eight parties, totalling thirty-nine 'fellows' were on the Grub Lane track, most of them happy to camp at the water-hole near the Barwon Heads turn-off, where they gathered so regularly that some had planted vegetables. Moving on restlessly all day in the hope of special finds they despoiled hundreds of nests for the eggs of fantails, canaries, diamond-hawks, jays, greenbacks, bronze and speckled cuckoos, chocolate-birds, diamond woodpeckers, mopokes, kooka-burras, crows, wattle-birds and curlews.* Eleven or twelve kilometres out, the Grub Lane nesting ground included an area later given to the school and now a wildlife sanctuary. More hardy characters, 'fellows of the true old breed', as 'tough as maple', made the 14 kilometres to Bream Creek before breakfast, while some went even further to Spring Creek or Jan Juc, where at that time the Otway forest began. It had wonderful scenery and the nests of the sphinx, the black magpie and the whistling jackass. Others tried the You Yangs, the Moorabool River and the north shore of Corio Bay. Cuthbertson saw them as Adams in paradise.

Charles Belcher, one of the few who continued an interest in birds throughout his life, reminisced in 1956, with some pangs of conscience, about the cult of nesting, which he defended as no more cruel than fishing. He contended that it was not—as he thought might be feared—spiritually damaging, by making boys callous. But it was environmentally disastrous, as Belcher knew by 1893 in the disappearance of the black-robin, duck and teal from Bream Creek. As a good haul was a hundred eggs for the season and the number of boarders averaged about seventy in the heyday of nesting, it is likely that five thousand eggs were taken each year from about 1870 to 1890, with special attention to rare species. Numbers, incidentally, seem to have been less important to boys than the thrill of the chase for uncommon varieties.

Days when nothing was found could be enjoyed for the tough-ness they developed, the fresh air, the bush food and the close companionship. Boys taught themselves and each other about nature and were scornful that masters were 'very weak about eggs'. Only Garrard, who had roamed the area as a boy, was really 'eggy'. Masters might know the common sorts but 'ask them to describe a Whistling Jack or Black Robin and they collapse at once'. In that sense nesting was a cult in which boys were the initiates and masters

THE NESTER'S SONG

To the dark-armed forest yonder,
    Ere the gray
  Crimsons with the dawn of day,
With our truest mates we wander
    And beside the camp we stay
      Till we hear
  Music of the magpie near.

Haunts of diamond hawk invite us,
    Robins black
  Offer plunder that we lack,
Yellow-breasted shrikes requite us,
    And the nest of 'whistling jack'
      From our gaze
  Hidden in the wattle sprays.

Brooding-place of grey-winged plover,
    Lowly laid,
  Find we in the tussocks' braid,
Or the dim retreat discover
    That the cunning sphinx has made
      High aloft
  With its woven fibres soft.

Firm to swaying branch that narrows
    Oft we cling,
  And our burden earthward fling,
While the parrots—azure arrows—
    Round us flutter, shriek, and sing,
      Till we come
  Sliding from the lofty gum.

Monarchs we of rarest treasure,
    Wealth untold,
  When the lake thrush egg we hold,
Finding ever keenest pleasure
    In the forest's green and gold,
      In the sea
  Sighted from the topmost tree.

Leave the river, leave the rowing—
    We but love
  Rustle of the leaves above,
Sunlight on the blue-gums glowing,
    Plaintive murmur of the dove,
      And the quest
  Of the deeply hidden nest.[4]

---

* The names are those they used.

[4] *Barwon Ballads*, pp. 195–6.

Charles F. Belcher, as a schoolboy, *c.* 1893.

just tagged along. It is hard to see masters developing a strategy like that of the big boys, who took the cox of the crew with them to climb right out in the tea-tree over Bream Creek and left him to scramble down and rush after them if he found no eggs.

Talking of masters, Belcher recalled outings in the 1880s with Bracebridge Wilson, who would hire Mickey Sheridan's cab on a good spring day and take two or three boys far afield, perhaps to the Point Lonsdale lakes, where he looked for algae. Against the advantage of being fresh for nesting on arrival, boys had to put up with a much later start and therefore a short day. Unless up front with Mickey, they had also to restrain themselves until the headmaster started a topic of conversation.

Among the few, like Belcher, in whom genuine scientific interest was kindled, H. M. R. Rupp began a lifelong study of Australian flora. When his collection of orchids was given to the Herbarium of New South Wales in the 1940s, it included two or three specimens gathered on far-off Saturdays near Geelong. In 1949 he became only the third Victorian, after von Mueller and Baldwin Spencer, to win the Clarke Memorial Medal of the Royal Society of New South Wales. His more hearty contemporaries brought back masses of pink and white heath from Anglesea and bouquets of orchids and native violets from Spring Creek and Jan Juc.

As photography became easier about 1890, after the invention of the dry plate had made cameras more portable and when printing techniques improved, the *Quarterly* became excited about the possibility of reproducing photographs like one of two crews at the Willows 'clustered on a tree' and a sunset at Connewarre. It also promised 'our friends in English schools' that they would be given views of the wild ocean coast.

It was probably also thought that English boys* would envy the fraternity of the Saturday Party and admire the rivalry to make the best winter pancakes, endure the longest tramp or row, find special nests and wildflowers, kill snakes, capture gliders and make pets of baby rosellas. In their eagerness to achieve legendary feats or get the best nesting territory, boys rose earlier and earlier—if indeed they went to bed at all—so that the headmaster had to put them on their honour in 1890 not to set out before 4 a.m.

As the country became more settled and the nesting and fishing less inviting, long drives in a strange assortment of vehicles, with which the grounds were studded on Friday nights, took over. Prodigious walks also became common. One old boy wrote proudly in 1939 of a succession of walks he made in the spring of 1909. One Saturday, with two companions, he covered 53 kilometres to the You Yangs and back, and the next week 54 to Barwon Heads. A month later the 48-kilometre round trip to Torquay seemed no distance. That was

---

* There were traditions of afternoon rambles, bird-nesting, squirrel hunts and shooting expeditions at English schools, but nothing like the full-day official outings of GGS.

eclipsed by a party who went right to the end of Queenscliff pier and back, a grinding 61 kilometres. Imagine his distress on visiting the school one Saturday in 1939 to find a majority of boys lazing about, none of whom, as far as he could tell, had ever heard of the Dog Rocks. If they did go out on Saturdays, ten to one would have mounted bicycles, which forty years before were beginning to transform the Saturday programme. By the turn of the century the 'safety' bicycle had become so strong and easy to ride that, hung with frying-pan, bag and billy, it often became the steed for Saturday Parties, not just the vehicle for stately rides about the town on Sunday afternoons as in the day of the Bicycle Club with its penny farthings in the 1880s.

The picture we get of Saturdays at the old school is one of young lords of creation running free in the bush. They seemed to extend the special world of the school to the whole Bellarine Peninsula. References to outsiders were few—Wilson's cabman, the Old Melburnian with the punt, a couple of 'witless rustics' in hob-nailed boots who took one of the boats from the Willows in 1886 and brought it clumsily back, badly scratched and half-full of water, and a typical Australian 'hatter', who screamed profanities at passing oarsmen from a bark hut near Barwon Heads. There must have been accidents and injuries and the chills for which Dr Pincott ordered a hot bath at the sanatorium in 1883, but no disasters were recorded during more than fifty years of Saturday outings from the gray school on the hill. Through Wilson's trust, boys had been given an amount of independence rare, if not unique, in the annals of education. They were exposed to all kinds of situations and sometimes to terrible weather. Witness a cart coming back from the You Yangs

The last Saturday Parties of 1910 or 1911, gathered at The Willows.

107

on a desperately wet and thundery night. After most of the party got on the train (probably at Lara), the two hardiest pressed on through a ten-minute burst of St Elmo's fire, the electricity sparking from their caps and dancing over the harness and wheels. The same night a crew was almost blinded by lightning at the Break; it took them a day fully to recover their sight.

Such a day, pressed like the best of Rupp's orchids into the pages of his *Barwon Ballads*, inspired one among many poems through which Cuthbertson celebrated unforgettable Saturdays:

Home in the Storm
All the day the summer sun had tried us,
    And our hope was in the evening cool,
In the southern wind, so long denied us,
    Sweeping over sea and river pool.

So we rowed and wrestled, happy-mated,
    Bathed in breakers at the burning noon,
And among the pale green lignums waited
    On the margin of the dark lagoon.

But at sunset, when the clouds were bright'ning
    And the lilac with the rose was wed,
Came the inky pall, the vivid lightning,
    And the angry thunder pealed o'erhead.

From above a rainy deluge spouted,
    Hissing white upon the dusky lake,
And, disconsolate, we gazed and doubted
    If the *Daphne* would regain the 'Break'.

But we turned and faced the stormy water,
    Though the oars were dipped far up the loom,
And we struggled till at last we brought her
    Through the channel in the gathering gloom.

Ever in the sky the steel-blue quiver
    Of the lightning showed the landscape weird,
Lit the rushes, lit the silent river,
    And amid the thunder disappeared.

But the storm passed and the calm succeeded,
    And the moonbeams pierced the fleecy gray,
And, with better omen, on we speeded
    Past the willows on our homeward way.[5]

Wilson's spirited approach is also seen in the picnic he arranged on 23 November 1867 at Queenscliff, to give those of his boys whose families were not themselves on the road a chance to greet the *Galatea* with Australia's first royal visitor, the Duke of Edinburgh, on board. 'We hired a monster coach, capable of carrying forty people and drawn by a team of six capital horses...' Despite a mishap which put them on foot for over an hour, while the coach returned to Geelong for repairs, the party arrived at Queenscliff at 11 a.m. and chose a spot for a 'bivuac'. 'In ten minutes', Wilson

[5] *Barwon Ballads*, pp. 141–2.

108

wrote to his father, 'I had our little tent pitched and all the stores, solid and liquid, stowed away in it under charge of our manservant'. From a nearby cliff the GGS contingent watched the *Galatea* join the Victorian fleet. When she had gone they scattered all over the place to explore 'the pretty little township'.

Queenscliff, about 1870, taken by Oriana Wilson.

On field and river
The flag presented to the school by Wilson's daughters in 1887 (see p. 100) was no idle piece of bunting, but an emblem charged with the rhetoric of 'play up, play up and play the game'. The sinews of English muscular Christianity were strongly in evidence in the sports-mad provinces of Australia, where games between schools were often important middle-class social events, helping undecided parents to choose schools for their sons. A tiny flag always fluttered at the bow of the racing boat when Cuthbertson celebrated in verse the exploits of light-blue crews, and peacetime football contests were given the flavour of wartime gallantry in lines like:

> These are the men to be trusted
> Who grimly the colours defend.[6]

In front of at least a thousand spectators at annual football matches with Geelong College, or more at Melbourne games, and

[6] *Barwon Ballads*, p. 135.

109

many thousands at the Head of the River or the United Athletic Sports, Geelong Grammar boys carried a burden of expectation that they would keep on until exhausted and never do a mean thing. *Noblesse oblige*, no less. How well the action matched the rhetoric it is hard to say, but what can be seen is a 'holier than thou' treatment of the many disputes with other schools about the way a race was run or the age and eligibility of competitors. A long-standing gripe was the unwillingness of Melbourne schools to bring their boats to the Barwon, when GGS held the challenge cup and therefore had the choice of water. The Melbourne schools also insisted on using the Upper Yarra course when the race was in Melbourne which was difficult for a foreigner to steer and where the result might be determined by the toss for stations. At least one Geelong Grammar cox ran his crew into an obstruction on the side of the course. To the argument that few spectators would come to the Lower Yarra, GGS replied that given open water and a fair course it did not matter if the only spectators were the starter, umpire and judge.

Copies of opponents' magazines, if they had them, were combed for slights. In 1882 and 1883 the *Quarterly* and the *Melburnian* sniped at each other about which of the two schools was entitled to the football premiership, and in 1886 the *Quarterly* accused its rival of quibbling about the boat race:

When M.G.S. was beaten at cricket the *Melburnian* abused our wicket or the hue of our shirts. Now it says that we were moving at the start of the race and that the judge's verdict was wrong by half a length.[7]

Most shrill were complaints about the stacking of teams. After defeat by St Ignatius in an intercolonial rowing match in Sydney in 1889, it was asserted that the Ignatius stroke had left school three years before and that No. 2 had been attending university lectures. That was the last race against such dissemblers; more honourable opponents were found at St Peter's, Adelaide, in 1895. Cricket and football matches with Geelong College were suspended for two years following accusations in 1881 that the College was stacking its football team, and even after hostilities resumed there was talk of College boys returning to school just before a match and leaving immediately afterwards. The *Quarterly* and the *Melburnian* joined forces against Scotch in 1890, complaining that the Scotch twenty was 'recruited too freely during the season'. Apart from the usual old boy dropping in for a game, Scotch is said to have fielded one undergraduate, one Wesley old boy and a private-school league player.

Backbiting of this sort became so bad that the five 'Public Schools'—MGS, GGS, Scotch, Wesley and St Patrick's*—adopted a set of rules in 1890. 'Boys' had to be under twenty-one on the first of January in the following year and were to be genuinely attending

---

[7] *Quarterly*, Oct. 1886, p. 33.

* St Patrick's played only one game (in 1891 at cricket) against Geelong Grammar between 1891 and 1901, when Xavier replaced it.

school. Headmasters were required personally to write out and sign as bona fide all team lists, which were solemnly exchanged before each encounter. Formal cricket and football premierships, with a points table, were introduced, based at first on one home and one away game with each school, but after 1901 on a single game with each. Football was to be played on public grounds unless both teams agreed to the use of a school ground. In rowing the schools were given choice of water in rotation, but to Geelong's distress (having a wealthy and progressive boat club) the boats were to be old-fashioned, heavy, fixed-seat fours with no outriggers.

The *Quarterly* found the rules strict, but although repulsive 'to those who had never attempted to play a doubtful boy', they were better than constant wrangling.

Not that they abolished disputes and sharp practice. After a public outcry over the boat race in 1910 and accusations and counter-accusations of professionalism and mean-spiritedness, a conference of headmasters and representatives of their councils (including the new-comer of 1908, Geelong College) tightened the rules by reducing the age limit to nineteen on 1 March in the current year, forbidding professional coaches and rubbers-down and expressing the opinion that schoolboys should not play in adult competition. Interestingly, the conference, in debating the emphasis placed on games, was satisfied that too much time was not given to them.

That was not what defeated opponents in the 1880s thought about Geelong Grammar School, where sport seemed to be the unofficial religion, with Cuthbertson its high priest. In rowing, football, athletics and rifle-shooting the school was pre-eminent and sometimes the cricket team was also strong. Bracebridge Wilson argued almost vehemently that studies were not neglected. On the contrary, he believed that because they were fit and happy his boys worked well. Their success at team games was merely evidence that they were making the most of the incomparable opportunities of boarding-school life to develop bodily strength and moral character. Neither he nor Cuthbertson exhorted boys to play just to win—far from it—but their belief in games and their boyish delight in victory acted as great spurs to sporting activity. In farewelling his old friend in December 1895, Canon Goodman observed that Wilson's genius showed out above all in regulating the sports of the school. He rode brilliantly on the crest of public opinion and was happy to take the risk that physical prowess might seem to be placed above mental attainment.

A string of magnificent crews followed wins in 1878, 1880 and 1882 with six straight victories from 1885 to 1890. Angus Greenfield believed that hard Saturdays on the river so tired their arms that they learnt to use legs and backs as second nature. Even young boys tackled and survived the 60-kilometre round trip to Barwon Heads. Opponents pointed to the sheer weight of Geelong Grammar crews, but the *Quarterly* retorted that the weight they won by was the long

111

The cup won by A. F. Garrard in 1890 for the Maiden Sculls at the Ballarat Regatta.

Saturday row and the quick catch, hard drive and clean finish drilled into them by Cuthbertson. In football, similarly, they could run all day and in the 1880s had a great record against the Melbourne schools, not losing to Scotch or Wesley and beating MGS sixteen times in twenty games. Their tally was vastly superior; against MGS in the 1880s they kicked 84 goals to 30 and against Wesley 109 to 15. In those days of low scoring, before behinds were introduced in 1897 and when seven or eight goals was a large score, GGS beat Wesley 30–0 in 1890.

They so dominated athletics in 1880, after a narrow win in 1879, that the other schools excused themselves from the competition in 1881 and allowed the challenge cup to go permanently to roost on a bracket in the Geelong Grammar dining room. Perhaps the strongest measure of their determination is the performance of the 1887 football team who won 'first place in the football field, in the face of the greatest difficulties that ever assailed a school team'. Although typhoid had raged in the boarding-house since the beginning of May (see p. 88) they had beaten College, trounced Wesley and shared the honours in two matches with MGS. Most schools would have cancelled the fixtures.

The only problem confronting a neat thesis about Saturday Parties giving unbeatable strength and stamina is that in football against Geelong College, when they were not arguing about the eligibility of players, and after what were usually close, hard-fought encounters, they won six games and lost seven in the 1880s, scoring 27 goals to 41. For that reason, in addition to their longstanding rivalry in the town, the College match was always the match of the year. In the period from 1868 to 1914 honours were about even and neither school gained the upper hand for more than a couple of years. An epic quality was built into the rivalry in 1878 when after two drawn games, on top of two drawn in 1877, the schools were persuaded to play a decider. By special dispensation, for that final encounter they were allowed to use the Corio ground, the home of the Geelong Football Club, and drew again. Great then was the excitement in 1879 when Grammar beat College twice. As a sort of coming of age, we are told that after the 1870s the school always played on the senior ground rather than, as previously, on the Argyle, an unformed rectangular space, 157 metres by 95 metres, bounded on the south by Aberdeen Street and on the west by Pakington Street. The use of the Corio Oval may have been granted because many of the Geelong team were College and Grammar boys. Angus Greenfield (1892–93) said that several besides himself in his year played for Geelong. He mentioned practice matches in which twenty or twenty-five from the school would take on fifteen or sixteen of the Geelong team.

Despite English precedents, powerful at GGS, this strange Victorian game, its heroes glistening with pungent eucalyptus oil, carried all before it. The *Quarterly* was flooded with quaint jargon like 'sending the oval along the lower wing' and 'piloted the leather

112

through the posts'. At first draws were not uncommon and in 1877 there was an unfinished match. In the second drawn game with MGS in 1878, which Cuthbertson replayed in verse, the two sides charged and counter-charged each other's goals throughout two halves of an hour without scoring. So accustomed was GGS to winning in the 1880s that a long postmortem was found necessary after a defeat by MGS in 1885. Old Geelong Grammarians were appealed to witness the fact that success had been based on well-organized practice matches 'under good captaining' and on the discipline shown by stalwarts like R. S. Thomson and T. Manifold, who thought only of the side, never of themselves. That moral principle was a golden thread running through all accounts of football matches.

Moral principles, of course, are all very well until actions confound them. A reminiscence about Steve Fairbairn, printed in the *Corian* of June 1975, suggests that GGS sporting heroes were not always ethical models. He is said to have owned a short-odds favourite at a local race meeting in western Queensland. Having bet heavily against his own horse, he ordered the jockey to throw the race, but, that having failed, told him to weigh-in light. This was also frustrated: the stewards thought Mr Fairbairn such a good sport that they gave him the race. He was later seen pondering what such a win would cost him on a yearly basis. His personality is described as complex, yet simple. He never grew up and was inordinately proud of his physique. Asked to coach the Cambridge eight by a president who later became a bishop, he lasted two days: his earthy language offended. When he coached his son Ian in a pair at Eton only two small boys appeared for his first visit, the whole school on his second and after the third the provost asked him not to return.

In cricket, where skill was more important than strength, GGS fared better against Geelong College than against Scotch and Melbourne Grammar. Again, until a bright patch in the early twentieth century, they were more successful in the 1880s than in other decades, and were undefeated in 1886 and 1887. It seems that L. H. Lindon, himself a very good player, was responsible for the revival of cricket in 1896. He arranged a practice wicket at the main school playground and could often be found coaching boys in the nets. Whereas rowing and football, except for the 1902 champion team, suffered a drought in the new century, the cricketers were equal premiers in 1902, premiers and champions (being unbeaten) in 1903 and premiers again in 1906.

One explanation of weakening sporting performances is the failure of the school to grow. With about 180 boys in 1907 it was not much bigger than it had been in 1880, whereas Melbourne Grammar had grown from 250 to 435, Wesley from about 130 to over 300 and Scotch from 220 to 390. In contrast to the immense growth of Melbourne in the 1880s, which provided the basis for a strong middle class in the new century, the potential intake of country boys remained small and the population of Geelong was stagnant. Apart

The crew in 1880; Steve Fairbairn is standing on the left.

GEELONG.

ATHLETIC SPORTS,

CORIO CRICKET GROUND,

WEDNESDAY, NOVEMBER 8, 1876.

COMMITTEE:

Mr. R. B. CHATER.   C. N. ARMYTAGE.
Mr. J. L. CUTHBERTSON. W. J. AUSTIN.
Mr. J. O. THOMAS.   D. S. WALKER.
A. J BLACK.

JUDGES:

Mr. J. L. CUTHBERTSON.   Mr. J. O. THOMAS.

STARTER:

Mr. R. B. CHATER.

HANDICAPPERS:

Mr. R. B. CHATER.   C. N. ARMYTAGE.
W. J. AUSTIN.

SPORTS TO COMMENCE AT TWELVE (NOON).

N.B.—In the "Grammar School Cup" the winner of each of the events is to receive Five points, the second Three points, and the third Two points.

D. S. WALKER, Hon. Sec.

A light blue twenty, the football team of 1909.

from that, a new spirit animated rival schools.

Melbourne Grammar had been revived by Blanch, Scotch by Littlejohn and Wesley's headmaster, Adamson, supported by excellent coaches, rivalled Cuthbertson as poet and sporting enthusiast. Under Charlie Donald, Wesley crews won the Head of the River six times running between 1901 and 1906, Wesley footballers humbled the light blue twice (1904–05) by margins of ten goals and once (1907) by twenty, and even in cricket (1907) the boys with purple blazers plundered 523 runs in an innings from a GGS team which made only 148 and 32. Following the celebration of nineteenth-century sporting prowess at the jubilee in 1907, there were to be many parched years in which to practise the virtue of playing without winning.

With its broad horizons, wealthy boarders and romantic spirit, GGS embraced intercolonial competition by rowing against St Ignatius (Riverview) on the Barwon in 1888 and on Sydney's Lane Cove River in 1889 for one win each. Then, more successfully, crews exchanged visits almost annually from 1895 with St Peter's, Adelaide. Noel Learmonth recalled J. B. Wilson's excitement on hearing of victory in the first race against St Peter's and the arrival back at school of 'Cuth' and the victorious crew several days after everyone else had returned from the Easter holidays. Cricket was played without success against Sydney Grammar in 1889, 1893, 1895 and 1905—bad years in which to compete, because in the first three of them GGS had not won a match in Victoria.

The history of games is notable for the formalization of rules, the perfection of techniques, the improvement of grounds and the standardization of uniforms. 'The Victorian game of football is the game most loved by the great majority of Victorian schoolboys', remarked a writer in the *Jubilee History*, but for decades after the code began with a school match between Scotch and MGS in 1858 the rules were in flux. Bishop Stretch remembered that in the 1870s the rules were so vague that 'no one would risk taking on the duties of referee'. Boys tore at each other in long, low-scoring games on rough grounds with indeterminate boundaries. Goals alone were scored until 1897 when behinds were introduced and an extra set of posts appeared. 'Little marks' were abolished at the same time. Play was deliberate, with long drop-kicking and the frequent placing of the ball when shooting for goal. The first uniforms, including long silk jerseys, were too flimsy for the fray, causing frequent retreats 'under cover of an overcoat'. Later we see knicker-bockers and jumpers laced at the back; and later again, as in 1907, some boys wore short and some long-sleeved, finely woven light-blue jumpers with long shorts, dark socks and (mostly) white buckskin boots. In team photographs almost all wore caps.

For cricket as for football in the 1860s the ground was a patch of common in South Geelong. It was too dangerous for wicket-keeping, too rough for good batting and had no boundaries: you ran for every run. The school's own 4 hectares, at the far end of

The cricket XI, 1913, the last to play at the old school ground.

114

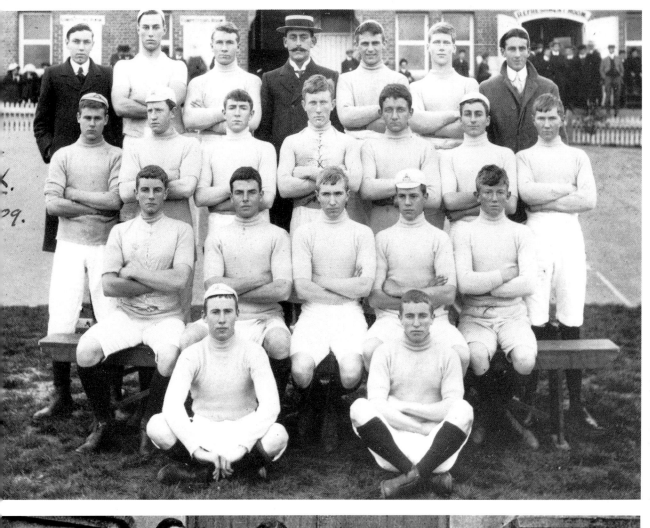

McKillop Street, bought in 1877 through the generosity of Sir Charles Sladen and Mr S. V. Buckland, was little better. Fast bowling was lethal. Despite considerable levelling, the provision of water, the planting of trees, the building of a shed and a good picket fence, boys preferred to play elsewhere. As it was like a lake in winter, football was impossible. The wisdom of the original purchase must be doubted. It was not until 1907, after an immense amount of work (costing £1300) was put into regrading and resowing the area, that it was satisfactory for cricket, with a senior ground and two junior ones.

The state of pitches may have had something to do with low batting and bowling averages. Only five batsmen averaged over fifty between 1876 and 1907, and a majority of bowlers conceded fewer than ten runs per wicket. Outstanding performances with the bat were those of C. Jessop and D. Elder, who from eight innings in 1899 averaged 54.5 and 52.9 respectively, though H. Youngman with 71 from three innings in 1878 and G. Moffat with 63.5 from four in 1881 had better averages. Despite record totals of 326 and 337 against Wesley in 1880 and 1881, no century was scored until 1891 when A. Green made two and averaged 45.7 runs in eleven innings. Jessop and Elder each scored two centuries in 1899 and J. H. Lindon made a century each year from 1902 to 1905. Among the bowlers Steve Fairbairn, who was also a useful batsman, stood alone. In 1879 he captured 55 wickets at an average of 7.05 (including 13 for 54 in a match against Wesley) and in 1880 took 57 at an average of 8.5. The closest to that was E. R. White with 44 at 10.4 in 1900.

During the period bowling progressed from underarm, through round arm to overarm delivery. At first overarm seemed a difficult technique, inspiring a set of instructional pictures on the wall of the prefects' room at about the turn of the century. In deference to the old-timer, Bishop Stretch, who opened the improved ground in 1907 decked out in his best clerical garb of frock coat, knee-breeches, gaiters and top hat, the ceremonial ball was underarm. A slow yorker, it bowled him, perhaps as an omen that the school would not use the ground for very long.

Unlike the bishop, the cricketers at the end of the era were clad in white flannels. In their team photograph of 1906 they look splendid in caps and blazers on which those who had won them wore the school colours. Triple-colour men, who were entitled to display the school coat of arms on blazer pockets, stood out magnificently, true heirs of a fine sartorial tradition. There had been earnest discussion in 1887 about distinctive and inexpensive colours, as an advance on just wearing the badge on the cap. 'Everyone knows the comfort of good sweaters and blazers at the lakes or a match', said the *Quarterly*, sounding just like the immaculate Cuthbertson persuading his charges to take yet another step towards his ideal. It announced that a committee was looking for one blazer to be used in all sports and yet to be distinctive for each, and floated the suggestion that the first eleven blazers be plain blue, that the first twenty have a mitre on the breast and that the first crew add crossed oars to the mitre. If that were done a boy in several first teams would need only one blazer. In case it seemed to be too caught up in the sartorial, the article concluded:

After all, dress and badges are secondary. What we want are good oars, shots,* cricketers and footballers and not a lot of fellows with beautiful blazers, who can neither kick, shoot or row...[8]

The *Jubilee History* indicates that in the outcome the blue blazer was reserved for first teams. The rest of the school wore white with light-blue trimmings and had a plain badge on the cap.

School Colours

MEMBERS of teams win their colours, which are:—
ROWING.—Light blue cap with gold bullion mitre over crossed oars. Light blue blazer, faced with silver blue trimmings, mitre and crossed oars on pocket.
CRICKET.—Light blue cap with gold silk mitre over XI. Light blue blazer with large silk mitre over XI on pocket.
FOOTBALL.—Light blue cap with gold silk mitre over XVIII. Light blue blazer with large silk mitre over XVIII on pocket.
TRIPLE COLOURS.—(Crew, XI and XVIII). Light blue blazer with silver blue trimmings and School coat of arms on pocket.

SCHOOL COLOURS.—Light blue cap with metal mitre. White blazer with light blue trimmings.[9]

A penchant for dressing well had been brought to school by the young bucks of the Western District, whose gold rings, tie-pins and watch-chains were their badges of wealth (see p. 56). On Saturdays before blazers were in vogue, and apparently with permission to be absent from Saturday Parties, they waited around the quad all morning and then, bedecked with elegant white waistcoats, a profusion of jewellery and beautiful silver-knobbed sticks, went off to watch Geelong play football, for all the world like the sons of English gentlemen.

Any resemblance to English toffs was nevertheless superficial. As no English public school boy would have associated with a town team, either as player or spectator, Geelong Grammar boys put on the mental garb of Australian democracy in a free and easy mixing with Jack who was as good as his master. But only in football. In cricket and rowing there was a gulf of imported snobbery; particularly in rowing, which was an expensive sport dominated by middle-class clubs, which were loathe to contend against labourers. The cost of boats and equipment ruled out the working class (except at Ballarat) and made the river the preserve of the wealthy. Afloat the GGS boarders—the school having ruled out the day-boy town-dwellers—were like young gods in the paradise of the Barwon. Both upstream and down there were great rows, and for the first eight months of the

---

* The article suggested that crossed rifles would be too military for a blazer and should therefore be worn on the cadet uniform.

[8] *Quarterly*, April 1887, p. 28.
[9] *History and Register*, 1907, ch. xvi, final page.

year—before nesting claimed everyone's attention—the river was the chief relaxation. Part of the headmaster's report of 1878 frames the picture:

When Mr Robert Hood,* of Hexham, presented to the school the beautiful racing four-oar, the Alexandra—invicta Alexandra, as we love to call her, for she has carried her crew to victory in every race they have rowed in her—he could hardly have anticipated the splendid result that has sprung from his well-timed generosity. Our Boat Club numbers thirty-one members;** it has a capital boat shed of its own on the Barwon, with four four oars, two pleasure boats and a racing eight oar—the first school eight in Victoria.[10]

Saturday Parties on the river, when the boats were most in demand, have already been discussed. They were the backbone of school rowing, its major raison d'être, upon which, especially after Cuthbertson's arrival, competitive rowing was based. Rowing nevertheless began at GGS as a response to an event for scratch fours at the Barwon Rowing Club regatta in 1870, which F. McLeod, W. Guthrie, G. Henty and R. B. Chater[†] decided to enter. For a few years school crews rowed in borrowed boats and then in 1874 the Boat Club was formed, a racing four was purchased (with considerable assistance from Mr Hood) and a successful challenge was issued to Wesley, who had won the Melbourne head of the river race.

The Boat Club, exclusive to those boarders who could afford its high subscription, was the most conspicuous display of wealth at the school. So great was its backing that when the shed and the whole fleet were swept away in a flood in 1880, only a few months elapsed before a better shed and a finer fleet appeared. Cuthbertson is said to have rounded up the necessary funds within a week of the disaster. By 1907 there were three eights, ten fours, two pairs and a pleasure-boat. The club was as progressive as it was wealthy, and was often frustrated that the other schools clung to heavy, outmoded boats. The possession of an eight in 1878, twenty-three years before eights were used in the Head of the River, was typical. Cuthbertson spoke earnestly to anyone who would listen about the fact that English schools like Eton and Radley rowed in sliding, outrigged eights and he wanted at least an experimental race in eights as early as 1881. For many years before sliding, outrigged fours were adopted in 1898 the rowing fraternity at GGS campaigned against the 'absurd and obsolete' fixed-seat gigs then in use. They enjoyed the St Peter's race particularly because it was in outriggers. Success no doubt gave them the right to criticize. From 1875, when they entered their first head of the river, until 1900, when the tide began flowing against them, GGS crews won thirteen races to Scotch's nine, Melbourne Grammar's

---

* A prominent pastoralist, Hood gave the four-oar gig 'of best construction' early in 1877. (Minutes 9 March)

** There were about eighty boarders that year.

[10] *Prospectus*, 1878, p. 11. † Master from 1868 to 1878.

118

three and Wesley's one. Their six victories in a row from 1885 to 1890 made them a legendary force on the river. Apart from that, in 1881 they collared permanently the Robertson Cup, presented for competition between school crews at the Upper Yarra Regatta (later Henley on Yarra), by winning it straight off for three years. From

The crew of 1911, immaculate in caps and blazers, unlike earlier crews.

The Boat Club, all afloat on the Barwon, *c.* 1900

119

such a rowing school numerous senior oarsmen emerged. In the nineteenth century the Jesus College, Cambridge, contingent was most notable. G. F. and C. N. Armytage and C. and S. Fairbairn (the latter four times) rowed for Cambridge, as did N. L. Calvert of Trinity Hall; only W. and W. St L. Robertson of Wadham represented Oxford. Melbourne University and Victorian interstate crews were also strengthened by the light blue. Across the country, especially on pastoral properties, the emblazoned oars won by members of victorious crews may still be seen,* the custom of presenting them stemming from the Robertson Cup race of 1881 when 'after the home university fashion', instead of the usual trophies, the crew received their oars and the cox was given a little silver rudder by the crew.

Other mementos, cherished by those whom they addressed, were Cuthbertson's poems, celebrating famous races like that of 1878 when:

> Not so fast, not so fast,
> There's a buoy to be past.[11]

Number two's oar crashed into the obstacle, bringing the boat to a standstill—yet they won, and again and again. After the *Alice*, bought from Ormond College in 1885, carried a succession of victorious crews, the myth-making rowing bard could say (in 1889) that the river belonged to the school.

> And we, who love the river best
>   of all Australian boys;
> We, nursed upon the Barwon's breast,
>   and cradled in its joys;
> Who—through the summer's fiery heat,
>   or winter's nipping cold—
> Still to the river that we own
>   together firmly hold:
>
> We will not leave the shed at morn
>   to seek the camp below,
> The Willows' welcome shelter,
>   or the fire-light's friendly glow,
> Before we cast a glance of pride
>   at the long victorious line
> That holds the names of those who rowed
>   and won in eighty-nine.[12]

In running as in football they were happy to challenge derivative English values by adopting wholeheartedly a peculiarly colonial event, the United Athletic Sports. 'The boys wouldn't care a brass farthing for the fact that English Public Schools don't have such a meeting', said the *Quarterly* in 1887, trying hard to persuade the other schools to return to the fray that had lapsed after GGS carried off the first challenge cup permanently in 1881. Except for the absence of a greasy pole or pig, the sports, when founded in 1872, had resembled picnic meetings held on public holidays throughout the country. Thousands of spectators turned up. Gold or silver medals were given to the winners of individual events and after 1875 a champion's cup was awarded on a points system for the best overall performance. To that date Geelong Grammar boys had won medals, the drop-kick at football and the weight putt being their specialty, but they did not produce an all-rounder to take the cup.

What they did notice in 1877 was that as a school they gained the highest aggregate of individual points. Coupled with Cuthbertson's interest in stimulating the true public-school team spirit, instead of pot-hunting, this led to the suggestion that an additional cup might be awarded to the outstanding school. As a result, in 1878 Geelong Grammar went expectantly to the Melbourne Cricket Ground by special train to do battle for a challenge cup which was to be held

---

[11] *Barwon Ballads*, p. 296.
[12] *Barwon Ballads*, pp. 287–8.

* Except for many presented by descendants for display in the school's boatshed.

120

permanently by the first school to win it three times. In fact they went twice, the original fixture having been washed out by a 'dismal downpour', the contingent of eighty straggling home 'not sorry to get into our mia-mias after a good grumble'. Although Tom and Steve Fairbairn were first and second in the weight, MGS took the cup. Then narrowly in 1879 and overwhelmingly in 1880 GGS won, and was awarded the cup permanently by default in 1881 when Wesley (whose headmaster was its joint donor) pleaded that the sports interfered with work and MGS also withdrew. The light blue, as usual, were ready to go almost anywhere at almost any time to compete. In 1897 they offered to put the cup forward for perpetual competition and suggested doing away with individual prizes if expense was a barrier to revival, but nothing happened until 1905.

In the interim, athletes from public schools were invited to compete in specific events at each other's sports. At GGS interest focussed on the competition for the school cup, awarded to the athlete who won most points in individual events, for which there were the usual medals. From 1873, when the sports commenced, until 1880, the cup was awarded to the competitor with the best aggregate in open handicap races over 100, 200 and 440 yards, but after that (with some variations) it was awarded for the best aggregate in nine championship events—100, 200 and 440 yards, 1 mile, 120 yards hurdles, weight putt, pole vault, long jump and high jump. The drop-kick at football for which W. Hopkins set the record of 75 yards in 1873 and throwing the cricket ball, which A. Green hurled over 107 yards in 1892, were apparently novelty events. Steve Fairbairn, Tom Parkin, H. M. R. Rupp, A. J. B. Reed, J. S. Agnew and A. G. Bagot each won the cup twice, but the outstanding athlete was Angus Greenfield, who scored a magnificent 23½ of a possible 24 points in 1893, having won seven events outright and dead-heating in the mile with E. A. Austin. In the triumphant team at the United Sports in 1880, when GGS scored 51 points, MGS 15 and Wesley 12, Steve Fairbairn won the 440, high jump and hurdles, and W. Moffatt the 100, weight and long jump. Fairbairn was second in each of Moffatt's events and Moffatt second in the hurdles.

Of the school records up to 1907, only one, a ten-second hundred yards by A. J. B. Reed in 1902, was impressive by later standards. The high jump stood at 5′ 6¾″, the long jump at 20′ 6″, the mile at 4 min 55 2/5 s and the 440 yards at 53 3/4 s. Better tracks, better spikes, better techniques were to make such performances look second rate as the century progressed. There were even better togs, like the advance Cuthbertson made in 1877 by having English university style singlets and shorts adopted by the public schools in place of restrictive tights and trunks.

In a flexible approach to the programme, after the school's bicycle club was founded in 1881 two bike races (they would have been penny farthings) were included in the sports. They were the first bicycle races in Geelong. For the younger boys a kangaroo race was held, which was won in 1885 by W. H. Pincott, later the

Silver medals for achievement at sport.

121

Sports (athletics) team, 1906.

school's famous rowing coach. They did not ride kangaroos. As the *Quarterly* reported:

The spectacle of the youngsters with legs strapped together and arms tied back, and adorned *a posteriori* with stuffed tails, was certainly amusing. Pincott hopped comfortably in.[13]

Swimming was the most popular of minor sports. Based on the morning dip and the rule that no boy should row unless he could swim 80 yards, it was stimulated by annual sports, with the usual cup for the champion swimmer and medals for other winners. In December 1885, when repeated cold weather caused the postponement of the swimming sports until the following term, it was decided that boys who had left school would be entitled to compete and should scan the *Australasian* and *Geelong Advertiser* for notice of the date. A delay like that would have saved Wilson some embarrassment at one swimming sports in the 1870s, when he noticed fearful bruises on the back and legs of young Ernest Jackson and learnt to his horror that they were the marks of his own tawse. 'I always bruised very easily', Jackson wrote later.

Swimming was Wilson's special interest, and was the only sport in which day boys figured more prominently than boarders (see p. 50). Pastoralists' names are rare on the list of champion swimmers, which was dominated from 1900 to 1907 by R. I., E. T. W. and V. H. Carr, each twice and the last three times the winner. An enlightened innovation in 1878 was a life-saving competition during which a dummy was thrown from a boat in deep water and retrieved by competitors. Here was a way to save lives, 'for no swimmer who has pulled that heavy figure a few times out of deep water would have fear or difficulty with a real person'.

Every afternoon in hot weather resident masters were pestered to take boys swimming. In summer every crew looked forward to leaping into the river from the elastic willows at their famous camping spot. Most of all, the long haul to Barwon Heads was lightened by the prospect of a tussle with the great Southern Ocean:

> But sweetest to dive in the breakers,
>   To spring to their emerald crest,
> To rise on the rainbow-arch-makers,
>   To be tossed on their billowy breast—
> In the rush and the foam of the breakers
>   It is there that the bathing is best.[14]

They were happy to row for four hours out and five hours home for the exhilaration of beach and sky and surf—like today's board-riders chasing epic waves along the coast.

In a form of censorship that turned to discrimination in verses like:

> The bat, the oar and football's hardy sport
> Have put the game of tennis out of court [15]

Cuthbertson poured scorn on what had originally been an aristocratic game that might have been expected to arouse in him something like his love of fives. He wanted it banned, as it was at some schools, because of its threat to other sports. He made sure that it was only mentioned with a sneer, as in 1881 when the *Quarterly* pointed to half-hours morning and evening that could be used for music rather than everlasting lawn tennis. In 1884, a projected match with a Melbourne school (just the competition he loved) prompted the observation that if the muscular energy used knocking balls around the excellent court in the previous year had been harnessed it would have produced stupendous results. We have to wait for the *Jubilee History* to discover that there was an annual championship and that in 1885 an exceptionally strong four was regarded as the best school team in Victoria. Like swimming, one assumes, tennis must have been one of Wilson's loves. It would have needed a strong supporter to become established in the face of the considerable cost of the asphalt court laid down in 1881, less than ten years after the modern game was invented and only four years after the first Wimbledon championship.

Among other games and diversions, we know of fives, with which Cuthbertson persevered on unsuitable walls in the quad, despite Wilson's antipathy (see p. 49) and which was given a fillip by the asphalting of the quad in 1880. With a chance remark in *Fairbairn of Jesus*, Steve Fairbairn revealed that at least in the late 1870s there was also a cross-country paper chase. Despite a bad headache, which might have signalled the approach of scarlet fever, he slipped out of a sanatorium window, joined another hare, grabbed a sack of paper and went 10 kilometres before being caught. There was an attempt to get hockey going in 1879 and squash was successfully introduced (on outside courts) in 1881.

TENNIS AND COLOURS.

Tennis.

TENNIS has been played at the School for many years, and the court is always kept in first-class order. As there are no regular inter-school contests the game has not been placed on the same level as football, cricket, rowing, athletic sports, and rifle shooting, and the School has no tennis colours. In 1885 we had an exceptionally fine four, consisting of S. F. Mann, A. E. Tyson, H. Matson and H. Crabbe. They played and won many matches, and were regarded as the champion school team in Victoria. Tournaments are held each year at the school, and the annual contest for the championship creates a good deal of enthusiasm. Perhaps the following couplet taken from the School *Quarterly* appropriately defines the position—

> " The bat, the oar, and football's hardy sport
> Have put the game of Tennis ' out of court.' "

[14] *History and Register*, 1907, ch. xvi, Swimming.
[15] Quoted in *History and Register*, 1907, at end of ch. xvi.

123

From a beginning in the playground, with Indian clubs swung at the peril of the boy next door, gymnastics moved into the new gymnasium in 1872. Weekly classes were conducted by Herr Reichman and later Mr Metzger, who supervised traditional European work on the vaulting horse, parallel and horizontal bars, ladder, trapeze and so on. Lindon engineered a change in 1896 when the Bracebridge Wilson Hall became available and the old gym, later converted to a carpentry shop, was used just for the ladder and trapeze. Under the full-time care of ex-British Army instructors G. H. and J. Webb, and in sympathy with Garrard's very strong cadet corps, in which they served, a broader course of exercises, bayonet drill, gymnastics and boxing was introduced from which stemmed an annual assault-at-arms, described at its best in the jubilee year:

The programme consisted of running exercises, parallel bars (with tableaux) bayonet exercises, musical dumb bells, free gymnastics (with tableaux), horizontal bars, exhibition of boxing, physical drill with arms, Indian clubs, vaulting horses (with tableaux). Some clowns in grotesque attire added to the amusement of the company with their vagaries.[16]

Imagine the patterns of bodies clad in black tights, white shorts and singlets, the rush of sandshoed feet, the strain, the leaps, the sweat of fifty boys, the twitching of the walrus moustaches of the brothers Webb (the larger of whom was an immense figure shaped like a medicine ball) and the relief of watching mothers when the last thump was over. For serious cases of gymnastic fervour a championship was conducted each year for the usual cup and the immortality of having one's name recorded in the *Quarterly*.

Gymnastics display for the Jubilee, 1907.

[16] *History and Register*, appendix, 'Assault at Arms'.

124

The assault-at-arms was an expression of a well-established martial spirit, stemming from a colonial pride in being British, which was especially strong among the privileged class. Typical of the resultant hyperbole was Canon Goodman's remark at the opening of fund-raising for the new hall and drill room in 1893 that the loss of the warship *Victoria* in the Mediterranean had the whole empire in tears in sympathy with the Queen, for whom every boy in the corps would shed his last drop of blood. They were proud to be Victorians (not yet quite Australians) according to Charles Belcher, but that did not obscure or diminish loyalty to England. To argue against Britain was to cause a riot. In 1897 boys proudly wore medals of aluminium—bronze struck by the Geelong Town Council (the Honourable Sidney Austin, father of several old boys, was mayor) to commemorate Victoria's sixtieth anniversary as Queen and they listened to Alderman Bostock (later a key council member) explain how they should learn to transfer their loyalty from school to country. This should not have been difficult in a place where putting school before self was a cardinal virtue and where the discipline of the cadet corps was seen as a powerful educational instrument. Wilson, we are told, was a natural in command—straight, firm, a fine marksman and a good military organizer, yet no jingoist.

Wilson made his most complete statement about cadets at Speech Day 1894 when, in response to rumours that the government intended to retrench them, and in answer to criticisms that they were a useless luxury, he said that he regarded cadets as vital in developing habits of prompt attention and subordination to authority. Besides, he warned, no one could tell how soon a great war might burst and reveal the ineffectiveness of geographical isolation and a few coastal forts. At such a time, these young men, the flower of the colony, would rapidly become efficient soldiers. The *Quarterly* had said the same thing in April 1892, pleading with parents not to think that the corps was warlike.

Not such, we may be well assured, would be the spirit of those over whom waves the light blue flag. Not defiance or aggression would be their motto, but defence, and to the last cartridge.[17]

Wilson formed the corps in 1884 in step with 'a military spirit rife in Australia', as a result of Russian invasion scares and following initiatives taken by Sir Frederick Sargood in the Victorian government. It was soon sixty strong in a school of one hundred and was encouraging marksmanship among boys who were often already good shots. As in games, the *Jubilee History* could boast that every rifle match open to the corps had been contested. By 1891, with an enrolment of eighty in a school of 108, the cadets had their own bugle band and were shaping up like a championship team under Captain Garrard, that Australian-born schoolmaster with a passion for arms. As the *Quarterly* reported in 1892, the school was proud that its 'gallant cadet corps' had won the honour, in a drill competition with Scotch and Geelong College, of being placed in charge of the Queen's Colours,

[17] *Quarterly*, April 1892, p. 37.

and shrugged off a caricature of their excitement which appeared in a Melbourne paper:

They would all smile simultaneously with that peculiar smile of which only Geelong people are capable. The premier cadets hoisted their new won treasures as high as possible and eagerly thought of Pivot home and beauty.[18]

What it felt like to be there is conveyed by T. A. Brown, who tells of a train journey to Melbourne and a long, dusty march to the rifle range behind the Botanic Gardens, where a frenzy of polishing commenced. After months of preparation they were keyed up for the event, knowing that Garrard had set his heart on winning. No drill seemed too hard for them, so they waited confidently after their rivals had competed until suddenly the good news broke. F. W. S. Mawson, a Geelong dentist and coach of the school's rifle team, who was seated on horseback near the judges, heard the result and galloped madly towards them, waving his bell-topper. Describing the triumphal march back to school from the Geelong station, Brown strikes an epic note. The bugle band played almost without a break, but gradually their lips gave out. At Myers Street only the senior bugler was left. Then his lips also cracked in a spurt of blood as they wheeled into McKillop Street, a hundred yards from home. When ordered, 'Strike up, bugler!' he raised a bloody mouthpiece for

Cadets ready for action during camp, 1887.

126

Garrard to see. So two kettle drums played the victors into the school yard where 'the dear old head and his lady' received them, beaming with joy. Consistent with contemporary sentiment, the colours so seriously contested had been worked by the hands of the governor's daughters.

This martial atmosphere was a natural preparation for enlistment in the Boer War in 1899. Of at least forty-seven old boys who went, two were killed—Lieutenants Noel Calvert and William Skene—to whom the school's first war memorial, a brass plaque given by the Old Geelong Grammarians, was unveiled in Big School in December 1902, six months after the school bell had joined in a great peal to celebrate the end of the war. In celebration of nationhood and empire the corps grew in numbers and stature under Lindon. In 1907, with 108 members, it contained 'over ninety percent of the school who are eligible to join'. With Garrard advancing to colonel and with the Webb brothers' soldierly experience at hand, it was shaping bodies and minds to endure the catastrophe of the Great War. This called for the blood Canon Goodman believed they would willingly shed for Queen and country.

In the early years of the century the combined cadet corps of the Victorian schools went through their paces in camp at Queen's Park, Geelong. They were under the popular command of Lieutenant-Colonel Garrard. In preparation for Gallipoli and Flanders

The bugle band, 1892.

The camp layout, 1887.

Sargood Shield rifle team, 1892.

they learnt, among other things, to be good Australians by swimming the Barwon to go AWL. On Empire Day 1908 the might of the public schools—Grammar, Scotch, Wesley and the two Geelongs—marched past the colours in a big parade at Werribee.

To encourage good shooting, the Victorian Rifle Association held an annual cadet tournament at the Williamstown range. In the nineteenth century Geelong Grammar was frequently successful. In the twentieth however—as in rowing and football—the story was different. GGS won the teams' trophy ten times between 1884 and 1899 but only once in the decade after that. Perhaps they missed their coach—the Geelong dentist of the waving bell-topper, otherwise Sergeant Mawson of the Volunteer Mounted Rifles—who had been a Queen's Prize winner. Typically, for the period, good shooting brought gold and silver medals, shields and cups, some of substantial value. Ten guineas given by the cadet corps to the Old Soldiers' Home in 1891 was largely made up of the £7 worth of prizes won by the shooting team.

The chief prize in all the boys' activities on field and river was prestige. They were helping to create a Victorian tradition in private education that has remained very strong and strongly sporting. Determined to achieve at least a flavour of their English counterparts, the Associated Public Schools, though envious of Geelong Grammar's assumed gentility, followed the school of Cuthbertson and Wilson (note the order) into the field of honour they had chosen. As we have seen, it was not entirely bordered by English precedent and there was a great deal of new-world vigour and a democratic bravado about the way they performed. Premierships were introduced that would have been scorned at places like Eton, Rugby, Winchester, Shrewsbury, Marlborough or Cuthbertson's own Glenalmond, among which there was less need to define an in-group or establish standards of behaviour. In the colonial arena carefully-selected opponents helped to set the elite schools of the 1890 agreement in a class apart.

Public rivalries gave spice to sporting life. Because their games, not their scholarship, bathed them in the warm glow of middle-class approval, public school boys were inclined to see themselves as the local equivalent of English sporting gentlemen. With Cuthbertson's help, Geelong Grammar did all it could to foster that image as a group image. He was tireless, as Adamson of Wesley acknowledged, in promoting the 'public school spirit', through which the greatest sporting rivals became the most cherished social allies. Dear to his heart was the fraternity of 1880 when, in the school holidays, the Grammar and the College at Geelong combined to send a football team, called the Aboriginals, to tour the illustrious Western District. They were so well connected that they could afford the joke of the name. The following year, when cricketers also toured, a number of Melbourne Grammar boys were included in the side.

PART II

Corio and a wider world

An artist's impression of a
dream fulfilled, 1923.

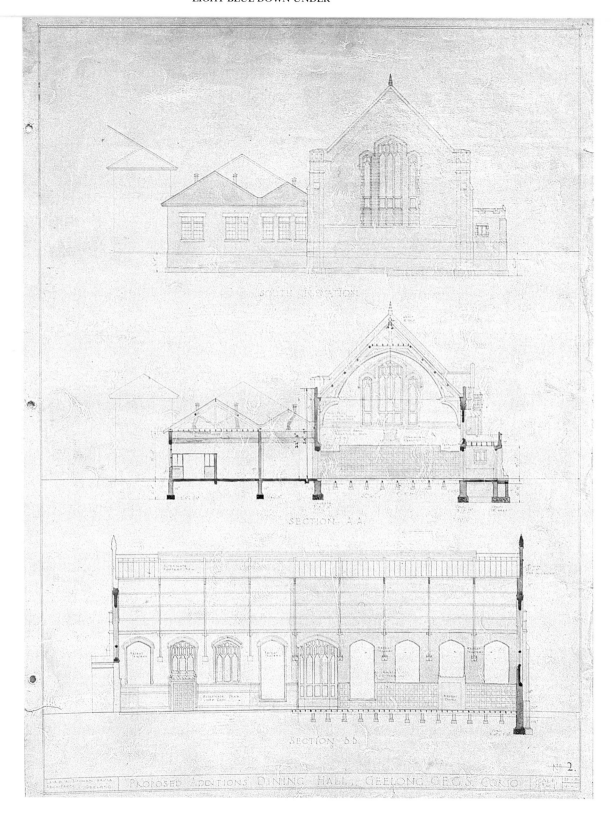

8

The move to Corio under Francis Brown

TRANSPLANTED

The undercurrent in the school's affairs, which became the main stream and swept Lindon away, was soon to tear it from its old buildings and deposit it on a new site. Fearing a negative reaction because of sentimental attachments to the old gray school and its place within the town, the council at first kept secret a more logical but far more ambitious plan than the 1909 proposal to develop separately at the two ends of McKillop Street. They wanted to move across the river and consolidate all facilities in a paddock at Belmont. They probably dreamed of a place that would kindle feelings they associated with self-contained English schools, and provide a backdrop against which schoolboy heroes could 'Play up! Play up! and play the game!'—an intimate, all-embracing, private world, where in the drama of games there would be moments like Newbolt's:

There's a breathless hush in the Close tonight—
Ten to make and the match to win—.[1]

In his own name, hoping for such an outcome, W. T. Manifold had already paid £4055 for 30 acres near the highway on Roslyn Road and was holding them for the school.

The council hesitated for over a year before adopting the great project and making it public. In a dramatic session on 31 October 1910, encouraged by successful fund-raising, they decided unanimously that 'the scheme at Belmont be proceeded with', and that the Maude Street site, the sports-ground and the recently-acquired hectares be sold. They believed that the advantages of consolidation on the new site far outweighed the disadvantages. Although sea-bathing, for instance, would not be easy from Belmont, the river would be almost as close, the playing-fields adjacent and the treasured countryside at the very doorstep.

Ambition for the school ran strong. On its cramped main site and distant grounds, there could be no focus and none of the sense

Francis Brown

[1] Sir Henry Newbolt, 'Vitae Lampeda'.

131

of space achieved through their rural settings by most English public schools. Manifold even suggested that William Guilfoyle, well known for his landscaping at the Melbourne Botanic Gardens and at many Western District properties, should be the first person consulted about plans for the new property. This aristocratic dream was passed over in favour of Donald Mackinnon's equally English and more material suggestion recommended by Ankatel Henderson, president of the Royal Victorian Institute of Architects, that the council run a major architectural competition. There would be two stages, the first to establish the position of the various buildings, the second to allow selected competitors to detail their schemes. The school was to be planned as a coherent array of buildings in which a group of separate boarding-houses was to be associated with a large classroom block, hall, chapel, headmaster's house and so on. Nothing like it had been contemplated in Australia. The larger ideas, the greater confidence and the broader perspectives of the new council, several of whom were proprietors of great estates, had lifted the little school at Geelong into a new dimension.

There was, nevertheless, considerable anxiety about the response of the school community, from whom the bulk of the funds would have to come. In the same *Quarterly* in which they published the plan as a leading article headed 'School Development Scheme', the council wrote an open letter to old boys, explaining the decision and attempting to placate those who might react adversely. 'We are aware that a strong and very natural sentiment may at first lead those who have been educated at the school to be disinclined to approve of a change', the letter began. It went on to say that unless there was positive notification to the contrary the council would assume that donations to the fund for the improvement of the school could be used as council saw fit. There were grounds for optimism because, through Chirnside, Douglass, Mackinnon, Manifold and the Austins, council had a majority on the committee of the Old Geelong Grammarians and easy access to old boys. For all that it is surprising and significant that opposition was negligible. They had touched a vital chord in the minds of those who loved the school and who wished, boyishly perhaps, in the spirit of Cuthbertson's poems, to see it second to none. An excited group surrounded the chairman, W. T. Manifold, on 21 October 1910, as he drove a pair of horses across the ground at Belmont to turn the first sod of the new era.

The great idea now possessed them. In November 1910 Mackinnon reported further conversations with Henderson, confirming the possibility of a two-stage architectural competition. Council decided to split £100 among those who submitted the best general plans, at the same time asking them to compete in a second detailed stage, the winner of which would become the school's architect. Henderson also influenced the decision about building material. He persuaded the council that the local Barrabool stone did not chisel well and that, as bluestone was too expensive, they should opt for brick with stone facings. Brick being fashionable among architects at the time, he dismissed as unsuitable an offer of bluestone from the Austins at Barwon Park after merely viewing photographs of the estate.

In April 1911 members of council puzzled over twenty-one sets of first-stage drawings. Somewhat bewildered, they decided which architects would be asked for detailed designs. Those chosen were Hall and Durran of Geelong and three Melbourne firms—H. Desbrowe-Annear, A. & H. Henderson and Wight and Hudson. Council's decision was confirmed by the architect of St Peter's Collegiate School, Adelaide, who happened to be visiting Geelong. He also helped to prepare the conditions for Stage 2, which were duly approved by the Institute of Architects and sent out to the competitors. The final drawings, which came back at the end of June, gave the council another headache. On the advice of Soward, their Adelaide contact, they decided to award points for various elements of the design and at the end of a long meeting, during which A. F. Garrard gave his report on each submission, they adjourned for a week.

When the points were totted up Gerard Wight and Philip B. Hudson were the winners. The former was a well-established Melbourne architect, the latter almost a beginner. It was to be Hudson's first major commission and Wight's last. Hudson, who later designed buildings for Brighton and Ivanhoe Grammar Schools and Geelong College, is best known (with James Wardrop) for the Shrine of Remembrance in Melbourne. The winning architects responded to the GGS council's interest in flexibility and future development with six alternative treatments of the site and numerous sets of plans and elevations for individual buildings. It was a system the council could play with rather than a prescriptive plan, so it is no surprise that the final design was stitched together by the council and the architects, with clandestine reference to other competition designs, comments from Soward in Adelaide and a lengthy report from Garrard.

A final version was almost complete in August 1911 when the free-enterprise world, to which they were all committed, took the edge off their delight. Following the school's announcement of its plans, the land agents W. P. Carr and Sons had stepped in. Despite prior and, it was thought, firm negotiations by Manifold with the neighbouring farmer, they purchased an adjoining 37 acres for residential subdivision. The first the council knew of their action was a newspaper advertisement for a 'Belmont Hill Sub-divisional Sale', which took place very successfully on 19 August 1911. Ironically, proximity to the school's new site and to a proposed tramway up Belmont Hill, which council had noted as a distinct advantage in getting boys to the sea baths, helped to sell 130 out of 201 allotments. Manifold and others had failed, despite the full support of the Shire Council, to prevent the sale going ahead, and the agents had refused an offer of £750 above the original price. It left a nasty taste in the mouth that

133

the Carr boys had been prominent at the school in recent years.

From their hostile reaction to that subdivision, which was regarded as skimpy and unsympathetic, it is obvious that the 30 acres of the initial purchase, so large in comparison to existing facilities, was far too small an area to contain the council's dream. They indicated also that an adjacent, especially lower-middle-class, suburban subdivision was an anathema. They wanted boarders, not day boys. Their view of the tram as getting boys to the baths rather than connecting home and school quite clearly revealed that bias. How little day boys were under consideration is also clear from their swift decision to give up Belmont and buy land on the opposite side of Geelong, remote from any habitation or public transport, though marvellously situated for bathing.

Angered by the Carrs' intransigence and, like a rejected suitor, finding a new love on the rebound, council was soon to receive with enthusiasm the report of its Works Committee (who spent only three days on the quest) that a suitable site lay across Corio Bay, with a magnificent water frontage that took in the peaceful Limeburners' Bay lagoon. On Wednesday 20 September the council, graced by the rare appearance of its president, Archbishop Clarke, gathered in Geelong and drove out as a body to see the promised land.

The day was beautiful. Geelong looked romantic and unthreateningly distant across the water, but just to make sure that they were secure against development, the council purchased two large blocks of farming land for £7353.8.0. One portion of 120 acres fronting Limeburners' Bay was obtained at £25 per acre from John Thompson, the other of 85 acres at £50.5.0 per acre from Joseph Michel and his sons. In addition, with a caution that was almost paranoid, W. T. Manifold put his name, on the school's behalf, to another 57 acres to the west between the principal purchase and the Melbourne—Geelong railway. On the east there was safety in Austin's Avalon, where the light blue was revered. From its 22 scattered acres in South Geelong and the abortive 30 at Belmont, ambition had moved the school to 262 acres at Corio. The new property stretched from Limeburners' Bay to the railway-station at Cowie—a name that was changed to Corio once the school had given the place a new identity.

The speed of the decision was remarkable. The transfer documents were signed on the same day and the happy council drove homewards with the archbishop's blessing:

Gentlemen, I congratulate you. In faith you have done today a work, the wisdom of which, I have no doubt, will become more and more manifest through succeeding generations.[2]

They had certainly cast their bread upon the waters with a project that would take decades to mature, which would probably never exhaust the possibilities of those 262 acres, limited though they were to appear later for the full development of a challenging education.

[2] Minutes, 20 Sept. 1911.

There was plenty of room now for Wight and Hudson's scheme. The major question was how to relate the buildings to the water frontage. An amended set of drawings was shown to council on 9 October 1911, and on 18 October council's view of how the various buildings should be located was pointed out to the architects during their first visit to the site. There were to be four boarding-houses, the main school, a chapel, headmaster's lodge, science laboratory and laundry. For six months council and architects amended the plans, then called for tenders in May 1912. Builders were wary. Dismayed at the size of the quotes of the few who responded, Wight and Hudson extended the time limit for tenders and reduced the deposit, without success. Their estimate of £42 000 had been exceeded by over 50 per cent. Council was dismayed. After further discussions with the architects about pruning expenditure, they decided not to downgrade the project (except by using concrete facings instead of stone) but to build in stages. After some haggling they reached agreement, on 11 November 1912, with Thomas Quayle of Brighton for the construction of the main school and just one house for a little over £30 000. The work was to be finished on 5 February 1914.

Early optimism about the move was shaken by the unexpectedly high cost. Council might have hesitated further if the old boys had not stood firm when consulted prior to the letting of revised tenders. They gathered on 6 September at Scott's Hotel in Melbourne (another indication of the movement of the school beyond Geelong) and gave overwhelming support. A committee was formed to raise the £30 000 by gifts or loans and £8000 was promised on the spot.

The archbishop and members of the school council surveyed the promised land of Corio on 20 September, 1911, then held on the spot a meeting at which they decided to purchase. Council members present were, from left: E. A. Austin, H. P. Douglass, W. F. Volum, Archbishop Lowther Clarke, H. A. Austin, T. E. Bostock.

Appropriately, in terms of the school's national ambitions, the first citizen of Australia, the governor-general, Lord Denman, left Government House, Melbourne, on 3 April 1913 to take a train to Cowie station to lay the foundation stone of Geelong Church of England Grammar School, Corio. Cars were waiting to ferry him and his party, who were joined by the president of Corio Shire, the chairman of the school council and the new headmaster, to a windswept paddock by the bay. Under a clear sky a crowd, including the whole school, was waiting where Quayle's men had the engraved stone ready for this courageous transplanting. Flourishing already, its Englishness was increased by the event, which, in Lord Denman's judgement, made it the first Australian public school to be set up on truly English lines. It could certainly no longer, in any sense, be the local school of its original foundation and, because access to the capital by road and railway was much easier than before, it was to be linked more and more strongly to Melbourne. A link with the old school was preserved. A. A. O. Davenport, the senior prefect re-laid the inscribed section of the original foundation stone, using (as Lord Denman had also) the silver trowel presented to Sir Henry Barkly in 1857.

As the first fruits of the move, new enrolments in 1914 leapt from the thirty-six of 1913 to eighty-seven. Country and interstate enrolments increased dramatically. The school's pastoral base was strengthened. Then in 1915 the sons of Melbourne business and professional men came in a rush. With its new buildings, its new site and its elite tradition, the school attracted fresh attention right across Australia. The council's gamble had paid off.

Entries 1912–15

Place of residence	1912	1913	1914	1915
Melbourne	9	9	18	35
Geelong	9	9	11	4
Corio			5	
Werribee, Lara, etc.			7	
Victorian country	10	8	20	22
Interstate	6	9	25	8
Overseas		1	1	
Total	34	36	87	69

Such a striking result deserves explanation. Why should so many families suddenly decide that the transplanted school, remote from most of their homes, was the place to send their sons? As its headmaster, staff and academic reputation had not changed, it seems that the new buildings and grounds and what the governor-general commended as its Englishness were what mattered. In the

136

anglophile world of those who sought to be paramount in Australian society and in a materialistic community that has always valued impressive structures, that is understandable. In addition, the distinct waves of newcomers, strongest at first from the country and interstate, then Melbourne, suggest that there was a snowballing effect in which that strong financial commitment of the old boys in September 1912 was crucial. They were the school's best publicists and, because of their fund-raising, they had an investment to defend. On their grapevine from its original Western District roots, through tendrils stretching strongly into the New South Wales Riverina and outback in Queensland, they sent the message that the old gray school was being dramatically reborn. The response they got, as well as their influence in the Victorian capital, probably ensured that Melbourne families would follow.

Despite its success the school was incomplete; of the projected boarding-houses only Manifold and Cuthbertson were to be seen; and that was an achievement because, after the original tender, only one house was thought possible. Perry temporarily occupied part of the main, quadrangular, classroom block and half the chapel and half the dining hall were erected, although further enrolments justified the construction of Bracebridge Wilson House especially for junior

The school as village, linked to the outside world by a ribbon of road that led to the station and the highway. The first stage of the dining hall, the kitchens and boiler-house are in the foreground, 1925.

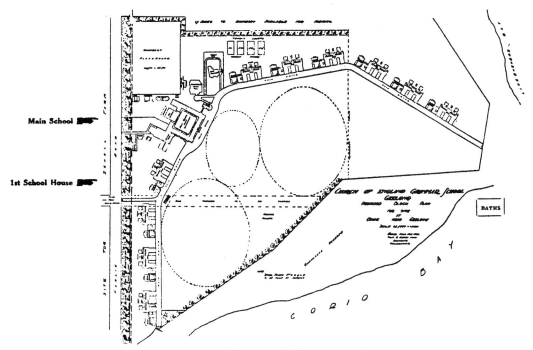

boys in 1916. That was a significant addition, fulfilling the architect's dream of a sweep of buildings facing the ovals.

As a result of its move, the school had become more distinctive. Geelong Grammar School, Corio, was a place unto itself. So much so that the sleepy Cowie siding, as the station for 'The Grammar School', changed its identity, the size of its platform and then its name.

OUT OF THIS WORLD

What had seemed an idyllic spot when the council first inspected it on that beautiful spring day in 1911, proved bare and vulnerable to the strong northerlies of summer and the winter south-westerlies that prevailed in the district. During the winter of 1913 no vegetation prevented travellers, passing through Cowie in the train, from seeing brick walls rising in the wilderness. Their backs to the railway, the buildings looked east across the beginnings of two large playing-fields between which a track soon led to Limeburners' Bay, the lagoon on which rowing was to take place and where baths would be erected. Bracebridge Wilson would have warmed to the possibilities of using the bay, filling his yacht with boys or ready to dredge for still unknown marine plants during the holidays. Guilfoyle's death precluded sensitive landscaping. Instead, hundreds of cypresses, so effective as windbreaks in the Western District, were planted in straight lines, their tiny spires of green soon easily distinguished among the swaying grasses during summer's tan. No attempt was made to soften the environment; instead, shell-grit paths, natural to the area and cheap, intensified the glare of the sun. During the first, terribly dry, summer, fourteen-year-old Leonard Fell thought that he must have been sent to Simpson's Stony Desert.

When it moved early in 1914, the school was suddenly and completely on its own. Without the atmosphere and close support of the large and relatively complex Geelong community, it seemed withdrawn from the world, especially as a lack of housing contributed a monastic flavour. Besides the headmaster's house the school provided only two dwellings, both iron boxes into whose wall cavities seaweed had been stuffed for insulation. One was for the bursar, the other a prize for some favoured member of staff. Married men seem to have found commuting from Geelong irksome, so bachelors predominated; but unlike monks, although provided with similar cell-like rooms, they were a footloose lot who rarely stayed for more than a few years. Even so, C. A. Cameron believed that the new headmaster, Francis Brown, had an almost infinite capacity to tolerate fools, some of whose behaviour was hilarious. Between 1912 and 1929 the average period of employment of staff at GGS was four years, compared with eleven years during the same period at Melbourne Grammar. If a man wanted to marry, as one of Lindon's former pupils, the energetic sportsman E. C. H. ('Bully') Taylor was to discover, he was obliged to get out. (So Melbourne Grammar gained the man who made its football team famous.)

If not in villages or small towns, English public schools were rarely so isolated and never so devoid of the family life of their own teaching and domestic staff as was Geelong Grammar. While funds were tight and salaries were low, distance was obstructive. Schoolmasters could not afford motor cars and the headmaster, who might have bought one, had no inclination to do so. The open car of the rich (unsalaried) bursar, Edward Austin, bumping between Geelong and Corio on the rough roads of the day, was unique at first. Brown committed himself entirely to Corio, hobbled by his concern that the whole venture might fail if he was not prudent. As he said to his son Philip at the end of his career:

We have to be thankful that each year from 1912 there has never been a loss, but always a profit which has enabled the council to do things which were urgently required. This is my reason for concentrating my thoughts and energies on the school to the exclusion to a large extent of other matters in which I should gladly have interested myself had I been able.[3]

He mentioned his fear that, if the school failed, its heavy debts might have crippled the diocese of Melbourne. He had none of the flamboyance and risk-taking zest of his council. On the contrary, his penny-pinching habit of mind contracted the school's life within its boundaries like a tortoise huddling within its shell. John Manifold observed that Brown seldom left the school and invariably worked far into the holidays.

It is likely that Brown's outlook and temperament stemmed from straitened family circumstances. Born in 1869, he was the eighth child of Eliza, wife of James Brown, a master hatter, whose declining business prompted a move from rural Gloucestershire to the city of

[3] F. E. Brown, private correspondence, archives.

Bristol, where he was little better off. James died quite young, leaving Eliza to prune the business into a small retail operation. Francis and his brother William, who also became a clergyman-headmaster (at Norwich Grammar School), were accepted into Queen Elizabeth's Hospital, a Blue Coat school at Bristol charged with the education of poor children and orphans. Later they both entered Bristol Grammar School and then Hertford College, Oxford, on mathematical scholarships.

A tall thin man, with a pleasant face, Francis graduated with second-class honours in 1892 and was ordained in 1896, the year after he married his childhood sweetheart, Ada Hancock, whose father was a Bristol linen draper. From graduation until 1904 Francis was senior mathematics master at Hulme Grammar School, near Manchester. After ordination, taking on a big commitment, he was also a curate in Manchester. From 1905 to 1911, he was in charge of mathematics and became second master at King Edward VII Grammar School, Sheffield.

At the age of forty-two, Francis Brown applied in succession for headmasterships at Preston in Lancashire and at Geelong. He accepted the first on the understanding that he would be released if successful for the second and was at Preston Grammar for only a term before migrating with his young family.

For that large step he was both well- and ill-prepared. Although a good scholar, a fine teacher, a firm disciplinarian and a meticulous administrator, he lacked experience of boarding-schools, being especially ignorant of the house system he was called to inaugurate. Similarly, of course, Wilson had been inexperienced at first, but had found his way by intuition based on a whole-hearted delight in boys that was lacking in the pioneer of Corio. An honest, God-fearing and very painstaking man, in whom modesty and humility were harnessed to a strong Christian purpose, Brown searched for enlightenment about God's will and acted upon it resolutely. No one could see a selfish element in his motivation, but there was an immovable base to his character that, once his opinion became law at GGS, tied the school to his inflexibility.

Keith Angas, a prefect in 1918, thought that Brown tried to cover up an intense shyness and sensitivity with a facade of austerity. His dark, clerical garb alone (a cartoonist might have set him against those shell-grit paths) would have suggested his nickname 'the crow', but in addition he had jet-black hair, a beaky nose and rather bushy (though light-coloured) eyebrows. Tall and straight under his mortar-board, he took long strides, gripping his gown at shoulder height.

As we have seen, Brown justified the monastic situation he helped to create at Corio by referring to financial stringencies. They were, however, temperamentally attractive to him. His boyhood poverty and grammar-school experience cut him off from the expansive world of those born rich or well connected. Although he moved with dignity and perfect manners among them, and earned their respect,

141

he was never relaxed with wealthy parents and, much though he admired English public schools, he had no personal experience of them. Despite the rudimentary house system, and the emphasis on prefects, games and good manners which he had inherited, he was not, as the *Corian* claimed at his retirement, 'imbued with the best English Public School traditions'. Lost in its own world, until J. R. Darling came, the school lived happily with such illusions.

Distance could anyway only be nibbled at during the early years at Corio. Before a bus was chartered in 1922 about forty day boys and several staff, including Cameron, Pinner and Morris, gathered each morning at 8.20 in a shed at the Moorabool Street pier to take the school's motor-boat *Avalon* for forty minutes across the changeable bay. A one-eyed Boer War veteran, Jack Messervey, was usually at the helm. By the time the Gardiner four-cylinder, twelve-inch bore, in-line engine (which started on petrol) had switched to kerosene, the boys had begun a study period. School, for them, began just off the end of the pier. The return journey at 5.10 ruled them out of the full sporting life of the school unless they accepted the extra time and expense of taking the school cab to Corio station and catching the 6 p.m. train. During the appropriate term, day-boy members of the first cricket and football teams often used bikes to link the school to the train. When storms raged everyone faced the rail alternative. Morning fogs could also be tricky. Messervey would grope his way by dead-reckoning, run aground somewhere near the school and try to make out just where they were. Once 'Jarps' Morris was left clinging to a pole after some desperate manoeuvres in a fog.

Movement the other way, from the school to Geelong, was negligible. R. R. Andrew commented that even in the later 1920s school life was a sort of academic apartheid—quite separate from normal life and living. A tradition of involvement in the life of the town, built up in the days when Geelong Grammar provided many players for the Geelong Football Club, was over, even on the simple level of carousings like Cuthbertson's, the progress of the baths' crocodile, informal afternoon strolls, cycling through the streets and Sunday services at Christ Church. Annual sporting clashes with Geelong College lost little of their public appeal, but there was a palpable gap where the Grammar School had been. Handicapped, particularly at first, by the transport system, neither masters nor boys, with a few exceptions, could make a regular contribution to the life of Geelong. They were not encouraged to do so—the school lived for itself. As Ross Cameron observed, when talking of his father Charles's career,

We moved out to Corio to live in No 1 Biddlecombe Avenue, in 1921, and this move in a day of primitive transport was a move that put my father beyond distractions, and bound him to the school on a twenty-four hours a day, seven days a week, schedule.[4]

4 *Corian*, June 1976, pp. 377–8.

The strongest regular contact boarders had with the outside

world was the store near the railway station, lovingly dubbed 'the belfry' when 'Joe Bat' (Batterham) kept it. After school, despite the provision of a tuckshop (a new Cale) on site, the doorway under Joe's broad verandah was often choked with the bicycles of boys filling their stomachs. Here they kept in touch with real life through aniseed balls, all-day suckers, soft drinks, ice-cream, potato crisps and more stodgy fare for the really hungry.

For some the sight of the railway was a reassurance that exeats and term holidays would come. Then Corio was like an ant heap on the move, the school wagon or truck ferrying baggage and the station platform swarming with grey-blue bodies. The local cab, brought into being by the school, may have delivered some of them. The road from the highway past the station and the 'belfry' to the school was as awful as its companion, the rickety tramway along which a horse-drawn coal truck plied, taking coal (later briquettes) from the railway siding to the school's big boiler. On the slight slope to the sea the horse was unhitched and the wagon was left to run tipsily down to regular derailments.

The boiler indicated one point of focus. Placed near the service road behind the school, it tied together the central kitchen, the dispersed boarding-houses and the headmaster's house. As building continued and the junior school was added, hot water pipes ran along the main axis, showing as dark lines through winter frosts.

Not everything was new. Jacked off its stumps and secured in pieces to low loaders, like a number of other timber structures, the fortuitously timbered Bracebridge Wilson Hall was dragged by horse teams from the old site. Set up again behind the main quadrangle, it was maid of all work, variously used over the years as assembly hall, theatre and gym as well as providing smaller spaces for the armory, museum and visitors' tog rooms.

Avalon moored at the jetty at the baths, waiting to take day boys home to Geelong after school.

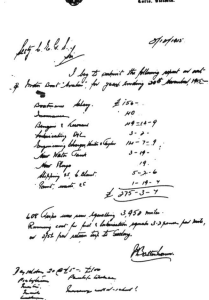

The initial rawness continued for a long time. The jubilee oak, planted by Bishop Stretch near the cricket ground in 1907, was brought to a similar site between the ovals, but, blasted by seemingly eternal winds, trees grew slowly and shrubs and flowers struggled to survive. Salt-tolerant native plants were neither available nor valued. This barren landscape suited, if it did not actually encourage, Spartan behaviour. Boys loved its spaciousness and feeling of freedom. A male heartiness, already part of the school's tradition and strong because of its rural roots, seems to have been heightened. The headmaster told parents that he had no place for a disabled student or one who hated games.

Intellectual disabilities were not so important. C. A. Cameron had to advise an eighteen-year-old not to sign himself 'Capitan of Botes'. He also spoke of a school captain aged twenty who, when he told the headmaster that his work programme of two periods of divinity and two of algebra was too heavy, was allowed to drop the algebra. Brown asked R. L. C. Hunt to come back to school just for the rowing in 1914. In the absence of intellectual and cultural stimuli, the mass of boys filled in their time with physical activity, hitting and kicking balls about in any spare minute. Organized games, strongly sponsored by the boarding-houses, whose 'healthy competition' Brown thoroughly approved, became the staple out-of-school activity. In a small school, usually beaten by other public schools, house matches were also an enjoyable retreat into a private world.

That hearty activity was extended, especially at weekends, into rambles on foot and, more often, by bicycle. Placed as they were on the Werribee plain, the boys had much further to travel before they found country as pleasant as the Barrabools or the Bellarine Peninsula. The gentle Barwon River now flowed less strongly through their lives. By contrast the You Yangs presented a rugged challenge and Saturday Parties making for the Brisbane Ranges became involved in another physical competition by vying with each other to reach the Lal Lal Falls on the Moorabool or to go as far as the Leigh at Shelford, near Golf Hill. There, from time to time, the headmaster and his family were guests of George Russell's daughter and her husband, Commander Biddlecombe—an association that probably inspired Biddlecombe's gift of six masters' residences between 1920 and 1925.

Those residences softened the social situation at Corio, but scarcely decreased incipient sexual tensions. Four out of twenty-nine staff during Brown's period were women, three of whom were successive art teachers. In that closed community bachelor masters were thrown into the company of spinster matrons in an unending skirmish leading to matrimony. Liaisons were hard to conceal and morals strict, so marriage was a predictable outcome, except where one of the numerous maids, lonely herself, fell into the arms of some desperate man. The bachelor quarters for domestic and outdoor male staff were like a

bomb awaiting detonation. Boys talked about liaisons, sometimes boasting intimacy. A Cuthbertson boy, caught during an assignation with 'one of the biddies' behind the Bracebridge Wilson Hall in 1918, was saved from expulsion by his house-captain, Keith Angas, who says he summoned up moral courage unequalled in his lifetime to plead with Francis Brown that the offender was only trying to 'cut a dash'. To his relief he found inside the austere headmaster a charming, sympathetic priest.

Masturbation, as elsewhere, was widespread according to old boys. Homosexuality, feared but not talked about, resulted sometimes in the sudden disappearance of teacher or boy. E. L. Nall's greatest concern as housemaster of Cuthbertson was said to be an outbreak of homosexuality. 'Find something definite to do', he pleaded constantly. When his suspicions were aroused one year, according to A. S. Ellis, he started 'a terrific witch-hunt'. Everyone was called down to be questioned about his sexual habits. On reflection Ellis sensed that the school authorities were concerned that such behaviour would sap national vigour.

Masculinity was at a high pitch in the boarding-houses, where prefects ruled supreme and often inflicted corporal punishment. Its results were visible in summer at the school baths where boys, by tradition naked, often wore ugly stripes. Privacy was not valued.

The view from the tower looking towards the freezing works at north shore Geelong, 1925. Shell-grit paths and iron roofs blaze in the sun. Behind Manifold and Junior Houses, across the avenue named after him, are residences given by Commander Biddlecombe. The school cab attracts custom near Manifold. A car is parked in a favoured spot beside the jubilee oak.

145

Because Wight and Hudson's dormitories and prep rooms were bare and large, a kind of herd behaviour was in the ascendant. Life was miserable for sensitive and intellectual boys and for those whose parents skimped and scraped to keep them at school. They were humiliated with shows of wealth in clothes and gear and tales of luxurious living at home and abroad. Dr. Brown did what he could to combat such values—he tried to keep pocket-money within limits—yet often felt defeated. Those who clutched too eagerly at the pleasures of this world found him adamant. Their warm blood sent his cold. Three boys who prepared for their return to school after the holidays with a good dinner at the Francatelli Cafe in Melbourne and who then boarded the train for Cowie with a further bottle of claret were given their marching orders, especially as they blustered self-righteously when the headmaster interviewed them. He felt strongly that he and the school were pitted against worldly parental attitudes.

To allow a boy so much money that he can spend nearly 10/- on a dinner encourages extravagance and self-indulgence. It puts temptation in the boy's way and does not give the school a chance.[5]

A recurring theme in Brown's letters was the antithesis of city and country, the first as suspect and evil, the second as wholesome and good. To him, isolation from Geelong and especially from Melbourne was one of the school's great assets: boys could be rescued from their soft lives like alcoholics drying out after a binge. He thought that boys who were distracted by easy city ways should be sent to toughen up with really hard work in the country. These attitudes and his role as cleric and headmaster helped to hide the gentle person underneath. Like many of his contemporaries he let duty harden him into the headmaster role. When giving the cane he made boys lean over the back of a chair and put their elbows on the seat. Each stroke was accompanied by a lecture.

It is interesting that a rich man's school, with the warm traditions of Wilson and Cuthbertson, should have come so completely under Brown's spell that by 1929 it was hard for those in it to see it without him and his values, summed up in his aims for the school: 'To teach religion first, then character—which is impossible without industry and trained intelligence.' Yet, what the *Corian* noticed in December 1929 as his 'constant insistence upon the high importance of a right attitude towards life', which put character before brain and brawn, was precisely what Wilson had done. The difference between them was Wilson's relaxed approach to the upper class, his joy in everything, his quick temper and humanity. Apart from that critical difference in temperament the two founding headmasters—one (virtually) at the old school in Geelong, the other at Corio—had surprisingly similar characteristics. The editorial farewell to Brown looked back on his singlemindedness and immense diligence, his flair for organization, quiet courtesy, punctilious regard for detail and calm unhurrying

[5] F. E. Brown to Mrs Burston, 11 Apr. 1925, correspondence, archives.

146

The first Corio prefects with the headmaster, 1914.

judgement, to which others deferred because they knew that 'the highest interests of the school were his only motive'.

In stressing conformity and discipline Brown found his most valuable ally in Reginald Gellibrand Jennings, appointed in 1914 as the first housemaster of Junior House.* Jennings became a legend in his lifetime. By an intuitive use of games theory, he yoked pre-adolescent youths to a manners-maketh-man philosophy.

Rather than Francis Brown, it seems, he was the drawcard at Corio, attracting at junior level an intake upon which the growth and distinctiveness of the school were based. For although Junior House was, as Philip Brown has suggested, his father's masterstroke, as unusual and significant as Darling's later creation of Timbertop, it was Jennings' regime, not its location or structure, that gave it character. Like the new school itself as a completely boarding junior school it was, with The King's School, Parramatta, one of only two in Australia and was a departure from the separate preparatory boarding-schools of the English tradition. Semi-detached like the preparatory

---

* Jennings (1879–1943) was educated at Cumloden in St Kilda and St Peter's, Adelaide. After a brief period in business, he taught at Queen's School, Adelaide and from 1909 to 1913 at Melbourne Grammar School.

Junior House in the early days
at Corio, probably 1915.

operations run by Melbourne schools and its own predecessor in Geelong, it began in 1914 with nineteen boys, 'awkwardly lodged upstairs, behind swing doors, at the north end of Manifold House'.*

After a year there were forty Junior House boys and in 1917, when the newly erected Bracebridge Wilson House first held them, seventy were on the rolls. Aged between ten and thirteen years, they ranged from grade 6 to form 2. By the 1920s about a hundred could be seen before and after school engaged in multifarious activities organized by Jennings. He took them out for bat drill on summer evenings, crunching the shell-grit triangle around the jubilee oak, and wallowed in the baths on warm afternoons among circling 'little beasts' trying to duck him. At other times he looked the English gentleman, walking through the grounds with his stick and spaniels. Always perfectly dressed for the occasion, he was a wiry athletic man who had been a considerable cricketer—but no extrovert. Like Cuthbertson, he made school life his whole world and wrote about it, though not as intensely as the poet, with warmth and sentimentality in *The Human Pedagogue* (1924) and *Threads of Yesterday* (1932). Stories from his first book, *Told in the Dormitory* (1911), were related quietly from memory to the first generation of Junior House after lights out. They left an indelible impression on the headmaster's son, Philip, who, with his younger brother, Martin, was a new boy in 1914.

Like Cuthbertson, Jennings encouraged self-expression (within the limits of his credo) and had the same ability to move easily, even magically, from precept to example, from seriousness to fun and from the group to the individual. In Philip Brown's view:

Fitting small boys for life in the round became his vocation. He reached Corio as a sound, systematic, sympathetic and interesting primary teacher, proof against the sidetracker but with an ear for each boy. Whether in class or not, he usually had the knack of unforced control based on his clear distinction between formal and informal occasions and manners.[6]

Fitting boys for the navy was a natural outcome from his system. When two gained entry to Jervis Bay in 1929 the *Corian* commented that the same thing had happened in 1924 and that no Junior House boy who had tried for entry to the Naval College had failed. Jennings reminded Ian Downs of that tradition when the latter went for an interview in 1928. Looking the selectors straight in the eye and answering all questions smartly and briefly was said to be the secret of success. One of the 1929 pair, R. J. Robertson, who was cleared of blame, made national headlines in the 1970s in the aftermath of a collision between his ship, the aircraft carrier *Melbourne*, and the destroyer *Voyager*. Rod Andrew lost a friend, the future painter C. R. ('Peter') Purves-Smith, to the navy in 1925. His departure also

[6] *Corian*, May 1979, pp. 89–90.

* In 1924, a quite separate Geelong Preparatory Grammar School, which fed Corio with day boys and some boarders, was started independently in Geelong.

cut off what would have been an important association with Russell Drysdale.

Against the formalities of the time and in contrast to life at the senior school, Jennings invented challenges like the annual Great Push, in which half of Junior House defended the You Yangs against the other half. He also gave young boys important responsibilities in running things and reporting them in the *Junior House Gazette*, which carried their original writing as well. A good library and an emphasis on art and the performance of music and drama helped their emotional development.

At the same time Jennings was conservative, but in a radical way that may have induced upwardly-mobile parents to see Junior House as a social polishing school. Russel Ward, who worked under him in 1937 and 1938, found Jennings to be 'the greatest snob I ever knew, and the most successful cultivator of a pseudo-Oxbridge accent'. He insisted on good manners, was rigorous about dress, and organized elocution classes for boys whose crude Australian speech offended his anglophile taste. Junior House pants were made without side pockets to prevent lounging and an upper-class tone was achieved on Sundays and formal occasions by the introduction of starched, white, expansive 'bomb-proof' Eton collars. Some parents loved to parade with their distinctive young gentlemen and some boys never forgot the humiliation of being so un-Australian. Colin Officer long remembered the hisses such dress provoked when trains packed at Corio steamed through Footscray station.

Within an unyielding system of discipline tempered by Jennings' sense of fun every element of life at Junior House was competitive. Three sections, called Barwon, Barrabool and Connewarre, vied against each other. A giant points system, focussing down to the most minute items of apparel and equipment, controlled behaviour. One of his boys, looking back, noted this substitution of discipline for reason as the characteristic of Jennings' rule. He arrived at Corio at the age of nine years in 1921, intellectually and socially ill-equipped by his free-wheeling Sydney prep school. The getting of wisdom was slow and painful.

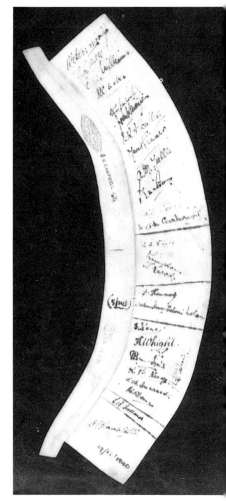

Eton collar with Grammar School signatures.

In those times there was a morning inspection of dress and cleanliness of all the boys in the Junior House. Any failure in either regard was punished by the reward of a bad point. Even one bad point was very bad. Two bad points were a disgrace. Three bad points were almost unheard of. In my first term I was awarded six bad points. I was paraded before the house and Mr Jenner [*sic*] the housemaster announced that I was the dirtiest and most untidy boy the school had ever seen. I was a disgrace to the school, to the house, to my section, and to my brothers.

Next term I was determined that I would do something which was correct. I decided that I would not lose my front stud. I bought a penny brass front stud and come what may, I managed not to lose it. That was 52 years ago and I still have that brass stud. It was a start and from there I progressed. I bought a back brass stud and kept that until someone stole it while I was in camp at Puckapunyal. Perhaps they thought it was gold but it was more than gold to me. I went on in this fashion to a point at which I was no longer awarded bad marks.

I do not know whether they still have the same sort of habits and customs at school. The Junior House then had a points system—maximum 100. These were

149

awarded for work, sport and leadership. Those with no points were known as 'minnows'. I was a minnow for a record number of years but rectified that during my last Junior House year.

As I look back on the Junior House my main recollections are the 'polishing' by Mr Jenner and the firm impression I had and still have that he was the man who substituted discipline for reason.[7]

Some boys did not respond at all to the Jennings treatment. John Manifold, the poet, loathed GGS 'perfectly consistently' for six years after his arrival at the age of nine in 1925. Geoffrey Fairbairn (later an authority on insurgency) found the first day the worst, 'submitting to tricks regularly played on new boys and listening to the cold, cruel eyes of the Junior School's Master as he raved on about the bishop's mitre on one's breast'. His father, J. V. (chairman of council 1937–40) who disliked Jennings intensely, had warned him against maladjusted OGGs who thought that their schooldays were their happiest.

Brown's rhetoric supported Jennings' socialization. He spoke constantly of the 'tone' of the school, lamenting any falling away from moral and social perfection. Onto the easy grace of Bracebridge Wilson's gentlemanly *noblesse oblige* ideal and Cuthbertson's relaxed cult of boyish exuberance and joy in achievement was grafted (or rather clamped) a concern for the proprieties best expressed by Brown's concern that it was not possible to assimilate more than a few boys with imperfect manners and accents. He did not lessen the sense of social superiority at Corio, but preached a greater reliance on formal duty.

Francis Brown insisted that he was both the keystone and the arch of government. He was a centralizing headmaster; no detail was too small to claim his attention. His letters show that he interposed himself between housemasters and parents so that there was little balancing of the power of 'king' and 'barons' as at most English schools, where boys were recruited not by the school but by housemasters, under whose special care they remained. Fearing their financial implications, he neglected cultural and artistic programmes, and committed the school not only to young and transient bachelor masters but also to a grim philosophy that denied them private lives. In April 1912 he had written to his brother at Norwich asking for his help in finding men who wanted educational work of a missionary kind.

One test of how palatable Geelong Grammar was to Englishmen with boarding-school experience came through the exciting appointment in 1921 of G. C. T. Giles, an Etonian who had won first class honours in the classical tripos at King's College, Cambridge, and had been tutor to Queen Mary's nephew, the Duke of Teck, and 'Professor of English' at the Public Commercial School in Athens. He was a swan among ducks at Corio, making an impact in some ways similar to the young Cuthbertson. As Brian Jones remembered:

Anyone less like a communist in general appearance and demeanour than Granville Charles Trelawny Giles, elegant product of Eton and King's College, Cambridge, it

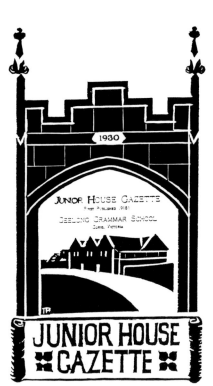

JUNIOR HOUSE GAZETTE

[7] Anonymous respondent to a questionnaire from Jane Carolan, 'A History of Geelong Grammar School, 1912–1929', MA thesis, University of Melbourne, pp. 244–5.

would have been hard to imagine. He looked much more like one's idea of a typical English country gentleman of that time, president perhaps of the local Conservative Association, and a life member of the M.C.C. (which in fact he was), usually wearing a tweed country suit, a silk shirt, Eton Ramblers' tie, and (what made a particular impression on some of us) white socks.

For the first time in my life I began to think of Latin as something other than a linguistic grind. In fact I began positively to enjoy it and to look forward to our sessions with him (the Latin VIth consisting of Paul Radford, Ken Mackinnon, and myself) in his study in Perry House.

Giles had the nicest manners which showed themselves for example in his treatment of wrongdoing. Before his arrival no one could have imagined a boy being caught using the housemaster's bath without permission and not being severely punished. But one day when Giles found a boy having a hot bath in his bathroom he merely said, 'I beg your pardon,' and went away. Similarly, when one night he came along to see what all the row was about in the middle dorm. and found us, having been alerted of his approach, all kneeling silently by our beds in prayer, he turned round and tiptoed reverently out.[8]

Giles was selected personally by Brown, during his visit to England in 1920, to fill Donald Mackinnon's generous gift of a classics mastership. Mackinnon, like his father Daniel before him, believed that education should be based on the classics, which had not been strong at GGS since Cuthbertson's day. The salary was £700 per year, well above any but Brown's, and over and above that Giles received board and residence and a generous contribution towards his fare. Despite the special treatment Giles complained that he was out of pocket; that Corio was a wilderness, culturally and physically; that he was thwarted in his attempts to stimulate activity in literature and the arts, as was stipulated in Mackinnon's gift; and that his accommodation was unsuitable.

Having had to refuse one of the new masters' houses because, so he said, he could not afford to furnish it, Giles lived in bachelor accommodation while his wife, who became more and more restless, found somewhere to live in Melbourne. For all these reasons, mostly related to the limitations of life at Corio, he was unwilling to make a long-term commitment, stayed an obligatory two years, to avoid repaying his fare, resigned and returned to England. Even though he had made him housemaster of Perry in 1922, Brown might have been glad to see him go. It turned out that the clever classicist from Eton and Cambridge was unorthodox in religion and a left-wing thinker, even a communist, sworn to bite the privileged hand that fed him. In 1926 he became headmaster of Acton County School and in 1944 was president of the National Union of Teachers, on whose executive he served from 1937 to 1949.

How privileged was the school? How ratified a social atmosphere did it contain? Those are seminal but difficult questions. Certainly it seems that by breaking its close ties with Geelong, although day boys had for many years been few, the school lost a corrective to social elitism, which now flourished more than ever because of the high fees made necessary by the expensive new buildings and because of the school's stronger image as the nearest Australian approach to an

[8] *Corian*, June 1977, pp. 245–6.

151

English public school. In the minds of its clientele it was a world apart—selected for its uniqueness and good social connections and, by some, for job-advantages attendance would bring. The rush by Melbourne professional and business families to enter the transplanted school in 1915 is an indication of what was happening. They may have been influenced by the remarks of Sir Arthur Stanley, Governor of Victoria, at the first speech day at Corio in December 1914. When he saw the school colours, 'the old light blue' he said that he felt 'once again in the upper school at Eton'.

Links between the school and a wider Australian reality were tenuous. On one level within the school a slice of the Australian ruling class among the pupils was sustaining its own mores in an amplification on the new site of the gentlemanly prestige achieved in the nineteenth century. On another level many teachers lacked the social background and experience to influence their charges outside the classroom or hold their own with parents. Even in Australian terms Brown's staff was not distinguished. Forty-seven per cent were recruited from second-string independent schools and 15 per cent from state high schools; only 34 per cent came from the most established independent schools like Melbourne Grammar, Scotch and Wesley. A mere handful were aware of what the English boarding-schools they were meant to be copying were like.

TRADITION

Although the new start at Corio emphasized the school's boarding tradition, it was a shock to other elements of its identity. While responding formally to the council's pressure in the direction of English public-school life, GGS faltered in one very significant respect and failed to achieve continuity of vision. Staff turnover in the first four years of Brown's headmastership was enormous. The new buildings housed practically a fresh group of teachers. Whereas in 1912 there had been no newcomer except Brown, there were four in 1913, four in 1914 and four again in 1915. Of Lindon's nine appointments E. T. Williams alone survived the transplanting and only two men, 'Jarps' Morris and George Steedman, remained from Wilson's day. In each of the two-year periods, 1913–14 and 1915–16, helped by the Great War, three-quarters of the staff changed. It was an ideal opportunity for a new headmaster to sweep clean, but there was a groundswell of sentiment for the days of Wilson and Cuthbertson which, in the absence of positive new ideas, gave the school much of its social meaning. This was expressed not only through old boys, so strong on council, but through their sons and grandsons, who came to Corio to emulate legendary heroes.

The acceptance of the move by the school family as a desirable retreat into a private English world reinforced an aristocratic ethos to which only the sons of pastoralists could naturally aspire. In an important sense they became the main exemplars of tradition. As Graham McInnes noticed from the social rough and tumble of

Scotch College in the 1920s, GGS, because of its pastoral connections, was *sui generis*:

situated on a bay about five miles outside Geelong was what all of us recognized as *the* public school of Victoria, a quite different institution from ours and one that you really didn't compare yourself with at all, because it was not a question of rival excellences but of a difference in category. Geelong Grammar was of course C of E but it drew the bulk of its pupils from the sons of wealthy squatters and sheep station owners of the Western District. There must have been more money per square inch of pale blue Geelong Grammar school cap than in that of any other colour. The great pastoral names of Victoria, the Fairbairns, the Manifolds, the Baillieus,* the Staughtons, the Russells, attended Geelong Grammar. To us it was less a school than an institution, a belief, a state of mind (or if you like, of grace), into which you were born and to which you could not and perhaps did not wish to aspire.[9]

One outcome of this myth was the assumption, both within the school and outside, that it still catered mainly for rural property interests, especially those from the Western District and the Riverina. Even though during Brown's headmastership as many boys entered the school from capital cities as from country properties, the prestige of that pastoral connection remained; so much so that more old boys went into rural occupations than came from them. The bloods in the school were the rural elite concentrated in Manifold House. Their values permeated the school, their muscular extroverted activities set the pace and their lack of scholarship explained and excused the school's poor academic record.

It may be oversimple to suggest that boys' values were so pervasive. Yet otherwise the school was claiming to be part of the English public-school tradition with hardly any knowledge of it. Brown was a strange choice for that aspect of the council's mission. He had been a day boy in a city school, had had no teaching experience in boarding-schools and could boast no public-school connections at all. His staff was almost as unprepared; especially as he was unable to make good the deficiency by attracting men with appropriate experience from Britain.

Building on Lindon's reforms, Brown made the school more formal. His punctiliousness and Jennings' training ensured high standards of politeness and good form and his strictness and hard work kept everything in place. He made himself boss more forcefully than Wilson or Lindon before him, and to the council's admiration and relief kept the budget firmly under control. Because this emphasis on the letter of the law offended him, the most dedicated proponent of the old warm-hearted way, Bracebridge Wilson's son-in-law, the bursar A. F. Garrard, shaped up as a critic of the new headmaster. Their personality clash and power struggle added so much tension to the early days at Corio that the council was forced to decide between them.

---

* A Scotch boy could perhaps be excused for including such urban Johnny-come-latelys. In fact, no Baillieu attended GGS before 1925.

[9] G. McInnes, *The Road to Gundagai*, London, 1965, p. 93.

Lindon's financial inadequacy in the face of the large undertaking proposed at Belmont in 1911 seems to have led the council to appoint Garrard as secretary-bursar. He had been largely responsible for inspiring confidence among old boys in the 1908 development scheme and in collecting gifts for it. Independent of the headmaster, he was responsible directly to council for the domestic and ground staff. If the two areas of control had been distinct no great harm would have resulted, but they were not—the school was one community. Brown found the situation irksome, but rather than tackle council about the principle, if indeed he recognized a constitutional issue, he drew the chairman's attention to what he characterized as Garrard's wilfulness:

The trouble arises chiefly, I think, from the fact that the bursar does not understand his position. He regards himself as the servant of the Council, quite detached from the Headmaster. Consequently he does not consider the wishes of the Headmaster or show desire to work loyally with him for the welfare of the school. Matters are not submitted to me for my consideration or approval but the bursar's object appears to work *independently* on his own lines and to establish a system of dual control which is bound to be disastrous. I am also conscious of a spirit of *opposition*.[10]

The suggestion that the bursar did not understand his position and was acting outside the terms of his appointment was clearly incorrect. Garrard was given massive responsibilities during the move from Geelong, especially in the supervision of construction on the new site. He was the eyes and ears of the council, the man most directly involved with the architects and builders, the keeper of the purse. But a spirit of opposition was indeed evident and was heightened by lack of sympathy from the outset between the Brown and Garrard families. Endeavouring to be hospitable when the newcomers arrived, the Garrards found the Browns cold and standoffish, while the headmaster was deeply upset by what he called Mrs Garrard's disloyalty. During 1915 these feelings were on the boil. Garrard's daughter has claimed that the headmaster refused to allow her mother or herself to swim during vacations in the school baths and, despite Mrs Garrard's traditional assistance with concerts and chapel, restricted their use of the school's piano and organ.

Divided authority amplified the 'spirit of opposition'. In March 1915 and again in September, Barry, one of Garrard's men, whose duties included ringing the school bell, muddled the times of periods. All was at sixes and sevens. The headmaster was so angry on the second occasion, which he believed was deliberate, that he called for Barry's dismissal for insubordination. Garrard countered by protesting his man's innocence and offering to resign himself if Barry was dismissed. The matter rankled so deeply with Brown that he returned to it in his regular report to council in February 1916, claiming in addition that it was under instructions from Sergeant-Major Batterham, the school's foreman, and Garrard's henchman, that Barry had rung at the wrong times.

The demarcation dispute produced other bitterness and, put

[10] F. E. Brown to W. Manifold, 2 May 1915, correspondence, archives.

154

under pressure by Brown, and no doubt aware of the bad feeling between the Browns and Garrards, the council sought to resolve the situation by separating the two families. Garrard was told that he must give up his house, one of only two school residences apart from the headmaster's. He would be allowed £50 per annum, but would have to live in Geelong. That he refused and resigned was natural in the circumstances. As the organizer of all building activity, needing often to make an early start, he would have been hamstrung by the move. The war was gathering momentum and he was a military man, so he gave up the struggle with Brown for the heart of GGS and became commandant of Broadmeadows training camp.

Council must have been torn over the issue, but voted in favour of the headmaster who later confided to his son Philip that, despite his good work, Garrard had too exalted an idea of his position.

He seemed to consider that the school should be controlled from the secretary's office instead of the headmaster's study. As I naturally held a quite different opinion the position became strained and ultimately he resigned to my great relief and the intense satisfaction of the School Council who recognised how impossible the position had become. The resignation must have come in any case (unless my own had preceded it...)[11]

Feeling as he did, Brown would have been galled by Garrard's public image. The *Australasian* of 16 October 1915 carried an article on the school which sums up the threat the bursar posed to a headmaster who could not work with him.

As we swung into the main drive we passed the cottage of Colonel A. F. Garrard who seems to be the centre of activity. He is the secretary of the Council, the organizer of much of the development, the executive officer of the Old Geelong Grammarians known to all generations of the school as a keen, thorough, tactful administrator...[12]

The war gave the colonel a way out and saved the council from an embarrassing showdown. Brown's victory, if it was his, established the pre-eminence of the headmaster. He indicated the seriousness of the division within the school by claiming that the boys and a majority of parents were with him and that staff were involved. 'Some I know', he said, 'were loyal to the core, whilst others looked on watching developments with an amused interest'. If that were so, his authority had certainly been at risk, but how virulently either man had pursued the issue is unclear, except that Brown seemed determined to get rid of the remaining signs of the cancer—Barry and Batterham—after Garrard left. So strong was Brown's position thereafter that J. R. Darling, his successor, acknowledged an important debt to the man who had made the headmaster's position one of absolute authority.

The mere demise of Garrard was not sufficient for that. It was the attitude of his successor, Edward Arthur Austin (who had been a council member since 1909), which cemented Brown on a pedestal.

[11] F. E. Brown, correspondence, archives.
[12] *Australasian*, 16 Oct. 1915.

Ned Austin

While Garrard's feeling for the school was at odds with Brown's, Austin was fully in tune with the headmaster. He was certainly never seen at work in his office, as Garrard had been, during chapel services. Quite the contrary. He earned the nicknames 'Pie' (meaning piety) and 'Holy Ned', not just for twenty-five years service as churchwarden at St Paul's, Geelong, and thirty-four as lay reader at St Luke's, Fyansford, but for constant mental genuflexion. A synodsman, he was appointed to the council of the diocese of Melbourne in 1918. Closer to the spirit of Wilson (and later Darling) than Brown, he founded a club at St Paul's for underprivileged boys and took them away in groups to his own holiday house at Lorne. He was a religious rock on whom Brown could rely absolutely and from whom he received constant affirmations. When on leave in England in 1920 Brown learnt from Austin that he remembered the headmaster keenly as he knelt on Easter Day beside Brown's eldest son, to 'partake of the Bread of Life and the Cup of Salvation. Ah, Yes, there is wonderful strength and joy in the full realization of the living reality of the Communion of Saints'.

A bachelor, Ned Austin lived for the school and served without pay. He had been so anxious to interpret it for Brown, right from the new headmaster's appointment, that in September 1911 he had sent him in England a sizeable parcel of books about GGS. There were the 1907 *School History and Register*, the October 1910 issue of *The Geelong Grammar School Quarterly* and Cuthbertson's *Barwon Ballads*. He described the ballads as the work of a man who 'did much to build up the tone that exists in the school today', and might have added that he himself hoped, through verse like Cuthbertson's, to strengthen and enlarge tradition. In 1927 he published *Light Blue Days*, an anthology of school and nature poems, to which Brown responded with warm appreciation. Although a modern reading suggests that there were thousands of verses but not a memorable line, he told council that it was a wonderful work.

Outstanding among the many features of this anthology is the spirit of Cuthbertson that pervades it. The school cannot afford to lose Cuthbertson's spirit and ideals and we owe much to Edward Arthur Austin for thus helping to perpetuate them amongst the present and future generations of boys.[13]

How long he would have been able to tolerate the errant Cuthbertson in the flesh, or to find an honoured place for him without Austin is problematical.

Brown and Austin were also as one through their total inwardness about the school. They helped each other make it, sentimentally, a world sufficient unto itself. Born across the highway at Lara in July 1875, ('Ned') Austin and his twin brother, Arthur, were at GGS during the later Wilson years. Sons of Sidney Austin, a pastoral pioneer, they joined their father in the wool-broking business of Dennys, Lascelles and Austin in Geelong, where Sidney was three times mayor. Even before he left the firm, aged forty-one, to become bursar, Ned's heart was at the school. As a boy he had been senior

13 Minutes, 2 Sept. 1927.

156

prefect, a member of the first eleven and second eight and had run equal first in the school mile. Like most of the Austins, he had been a stalwart old boy, vigorous in the Old Geelong Grammarians' association since its inception. With his Uncle Herbert he joined the reconstituted council in 1909. Unlike Garrard, who was a schoolmaster by profession and an Old Geelong Collegian, Austin could speak like an amateur of the school, which was not his livelihood. Not being married, he could give himself to it like a husband. He acted in the spirit in which he had initially recommended the school community to Brown.

In the School Council you will possess a body of men seven of whom are Old Geelong Grammarians—who will back your efforts in every way, and the old boys of the school you will find them very staunch and loyal supporters of the school...[14]

Better than that, for Brown, he was deferential both to the office and to the person of the headmaster. Garrard's 'spirit of opposition' was replaced by a will to please and, within a few years, by unfailing support based on deep affection. After Brown left for his furlough in 1920 Austin broke his customary reticence to write:

All through today you have been very greatly in my mind. There are times when through deep emotion one is powerless to express in words all that one feels at heart, and yesterday at Corio station, and in the evening when I placed my hands in yours and bade you farewell were such times. I never can adequately express all that you have been to me during the past four years of most intimate and loved association.[15]

Two days later he wrote again, acknowledging a milestone in their relationship. The headmaster had asked the bursar if he might call him by his Christian name. Austin was overjoyed, but, as in a formal dance, he kept a proper distance. He did not use the headmaster's first name in correspondence but trod a slightly relaxed measure with a 'My dear Mr (later Dr) Brown', which was full of intimacy in those starchy days.

On the one hand Austin became Brown's plenipotentiary with council and staff; on the other he was the eyes and ears of the old boys within the school. In an uncanny way he married the ideals of the headmaster to the ambitions of the Western District old boys who called the tune. He was the epitome of the old school giving itself to the new. His belief in Brown must have carried great weight in council, as when he told them in 1923:

Dr Brown with unfailing tact, a wise discretion and above all with truest sympathy reaches the hearts of the boys and makes them feel that their troubles as well as their joys are his own.[16]

He was able to alert Brown to danger and help with inside advice, like the warning he gave in 1920, when the Brice Mackinnon Mastership was being filled, that the donor (Donald Mackinnon) would not welcome the appointment of a cleric.

By the early 1920s Brown was secure. With Austin's support and

[14] E. A. Austin to F. E. Brown, 19 Sept. 1911, F. E. Brown, correspondence, archives.
[15] E. A. Austin to F. E. Brown, 10 Mar. 1920, F. E. Brown, correspondence, archives.
[16] Minutes, 7 Apr. 1923.

thanks to Jennings' success with Junior House, he had a full roll and was master of the scene. The cypress trees were taller than he was and the buildings had lost their first raw look. The harsh winds and the hard light had been tempered. Pride in the school, thus transplanted and reinvigorated, carried its name throughout Australia and far overseas. The council, who had taken over in 1908 and had moved the school so energetically to Corio, savoured the prestige of founders. They liked what they had done.

But there was a nagging doubt in the minds of two newcomers to council, John Manifold and W. Max Bell, that the school did not stand as tall in Britain as it might and should. They felt that it was socially downgraded by the 'Grammar' and they proposed that like Harrow, Shrewsbury and similar foundations, it should be known simply as Corio School. Manifold placed the issue clearly within that English tradition, where public schools were quite distinct from grammar schools. It hurt him that Geelong College was more felicitously named and therefore might automatically stand higher in the eyes of Englishmen, whose slights he seems to have experienced. Bell said he had heard that there were moves, for similar reasons, to change Melbourne Church of England Grammar School to 'Melbournia', although the change, similarly motivated, had been turned down in 1911.

Despite support from the English-born archbishop, the change was not pursued by council when it was first suggested in 1925. That it would not go down with old boys as easily as the move from Geelong was clear from the negative response when Dr Brown briefly mentioned the possibility at an Old Boys' Smoke Night in May 1925. Similarly, when the issue was put seriously to the school community in the August and December *Corians* of 1926, first by 'Clematis' (probably Manifold) and then by 'Watch Dog', there were passionate rejoinders, indicating that a strong tide of sentiment was running against the proposal. Australian nationalism and, even in such an elite school, Australian democracy were involved. Many old boys felt that what the school had done was good and could stand by itself without further Englishness to set it off. They feared for the place of GGS in Australian society and thought that Manifold's desire to rid the school of a name that diminished it in English eyes might strip it of its proud history and great associations.

Still convinced that the name was an indignity and a blight on the careers of old boys in Britain, Manifold tried again after three years. Pleading urgency and, significantly, with Donald Mackinnon's support, he gained a quick and unanimous vote from the school council and expected an easy passage through the diocesan council on which E. A. Austin sat. Within a month the depreciated grammar would be Corio School. Unfortunately for Manifold, however, it was decided that as the school was governed by an act of synod, that representative body would have to be consulted. As a result, the high-handed action backfired. Disturbed not only by the substance of the proposal, but also by the chilling fact that the first they knew of the matter was from reports in the *Argus* and *Geelong Advertiser*, the Old Geelong Grammarians asked council for an explanation.

This shot across the bows was not enough for John Race Godfrey, Inspector of Mines at Bathurst, NSW, who told the council to keep their hands off the old school. Although due to retire, Godfrey was full of fight. On 7 June 1929 he peppered 250 of his school contemporaries and acquaintances with a circular letter and a trenchant petition. Not everyone liked his words but most shared his views. Only a quarter failed to reply and only two who did so refused their support. As well as signing the petition many wrote nostalgically, like R. O. Moore from Blackall in Queensland:

I must add a line to the enclosed to congratulate you on taking the matter up. As I do not get the Argus I had not seen the notice you quote. I think it would be a rotten shame to alter the name of the old school. What would dear old Cuthbertson say? Hope your protest will be successful in blocking the proposition.—Don't think I've met you since the days at the old Grey School—but if you come to C. W. Queensland, call here and get a warm welcome.[17]

In a file headed 'Hands Off', the replies (but not the original letter or petition) have been preserved in the school archives. Godfrey had tapped an artesian basin of sentiment. Without its name, most of Godfrey's contemporaries believed, the school would lose its tradition. Like him, they felt alienated from the new school and distrusted its administration. Younger old boys threatened to remove their sons, dissociate themselves from the school and ignore Brown's farewell testimonial.

Council, with Manifold acting as chairman for a vital six months from April to October 1929, was moved neither by Godfrey's petition nor by the protest of the New South Wales branch of the OGGs, whose president, F. B. S. Falkiner, and his brother had given the school its chapel. Instead, Manifold, Turnbull and G. A. Fairbairn, who were also on the OGG committee, persuaded that body to accept the council's explanation and dissociate themselves from Godfrey's circular.

So far so good, but at least four of the OGG committee still had serious doubts about the change of name and one of them, Norman Belcher, joined Godfrey in appealing beyond council to synod by canvassing every synodsman connected with the school. Belcher formed a defence committee of people who had responded to Godfrey's circular and, cutting out any criticism of council or denigration of the new school, published a booklet entitled *Protest and Reasons against Change of Name*. It was mild and skilful, setting at its masthead one of Cuthbertson's nostalgic poems. At his own expense Belcher posted the booklet to 1100 old boys and received an overwhelming response. An enclosed petition was signed by two-thirds of the recipients. Even if all of the other third, who did not respond, had favoured change the protesters had a vast majority.* Letters

---

* In a separate enquiry in 1974 Jane Carolan found that the boys of Brown's day were (had been) 86 per cent against and 14 per cent in favour of change.

[17] R. O. Moore to J. R. Godfrey, 13 June 1929, 'Hands Off!' file, archives.

poured in castigating the council and promising Belcher support.

Through all this, the school's tradition and identity were thought to be at stake. In essence, though, the argument was about English and Australian taste, and the direction it took is an indication of the hardening of Australian sentiment. For the Geelong Grammar community to resist so strongly a logical change, bringing increased status within the English social hierarchy, suggests a democratic belief that the true context for Australian lives was not to be found at Oxford and Cambridge. As a result, the hottest issue in the debate was about the social stigma of the term 'grammar'. Old boys argued at length about the validity of their own experience. John Manifold and his sympathizers said that they had been embarrassed and ashamed; but a surprising number, including Godfrey, remembered an advantage, not a disability. A particularly strong view came from W. G. Hawker, who told Belcher:

as one who has spent the last three years at Cambridge I should like to assure the Council that there is no disadvantage in the title 'Geelong Grammar' as far as England is concerned and that the school would lose to a great extent her identity and present high reputation if the name were changed.[18]

It should be remembered that old boys were not unswervingly conservative. Strong though their sentimental attachments, few had doubted the wisdom of moving from the 'old Gray School'. The former headmaster, L. H. Lindon, chipped in with the majority, stating particularly that he had never been conscious of confusion between Geelong College and Geelong Grammar School.

Manifold was not persuaded. On the contrary, he thought council would show weakness if it dropped the matter. Then he changed his mind. Shortly after the enabling bill went to synod in August 1929, it was withdrawn because of the prospect of a humiliating defeat resulting from Godfrey's and Belcher's lobbying. The *coup de grâce* came at the annual meeting of the OGGs on 22 November, when Belcher outlined what he had done, stressing his restraint in avoiding publicity and pointing to the overwhelming rejection of the new name. He asked for a guarantee that the matter would not be raised again so that the 'Old Boys of tomorrow shall know their school by its right name and not have any foreign ideas put into their heads'. The meeting did not go as far as that but it did pass unanimously and send to the school council and synod the following motion: 'That this meeting emphatically protests against the name of the school being changed'.

Even after 10 March 1930, when the school council resolved to defer the proposal to change the name, old boys were uneasy. Godfrey and others continued to protest. In defence of the old name they consolidated the old tradition, which they had shown to be stronger than the powerful group of old boys who had guided the school to its new site.

18 W. G. Hawker, to N. Belcher, 23 Oct. 1929, 'Hands Off' file, archives.

EMPIRE

During 1914, when the school was settling in at Corio, the frenzy and dislocation of World War I began. Bonds of empire, proved during the Boer War, were to be tested again and strengthened as the school sealed with blood its right to share the burden assigned in British rhetoric to the public schools. Old boys marched to the slaughter willingly and in larger numbers, relatively, than men in the population as a whole. From August 1914 to May 1917 they enlisted at the rate of about ten per month, with an acceleration early in each year as school leavers joined the ranks. After May 1917, when the nation hesitated as a result of the conscription controversy, the rate slowed to three per month. Francis Brown studied the rolls and concluded that fewer than forty of the boys who passed through the school between 1908 and 1918 had not enlisted.

Squatters' sons were no more likely to enlist than city boys. The least enthusiastic were those from country towns, whose enlistment rate was more than a third below the average. Love of school ran parallel to love of king and country: 71 per cent of those who enlisted were members of the Old Geelong Grammarians. Some were so enthusiastic that, distrusting the speed with which an Australian force might be in action, or hoping to join famous regiments, they sailed for 'Home', where they met another group of old boys who had given up their studies at Oxford and Cambridge in order to enlist. At the outset Australia was less in their minds than the empire. As the *Corian* put it:

Everywhere the subjects of Great Britain at home and across the sea are rallying to the flag. The Empire is united and determined and is fighting in a just cause. The issue is with God.[19]

The war conferred on the public schools a new sense of their importance within the nation. It was a time to act upon their beliefs, not just to listen to people like Dr Leeper, Warden of Trinity College, Melbourne, who had reminded the school just after the Boer War that the empire would only be retained if its governing classes had strength of character. He had urged them to prepare themselves for the tasks of citizenship and government. With that in mind some had joined the British colonial service, but nothing justified their place in society so clearly as war. Fifteen years on, Dr Leeper went everywhere exhorting young men, especially of the middle class, to do their duty. The myth that Waterloo had been won on the playing-fields of Eton was powerful at Corio. If GGS was to be a true public school, the *Corian* said repeatedly, it must respond with fervour and resolution to the most challenging *game* of all. In this sense, however good the drill, fieldcraft and small arms training (their shooting was indeed excellent) they had received from Colonel Garrard in the school cadets, Geelong Grammarians were better prepared for the occasion than the activity.

Every old boy who enlisted went off to war with the blessing of the Old Geelong Grammarians association. In 1916 a special letter

[19] *Corian*, Aug. 1914, p. 3.

Officers and NCOs, 1916.
E. C. H. ('Bully') Taylor is in
the centre.

was drafted placing on record the 'deep sense of indebtedness' of the association:

to every old boy who in response to the call of duty is serving his king and country in defence of all that the British Empire holds most dear—honour, right, justice and liberty...[20]

It concluded with a metaphor of Cuthbertson's which likened school-boy games-players to the warrior heroes they were now being asked to become:

> For you are the men to be trusted
> Who grimly the colours defend,
> The warriors, battle be-dusted
> Too lofty of spirit to bend...[21]

A high proportion, of course, as they were to discover in combat, were natural soldiers—boys bred in the bush and used to riding, shooting and taking physical risks. Tough characters—made even tougher by boarding-school life—many were fearless, even reckless, in the face of danger. All but two of the 1914 champion eight were lost. Among Victorian schools, the highest casualty rates seem to have been at Ballarat College and Geelong Grammar School—from Ballarat, the most empire-conscious of towns, and Geelong Grammar, the most empire-conscious of schools. At GGS one in five of those who enlisted was killed, and 10 per cent of the 417 who served won Military Crosses.

Among the Associated Public Schools of Victoria, Geelong Grammar and Melbourne Grammar, with 52 per cent, had easily the highest proportion of officers to total enlistments. Xavier had 34 per cent, Wesley 29 per cent and Scotch 22 per cent. At the end of the war no Old Geelong Grammarian was a private. Of the 417 who enlisted 216 became officers, including a brigadier-general, 10 colonels, 24 majors, 53 captains and 110 lieutenants. Although the AIF was free from many traditional British attitudes it was taken for granted in the public schools that they would provide leaders. Although the most important factor in gaining their commissions was probably their comparative literacy, the frequency of their promotion seems to have strengthened their leadership assumptions. One of them wrote from the front in 1916 in a vein the school authorities would have been glad to hear:

From a boy's album, the march-past of a drill platoon, 1918.

It must often be asked how it is that England has been able to find amateur officers for an army of millions she has been able to raise. I think the Universities and Public Schools are responsible for training them. Here a man is inspired with the spirit that fits him for leadership. His associations and education have trained him for it and he falls into his place as naturally on the battlefield as he does on the football ground. He has learned which is the right thing not necessarily from his religious knowledge but from seeing and doing in sports and...is afraid of doing wrong...[22]

But who were 'the men to be trusted'? It is interesting that leadership training at GGS was not predictive. Being a prefect at

[20] OGG Minutes, 13 Oct., 1916.
[21] OGG Minutes, 13 Oct., 1916.
[22] *Corian*, Aug. 1916, p. 52.

school scarcely increased one's chances of promotion. Among thirty-six of Brown's prefects (appointed prior to October 1917) twenty-nine enlisted and sixteen (55 per cent) were commissioned, which was only 3 per cent more than for the school as a whole. Prefects, indeed, on Brown's calculation of the enlistment rate, were less likely to join up than their fellows. Once in, however, they defended the colours so grimly that one out of three of them was killed.

The wider school community was also deeply involved. As we have seen, Colonel Garrard resigned as bursar in 1915, and soon became commandant of Broadmeadows training camp. Most members of council were too old to serve, but John Turnbull and Percy Chirnside enlisted. Captain Chirnside, who had raised and equipped the second battery of Victorian Horse Artillery in 1889, provided his own little army. Donald Mackinnon was often in the news, first as chairman of the Victorian recruiting committee, later as director-general of recruiting for the Commonwealth. He travelled the country, whipping up enthusiasm and, by sharing Billy Hughes' passion for conscription, became a controversial figure. The death of his son Brice only increased his ardour. Early in the war and again in 1917, when enlistments were flagging, he pressed upon all old boys' associations the idea of a public-school contingent, the brainchild of a former Wesley master, Captain Harvey Carter. In 1917 the Victorian headmasters were also approached. All six agreed, and the *Corian* commented:

We know that most of our eligibles have already enlisted but when Mr Mackinnon asks for more of the same mettle the honour of our school is involved in giving him the fresh one hundred and fifty needed.[23]

The war was embraced strongly by all public schools, but each responded in its own way to the spiritual and social challenges. For instance, Wesley's headmaster, L. A. Adamson, trod numerous platforms exhorting men to enlist, appealing to jingo and lambasting the hun. He was an outgoing man, according to a history of Wesley:

a confirmed theatre-goer, song-singer, and poetry-writer, he loved sporting victories, military prowess, aeroplanes, and success of any sort.[24]

Brown was quite different. He focussed on the moral issue and was proud for the school's sake of those who joined up. Their autographed portraits occupied every vantage point in his study. He recognized that they went

to prevent a great wrong, to stand for what is just and true, to preserve our liberties and to save the world from bondage for a cruel, crafty and unscrupulous foe. They went forth in the spirit of crusaders of old, to do battle for Right against Wrong, Good against Evil, for Humanity against Cruelty, for Christ against Anti-Christ.[25]

[23] ibid., May 1917, p. 59.
[24] Blainey, G., Morrissey, J. & Hulme, S. E. K., *Wesley College*, Melbourne 1967, p. 149.
[25] *Corian*, Dec. 1919, p. 8.

Unlike Adamson, however, he put pressure on no one to enlist. He came to know the war, and to be known himself because of it, through the casualty lists. After those whose portraits lined his study were sent to oblivion, his memorable bidding prayers for the dead quietened the last whisper in chapel. The leanly-spoken, solemn words were his charge to the school to keep the awful sacrifice sacred.

Under E. T. Williams as editor the *Corian* was also influential in giving a relatively mild tone to the school's response. The editorials were optimistic but restrained comments on the course of the war and measured exhortations to support the empire. The passion of schoolboy editors like J. D. Burns of the *Scotch Collegian* was missing. Burns' poem, 'The Bugles of England', which contained the lines:

> O, England, I heard the cry of those that died for thee,
> Sounding like an organ-voice across the winter sea;[26]

had no parallel at Corio. Williams relied for strong effects on material from English newspapers and school magazines, thereby aligning Geelong Grammar with metropolitan opinion. Winchester was the paradigm and patriotic poems by warrior Wykehamists were quoted for emulation. In a typical passage, Williams also paraphrased Field Marshal Lord Roberts' 'Last message to the Public Schools' and included it in the December 1914 issue as if it were addressed specifically to Geelong Grammar School.

There is not one of you boys who may not take his part in this great struggle and now is the time to show what you are made of. Preach to all around you the 'glorious right' of this war in which we had to take our part or else for ever hide our heads in shame.[27]

That 'glorious right' of the war seems never to have been doubted at Corio. And its power was felt in the *Corian* through page after page of shatteringly brave and matter-of-fact soldiers' letters, which treated as routine the foul trenches, the lack of food and sleep, the inability to wash and the fear of shrapnel and poison gas. More than ever the magazine became the organ of the whole school community, past and present. It stamped the war indelibly on schoolboy minds. Because they had just supported the move to Corio, more old boys than ever were known to the school and eager to keep in touch. In the old boys' section of the magazine an honour roll, kept constantly up-to-date, reported enlistments, postings, promotions, wounds, decorations and deaths. Because of censorship and the editor's blue pencil, the printed letters no doubt diminish the experience, but their everyday prose was surprisingly moving. They faced the ultimate test of their manhood without pretence and emphasized simple values of mateship, honour and courage they associated with their schooldays. Naturally, in writing to the *Corian*, chance meetings and organized reunions with other old boys were given more emphasis than the bloodshed and the horror, but an eager cheerfulness and a sense of playing a game, even as they moved back to the front after leave were as true of letters not written for publication. They could thank the school and the strength of Australian sporting traditions

26 *Scotch Collegian*, May, 1915.
27 *Corian*, Dec. 1914, pp. 1–2.

for a romantic emphasis on games that gave them a marvellous mental safety-valve at the time of greatest terror. The playing-fields of Eton could not have offered more.

The effect overall was to unite them in a mystery they called others to share, though with a brotherly concern that fellows just leaving school were too young to withstand the strain. Warrior Australians for the first time at Gallipoli and then in France, they linked Geelong Grammar easily with the bush associations of the digger legend and with the heroism of Anzac. Old boys at the front felt that they were writing a chapter of the school's history as well as the nation's and old boys at home saluted that role. In that sense, the war, which had initially drawn the school strongly towards Britain, left it more than ever Australian. Soldiers discovered an Australian ethos that was validated and enlarged by their fame as fighting men, for they knew that they had outclassed the British in the most ancient and brutal of games.

The effect on those who remained was profound. During the bloodbath in France in 1916, when familiar names appeared in increasing numbers on the honour roll in the *Corian*, the Old Geelong Grammarians cancelled their Old Boys' Day smoke social and dinner. It was the same in 1917—the school's sixtieth birthday* on 24 June 1917 was allowed to pass without ceremony. The mood was solemn. At the annual meeting of the association on 5 November 1917 a war memorial was proposed:

let it indeed be worthy of these our brave sons who by sacrificing their lives for a great and noble cause have won themselves enduring fame and shall receive from their country, their home and their old school enduring gratitude that can never die.[28]

Initially, in common with Scotch, Melbourne Grammar, Wesley, Geelong College, Ballarat College and other schools across the nation, the idea was to build a memorial hall, something on a grand scale that would strike the imagination and 'remind future generations every day and every year of those who went forth from the school to fight and to bleed and to die, that the world might be free'. The walls would carry the photographs and names of every old boy who had enlisted, while a separate monument in the grounds and a special tablet in the chapel would be inscribed with the names of the fallen. A massive £15 000 was needed.

Despite an enthusiastic launching at Scott's Hotel early in 1918, when £2641 was promised, the target proved too high for a group who had so recently given massively to the school, or else the old boys failed to match the rhetoric of the *Corian*. In August 1921 only £9404 was in hand and the association's sub-committee, comprising the headmaster and its president and secretary, recommended a monument rather than a hall. They may have reasoned that, as the

---

[28] OGG Minutes, 5 Nov. 1917.

* In the sense of the laying of the foundation stone on 24 June 1857.

The school cheers the end of World War I, November 1918.

Bracebridge Wilson Hall was still serviceable, a more sacred place, befitting the sacrifice, should be created. Brown was impressed with what was happening at Winchester, where memorial cloisters costing £100 000 were being constructed. So the sub-committee commissioned the architect Harold Desbrowe Annear and the artist George Lambert to submit plans for cloisters and a monument. The old boys and the council agreed.

Annear was best known for fine domestic work and for a social conscience that led him to become editor of *Every Man His Home*. This was to be his only war memorial and was one of just two religious commissions he accepted. Gothic in inspiration but sympathetic to the space they occupied between the main quadrangle and the chapel, the eleven arcades sit quietly in the lawn, as if sharing the AIF's penchant for understatement, and welcoming the rule of silence that has been observed in them.

By contrast, Lambert, a war artist who knew his subject well, emphasized secular and mythological qualities. His portrait 'A Sergeant of the Light Horse' had been acclaimed one of the finest of the war and he was used to working in bronze. As the cloister linked the temporal and spiritual elements of the school, so Lambert's sculpture offered the secular a place within the divine. Two weary soldiers, one fully equipped for the French trenches, the other a light-horseman of Palestine, shoulder the burden of the huge carrion bird of evil which has at last been struck down by the spirit of heroism and justice, represented by a youth no older than those who, during the war, had awaited their turn to leave school and enlist.

W. Beasley. 80.

There was another memorial, also symbolic. Donald Mackinnon, that man of great wealth and patriotism, to whom Geelong Grammar was like a religion, gave a large benefaction to endow a classics mastership in memory of his son Brice, who was killed in France. He chose to prepare the way for good learning rather than godliness, to help secure Geelong Grammar a place in the world of scholarship.

For the chapel, where prayers had been offered upon news of each death, the headmaster encouraged relatives to fund personal memorials to the fallen. Six new stained-glass windows transformed the bare space, echoing the words of Cuthbertson with which Dr Brown welcomed old boys home from the war:

> And such was he whose name we keep
> Alive among us still,
> Who is not dead, although he sleep
> On yonder wind-swept hill—
> Whose voice is like a bugle call
> That summons us to be
> Unswerving soldiers, one and all,
> In life's Thermopylae.[29]

True to that traditional linking of God, school and country— it was a great moment during his last year, for Brown—the chapel was completed in 1929. On Sunday 22 September its new nave, with space for more memorial windows, added resonance to the singing of the first chapel services for several months. Two days later forty-six candidates lined up for confirmation. Then, at the patronal festival on All Saints' Day, 1 November, Bishop Reginald Stephen, assisted by Bishop Thomas Armstrong, both old boys of the school, conse-crated the nave and presented the whole chapel to the glory of God. After a loud knocking at the door, the procession had been admitted by Leslie Falkiner of the grazing family who gave the original funds and most of those for the extension. Bishop Stephen reminded the congregation (swelled by the school council, many clerics, fellow Anglican headmasters, the Falkiner family, parents and old boys) of an educational tradition stemming from William of Wykeham's objective in founding Winchester College in the fourteenth century: 'that the strength and fervour of the Christian religion may grow hotter'. He pointed boys beyond the average religious observance contained in saying one's prayers, attending services and behaving honourably, to the path of faith leading towards an inner life full of the love symbolized by the cross of Christ.

Ten days later, as usual on Armistice Day, the school went to the chapel at eleven o'clock. Following two minutes silence there was a short service during which the headmaster read the long roll of those who had fallen in the Great War. Then the Last Post sounded, the National Anthem was sung and in single file, according to the rule associated with that sacred place, the school moved silently through the memorial cloisters back to work.

ROUTINE

Just as Wilson's personality had created a warm, supportive school family, Brown moved Corio to greater formality and routine. His fairness, diligence and attention to detail reinforced an impersonal moral tone. Students felt that he was almost as omnipotent as God, and nearly as distant except on Monday mornings, when a large contingent of backsliders knew his wrath at close quarters through

[29] *Corian*. Dec. 1919, p. 8.

Donald Mackinnon, chairman of council, escorts the Governor-General, Lord Stonehaven, to the ceremony at the war memorial, 24 June 1927.

At the dedication of the war memorial, by Archbishop Lees of Melbourne, and the unveiling of the bronze statue by the Governor-General, Lord Stonehaven, 24 June 1927.

the cane. In easier financial circumstances the softer side of his nature might have been more apparent, but to one so dutiful the school's heavy debt became a mental block. He could not relax with it, so he pruned and skimped until thrift became an end in itself and a virtue he expected others to share. Above all, he felt that he must be its chief exemplar. It was not entirely his fault. In their almost reckless quest for greatness, the council had tethered him to a huge financial responsibility, which was a first charge on his middle-class sense of propriety.

In this way a rich man's school came under the spell of a miser, who paid lower salaries and expected greater effort than any of his contemporaries. He was quite aware that men frequently left for better pay. Edgar Robin, BA (Melb.), was a classic case. He became restless on £250 a year in 1925, asked for a rise, was refused and went elsewhere. Having fought in the AIF, he was not a beginner, and was just the type of scholar-sportsman needed by GGS, which his father P. A. Robin* (acting headmaster in 1920) served with distinction from 1919 to 1927. Brown reported Robin's progress a year later with dismay:

A master left me at the end of last year because I was not prepared to increase his salary from £250–£300 p.a. He was appointed to Ballarat Grammar School at £300 p.a. At the end of this year, I understand, he is leaving Ballarat to take up an appointment in one of our public schools at a salary of £420 p.a. with board and residence. In the face of these facts if we are to obtain as good a staff as other public schools or to maintain the present standard of efficiency we must be prepared to pay larger salaries.[30]

Yet, although council was happy for him to negotiate whatever salaries he saw fit, he could not bring himself to compete. It was apparently enough for him that he was paying above the minimum acceptable to the Assistant Masters' Association, so schools like Scotch, Wesley, Melbourne Grammar, Shore, St Peter's and even Ballarat Grammar outbid him for staff. When his bottom salary was £250 in 1920, Scotch and Wesley paid £400 and Melbourne Grammar an additional bonus of £100; and in 1925 after the Robin case, when his top position (only available to a housemaster) was £450, Melbourne Grammar had several (not housemasters) at £600. There was no built-in movement up the scale, as at Shore in 1925, where a teacher received £250 in the first year, £300 in the second, then annual increments of £20 to £500 and £10 to £600. By the end of his headmastership, Brown's salaries had fallen far behind those at St Peter's, Adelaide; his most highly paid assistant master (apart from the specially-funded Brice Mackinnon master), with £500, earned little more than the base salary at St Peter's, where four men received

---

* P. A. Robin was the most highly qualified of Brown's staff. He had BAs from both Adelaide and Cambridge and a Doctorate from London University. He taught at the Leys School, Cambridge, and several Australian schools and was founding headmaster at Ballarat Grammar from 1911 to 1918 before coming to Corio to teach languages and literature. He wrote several books, and edited the *Corian* after Williams' death in 1922.

£1000 or more, and where Englishmen from the public schools were numerous.

Salaries were only the beginning of stringency. He trimmed the staff to a minimum, deciding, for instance, to get by with one fewer in 1923, when enrolments were down slightly. He used prefects as junior masters when short of staff in 1918. Men were also expected to shoulder very heavy loads of games and boarding supervision. Their private lives were suspended in term time. Brown was also unwilling to pay for scholarship. Senior subject masters received little more than their juniors and were miserably off in comparison with housemasters. In that context, Donald Mackinnon's generous funding of the Brice Mackinnon mastership, as a means of raising the standard of scholarship, was a *de facto* criticism of the appalling salaries. It was also only a token of what was needed. To Giles, the first Brice Mackinnon master, who found himself intellectually alone in Brown's cultural backwater, the concept of improved scholarship must have appeared almost ludicrous.

By keeping salaries low, Brown seems to have been saying that he preferred a sacrificial atmosphere. In that respect it was a triumph to get R. G. Jennings as head of Junior House at half the salary he had been offered in Melbourne. The overall outcome was rapid staff turnover and a lack of sympathy between many of the staff and the headmaster that led to an even greater emphasis on formality and routine and reduced the likelihood that GGS would achieve the atmosphere of its English models. Brown had Thomas Arnold's high moral purpose, he espoused the same combination of religion, scholarship and manly games, but he found it hard to commit others, on his terms, to the great task. He tried time and again to recruit from England through Oxford and Cambridge agencies, but only gained five men that way. He had no personal connections with English public schools like those available to his successor. You might say that he was too honest, that in pointing out the difficulties as he saw them he was only being fair; and that is true. He told G. A. Hancock in 1915 and T. Thompson in 1922 that the work would be hard, but pleasant for someone who made it his chief concern. By writing in terms no masochist could refuse, he indicated that he preferred men of zeal like himself, who wanted nothing but work satisfaction and who sought nothing in this world beyond the school. If they were married he expected their wives to live elsewhere. It was almost as if he did not want the kind of men who could have achieved the council's aims, so perverse was he in not paying attractive salaries or making concessions to human needs. But the council was also to blame in providing facilities for boys rather than staff and for accepting the headmaster's penny-pinching over salaries.

In the outcome, though, what was the staff like? In line with C. A. Cameron's cutting assessment that Brown employed many fools, one thing is clear. While the council hoped for an English public school and the *Corian* used Eton, Harrow and especially Winchester as models, and summed up Brown in 1929 as having been 'imbued with the best English Public School traditions', neither the headmaster nor the majority of his staff had any direct experience of what that meant, or precise idea of how to achieve it. Of sixty-four staff members for whom details are known (among seventy-nine who worked under Brown) only three had taught in English public schools, and one of those, Eric Nall, spent just one year at Cheltenham. As we have seen, thirty, or almost half, had been appointed from the smaller grammar schools at the second level of the Australian pecking order and ten from State schools. Only twenty-two came from the larger Australian public schools of Adelaide, Melbourne and Sydney. Whereas in English public schools an honours degree was desirable, only 14 per cent of Brown's staff were so qualified. Over a third held no degree at all.

Some flavour of England was, however, represented in the possession by eighteen staff (mostly Australian-born) of degrees from Oxford, Cambridge and other English universities. As an unusual mark of distinction, four of these had held Rhodes Scholarships. Even so, a majority (twenty-eight) of those with degrees had obtained them in Australia. Again in contrast to English schools, Brown (for any length of time) had only one clergyman on his staff. On the other hand, in achieving Arnold's objectives in manly games the presence of eight university blues and one Olympian was more than might have been expected and suggests that the school was attractive to sportsmen.

The war cut down some of the most promising of Brown's early appointments, but unlike the situation after World War II, few who survived came back to Corio. H. L. Harvey, a Queensland Rhodes

Headmaster and staff, 1929. Standing: J. Webb, B. R. A. Coulter, F. C. Hancock, Rev. E. A. Hunt, F. N. B. Newman, E. C. Marchant, C. R. Bull, W. N. Jaffray, A. S. Marshall, E. de J. Robin.

Seated: E. W. H. Pinner, Rev. J. H. Allen, R. G. Jennings, A. Morris, Rev. Dr. F. E. Brown, C. A. Cameron, E. L. Nall, K. C. Masterman, A. H. Lowe.

Scholar with an honours degree in chemistry from Oxford, who had been appointed senior science master in 1913, was one of four science masters who joined up and did not return. Yet, in the war years several men were appointed who were to become veterans under Darling. Indeed, despite the general transiency of Brown's staff, there was a core who gave long and valuable service. R. G. Jennings (1914−41), C. A. Cameron (1916−47), Rev. J. H. Allen (1917−45) and E. L. Nall (1917−48) remained on the staff until or beyond a second world war. They were joined in the 1920s by E. W. H. Pinner (1921−50), W. N. Jaffray (1922−56), A. S. Marshall (1923−59), C. R. Bull (1927−39), Miss O. M. Finnin (1928−44), K. C. Masterman (1929−55), F. N. B. Newman (1929−66) and B. R. A. Coulter (1929−32 and 1936−71).

Overall, intellect and culture, though present, were in short supply. Brian Jones, who was school captain in 1924 and a member of staff in Brown's second last year, has reinforced Jennings' dismissive view that his colleagues were 'educated nonentities'. Jones, who admired Brown and considered the school to be a very happy place, believed that with the exception of Williams, Gardner, Cameron, Allen and Morris (he did not include the latecomers Bull and Masterman, and seems to have been hard on Robin, Giles and Pinner), the staff were indeed nonentities, lacking influence with Brown and making no contribution out of school. In his view they were not even educated.

Few were academically adequate, if that was what Jennings (who himself had no degree) meant by educated, and most were philistines. In the early 1920s, except for Giles, none was a scholar— not even Robin, who was drearily academic. Jones thought that, because so many boys were destined for the land, the school had the teachers it deserved. Pinner, for instance, had come as a swimming instructor. Jaffray managed to teach very little. 'Bully' Taylor perhaps sums up the style. He wore his old GGS blazer most of the time, as if the meaning of the school lay in it. A disciple of Cuthbertson, but without his intellect, he put personal rapport above all else. With a predictability for which boys loved him he paraded his stock joke.
Bully (to a boy caught chewing his pen): 'Don't you know you will get a terrible disease?'
Class: 'No, sir, what's that?'
Bully: 'Why, appendicitis.'
The joke is said never to have failed. At best, as teachers the staff were good tradesmen. 'Jarps' Morris passed off as scholarship an ability to recite, with his inevitable whistle and without looking at a map, the names of towns, seaports, rivers, capes, bays, promontories, etc. in any part of the world. Brown's own approach was cut and dried: he would allow no questioning of religion.

A boy's eye could pin masters and store them like exotic insects. Ian Nicholson remembered 'Billy Lop' Williams quoting his favourite poem, 'Drake's Drum', in one of the dormitories. When he came to 'Captain, art thou sleeping there below?', a voice from under a bed responded, 'Aye, Aye, sir!' The offender soon felt six of the best, but then, as always happened when he caned one of his favourites, Billy made it up to him with coffee and Banbury tarts. E. V. Butler, housemaster of Cuthbertson (1914–18), was renowned for his sense of fun, which led him to imitate his colleagues during class. If you did anything wrong you would be stood on your desk, while he leaned back, almost overbalancing, in his chair. If 'the crow' looked in they would exchange a smile. Nall's nickname was 'enthusiastic', Hancock's was 'gravy face' (it was mottled yellow as a result of malaria). Gardner was 'Jackey' or 'What? What?'. Scott, a larrikin, loved grand opera, played football for St Kilda and told 'Cac' Cameron, who had also been a league player, that his coaching had whiskers on it. The boys agreed. Vizard, a foreigner thought to be a German spy, had such prominent teeth that, when he raised a metal bar to show that he was preparing to test its expansion over the flame of a Bunsen burner, he seemed quite logically to say, 'Now we will eat the bar'. Just as deceptive was Captain 'Jick' Webb's invitation to his boxing pupils. 'Hit me! Come on, hit me!' he would say, but give them a good belting if they succeeded.

Formal attempts to improve the quality of students, although just as necessary, were no more successful than attempts to improve the quality of staff. Geelong Grammar had no entrance test and its rural base and reputation for pastoral care made it a haven for slow learners, only the most retarded of whom were ever asked to leave. It is unlikely that the eleven additional scholarships awarded during Brown's period brought more than five new faces. Of 139 scholars between 1912 and 1929 59 per cent were boys already in the school, which because of its social exclusiveness, expensive extras, moderate academic reputation and inaccessibility could not compete for very bright boys with schools like Scotch College and Melbourne Grammar. Only 17 per cent of scholarship boys came from State schools: there was little of the infusion of outstanding students which flowed into Melbourne public schools from famous central schools in middle-class areas. Such pupils might anyway have been admitted grudgingly by a headmaster who told his council in 1918 of an unadvertised entrance test:

It is undesirable to introduce too large a number of boys with imperfect manners and accents amongst a form of small boys. Only a small proportion can be properly assimilated.[31]

That hidden curriculum, whose most devoted adherent, apart from Brown, was R. G. Jennings of Junior House, espoused a thorough-going gentrification—collars starched, studs in place, hands clean, voices tuned, eyes alert for the moment for raising caps or opening doors for ladies.

Even so, when enrolments fell, risks had to be taken and not only with accents. In 1924, as an indication of importunity, council even sanctioned—when there were no other suitable applicants—the entry of Roman Catholics, who had been barred since 1912. Jews were always slightly more acceptable. The headmaster was free to decide each case on its merits, but Japanese were ruled out in 1925 when Brown enquired of council whether he would be allowed to enrol some Japanese boys from the C. of E. Preparatory School in Geelong. In the event, few such outsiders were accepted. In a representative survey of old boys of Brown's period conducted in 1973, no Catholic or Jew was identified, although there were some of both groups. The majority (79.5 per cent) was Church of England, 14.7 per cent were Presbyterian, 1 per cent were Methodist and 4.5 per cent had no religion at all.

Despite its disabilities, the school had, thanks to its prestige and probably to Jennings, attracted an impressive array of talent. When Rod Andrew, dean of medicine at Monash University, was summoned by his schoolboy friend the artist Russell Drysdale to provide an introduction to a collection of Drysdale's work, he wrote revealingly about their life at Corio during the 1920s, in the company of boys who were to take an important place in Australian life and letters.

The first thing he wanted Drysdale to remember was that they both enjoyed themselves immensely, despite the ill-paid and mainly undistinguished staff, living on a thin layer of pedagogical fat; despite the sad figure of the headmaster—apotheosis of the Protestant work-ethic—the dominance of religion, the hideous, red-brick buildings, the grinding discomfort and rugged routine. 'Corio is a godforsaken unlovely spot', he had written in his 1929 diary.

It was the boys who made it. Among Drysdale's contemporaries—they were a year younger—Andrew remembered especially Jerry Backhouse, Bill Landale and Alan Mann. And in his own stream, Alan Brown, Dickie Downer, John Dunlop, 'Beaky' Fairfax, Jack Gorton, Jo Gullett, John Hackett and John Rivett. Hackett, whom he described like Gullett, as a man of action and thought, was considered by Andrew to be 'the brightest of our time'. Rivett read Eliot, Flecker and Hopkins and Andrew himself, as captain of Perry House under Masterman, imposed a two-shilling levy to buy Medici Society prints for the walls.

Obviously talent and sensitivity were there. What was needed was an extension of the stimulation already provided by Bull and Masterman. It came in the exciting years that followed, when the appointment of a very young and visionary headmaster opened floodgates of change.

The prefects and headmaster in Francis Brown's final year, 1929.

NAME *George Russell Drysdale*
Date of Birth *7ᵗʰ Feb'. 1912*
Date of Admission *15ᵗʰ Sept. 1923*
Previous Education
Boarder or Day Boy *Boarder*
House *Junior House : Perry. Feb/26*
Religion *Church of England*
Parent's Name *G. R. Drysdale*
Parent's Address *To Union Bank of Australia. Melbourne*

Sicknesses

Date of Confirmation *July 4ᵗʰ 1928.*
Date of Leaving *May 1930*

9

From kingdom to empire—the Darling era

J. R. Darling

THE SUCCESSION

In 1929 the school council was looking for a married Anglican clergyman (though the conditions for the appointment specified that he need not necessarily be in Holy Orders), about forty years old, to become the new headmaster. Committees were set up in Australia and England to identify and claim him from a hoped-for mass of applicants. Just as Volum had gone 'Home' to represent the council in 1911, its chairman Donald Mackinnon voyaged to Britain towards the end of 1929 to join the English selection committee, chaired by the famous 'Monty' Rendall, who was formerly headmaster of Winchester College. Notables in the motherland were often used in this way for the task of finding governors, bishops, judges and administrators for the far-flung empire on which so much of Britain's wealth and pride were based. However, apart from Rendall, an experienced kingmaker, this committee comprised two middling officials of the Board of Education and a florid clergyman who was headmaster of Norwich School and a brother of the retiring headmaster.

A quite presentable cleric did sit among the short-listed candidates mustered in an ante-room for ordeal by committee, but he was not chosen. Against the council's preconceptions and despite sharp questioning by the Reverend Brown about his lack of a wife and a clerical collar, and despite his inexperience (he was only thirty years old), the committee voted for a tall, thin, energetic and ambitious schoolmaster, James Ralph Darling, who was eventually selected in preference to various Australian applicants by the council at Corio.

The boldness of the move can best be explained, at council level, in terms of Donald Mackinnon's vision and power. He warmed to the possibilities of a school under Darling furthering his own ideals of humane scholarship, expressed already in his endowment of the Brice Mackinnon mastership. As a representative of that breed of Western District squatter who knew Oxford

176

and Cambridge for their culture as well as their prestige and sporting activities, Mackinnon hoped for the development of art and music and above all for a school which was prepared to accept the responsibilities of leadership within the Australian community. As a Presbyterian he was insulated against the lobby who put their faith in the power of a Church of England clerical collar. Against those who wavered because Darling seemed a risk, untried in command, he mustered close friends like John Turnbull, also a Presbyterian, and convinced others that a drastic change was needed. 'It was he who chose me', Darling said later.

On the other hand it would have been a bold move to overlook him. Although apparently a long shot, Darling had the strong support of William Temple and Geoffrey Fisher, both former headmasters of Repton and future archbishops of Canterbury, as well as Frank Fletcher of Charterhouse and L. R. Phelps, the remarkable provost of Oriel. Temple, then archbishop of York, was his friend and mentor; under Fisher he had been head scholar at Repton in 1917 and, apart from his personal support for a promising member of staff, Fletcher was useful to Darling because of his effectiveness as a layman in charge of a great school (he was one of the most respected English headmasters of the day). Even if some members of the council at Geelong were reluctant to accept Mackinnon's enthusiasm for the young, unmarried, unfrocked candidate, they would have found it difficult to challenge the reports of such unassailable Anglican referees. Besides, Darling was quite well known to Rendall, who had earlier advised him to forget about GGS because, as a Labour man, he would not go down at the Melbourne Club. (He later became its president.)

Darling's recollections of his mood at the time are revealing. He saw himself as a fish being played by God; challenged to take religion and culture to Australia in the service of the empire but deterred by the distance and the magnitude of the task; set on by the thought that success at Corio could overcome his lack of a first-class honours degree* and prepare him for the headmastership of a great English school, but set back by worries about the status of an Australian appointment; inspired by a telegram from Julian Bickersteth of St Peter's, Adelaide, urging him to apply, but put off by the revelation from Fletcher at Charterhouse that a married cleric, forty years old, was being sought. During a Mallorca holiday he thought it all through and decided against it, but applied after a casual visit to Rendall, from whom he gained the impression that the field was not strong.

At the interview he was relaxed and debonair because he had decided not to care one way or the other. Then, hating the idea of being rejected, he waited in agonies for a telegram during the long weeks it took Mackinnon to return to Australia and complete the business at that end. The impatience suggests the blending in

J. R. Darling's first day

---

* He had gained a pass with distinction in the shortened course for ex-servicemen.

Darling of a strong will and the Christian desire to lose and yet find himself in the service of high ideals. Unconventionally for an Englishman of his day, he was putting himself and his prospects to a spiritual test.

Why was he like that? In part because he was a complex man, during whose development contradictory impulses had been at war. In part because he possessed few inherited advantages in an Edwardian England where family and social class were powerful orientations. Apart from intelligence and a privileged education he had no claims to occupy a position in the realm of his ideal, the civilized man. His ancestry ended in an apparent cul-de-sac at his great grandfather, Ralph Darling, who served as a corporal in the cavalry during the Peninsular War and at Waterloo. Ralph's brilliant son, James George, however, through the patronage of Lord Derby, entered Trinity College, Dublin, and emerged many ranks up the social ladder as a clergyman, later rector of Eyke in Suffolk.

Nevertheless, not only because he was the son of a corporal, but also because his wife's family were in trade, Darling's grandfather was accepted uneasily by the sporting gentry. His father, Austin, in turn, despite the credentials of Winchester and Oriel College, Oxford, and a fine sporting record, stood precariously in the ranks of polite society. His thoughtful wife, who came from a Lowland Scots business family, brought him no social prestige, although her money may have helped him purchase a minor preparatory school at Tonbridge in Kent, where he was headmaster and lived in comfort with five children, six or seven servants, a fine rose garden and shooting in Scotland, Ireland, Sweden or Suffolk according to the season. In James's view family life revolved around his father's shooting; to afford it, perhaps, or from another side of his nature, he enforced strict austerity.

There was a contrast between the parents that fostered two contending sets of values within their son. The father, warm, handsome and self-centred, generated ideas of worldly success and social prestige. The mother, who had hoped to be a missionary, lived and preached duty and self-sacrifice. Public spirit carried her to a three-year term on the Tonbridge Town Council—one of the first women in England to hold such a position. No wonder that James was torn between ambition and conscience. Scarred from working inordinately hard for a Winchester scholarship and yet failing, he tended to see himself as having a second-class mind. Repton, to which he won the top scholarship in 1913, was a hearty school with a great cricketing tradition, but purgatory for an intellectual without sporting talents.

Darling says his insecurity fostered an existing tendency to talk too much. Then, at the same time as he was being toughened into the view that in life one stands substantially alone, he emerged from the brutality of the upper fifth to one of the major experiences of his life, the teaching of Victor Gollancz.

William Temple had set off an explosion of Christian social ideas at Repton during his headmastership from 1910 to 1914, and it was in that tradition that the young socialist Victor Gollancz appeared. Later a world figure through the Left Book Club, he swept into the sixth form pouring out the latest thing on his mind, whether it was China, Peru, Isaiah, Lloyd George, Periclean Athens, Italian Renaissance art or European romantic music. His ideas and enthusiasm won him a group of young disciples to whom (it was 1917) the remaking of Britain and the world after the war became a great crusade. The school was split into opponents and supporters whose battleground was the debating society of which Darling was president in his final term. Geoffrey Fisher, the headmaster, had to cope with a group of prefects, including Darling, his brightest student and editor of the school magazine, who were listening more intently to an assistant master than they were to him and who were challenging not only the values of the school but also those of the social groups and national traditions it represented. A term later Gollancz was abruptly dismissed.

Had Darling gone to Winchester on a scholarship and still become headmaster of Geelong Grammar School his views would have been quite different; for he gained through Repton, from Temple and Gollancz, the framework of ideas and attitudes on which he was to build. A love of history, given to him by D. C. Somervell, and an indelible insight into true scholarship from L. A. Burd, remarkable though they were, might have been experienced elsewhere. For if we look for Darling's character, in the boy who was father to the headmaster, that blending of Christian and socialist ideology is of critical importance. When linked to his earlier feelings of failure in not qualifying for his father's Wykehamist and sporting world and an even more distressing failure to win an Oxford scholarship in 1917, it seems to provide the clue to his passionate pursuit of meaning through communal effort and service to those less fortunate than himself. His admiration for Temple's breadth of view and Gollancz's intensity led to the concept of the rounded man of action, a kind of Renaissance figure with a social conscience.

The desire, so like his mother's, to dedicate himself to the improvement of the world, was strengthened by the Great War, in which he served during 1918 as a raw lieutenant in the field artillery in charge of a bunch of Durham miners. His war service toughened and filled him out and gave him a sense of having the right to put the world in order; indeed, like many of his contemporaries and especially those who went into teaching, he thought he should work twice as hard to make up for the loss of the finest spirits of the age. There was something else: a profound religious experience related to the providential calming of an ungovernable horse. At a low point in his self-regard, he thought that his failure to manage it would put him out of officer school. After that he felt called to make good use of his life, thus adding emotional power to his intellectual convictions about social responsibility. As with his unquestioning acceptance of the role of an officer leading ill-educated Durham miners, he saw himself as part of an intellectual leadership offering, through *noblesse oblige*, to attend to the needs of the people, not as socialists but as heirs to the old liberals, turning to the education of the common man rather than to the direct redistribution of wealth.

That mood was confirmed at Oxford, where he was a member of the Labour Club and chairman of its literary committee. Delighted though he was with Oxford's traditions, its characters and its social networks, Darling was excited to go to Liverpool as a student teacher in 1922. He joined the staff of Merchant Taylors' School, a lower-middle-class preserve and a far cry from Repton. It was a bruising experience. In many ways he felt like a pioneer and in the time left after participating in almost every aspect of the school's activities he ran a boys' club in a Liverpool slum that was like Belfast for the violence of its religious bigotry. Once a term he stayed with Temple at Manchester.

His decision to leave Merchant Taylors' in 1924, to forsake the industrial north in favour of Charterhouse School in stockbroker country near Godalming south-west of London, brought to life a basic conflict between Darling's ambition and his social conscience. 'Don't spare yourself' was one of his maxims, but here he was running away from a duty. His expiation was an exhausting programme of Worker Education lectures, the chairmanship of the local branch of the Labour Party and service as a Labour member on the Godalming Borough Council. Temple helped him to resolve the basic dilemma by counselling patience in teaching ideals at a rich man's school and Frank Fletcher, the headmaster, challenged him to a greater understanding of boys. Fletcher was always asking 'why?' and always insisting upon one fixed point: that the school did not kill boys or prevent them from being themselves. No one fussed about 'the good of the school' at Charterhouse.

In 1929 Darling responded to an emergency call to replace an Eton master in charge of forty-five public-school boys on a tour of New Zealand. He was a success, and that and the thrill of command and constant public speaking kindled a missionary zeal that linked the needs of Australia and New Zealand with his own ambitions. 'Let me know of any openings', he said to Bickersteth of St Peter's, Adelaide, thinking that an Australian headmastership would be an interesting duty as well as a stepping-stone to a good school in England.

What did he have to offer to Geelong Grammar School? First and foremost, a rich experience of the English public-school system that was lacking in his predecessor. He also had, if not a philosophy of education, at least a set of ideas, ideals and prejudices that had as their centre the concept of the civilized man, who played games for the love of them, who studied without cramming, who valued music, art, literature, religion, politics and history above material success. Temperamentally he was an entrepreneur, prepared to take risks, but prepared also to work hard to minimize them, a strategist who kept his eye on the whole chess board. There were creative tensions

Headmaster and staff, 1933

Standing: H. McKnight, J. W. Glover, A. S. Marshall, H. D. L. Fraser, V. J. H. Turnbridge, G. C. W. Dicker, C. E. S. Gordon, F. N. B. Newman, J. J. Mckinnell, Rev. H. W. Baker, J. S. Cook, R. J. R. Mayne, W. J. Howard, D. I. Maclean.

Seated: G. E. Green, W. N. Jaffray, Rev. J. H. Allen, E. L. Nall, C. A. Cameron, J. R. Darling, R. G. Jennings, K. C. Masterman, E. W. Pinner, C. R. Bull, P. Fletcher.

within him, such as the struggle between ambition and humility that made him deeply aware of the contradictions in life. His closeness to Temple, the Christian and the thinker, meant that while the school missed out on a cleric, it gained a man of faith who had the courage to act on his beliefs. During his time at Charterhouse his faith had strengthened and his confidence grew as boys responded to his charisma.

LONG LIVE THE KING

Taking charge

To a school which had focussed its energies inwards upon traditional muscular Christianity for so long, Darling's first years were both threatening and exhilarating. Very little was left in place. Like a new king in the era before constitutional monarchy, the young headmaster swept away old relationships and introduced new concepts, new approaches, new values and new favourites. In a burst of energy unparallelled in the school's history, he challenged almost every element in its taken-for-granted world. It could be said that everything he did was related to his goal of the civilized man, but that, or any other summation, does little justice to the inventiveness and range of

181

his methods or to his powers of coercion and persuasion. He believed so strongly in what he was doing that he lived and breathed it; his power and enthusiasm either carried along or swept aside, at least temporarily, any doubters. Apart from that, his predecessor had bequeathed him a strongly hierarchical structure, in which the headmaster was nearly as infallible as the Pope. Defenders of the old order licked their wounds and clung precariously to their jobs, but were able to make no stand against him. If his eloquence could not disarm them, his grasp of detail snared reaction before it began to run.

Most important of all, he tutored the council in the fundamentals of the English public-school system, to which as provincials they bowed with respect. Their support was his lynch pin, and Donald Mackinnon, the chairman, became almost as important as Darling in the transformation of the school. He was the elder statesman, respected without question by old boys and parents, the only man able to get away with what Darling's policies most required, the spending of money. Darling needed it for new buildings, better staff, scholarships to attract clever boys, and for the support of creative leisure activities, including the entertainment of interesting visitors, who came like irrigation to the cultural desert. Darling told a friend at the end of his first year that the council had refused him only one thing. They continued that way and he made the most of his honeymoon.

Honeymoon? Well, yes, in the sense that his initiatives were supported even after Donald Mackinnon's death in 1932, when the new chairman, John Manifold, although less adventurous, was his friend and ally. Looking back, Darling has called the period 1930–34 'Halcyon Years'. Because his coming triggered something like the release of nutriments in Lake Eucumbene in the Snowy Mountains, which for a few years after it filled produced exceptional fish, staff and boys discovered new dimensions in the school and in themselves. Little seemed impossible. Darling himself experienced the flowering of qualities previously held in the bud by self-doubt and subordinate status—a probing and constructive mind, moral courage, stamina, sustained eloquence and vision. New for him also was the companionship, on paternal terms, of senior boys. As headmaster he could draw out young hearts and minds as never before. He tasted the joys of the giver of great gifts.

He tasted also, during that honeymoon, the bitterness of unripe fruit: some prefects were unworthy. He was appalled by the flies and mosquitos, the materialism, the raw school buildings and the cultural desert. He wanted English schoolmaster friends to come out to help him, but wrote to say he would not wish such a fate on anyone. 'Education here is a farce', he told Monty Rendall in December 1930. Relief came in unburdening himself to his mother in terms that later struck him as unpleasantly superior and priggish, and in escape during the holidays to the pastoral eminences of Golf Hill and Camden Park among anglophile Australians and fellow expatriate Englishmen. A few friends at Corio helped to keep him sane, but work left little time for socializing. With his mother's dedication and with a bachelor's monastic zeal, he buried himself in the great task. Of course, within Darling's definition of education, work embraced a variety of activities and brought many satisfactions. In spirit, the clearest Australian parallel is with the Whitlam era in federal politics: pent-up energy and idealism were having a fling. But in outcomes the comparison breaks down. Darling's innovations were hallowed at Corio by their Englishness and, his power being nearly absolute, opponents had difficulty in holding ground against him.

Even so, there was enough residual Australian philistinism and anglophobia, enough care for the inwardness of the Brown era, for the new broom to sweep up piles of discontent among the staff. Darling needed teachers who were much more than technically competent, and Brown had bequeathed him very few. He wanted civilized men, versed in the ways of boarding-schools, for whom there was obviously only one source. Rendall was given a standing order for information about likely candidates. The problem of making room for newcomers had to be solved 'by the painful exercise of my headmagisterial prerogative'. The Australian system of day schools, natural to a population huddled in the commercial capital cities of the various states, had encouraged a nine-to-five mentality and a coarse, petit-bourgeois tone, valuing the winning of premierships and the eye on the main chance. Only in the more secure gentlemanly world of the English public school would he find kindred spirits with whom to share his vision.

First it was necessary to convince Donald Mackinnon and the council that he should be able to offer attractive salaries, secondly to challenge friends and acquaintances to join him in the great imperial task of civilizing Australia, and finally to face and subdue the hostility his policy aroused. 'Move up, I don't want to sit by that b—', greeted Darling at a special occasion, a predictable response to his ruthlessness in sacking five of the staff in his first year. In came C. E. S. Gordon (a former pupil of Darling's) from Charterhouse and Philip Fletcher, then Gerry Dicker from Winchester (after sharp bargaining over salary) and J. J. McKinnell from Rugby as director of music. Fletcher and Dicker came temporarily, as Darling invigorated the existing practice of teacher exchange. Concern for their registration for the sensible term of two years brought a confrontation with M. G. Hansen, the Victorian Director of Education who, unless they passed a teaching test, refused to accept them for more than a year because they had no formal teacher training.

Here was another clash, natural to Darling's presuppositions, between English gentlemanly amateurism and Australian credentialism, the latter the product of a society needing to ensure the survival of teachers recruited from the people for the people. Darling justified the English practice of taking honours graduates straight from Oxford and Cambridge by saying that knowing what to teach was more important than knowing how. He also pleaded the special

183

needs of GGS for men of character capable of being housemasters. Australian positions did not attract them; apart from the distance, the meagre pay, the lower scholastic standards and poor career opportunities, they would feel degraded socially. In his first year in the country Darling was articulating views about the status of teachers that led to the foundation (largely at his instigation) of the Australian College of Education three decades later.

'You realise, I am sure', he wrote to Hansen, 'how much I feel the necessity for raising the status of assistant masters in Australia. It is the most valuable work that any man could do for this country'. He wished that people would remember that Australia and England were part of the same empire and would give up 'safeguarding instincts'. Hansen was not put off. He saw the anomaly another way. Darling's proposal gave honours men from Oxford, Cambridge and other Australian states an advantage over Melbourne honours graduates. Besides, the Education Act requirement that teachers should be trained could not be set aside. Darling had found out already that even headmasters came under its provisions. On 13 March in his first year he was given permission to teach and was sent the forms that led a month later to a teaching test by J. A. Seitz, Chief Inspector of Secondary Schools. Darling told him bluntly that his week was unpleasantly full, but offered him Leaving honours history, then lunch and something for the afternoon. The story goes that after one of the lessons the tall candidate moved out past the diminutive inspector, saying imperiously, 'That's the way I teach!'

In his impatience to change his own school, Darling fretted over such restrictions and found allies among assistant masters at Melbourne schools, who found his stimulating and prophetic ideas a call to higher levels of discussion. They encouraged him to speak and to publish, and recruited him for the fight against the conservatism of the public-school establishment he was supposed to represent. He became a phenomenon across the country, causing W. D. Kennedy of Wesley, the secretary of the Assistant Masters' Association, to chuckle about the contrast with Brown, who had never been seen or heard in public. At this time, too, with another energetic young headmaster, Leonard Robson of Shore in Sydney, he was recruited by Julian Bickersteth of St Peter's, Adelaide, to help transform into a separate Australian conference the existing loose connection of head-masters from individual schools with the Headmasters' Conference in England. In doing so they created a platform from which Darling's ideas were to permeate independent schools. Geelong Grammar was put firmly on the educational map when the first meeting of the Headmasters' Conference of Australia was held at Corio on 21 and 22 December 1931.

Almost as important as the masters in the transformation of the school were the prefects. In the tradition of Edward Thring, modified by his experience at Repton and Charterhouse, Darling not only used the prefects as junior executives under his direct command, but also expected them to absorb and exemplify his ideas and ideals.

The prefects' table.

Darling looked ahead to 1934 when there would be prefects who had grown up under his influence. They were to be conscientious and civilized, expressing to the school the value placed on articulate all-rounders by participating with equal enthusiasm in games, studies, poetry, art and music. For the most part they received this message with the rest of the school in chapel or assemblies, but there were special prefects' camps. Sometimes they were taken aside at the cricket nets or on the golf course and unfailingly he met them over lunch at the prefects' table. Many were encouraged to return for an extra year at school to be his lieutenants, both for their own benefit and, as he put it, to give something back to the school.

Cleverly he used the same argument to reinforce the sixth form, previously a handful of boys. They were given a pleasant room of their own alongside his study, whence he would descend on them for divinity and English, or, in the manner of Victor Gollancz, for a discussion of the latest thing on his mind, especially if it was an idea for the school about which he wanted feedback. He set out to win them and through them the school, and through the school Australia, to the notion of a well-tuned mind at ease with all knowledge, and he directed them to use their privileged position for the service of their country. As he said to the Old Geelong Grammarians on Old Boys' Day in April 1930, in a speech which delighted Donald Mackinnon:

I do not think it is extravagant to say that the opportunity which the Council of the School has given me is as big a responsibility as any in this country, or even further afield than that. I do not know whether you have realised the influence and importance a school of this kind can have in a country which is, after all, still growing. No other school in Australia has quite the same connection with all the other States.[1]

He told them that they should be forming the public opinion of the country.

This was a more sensitive point than he knew. Claiming the right to lead by virtue of Englishness, or by right of wealth or class, ran counter to an established democratic nationalism. So, radical though he was in certain ways, once he had adopted that picture of the school, Darling was caught in the mainstream of Australian conservatism. Donald Mackinnon's enthusiastic judgement in April 1930, that he had captured the old boys, might in a subtle way have meant that he had given himself to them.

There was also the risk, in the leadership rhetoric, of sanctifying individuals who subsequently failed to develop and blighting those not chosen. Stephen Murray-Smith later put it to Darling that the choice of school leaders in his day had not been justified by their careers. 'My dear fellow', Darling replied, 'you don't choose boys to run a school because you think they'll be leaders in later life'. Choosing them, though, could be damaging. One of his head prefects noticed that the boys being used so vigorously could become pompous and self-righteous. Masterman wrote from leave in England during 1934 about the danger as well as convenience of the prefect system,

[1] *Corian*, May 1930, p. 93.

Julius Caesar, 1945

The Trojan ship, constructed by C. A. Cameron, under sail during the Virgil play in October 1931.

Doug Fraser, from a portrait by William Dargie.

doubting whether it had worked as well as people liked to think.

That system of hierarchical government was softened by attempts to involve the whole school community—boys, masters, matrons, wives, indoor and outdoor staff—in drama, music and art, all brought together by a series of pageant plays in the 1930s (see chapter 12). The bimillenary of Virgil's birth prompted Masterman to suggest a celebration upon which Darling seized as a means of feeding his philistine herd a classical diet and giving them at the same time a radically new sense of teamwork and achievement. By bringing Aeneas ashore at Limeburners' Bay, Darling was fighting the traditional idea that games provided the only worthwhile out-of-school challenge. He had been interested in acting since childhood.

In 1933 a radical adaptation of Hardy's *The Dynasts* and in 1936 a home-grown religious pageant 'Alpha and Omega' were performed with casts of hundreds. An army of helpers prepared the scenes and props. After that, because, perhaps, the community-building task and his demonstration of the significance of cultural activities had been achieved, Darling turned to formal drama. In 1945, with *Julius Caesar*, he began a succession of Shakespearean plays in which Ken Mappin (from 1948) joined him as producer. They achieved a standard unthinkable before his time.

The new regime gave heart to Bull and Masterman, the senior masters, respectively, in English and classics. As Darling's chief allies in the fight against philistinism their influence grew appreciably. His own recruits added new dimensions. Most were educated and few were nonentities. In contrast to Brown's appointments they stayed, on average, over ten years. Many grew old with the headmaster. His charisma attracted unusual men. Russel Ward, a radical young historian, destined for fame as a scholar,* remembered walking a few times across the oval at St Peter's College, Adelaide, with the 'tall, slim, engaging young Englishman' who in 1937 became 'the first and incomparably the most humane, liberal and best employer' he ever had. Like Ian Weber (1939—78), Leslie Tomkinson (1935—67), John Brazier (1934—65), Jimmy Neil (1939—66) and Bill Cartwright (1936—71), Russel Ward (1937—39) was recruited at junior level. He moved to the senior school in 1939. A left-wing thinker, he was encouraged to hear Darling say with passion that the school would not be doing its job until it sent Labor members to parliament.**

Darling's concern to improve Australian education, and the liveliness he brought to Corio, attracted men who previously would not have considered teaching there, even with the larger salaries he was able to offer. He wrote indefatigably far and wide in the search for good staff and especially for the right people for particular tasks,

---

* His seminal book, *The Australian Legend*, was published in 1958.

** It has not, though technically John Cain, Victoria's Labor premier, is an old boy. He spent two weeks or so in Manifold House at the beginning of 1947, then left for Scotch.

finding J. C. Nield (1935–38)* in Sydney for the social studies fifth form and J. J. McKinnell (1931–34), for music, at Rugby School. But for Darling, the great talent of William McKie (1934–38), who joined McKinnell and then succeeded him, would probably have been considered out of place. In a male-chauvinist way, perhaps, he next looked for a *man* to give greater practical emphasis to art, through forge and workshop. When J. S. Derrick (1935–40) was appointed, Mary Finnin (1928–44), the charming painter and poet who had inspired Russell Drysdale, was moved to the junior school.

Other appointments of the early 1930s included H. D. L. (Doug) Fraser (1931–63), who from 1945 became just as successful but gentler and less dogmatic than Jennings as head of the junior school; John Glover (1933–69), a modern languages specialist; Raynor Dart (1934–61), who made his name as housemaster of Manifold; A . J. (Lex) Spear (1935–70), urbane and thorough; W. J. ('Bushranger Bill', usually just 'Bushy') Howard (1931–55), a Tasmanian Rhodes Scholar before World War I and senior science master after Cameron retired in 1947; J. B. ('Lep'**) Ponder (1934–65), one of the most learned and variously accomplished members of staff, a great bird photographer, prodigious overland cyclist, and perhaps the only schoolmaster ever to have illustrated Platonic themes by playing Bach on a clavicord. In 1937 H. B. ('Barney') Hutton arrived from England to teach French. True to the label 'scholar and gentleman', he was housemaster material and in the late 1940s inaugurated the special administrative role of 'assistant to the headmaster'. When Darling was in England in 1939 the senior English master, Bull, was replaced on the staff by P. L. J. Westcott (1940–69), whose keen mind, wide reading and trenchant comments kept his colleagues on their toes. His regular newspaper columns on literary, historical and educational matters, although anonymous, gained him a large following in Victoria. Pique at the loss of Bull led Darling to warn Westcott, at their first meeting, that he might have trouble justifying his appointment. Also in 1939, although briefly, through the science teaching of H. Bower and H. B. Mendel, the school benefited from Hitler's persecution of intellectuals and Jews.

Among relatively few old boys to join the staff at this time (the reservoir of potential teachers was small at GGS until the 1920s) were John Cook (1931–58) and Vic Tunbridge (1933–67). Jaffray, who had fought with Cook in France, suggested him to Darling when he was looking for someone in 1931 to run agricultural courses and to act as secretary of the Old Geelong Grammarians. Cook was a school prefect in 1914, completed a science degree after the war, and then worked for a gas company. Samuel Wadham (professor of

Peter Westcott

'Barney' Hutton

---

* An innovator, later famous as the founder of Koornong, an experimental school.

** As an illustration of the strange genesis of nicknames he was naturally 'Panda', but when Dart described a panda as 'a leopard kind of thing', the abbreviation Lep was coined, and stuck.

187

John Glover

Eric Nall

agriculture, later one of Darling's allies on the council) helped him to plough his new furrow. His own and his wife's enthusiasm* strengthened a school tradition of keeping in touch with old boys—their home in Biddlecombe Avenue was open house.

A prefect ten years after Cook, Tunbridge was outstanding at cricket, football and athletics. He graduated in civil engineering but, failing to get work during the depression, tried teaching at Wesley before returning in 1933 to Corio, where he taught maths and physics, coached his favourite sports and put into practice (in Perry from 1937) all the skills Darling hoped for in a housemaster.

Whereas day schools were run through senior subject masters, Darling increased the emphasis on pastoral care and character building at GGS by filtering his major decisions through the housemasters. In all his appointments he looked for 'men of character capable of being housemasters', but his hopes of finding a number ready-made in England were dashed. At first only C. E. S. Gordon, his former student at Charterhouse, filled the bill. Gordon took over Manifold from C. A. Cameron, who became second master in 1935. Masterman ran Perry with a civilized air until 1936, when Tunbridge succeeded him.

When Nall was moved to Barwon House at the junior school in 1935, Pinner was given Cuthbertson. Joe Pinner was laconic and so characteristically Australian that it may seem strange that Darling should have chosen him. They were in some ways opposites. The choice was justified because Pinner became an exceptionally skilful housemaster whose senior boys, moving closely also in Darling's orbit, were put out by what they felt was 'Ralphie's' failure to value Pinner as they did.** The best illustration of Pinner's style concerns David Burns, who managed, apparently without being missed, to attend the Melbourne Cup in 1944. Two years later, when he was saying goodbye to Pinner, the housemaster enquired gently of Burns if he had enjoyed the cup that year. Similarly, it is said, Rupert Murdoch would slip away to the races. At Flemington one Saturday he was placing a bet when Pinner appeared. Was he seen? He did not know until he was in hall near Pinner a fortnight later. The conversation turned to racing. 'We know about it, don't we Murdoch?', the housemaster said. Boys trusted Pinner, sensing that although a step ahead he did not take advantage of them. They liked him for not pretending to know all the answers and preach to them as Darling was tempted to do. In this way, like Bracebridge Wilson, Pinner was, as one old boy put it, 'stable, penetrating and supportive'.

Two new houses were created in the 1930s. Although lack of numbers precluded their participation in inter-house games, the flotsam and jetsam of day boys, whose identity had always been

---

* The *Corian* reported in December 1958 that she wrote at least 300 birthday letters to OGGs each year.

** In fact, Darling believed that Pinner should be his replacement when he seemed likely to stay in England in 1939.

precarious at GGS, were given a stronger focus through Geelong House in 1931. Since it was also possible, because the school had a bus, for them to stay for tea and prep (after Darling had persuaded parents to pay for the privilege), they felt much more part of the place. 'Joey' Allen, the chaplain, was appointed housemaster. Six years later his old colleague W. N. Jaffray took charge of the new Francis Brown House, through which house competition was considerably expanded. Although not returning to the small bedrooms of Wilson's school, Francis Brown House offered boys privacy and comfort previously unknown at Corio.

Bachelor masters were also given privacy and an important release from the herd at meal times. Those not on duty enjoyed better food and a drink with dinner when the matrons' dining room was converted to their use in 1931. Renamed the Morris Room after 'Jarps', it became their club and one of Darling's happiest innovations.

'Joe' Pinner

How completely the personality of the headmaster influenced the school is seen in the transformation of the business and secretarial side and in greater informality. Among Darling's first acts (it was self-preservation) was the hiring of a secretary. Vi Moden occupied the dingy ante-room, where boys and parents had languished, and transformed it into a cheerful, busy place, full of evidence of the system Darling was creating. She sat at her typewriter surrounded by correspondence files, timetable forms, homework cards, school lists, calendars and other new-fangled things. His approachability within it and his activity outside the school made the keeping of the headmaster's diary a major activity and his correspondence, as the files testify, was endless. He found it hard to forego the gentlemanly convention of writing to his friends and to important people in his own hand, but increasingly pleaded pressure of work and signed as Jim or J. R. Darling under Miss Moden's tic-a-tac. The easy style and pleasant atmosphere tempered the violence of the changes he made. An old boy received the message 'from a good authority within the school' that he was 'open, careless, free in manner and speech, a complete contrast to the old head, yet firm and mixed freely with the boys'. He was in fact more in tune with Australia than he at first thought. By June 1933 he noticed a 'distressing tendency' in himself to get offended by the superior attitudes of Englishmen and their extraordinary voices.

Impersonality offended him, and that was so unexpected in an Englishmen that it gave him an easy conquest of the people 'out the back'. Furphies spread quickly among maintenance and groundstaff. From Tom Judd Jr, the school porter, came the story on Darling's first day, that instead of the cold 'Nothing Judd', which usually greeted his dutiful morning knock at the headmaster's study door, he heard a cheerful 'Come in' and 'Oh, hello', from which it took him a week to recover. Others found that the headmaster spoke directly to them and did not expect or welcome a diffident tug at their caps when he appeared. 'For a pommie, he'll make a bloody good Aussie', said Perc Trebilcock, the labourer.

Nevertheless, Darling also expected a devotion to duty equal to his own. Matrons, bursar, ground-staff and all were drawn into unquestioning service to the good of the school. He did not preach it at them—that anyway was not good form—but his actions, his precepts and his expectations quite apart from specific requirements, committed them. Only the brave demurred. One of Tom Judd's early experiences is probably typical. He found the courage to tell the head that he was being asked to give up his lunch hour. 'Tom', said Darling (it was the first time anyone in authority had used his first name), 'I've noticed that you have a tendency to stick up for your rights too much'. The diplomacy of the 'Tom' or, on occasions of special effort, an appreciative 'Tom, you're a genius', expressed Darling's underlying awareness of fellowship in the cause, tangled though it was with *noblesse oblige* and with an intuitive approach to the art of managing people. With those more nearly his equal, such as the bursar, he achieved a close relationship through his grasp of issues and by his watchfulness and concern about details of administration, as far as they affected the schemes he had in mind. So much more was happening at the school that the petticoat revolution extended to the bursar's office and the number of general staff grew quite rapidly.

New facilities

Two sentences from the headmaster on Old Boys' Day 1930, which he more or less repeated in his report at the end of the year, foreshadowed his dynamic approach. Shrewdly he cast himself in the role of the young man given the opportunity to fulfil the hopes of his predecessor:

I feel that Dr. Brown has left here a foundation upon which any man ought to be proud to build. A most remarkable feature about him was the way he must have withheld himself from doing the things he wanted to do, and which it was not advisable to do at the moment.[2]

Darling spoke and acted as if the advisable moment had come, a general moment and not just his own, despite the fact that a world depression had struck Australia with particular savagery and that the same *Corian* that reported his statement to the old boys carried an account of an address by the distinguished economist, Professor L. F. Giblin, who likened the Australian nation to an extravagant family forced now to deny itself in order to pay for having borrowed too much.

Darling shared that view. In a world economy out of control, he believed that Australia was paralysed by materialism and selfishness, two vices which had been rotting the community for ten years, and which were, he felt, more the result of a moral failure among the educated than among the labouring classes. So he challenged the school from the pulpit in 1931, as unemployment rose to over 30 per

[2] *Corian*, May 1930, p. 93.

cent and he became fearful of some kind of civil war. 'To you is given as great a chance as ever came to a generation of men', he told them, and before long was calling them to share in the founding of an Unemployed Boys' Centre in Geelong, to do more for themselves around the school and to take a broader view of life through a more sympathetic education. This *was* his moment, for his goals were spiritual not material. Geelong Grammar must show Australia the way by producing rounded and unselfish leaders, not the gamesplaying kind who, under Brown, had returned to school as if into a holding paddock, wasting their potential in as many as twenty-one spare periods a week. In a speech to the Teachers' Union at Sydney in 1931, he stressed the importance of values in education, especially the need to cater for all individuals and to develop character by replacing laziness and self-interest with energy, continence, altruism and thoroughness. That kind of individual could find happiness only in social action, so the nation would be remade. Temple and Gollancz were speaking together through their ardent disciple.

Such important work could not wait for the depression to end. In fact Darling had begun it as soon as he arrived, well before the moral issue was raised. Whatever might have been said politely about Brown's foundation, the school needed shaking into life. Darling saw that modern science laboratories were fundamental, that other new classrooms would release space for an art room, a sixth form room and a comfortable library, while new dormitories in Perry House would enlarge the school and increase its income. On 29 March 1930 he gained Donald Mackinnon's support for a second storey over part of the quadrangle, where the new dormitories and classrooms would be located, as well as for the £5000 science wing. Mackinnon softened up the council, instructed the architect to draw up plans and cheered Darling by his optimism about the low cost of building and the availability of funds through the AMP Society. Indeed, he thought finance would be quite easy by the end of the year, when a large benefaction from the Whittingham Estate in Queensland was expected.* In the meantime John Turnbull, another of Darling's champions on the council, persuaded one of his brothers to lend the money for the science wing, the plans of which had been much improved after advice from Professor Wadham. The *Corian* was delighted. Funds had also been found for seats in the Bracebridge Wilson Hall (ending the regular sweat of moving chairs from the dining hall), for a hobby room in the drill hall and for beautifying the grounds.

The pragmatist, the planner and the entrepreneur in the headmaster were stimulated by this success. It was his own solution, in concept and in detail, worried over and gradually given form during the hectic months after his arrival. He often worked on it late at

---

* It was not to be available for building. Arthur Herbert Whittingham (1869–1927), Queensland pastoralist, businessman and politician, was at GGS from 1885 to 1888. He left the A. H. Whittingham Fund to promote education in the school. About £100 000 initially and about $222 000 on the death of his widow in 1972, has provided many scholarships.

night, at the same time as he thought out a general strategy for changing the school, coped with day-to-day administration and wondered whether it was all worth while. In terms of his career, he was compelled to build in order to make his mark and gain release from the unpromising outpost of empire. He little knew, of course, that such pioneering, as had happened to many of the founders of the Western District, whose descendants were the backbone of the school, might eventually hold him by the heartstrings.

After a quiet year in 1931, when the initial improvements were being enjoyed and new ones were confined to the planting of trees and hundreds of daffodil bulbs, and as the depression deepened, bringing all sorts of economies, Darling returned to the attack. Despite a harrowing time looking at the finances in August 1931 and deciding to retrench two of the staff and accept a voluntary 5 per cent salary cut from the rest, Darling bounced back in March 1932. An expected drop of thirty in the number of boarders had not occurred. The school was 'disgustingly full', he told Archbishop Head in April, possibly hoping to get support from his fellow Old Reptonian for the spending of £60 000 on new buildings. In a three-stage plan he wanted a new junior house, several more classrooms, two senior houses, an extended dining hall, a better laundry, new domestic quarters, sewerage and a library. In a long letter to Donald Mackinnon in March, he had set out the implications of his success. The drawing power of the school was proving extraordinary and, believing that it was bad policy to turn boys away, he had committed it beyond the limit of its facilities. In June the position worsened. Eight extra boys had been crammed into Perry, several more were to go into R. G. Jennings' spare bedroom and still there were fifteen floating about.

As an expansionist he naturally found it hard to refuse new boys. The pressure was probably useful in council, but the preference for numbers rather than quality contradicted his desire to raise the standard of scholarship. His statement to Mackinnon in March 1932, that it was not possible to be selective, seems quaint and perverse. The opportunity might have been used to move towards an Australian Winchester, with tough entry standards, so the fact that he did not explore that possibility suggests that Darling still carried the wounds of his childhood failure and was determined as a Christian and quasi socialist to accept all comers into his kingdom. Apart from that, there was the political problem that selection would have excluded a high proportion of the traditional Western District clientele and brought a confrontation with the old boys. Perhaps, though, he was right to argue that the first priority was numbers, in order to support the specialist staffing of music, art and manual work and the development of a strong sixth form. He was able to pay more to his staff and was deploying them in areas previously considered impossibly extravagant. He was also attracting in the new entry a further and disproportionate number of the sons of professional and business men from Melbourne.

The effort might have borne fruit if he had not lost his strongest supporter in April 1932. Although sceptical, the council did ask for estimates of the whole scheme and Darling found Bell and Fairbairn sympathetic. Then, just as Mackinnon, who had been taken to hospital for the first time in his seventy-two years, was pondering the estimates and beginning to see daylight for Darling's £60 000 plan, his own darkness came down. Had he lived, the scheme might have survived. It needed the courage of an elder statesman who did not have to count his own pennies in the way that his successor, John Manifold, did.

In every other way, 'My dear John' brought joy to Darling. They were already friends, so he could write openly about his hopes and fears. In a June letter he expounded a temporary solution, a few classrooms and a library. Then in August, with the help of Milton Thewlis, who was bursar and a great ally, he went once again, frightened but compelled, into the big plan. More and more he sensed that his choice was between everything and nothing. If it was to be everything, the risks for the council were so great and the plan so dependent on his own vision and drive that he might have to make a permanent commitment; in which case the council would probably have to decide between him and the scheme. He was sure that he could not carry on indefinitely without the facilities he wanted. Much now depended on the support of Jim Fairbairn and the old boys, and to a lesser but important extent on the detached voice of Sam Wadham, professor of agriculture, who had joined the council at the headmaster's suggestion.

Darling and Thewlis had looked with growing optimism at every element of the budget. The risks of a decline in enrolments, a national financial crash and problems with the Whittingham Estate bequest seemed to be balanced by the advantages of low building costs, available finance and the current rush for places. Darling urged Manifold to take a long view, to work for the school's centenary in 1957.* He pictured a great school, blessed not only with adequate buildings but with a substantial endowment fund. It was so fine a dream that when the council said no, Darling's bubble of optimism was pricked. He wrote to an acquaintance, 'I am getting very much weary of this job, or the age, or myself, or something'. His proposal that affluent parents and friends of the school, such as Sidney Myer and Sir George Fairbairn, should be asked to lend £10 000 each at 4 per cent interest (bank rate was 5½ per cent) was considered inadequate and possibly undesirable. John Manifold was happy about those gentlemen, but others might not be acceptable. He knew of some people called Connibiere who were rolling in money and had nothing to do with it except turn it into more, yet thought there might be awkward repercussions from such a borrowing.

---

* It was in that year, on the eve of the centenary pageant, that John Manifold died.

Darling had to be content with £18 000. As Manifold told him on 1 October (when £14 000 was the target), the council would think it such a paltry sum after the other figures that they would have a dash at it. He would ginger up Jim Fairbairn to come to the next meeting with at least some money in his pocket. Darling also decided to 'ginger' Jim Fairbairn—about the pressures on accommodation and the immediate difficulties that could be overcome by building. He was starting a hare that he hoped would run strongly past other members of council to old boys and parents. The £18 000 was to be privately borrowed to provide new classrooms, new masters' residences, an extended dining hall and alterations to Manifold and Cuthbertson houses.

The strain that would have attended a £60 000 borrowing is suggested in John Manifold's relief when £18 000 was achieved. He had been obliged to guarantee the original £14 000 to get work started, and was deeply concerned about his bond. Darling was also relieved; even now GGS could claim to be providing the best educational opportunities in the country, and after that beginning he told 'My dear John', that they could not stand still. He gave warning that Junior House, 'scandalously crammed' with 130, must be given new classrooms and boarding accommodation.

So it went on into 1933, with phases of thought favouring first an expansion of Junior House, with extra dormitories as well as a separate classroom block, then an intermediate house and then a junior house cutting off at age thirteen rather than fourteen. Educational needs had to be balanced against financial possibilities. Council approved a new Junior House in July but failed to persuade the AMP to fund it and threw out Darling's contingent request for a senior boarding-house to allow promotion from the junior school at thirteen. The headmaster, his confidence increased by warm professional tributes to the school during 1933, weaved and swayed like a prize fighter seeking an opening. His principle was senior houses of a maximum size of sixty-five, but to achieve a new one he was prepared to keep them at eighty-five—a figure condemned in all his arguments.

Many possibilities for fund-raising were explored. One of them envisaged lining up old boys for life assurance through the AMP. Jennings, eager for his own domain, thought it would be possible to borrow from Junior House parents and even boys, and Darling, the chairman of the council and the president of the OGG drafted letters to old boys urging them to contribute. The result was a separate junior school of eight classrooms, a hall, music rooms, engineering shops, art school and enlarged library. The original Junior House, renamed Barrabool, and the dining hall were altered and enlarged, and two new houses, Connewarre and Barwon, were added, giving accommodation for 150 boys. At the same time new playing-fields were laid out beyond Biddlecombe Avenue. To the delight of the building industry in Geelong, the construction took place towards the end of that terrible depression year 1933, and the buildings were

The Junior School Library, 1939.

194

available for first term 1934. They released several classrooms in the senior school and represented one of the largest steps forward of Darling's period. The junior school started 1934 with its own staff and timetable.

A loss of £5000 in 1934 and a further loss in 1935 applied a damper to development before steam was raised again in 1936, when the survey pegs for another senior house, Francis Brown, were driven into the chapel oval. 'FB' opened in first term 1937 and, despite economies that denied it an attractive finish, was one of Darling's dreams come true. The layout and furnishing expressed his ideas about boarding life. It also completed his basic needs, about £80 000 having been spent on extensions and reorganization since his arrival. As basic needs were only the beginning, in the December *Corian* of 1936 he floated ambitious plans for self-contained art and music schools in the hope that someone would provide the funds. They did. The art school was completed in third term 1937, with Whittingham Estate money; and the music school, costing £10 000, the gift of the Bell family in the next year. Mrs Biddlecombe, Miss M. G. Bell, Mr A. C. Bell and Mr W. Max Bell (a council member) handed the music school over in the presence of Dr Malcolm Sargent on Sunday 14 August 1938, a much superior building in materials and workmanship to any other at Corio.

The building programme is a major indicator of Darling's achievement in the pre-war period; without it there would have been much less chance of a revolution in the curriculum and in attitudes towards school life. He acknowledged in December 1936 that he had been given what he needed:

I am in the position now in which I must take full responsibility for what this School is, and blame myself and no other for its deficiencies.[3]

The achievement was so much his own that it strengthened his paternal role and made him a hero. In recognition of what he had done and possibly in fear of losing him in 1936 (while he was considering the possibility of becoming Director-General of Education) the council raised his salary to £2000, plus ten annual increments of £100. Manifold was convinced that 'under the cloak of his genius' the 'mere development of a school had become a work of national importance'.

Darling hoped for a national impact and believed that it was necessary. He argued that each year's delay in the building programme at Corio denied one group of boys a better chance to prepare for the political and social responsibilities of leading the world along happier paths again. It is difficult to know, in this matter, whether his idealism or his ambition was stronger. Anyway, both blended with the desire of the council and the Old Geelong Grammarians that the school should be famous not only in Australia but in Britain. The result was a shared rhetoric about GGS holding its position 'with the other great schools of the world'.

The School Library, 1939.

[3] *Corian*, Dec. 1936, p. 196.

195

That self-image of the great boarding-school, polished by Darling's reforms and acknowledged in the British world league, moved Geelong Grammar even further away from the Australian norm. Quite early in Darling's period day fees had been raised to cover the evening meal and homework supervision. Day boys stayed until 8.30 p.m. and only slept at home. Although achieving greater integration, it was a paternalistic, even anti-family, move by which the school asserted primacy in their lives in a way no day-school could attempt, and was fascinatingly close to the desire expressed by Bracebridge Wilson in 1863 that he should be given full charge of boys' lives (see p.50). J.R.D. was, for a time, in 1937. During a polio epidemic, rather than exclude them, he arranged for day boys to stay in the Bracebridge Wilson Hall. In his addresses at speech days, also, Darling developed the position that the school knew best and his decision to provide 'honest' reports on boys' progress and behaviour asserted the same thing. It was not, however, a bald, take-it-or-leave-it situation for parents; he was happy to see them and talk about problems, though probably within an atmosphere favouring his view of the case. When boys were in serious trouble he was usually optimistic about the chances of helping them, although housemasters often felt that they shouldered the greater part of the resultant pastoral care. He was also flexible and paternal in going to council to get concessions for those who were embarrassed by rising fees made necessary by the costs of the building programme.

In all the struggles for improved facilities Darling's contribution was immense. Ewan Laird, the school architect, credited him with having a mind any architect would envy, and described him as a planner who could lead and inspire architects to produce the result he envisaged. He was also a great improviser and blended political cunning with statesmanship; while he did not deviate from his major objectives, he was never still in the pursuit of ways to achieve them. Above all, he was not guilty of building for its own sake. What really mattered was the life not the fabric of the school, its curriculum not its appearance.

To the chapel, which had given Brown so much joy, Darling, the layman, who came to think of the school as his parish, brought a concern derived from Temple that the gospel should be first understood and then put widely into action. Although some have said that a glass wall might as well have descended the moment any sermon began, many boys were committed by his faith and eloquence to see the world and themselves differently. Even sceptics were affected. 'If you have been to Geelong Grammar you may drift', one boy said, 'but you cannot drift with a clear conscience'. Darling put himself on the line in his sermons, summoning all his skills to make them works of art with which to capture and hold that difficult audience. Not all the three hundred or more he delivered at GGS were successful; sometimes they were too long and occasionally lacked form. Usually, though, by finding their level skilfully, he lifted boys to stronger insights into their humanity and the meaning of God. Through wit

196

and humour, candour, pungency and a vivid imagination, according to Michael Persse, he expressed uncompromising hostility to complacency and inertia. He wanted boys' lives to be as active as his own.

So the council gained the spirituality which was part of its 1930 blueprint for a forty-year-old, married, clergyman headmaster. Then, in October 1934, although still lacking in years, Darling informed them that he was ready to remedy the conjugal shortcoming. He was engaged to be married to Margaret Campbell of Melbourne. Getting engaged, he observed to a headmaster colleague, was rather a disorganizing process, but he put up with it impatiently until the marriage day in August 1935. Already, no doubt, the council knew that his choice had transformed him. Old boys heard on the grapevine from a senior boy that his trip away in 1934 had changed him both personally and professionally for the better, without realizing, until the engagement was announced, that love may have been largely responsible.

The Bracebridge Wilson Hall in the 1930s.

Margaret, who was just twenty when they were married, and a friend from childhood of some of the senior boys, shared with him the unceasing activity he brought to Corio. She received, with warmth and efficiency beyond the scope of a bachelor, his army of interesting and important guests. She and their children became a self-sufficient community in which the headmaster's wife, as much as the headmaster, set the tone and nurtured creative relationships. His life belonged professionally to the school; hers, although it was she who gave, can be seen as one of his greatest gifts to it. She was able, because of the transformation he achieved, to contribute in a way not possible for the wife of any previous headmaster and, because of her own talents, to make a mark unusual for headmasters' wives anywhere.

War

It might be thought that the 1939—45 war was an interlude between phases in the development of the curriculum and facilities at Corio. And so it was, as well as being a special experience in the everyday life of the school. But, as happened to the nation as a whole, for instance through the expansion of manufacturing and the altered role of women, there were fundamental changes requiring new attitudes and administrative structures. The freezing of fees for seven years, the huge backlog of maintenance and the sharp escalation in teachers' salaries after the war, presented Geelong Grammar School with a crisis from which it emerged a different school. In fact the war was a fulcrum for forces generating the 'imperial' expansion that characterizes this section of the history.

Yet not just the war: a turning point in Darling's leadership that coincided with the outbreak of hostilities and was enlarged by them would have happened anyway. The school made a serious loss in 1938 and, while the headmaster was holidaying in England during 1939, the council in consultation with his deputy, C. A. Cameron, introduced severe economies. Rather than increase fees, they pruned

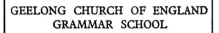

GEELONG CHURCH OF ENGLAND
GRAMMAR SCHOOL

DIARY

1939

BROWN, PRIOR, ANDERSON PTY. LTD., PRINTERS.
PRINTCRAFT HOUSE, 430 LITTLE BOURKE STREET,
MELBOURNE, C.1.
A

Scout.   T. E. S. Stewart.
No 78460.

APRIL

Thursday, 20

Militia - Band turnout lousy.
Let go at 5 min to 6.!!!! Absolutely
blown- everything seemed to go
wrong=
Very little turnout.

Friday, 21

Footer. Not to good. Gym
+ push up taped. Bath. Read.
Beaut day. — Life tomorrow is
like this — will try to get to B.H
Pat ran up.

Saturday, 22

Sat. Peat to Batesford. Swim. v. cold.
Very tired at Night — Read.
Richemonts.

Sunday, 23

Symall awo - Rehearsals - Read.

41

what they considered to be Darling's extravagances and dealt heavy blows to the morale of his supporters. The tone of Cameron's end-of-year report indicates a clash of values. He praised things Darling would not have mentioned—traditional approaches to teaching, the playing of games to win and loyalty to the school. It seems that Cameron, E. A. Austin, other old-boy members of council and even its new chairman, J. V. Fairbairn, who had taken office in December 1937, were reacting against Darling's progressive attitudes and especially to the financial risks attached to his policies. They probably resented the forceful way he had committed the school to his personal vision of education, in contrast to his predecessor who had put the good of the school before personal ambition or convenience.

The circumstances of both of Darling's visits to England raised doubts about his commitment to the school. He had been frank with John Manifold in 1934 about his desire for an English appointment, which Manifold quite understood; but in 1939, because no one at Corio seemed to know what his intentions were and because in his absence it appeared that Cameron was dismantling treasured policies, his supporters were in disarray, disturbed by economies that threatened Darling's educational goals. They wrote to tell him so and he, not being in tune with Cameron, and possibly not realizing how important his own charisma was in influencing the council, felt that his deputy had failed him in not preventing the economies, which he believed led to the resignation of two of his finest masters, C. R. Bull and C. E. S. Gordon. There is a problem of interpretation here. Whereas Darling considered that Cameron was being disloyal to him, John Manifold thought that Darling was disloyal to the council by criticizing the cuts and disloyal to his deputy by supporting the complaints of staff members.

The lack of trust was compounded by distance and by Darling's uncertainties. If he had shown that Corio was the only place that mattered to him, the tension might have eased, but on the contrary there were rumours that he had refused the headmastership of Marlborough—an unlikely story considering his ambition, but consistent with the view that he was very busy sounding out the possibilities of an English appointment.* Moreover, when war broke out he offered himself to the British army and when rejected took a position in the ministry of information. Until late in 1939 he had not made up his mind to return, partly from feelings of duty towards his homeland, partly from concern for the safety of his wife and two daughters on U-Boat-infested seas, and partly, perhaps, because of the frustrations of missionary work in the cultural desert. The uncertainty was expressed in a speech day announcement by the deputy chairman that the headmaster 'expected' to return for the commencement of first term 1940, and in the concern among Darling's supporters to preserve his image against attack. This was summed up in C. R. Bull's decision, as master-in-charge of the *Corian*, to reprint in

---

* He might have had Marlborough if Fletcher had backed him. He refused Bradfield.

December, as the frontispiece to the magazine, a portrait of Darling used in the same place in the May issue.

Darling might have delayed further if Professor Giblin had not alerted him early in September to the extent of the crisis, though Giblin, like his other supporters, did not know whether Darling intended to return or not. If he did, Giblin thought he would have to 'take time from other things to build up again the apostolic touch' of his early years and reverse the return to old ways. In a sharp analysis Giblin detected 'a move—perhaps half-conscious—of the Old Guard (including old boys generally) to prepare for a reversal of policy if you don't return: with financial considerations as an excuse or a blind'. He predicted a problem of masters' loyalty.

The staff was split. Some older men, especially, opposed his changes because they disturbed their routines and stretched them beyond their capacities; conservatives considered him a socialist and a meddler whose educational philosophy was hopelessly unrealistic; and nationalists resented the hallowing of English cultural attitudes and the appointment of Englishmen. Of course, most of the old and conservative were Australian and the young and progressive English, or at least anglophile, so that the war, by taking the young men and replacing them with retired or temporary or women teachers, gave the old guard much more say within the common room and exacerbated the clash between Darling and Cameron, whose relationship was stiff and purely formal from that time onwards. The open rift with Cameron and others, however dutiful they remained, made Darling's task, when he did return, more difficult, especially while there was no counter force on which he could rely. Cameron, known to generations of boys as a great character and effective teacher, was a formidable critic.

Had it not been for this situation Darling might have called more staff meetings and softened the autocratic element in his paternal style. He was also older, and the loss of Bull and Gordon, together with the absence of his own long-term appointments at the war, meant that the gulf between headmaster and staff widened. There was less of the quality of adventuring together that had distinguished the early 1930s.

On the other hand, the school as a whole became more cohesive. Petrol rationing and general restrictions on transport forced it in upon itself and gave Darling an unparalleled opportunity to practise the self-reliance he often preached. In 1938, having decided that a national crisis was imminent, he sought to strengthen the moral fibre of the school through a programme called National Service. The idea probably came from discussions he had over several years with W. Kent Hughes and G. S. Browne, who were enthusiastic about the training of Nazi youth. Although he hated fascism, Darling believed that young Australians needed a more disciplined approach towards service to their country. Schools like Geelong Grammar lacked credibility, he believed, if they did not show the country that they could be tough, self-sufficient and ready to respond flexibly to national needs.

Geelong Church of England Grammar School
CORIO :: VICTORIA

SALARY SCALES AS FROM THE BEGINNING OF 1939

[The School Council reserves the right 'to vary the terms of the appointment in cases of emergency at three months' notice. Nothing in this statement, moreover, affects the Headmaster's ordinary right of dismissal or the right on both sides to terminate the agreement at half a term's notice.]

COMMENCING SALARY:

For men with University degree, or its equivalent ...... £250 per annum
(with board and residence)
For men without degree .... £200 per annum
rising by £25 a year to £300 (or £250) at the commencement of the third year.

After the third year the master becomes eligible for membership of the permanent staff (provided that he has satisfactorily obtained registration).

On appointment to the permanent staff, a master must enter the superannuation scheme, towards which, if he is under thirty-six, the School Council and master make equal contributions of £20 per annum; if over thirty-six, of £30 per annum.

INCREMENTS:

Increments hereafter are at the rate of £30 every second year up to £600 per annum, or, in the case of men without degree, £550.

In special cases masters may be appointed on to the permanent staff after one year's service, or recognition of past experience may be made by appointment at some stage in the salary scheme other than the beginning.

HOUSEMASTERSHIPS:

Appointment to these positions is in the absolute discretion of the Headmaster, without consideration of seniority, and is for a period of not more than 15 years, during which the housemaster is entitled to an extra amount of £150 per annum in the Senior School, or £50 in the Junior School.

The School Council will, if it is possible, provide married masters with a residence free of rent and rates in lieu of board-residence, but this provision cannot be guaranteed in all cases.

The following special appointments do not come under the above scheme:—
SECOND MASTER.
MASTER OF THE JUNIOR SCHOOL.
BRICE MACKINNON CLASSICAL MASTER.

RETIRING AGE:

The official retiring age is sixty, at which the superannuation pension becomes payable: but the Headmaster may, if he desires, invite a master to remain on the staff until he reaches sixty-five.

199

Thus the international situation, which was rapidly deteriorating into war in 1938, provided further motivation towards the development of the school as a community in terms already explored through the pageants. What Darling has described as his pragmatism appears in this context to have been much more than a seizing of chances. He had the vision and courage to declare that the international emergency required action, which he then took and stuck to, not for itself but for the principle underlying it. That principle, the challenging of individuals to serve not seek, was strongly expressed in what the school, because of the war, began to do for itself. It is a tribute to the idea and to the understanding that had been built up between Darling and his senior English master, that C. R. Bull initiated the scheme successfully in the headmaster's absence.

Darling's belief that GGS should lead and produce leaders was fundamental to the National Service idea. He described it as 'an organized effort to develop all kinds of usefulness and it is in the hope of some such national movement that we are going to attempt to train ourselves next year'. He wanted boys to become skilled so that they could pass on those skills to the community:

All schemes on a large scale break down at present for a lack of sufficient numbers of trained instructors. The intensive training of potential instructors will be part of Tuesday afternoon's work next year. The Scout movement is always in need of Scout masters: we can do much more than we have hitherto done. First aid units, fire-fighting squads, practical experiments in draining and in the prevention of soil erosion, elementary surveying and map-making, and training in the making of miniature rifle ranges, and of rough permanent camps: these are some of the ideas for developing usefulness which have been suggested.[4]

The response of staff and boys and the frustrations and fun of National Service can be savoured later in this chapter. What is important for the present discussion is that its initiation helped the school to move along a self-defining path to Timbertop (see pp. 219–24), which is usually regarded as Darling's major innovation.* Yet educational objectives were not the only ones. National Service had financial implications not mentioned in the rhetoric used to convince boys of their duty to school and country. As well as its patriotic aspects, the scheme was a great money-saver at a time when fees were frozen and labour was expensive. In that sense it was as much the child of the 1938 financial crisis at Corio as of the international situation.

The strongest antecedent of Timbertop, as a do-it-yourself operation, came in 1941 from two building projects in which boys assisted the school's skilled tradesmen. The first, a hut 9 × 4.5 metres for the newly formed Yacht Club (itself part of National Service), was almost completed one Saturday in first term by eight school carpenters and forty boys under the direction of the bursar, Milton Thewlis. The second followed a fire which destroyed the mechanics and

---

[4] *Corian*, Dec. 1938, p. 215.

* It was already, of course, pointed in that direction through the Saturday Party tradition.

carpentry workshops, a vital element in National Service training, on 23 August 1941. As the editor of the *Corian* said soon afterwards:

More than one good thing has come from the fire, though the damage seemed at one time to be irreplaceable. Though the fire itself destroyed much well used machinery, and, in many cases wrecked the work of years, yet we have got something more valuable, I think, from it. The old spirit of the Mechanics Room was good—a group of boys perfecting themselves in a very worthwhile craft, and using their knowledge for the School rather than for themselves, but they were only a group, only a part of the School. And the rest of us, I fear, watched, admired, and kept apart.

Then came the night of Saturday, 23rd August, and the Mechanics Shop was destroyed. But the School, next day, was no longer a spectator. When volunteers were called for, to give up three days of their holidays and build a new shop, the call was made for sixty boys. Over 100 boys volunteered.[5]

The experience of building the Yacht Club was repeated on a larger scale by bursar, workmen, headmaster, masters and boys, who were indeed, as the editorial suggests, building with themselves as well as with timber. Nothing could have made the whole point of the National Service scheme more clearly than that purposeful co-operation of all elements of the school. Relationships between 'front' and 'out the back' could never be distant again. The moment was one of great pride, something on which to build a new tradition. As the *Corian* put it:

Last holidays saw an addition to the School buildings, which, if the circumstances of its construction are taken into account, is probably the most impressive achievement of this School.[6]

The headmaster emphasized the tradition at Speech Day 1942, after mentioning the building of a carpentry shop at Bostock House:

These enterprises have become a feature of the School, and no one who has taken part in them will question that they are amongst the most satisfying experiences of their life here, or anywhere else, for that matter.[7]

He might justifiably have boasted about his own contribution, not just in daring to think that way, not just in securing support, but especially in adopting the fundamental approach of the Geelong Unemployed Boys' Centre, also his brainchild, where craftsmen were used as mentors. It was a levelling exercise that put the headmaster under instruction and gave an unprecedented prestige to the boys (not many) who could drive nails straight.

Almost every term until the end of the war as many as fifty boys gave up a week of their holidays to help with building ventures, such as a cottage for the Brotherhood of St Laurence at Carrum Downs, dormitories at Bostock House and a church at Mt Duneed. During term, as well, they worked on weekdays and Saturdays. In 1944, for instance, two six-roomed masters' houses were under construction at Corio (using the best boy carpenters to minimize supervision) while cow sheds, dairies and fences were put up at Mt Duneed to replace those destroyed in a bushfire that had also burnt St Wilfrid's Church.

[5] *Corian*, Aug. 1941, p. 113.
[6] *Corian*, Dec. 1941, p. 189.
[7] *Corian*, Dec. 1942, p. 144.

Like the scaffolding for a new tradition, boys and some staff joined the experts from 'out the back' to rebuild the burnt-out carpentry shop in 1941.

Thus, building activity and National Service training established the workshops more firmly in the life of the school than had been possible before, while wartime shortages of parts and materials encouraged the ingenuity and skill by which tools and equipment were maintained. Attitudes to manual labour were radically changed.

Then the war brought Ludwig Hirschfeld-Mack, a member of the famous Bauhaus, to the art school and Geelong Grammar was given a rare and transforming injection of non-British ideas. A Quaker, but of partly Jewish descent, Hirschfeld (as they called him at GGS) fled to England with Walter Gropius in 1934, when Hitler condemned the Bauhaus. Interned after Dunkirk, he was sent to Australia on the *Dunera* and was prominent among those gifted internees at Tatura when Darling heard about him and 'took steps to extract him' for first term 1942. Under Hirschfeld the art school became a general resource centre and centre for resourcefulness. He introduced boys to avant-garde painting techniques and encouraged wood-carving, weaving, musical instrument making, leatherwork and other crafts as well as co-operating with the producers of plays and exhibitions in the provision of scenery, lighting and displays which were of a quality that made previous efforts look clumsy. Both the Bauhaus approach to applied art and its emphasis on teamwork confirmed and enriched the new tradition at Corio.

One thing the war did not do at GGS, whatever may have happened in the country as a whole, was divert its official loyalties from imperial Britain. The expression British Commonwealth was not used in the *Corian*. Although American Independence Day was celebrated with a special assembly in 1944 and Roosevelt's death was marked with an editorial in May 1945, and although impressive Airacrobras and Kittyhawks emerged from the International Harvester works to zoom over the school, attitudes expressed in the school magazine reflect chronic anglophilia, enshrined in remarks like 'an English picture and therefore very competently handled'. Indeed, as the war progressed the school became more and more English. The enlistment of their fathers and the disruption of travel to Britain, as

202

well as danger there, meant that by May 1941, as well as boys from all six Australian states, 'ten other sections of the British Empire' were represented at Corio. Seizing the role of mother to the motherland, Geelong Grammar initiated scholarships to give fatherless English boys places at Corio. Others came without assistance, so that by December 1941 Junior School alone contained forty boys (over 25 per cent) from outside Australia. Although many returned home after the war, Geelong Grammar was so firmly on the map for Britons abroad that in December 1946 the headmaster appealed for families to accommodate boys from Malaya, India and the Far East during vacations.

Another sense in which the war was a turning point stemmed from full employment and general prosperity. Costs rose dramatically, especially because the post-war view that secondary education for all was the key to social justice created a special demand for teachers and an escalation in their salaries and superannuation. The State took the initiative and independent schools had to raise fees rapidly to compete. This brought a bruising financial situation at Corio where the backlog of maintenance was an extra burden. Despite the continuance of self-help economies the school seemed unlikely ever to achieve the extra boarding-house it needed for optimum numbers. Darling was frustrated and looked once again for an opportunity in England, where he spent most of 1948. At Oxford he received the rare distinction of an honorary DCL (Doctor of Civil Law), and was greeted there and at Cambridge by large numbers of OGGs, whose presence expressed his great achievement at Corio.

A few years later, partly as an economy, partly as an extension of the National Service idea, partly as an outcome of wartime building ventures and partly in response to new ideas in education, Dr Darling proposed a build-it-ourselves bush outpost of the school. Its creation was not in itself a turning point but, in association with other organizational and personal developments, it meant that neither he nor the school could return to the comparatively simple life of the Corio of the 1930s.

A REVISED CURRICULUM

It is important now to backtrack and examine the way in which Darling's educational philosophy altered and invigorated classroom practice. Although the drive for new buildings was the most obvious expression of the desire of Darling and Mackinnon to enlarge Geelong Grammar School and make it a true public school, what went on in them was vital. Until he had a sixth form with economically viable specialist classes, not two or three boys eating up the time of his most valued staff, Darling saw no hope of the kind of leadership and stimulation he remembered at Repton and Charterhouse. Time and again in his first years he wrote to parents about the importance to their sons of another year at school, for the intellectual or leadership experience it could give, and for the opportunity to pay back what

203

was owed to the school. He preached community, responsibility and self-sacrifice, shaped by notions of gentlemanly *noblesse oblige*, especially among sixth-formers. Sloth and complacency were attacked, not only on principle but also in order to improve the school's abysmal examination record and to feed more boys into the sixth form. Yet Darling was a realist. He dared not alienate the pastoralists upon whom the school's finances and traditions depended by threatening the entry of their often backward sons with an academic test. He had to put up with them and somehow stimulate them. A cleverer element would have to be attracted by scholarships and the improved public image of the place. So he made a virtue of necessity and hammered out in his first ten years a new, comprehensive approach to secondary education. In the process, though for different reasons, he felt just as Brown had, that Geelong Grammar needed to be regarded as distinct from the Melbourne day-schools. In the process, too, he emerged as the inheritor of Wilson and Cuthbertson. Through his love for the most difficult boys he set a new pattern of humanity in the school—and that affected the curriculum.

Darling had options. He could have stood out for scholarly standards and risked a backlash from old boys and parents, but he could not have done so quickly enough to impress the English selection committees he was hoping to meet within four or five years. As a result, and possibly without realizing it, he was caught like a ram in the thicket by Geelong Grammar School traditions. The need to make a mark quickly led him away from scholarship to general educational objectives that were, incidentally, more in keeping with Australian tradition and in line with his own beliefs, derived through Temple from the great Edward Thring of Uppingham.

This does not mean that he accepted the poor academic performance of the school; it was in fact the starting point for his reforms. 'Collect some ideas about education...We are in darkness', he told Gerry Dicker, who was about to come out on exchange in 1932. A comparison of results with those of Melbourne Grammar revealed that proportionately only half as many Geelong Grammar boys passed Leaving Certificate, and the humiliation of a rebuff from his own Oxford college to one of his best boys because his subjects were quite wrong, confirmed the need for a major attack on the curriculum and old-fashioned teaching methods. He was determined to improve performance overall, not just with bright boys or with the university in mind.

The days of spare periods were over. The old-style sportsman-hero would have to suffer long hours for his moments of glory, quite apart from the fact that the spotlight he had occupied was dimmed so that attention could be focussed on the cultural all-rounder. Hard work was the maxim; it nurtured a disciplined mind. Motives of fear and duty were to be outweighed by interest. Learning was to be relevant and exciting, set in a broader, more human context than the classroom. With that in mind the pageant plays instituted in this period (see p. 279) were vehicles of an educational philosophy that found a focus for school work in communal activity. C. R. Bull commented later:

As an educationist, J. R. Darling had two outstanding fields of vision. He saw the need for incentive, interest and perspective in school work if it was to be more than superficial, and he saw the vital need for individual and group participation in activities designed to develop that incentive, interest and perspective.[8]

The new philosophy was put to the school community at Speech Day 1930 in a statement that laid the foundation for curriculum development in Darling's period. He began by referring to the stimulus of the depression and the school's responsibility to help boys take life seriously—not vocationally, for it was nonsense to try to prepare them specifically for a great variety of occupations, but by developing qualities of mind. From experience on a committee of the Melbourne Chamber of Commerce, Darling could say that leading businessmen wanted boys to stay at school longer to get a better general education. Of course they should not waste their time:

A last year at school devoted to a dull idleness in school hours is far worse than valueless, and I hope I have made that sufficiently clear to everyone.[9]

He challenged parents to think about their responsibilities and pointed to the damage done to boys and to the school by 'habits of indolence and slovenliness, lack of discipline and indulgence, learnt in the nursery and at home'. Illiterates of ten were no longer acceptable and teenagers would face an entrance test. 'The spelling and writing and grammar of this school was disgraceful, but those should have been taught by a governess years ago'. This bold moral tone was extended to a challenge to parents to accept the school's values and not indulge boys during exeats and holidays, for although Darling was saddled with them, he was not going to let the rich and idle (those who could afford governesses) provide the ethos of Geelong Grammar School. He made a frank reference to the need for much more knowledge and skill among people on the land in Australia, and in his policy of honest reports broke away from that cautious spirit, that fear of hurting parents' feelings, that had characterized previous comments about boys. He was toughening up the ruling class to face its responsibilities, and here again the support of Donald Mackinnon was timely. Mackinnon told Darling not to fuss about parents who were angered by the new frankness. 'If necessary some of us might change their outlook', he wrote.

By 1933 a revised timetable was in place. It simplified subject choices at the bottom of the school. Of the thirty-four periods, forms 1 and 2 spent ten in English, eight in arithmetic, three each in geography, history and drawing, five in drill and two in divinity, while in form 3 there was the choice between three periods of geography, Greek or German after seven each in English and mathematics, five Latin, four French, three history, two drawing, two drill and one divinity. Up to that level no science was taught.

[8] *Thirty Two years*, p. 131.
[9] *Corian*, Dec. 1930, p. 186.

Wider choice began at form 4, where physics and chemistry (five periods) were introduced. Mathematics (eight) now took periods from English (five) and, in addition to the choice between the three Gs of form 3, biology or German could be substituted for Latin and agriculture for French. This was the Intermediate Certificate year at which the examination sheep (three out of six classes) were drafted from the unacademic goats, most of whom, even if they remained at school, would proceed no further. Public exams were not their forte, and even among those who sat for Intermediate there could be a distressing desperation. In 1932 the Registrar of the University of Melbourne returned the papers of two facetious boys with the comment that 'similar effusions' in previous years threatened to establish a tradition at Geelong Grammar School that this was the right thing to do when unable to deal with an examination.

To cater for this group, who in his opinion appeared dull largely because they were uninterested, and who were to a great extent from rural backgrounds, Darling introduced an agricultural science course with J. S. Cook in charge. It included English, a more practical arithmetic, history, geography and a large amount of science, particularly agricultural chemistry and biology (which could not have gone ahead without the new laboratories). Less convincingly, the substitution of German for Latin was supposed to cater for future businessmen. In a brisk correspondence, Sir Maynard Hedstrom of Fiji exposed the thinness of the claim that Geelong Grammar School was now providing commercial as well as professional and agricultural courses. He criticized the academic bias of English public-school education from which the curriculum was derived, and countered Darling's comment that schools should only teach boys how to think, by citing his own valuable experience on the commercial side forty years before at Wesley. The headmaster replied adamantly, '...our ambition is to stimulate the interest of boys so that they use their brains'. This was a direct rebuff, though politer than the observation to G. S. Moffat's mother that the value of commercial subjects (here he was thinking of a clever boy) was nil. The gentry notion of 'trade' as demeaning had clearly survived Darling's long sea voyage, as had a general English emphasis on book-learning that was not entirely taken for granted in Australia.

Quite apart from the fact that half the boys were slow to respond, Darling's emphasis on the stimulation of intellectual activity was regarded sceptically by many masters, including C. A. Cameron. At Speech Day 1939 Cameron spoke strongly about the need for old-fashioned 'chalk and talk' instead of the 'scissors and paste' of the project method. Cameron's son believed that his powerful father was complementing Darling's strengths with his quite opposite approach.

What was considered the main innovation in 1933 concerned the brighter stream, who were now to take the Leaving Certificate examination in a larger variety of subjects over two years rather than one. Too many, it was thought, had scraped through a minimum of subjects one year, then dropped them and concentrated on a few more the year afterwards. Despite cramming and many spare periods, the failure rate was about 50 per cent. Again, Darling believed that the educational goals were short-sighted; there was little training of the mind because the exam itself had become the objective. He warned that he would demand higher standards but also offered the reward of a proper sixth form, with a pleasant classroom, to those who passed Leaving.

At the Leaving level maths and English were compulsory, then a selection of subjects could be made, leading either to specific university courses or to business and agricultural careers. The degree of specialization was not great. The landed stream was offered biology, agriculture, chemistry and European history, 'the latter being a subject which will provide a background for much interesting reading in the future', while the business types did geography, economics, chemistry and European history. In the sixth form the university was the only goal. Apart from English and a period a week each of political problems and the history of science, boys could choose between five streams—classical, moderns, history, sciences/medicine and engineering. The introduction of political problems and history of science was an expression of Darling's concern to extend debate and discussion beyond routine classroom topics. He hoped they would also flourish in revitalized out-of-school societies.

The assumption in the new curriculum that every boy would be kept hard at work placed extra strains on staff and space. An expanded library was essential for a more self-directed, more wide-ranging education and the new science laboratories, apart from their importance for the agriculture classes, were seen by Darling as a means of combating cramming by emphasizing observation and experiment. He asked Dicker, who was about to come from Winchester, to discuss science teaching with his colleagues and bring some modern texts, and gained Cameron's agreement in principle to change the approach to chemistry, especially with the much better students who were coming through to the honours year. The comprehensiveness of his school made him fight against the stereotyped academic education induced by university entrance requirements and against elitists who delighted in the examination straitjacket and belittled that training of mind and breadth of knowledge he espoused. He valued all-rounders and urged Bob Southey, for instance, to balance his classical diet with a dose of physics. He might have gone further but for external pressures. When R. E. Thwaites criticized the inclusion of maths at the expense of humanities for the sixth form medical stream, Darling referred to the opinion of the noted Melbourne surgeon, Sir Alan Newton, that maths was becoming essential for medicine. Broader cultural and pastoral goals did not interest university faculties.

Darling's missionary zeal, fed by his sense of achievement within the school, led him to state his philosophy publicly. His trenchant criticism of sporting premierships and his desire to remove public-school events from the limelight helped to spread his general views. In addition, he won the support of G. S. Browne, principal of the Melbourne Teachers' College and then foundation professor of education at the University of Melbourne. After a visit to Corio at the beginning of 1933, Browne said that Darling's work and idealism had strengthened him for the fight against the deficiencies of education in Victoria. Geelong Grammar School had suddenly become a show-place. In a two-day visit Browne said he saw more sound modern methods than for months before. It made him wish that Darling could be Director of Education for a year or two.

Sweet though he found such praise, after five years at Corio in 1934 Darling felt that the curriculum was still inadequate. He was ready for further reform. Examination results were better, boys were at last working harder, but they were not being offered relevant courses and were not becoming the thinking citizens needed by the nation. Isolation had to be overcome and schoolwork more clearly related to later life:

> Leadership in a democratic community must come from a full sharing in the life of the community. It is our function as a School in this Commonwealth to overcome any remoteness from life which our geography may tend towards, and that can be done partly by making work in school fit more into ordinary living. Moreover, it is our function to educate all boys for the position in life which they are intending to occupy. Now, I calculate that forty percent of our boys at least go on to the land, and forty percent go into business, and only about twenty percent to the university, whether at Home or in Australia. It is our duty to provide for these groups the education which will fit them best to be happy and effective in their respective spheres, and I do not believe that secondary education as at present designed does this at all...The resultant scheme which I now propose to explain is designed to insist upon the minimum basis of a secondary education and to allow the individual a facility which he has not previously possessed of developing his peculiar capacities according to his peculiar tastes. It ought to prevent any boy from feeling that he is a failure, because he finds academic work difficult. If it does this, it will have gone a long way towards solving the problem of the secondary school.[10]

During the first three years of secondary education Latin, mathematics and German,* 'for the training of the brain', and general science and English composition, to give 'a general understanding of the world', were made compulsory. Freedom of choice, which it was hoped would stimulate interest and lead to important student-centred activity, was given on three afternoons a week, when it was possible to do music, art and manual work, or through projects, to extend the more formal experience gained in academic subjects.

The approach was that of the Dalton Plan (which emphasized individual learning), modified to suit the style of the school and the level of staffing. Historically it provides an interesting parallel to Bracebridge Wilson's attempt, early in his headmastership, to overcome the problem of the great range of abilities among his pupils.

In that forbidding trio—Latin, maths and German—boys had

[10] *Corian*, Dec. 1934, pp. 195–6.   * Years 2 and 3 only.

to achieve satisfactorily each month before moving ahead. Those who had missed work or were unusually dull or bright moved into special sets at each level, and a final escape clause enabled the completely unacademic to take something more practical.

In keeping with Darling's earlier views, the Intermediate examination was abolished in favour of a two-year programme based on the existing Leaving Certificate curriculum. This was undoubtedly still too academic for such a mixed school, and the tokenism of the business course was not reduced. On the other hand, boys not needing the Leaving Certificate were encouraged to join the Public Affairs Sixth Form, 'specially planned as a preparation for citizenship in a democratic country'. Otherwise the fifth and sixth form programmes were unchanged. The whole programme was shown in a diagram which accompanied the headmaster's report in the *Corian* of December 1934.

The new courses were a high point for Darling, the educational strategist. Although still much more directed towards university work than was justified by the 20 per cent who were destined for it, the courses did put Darling's major precepts into action and were an important basis of John Manifold's claim at Speech Day 1935 that Geelong Grammar School led Australia. Confidence in the scheme was strengthened by comments like the following from G. S. Browne, who offered Darling the chance to spread his educational gospel by delivering the John Smythe Memorial Lecture in 1935:

I am perfectly sure that your scheme of organisation is the most important educational experiment being carried out in Australia at present...Australian education is at the crossroads and your school will have a great deal to do with determining future directions.[11]

Browne used Geelong Grammar as much as he could for visits by about two hundred Dip. Ed. and Teachers' College students at a time. Its progress so delighted him that in October 1936 he let fly with the thought that, if only someone like Darling could be found for Melbourne Grammar School, the future of education in Victoria would be very promising.

[11] G. S. Browne to J. R. Darling, 27 Feb. 1935, Darling's official correspondence.

Darling felt tense in February 1935, when the scheme was being put into action. The acknowledgement of his leadership brought a strange penalty. He felt overwhelmed by the ease with which he had been able to carry out his ideas and was concerned that they had not been given critical enough treatment. Eileen Kellaway pleaded with him to put up with the colonial cringe—'bear gently with our approval'—because the hoots of joy that greeted his efforts were in large part relief that he was not another of the 'duds unloaded from the other side'. She saw him as a fair exchange for the many talented expatriate Australians in Britain.

Stronger criticism might have emerged if deference to Britain had not been habitual. It took an American, Professor I. L. Kandel of Columbia University, to cast doubt on the emphasis on Latin, which held so central a place in English public schools and in entrance to Oxford and Cambridge, as well as in the development of his own intellect, that Darling rationalized its inclusion at the heart of his curriculum as the basis of clear thinking and writing. He closed his eyes to his experience at Charterhouse, where only the scholars really benefited from it, and overlooked the contradiction between its rigour and the broadening experience he championed. Looking back in 1960 he did not advocate

a return to the sort of education to which, in spite of the appalling gaps in knowledge which it left, I personally feel that I owe much, that close study of classical grammar and thought whose main virtue lay, perhaps, in its main defect, that it had to be so thorough that it left no time at all for any other studies.[12]

Probably nothing was more inappropriate than Latin for the rural ruck of his Australian school. It seems incongruous that he welcomed its toughness and precision when he was trying to establish 'interest' as the chief motivation for study. The picture painted by one of Masterman's pupils of that delightful, cultured man grinding his young class through Latin distinctions such as that between 'few Greeks' and 'a few Greeks', until the boy near the bottom got it right and was sent to the top of the class, is beautifully British. It is also frightening; for it seems probable that, to ensure the entrance of a minority to the great English universities, almost the whole school was subjected to Latin.

Against the tendency for contemporary disciplines, especially science, to replace classics, Darling stood firm. Moreover, according to John Béchervaise, his belief in the importance of concentrating on the meaning and purpose of man, rather than keeping abreast of the expanding universe, added further bias to the curriculum. He put more effort into the development of art and music than into science and mathematics, notwithstanding his initial drive for laboratories and the introduction of general science in the lower part of the school. As a consequence the school was often out of step with the trend towards science as a career. What it was to do, with remarkable success in the 1950s especially, was produce acceptable applicants for

12 *The Education of a Civilized Man*, p. 24.

W. B. McINNES

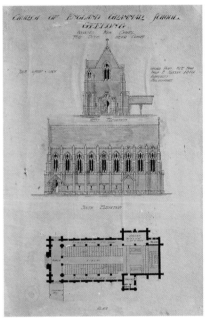

Top: great ideas in 1911. A proposal for the new school at Belmont, submitted unsuccessfully as part of the architectural competition from which emerged the plans for Corio.

The plan and elevation for the chapel at Corio, by the successful architects Wight and Hudson.

The Reverend Francis Ernest Brown, Headmaster 1912–29.

Australia's foreign service. Just as Jennings' disciplined boy was a naval officer in embryo, Darling's civilized young man carried a diplomatic pouch in his suitcase.

In 1934, during a conversation on Sydney Harbour Bridge (then only two years old and equally a symbol of science and human aspiration), Darling apprised J. C. Nield of the most imaginative experiment of the new curriculum. The young Sydney graduate was to take charge of the public affairs form, an interesting mixture of scholars who had completed sixth form and dropouts from fifth. They were to continue with some normal subjects, including English with the headmaster, but for the most part were to combine theoretical studies of society, such as economics and political science, with practical involvement. Fired by Darling's social conscience, the public affairs form undertook, for instance, a social survey of Port Melbourne, which led to a general involvement of the public schools in a boys' club there. They went on heart-rending study tours of slums still in the grip of the depression, listened to protagonists of contemporary political and social issues, both local and international, and in 1937 mounted an impressive exhibition on land utilization in Australia. 'The Public Affairs Form', Nield said later, 'was out to learn from Australia and to teach Australia'. What began as a pragmatic exercise to occupy the time of about twenty boys had become an important innovation.

Because of his concern to free the curriculum from the tyranny of examinations (or was it examiners?), Darling was, from 1932, a restless member of the Victorian Schools' Board, that body of academics and schoolteachers which virtually controlled the direction of secondary education in Victoria through the Intermediate and Leaving Certificate syllabuses. In his first year he tried to have the exams shortened, especially for Intermediate, from a marathon three hours. He failed, as he did again in 1936 when, with the support of the vice-chancellor and Professors Browne and Wadham, he proposed a radical simplification of university entrance procedures. His correspondence reflects the endemic conflict between the different goals and expectations of schools and universities, as well as the conflicting interpretations placed on the same event by different people. Wadham expected the professorial board to prove the greatest stumbling block, whereas Darling was more hopeful of converting professors or even the education department than his schoolteacher colleagues, so wedded were they to existing syllabuses. The idea of teaching Australian history, for instance, which Professor Ernest Scott suggested in 1931, was greeted with horror—especially by Darling.

One issue related to curriculum was ignored at Corio. The examination chains could have been largely broken if Darling had wanted to move into the Class A system by which schools were authorized, subject to periodic inspection, to conduct internal Intermediate and Leaving examinations. Why he did not, when he was so critical of university domination, is hard to understand, except that by putting examination students to the external test he retained

James Ralph Darling, Headmaster 1930–61.

HILDA RIX NICHOLAS

One of the stained glass panels incorporated in the windows of the school library (later the Hawker Library) commemorates Charlemagne, 'Monastic, Cathedral and Schools Founder'.

The Timbertop Chapel.

211

John Manifold

NAME *John Streeter Manifold*

Date of Birth 21ʰ April, 1915

Date of Admission 15ʰ Sept. 1925

Previous Education Home Tuition.

Boarder or Day Boy Boarder

House Junior — Manifold, Feb/29

Religion Church of England.

Parent's Name John Manifold.

Parent's Address Purrumbete, Weerite, Victoria

Sicknesses

Date of Confirmation Sept. 23ʳᵈ 1929.

Date of Leaving

complete control of the syllabus for the large proportion of students who took more practical options.

Whatever their tastes and talents, the students of the 1930s were given an unusual opportunity for self-fulfilment. Bright boys, in particular, felt an excitement that had not existed in the school before. Darling set the pace with his sixth form divinity and English. He treated them like undergraduates, stretching and goading them into critical awareness. Colin Officer remembered 4000-word essays on topics like: 'Authority has its source in God and not in man; no man and no group of men has in itself the right to govern others'. The top mark for their efforts was about 50 per cent: 42 was labelled 'very good'. Darling explained that on his scale perfection was unattainable and that a great essayist like Charles Lamb would get perhaps 85. Bull, Masterman, Gordon and others, each in his own style, provided similar challenges. When Westcott later observed one of Masterman's 'admittedly brilliant' little classes, he saw 'approbation and disagreement, loyalty and rebellion, humour and severity, commonsense and eccentricity' appear in both master and pupils within forty minutes. Boarding-school life presented opportunities for such stimulus to continue out of class, at informal gatherings in masters' houses and through clubs and societies. The literary magazine *If* gave young poets like John Manifold and Michael Thwaites the motivation to polish their work for publication.

When he was in England in 1939 Darling bequeathed his sixth-form English, though not his marking scale, to Russel Ward. If he had known Darling's scale Ward would not have thought his own standard 'absurdly high'. For one essay the best marks he gave were 76, 65 and 63, with most of the remainder in the low 50s. He should, he thought later, have given the top student, Geoffrey Dutton (future poet and writer) over 90 and Bob Southey (later president of the Australian Liberal Party) close to that. In the same vintage at GGS Ward found Stephen Murray-Smith (editor of *Overland*), Frank Kellaway (poet and librarian) and Stuart Sayers (long-time literary editor of the *Age*) and they stimulated each other. Kellaway remembered learning as much in discussions about literature and from swapping poems with Dutton as he did in class. The school charged them with intellectual energy, if not with the radicalism many old boys and staff were worried about.

Despite his involvement, as secretary of the Public Affairs Society, with Ward, its communist president, Murray-Smith was astonished on looking back at how little he knew about social and political issues.* When he met them at university, radicals from Scotch, Melbourne High and Geelong College were far better read. Yet, by and large, it seems, the GGS boys of that era took into the world a strong social awareness. Apart from a few like Manifold and

---

* Later Murray-Smith was also a member of the Communist Party. Believing that the absent Darling would have concurred, Ward alienated most of the staff in 1939 by inviting the communist Ralph Gibson to address the Public Affairs Society.

Murray-Smith they may have remained conservative and some even patronizing (there was that danger in the whole approach), but a surprising number carried a new idealism into business, government and the arts. In addition to those already mentioned in the last few pages a long list of the 'products' of Darling's early burst of enlightenment might be compiled. Prominent in later life were Alan Brock Brown, Michael Duffield, John Gorton, Rupert (Dick), Alan and David Hamer, David Hay, Sam McCulloch, Jim Mann, Ken Myer and Peter Thwaites. Three of the six Rhodes Scholars educated at GGS up to 1954 were at school in the early 1930s—J. G. Mann (left 1931), M. R. Thwaites (left 1933) and A. W. Hamer (left 1935). Many who would have become well known were killed in World War II. The greatest loss to Darling was of Bill Lloyd, senior prefect in 1933, in whose career he had taken an inordinate interest.

In the hope that, like Gollancz at Repton, he would present challenging ideas to the school, Darling added Charles Manning Hope Clark to the staff in 1940. Passionately agnostic, with a quizzical look, a throaty warble to his voice and his pyjamas often showing under his clothes, Clark had the brilliance of Masterman and something extra—a mind that seemed always to be grappling with mysteries and setting issues at GGS within global perspectives and the time-frame of civilization itself. Almost tortured by the evil of the world, he found release in the ideas of the great Russian novelist, Dostoevsky. He spoke to the various out-of-school societies on a wide range of topics and as president of his own creation, the Philosophical and Historical Society, invited bright young university lecturer friends like A. C. Jackson, George Paul and A. G. L. Shaw to talk about Marx, ethics, psychology, Plato, the Soviet Union and other abstruse subjects. Despite being unfit for war service he had physical as well as mental gifts and, having been a fine schoolboy and then university cricketer, coached the first eleven very successfully (p. 350). When Clark left after first term 1944 to accept a lectureship in political science at the University of Melbourne,* Darling was not entirely sorry to lose him. Clark's forthrightness about the futility of war, carried home for instance by Geoffrey Fairbairn in 1940, and not softened later when Australia was facing disaster, was seen as defeatism if not subversion. He also spoke irreverently of chapel as 'that Jesus business'. Complaints echoed around the Western District and flew back to the council. If Darling had not known of Gollancz's dismissal from Repton under similar circumstances in World War I, he might have found it harder to stand on his high horse, as he says he did, and defend freedom of speech.

Among other recruits to the common room in the early 1940s were two bachelors, R. R. Baldwin (1940−71) and E. H. Montgomery

Michael Thwaites

* In 1946, after moving to the department of history, Clark inaugurated the first full-year course in Australian history. Later, like Ward (at the University of New England) he became a professor of history (at the Australian National University). Masterman, who held the chair of classics there, again became his colleague. With prodigious energy Clark has written a six-volume history of Australia for which he is known world wide.

Rolf Baldwin

(1941–64). Rolf Baldwin was a red-cheeked, cheerful lover of the bush; his no-nonsense but friendly approach to his pupils was shared by 'Monty', a large matter-of-fact man who proved very resourceful and relaxed when given the task of founding Timbertop. H. R. McWilliam (1941–61) grappled more seriously with educational ideas; he became the first Master of Glamorgan in 1947 and left to become principal of the teacher-training institution Mercer House. J. E. L. Barber (1942–72), an old-boy oarsman, taught history and English.

The war forced many changes. Eighteen members of staff were on active service in May 1943, when the *Corian* published the following list: R. R. Baldwin, B. R. A. Coulter, C. W. R. Dart, J. S. Derrick, Miss O. M. Finnin, H. D. L. Fraser, L. A. Hardy, W. J. Howard, H. B. Hutton, W. N. Jaffray, Rev. N. A. Keen, T. F. McGrath, J. W. Neil, A. J. Spear, L. N. Tomkinson, V. J. H. Tunbridge, I. R. C. Weber and E. A. Williams. Numerous short-term replacements were made and when the war ended—or even before that—those returning had to be absorbed. Howard and Jaffray were back in January 1944 and Tunbridge, one of the 'rats of Tobruk', in May 1944. For two terms there were two Tunbridges on the staff: Vic's wife Marjorie, who had replaced him in 1941, remained until the end of 1944. She shared a rare female presence (except in art there had been no woman on the senior school staff and few at the junior school) with Mrs F. K. Wilson (1942–45), a graduate of Oxford who taught senior French.

Later in the 1940s openings for new staff were rare. When 'Joey' Allen retired to be vicar of Gisborne in 1945 Mervyn Britten (1946–48) came as chaplain from a similar position (after war service) at the Royal Military College, Duntroon. Cameron was replaced on the staff by K. J. Mappin (1948–67), a lean, thoughtful and thoroughly humane scientist, without whose spectacular contribution to drama the era would have lost much colour. P. N. Thwaites (OGG), later principal of Geelong College, spent 1946–48 at Corio, and in 1949 A. D. Hickinbotham (1949–51) and P. M. Moyes (1949–50) appeared.

There were other changes. When Cameron retired in 1947 Pinner became acting second master for a year while still in charge of 'Cuthy', before Hutton, significantly a much younger man, was given the new and probably long-overdue role of assistant to the headmaster. At the junior school there had been a post of supervisor of studies since 1935, but Darling may not have seen its potential until it was held with distinction by A. Todd (1943–47) from 1945 to 1947. Nall, who had been the first supervisor of studies and was Master of Junior School from 1942 to 1945, was replaced by H. D. L. Fraser early in 1945.

NEW TERRITORY
The last decade or so of J. R. Darling's headmastership spawns contradictory judgements. In one view he neglected the school; in

another he put it on the map. He withdrew, in part, from its everyday life in favour of more general community activity, yet achieved his best-known initiatives—the establishment of Timbertop and the planning of a new school and farm management college at Highton. The contradiction is more apparent than real. It disappears if the 1950s are viewed as a phase of Darling's general mission to Australia. In that perspective he had shown during the 1930s what ought to be done and valued throughout the country and had established the contacts and the reputation that were later to give him the opportunity to move out from the school and influence profoundly post-war social and educational thought. His prominence in the foundation of the Australian College of Education is a case in point. There was no change of direction, just a greater sphere of influence.

Indeed, Darling is remarkable for the consistency of his actions and ideas, which were those of a statesman. Not only had he become known nationally by his work at GGS during the 1930s but, in keeping with his philosophy of bringing the world into the school, he thought on a national and international scale. His preoccupation with the conduct and future of the British Commonwealth (always 'The Empire' to him—with *England* as its unchallengeable centre) made him a severe critic of Australian insularity and provincialism. His ambition was to see his old boys revitalize Australia through the British tradition and show other schools right across the world how ideals of service to humanity could be put into practice. He wanted his school to be *par excellence* the place of conscience and responsibility and he exemplified his own idea of leadership in the way he bullied and cajoled less committed and less energetic spirits. Christian convictions kept him going in the face of parental, staff and pupil apathy. For him, unselfish service to others had always been and always would be the hallmark of a civilized society, linked, of course, as it was in the classical tradition of the English public schools, to the development of intellect.

Education for democracy was not one of his strong priorities, but in 1939 he initiated a School Representative Council which lasted, at least as a list in the *Corian*, until 1944. In the first year no prefect could be a member: in the second and thereafter the senior prefect was included as chairman. Official recognition seems to have been slight. No mention of the council's proceedings, as happened with school societies, appeared in the *Corian*. That was understandable for 1940 when, angered from the outset by their directive chairman (reputed to be more royalist than the King), a critical and then disruptive group of left-wing sixth formers led a walk-out that halted proceedings for the year.

Darling did not keep silent on public questions. Early in the prelude to World War II he warned about the dangers of a compromise with Hitler. Soon after hostilities began he stimulated discussion about the kind of post-war world people should be fighting for, and in the 1950s he was fiercely determined to make the school and the country face up to their responsibilities. His aims throughout were

Rutter Badge

1948

Tony Gilder
Mark Lyon
Tony Dowling
James Norman
John Palfreyman
Tim Murray
John Dehlsen
Neil Lawrance
Warwick Dubois
Bill Moore
Rob Patterson
Eddy Dickson

Alan Cash

the same: the world, the nation, the school must be redeemed from materialism and small-mindedness by strong-willed, well-informed, unselfish people, dedicated, as he was, to great works. In an important sense this was an elitist position: he valued his own role as an opinion-maker and did not expect the task to be within the capacities of the rank and file. They would, he hoped, be a general influence for good. Only his best boys, energetic, civilized, selfless, could cope with the challenge. So, as he confessed in *Richly Rewarding*, he concentrated on them and neglected the ruck; worked hard in the community and left the routines of GGS to his special assistants Barney Hutton and Alan Cash,* to housemasters, and to the heads of the junior and preparatory schools. His conscience about it reflects the romantic tug at his sleeve of an earlier phase of life at the school (when he could be in touch with all its activities) rather than the needs of that larger and more complicated institution that his vision and energy had brought forth. What he might have done, had he not been so steeped in the god-headmaster tradition, and so paternal by temperament, was reorganize the school in response to its greater size and complexity. Geelong Grammar had become an empire, but, although diverted by his larger mission to Australia from keeping in close touch with things, he wanted to retain the atmosphere of personal rule. Boys who knew of his earlier magic with his special sixth-form class felt cheated (even in the 1940s) by his frequent absences and obvious lack of preparation. He had not stopped caring. To the annoyance of housemasters, boys in trouble found him warm and forgiving. His door was always open to them, despite his wife's desire that he should impose an embargo on two nights a week.

He had, of course, changed. The tall, thin, sallow young man had filled out, become ruddy, stooped a little. Lofty and Olympian now, rather than restless and participatory, he was more introspective and occasionally jaded; still bubbling with humour but more sardonic; still the generous host but more formally hospitable; still sensitive but a giver rather than a sharer. Peter King, senior prefect in 1954, found him the centre of the moral universe, but distant. Rarely, he thinks, was rule so remote. To retain personal control Darling concentrated decision-making in the hands of the housemasters and his special assistant. He lost contact with young staff, to some of whom he seemed imperious, almost a dictator. Many senior masters saw little of him outside chapel. It was left to his aura, the sense of his greatness and his eloquence on formal occasions, to provide coherence.

It was also left to his staff! Any falling away of the headmaster's earlier vitality was masked to a great extent by the quality of people who wanted to come to GGS. The 1950s were a rich period of recruitment. Nearly every year someone arrived who was to give important long-term service—Alan Cash (1950–61), Ivan Sutherland (1950–   ), Bill Lester (1952–85), Bertie Eyre-Walker (1952–79),

---

* Cash joined the staff in 1950. He took over from Hutton as Darling's special assistant in 1956. Hutton, who had held that position from 1949, succeeded Jaffray in 1957 as housemaster of Francis Brown.

216

Bill Panckridge (1953—87), Don Marles (1955—78), Frank Covill (1955—   ), Dick Weigall (1955—56, 1960—   ), Hubert Ward (1955—67), Michael (Collins) Persse (1955—   ), John Bedggood (1956 and 1960—   ), Ian Edwards (1957—   ), John Béchervaise (1957—72), David Happell (1959—76), Tim Murray (1959—77), Graeme Renney (1959—70), and Peter Thomson (1959, 69—72 and 74—83). Most were Australian born and a few more than in earlier years were OGGs. The early 1960s saw the arrival of Peter Graham (1960—   ), who was to serve the school on three sites, and in Darling's final term Peter Jardine (1961—   ), shaper of boys and wood.

For shorter terms, but often excitingly, there were men like Ken Leslie (1953—56), John Landy (1955—57), Paul McKeown (1955—58), Ivo Dean (1959—61), Peter Gebhardt (1959—60), and Barry Connell (1951—57), as well as exchanges like Peter Hare (1949—50) from Rugby and Michael Charlesworth (1953—54) from Shrewsbury. Among Darling's late crop were fourteen who became headmasters—including Cash at Armidale, Marles at Trinity, McKeown at Canberra, Ward at Ely in England, Gebhardt at Bathurst then Geelong College, Murray at Hamilton then Canberra and Renney at Ballarat then Scots in Sydney. In addition Ivo Dean was the first head of the Marcus Oldham Farm Management College.

More or less behind the scenes, but at the headmaster's right hand in his dealings with council, the bursar continued to be a key figure, whose headaches multiplied with the expansion of the school. Without the tact and energy of stocky Milton Thewlis (1932—53),* who organized Darling's self-help construction schemes and sympathized with his plans to stimulate and civilize, the school community would have been less unified and content. He was never arbitrary or capricious in keeping the worn purse strings tight. It was the same with his successor Peter Desborough (1929—72), an immense man whom even Darling and Westcott had to crane their necks to address. Proportional to his bulk, he tackled the huge backlog of maintenance covered by the centenary appeal of 1957 when, most noticeably, rusting iron roofs were replaced with non-corroding plastic.

In explaining the changes of the 1950s and especially the creation of a fourth-form outpost of the school in the mountains near Mansfield in 1953, it is necessary to consider established policies and attitudes within the school in conjunction with post-war social and economic conditions, for the new move was almost equally derived from both. Financial difficulties were its mainspring. In addition to the crisis of 1939, when the school lost over £2000, and the backlog of maintenance, inflation was a killer. Between 1938 and 1949 wages jumped by 96 per cent and materials 60 per cent, whereas fees (controlled until 1946) could not realistically be pushed beyond 45 per cent. The books were balanced at the expense of masters' salaries, which rose

J. R. Darling inspecting progress during the replacement of rusty iron by fibro-cement roofing, 1955. The funds came from the centenary appeal.

---

* He came as accountant in 1916.

only 20 per cent, but which could not be contained in the 1950s. There was then a long overdue rise in the salaries of all teachers, who were in short supply for the rapidly expanding State secondary system, which reflected the community's awareness that white-collar jobs were more desirable and knowledge and skill more necessary in a technological age.

The State not only put a premium on the recruitment of teachers but provided many new high schools, particularly in the country, where they offered an alternative to boarding-schools. These were long overdue reforms, which Darling did not begrudge—he would no longer have to apologize to Englishmen for the inadequacy of Australian salaries—but which threatened the staffing of private schools. How much more could parents pay? Would private schools have to fold or become more elitist than ever? These questions were a nightmare which drove headmasters, school councils and parents into the political arena. Their major objective, which Darling had suggested early in 1946, and which the Headmasters' Conference adopted later in the year, was an income tax rebate for school fees. For Darling it was imperative that something be done: fees at GGS were already a pastoralist's ransom when they were raised 20 per cent in 1946. The Liberal Party responded. During twenty-three years in power, after an historic victory over Labor in 1949, Liberal governments introduced first a tax concession on fees, then tax deductibility for approved building funds and finally direct grants for specific projects such as libraries and laboratories. Thus costs were contained and capital was attracted for expansion.

Until all these concessions were achieved, lack of money was a powerful constraint at GGS. The debt incurred in the 1930s still prevented expansion in 1950. Although another boarding-house was essential to reduce by twenty the eighty-five boys incarcerated in what Darling called 'those monstrosities' Manifold, Perry and Cuthbertson, it would cost a crippling £60 000. Darling felt trapped. He could not have the school he wanted. More was needed than the excellent range of out-of-school activities and something bolder than a revision of the curriculum, which he carried out in 1949. The place needed new life. Darling was distressed by the apathy of the majority of boys and, after a very difficult third term in 1949, he launched a sharp attack on declining moral standards. Senior boys had not 'put the school above their own tastes and impulses'. At Speech Day 1950, in perhaps the most significant of all his utterances, he expressed despair about the lack of academic excellence. The examination results of the best boys suffered from the dissipation of their energies in a plethora of activity, while the worst boys dodged everything in favour of the national vices of sunbathing and listening to the wireless.

He was determined to destroy or starve some activities, but knew from past experience that he would be blocked at every turn by the conservatism of boys and masters, as well as old boys, who would throw his own innovations at him as if they were unalterable school traditions. Most of all he despaired about organized games.

He told the assembled dignataries and parents that it was a grievous tyranny to take seriously both school and house sport, so unreasonably imposed in a school which provided so many other activities. Then, although he was only fifty-one, he likened himself to Tennyson's Ulysses, summoning the strength for a final effort at being effective:

We are not now that strength which in old days moved Heaven and Earth...but something ere the end, some work of noble note may yet be done.[13]

That consciousness of the need for a supreme effort to strike at materialism, self-interest and convenience welled up within him as he spoke of the kind of man needed to save Australia and humanity:

We need in this generation as we have had them in the past, men of conscience, driven, even against their wills, certainly against their own interests, to take a stand for principles. Men not afraid of facing unpleasant facts, not afraid of being different in their views from other people, men who cannot rest so long as opportunities remain to work for the really great human objectives—peace, justice, honesty and decency between men.[14]

After warning parents to be careful not to destroy the precious growth of conscience in a boy (and thus destroy the boy himself and the possibility of civilized society) he went on to his inevitable peroration—the great fixed point in his philosophy:

For selfishness is, as it has ever been, the ultimately destructive force in a society, and there are only two cures for selfishness—the regimented state which we all profess to dislike, and the change of heart, which we refuse to make. That is the choice, believe me, for each one of us, and we have not much time in which to make it. The need for decision is serious and urgent and the sands are running out. If as a school we can do even a little to help boys to make the decision aright, then we have some right to exist; if not, we do not matter at all.[15]

Timbertop

That desire to help boys make the decision aright led to Darling's 'work of noble note'. Two tracks joined in his mind and became a road to the mountains, penetrating a realm beyond the control of money, power and comfort. A place in the bush would answer both his needs. First, it could be constructed cheaply, even (as he had shown) by boys themselves. Secondly, it would provide those challenges from which stamina, self-reliance, courage, adaptability, persistence, enterprise, responsibility and sensitivity could be developed in a boy, especially at puberty, when the adult within him was looking for room to grow. Darling had been thinking that way for twenty years. He had written to the Victorian Director of Education in 1936 about the inadequacy of secondary education in providing challenges for adolescents.

Speech Day 1951, when the headmaster announced that a section of the school would be transferred to the mountains, was the most dramatic since 1937. Darling's creative energy had broken loose again. Following the setback of 1939, which left its marks in a

13 *Corian*, Dec. 1950, p. 177.
14 *Corian*, Dec. 1950, p. 178.
15 *Corian*, Dec. 1950, p. 179.

confrontation with the council in 1940 and some subsequent distrust, and after the frustrations of the war years, he had had to bear with patience the struggle against inflation. Expansion was out of the question. Under Labor governments until 1949, middle-class dominance in Australia was challenged and international as well as national tides seemed to be tearing at those roots of privilege which sustained the school. Even in 1952 there were great risks: as in the 1930s, the headmaster pressed the governing body into large commitments to an unorthodox development and overcame their objections with a mixture of pragmatism and theory. How fully they had listened to him on educational, administrative, financial and planning grounds is revealed in their statement to the school community in December 1951:

The School Council has made arrangements to acquire a country property upon which will be built accommodation for about 120 boys. To this new auxiliary part of the School will be sent all boys during the calendar year, generally known as Middle Dormitory year, that is, the second year in Senior School, when the ages (at the beginning of the year) will be between 14¼ and 15¼. The new establishment will differ from the main school in three main ways: First, it will be in a locality and environment in which largely the physical and moral development of the boy will be encouraged through the challenge of the natural conditions; secondly, it will be planned in such a way as to make it easily run by the boys themselves without dependence upon a large supply of employed domestic and other labour; and, thirdly, it will be as nearly as possible self-supporting, or, at least planned in such a way as to become so.[16]

To quieten doubters, reference was made to Kurt Hahn's successful precedents at Salem and Gordonstoun and to the Outward Bound schools in Britain. Those who feared loss of academic experience were especially reassured that, far from weakening examination performance, 'a concentration on fundamentals and a freedom from distractions' might help boys to spend the year more valuably than at Corio. But the central point, related to the malaise in 1948 and 1949, was diagnosed here as a function of the complexity of the ordinary school:

The mere existence of the complicated machinery necessary in a large school militates against independence and initiative, and encourages a negative conformity. This danger is accentuated in this School, of which many boys are members without intermission for ten or more years.

The new establishment should throw the emphasis back upon the individual. Boys will have to learn to look after themselves, to find their own occupation, and develop their own capacities. The rather harder conditions and the challenge of the environment will convince all boys, even those who are physically undeveloped, of their capacity to surmount difficulties and overcome the weakness of their bodies. The absence of paid assistance will teach boys to be independent and give them the confidence derived from the knowledge that they can be so. It is believed that this self-confidence will be transferred into all departments of their lives, giving them courage in tackling difficulties in school work and, later, to take the responsibility of leadership in all sorts of public opinion.[17]

This emphasis contradicted many of Darling's earlier objectives

[16] *Corian*, Dec. 1951, p. 160.
[17] *Corian*, Dec. 1951, p. 160.

and was possibly a sign of reluctance to grapple with more fundamental questions. They might even disappear within the ambit of
a spectacular novelty. Although not a confession of failure, the
Timbertop move replaced to a great extent the influence of high
culture with that of nature and increased the emphasis on character
rather than intellect. That it was planned to achieve a fundamental
change of attitude within a single year of a boy's life indicates
Darling's idealism. Timbertop was to be the equivalent of the biblical
wilderness, where a change of heart or the tempering of resolution in
a boy about to become a man might best be attempted. He seized the
chance to send the fourteen- to fifteen-year-olds, so that the sexual
and psychological drives of puberty might be directed into socially-
acceptable channels. For he believed with Kurt Hahn that the
loutishness usually associated with adolescence could be constrained
and the undefeatable spirit of childhood preserved at the onset of
puberty by kindling and sustaining 'the non-poisonous passions, the
zest for building, the craving for great adventure, the joy of research,
the love of painting, music or writing, the devotion to any skill
demanding care and victorious patience'.

The council had stifled Darling's first approach to Kurt Hahn's
ideas a decade before, when wartime shortages and the 1939 economic
crisis prompted him to suggest upgrading the school farm and using
it educationally as at Gordonstoun. They regarded his initial suggestion
as inappropriate: he wanted to use only the duller boys, for whom,
because they came mostly from rural backgrounds, it would, at great
cost to their parents, have been no new experience. Later he had
more ambitious plans with which, from the dual perspective of
professor of agriculture and member of the school council, Sam
Wadham agreed, to use the farm to give a more meaningful education to
the high proportion of unacademic and difficult boys in the school.
Eventually, along these lines and with remarkable success, from a
concept and energy of his own, he had instituted the National
Service scheme; he had stimulated the zest for building considered
so important by Kurt Hahn and was now ready, by challenging them
at fourth form, to launch the school as a whole into a great adventure
that promised to give generations to come the sublime experience of
the mountains.

These strands of idealism and educational planning, despite
their importance in getting a favourable decision from the council,
were probably less significant in the Timbertop decision than administrative and economic expediency. Although Darling's initiative coincided and accorded with a plaintive *Call to the Nation*, issued by
establishment figures in 1951, it was based on the economics of
Corio. The boarding-houses had been grossly overcrowded, yet new
residential facilities could only be paid for by an expansion in numbers, which would in turn require expensive additions to classrooms,
chapel, dining hall and science block, which could only be paid for
by further overcrowding. This would merely repeat the existing
situation, for the poor morale of the late 1940s, which had generated

.J. Beasley. 80.

the crisis, was itself the product of overcrowding in an attempt to service capital borrowed in the 1930s.

When the council found that an exciting fourth-form branch of the school, to hold 120 boys, could be constructed for the cost of accommodating sixty-five at Corio, Timbertop was born. Because the structures would be simple and the labour force largely unpaid, the books would balance even without donations. Besides, the new site would prove an investment, not only in terms of an expected appreciation in value and its use for a forestry operation, but also as a possible retreat for the whole school from the advance of industrial Geelong. The advent of the Shell refinery in 1952 had frightened the council, but increased property values indicated that there would be assets to back a move elsewhere.

His eloquence in promoting it at Speech Day 1951 suggests that Darling sensed that Timbertop was a natural for fund-raising. By comparison, additions at Corio would have been flat beer. After explaining what the project would mean to the school, he urged parents to support it, especially with money. In the pamphlet they were holding there was a tear-off slip (repeated in the *Corian* for the benefit of absentees) which called urgently for an indication of support, preferably by donation or interest-free loan but also at various rates of interest from 2 per cent for ten years to 4 per cent for thirty.

Everything he said expressed Darling's view that the new move was a masterstroke. His enthusiasm for its shrewdness and idealism, its blending of educational and economic goals, and his great pride of authorship, is revealed in the following extract from his address:

In one glorious hit we really solve in the only possible way the desperate problem of too great numbers in the Houses at Corio and the consequent pressure upon other buildings—Chapel, classrooms, Dining Hall, and so on. No other solution except a reduction in numbers will solve this problem; and a reduction in numbers would inevitably imply a large increase in fees. By sending about 100 boys to 'Timbertop' we shall be able to make the building operations a major school project, in which all can take their part and learn from the experience, and we can at the same time take the first step in the direction of a simpler and cheaper school economy. Again, I cannot here explain in detail how all this works out, but I do assure you that from this aspect 'Timbertop' is not only desirable—it is absolutely necessary for the School—and the only practicable solution of difficulties and weaknesses in the School of which I hope that you will remain slightly less conscious than ourselves.[18]

'In one glorious hit', that was the keynote. There was something magical in achieving an educational masterstroke as the solution to an intransigent financial—managerial problem. It was as if Darling, the golfer, had hit through trees from deep rough to a barely visible green and had holed out.

Easily overlooked in information about Timbertop was a reference to the maintenance of contacts between Corio and its outpost. The headmaster each term, and housemasters once a year, were expected to spend a week (or at least a long weekend) consolidating the empire. How academic continuity was to be maintained was not

[18] *Corian*, Dec. 1951, pp. 150–1.

spelled out: indeed, intellectual goals had hardly been considered. The school was geared to pastoral care, dominated by housemasters, and the emphasis on character-building at Timbertop, which was beyond the purview of subject heads, meant greater difficulty in achieving a coherent curriculum. A rare type of schoolmaster was needed—one who combined scholarship with zest for the outdoors. There was a danger of repeating the kind of mistake made when the new school was launched at Corio without men experienced in the various roles of boarding-house care. Finding appropriate staff and maintaining effective communication became a formidable task for the headmaster. Timbertop was neither a separate school, able to go its own way, nor a branch that could be closely supervised.

E. H. Montgomery

The success of Timbertop is revealed in the triumph of that indigenous name over the restrictive and repellent 'Sparta' that had been allowed initially to sum up what was expected. It grew free of traditional boarding-school discipline and leadership rhetoric and free of any rigid plan, thanks to the zest and insight of E. H. Montgomery, who was in charge for eleven years from late 1952, and who can be ranked with Jennings and Cuthbertson among assistant masters responsible for the creation of a special element of the school's tradition. Nothing was stereotyped with 'Monty'. He did not fuss over trifles and was undaunted by the continuous, unexpected and intransigent problems of the first few years. The bush around Mt Timbertop took charge in a way that often gave the man on the spot the only possible initiative, and the fact that he was flexible and gained the respect and support of locals full of bush 'know-how' had an indelible influence. When an abominably wet winter in 1952 set back construction so that the 1953 fourth formers had to be taken in two stages (35 for the first half-year, 63 for the second) and nothing was complete, a pioneering ethos was secure. Despite the heritage of enthusiasm and skill from earlier GGS building ventures, despite the excellence of the effort put into them, the garages prefabricated at Corio early in 1952 and the first boys' units, made on the spot by boys and school workmen late in that year, as well as the larger contracted buildings, were mere artifacts in a saga dominated by the weather and the site. Even more than had been hoped, the Australian bush was providing a formative challenge.

By the end of 1953, after Homeric adventures (as well as Spartan rigours) the basic plans had been achieved. There was a dining hall, sanatorium, single masters' quarters, several married masters' houses, a mechanics shop, classroom block, men's quarters, electricity generator, dam and water supply, a proper access road and five completed units in which the boys were housed. Those units— no better name could be found for them—as well as the way they were organized, expressed most of the difference between Timbertop and Corio. Each had a dormitory, living room, pantry, boiler room, tog room, bathroom and lavatory, and each held between twelve and fifteen boys who formed their own democracy. They took executive responsibility by monthly rotation, after an exhaustive ballot along

Timbertop
Magazine

Written by
The Boys of Geelong Grammar School
TIMBERTOP, MANSFIELD

EDITOR:

P. J. McKeown, Esq.

No. 3   FEBRUARY, 1958

the lines (was it one of Monty's jokes?) of the Australian Labor Party's voting system. Unit leaders and their seconds were responsible for organizing the unit housekeeping, such as cutting their own wood, stoking the boiler, landscaping the surrounds and cleaning and tidying. Each week they met Monty for what he found a valuable discussion of the running of the school. Even so it was far from a free and easy democracy; routines were strict and classes little different from those at Corio, though with an iconoclastic air three different 'bells' were adopted. A ploughshare was struck for special assemblies, a shell case sounded for school periods and a real bell rang for evening study time and lights out.

Montgomery says that he saw little of Darling during January 1953, so Timbertop started without many detailed prescriptions. How different it might have been if it had been closer, or if the headmaster had had more time, is anyone's guess. A straw in the wind was the experience of the original units during the first of Darling's visits. All their furniture was rearranged where he, rather than they, thought it should go. Of course, when his back was turned...! By contrast, Montgomery's willingness to let boys make their own decisions was essential if the aims of self-dependence, initiative and responsibility were to be achieved.

Bostock House

With the opening of Timbertop, the school had three subsidiaries. The closest to Corio was Bostock House in Geelong, formerly Geelong Preparatory Grammar School, which had been founded in 1924 and which was taken over and renamed at Darling's instigation in 1933. Light blue replaced dark red in its uniform, except for the tie, and at roll-call boarders soon outnumbered day boys. The strengthening of the boarding side had begun in 1930. Governesses were becoming hard to find, so Old Geelong Grammarians were glad to hear from the new headmaster that the Reverend P. H. Dicker's Prep. provided excellent care and continuity; they were encouraged to enrol simultaneously for both schools. In the years 1926—29 Dicker had supplied Corio with about twenty-five boys each year but in 1930 there were about sixty. During the 1940s, when many fathers were overseas, a further strengthening of boarders occurred, but the trend was reversed after the war. After Dicker (until 1933) the Reverend P. A. Wisewould (1934—43), the Reverend E. D. Kent (1943—45) and Mr W. G. L. (Bill) Cartwright (1945—71) were Darling's lieutenants at Bostock.*

Glamorgan

Distance was not a great problem there, and the transition of students to Corio, as well as staff liaison between the two schools, was relatively easy. Not so with Glamorgan, taken over in 1947 from Miss Isabel

---

* Long and outstanding service was given by Peg Steel (1945—71), John Ellis Jones (1946—63), Ralph Davies (1952—80), Lilias Burns (1954—72) and Nona Eyre-Walker (1955—78) on the teaching staff, and on the domestic side by Josie Woods (1935—75) and Marie Webster (1957—84).

McComas to secure a permanent and strong entry of boys from Melbourne. All the metropolitan schools had their own preps, so Glamorgan, founded in 1887 and situated in Douglas Street, Toorak, had had to seek financial security as the chief Melbourne feeder for GGS. In the 1930s Darling had preferred the preparation given by Miss Adderley of Adwalton and had tried, without success, to help her move closer to the Toorak and South Yarra homes of his Melbourne clientele. Glamorgan remained the most convenient prep. So, when Miss McComas, then aged eighty-six, was persuaded to retire after sixty years in charge, GGS connections made great efforts to secure the school, although it provided only 3 per cent of the Corio intake at that time. Darling expected that the purchase would be significant in keeping up enrolments, and critical for the proper development of character and intellect. Control from Corio would ensure high standards lacking in Miss McComas's later years. But control from Corio also meant the further dissipation of the headmaster's energies. As the dynamo within the school machine he was committed to regular visits to Douglas Street and was involved at an additional level with educational ideas, planning and administration. Added to his community commitments and social life, this activity kept his chauffeured black Morris buzzing up the Princes Highway, Darling's tall figure bent over letters and notes related to innumerable meetings and talks.*

Glamorgan   J. Beasley.   80.

THE CONNELL REPORT

Timbertop was four years old at the end of 1956, and Geelong Grammar was about to celebrate its centenary, when the headmaster announced that during 1957 Professor W. F. Connell and members of his staff from the faculty of education at Sydney University were to conduct an inspection of all aspects of life at GGS. As often, he was ahead of his Australian contemporaries—it was twenty years before such evaluations became common. With Connell's assistance in pinpointing weaknesses of organization and scholarship, Darling hoped for a renewal similar to that contemplated for the fabric at Corio through a centenary appeal. He was oppressed by the shortage of dedicated young staff, especially at Timbertop, and recognized ruefully that instead of the small and simple establishment he had taken over from Francis Brown, GGS had become a 'large, highly complex and, I sometimes fear, unmanageable heterogeny of schools'.

Darling was to regret the invitation to Connell, despite great stimulation from the visitors. He looked back on the inspection as the most honourable and possibly the most stupid thing he had done in his life. If he had been hoping for the kind of praise so frequently

---

* Meanwhile, under his lieutenant there, Ron McWilliam (1947–61), the long and distinguished service at Glamorgan of Katherine Alexander ('Miss Allie') (1909–50), and that of Marjorie Whiteside ('Miss Whitey') (1924–64), continued, bringing two more legendary figures into the GGS community; and Dorothy Evans in 1952 began thirty years' work in charge of the Glamorgan kitchens.

Thomas Ronald Garnett,
Headmaster 1963–73.

The Hon. Charles Fisher,
Headmaster 1974–8.

CHARLES BUSH

heaped on the school in the 1930s by Professor G. S. Browne, he must have been shocked. The report was shattering, especially to his ego, for it found much to criticize in a school for which since the mid-1930s he had consistently claimed personal responsibility and about which he had boasted that he knew 'better than any other critic the weaknesses of the organization and the gap between what we should like to do and what we actually do'. 'We are none of us', he had added, 'self-satisfied with the School'. Yet he accepted few of Connell's criticisms and in particular made no effort to alter the centralized structure of command which, because of his other preoccupations, reduced responsiveness and flexibility throughout the organization. That affirmation of old ways and the rallying of Darling's staff against outside criticism was to heap up troubles for his immediate successor, T. R. Garnett, and the constant travel required to hold together that far-flung empire was to contribute to the early death of Charles Fisher, who followed him.

Darling's dismissal of the Connell report is hard to understand. Time and again he had complained at speech days that he was at his wits' end in trying to deal with the complexity of GGS and the apathy of a majority of boys. Time and again he had tried to solve the problem of a very mixed clientele, and had been especially concerned, as Connell was, with lack of scholarship. He was offended, and justifiably that the excellences of the school—its freedoms and friendliness, artistic vitality and tradition of pastoral care—seemed to be taken for granted.

Did Connell offer a way out? That will have to be judged later in this history, as part of a discussion of Garnett's headmastership, when many of the professor's suggestions were implemented. What remains to be said here is that, on most of the critical issues, the difference between Darling's practice and Connell's suggestions was one of values. Connell was Australian born and his team was expressing an Australian educational tradition distinct from Darling's English heritage. Connell questioned the deeply-ingrained, taken-for-granted values of the English boarding-school, especially its pedagogical amateurism and leadership rhetoric. He was not prepared to excuse inadequate classroom teaching and a poorly developed curriculum on the grounds that the true purpose of the school was character-building, and he could look dispassionately at Darling's empire. Whereas the headmaster saw it in heroic terms, as the outcome of struggles against immense financial odds and against Australian materialism, the professor diagnosed rampant pragmatism and a lack of concentration upon essentials. There must also have been a political difference. Darling wanted to defend the existing order, Connell to allow for change. It is ironic that on the same day as he announced the inspection, Darling lamented Britain's difficulties over Suez. As the tides of empire, on which he had voyaged to Australia, drew back, he joined Robert Menzies on ground that would gradually be deserted by Australians, who were learning by experience what he had often told them, that they would have to stand on their own feet.

Corio from the air in the early 1980s.

PHOTOGRAPH BY
RICHARD MADDEVER

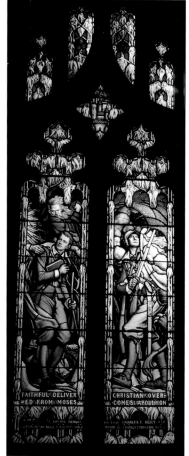

Memorial windows in the Chapel of All Saints; *left*, for Lieutenant Charles C. Kelly, AIF; *right*, for Leading Aircraftsman Leigh Brereton Sadleir Falkiner and John Alexander Falkiner.

He meant, of course, that they should stand on their own feet within the British tradition, that the school and nation should shoulder Britain's responsibilities in the world. How hard it was for GGS to do so was exemplified in the stresses placed on the school by its expansion under Darling and under old-boy dominated councils, who had been preoccupied since 1914 with their dream of creating a school equal to its British progenitors. Provincials, irked during their university days by the condescension of Oxford and Cambridge men, who assumed the superiority of English public schools over colonial foundations, they were determined to show their mettle and were happy to be led by an ambitious young headmaster who had his own reasons for wanting to make their dream come true. So, like a cat chasing its tail, they continued to expand from an inadequate financial base, never stopping to question the original ambition, though pausing occasionally to wonder if they could keep going, and even to wonder if they still belonged to Australian society. That was the rub: the high fees necessary to maintain an English upper-class boarding-school atmosphere distanced the school from the community it hoped to lead.

Early in his headmastership it had not been in Darling's interest to point to the endemic nature of financial constraints on the school. He wanted action, not reflection. His first public exposition of the situation did not come until December 1956, when, with the centenary appeal under way, he hoped to dispense with the problem by stimulating large donations. Its size, however, made that a remote possibility. He showed that the immense and unusual overheads of the establishment at Corio put the school in a straitjacket from which Houdini could not have escaped:

It would be wonderful to have a great endowment which I was free to use in order to do all the things that I know should be done; but I suppose that no school outside America can expect to have such resources. I wonder, however, whether those who are critical ever understand just how much of a compromise between the ideal and the possible it all has to be. By its very nature a boarding school which has in some way to look after boys for the whole twenty-four hours of the day and for week-ends makes demands upon masters greater than a day school. This means, as masters are only human, that a boarding school must have a higher staff—student ratio; that is, fewer boys to a master than a day school. In these days of early marriages and because of our comparatively isolated position, that means accommodation for masters and other staff on the School property and the upkeep of these houses. All our financial troubles stem from these two sources—the fact of being a boarding school and the fact that we placed ourselves out here away from any organic settlement.* Everything that is here at Corio—except of course, the Shell Company—we have had to make for ourselves. There is much else that I can see should have been or should be done. I could make good use of considerably more masters, particularly young ones: I know that our science laboratories are inadequate for the task that they are now called upon to perform. I know better than any other critic the weaknesses of organisation and the gap between what we should like to do and what we actually do. We are, none of us, self-satisfied with the School. We make mistakes, and we fail to do our best, like other human institutions, but much

---

* Nearly all similar English schools are at least in villages or small country towns.

227

OPENED BY
Mrs J.R. DARLING
29th JULY 1961

As one of the last acts in her long stay at Corio, Margaret Darling opened a drawing annexe for the carpentry and mechanics shop, 29 July 1961.

of our failure as I see it, is the inescapable consequence of having to cut our coat more or less according to our cloth, and though we have more cloth than many schools, we also have a larger frame to cover.[19]

According to that analysis, the original move to Corio had imposed a fatal financial burden. Brown, in trying to contain it, had to put aside the great aims of the move, while Darling, by struggling to escape, and achieve those aims, had brought territorial expansion and international fame at the expense of unmanageable complexity.

FINALE

Even so, Timbertop was not his last fling. J. R. D. broke out again in 1959, with plans for a joint project in the Barrabool Hills, beyond Geelong's expanding suburban fringe at Highton. As a further answer to the needs of country boys for whom he had made special provision at fifth form (see p. 206), he had found common cause with the trustees of Marcus Oldham, who offered to fund a farm management college, where boys with rural backgrounds would be given further education. Capital costs would be minimized by sharing the £20 000 site and major facilities like a hall, chapel and playing-fields with The Hermitage* and Geelong Grammar, both of whom saw benefits in moving their primary operations out of inadequate buildings and cramped sites in Newtown. Provision was also made for a new Geelong secondary school at some later date. For GGS the scheme was a replay of the original attempt to move the old gray school to Belmont.

The hope that the costs to GGS of land and buildings would be covered by the sale of Bostock's Pakington Street premises proved false. There was only £47 000 to set against an initial expenditure of £72 000. Worse than that, financially, Bostock's numbers were eroded by the move, which produced nothing but losses during the 1960s. The site was inaccessible. The trough of enrolments entered the senior school in 1968 and jeopardized the future of Geelong House as well as contributing to an overall weakness that assisted the introduction of co-education. In that way Darling and the council bequeathed to their successors a problem that was to bring a further and more fundamental change. Neither that nor the struggle that later faced The Hermitage and GGS at Highton should be allowed to dim the creative vision. Marcus Oldham Farm Management College, whose first principal, Ivo Dean, had previously been in charge of the agricultural students at GGS, has given hundreds of Old Geelong Grammarians among its many graduates an important injection of new ideas on their way to family properties and other rural careers.

After a lifetime of concern about the future of other people, J. R. Darling looked to his own during 1961. There were, of course, strands of interest and commitment that would remain unbroken.

[19] *Corian*, Dec. 1956, pp. 193–4.   * Geelong Church of England Girls' School.

They had, indeed, as he knew, called him more frequently from the school in the 1950s than was good for it. Early in his headmastership his mission to Australia had been focused on GGS, with forays in pursuit of largely educational goals, like the establishment and nurturing of the Headmasters' Conference of Australia, of which he was one of the three founders in 1931. Now he was widely and deeply involved elsewhere, though without realizing the extent of it until his wife pointed to the evidence in his diary. Jostling for room with his many speaking engagements were the meetings of committees like the Australian Broadcasting Control Board, the Australian Road Safety Council (of which on retirement he became chairman), the Australian Elizabethan Theatre Trust, the Council of the University of Melbourne, Australian Frontier and the Australian College of Education, which he had been instrumental in founding at Corio in 1959, and of which he was president from then until 1963.* The College of Education expressed a fixed point in his philosophy, visible earlier in his efforts first in Victoria and then nationwide, to have State high school headmasters join their independent colleagues in conference, and in his determination, almost upon arrival, to raise the standing of teachers (p. 184). Like the College of Surgeons it was to be a means of improving the profession and projecting it more positively to the wider community.

These interests would have sustained him while he looked for a further major commitment, at a time of life when others would have been glad of more golf and reading. He was pondering the possibilities, said to be open to him, of becoming a Liberal Party senator, or taking holy orders and working as a suffragan bishop of Melbourne, when the government of his old friend, Sir Robert Menzies, stepped in and asked him, towards the end of June 1961, to become chairman of the Australian Broadcasting Commission. He still had most of his final term at Corio to complete.

So long and so memorable a headmastership, ending with the prospect of a vigorous new career, was unique in Australian history. To capture its flavours and to offer their tribute, a selection of those who had known him best anticipated Darling's retirement during 1961 with the research and writing of *Thirty-two Years*, in which their 'recollections and impressions' reveal the range of his interests, the depth of his influence and the power of his personality.

The end of his long career was marked in many ways, public and private, at Corio. At an open day on Saturday 29 July, amid numerous displays and activities of a kind unknown before he came, two projects completed by masters and boys, in the tradition of building he had begun, and for purposes he had introduced, were formally opened. One was a drawing annexe to the carpentry and mechanics shops, the other provided four additional holes for the golf course.

The subject looks at the object. J. R. D. examines 'Thirty Two Years' shortly after it was presented to him.

THIRTY TWO YEARS

Presented to JAMES RALPH DARLING Headmaster, GEELONG CHURCH of ENGLAND GRAMMAR SCHOOL 1930 — 1961

---

* His many and profound achievements had been recognized with an OBE in 1953 and a CMG in 1958. He was knighted in 1968.

The dining hall crowded for
J. R. D.'s farewell by the Old
Geelong Grammarians, 1961.

Appropriately, the day finished in the dining hall with a production of *King Henry the Fifth*. Appropriately, too, a major item on
exhibition was *Thirty Two Years*, typed on hand-made paper and
with a rich, red, Nigerian goat-skin binding designed by Denny
Evans. After a brief foreword, a poem by Michael Thwaites took
readers back to the halcyon days. The poem began:

> In that keen morning it was good to wake.
> The sun that roused the swans on the lagoon
> And caught the clocktower in his kindly beam
> Made every day a lordlier circuit. Wide
> The sky of our expanding universe.
> The air had tingle. In that heady spring
> Music and drama, art and poetry
> Flowered from the ground, with handicrafts
> and skills
> Buried till then. A pulse and pain of growth
> Set the blood coursing, and the earth
> was young.[20]

Whereas Michael Thwaites had known 'the boss' in that morning
light, the way, despite his warmth, he had grown more aloof because
of the school's complexity, was expressed by M. A. S. Landale, head
prefect of 1961. Landale spoke the formal words of farewell on
behalf of the boys at a dinner to honour the Darlings on the last
night of term. 'To many of us you are a person we know about
rather than know', he said, and added later, somewhat longingly,

In the days of our fathers—and I've heard my father say it—your relation with each
boy was as friend to friend. These were your creative days; they must have been
exciting days.[21]

Multitudes, multitudes, how the
staff had grown by the end of
Darling's thirty-two years.

After receiving gifts from the school and thanking them with his
usual wit and power, the headmaster, with a touch of humour, to
everyone's delight, broke his cane and threw down his mortar board.

[20] *Thirty Two Years*, p. 3
[21] *Corian*, Aug. 1961, p. 116.

10

Tradition under review through Tommy Garnett

The idea of the headmastership as the seat of power and the cutting edge of change in such schools as Geelong Grammar, whose traditions otherwise are often projected as immutable, is a delightful paradox that lifts the heart of the historian from the apparent changelessness of teams, clubs, concerts, plays and the long, smiling, scowling processions of staff and boys. Paradoxical, too, is the thoroughness with which T. R. Garnett, the gentlest headmaster since Bracebridge Wilson, set about the task of transforming Darling's school. Although a classical scholar, he shared Wilson's great love of nature, and there was a flavour of the scientist about the way he bared his emotions to the logic of his mind as he pruned back authoritarian tendencies generated by Brown and consolidated by Darling. The size and complexity of the school made it impossible for a newcomer to stamp it as quickly with his personality as previous headmasters had done, but what was to emerge from the twelve years of his regime was an institution expressing his values. It was less conservative and was more concerned about the feelings and rights of individuals.

Tommy Garnett (he was universally Tommy) came to GGS in 1962 from the headmastership* of Marlborough (the pinnacle of any reasonable ambition), as a result of his firm belief that a headmaster should spend only ten years or so in a school. He was forty-six. Ready for a change, and looking forward also, as an amateur botanist and ornithologist, to new horizons, he provided impossible competition for younger, less-experienced applicants.

He came from a family that was as remarkable over many generations as the Darwins, the Huxleys and the Stephens for breadth of vision, variety of talents and intellectual power. His own experience was of a country boyhood and schooldays at Charterhouse, where his superb batting was long remembered. In one season he made over 1000 runs at an average of 91. He won a scholarship in classics to Magdalene College, Cambridge, in 1933, where he excelled at cricket,

Tommy Garnett at Marlborough

---

* The title was Master of Marlborough.

231

hockey and Eton fives and after graduating with high honours taught briefly at Westminster school and then Charterhouse. In 1939 he played cricket for Somerset. During the war he served in the RAF, becoming a squadron-leader, then returned to Charterhouse where he virtually ran (as his deputy) the headmaster's house, coached the eleven, organized the Natural History Society and developed a school farm. In 1951 he was appointed Master of Marlborough, a great school at which he was much admired for his farsightedness and humanity, and where one of the parents was Frank Woods, later Archbishop of Melbourne and president of the GGS council. When casting about for a successor to Darling, the archbishop wrote to ask Garnett if he knew of anyone who would do. It was a fateful letter.

The presence of Woods was an attraction to Garnett, just as the complexity of the school was a challenge. With its preparatory branches and its mountain outpost, nothing like it existed in England. How would he cope? The council and the retiring headmaster had confidence that this seasoned campaigner had the flexibility to adjust to Australia and the capacity to rejuvenate the school. He was young in spirit and loved the outdoors. With his wife, Penelope, and five children, the eldest of whom was twelve, he had often camped out in Europe and Scotland. He was a universal rather than a national type. The willingness of such a man to come to what was still in some ways a province was flattering to GGS.

What exactly the council expected of him is not clear, but they knew they had a thinker and some were aware that the school was stagnant. He, for his part, was shocked by what he found, though not as much as Darling had been in 1930 and for different reasons. Corio was far from a cultural desert, but Garnett believed that it lagged well behind places like Marlborough in scholarship. Too few boys were self-propelled and there was a large ruck reconciled to failure in the classroom. He felt the same way about that as Lindon and Darling had when they took over. One of his great worries was the inertia of staff who had grown old with Darling.

He found decision-making centred upon himself. Yet, unlike Darling, he did not want to be the expression of all wisdom or the central figure in an oligarchy of housemasters through whom important decisions were filtered. His strength was not in rhetoric and his ideal was a co-operative one in which individuals made decisions appropriate to their level of power, and learnt by the experience. So concerned was he that he read the 1957 Connell report with a growing appreciation for its analysis and a mounting determination to achieve greater administrative devolution.* He persuaded council to have management consultants look at the situation and then gained approval for the appointment of a Master of Corio, who would be in charge of all activities at the main school. His own role thereafter he liked to describe as resembling that of the admiral of a fleet. The Master of

F.Fletcher to J.R.Darling, 12 August 1933.

Extract from pp6-7:

'The cricket season was amusing, mainly owing to T.R.Garnett, who made 1023 runs for the school in 11 completed innings – centuries agst. every school except (alas!) Winchester as well as in 3 or 4 other matches. He then ended the quarter by being equal top of the Sixth. He goes to Magdalene Cambridge as a scholar with leaving exhibitions & a grant from the Tercentenary Fund to see him through. His father has 5 or 6 children & no money; he was in cotton like all the family. But the boy thrives on it; he's one of the very best. His elder brother is on his way Home from Canada on a cattle boat as a Rhodes Scholar from Ontario; he left Pageites early to join his father in Canada'.

(Darling Papers.)

---

* In November 1972 council noted that a remarkable number of the suggestions of the Connell report had been adopted.

Corio was the captain in whose ship he happened to fly his flag and from which he organized his fleet operations, involving overall policy for the separate masterships of Highton, Glamorgan, Timbertop and Corio. Darling's centralized empire, like Britain's, was to become a co-operative commonwealth.

All this was not just an outcome of the headmaster's personality. It was a generational change, expressing social and political concepts that played down the leadership role of the privileged and valued wider access to power. Within the school it meant the rejection of conformities. As he was later to sum it up:

> True education must involve the making of choices, and if the choices are to be real choices some of them will be wrong or at least regarded as wrong. A very important part of education, of the education we aim to revive, is concerned with this making of choices, not the imposition of a brittle mould.[1]

A corollary was the acceptance of responsibility. He looked outwards at the endemic Australian tendency to knock authority, yet keep it to be knocked. Describing the habit as blame avoidance, he noted that Connell's team had been concerned that the concentration of responsibility within the school might breed a reciprocal irresponsibility.

In a community which had waited for the headmaster to give the nod, or had feared his frank rebuke, this new approach was perplexing. Staff felt uncertain about what Garnett wanted, when what he most wanted was for them to take initiatives. He also warned those parents who believed that the way to get things done was to go right to the top, that they would have to look more widely for assistance. At the same time his deafness and his shyness, which were enlarged in many minds to an inability to communicate, became talking points among those who preferred Darling's rhetorical style. Alienated and confused, their ears were half-deaf, their minds partly closed to change. Some felt that he was destroying the school. Among old boys, to whom the position was garbled, and even in the council, there was opposition and distrust. One Western District grazier depicted him (as Darling had originally been perceived by similar men) as a dangerous leftist. Because Darling himself was shocked by what he thought his successor was doing and because he made his concern known, his disappointment also hung like a black cloud over the scene: it was thought at the time that Garnett's proposals for change at Corio were known at the Melbourne Club long before they were general knowledge in the school. Feelings were especially strong after Garnett circulated among staff a book called *The Lanchester Tradition*, which cut close to the bone in exploration of the power of precedent. It was hard to tell whether the action was deliberately hurtful or a brave attempt to make people face a serious situation—in line with Garnett's practice of enlivening members of staff constantly with ideas, articles and suggested reading.

In what was also a generational conflict, the philosophy of *noblesse oblige* and Darling's hope that the products of GGS would purify the

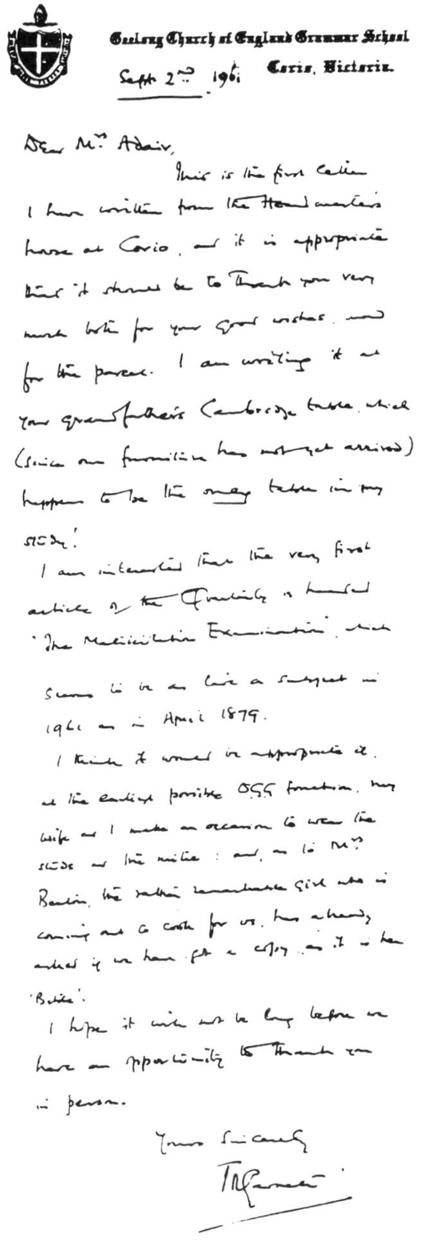
Geelong Church of England Grammar School
Corio, Victoria.
Sept 2nd 1961

Dear Mr Adair,

This is the first letter I have written from the Headmaster's house at Corio, and it is appropriate that it should be to thank you very much both for your good wishes and for the present. I am writing it at your grandfather's Cambridge table, which (since our furniture has not yet arrived) happens to be the only table in my study!

I am interested that the very first article of the Quarterly is headed 'The Matriculation Examination', which seems to be as live a subject in 1961 as in April 1879.

I think it would be appropriate if, at the earliest possible GGS function, my wife and I make an occasion to wear the scarf and the necktie: and, as to Mrs Beattie, the rather remarkable girl who is coming out to cook for us, has already asked if we have got a copy, and it is her 'Bible'.

I hope it will not be long before we have an opportunity to thank you in person.

Yours sincerely

T R Garnett

[1] *Corian*, June 1972, p. 285.

power structures of the nation and give leadership to Australia were replaced by the idea of the creative rebel participating at lower levels in a more thoroughgoing transformation of society.

One starting point for restructuring was the administration. Rather than being tied to the headmaster as *his* assistants, the positions already in place of second master, director of studies and assistant to the headmaster became more specifically defined, with their own distinct, full-time responsibilities and powers. The second master became Master of Corio, with room for initiative and self-fulfilment rarely accorded to deputies. The assistant to the headmaster was restyled Administrator and given a large brief covering enrolments, space allocation and extra-curricular activities. The responsibility of the Director of Studies extended to the co-ordination of the curriculum, development of syllabuses and the oversight of complicated subject choices. Housemasters were less dominant than before.

Garnett took the opportunity to introduce new and young blood at the top of the school by appointing Bill Hayward from Fort Street High School, Sydney, as Master of Corio in 1966. A boy at St Peter's, Adelaide, and a Cambridge arts graduate, Hayward had a Sydney MEd and had taught at The King's School, Parramatta, before making an unusual move out of independent schools to famous Fort Street. Relaxed, urbane, conscientious, clear-headed, he became skilful at interpreting the admiral's plans and putting them into effect at Corio. Alongside as Director of Studies was John Béchervaise, whose patience, hard work, resourcefulness and detachment were legendary. Before an electronic card sorter (invented in 1968 by Richard Maddever) and then computers made the task much easier, Béchervaise endlessly shuffled the pieces of paper that represented boys' interests, expressed as subject choices, and matched them with staff skills and availability (indicated by coloured pins) to produce the first GGS timetables since the early days of Bracebridge Wilson to attempt a separate programme for every individual. Council was given a demonstration of the method in November 1964.

The complicated procedure was necessary because, in 1963, Garnett decided to organize teaching through sets rather than forms, allowing boys to work at their own pace in each subject of the curriculum:

We get many country boys who, by the accident of birth, are a year behind—they have only done Vth grade work. We put them in a low set in the First Form and push them on as fast as they can go.[2]

Bright boys could also be extended; Garnett envisaged many fourth formers being ready a year early for the Leaving Certificate. The reason was social and psychological. It matched his decision to let all boys sit the Leaving examination rather than allow those at the bottom of the stream to label themselves as 'no-hopers':

A boy who is slow at his work and is kept behind his age group is often very conscious of the fact; not unnaturally, he tries to compensate for his feelings of

[2] *Corian*, Dec. 1963, p. 191.

inferiority by throwing his weight about. He so often is the trouble-maker.[3]

Tommy Garnett, Bill Hayward and prefects, 1967.

This was the kind who had just kicked footballs about in Brown's day and who had been the target of Darling's extra-curricular innovations and the members of his agricultural and special sixth forms. Indeed, in the smaller school of the 1930s and 1940s, Darling's timetables had also given a fair range of choice.

The aim of the new system was that its flexibility would make any special groupings unnecessary and any collective stigma therefore impossible. Above all, scholarship was to be strengthened without disadvantaging the less intelligent. But the changes were unsettling, especially to older members of staff. Opponents who remained must have said, 'I told you so', when sets gradually became less important, though Garnett maintained that they had done their work in moving the school away from graded forms.

Similar social concern, as well as declining junior school enrolments, framed another fundamental change. When Garnett learnt that many fifth formers felt insecure after their return from Timbertop and that some of them compensated for it by bullying the third form, ready to hand in the senior boarding-houses, he decided to remove the younger boys to the junior school in a house of their own

[3] *Corian*, Dec. 1933, p. 191.

called Otway*. They worked in portable structures because of uncertainty about the future of the school at Corio. The Geelong Harbour Trust had ambitious plans for the expansion of the port by dredging the lagoon and encouraging industrial development. In response to the threat the council considered alternative sites. Garnett camped at Purrumbete during the 1961 Christmas holidays and talked to members of the Manifold family about the possibility of moving the school to Camperdown where there was a fine stretch of water for rowing. Although, in the end, the power-brokers of Geelong preferred GGS to industry, the short-term uncertainly proved damaging.

The Otway decision, made in Garnett's first term, was not popular. When he also gained council approval for the construction of special accommodation, fifteen to a dormitory, for the newcomers of form 1, it seemed as though the traditional house system was being replaced by age groupings. A widespread feeling that the new man had gone mad and was being sadistically destructive undermined confidence in his judgement and cut him off from a powerful element in the staff. Many felt that they had not been consulted, that the headmaster did not understand the school and had shown poor judgement in re-shuffling staff. It took him five years to repair the damage.

Otway became part of a new academic division called middle school, in which form 1 was also included, although otherwise separate. While forms 2 and 3—as Barrabool, Barwon, Connewarre and Otway—were involved in house competitions, form 1 became a new, self-contained junior house. It was renamed Fraser in 1967 after Doug, who had made so memorable a contribution at that level.

In 1965 Bostock was cut back to form 1 and day boys in forms 2 and 3 joined the middle-school houses. The numbers game was being played with interesting results; principle and pragmatism kissed again. The strong trend for country boys to start later provided an opportunity to give day boys firmer roots in the school.

Although hampered by the split his policies caused among them, Garnett inherited a capable staff. There was no need to cry out, as the young Darling had done, for skilled teachers interested in innovation. As well as experienced masters of the calibre of Béchervaise, Glover, Hutton, Lester, Mappin, Ponder and Westcott there were promising younger men like Covill, Happell, Marles, Murray, Persse, Renney and Ward. But he needed to gain their support; the school was now too big for new appointments to make a great difference, except in specialist areas like music and art or at the separate world of Timbertop. As will be discussed in chapter 12, Garnett was more successful in stimulating music through A. W. Tomalin (1963—70) and Mervyn Callaghan (1966—74) than in sustaining the art school. Timbertop was ready for new ideas and the retirement of 'Monty' in second term 1963 left an important position

---

* They formed middle school, but for two years occupied the old junior dorms in the senior houses.

open. It was filled for over five years by Mike Hanley, a South African with war experience and broad interests who had been teaching at Caulfield Grammar School. Hanley arrived at the beginning of 1963, at the same time as Arthur Mitchell, who had been farming near Mansfield and teaching at Alexandra High School after a long and successful career at Scotch College. Mitchell crowned that by taking over from Hanley in 1969 and serving until 1972. They both helped to raise standards of scholarship without any loss of outdoor challenges, and were assisted by a stream of active men like Glen Bechly, John Bedggood, Ian Collier, Einar Hay and Chris Roberts-Wray.

'Boz' and Barbara Parsons

Size and complexity brought flexibility, evident in the movement of staff between Highton, Glamorgan, Timbertop and Corio, and backed up by a policy that men destined to be housemasters should have had a wider experience (especially at Timbertop) than just at the main school. Life experience also counted. Rapid promotion awaited C. E. R. ('Boz') Parsons who, after his schooldays at Corio ended in 1936, had taken a science degree then served from 1940 to 1946 in the RAAF, to which he returned for four more years after a stint of commercial flying. For ten years after that he farmed in South Australia. He joined the science staff in 1962 and became house master of Manifold in 1965. Among others who came straight into the senior school in the 1960s were John H. Buckley and Adrian Monger. When Graeme Renney, who became Master of Bostock after Bill Cartwright in 1967, moved on to a headmastership in 1971, Garnett appointed as his successor John Herbert, a former rugby international who had come in 1969 from Fettes in Edinburgh. He had spent a year each at Corio and Timbertop.

Don Marles

In general such positions were filled internally. During an extraordinary reshuffle in 1972 Frank Covill became housemaster of Perry, releasing Don Marles (after a year's long-service leave) to become Master of Corio; Brian Coulter was succeeded as Master of Glamorgan by E. V. Butler, Master of Middle School; Ian Collier, the new Master of Middle School, left Cuthbertson House to Chris Roberts-Wray; Tim Murray became the housemaster of Allen (the former Geelong) House and Ian Edwards the warden of newly-created Lindon.

As Darling had, Garnett recruited carefully from England, using personal connections and the public-school network. Some newcomers came briefly through the (later) facetiously named 'rent-a-pom' process by which young men (including, perhaps, Prince Charles) became the equivalents of 'colonial experiencers' of the nineteenth century. Most were filling in profitably the gap between school and university. More significantly, in the final era of easy movement between Australia and the EEC-bound motherland, before the barrier of work permits cut exchange and recruitment, there was an influx of mature Englishmen. Not all became permanent. The *Corian* lamented the departure in 1968 of John Fison, Bill Goldstraw and Chris Goodwin. Only one of the lively migrants of

237

1964—66, Dick Johnson, was left to stand up for English cricket during breakfast and dinner in the Morris Room. Later he was reinforced by Roger More and Jonathan Harvey. The former, who had been a boy at Marlborough under Garnett, had been teaching at Haileybury in England, and the latter, who had spent two terms at Corio in 1969, after a career including a stint at Haileybury and some police experience, returned to become head of mathematics. Peter Henham, a barrister of Lincoln's Inn, stayed eleven years, all but the first of them (1962 at Timbertop) at Corio. As careers master and house tutor, in rowing and through his modern languages teaching, his large figure was highly visible.

Among those who had greatly enriched life at GGS and reached retirement age during this period were the irreplaceable Peter Westcott (1940—69) and the calm but still bright-eyed Brian Coulter (1929—32, 1936—71). Coulter's Mastership of Glamorgan capped a career almost as long as 'Jarps' Morris's forty-one years on the staff. John Glover (1933—69), Rolf Baldwin (1940—71), John Béchervaise (1957—72) and John Barber (1942—72) also retired. The wisdom and flair of Ken Mappin were transplanted to Clyde School when he resigned in 1967 after twenty years on the staff, but he avoided the irony of a possible move back with Clyde to Corio by moving to Scotch in 1969.

Garnett, as scholar and amateur scientist, was appalled by the state of the laboratories and the general level of science teaching. According to a boy from the 1930s who returned in the early 1960s as a member of staff, the provision for physics was atrocious. Nothing had changed since his day. This outweighed for Garnett the force of social conscience that had prevented Darling from seeking federal government funds for new laboratories in his supposedly rich school. It was a time of ferment in the scientific world. The boundaries between the disciplines were breaking down. In biochemistry and nuclear physics, in the first intimations of DNA, in the conquest of space and in new theories about the origins of the universe, the nature of matter and the meaning of life, old orthodoxies were being swept away faster than ever before. So great was the speed of change that the generational gap between the headmasters seemed enormous. From Brown to Darling had by contrast been a simple transition.

A set routine of learning laws and conducting orchestrated and unvarying experiments to demonstrate the neatness and rationality of everything was replaced in the 1960s by new syllabuses whose emphasis was on students finding out for themselves the relationship between experimental observations and less rigid general theories. Flux in the scientific world was accompanied by a new openness in the classroom and a conceptual revolution in mathematics. The 'new maths', introduced at form 1 in 1965, totally confused parents brought up on certainties like $2 + 2 = 4$. Chemistry and biology were in step a pace or two behind.

Garnett would have gone further. He would have liked the new

238

science building to contain a specialist laboratory to attract and stimulate a scientist, like the senior biology master at Marlborough (impossible man though he was) who kept up his research and nurtured an astonishing succession of academic scientists. In the Australian context of a generally low priority for research, he had to be content with separate spaces where keen sixth formers could develop their own projects. The Science Teachers' Association of Victoria had begun to sponsor a series of awards for independent enquiry by schoolchildren, which produced remarkable entries and provided important challenges, to which GGS boys responded with great success. They were stimulated by Richard Maddever, one of the few Doctors of Philosophy teaching in schools at that time. He had followed Garnett to Geelong from Marlborough.

The Darling Hall under construction, 1966. The open space, created by the removal of the Bracebridge Wilson Hall, was called the Darling Quadrangle. At the far end can be seen the Science Wing of 1965.

Tim Murray teaching in the round at the history centre, the old sanitorium, in 1970.

The new science wing, opened by Sir Frederick White, the head of CSIRO, on Old Boys' Day, 27 March 1965, was a cultural achievement equivalent to the building of the music school during Darling's initial burst of activity, and had a significance similar to Wilson's pioneering laboratory of 1879. Appropriately, Sir Frederick spoke of the need to consider science as a culture deserving greater emphasis, especially in Australia, and balancing the humanities. Darling's notion of balance had been to make sure that schoolboy scientists had artistic and literary experiences—not often the other way round. His position was formed in youth when he had found science 'almost an excrescence, a technical achievement, perhaps, for those whose minds were made that way', and was strengthened in later tussles between science and religion, where he continued to see the real issue. He had no enthusiasm for science like his passion for religion, literature and drama and was possibly rationalizing that lack of commitment in finding scruples for not seeking government funds for new science facilities.

In this context there was a kind of generational poetry in the winching across the road on steel rollers of the Bracebridge Wilson Hall, home of drama and debate, to make way within the core of the school's classrooms for large new laboratories that gave the second culture a prominent place. As Sir Frederick White concluded:

The boys at this school have excellent facilities for their studies, for sport, and to enjoy workshop practice, handicrafts, the arts and music. With these new science laboratories, I hope you will be able to stimulate a wide interest in science.[4]

To help the science teachers achieve that goal, the science building, like the art school, had its own reference library. In no part of the school could the speed of change towards a technological society be more clearly seen. Masters were treating concepts, and some boys were using methods and materials, known only at the frontiers of science a few years before. At the same time the classical tradition, which had been given prominence until the early twentieth century, and was later stimulated by the Brice Mackinnon mastership, fell right away. Garnett organized an amendment to the Mackinnon trust deed enabling the title to be given to the head of the language department.

Possibly the physical upgrading of science helped the focus on academic areas which led to the appointment of heads of subjects, with salary loadings similar to those of housemasters, in 1967, and which in subsequent years fostered the consolidation of teaching around specialist resources like the history library which had been founded in 1960. These became more fashionable as individual learning gathered strength. Class sets of a dozen or more books were found essential in subjects like literature, history, geography and social studies as students were challenged to read widely and think for themselves.

The Hawker Library, another key indicator of change, was reorganized in 1963 through the creation of a separate reference section. Numbered according to Dewey and catalogued under subject, title and author it enabled readers to identify relevant material quickly. A larger budget was provided for new books and old ones were made more attractive through culling, labelling and by covering their colourful dustjackets with polyethylene. Even so, it was not until 1967 with Rolf Baldwin as master in charge and Miss M. R. Capon as full-time librarian (a step up from Tom Judd's valuable but necessarily restricted role as curator) that the library was funded at all adequately. The book grant was again increased, further culling took place, pamphlet files were started, regular displays began and shelves of rare books were glassed in. Although still a decade or two behind Scotch and, especially, Melbourne Grammar, the course had been set that led in the 1970s to a fully professional resource centre, within which individual learning would be accelerated.

The general approach was not new. Projects and enquiry had been what excited educationists like George Browne about GGS in the 1930s. Now, though, there was a greater tolerance of individual difference. At the end of the track in Darling's philosophy, concerned though he was to make boys think, there were immutable values and states of mind. Faith and service were paramount, but linked strongly to them was power. He admired those who made things happen. His sermons tended to be about certainties, about commitment leading to action, whereas Garnett embraced the genuineness of doubt. The future for which the here and now was the vehicle was, for Garnett, problematical. He hoped to help boys learn to find a way to find the way.

One boy whose life was largely predetermined was enrolled at GGS in first term 1966, after preliminary discussions with the prime minister, Sir Robert Menzies, who had been in touch with Buckingham Palace. Prince Charles came from Gordonstoun in Scotland and was sent by Garnett to its only Australian equivalent, Timbertop. It was not called Royal Timbertop thereafter, but the kudos of the visit was permanent. The school's status was lifted onto a new plane through patronage far above the 'by appointment' of others supplying services to the royal family. Indeed, true to his motto, 'I serve', the Prince of Wales, a sixth former, was more a staff member than a pupil among the Timbertop fourth formers, one of whom he was privileged to overhear call him a bloody pom.

The visit was extended from one to almost two terms. Charles spent most of the time at Timbertop, but made several visits each term to Corio, where masters supervising his studies for British examinations kept an eye on his progress. Michael Persse, who was his history tutor as well as being, through the *Corian*, an important chronicler and interpreter of the visit, believes that Prince Charles and his family regard the experience as a formative one—the best part of his schooldays.

Protocol and security arrangements threatened a hoped-for in-formality. The press contingent was given a preview on 24 January

... Geelong ...
Church of England Grammar School
Corio

School Lists

1966

SCHOOL LIST—Continued

A/c. No.	Hse.	NAME	Form	Date of Birth
770	Bn.	Brookes, J. W. C.	III	13.10.52
158	M.	Brown, L. J. H.	UVI	16.10.48
203	P.	Brown, M. G.	UVI	22.10.47
925	O.	Brown, N. J.	II	13.5.53
957	O.	Bruce, R. E.	III	15.3.52
T951	T.T.	Buchanan, A. G.	IV	10.2.51
101	M.	Bullock, L. L.	V	15.4.49
156	M.	Burchett, C. W.	V	24.10.49
031	J.	Butler; E. C. V.	I	15.9.54
624	Bl.	Burnell, B. R.	II	16.10.52
306	B.	Burnell, J. N.	V	26.9.50
T736	T.T.	Burnham, G. R.	IV	9.5.50
926	Ot.	Burnside, J. R.	II	13.6.53
803	Co.	Burrows, A. D.	II	25.4.53
804	Co.	Burston, D. G.	II	21.10.53
162	M.	Burston, J. V. T.	V	30.11.48
771	Bn.	Burston, M. J. T.	III	29.9.52
T719	T.T.	Buttner, R. J. A.	IV	15.2.51
032	J.	Cameron, D. J. J.	I	26.2.54
204	P.	Cameron, E. A.	UVI	5.6.48
307	B.	Cameron, G. D.	V	27.6.50
T623	T.T.	Cameron, S. A. R.	IV	15.2.51
402	C.	Cameron, W. St. C.	V	16.4.50
163	M.	Campbell, D. N.	V	23.3.49
T721	T.T.	Campbell, J. A.	IV	29.7.51
430	C.	Campbell, J. T. E.	V	30.9.48
169	M.	Campbell, M. T. A.	VI	26.8.49
161	M.	Campbell, P. N. A.	VI	24.3.48
668	Bl.	Carroll, C. E.	III	10.5.52
448	C.	Carter, G. M.	V	30.1.49
807	Co.	Carter, P. A.	II	4.9.53
T953	T.T.	Carter, W. M.	IV	13.2.51
625	Bl.	Carty, R. N.	II	12.3.53
033	J.	Cawley, B. J.	I	3.10.54
T951	T.T.	Censor, A. J.	IV	3.10.50
T989	T.T.	Chambers, J. F.	IV	15.1.52
308	B.	Chandler, A. A.	V	15.2.50
T785	T.T.	Charles, Prince	VI	14.11.48
927	O.	Charlton, M. S. S.	II	19.1.53
928	O.	Charlton, R. S. S.	II	19.1.53
403	C.	Chen, W.	V	6.3.50
334	B.	Cheong-Chop-Hon	V	28.11.49
717	Bn.	Chirnside, R. A. L.	II	28.7.53
881	Co.	Christensen, P. L.	III	1.1.52
854	Co.	Christie, R. R.	III	30.1.52

10

and on 3 February, the day after his arrival, they spent the morning trailing their quarry, his GGS companion Stuart McGregor and his bodyguards on an inspection of his new home. Five former Timbertop boys showed him the ropes. After that he settled down to participate vigorously, with his minders, in runs, hikes and other outdoor activities. At the same time, across the world, David Manton, who had been chosen from Corio as an exchange for the prince, settled quietly in at Gordonstoun. He was under less pressure, not having to make special arrangements for his studies as Charles did with three visits to Corio in first term. On the first of these visits the press poured in. In a set piece of school sentiment they recorded him meeting Frank Meyrick, Tom Judd and Stan Riddell, who between them had 124 years of service on the domestic and grounds staff. In the May holidays he joined a GGS party on a visit to Papua New Guinea, where his great interest in anthropology was kindled.

During second term Prince Charles, based at Cuthbertson House, was more often at Corio. He left Timbertop finally on Thursday morning, 28 July, read a careful paper that night to the Historical Society at Corio about the ill-fated reign of King Charles I and said goodbye next morning to staff and boys in front of the tower. During a final pause at the art school gates an inlaid stud box of Australian wood, the lid depicting Timbertop, was presented to him by its makers, Peter Jardine and three boys—Richard Haughton, Anthony Chandler and Norman Brien. It was borrowed back for display at Old Boys' Day on the thirtieth and was returned at Essendon Airport by John Davies, the senior prefect, who went with the headmaster on 1 August to see the Prince of Corio and Timbertop fly away.

The connection formed in 1966 bore fruit later. Charles came back in April 1970 to show Timbertop to his sister Anne. As prince, not schoolboy, he arrived in a cavalcade from Mansfield, accompanied by a swarm of press, the usual bodyguards, the headmaster, Mrs Garnett and the Hanleys, Hays, Bedggoods, Roberts-Wrays and Bechlys, who had been at Timbertop in 1966. There was time for morning tea and a brief talk to the boys. Similarly in October 1974, at the end of an Australian tour, Prince Charles had lunch at Corio, 'with unaccustomed cloths and napkins'. He was glad to sit in a big chair—not on one of those 'ghastly benches'—and expressed regret, as others had, that co-education had come too late for him. So that he would not forget the school, he was presented, during the Queen's Jubilee (see p. 299), with a Huon pine stud box. At the same time, so that they would not forget him, some of his fellow Old Geelong Grammarians presented the school with his portrait, painted by Paul Fitzgerald. He invited several of his friends from GGS to his investiture as Prince of Wales in 1969 and his wedding in 1981.

Among innovations in the 1960s which had major long-term consequences was the introduction of Japanese. Bill Lester was midwife at its birth by alerting Garnett to its possibilities. At first there was no specialist teacher. A group of sixth formers, who had already

matriculated, taught themselves with the help of recordings in 1964. It was fun but had only a superficial impact. By contrast, a cumulative effect followed the decision to concentrate on Japanese as the school's Asian language and the appointment of Miss T. Machida from Tokyo to the Bostock staff in January 1969. She stayed for two years and began a major programme. The school had decided to commence unusually early in grade 2. At Glamorgan a few years later under Mrs Inoue the four- and five-year-olds were said to count to ten better in their new language than in their old and to be proficient in courtly bows and formal greetings. By 1974 Japanese was taught at every level at Corio, including a record seven sitting for HSC. No one could have been more pleased than Syd Crawcour, Professor of Japanese at the Australian National University, who as an OGG had blessed the experiments and whose support had strengthened them.

To provide more local self-determination, especially in syllabus and examinations, Geelong Grammar changed over to Class A status in 1969, thus removing the need for students to sit external examinations before year 12. This was 'In keeping with modern educational

Prince Charles with Princess Anne and Arthur Mitchell on the diving-board at the Timbertop dam, during his return visit in 1970.

243

thought', the *Corian* reported, although Corio was years behind most large independent schools in making the move. A richer, wider curriculum and more regular and relevant assessment were the benefits, more paperwork and occasional Education Department inspections were the drawbacks.

Logical extensions of the emphasis on individual responsibility were experiments with student representation and the introduction of voluntary chapel for the senior school. The Student Representative Council (SRC) was heralded as a new and vital organ when it was inaugurated 'to provide a voice for the boys' on 16 June 1964. The voice might 'give opinions, state new ideas and suggest improvements' but was to remain silent if those in charge knocked them back. The school captain was chairman of a council made up of elected representatives from each of the three post-Timbertop years in every house. House captains belonged ex-officio, making a total of twenty-one members, who brought forward motions pressed upon them by their constituents, as well as their own ideas. They lent dignity to their proceedings by addressing each other as 'Mr' and proved their effectiveness during 1964 by having winter study hours changed, by achieving the award of school colours to the holders of Commonwealth scholarships, by having the honour boards in the quadrangle brought up to date and by extending the riding of bicycles to Thursday afternoons. Some motions they passed were knocked back, but not without being taken seriously. They conducted inquiries. At the headmaster's suggestion they discussed the abolition of caps and took a plebiscite which revealed that 200 out of 300 senior school boys had had enough of them. It was only a straw in the wind, however. The headmaster and his advisers were reluctant to have the light blue the first public-school cap to go; yet it was, a year or so later. Heart to heart with each other, SRC members looked beyond grievances and anomalies to the attitudes of their peers. They criticized particularly the lack of intellectual enterprise in the school, religious apathy, the absence of popular music societies and the worship of sport. 'The state of these things is quite deplorable', said the 1964 report of the SRC. While they continued, it added, no boy in the school was receiving an adequate education.

The SRC continued in that vein, chipping away like seamen with blunt tools at the rust on their ship's plates, and getting proverbial answers to proverbial questions about why things could not be done differently. Every now and then a food committee was formed, to put the consumer's view to Stan Riddell, the chef, or (after 1967) to the resident representative of Nationwide caterers, and achieve at least a temporary improvement. Every now and then the issue of exeats was raised, until an acceptable amendment was developed in 1968. By then there was cynicism in the school about the value of the debating shop, which suffered by comparison with the SRCs of universities. The right to criticize was pleasant, but the possibility of achieving changes seemed slight and the need for diplomacy and tact was irksome. To dispel apathy the SRC began to publish its minutes

244

in 1968, but that was no answer. Neither was a constitutional change by which meetings were thrown open to motions from the floor, with the council voting on them like a jury. In 1969 it was dead, 'mercifully', and 'after a prolonged decline in health', said the *Corian*, referring to a spate of trivial and ridiculous motions and poor attendance. Its 'sophisticated reincarnation', the School Committee, a mixture of boys and adults, was hailed as a step forward.

The School Committee, which first met on 13 October 1969, had teeth and was a stronger attempt to offer democratic participation in decision-making. It was only slightly tilted in favour of adults for, apart from the headmaster (chairman ex-officio with a casting vote), there were ten adults and ten students. While the student contingent of two elected representatives from each boarding-house and one from Geelong House, plus the head prefect, was traditional, they were joined by a cross-section of Corio society, mostly nominated by the headmaster. No such group had come together before. It comprised the deputy headmaster, a senior-school housemaster, a middle-school housemaster, the doctor or one of the chaplains, a representative of the maintenance staff, either the bursar, the director of studies or the administrator, a representative of the GGS Women's Guild and two nominated masters. The Hermitage had an observer. Its clout and respectability, as well as a strict agenda, published minutes and regular meetings, gave the committee prestige, while occasional open meetings made it seem accessible. Observers in March 1970 found it rather bogged down in sub-committees on alcohol, charities, clothing, school rules and food, as well as a steering committee.

The boy editor of the *Corian* was concerned on the one hand that the student representatives were simply airing private views and on the other that those in authority could not lose the habit of speaking from a pedestal 'placed under many of them by circumstances'. Yet, to soften frustration, any boy could propose a motion or submit a question. The agenda had three quite separate sections: an initial question time was followed by matters for decision and then expressions of opinion.

In its second year the headmaster (constitution-maker, procedure-definer) withdrew from active participation in the committee to become a non-voting observer, the Master of Corio succeeding him as chairman. The action sums up Garnett's approach—he liked to be facilitator and catalyst, eager for things to go right without him. Standing back a little, he could also make more use of the committee's decisions and opinions, as well as provide an extra dimension through his official contact with the council, parents and old boys. Radical in allowing them to be discussed, he said he wanted to be able to act like a second chamber of parliament over controversial issues. The publicity GGS attracted always worried him. In effect, though, he was an absolute monarch using parliament as a safety valve. Even so, the committee's deliberations produced dozens of reforms, and not just from matters scheduled for decision. Garnett took matters of opinion seriously. In June 1972 two members of the committee

House prayers at Manifold in 1969.

commented that they could find few instances of committee opinion not becoming school policy. Between May 1971 and April 1972 twenty-one matters of opinion and ten of decision had been implemented.

Important discussions had been held on alcohol and voluntary cadets. Drink, which had always been a sensitive matter at the interface between community mores and school policy, and one of the more frequent causes of expulsion throughout the school's history, was placed in a new perspective partly as a result of discussions in the school committee. Typical of Garnett's approach, the new policy on alcohol was set down as a statement of principles, not rules:

The problem of alcohol in contemporary Australian society is a difficult one, and schools cannot escape from it. After considerable discussions, involving members of the School Council, parents, masters, and boys themselves, we have come to the conclusion that the matter is best dealt with by a statement of principles, rather than by a list of rules, some of which might not be applicable in particular circumstances, while others might be unenforceable and therefore bad rules.

What is written below is such a statement of principles, and it rescinds a letter which was sent out in 1967 on the same subject.

1. The responsibility for educating a boy about alcohol must rest primarily with his parents who should make plain to their son and his housemaster what are their views. What can be done at school in this field is limited.

2. Alcohol is a drug, and abuse of it may lead to a psychological and physical dependence. If it is to be used at all—and nothing in this paper must be taken as an encouragement to use alcohol—this characteristic must not be forgotten. Education is given, in various forms, at the School concerning the whole question of drugs of which alcohol is one.

3. At any rate in the State of Victoria, it is illegal for alcohol to be served in a hotel to a boy until he is eighteen. It is unfortunate that it is also at that age that he can obtain a licence to drive a car. Failure to separate the two experiences can be disastrous.

4. What is permissible in a private home, a restaurant, or at a picnic, must be different from what is permissible at a school, particularly a boarding-school. Commonsense demands that, while a boy is at school or travelling to and from school, the possession of alcohol, except in the presence of a responsible adult, must be regarded as a breach of discipline.

5. It is impossible to define precisely the phrase 'a responsible adult'. Broadly, it is a person whom a boy's parents, or his housemaster, acting in loco parentis, judge to be responsible: few boys will be unable themselves to make such a judgement.

6. Bearing in mind what is said about parents' responsibility and the limitations of what can be done at school, we suggest as typical situations in which a boy, if he is to consume alcohol at all, might be permitted to do so:
   (i)   with parents on exeats;
   (ii) lunching with parents on boatrace or sports days;
   (iii) dining in a restaurant with a master after a day or other school outing;
   (iv) dining in adult company with the resident Corio community (e.g. at the Boat Club dinner or in a master's house).

7. It is strongly recommended to parents and staff that the drinks offered to boys on these occasions be limited to beer, wine, and sherry.

8. When a boy is a guest, it is the grossest bad manners for him to bring drinks with him, uninvited; to take any away; or to drink too much.

A breach of the spirit which lies behind these principles is as serious as a breach of the letter of them.

T. R. Garnett, Headmaster
December, 1969.[5]

[5] *Corian*, June 1970, p. 168.

Despite a credibility gap with students and the feeling of some adult members that it had been preoccupied with questions of dress and leave, the committee had justified its existence. While additional sub-committees had been formed to consider Founders Day, wastage prevention and Saturday evening entertainment, the burning issue remained food. Continuing the work of its predecessor, formed by the SRC in 1966, the food committee met regularly with the Master of Corio and the Nationwide representative. It black-listed Brussels sprouts and wanted tomato sauce to be available for almost every dish except Weeties.

In the atmosphere of parliamentary discussion, if not of democracy, there was a strong current of innovation. Voluntary school for the sixth form was seriously considered in 1971 and, central to the new ideology, voluntary chapel attendance for the senior school on Sundays was introduced in the same year. Chapel had been under review in 1968 and in 1969; rather than compulsory matins and evensong, boys were allowed to choose one of three services. The most popular was choral communion at 9.15 a.m. when the new English prayer book, with its more direct language and greater congregational participation, was used. In a spirit growing stronger in the church at large, but still experimental, there was an informal service at 6.30 p.m. with films, talks, discussion and jazz or rock music. Boys brought out guitars and tape-recorders blared. It was not a service at all, according to traditionalists, who filed in at seven for the 1662 prayer book evensong.

The senior chaplain commented that schools were no longer using Christianity to instil morality or esprit de corps. Honesty was demanded when faith had to be presented on its own merits to boys who came mostly from non-church backgrounds. He was encouraged by the freer atmosphere and in 1970 quoted a comment on the 9.15 communion from an old boy who had left five years before: 'I have never known such a wonderful atmosphere in the chapel'. Perhaps this kind of response led to the abolition of compulsory Sunday chapel for senior boys, but just as likely was the concern that only about 75 per cent were participating. Checking attendance across the three services was almost impossible. So, in 1971 the fifth and sixth forms were excused, if they so desired, and a second morning service was introduced. At 10.15 a.m., after the choral communion, a family service was held for unconfirmed members of the middle school and children of the Corio community. Commenting on the change, a master, Jonathan Harvey, expressed surprise that there were few empty pews at 9.15 a.m. and praised the 'act of faith' of the headmaster and chaplain. The atmosphere delighted him.

The innovation inspired Michael Collins Persse to give an overview of religion at GGS. He noticed a far from reactionary responsiveness to religious and intellectual influences from various headmasters, and, although concerned about the loss of a willy-nilly penetration of spiritual experience among those who now stayed away, described the decision as a courageous and trusting one. Although unsure about the voluntary chapel decision, he was whole-hearted about arrangements for Easter 1971, which, being relatively late, was spent for the first time at school, an extra week being added to the May holidays. He found the experiment inspiring, not just in the chapel on Good Friday and Easter Sunday, but throughout the school from the Thursday to the Sunday. Nearly half the staff gave lectures, conducted readings or played music on Friday morning and repeated the sessions so that every boy could go to two. Boys also attended two out of three dramatic productions, including a reading of Clive Sansom's *The Witnesses*, a recording of *Jesus Christ Superstar* and a production by Tim Murray, with middle-school boys, of William Golding's *Lord of the Flies*. *Lord of the Flies* drew most comment. Simon was seen, like Christ, as the scapegoat victim of the group he sought to enlighten. To put the drama in context, Collins Persse pointed back to the nineteenth-century community in which the school was founded, contrasting the faith in human progress and the decency of R. M. Ballantyne's *Coral Island* with Golding's pessimistic twentieth-century allegory.

In that sense Garnett was very much a twentieth-century man. He saw no certainties, had no mission for individuals or the school, except the development of sensitivity and the acquisition of knowledge, including that self-knowledge and awareness of the individuality of others that gave each person the strength to make ethical decisions. For him, God was not an out-there, interfering God, but a still-discovering spirit with whom one ventured into stimulating uncertainties.

THE COMING OF CO-EDUCATION

No uncertainty proved as stimulating at GGS as the introduction of girls into the school. The fulfilment was to come under his successor, but the wedge was placed and struck a ringing first blow by Tommy Garnett, who had been harbouring co-educational ideas for many years. At Marlborough an immense waiting list of boys and house-master control of entry had kept his interest theoretical. Here there was more chance.

With council's blessing, he talked to Mary Coggin, headmistress of The Hermitage and wife of one of his housemasters at Marlborough, about the possibility of Hermitage girls doing their sixth-form maths and science at Corio in 1968 but, failing that, he went on to suggest to council that GGS should enrol its own girls in 1969, beginning with the daughters of staff and the sisters of day boys. This startled The Hermitage into discussions which matured slowly during 1969 and culminated in the adoption for 1970 of the previously suggested co-operation over sixth-form maths and science. The Hermitage was to pay $1000 'for facilities used'—an amount which represented about one-eighth of the fees boys would have been charged.

This sharing of science facilities and teachers had minor precedents among Melbourne schools. It was a one-way traffic,

Feeding the experiment in co-education.

The spearhead of amalgamation, the experimental Hermitage group in 1970 with Mrs Butler, the Master of Corio and the Headmaster.

acknowledging the discrimination over science and maths in favour of boys, which had always run parallel to a community bias against women as doctors, engineers and scientists. It made sense to attack that discrimination by opening the new science laboratories at Corio to senior girls from the sister school. There was overlap between the councils and parents of GGS and The Hermitage as well as a history of co-operation. Combined orchestras had performed since the early 1960s and (for even longer) plays, socials and dances had brought boys and girls together at both school and house levels.

Because distance decreed that the girls would have to spend the day at Corio and join the boys for other subjects, this science arrangement went further than anything that had happened before in such schools in Victoria. On 19 August 1969 Garnett announced the plan, which had already caused a stir among Hermitage parents. A few Latin as well as science students were to be involved and the girls would have a woman to look after them and a 'home' in one of the staff residences. When necessary they would stay at Corio for orchestra and play rehearsals after school. Describing the experiment as one of mutual benefit, the councils expressed the new-found belief that the association of boys and girls of that age in normal everyday life had much to commend it as well as enabling the schools to make better use of resources. The Hermitage was struggling. Its involvement at middle school level since 1963 on the Highton site, with Bostock House and the Marcus Oldham Farm Management College, had helped to solve space problems but had split the school and added a high interest burden. To get hold of the girls, perhaps, the GGS council accepted that The Hermitage would be charged only a token amount.

The arrival of twenty-two matriculation girls at the beginning of first term 1970 made a big impact. Corio was no monastery, but this was a heady change. Women staff were so scarce that Mrs Butler, wife of the Master of Middle School, was put in charge of the welcome strangers. She reported to a meeting of the councils in March that after an initial diffidence the girls had settled in well and were finding the competition stimulating. Sad to relate, one of the hopes of co-education was not fulfilled: the Master of Corio observed that the girls had not proved a noticeable civilizing influence. Some months later he had to suspend three of them.

The joint meeting of the councils to which those reports were made in March was looking at the larger possibilities of combining the schools at various levels. It had before it the recommendations of a combined sub-committee that the schools should amalgamate and go co-educational in all forms except 2, 3 and part of 1. Hermitage girls in forms 4, 5 and 6 would go to Corio and the remainder to a joint establishment at Highton. The chairmen of both councils indicated reservations, which appeared stronger at The Hermitage. There was already a backlash from the sixth-form venture and fear that further experiments might lead to dismemberment and loss of identity. Like swimmers to whom the water seems cold at first, the councils agreed to seek further information from around the world about co-education and to explore the financial situation more thoroughly. Meanwhile they did wade in a considerable distance by deciding that from February 1971 grades 1 to 4 would be combined at Highton and that a decision on total immersion would be made within twelve months. Parents and press were told what was afoot, and the combined councils posed for an historic photograph.

That was as close as they came at that time. The Hermitage council had second thoughts after inspecting the boarding accommodation at Bostock from which extra classrooms were to be made and after a disagreement about parity of fees. In co-education in Australia and New Zealand, said The Hermitage, girls paid much lower fees; in Britain, according to Garnett, there was no difference. Parents and the *Geelong Advertiser* were told that the deal was off until at least 1972. The parties went away licking some wounds. GGS was startled by the possibility that educational consultants engaged by The Hermitage council to sort out all the courses open to it might probe embarrassingly into GGS finances.

The co-education wedge was struck more firmly and confidently in 1972, when, after two years, The Hermitage council withdrew from the sixth-form experiment. It was trying hard to keep the school viable and the gains from the GGS arrangement seemed to be negated by the effect on school life and the school's prestige of the loss of over half the sixth form. For GGS, on the other hand, the sixth form had been strengthened with little effort and co-education had a pleasant taste. So principle and pragmatism embraced again with the announcement that girls would be welcome 'in their own right' in 1972, not as guests from The Hermitage, but taken from the fifth and sixth forms of girls' schools across the country. Eleven came from The Hermitage, which was the most affected, and six from Morongo, while fears that Clyde, where there were strong family links with Corio, would suffer badly, proved groundless. In a total of thirty-three girls, about half were boarders, half day girls, half in the fifth and half in the sixth form. Garnett has denied strongly that the motivation was financial. Uppermost for him was the balance to be added to young lives. However the council noted the admission of girls as one of a number of decisions made at a time of inflation and rural recession, when it was essential that the maximum use should be made of resources. The fifteen girl boarders, incidentally, were absorbed without capital cost through the goodwill of masters' families, in whose homes they slept. They ate in hall and were 'full members' of boys' boarding-houses.

The chance to be the first fully-integrated girls at the most famous boys' school in the country (already given the seal of royal approval through the enrolment of Prince Charles) was taken up eagerly, considering the break involved at such a late stage of secondary education and despite a level of fees parents had not paid for girls before. There was excitement and uncertainty. Circulars sent to those who showed interest explained that no decision had been made about clothing, but that uniformity would apply only to skirts, blouses, jumpers and dresses. The first girls, it was thought, would be pressure enough without worry about clothes. Like the boys, they could wear whatever they chose on Saturdays. Most were overwhelmed by the sporting facilities. Tennis, swimming, sailing, badminton, golf, judo, karate, fencing, squash, basketball, hockey and even cricket and rowing were available. The choice of subjects was wide and the long list of out-of-school activities impressive, even without the suggestion that cooking and flower arrangement (to be offered also to boys) could be added. The excitement of sex bubbled beneath the surface of assurances that, if out after dark, a girl boarder would be escorted 'home' by a boy. Boys would have added to the criteria for selection (giving preference to sisters, daughters of OGGs, country and brotherless girls) a reference to good looks. The headmaster put average intelligences at ease by saying that, although hoping for some, the school did not want only the very clever. He was concerned that the mix should be as natural as possible and was aware of the risk that clever girls would be resented. Old boys were envious. 'In my day', said Professor Rod Andrew, talking of the late 1920s, 'next to a decent feed of course, we missed most the company of women'.

A study of the admission books reveals that the majority of the 130 girls who entered between 1972 and 1974 were from The Hermitage (34) and Morongo (29). Thirteen came from high schools, nine from interstate and eight overseas. Of seven Melbourne schools affected, only St Catherine's, which lost eight girls in the three years, would have noticed the competition.

In summing up his headmastership for the council, two years

later, Garnett included a paragraph on educational issues entitled, 'Head of the Rocket', in which he treated the entry of girls as part of the development of the whole person and asserted that co-education had ceased to be highly emotional. And so it had at Corio, thanks to the matter-of-fact way he had introduced it and the warmth of the school's response. Garnett could announce at his last speech day in 1973 that over seventy girls were already enrolled for 1974. Others were being turned away because the senior school was full. That such a revolution had occurred without bitterness contrasts with the turbulence attached to change in his first years. He felt secure, particularly with the council, to whom he paid a revealing tribute:

There were times early on when I wasn't sure that I was glad that they had appointed me: but their strength supported the school through difficult times (now quite a long way past), and it will support my successor when he goes through something similar, as assuredly he will.[6]

Lindon

The position of the headmaster as innovator and therefore threat, which has been both a strength and weakness of the independent schools, had been particularly painful for Garnett because he followed so famous and powerful a man as Darling. In that sense there is a parallel between Garnett and Lindon, who saw the need to tighten discipline and encourage scholarship after the reign of the first great headmaster, and suffered for it. Looking back at that transition, Garnett felt for Lindon and brought him back into the school's consciousness by naming his next innovation after him.

Lindon answered the charge that independent schools are not innovative by providing separate accommodation and a great deal of self-government for those in their third post-Timbertop year. By withdrawing them, except for games, from their original houses, it also gave more responsibility there to first-year sixth formers and lessened the pastoral burden on housemasters. Consistent with the spirit that lay behind it, the master in charge of Lindon was called warden, and the provision of individual study-bedrooms made it possible to include girls. This daring move was made in 1972, at a time when Melbourne University colleges (where many of Lindon's inhabitants could have been) were just introducing residential co-education. International House was the leader in 1972, then Ormond and Queen's in 1973. Trinity or Janet Clarke Hall, the goal of so many from GGS, seemed light years behind.

The move had practical advantages. As with the advent of girls, or Darling's conception of Timbertop, Garnett's philosophy pointed in the same direction as financial considerations. Fraser House, designed for sixty-four, held only forty-one first formers in 1971 (a fall from fifty-four in 1968) and it was a sensible rationalization to move the youngsters out to space available in a declining middle school and to refurbish the building along the lines of the experimental Perry House study-bedrooms of 1969. Notice the step up the ladder of improved accommodation from Darling's ideal boarding-house,

Lindon, 1972. Ian Edwards, the warden, is in the front row with his assistant Dick Johnson.

the largely dormitoried Francis Brown of the 1930s, to greater privacy at Perry in the 1960s and in the whole of Lindon in the 1970s. The integration of first formers with the rest of middle school was not calamitous; their needs were provided for in separate dormitories and greater continuity was achieved because they had the same housemaster for three years. The juggling of pros and cons was typical of the period. It was argued that as well as being advantageous educationally, the creation of Lindon allowed flexibility. The building could return to its former purpose if entry patterns changed or if the upper sixth idea proved to be a mistake.

Commenting in the *Corian*, Michael Collins Persse noticed the implication of Lindon that human beings should begin to take formal control of their lives at least as early as the final year at school and pointed out that there can be no formula for greatness, whether egalitarianism or the prefect system. That mention of the prefect system is suggestive. Whereas Darling had looked to his second-year sixth formers for the repayment of a debt to the school, Garnett wanted to break their adolescent ties and point them out towards the world.

The advent of girls was linked to other decisions and to an attempt to reduce the number of students for whom a senior house-master was responsible. Failing the availability of funds for another house (which had been attempted in the 1968 appeal) and after much debate, it seemed best to keep day pupils separate from boarders in senior school, despite the success of 'day boarders' in middle-school houses. The old Geelong House continued, although renamed to avoid imprecision now that many pupils were coming from Lara, Werribee, Williamstown and Altona. It was called Allen House after the former chaplain 'Joey' Allen, who had been house-master of Geelong House for many years. In a further recycling of old buildings it was located in a three-sided courtyard behind the medical centre. Symptomatic of the sexual and social revolution that

253

had taken place, girls shared with boys facilities that until the end of World War II had been the quarters of the thirty-seven single men employed around the buildings and grounds. The old Geelong House became a senior-school clubhouse, where boys and girls from all houses could meet.

Fascinated by the spectacle of co-education at what they stereo-typed as the country's most conservative school, newspapers reported the experiment with relish, one even going so far as to inflate a special evening of wine, cheese and drama for Lindon parents and their offspring into the existence of a permanent 'mixed-sex bar'. *Truth* was fed a true story of a mixed showering which, the headmaster pointed out to its inhabitants, was a serious threat to Lindon's continuance. A conservative backlash waited in the wings, but the only pregnancy in Garnett's period was linked to a boy from another school. The mixed-sex situation created occasional dramas. A capricious, unhappy girl threw her arms around startled partners at an internal social, crying for intimacy. A softer girl let two insensitive boys pull down her pants.

Changing attitudes in the outside world were an enormous challenge in this period. Although it moved with the times—boys' hair, for instance, visible in team photographs, reached previously unthinkable lengths in the early 1970s—Geelong Grammar was committed to lasting values. For Brown these had been much more dogmatic than for Darling, for Darling more prescriptive than for Garnett, in whose time the softness and immorality which dismayed Darling in the 1950s seemed to need new approaches. The consumerist Western world was not listening to old tunes.

Yet old methods were still needed when it became apparent during 1972 that drink was flowing into Lindon from the local pub. 'Mr Smith' would phone, requesting delivery at a convenient window, from which, according to the hotel van driver, a pair of dark arms gathered in the loot. No face could be seen. Not wishing to proceed on circumstantial evidence, although there was only one Indian in the house, the warden, Ian Edwards, and the Master of Corio, Bill Hayward, arranged to spend an evening at the pub when the next order was expected. To achieve an arrest, Ian would drive the van back to the school and Bill leap from its interior to help seize the offender. No phone call came, then or later.

To the challenge for personal morality of sexual liberation through the birth-control pill (without which co-educational boarding might not have been a practical policy) and the pressure on international morality of nuclear armaments, were added the corrosive community divisions of the Vietnam war. As the ideals of multiculturalism gained hold, along with increased drug-taking, greater individualism and affluence, society was often in turmoil and at its core parents were splitting up much more frequently than in previous generations. As a caring community GGS was singled out by many for healing from the wounds of broken homes. Although assailed itself by the same forces, it was expected to provide stability.

REINFORCING TRADITION

In the same year, 1972, as girls arrived in their own right, a classroom innovation hit Corio. First formers, displaced from Fraser House, yet kept separate as the 'Fraser Group' in middle school, were organized on the 'open plan'. Their classrooms took on a bustle and excitement that had gripped part of Glamorgan in 1970 and were adopted throughout in 1971. It was a rare case of innovation moving upwards from a prep to Corio, but by no means the first time that vitality at junior levels had influenced Geelong Grammar School. Jennings and Fraser had made sure of that. This move came from Bruce Wicking, housemaster at Glamorgan for ten years, who, with strong support from B. R. A. Coulter, the Master of Glamorgan, had begun the experiments which led, in the Christmas holidays of 1970, to a great noise of carpenters' hammers and the wonderful quiet of carpets. Classrooms were enlarged and sound-proofed.

Bruce Wicking's ideas, expressed in his book, *Let Them Run a Little*, were essentially derivative. As Tommy Garnett pointed out—to reassure conservatives—the open plan was operating in about half the primary schools of Britain. (It was also of long standing at Preshill in Kew and at experimental secondary schools like ERA at Donvale.) Garnett also cited an American free-enterprise prophet, Charles Silberman, editor of *Fortune*, who thought that the plight of US schools, where half the teachers' time was spent on discipline, would be relieved by the sort of thing that was now happening at Glamorgan. It was, of course, a free-enterprise classroom system, giving space to the individual in institutions whose traditional reliance on discipline rather than experiment had always contradicted the basic ideology of capitalist society.

It is noteworthy that an important side-effect at Glamorgan was the welcoming of parents into classrooms as teachers' aides. They came in surprising numbers and they came regularly. 'Each one is different!', was the cry as mothers, who needed no prompting about the individuality of their own children, joined the experience of sharing rather than competition.

Garnett challenged Glamorgan parents to recognize the ineffectiveness of spoon-fed information. It was an echo of Darling's call to the school to use project methods in the 1930s. Like an army commander, seeing the importance of a breakthrough by his leading columns, Garnett put seven critical questions to his audience at the Glamorgan Speech Day in 1970:

B. R. A. Coulter at Glamorgan, 1965.

Can he concentrate on something worthwhile without supervision?
Is he going at the pace—fast or slow—which suits *him*?
Has he maintained his curiosity—his appetite for experience?
Does he know where he can satisfy his curiosity?
Can he communicate in speech and writing?
Does he have scope for creation in music, paint or wood?
Does he understand the basis of what he is doing in Maths (this is the field that causes parents most anxiety because most of them don't)?[7]

[7] *Corian*, June 1971, p. 119.

255

He also asked parents to think about their involvement with their children—how much they played with them, what they talked about and what intellectual and artistic stimuli they provided for them. Tackling a central prejudice against programmes like the open plan, he expressed astonishment at the number of people who believed sincerely that something enjoyed could not be work.

Garnett's belief in getting enjoyment from activity and broadening oneself through a full awareness of others, reinforced the school's humane tradition. Much had been under review in his time but much was strengthened. Even Michael Collins Persse, custodian of the growing archives and heir to the mantle of Cuthbertson, although apprehensive and antagonistic at first, accepted Garnett's changes as expressions of a spirit long present at GGS. The research he had done in 1957 for the centenary pageant, *Their Succeeding Race*, had given him a sense of continuity that put the well-being of the school above particular individuals and short-term arrangements. He had begun to publish in the *Corian* a long series of articles, many his own, on personalities at the school since its inception and could be forgiven the strong scent of the narcissus that blew, as in all schools, among its necessary myths. In the context of the inauguration of Lindon, he also put Garnett into context:

Lindon is both the logical and the chronological end of the long series of surface changes that have marked the Head Mastership of Mr T. R. Garnett, who is to lay down the burden of his office next year. A concomitant change is that to Open Plan methods of study in the First Form, as at Glamorgan. Both changes, and co-education too, are less sudden that they might seem. We have been edging, even striding, in some such direction for many years, perhaps since the School began. They imply certain freedoms and certain opportunities that are among the permanently valid needs of man; and they involve a formal recognition and ratification of certain attitudes, and the provision of an appropriate environment for their expression at the present time, rather than a fundamental shift of thought and practice.

Probably no school has even approximated to the classical boarding-school concept ... If any school has so approximated, it is certainly not Geelong Grammar School, whether at Corio or before that in Geelong. A healthy contempt for petty rules, of form for form's sake, has always characterized us, as have a love of space, air, and light (mental, spiritual, and physical) and a desire for elbow-room that the individual may be himself. This is most patently true of the Wilson and Darling eras in our history: it seems to me true also of the intervening ones, of which the Lindon era comes under scrutiny in this issue of *The Corian* (as the Brown era will in another issue).[8]

The Garnett era, by then, had spoken for itself. Talking about Tommy at Speech Day 1972, when his 6½ years as chairman of the council were ending, Bob Southey summed up his impression of the man he had earlier described as a constant source of inspiration and one to whom you had to be close in order to realize how far he was ahead of you:

And in conclusion I speak of the Head Master himself; and, of all experiences since I joined the Council, I rate highest the satisfaction of getting to know Mr Garnett. He is not the easiest person to get to know, partly because of his deafness, partly

Geelong Grammar School Common Rooms Association

FAREWELL DINNER

For

Thomas Ronald Garnett
M.A. (Cantab.), F.A.C.E.

Head Master 1961 - 1973

18 October 1973

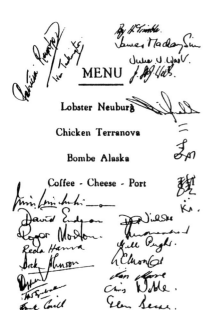

MENU

Lobster Neuburg

Chicken Terranova

Bombe Alaska

Coffee - Cheese - Port

[8] *Corian*, June 1972, p. 268.

because he has to be thinking of a dozen things at once, and partly, I suspect, because for all his deep understanding of psychology and his knowledge of human frailty, he has retained, more than most, intimations of immortality. He has never sought to make popular decisions; but his unpopular decisions have a curious habit of turning out popular in the end. He has incurred criticism for making changes which seemed to call into question well-established values; yet, when these changes have run their course, it is so often found that those values have emerged stronger than ever.

Not all of his decisions, no doubt, have been correct. Headmasters, like leaders in other spheres—war, politics, commerce—often have to take decisions quickly on inadequate facts. The true successful leader is the one who makes the fewest wrong decisions, and who, when a decision is proved wrong, is quick to admit it and to apply correction. In all, I believe that Mr Garnett has taken remarkably few wrong decisions: and those not of great consequence.[9]

Balcombe Griffiths

Other views existed. While those on the staff who were attracted to him and listened to Tommy shared Southey's admiration, many believed with Sir James Darling that Garnett's reforms were too radical for such a complex school and too unsettling in their own complexity. A final assessment is difficult to make, depending as it does on judgements about the state of the school when he took over, the nature and scale of the economic and social pressures to which he responded and the readiness of GGS, as a result of his reforms, to achieve consolidation under his successor. It is instructive that the council, which had been anxious to appoint a scholar after Darling, wanted to replace Garnett with someone who would reduce the uncertainties of his regime.

COUNCIL ACTIVITY

In summing up the Garnett period it is also important to comment that Tommy could have achieved little without the school council, who, after some initial misgivings, wholeheartedly supported him. Guided throughout by their ex-officio president Archbishop (later Sir) Frank Woods, who attended frequently and participated strongly, most of its members were used to sitting in major company boardrooms across Australia and, like their predecessors since the OGG takeover in the early twentieth century, were able to use their influence to obtain funds and gain prestige for the school. Outstanding chairmen in, first, W. Balcombe Griffiths, whose stint of sixteen years ended in 1966, and then Robert Southey, smoothed the path for difficult decisions during that era of challenging social and economic change.

The most worrying trend was a fall in boarding enrolments throughout the country. It had severe effects on a specialist boarding-school. Parallel to an improvement in State high schools and provincial independent schools, the share of the rural sector in national income was falling. At the end of Southey's term of office in 1972, council recognized that 'the precarious financial stability of a boarding school has been a constant anxiety'. Many traditional GGS parents had to rule out or delay sending their children to boarding-schools, especially in the late 1960s when rural incomes fell most rapidly and when, because of inflation, fees escalated.

[9] *Corian*, Apr. 1973, p. 27.

257

Boarding at Bostock and Glamorgan was hardly viable. In October 1967 the council asked the headmaster to visit South-East Asia, whence, it was hoped, more boarders might come.* It had already been advised of the need to defend its share of the market by improving its public relations. Quite apart from the changes Garnett wanted to make on educational grounds, the council was forced by declining enrolments to endorse his restructuring of the first form.

Nothing was so worrying as Bostock House where by 1965 the numbers in years one to seven had reached only eighty-two. An uneconomic fifteen were boarders. Pressures on the system had come most strongly just when the new venture was vulnerable. Plans to build communal facilities, such as a hall, in co-operation with The Hermitage and the Marcus Oldham Farm Management College were only a dream because those institutions were also struggling to become established on the joint site. Yet, although Bostock was not paying its way, the council was aware that the overall loss to the school would increase without the Highton branch. There was a strong inducement to combine with The Hermitage at primary level, or find some other way of reducing overheads. The Geelong middle class was not growing fast in numbers or wealth in contrast, for instance, to the Frankston-Mornington area where Peninsula Grammar School had been successfully established. So efforts to improve the accommodation and integration of day boys might not greatly increase the flowthrough to Corio, where distance and a late return home deterred people who lived on the Bellarine Peninsula.

All these problems were tackled constructively. As in Darling's day the council gave the headmaster room to move by finding the funds for new buildings. Massive injections of capital followed appeals in 1963 and 1968. The former, chaired energetically by Bob Southey, aimed at $150 000, then almost immediately raised the target to $250 000, which was oversubscribed within six months and by 1967 had produced $548 000 of a promised $707 000. Most promises were effective. Only 3 per cent instead of an expected 8 per cent of pledges were failing to mature. At Corio this bought Fraser House, the science block (which drew an additional $80 000 of Commonwealth funds), the Darling Hall and improvements to the staff common room; at Glamorgan, besides various improvements, an adjoining property was purchased and at Timbertop a library and quarters for outside staff were added.

The success of that appeal brought Southey onto the council in 1965 and helped, no doubt, to make him chairman the following year. A great-nephew of Isobel McComas, the founder of Glamorgan, he had been on the Glamorgan Committee for many years and his five sons went through the school. His reputation had always been high. One of that great crop of the early Darling period at GGS, he

---

* Strong connections with several countries of that region, especially Thailand, had been a notable development of the second half of the Darling era. (By the 1980s, heads of six Thai government departments were OGGs.)

had been editor of the *Corian*, a triple exhibitioner at matriculation, had won first-class honours at Oxford, served as a captain in the Coldstream Guards during five years' war service and had returned to a business career in Melbourne, primarily with William Haughton & Co., but later embracing many directorships. Not unexpectedly these connections and his effectiveness led to the chairmanship of the Liberal parties of Victoria in 1966 and Australia in 1970, while he was still (until 1972) chairman at GGS. He was knighted in 1976. His tolerance, breadth of vision and understanding of Garnett provided the school with a confident leadership that was perhaps unprecedented. Wilson and Lindon had had fights with council, Brown's relationship had been uncreatively formal and John Manifold, though a great friend, had often been worried by Darling's demands. The new mood was remarkable, too, for succeeding such an uneasy period, during which council members (particularly Bill Manifold, who resigned in 1965) often opposed Garnett's initiatives. Alongside Southey, Joe (E.O.B.) Grant played almost as big a part as chairman of the executive committee.

A strong indication of support was given in 1968, when an appeal was launched for $600000 to provide a new sanatorium, an extra senior house, a new Barwon boatshed, improvements to the middle school and, although there were already sixty, the perennial extra houses for staff.* John Darling was president and Martin Clemens chairman of the new appeal, which was launched in the presence of one of J. R. Darling's early prefects, John Gorton, the first OGG to be Prime Minister of Australia. With Southey chairman of the most important of the state Liberal parties, Gorton prime minister, and Prince Charles a recent old boy, GGS was riding a strong current of publicity. Even so, gifts did not reach the ambitious target. In May 1970 the chairman of the follow-on committee announced total promises of only $435000. There might have been greater concern if a pleasant financial bonus had not floated in a little earlier. In 1967 the Shell Company paid GGS $310000 for 47 hectares of land (not to be used industrially) across Woodstock Avenue, then being developed as a main feeder road from the highway to North Shore, Geelong.

The value of the Corio site was so high that for a time in the 1960s especially under the threat from the harbour trust, the council was tempted to move away. That consideration of alternative locations indicated how strongly its earlier isolation had been built into the school's ethos. The generation who had begun the GGS tradition on the Moorabool Street hill would have been puzzled by the insecurity of the late twentieth century, when their inheritors felt threatened despite the buffer of hundreds of hectares of land and a relatively quiet seafront. In 1968, although firm in the view that the amenity value at Corio was higher than the monetary, the council talked

Bob Southey, keeping the building appeal on the boil, 1963.

The fun of the fair, 1970.

---

* Garnett enunciated the principle that a new home should be built each year to keep pace with redundancy as well as expansion.

The school from the air, *c.* 1960.

anxiously to the Corio Shire and the Geelong Harbour Trust about long-term plans for industry and shipping. A few years earlier, when Victoria's third university was in prospect, they tried to convince a committee seeking its establishment in Geelong that a tertiary institution would be a welcome neighbour north of the lagoon. Any unsympathetic development of Avalon would be as disastrous as large-scale 'improvement' of the lagoon, which was already full of moored yachts. Despite Dick Austin's generous transfer to the school in 1963 of an extensive buffer of 104 hectares, a further subdivision of parts of Avalon into 20-hectare farmlets in 1968 raised the issue again. Assuming a long-term future on the site, the best course of action seemed to be the reservation of the lagoon area for natural history research.

To ensure the school's institutional viability the council in this period secured its incorporation. As a large business, with an annual turnover of several million dollars, borrowing, lending and dealing in land and machinery, it needed a precise legal entity. On 17 October 1972 a special council meeting approved articles of association, already agreed to by the archbishop in council, giving the school more freedom to run its own affairs. The galaxy who officially subscribed the articles were the archbishop, Sir James Darling and the successive chairmen, W. B. Griffiths, R. J. Southey and R. B. Ritchie (chairman-elect). The way had been prepared by the administrative rationalization which began early in Garnett's headmastership. As we have already seen (p. 232), his concern had sparked a series of reports from Associated Industrial Consultants, who had looked at the support for the headmaster and bursar. Similarly a council sub-committee had recommended an overdue amalgamation of the accounts of the four parts of the school.

As a far cry from the simplicity of Brown's regime, when the headmaster and bursar represented 'administration', there was an administrative staff of seventeen in 1972, when an Old Geelong Grammarian, Jim Winchester, succeeded Peter Desborough as bursar. He had been senior prefect, an outstanding chorister and captain of football in 1947. Typifying the greater complexity, even since Darling's day, the accountant was described as operating like a virtuoso pianist on a brand-new Burroughs L4000 Billing Computer with 80-column punched card input. It occupied the focal point of what was irreverently known as the Parkinson's Wing of the Perry Quad, where the bursar and his secretary, the accountant and his staff, the director of studies, administrator and Master of Corio with their secretaries, and the Old Geelong Grammarians' administration, had taken over space once occupied by classrooms.

In the same vein, in 1965 council procedures were streamlined by the creation of an executive and finance committee, modelled on arrangements at Melbourne Grammar School. Consisting of between six and ten members from a fifteen-member council, it acted as a steering committee and met eight times a year in Melbourne, where most members worked. Full council meetings, at Corio, were reduced to four per year, with more defined issues and more focussed debate. In addition, council sported a further ten sub-committees by 1969. The most important of these was concerned with salaries and super-annuation, which were, as always, critical in attracting and keeping staff. Just as Darling had found it necessary to improve Brown's salaries and conditions, especially with regard to housing, so Garnett, in the more competitive 1960s, pressed for higher pay, more security and still more houses. He regarded the establishment of proper conditions of service as one of his main achievements. In the early 1960s representatives of the Common Room Association bargained about salaries with a council committee. Then in 1966 a special salaries advisory committee was formed, consisting of the chairman and one other council member, the headmaster and a member of staff.

Whereas in 1962 the council-dominated committee had refused to guarantee automatic salary adjustments in keeping with those paid by the pace-setting State Education Department, its successor, though not bound to them, advocated conformity. Accommodation, if not a right, was to be provided, where available, for the better performance of duties. Because it was assumed to be compensation for extra involve-ment in the life of a boarding-school, a living-out allowance was to be paid in lieu of accommodation. Masters' sons would be educated for one-quarter of fees and half fees would be paid for their daughters enrolled at The Hermitage. No reference was made to female staff. His part as chairman of the Common Room Association in the complex and successful negotiations was Ken Mappin's farewell gift to his colleagues.

With the special loadings and, sometimes, entertainment allow-ances, paid-for responsibilities such as being Master of Corio, Timbertop, Middle School, Glamorgan or Bostock, Director of Studies, Administrator, a housemaster or (after 1966) head of a subject, there was something of a career structure within the school. In most positions, however, a great deal of work was expected. For the loads carried the remuneration was not, in fact, comparable to that in the State system, and Garnett issued warnings from time to time about the dangers of expecting too much of staff and allowing classes to become too large. He pointed to family difficulties associated with a long stay at Timbertop, where he expected anyone likely to become a senior housemaster to have had experience, and kept up a refrain about staffing pressures resulting from the school's compara-tively small size, non-selective entry and boarding emphasis. While wanting staff salaries hitched to the Education Department cart, he urged that staff levels should be related to those in English boarding-schools, and took the trouble in 1967 to bombard council with statistics (a whole book of them) showing that GGS was not, as some might think, extravagantly staffed. At his urging council tried to organize the school to bring the load of a senior housemaster down to fifty boys.

11

Takeovers and mergers—Charles Fisher and co-education

Charles Fisher

Corio, *c.* 1970.

Tommy Garnett's decision to retire at the end of 1973—to the beautiful garden Penelope and he were claiming from the bush at Blackwood—led to another search across the world for a headmaster. This time, although an Englishman, he was found in Australia, where he had been headmaster first at Scotch College, Adelaide, from 1962 to 1969, and then at the Church of England Grammar School, Brisbane. He was Charles Douglas Fisher, born in 1921, the third son of Geoffrey Fisher, J. R. Darling's second headmaster at Repton, who was Archbishop of Canterbury from 1945 to 1961.

Educated at Marlborough and having served from 1941 to 1945, with the final rank of captain, in the Royal Artillery, Charles Fisher read chemistry at Oxford, where he represented Keble College at rowing and rugby and was president of the junior common room. For seven years he taught at Harrow, then at Peterhouse in Rhodesia and at Sherborne. He had made a Rhodesian connection in 1952, when he married Anne Hammond, who contributed immensely at GGS and, after her husband's death, became secretary-companion to Lady Cowen, wife of the governor-general. The Fishers had two daughters and four sons.

Besides his family, Fisher brought an interest in organization to Corio, and a habit of mind that was in tune with Garnett's changes. Round-faced and strongly built, sharp, poised and businesslike, but warm and understanding, he had the qualities of a good managing director, well able to inaugurate full-scale co-education at GGS. For although he would probably not have initiated such a policy (he came as a sceptic), Fisher was quick to appreciate the new dimensions it gave. Once convinced, he used his special talent for public relations to promote what was happening at GGS as a great educational experiment.

The metaphor of the wedge, used to describe the initiation of co-education under Garnett, is inappropriate for its extension under his successor, but the idea of a splitting open of tradition to allow possibilities not considered before is essential to an understanding of

262

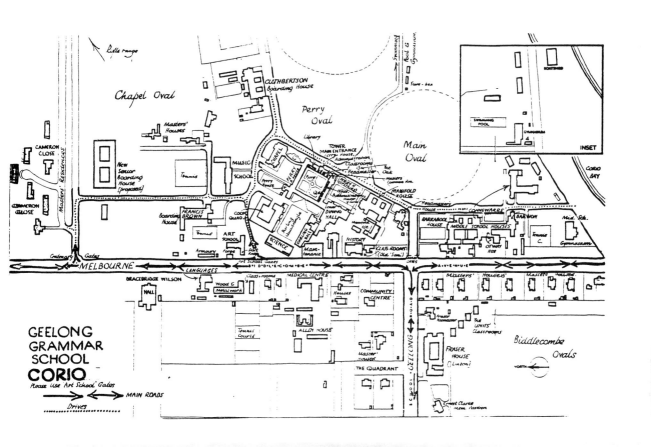

Rifle range

Chapel Oval

CLUTHBERTSON
Boarding House

Perry Oval

Main Oval

INSET

CORIO
BAY

CAMERON
CLOSE

Masters' Houses

New Senior
Boarding House
(proposed)

MUSIC
SCHOOL

Library

TOWER
MAIN ENTRANCE
Administration
Classrooms
Headmaster

The Oak

Masters'
Common Rm.

MANIFOLD
HOUSE

SWIMMING
POOL

CAMERON
CLOSE

Masters' Residences

Tennis

CHAPEL

PERRY HALL

Perry House

Office
Administration

BARRABOOL
HOUSE

CONNEWARRE

BARWON

Mid. Sch.

FRANCIS
BROWN

Boarding
House

COOK'S
QUAD.

Lower
DINING HALL

Headmasters'
House

MIDDLE SCHOOL HOUSES

Tennis
C.

Gymnasium

Tennis

ART
SCHOOL

SCIENCE

Main-
tenance

HISTORY

OTWAY
HSE

CLASS-ROOMS
('Old Tom')

Armoury

Forge

Art School Gates

B'DDLECOMBE

Gates

AVENUE

Centenary Gates

MELBOURNE

LANGUAGES

Class-rooms

BRACEBRIDGE WILSON

WALL

Wood &
Metalwork

Class-rooms

MEDICAL CENTRE

HOUSES

COMMUNITY
CENTRE

Masters'

Houses

Masters' Houses

Fraser
Headmaster

The UNITS
Classrooms

GEELONG
GRAMMAR
SCHOOL
CORIO

Please Use 'Art School' Gates

Tennis
Courts

ALLEN HOUSE

Masters
House

FRASER
HOUSE
(Linton)

Biddlecombe
Ovals

NORTH

SCHOOL

ROAD

GEELONG

MAIN ROADS

Drives

THE QUADRANT

Rust Clarke
Mem. Classroom

New head for top school

GEELONG Grammar, a leading Victorian boys' school has announced that Mr Charles Douglas Fisher will succeed Mr T. R. Garnett as headmaster when he retires at the end of next year after 12 years as principal.

Mr Fisher, 51, is headmaster of the Brisbane Church of England Grammar School and was formerly headmaster of Scotch College, Adelaide.

CHURCH OF ENGLAND GRAMMAR SCHOOL
OAKLANDS PARADE, EAST BRISBANE, Q. 4169
Telephone: 913751

27 · x · 7²

Dear Mr Judd,

How kind of you to write. I very much appreciated getting your letter.

I feel sure I shall have the pleasure of meeting you in 1974 even though no longer on active duty.

With my best orders,

Yours sincerely,

Charles Fisher

what happened. A token group of girls, a mere 70 in a senior school of 350 in 1974, was educationally undesirable. The council and the new headmaster recognized that something dramatic had to be done to achieve a better balance between the sexes. Members of staff were uncertain. After a two hour discussion late in Fisher's first term, their vote was split. The head told them that as they had given him no clear direction, he would advise council to go ahead with full co-education. So formal talks began in 1974 with the headmistress, Alice Pringle, and the council of Clyde School, Woodend, about the possibility of amalgamation.

Clyde was a natural partner. Founded in 1910 at St Kilda, it had moved to *Picnic at Hanging Rock* country as a specialist secondary boarding-school in 1919. In 1962, even though the Melbourne commuter zone had extended, it included only 10 per cent of day girls. Like GGS it had had fine leadership, originally from Isobel Henderson, later from Olga Hay, and during the 1960s from Joan Montgomery, who went to PLC in 1969, just as the rural recession cut numbers. Clyde's council came from the same social group as its counterpart at GGS; in the 1960s it included Dame Elisabeth Murdoch, Essington Lewis, Stephen and Roger Kimpton, Humphrey Champion de Crespigny and his wife Mary. In 1974 Sandford Nevile, a businessman and grazier, supported by Neil Walford, head of Repco, was chairman.

Following a disastrous year for enrolments in 1969, Clyde was hit heavily by inflation in the early 1970s. The figures were all red when put on the council table in September 1970. A deficit of $90 000 was anticipated for 1971 and because enrolments were running fifteen below the break-even point of 136 boarders and fifteen day girls, drastic action was needed. The old girls promised to help, the chief executives of large corporations were asked to identify possible pupils and Australian and foreign embassies were canvassed. Council members posted out an advertising brochure, and newspaper and magazine publicity was sought. Reluctantly fees were increased slightly, the school hoping for the option of greater enrolments. These did not come, but salaries leapt. So economies were made by dismissing staff and pruning the administration. When rumours flew about that the school was about to close, a counter-offensive was launched. Publicity was achieved through the ABC's 'This Day Tonight', and magazines like *Woman's Day* and *Home Beautiful*. A futile attempt was made to enrol day *boys* in forms 1 and 2.

The enrolment drive having failed, a loss of $80 000 was predicted for 1972 unless fees were raised by 23 per cent. Boarders in form 1 were to pay $715 per term and forms 2 to 6 $765. That seemed to bring stability, especially when state and commonwealth grants were greatly increased. But the situation deteriorated again in 1974. Fees were pushed to $1150 for senior boarders and $420 for day girls (more than double the 1971 rate) yet a loss of $68 000 was projected for 1975. It was time to do more than milk sentimental attachments to the school. The council looked at possible amalgamations.

264

The ground was well prepared for a close association with GGS. Both were predominantly boarding schools and had a similar clientele. In 1969 and 1970, when GGS stayed at school for Easter, Clyde followed suit. In 1971, at the first crisis, the headmistress initiated talks with the headmasters of Geelong and Essendon Grammars 'to seek areas of co-operation to fully utilize school facilities'. At Clyde German, economics, physics and chemistry were already studied by correspondence through the Department of Education. In 1972 unofficial approaches about co-operation were made to Melbourne and Geelong Grammars. This drew a positive response from Tommy Garnett, who said that if the 1972 experiment with co-education at Corio was successful he would like to assist.

So a formal dance began, the potential partners being aware of a mutual attraction. The council of the boys' school made the initial approach. Would Clyde be interested in amalgamation, its chairman, Robin Ritchie, asked in February 1974, or alternatively give places to GGS girls in forms 1 to 4? We might amalgamate, came the reply, but preserving our maiden name and only after long and serious negotiations. There was doubt at Clyde about the strength and sincerity of co-ed at GGS. Coquettishly, the Clyde council sounded out Scotch and PLC as alternative partners, but when they were reluctant to take the floor the thought of standing alone beside the ugly deficit projected for 1975 threw them into strong and friendly light-blue arms. Between 10 and 26 February 1975 a subcommittee, looking at the alternatives, received a further approach from the south and smiled on it.

Corio was eager. Ritchie, anxious about long-term viability, urged his colleagues to look ahead. At the beginning of 1974 there was a thorough review, later published as a booklet called *The School for the 1980s*, of where they were and where they wanted to go:

The Council, for the first time for this or any other Council as far as I know, made a statement about the aims of the School.[1]

From that base 'strategic decisions' and 'tactical choices' were outlined. Above all, greater size was contemplated. Ritchie saw the need to spread costs more widely. The school's educational aims precluded the alternatives of lowering drastically the staff—student ratio or reducing the commitment to out-of-school activities and pastoral care. He saw that they were stuck with a twelve-hour day.

In the circumstances, and with inflation running at 20 per cent, Geelong Grammar sensed the possibility of a fortuitous double marriage with The Hermitage as well as Clyde. The school's own enrolment of girls had slackened alarmingly. Because The Hermitage, which had thought of amalgamation earlier, was in grave financial trouble, a decision from Clyde might swing a further deal. So GGS emerged from the Clyde courtship early in March to tell The Hermitage that as Clyde was coming in, it should hurry or miss out. At the same time Clyde, which did not decide until 11 March, was

Geelong Church of England Grammar School

THE SCHOOL FOR THE 1980's

THE SCHOOL FOR THE 1980'S

The School must serve contemporary society.

A vital school will change in form and organisation from time to time but the essence and quality of the education derived over the years can be retained and enhanced.

Enrolment patterns deriving from new policy initiatives in recent years require that decisions about form and organisation be taken now.

Policy can properly be derived only from a statement of objectives: the following General Statement of Intention has been adopted by the School Council and provides the basis for policy decisions.

3.

[1] *Corian*, June 1975, pp. 294−6.

told of the almost certain inclusion of The Hermitage—even though, as we will see, The Hermitage did not decide in principle until 17 March. It seems that behind the scenes sub-committees of business-men were making business deals which the full councils would be persuaded to confirm.

Work began at GGS on a brochure, *Three Great Schools Make History*, while details of the Clyde treaty were hammered out. The main provisions were for the proceeds of the sale of Clyde to be used to build Clyde House, plus two tennis courts, and defray one-third of the cost of eight new classrooms. In an innovative plan for the new boarding-house, units each containing sixteen study-bedrooms were to be attached to an administrative core, including an assembly room where the school's honour-board would have pride of place. GGS agreed to accept all current and prospective pupils, dressed in Clyde uniforms until they were worn out;* it offered the headmistress a senior post with specific responsibility for Clyde in transition and began negotiations with four members of the teaching staff, only one of whom, Gemette Reid, accepted the offer to transfer. The Clyde curriculum was to be continued pro-tem and scholarships and sporting activities were to be maintained. Yet, although the Clyde family seemed to have accepted the inevitable, there was some loss of pupils. After a dispersion of others to Lindon, Timbertop and middle school, Clyde changed from a school of 140 to a house of 70.

Out of a special gathering of Clyde parents and old girls on 4 May 1975 further matters were raised for discussion with GGS. For instance, bursaries were granted to day girls, after a proposal for a bus from Gisborne was not considered practicable. Much of the old furniture, being inappropriate in the new house, was offered for sale to old girls as a means of preserving memories of the dismantled school. It was argued that the Isobel Henderson Library should be kept intact within the GGS library, but as that was not practicable all the books were embellished with a special bookplate and the reference works put in Clyde House. An early hope that three members of the Clyde council might transfer to GGS was ruled out on constitutional grounds. Only the chairman, Sandford Nevile, was taken aboard.

These details being cleared up, the Clyde council held its final meeting on 10 December 1975, with one important item of business incomplete. Efforts to sell the school had failed. Neither the state nor commonwealth government, as had been hoped, was interested. For the time being the premises were let to the new Braemar school for $10 000 per annum—a poor return on a valuation of $700 000. That hoped-for dowry of $700 000 did not eventuate. In the end Braemar paid only $420 000, which did not cover the expense incurred at GGS in accommodating Clyde.

As suggested already, Clyde's decision put pressure on The

---

* Ball and Welch, an ailing Melbourne store, protested at the possibility of being left with racks of unsaleable Clyde uniforms.

Hermitage, which had been trying to go it alone since withdrawing from the sixth-form deal at the end of 1971. Even before that the possibilities of amalgamation had been discussed. In March 1970 the two councils had agreed to exchange financial information, introduce co-education in grades 1 to 4 at Highton in 1971 and make a decision on a merger within twelve months. To help it decide, The Hermitage council engaged the Sydney consultants, Knight, Howard and Associates, to investigate both amalgamation and the preferred possibility of survival as a separate entity at Highton. Restricted space, antiquated buildings and deficient plant at the main site in Newtown made a new start imperative. At this juncture the failure of GGS to supply financial statements, as agreed, angered The Hermitage council. They could not work out the implications of amalgamation, or even a joint primary venture, without knowing relative costs. They suspected what indeed emerged, that Bostock House was run at what they regarded as an extravagant level. So in June 1970, scorning GGS, they decided to move the whole school by stages to Highton.

Nevertheless, during 1971 there was an exchange of letters between The Hermitage chairman, Archdeacon John Gason (who was also on the GGS council), and the GGS headmaster, Tommy Garnett, about plans to achieve at least a co-operative venture for primary grades 1 to 6 at Highton. Although both schools were in favour of some arrangement, these letters revealed huge anomalies between staffing and amenities in boys' and girls' schools and in the level of fees. If the joint venture was to be along GGS lines, Hermitage fees would have to rise unacceptably. If Hermitage fees were to be the basis of funding, Bostock staff would lose benefits and prestige. The figures showed that at primary level GGS boys each cost an average $1028 per annum and Hermitage girls only $581. A paper prepared in November 1971 for The Hermitage council declared that this difference in 'standard of living' made a combined primary operation unrealistic.

The Hermitage was proud that it was run on a shoe-string and, facing the future defiantly, clung to all its students, including the experimental twenty-two sixth formers who had spent the year at Corio. For fund-raising every parent was vital. In a school of 410 the loss of 100 to a combined school would have been disastrous. They were facing a bill of $520 000 for new buildings.

Brave talk could not get the school out of the hole it had dug for itself by moving to Highton. Instead of rising with the move, numbers continued to decrease. From 408 in 1971 they fell to 386 in 1974. With the ANZ Bank looking sourly at its loan arrangements, The Hermitage council was startled to find that GGS was considering primary co-education by itself at Bostock in 1973. A strong protest was made to the Archbishop of Melbourne, who was president, ex officio, of both councils. The threat was removed. In October 1973, however, the archbishop's mitre could not spike the decision of Geelong College to admit girls. College, having also lost boarders, was glad to imitate GGS and could offer many advantages to girls living in central Geelong who were inconvenienced by The Hermitage's move to the paddocks beyond Highton. It had extensive grounds and superior facilities for science, craft and music.

There was one bright spot for The Hermitage. In 1973 an old girl, Hazel Dauncey, left the school a marvellous nest-egg of $477 000. It probably helped to stiffen resistance to the erosion of pupils by Geelong College and Geelong Grammar, and put courage into the voice of the headmistress, Elizabeth Britten, when she reported to council on 5 June 1974 about the pros and cons of co-education. Her response to the nagging problem of declining numbers was to stress quality. Her reply to arguments that co-education was healthier was the quip that, if so, it was amazing that so many had been wrong for so long and had now got smart so fast. She stressed the difference between men and women and the need to nurture separately the compassionate, practical qualities of women so that they could go into the male-dominated community with confidence in their special talents.

Confidence in the school was another matter. A few months later, and less than a fortnight after The Hermitage resolved not to consider co-education but to bolster science and prepare a pamphlet on the virtues of single-sex schools, its finance committee revealed an estimated deficit of $40 000 for the year and projected a much gloomier result for 1975. The interest from the Dauncey estate was not enough to cover the shortfall; capital would have to be spent. In a situation of falling numbers this was disastrous.

As nothing else had, the gloomy prospect of making ends meet only by rapidly reducing their nest-egg, softened the council for another approach from GGS. Robin Ritchie, the new chairman at GGS, approached members of The Hermitage council in February 1975, telling them of Clyde's interest and offering terms. On 5 March the offer was reported to a full council and on 17 March Ritchie addressed an agonizing special meeting which lasted for four hours and which decided to give amalgamation favourable consideration. They were being hustled and some felt inadequate as a provincial Geelong group faced with the metropolitan clout of the Geelong Grammar council. Ritchie hoped for the basis of a merger decided within a month and operations to begin in 1976. Key issues were security for staff and a five-year period of transition from the girls' to the boys' level of fees. The official announcement was made late in April. Between May and August 1975 details were tidied up, including the provision of an array of Dauncey scholarships, the re-erection at Highton (as already planned) of memorial gates to Elsie Morres, the great first headmistress (1906–32), and preservation of The Hermitage flag in a glass case at Corio—no doubt as a reminder of obligations rather than as the spoils of war. To tell the world of their union, the brochure, *Three Great Schools Make History*, was published.

Throughout August 1975 John Herbert, the Master of Highton,

was busy with the ensuing diplomacy. He wrote to Hermitage parents and friends and arranged a cheese-and-wine party for anyone who was interested to get to know the new headmaster as well as the old headmistress and the probable staff members for 1976. A brochure, *Highton 1976*, carefully balancing pictures of boys and girls at the new site, was available at the offices of both schools. Six parents offered to conduct parents of prospective pupils around the school and in September and October there were open mornings.

The public at large was informed by newspaper advertisements of the new situation. Gossip flashed around Geelong about individual decisions and about the astonishing rearrangement that had taken place so quickly in three of Geelong's major Protestant schools. Morongo, the Presbyterian girls' school, was left alone among them flying the single-sex flag. Leakage from The Hermitage was strongest to Geelong College, not to Morongo, so it seems that co-education was generally acceptable. Miss Britten, at her final speech day, said that it had become clear that a number of parents were planning this extra dimension for their daughters. Of 277 Hermitage girls intending to continue school in 1976, 210 stayed with the new venture, 55 went to Geelong College and 12 to other schools. In forms 2 and 5 the proportion going to the College was 37 per cent, compared with 20 per cent overall; sisters could join brothers at the one school and avoid the late stay expected of day pupils at Corio.

In moving towards ratification of the draft amalgamation during October 1975 and at its final meeting, the Hermitage council expressed concern about certain easy-going attitudes of their partner and resolved that the present high standard of uniform *must* be maintained. That was not quite their last act: they had to stay alive until June 1976 in order to tie off the Dauncey estate. Indicating how serious their financial plight had been, they had to transfer $50 000 from capital to meet the deficit on 1975 operations. Even so, the reluctant bride brought a fine dowry to the marriage, which was officially recognized soon afterwards by an Act of Parliament. One Hermitage council member, J. F. Strachan, joined S. S. Nevile from Clyde on the takeover board. Typical of the less satisfactory terms obtained by The Hermitage, Elizabeth Britten* had a senior but unspecified position in the new venture. She stayed for a year to assist with the transfer, then took a break and was later appointed headmistress at Shelford Girls' Grammar School in Melbourne. Alice Pringle stayed two years at Clyde House. After that she was due to retire.

Involved as he was with the council as chief executive, Charles Fisher had played an important part in the negotiations over amalgamation, but when they were complete his major task began—to accommodate and organize a much larger and even more complex school. The headaches were innumerable, but Don Marles, who had been an impressive housemaster of Perry, and who had taken over as Master of Corio in January 1973, accepted many of the burdens.

---

* Her father, Mervyn Britten, had been chaplain and later a council member at GGS.

Even so, it was Fisher's confidence and energy that set doubters' minds at rest and his goodwill that snared troubles even before they began to run. As one parent discovered, he spent the first night of first term 1976 making newcomers feel at home:

> First of all was the night that all the new boys and girls arrived at Corio for the very first time. Cassie was in bed in the girls' dorm in the Middle School and Charles came in and sat on the edge of each of those children's beds and had a chat to them before they went to sleep. I later found out that not only did he talk to each of the little girls who had arrived for their first day at boarding-school, but he went right around the whole school, sat on every bed, and spoke to every boy and girl who had started at school that day.[2]

As he stood with the headmaster outside his house one Sunday night later in the year, when the boys and girls of Middle School and Jennings House were passing on their way to supper, the same parent observed the continuation of that relationship.

> I was amazed to hear Charles speak to every single child and call them by their first name—a feat that I have never seen a Head Master of Geelong Grammar do before. When I congratulated him on his ability to do this with all the boys and girls, he just laughed it off as part of his job.[3]

Whereas Darling in his later years had distanced himself from the general run of students because of his busy life, and Garnett had remained aloof through shyness and the habit of intellectualizing, Fisher captured their loyalty. His friendliness and concern were the stone that completed the arch of goodwill in the school and helped things to happen that Garnett had hoped for but had not been able to achieve.

The added complexity of co-education tested the stronger administrative structures now in place at Corio, through which the GGS empire was organized. The smoothness of the changeover to full co-education in 1976 was gratifying because it represented the efficient handling of many sensitive issues and innumerable details. The administrative objective was support rather than control. After Garnett's restructuring, the school was tuned to foster freedom and initiative in classrooms, houses and leisure activities. Although complex and bewildering to newcomers, it was caring and friendly.

At the top, though, it remained male-dominated. Few senior women were available as role models for girls. Apart from Alice Pringle in Clyde and Elizabeth Britten in her somewhat vague position, men decided almost everything. Pre-amalgamation there were five women on a staff of fifty at Corio; immediately afterwards there were ten among fifty-eight. It was not a large alteration. On the other hand at Highton, where there had been six men and five women in 1975, there was a dramatic change. Twenty-seven women outnumbered eleven men in 1976, and this led to uncertainty about meeting goals set by the male-dominated boarding-school tradition of Corio. Glamorgan remained unaffected, with a slight preponderance of women among a staff of twenty, and Timbertop was unashamedly

[2] *Corian*, May 1979, p. 15.
[3] *Corian*, May 1979, p. 15.

male until the late 1970s, when larger numbers of girls had to be provided for. The school council, where policy was framed, remained a male preserve until 1979, when Jocelyn Searby became a lonely representative of that other sex in the amalgamation.

Large-scale co-education added many dimensions. In a school which was used to strong generational patterns, there was a pleasant novelty in having boy—girl twins and an aunt—nephew combination in 1974. Clyde, in particular, brought further family relationships. On the social grapevine children were told to look out for distant cousins and the offspring of old acquaintances. Overall there was a deepening of identity. As newcomers, girls made comments about their experience which pinpointed characteristics of the school which had previously been taken for granted. One girl at Corio was impressed by the democratic, student-centred atmosphere; the emphasis on individuals regardless of their ability; the creative activities, the alternative sports and the vast freedom. 'This must be a health farm', she thought.

Other girls were alienated initially. Those who came from the little world of Clyde, despite the efforts of Alice Pringle, Gem Reid and their matron, Mary Brisbane, (who had been secretary at Woodend), felt that they had been thrust, physically as well as emotionally, into a large and cold environment. They lost their way. They were upstaged by the confidence of the original inhabitants. They blushed easily and remained embarrassingly silent in class. The sixth form, who had been at the top of the old tree, felt particularly disadvantaged at first. It was hard to belong, but interestingly the head of the river seemed to be a turning-point, by triggering an identity and a loyalty against outsiders. Gradually girls became absorbed into inter-house sport and out-of-school activities.

Hermitage girls, most of whom were not boarders, found the transition to Corio even more difficult. Unlike the Clyde contingent, their old identity was gone completely. If they were senior-school boarders, they felt dumped in Jennings House* with other girls from a great mixture of backgrounds. The concrete corridors and louvred windows of the building were unwelcoming and younger girls felt overwhelmed by the remorseless routines of the busy campus. Even though they soon knew that his heart was in the right place, and came to love him, they were startled by the great shouts of Glen Bechly, their housemaster, whose voice had been tuned to the hubbub of boys.

Day girls had to make a special adjustment to long and strenuous hours. One of them commented that at first it seemed a good idea not to break for afternoon travel, but later she noticed that fatigue set in and that few students used the evening study period properly. By the time she arrived home she had no energy for extra study. That was a rub. When J. R. Darling introduced extended hours for

---

* Named after R. G. Jennings it was his old Junior School classroom block, converted in 1970 for Connewarre and again in 1975 for a girls' residence.

271

day boys, the majority came from central Geelong. The Bellarine Peninsula was not a significant commuter zone. Now it was. Many Hermitage girls who joined the amalgamated school had long distances to travel. An hour in the bus at 9.30 p.m. was tough going.

The bruises suffered by The Hermitage would not go away. There was no house to carry on the name and provide support during the transition. At the senior school the huge organization swallowed up the newcomers. Elizabeth Britten could not be a rallying point, as Alice Pringle could in Clyde. Despite her war cry on the brink of the takeover about defending them, old standards were lost, and whereas Clyde was previously a secondary school, whose whole operation was transferred to Corio, The Hermitage, after earlier losses to GGS and Geelong College, had greater strength in the primary school at Highton, well away from the central policy-forming, image-making Corio core. The boards honouring senior girls, who had been captains and prize-winners since 1906, were raised on junior school walls. The Hermitage flag floated from the rafters of the Elsie Morres Hall over children to whom its meaning was marginal, while the former Hermitage and Bostock teachers struggled over the ideals and routines of the rearrangement. Significantly, in company with their former head, five Hermitage teachers from Highton opted out of the experiment at the end of 1976. All the care taken by John Herbert to unite the two operations could not lay to rest sharp differences that had prevented an earlier blending of the primary operations.

In terms most visible at Highton, the amalgamation was a takeover, scarcely sweetened by the inclusion of a few council members from the girls' school on the new governing body and scarcely affected by the presence of the former headmistress. It was, as planned, a step in achieving the goals of Geelong Grammar School. If any of the merging staff of 1976 had any illusions about that, the first few paragraphs of the chairman, Robin Ritchie, from the dining-hall terrace on Speech Day, Saturday 6 November 1976, would have put them right. He was prepared, he said, to pre-empt historians and declare the year notable. The council was preparing GGS financially and socially for its probable role as the only non-Catholic boarding-school in Victoria. As expected, the amalgamation had provided increased economic strength, better utilization of assets and a wider community from which to draw.

This large business looked to the future in another way in 1976 by launching an Endowment Trust, similar to foundations that were springing up at other independent schools. Sir Robert Southey was its first chairman. By the end of the year, after special lunches, dinners and an audio-visual presentation, $635 000 had been promised. The idea, as elsewhere, was to achieve a fund that would help to offset increasing fees and guarantee independence from governments. Government policies loomed larger in Charles Fisher's thinking than they had in that of any previous headmaster. During 1974 and 1975, the last years of the Whitlam Labor government in Canberra, he was

272

goaded into outspoken attacks on centralism and paternalism. Even when the Liberals returned, he reiterated at each speech day his strong belief that parents should be given the freedom to choose schools for their children. A voucher system, entitling them to a remission of fees, was his favourite recommendation. He was incensed in 1974 by the probings of the Commonwealth Schools Commission, which required schools to complete a questionnaire of forty-one foolscap pages so that calculations could be made about their affluence, to which recurrent grants were to be tied. Ideologically he sided with the Victorian Liberals, who had acted in 1972 to offset some of the federal pruning with strictly per-capita grants to schools.

The independent schools were caught in a difficult public-relations situation. Constant and rapid inflation made them uneasy with parents, whose natural resistance to increases in fees put school councils on the defensive. Throughout the 1970s there was a serious loss of confidence in Australian business. Wages seemed to be rising out of control and offshore capital threatened an Australian manufacturing sector weakened by many years of Liberal—Country Party tariff protection. Some parents were genuinely disadvantaged, but many who complained of high taxation were practising tax-minimization very effectively.

Professor (later Sir) Zelman Cowen, little knowing that he would quite soon be called to a peacemaking role as governor-general, warned against a strong reaction to government policy at Speech Day 1974. He saw the objective of the Labor government as equality of opportunity, achieved by 'the infusion of equalising re-source' into the whole education system. He was conscious that schools like GGS had been valued more for the status they conferred than for their educational philosophy and pointed to their identification in the public mind with social and economic privilege. Conscious as he was of the dilemma for a democratic society posed by an independence supported by and sustaining a privileged social group, he challenged the school to justify its independence with a distinctive quality of outlook and performance.

The linkage between privilege and independence implied that the less wealthy did not need that freedom. Charles Fisher confessed that he was tempted to think, even in Australia, that it was wrong to encourage independence of thought among those destined to work in hierarchical institutions. Yet he affirmed the Christian view that acts of conscience and free will, based on love, were bound to involve a state of tension with the world. He did not advocate an educated social conscience as strongly as Darling had done, nor seek constructive rebels, as Garnett had, but those possibilities were still there. He wanted the school to balance 'the wholesome development of the individual' by teaching 'the skills and responsibilities of contributing to community and national and world life'. How that balancing was to happen in a place so removed from wider social realities he did not say. He did not try, as Garnett had, to make it face up to itself as a self-aware, partly self-regulating community; but he and Anne, through their constructive relationships with people at all levels of its complicated world, gave it a focus that had long been lacking and stimulated a mood that was closer to its friendly traditions (and Australian attitudes) than Garnett's stirring.

That does not mean that Fisher was out of sympathy with Garnett's changes. He sought Garnett's advice and let him know that he appreciated his contribution and the struggle that went with it. His own assault on the old way was to move the Timbertop year from form 4 to form 3, which he believed suited the earlier maturing of teenagers and the addition of girls, as well as coming at a less critical time for their studies. The changeover was phased in during 1975 and 1976, at the same time as the first girls went into the mountains. Under Fisher, too, further experiments were made to focus out-of-school experience by taking advantage of the flexibility provided by the boarding-school. Several days in succession were set aside each term for extended activities (see p. 328).

Enrolments rose from 1000 to over 1600 upon amalgamation and the school became even more heterogeneous. The teaching staff, including an unprecedented number of women, increased from 87 to 132 between 1975 and 1979. There were almost as many teachers as there had been boys at the peak of nineteenth-century enrolments. While numbers of staff at Glamorgan were steady at 20, Corio moved from 48 to 65, Timbertop from 8 to 13 and Highton from 11 to 34. Problems of communication multiplied and, as well as the excitement of change, there were many uncertainties. To help staff get to know each other better and share the issues they faced, a two-day seminar was held at the beginning of third term 1978. Alongside discussions of the school's own programmes and procedures Sir Roderick Carnegie, an old boy council member and head of CRA, presented a picture of a colder future for Australia, in which self-reliant, risk-taking people, with flexible, well-trained minds would be needed more than ever.

That opinion confirmed the planning of the most stimulating building of the 1970s. Described during its germination as the resource centre, it was intended to promote self-sufficiency and stimulate a multi-media approach to education. In contrast to the carved bays and emphasis on books of the older Hawker Library, the spacious centre had many facilities for individual and group work and room not just for library professionals but for audio and video experts to support classroom teaching and out-of-school activities. It prompted the first strong expansion of ancillary teaching staff other than in the science laboratories. Completed early in 1979, the centre was located between the chapel and Cuthbertson House, deliberately close to the extra classrooms built in 1975 to help accommodate the influx of girls. Half the cost was covered unexpectedly by the Commonwealth government, the project having started before such centres were eligible for funding.

Just as modern, and as great a contrast to its ill-fated wooden

predecessor (see p. 91), the Bracebridge Wilson theatre was opened in 1978 as a venue for plays, speeches, seminars and social activities. Because there were many other facilities in the school it could be more specialized and much more comfortable than the marvellous (for its time) multi-purpose structure of the late nineteenth century. A long-term environmental problem of the Corio site was also resolved in 1978 when the school negotiated with the Shire of Corio for the development of school land on the shores of Limeburners' Bay lagoon as a public park which Robin Ritchie, the chairman of council, predicted would soon become a most attractive and effective buffer.

His busy fifth year almost completed, Charles Fisher drove alone on 5 December 1978 from Corio to Timbertop. Near Kanumbra in the foothills of the challenging mountains he seems to have fallen asleep. His car left the road and he was killed: not lost, like Bracebridge Wilson, at the end of his career, but snatched away at its peak. The shock to the school was enormous, releasing tributes that indicated how much he had achieved in so comparatively short a time. Letters of sympathy flooded in to Anne and her family and many official tributes were made. Robin Ritchie emphasized Fisher's warmth, enthusiasm and ebullience which carried others along, especially because he worked hard at personal relationships:

Charles was a more orthodox man than his predecessor. He was very good at names and worked at it. He knew how effective it was in allowing boys and girls and parents to develop a close relationship with him. Of course everyone knew who he was, but that he knew who everyone was was most unusual and endeared him to many.[4]

His appetite for experience impressed Don Marles who, like Ritchie, had been very close to him and who believed that Fisher's previous experience had prepared him well for his most demanding, but potentially most satisfying, assignment:

Charles liked being Head Master of Geelong Grammar School. He was not daunted by the prospect of being the chief executive of a system consisting of four schools, widely separated by distance, and catering for a wide range of age, interest and ability. He enjoyed his contacts with Council members, staff, parents, and Old Geelong Grammarians. He disliked the fact that the nature of his job lessened the amount of contact he had with boys and girls. There was still a great deal of the housemaster in him. He liked Corio as a place to live and enjoyed the community life of a boarding-school. He enjoyed entertaining, and he and Anne made their home the centre of Corio life. He was an excellent host. He arrived at Geelong with no experience or background of co-education and with uncertain attitudes about it. He quickly became converted and ultimately found it difficult to imagine how a school could be otherwise.[5]

At a service of thanksgiving for his life and work, in the school chapel on 8 December 1978, a fellow headmaster and former staff member, Paul McKeown of Canberra Grammar School, spoke also of the power, tenacity, goodness, energy, humour and humanity that

FISHER. — On December 5 (result of accident). Charles Douglas (Headmaster of Geelong Grammar School, Corio) dearly loved husband of Anne, loving father of Jane, Penelope, Geoffrey, Timothy, Matthew and Andrew.

PRIVATE FUNERAL

A Memorial Thanksgiving Service for the life of the late Mr. Charles Douglas Fisher will be held at All Saints Chapel, Geelong, Grammar School, Corio, on SUNDAY (December 10) at 2.30 p.m.

F. H. TUCKER & SON PTY. LTD., 55-57 Hope St., Geelong West. Phone 214788.

FISHER, the Hon. Charles D. — Our sincere regret and deepest sympathy to Mrs. Fisher and family on their tragic loss. —Geelong Grammar School, Highton, Parents and Friends Association.

[4] *Corian*, May 1979, p. 10.
[5] *Corian*, May 1979, p. 12.

had characterized Fisher's life. He finished with these words:

There are three broad divisions of souls, and they are expressed in these three prayers with which I finish. All of them have been part of the life of Charles Fisher:
1. I am a bow in your hands, Lord. Draw me, lest I rot.
2. Do not overdraw me, Lord. I shall break.
3. Overdraw me, Lord—and who cares if I break![6]

Fisher's death placed the school in an unusual position. Marles, who might have acted in his place, was leaving to take up the headmastership of Trinity Grammar School and his replacement A. A. (Alby) Twigg, although knowing the school well as an old boy, could hardly be expected suddenly to step in. So the council, with an eye to the business analogy Robin Ritchie was fond of using, appointed the chairman of council 'chief executive' and extended the term of C. E. R. (Boz) Parsons as 'senior master' to serve with him on what was called the committee of management. Sir Roderick Carnegie replaced Ritchie as chairman of the saddened council, one of whose first acts under his guidance was to rename the resource centre the Charles Fisher Library.*

In the interregnum year of 1979, Ritchie was determined to take stock. As well as farming his family property at Blackwood near Penshurst, he had had business experience in Melbourne, in that way covering the typical areas of activity from which the school had drawn its pupils since the move to Corio. He wanted to consolidate the amalgamation, look closely at management structures and review the use of material and human resources. To that end he organized an evaluation of the school by a team led by Dr Stephen Kemmis of Geelong's Deakin University. At the same time, through council, he set in train the procedures by which a new head would be chosen.

The evaluation confirmed the quality of pastoral care and the freedom of individuals within the school, but in pointing to a continuing weakness in scholarship it cast doubts on the effectiveness, despite the promise of the Fisher Library, of individual learning. This was to be in part the climate in which applications for the headmastership were assessed. They came from all over the world and among them the curriculum vitae and references of an outstanding New Zealander, John Lewis, who had excelled in classics at Cambridge and had been Master-in-College, in charge of the scholars at Eton since 1975. His appointment as headmaster was announced on 16 August 1979. He and his wife, Vibeke, also from New Zealand but Danish by birth, arrived at Corio a year later. John Lewis, the eighth headmaster, took up his office just 125 years after Vance had opened the school. The 1980s, on which it had set its sights six years earlier had many challenges in store.

PIERS HILL
WILLIAMSTOWN.
SOUTH AUSTRALIA 5351
TELEPHONE: (085) 65 3215

29 August 79

Dear Mr Persse

It was very kind of you to send the copies of *The Corian*. It was a most moving issue, and the range of the tributes, from all sorts and ages, was a wonderful testimony to Charles' character.

Yours sincerely,
Geoffrey Dutton

---

[6] *Corian*, May 1979, p. 32.

* Carnegie, Ritchie, Parsons, Twigg and the bursar, Jim Winchester had all been prefects under Darling.

12

A little Athens

THE PATH OF ENLIGHTENMENT

The first sixteen years at Corio continued the nineteenth-century pattern of activities beyond the classroom with desultory hobbies, an annual Pastime and some debating and literary discussion. Giles had done his best in the early 1920s to break the pattern, but it was only at the end of the period that Masterman and Bull, working more or less in harness, gave vitality to literature and debating. Under their influence A. S. Marshall made the huge leap in 1929 from the Pastimes of short farces and music hall to Sheridan's five-act comedy, *The Rivals*. To give it substance he played Sir Anthony Absolute himself, well supported as Mrs Malaprop by M. G. Duffield (later a distinguished professional actor) and J. G. Gorton, 'a rather diffident lover, caught in a masquerade'.

A day in the life of a boy at the end of Brown's period was a hearty communal experience. Disgorged from bare dorms in a slithering mass to the batteries of cold showers, swept into large house-rooms and the dining-hall, carried along in twenties and thirties during classes, drafted after that into traditional games, with an occasional less-organized swim in the warmer weather, and finally rounded up after tea for prep, there was little room for privacy and personal choice. Even at weekends, when the Saturday Parties set off, or when small groups gathered in the homes of rare spirits like Masterman or attended occasional concerts and films, the greater relaxation could spill into only a limited range of activities. Being different artistically was not easily accepted. Although Masterman drew boys aside for gramophone music and Bull had begun the literary magazine *If*, and had given the library a giant shake, the whole environment was as spartan as the dormitories: there were just two public art objects in the school—Lambert's war memorial bronze and the Christopher Whall window in chapel. Relieving 'the cramp induced by muscular Christianity', Rod Andrew remembered vividly the impact of Masterman's marvellous Dürer engravings, shelves of books and the four foot long papier mâché horn of his splendid gramophone.

DRAMATIS PERSONÆ

Chroniclers ... ... { J. H. LINDON
H. O. C. GILLETT
J. A. CARTWRIGHT }

TROJANS

AENEAS ... ... J. C. BARCLAY

CAPTAINS OF THE BOATS :—

Sergestus	K. M. BEGGS
Mnestheus	R. E. WHITE
Gyas	P. J. PARSONS
Cloanthus	W. W. G. MEECHAM
The Helmsman, Menoetes	N. C. A. CAMPBELL

COMPETITORS IN THE FOOTRACE :—

Euryalus	J. B. ALCOCK
Nisus	C. R. HOSE
Salius	W. R. C. McCULLOCH
Helymus	R. S. MORTON
Diores	M. A. NATHAN

DARES, the Boxer ... ... W. E. LLOYD

EURYTION ... ... K. L. BROUGHAM

and

R. B. ANDERSON	R. H. L. DUNN	H. D. STEWARD
A. F. CADDY	J. S. ELDER	J. B. STER
N. C. CARROLL	J. B. HOWSE	C. J. TAYLOR
W. B. CHAFFEY	W. H. LATCOCK	J. C. THOMAS
R. N. CLARK	B. H. O'BEIRNE	M. R. THWAITES
A. V. CRASKE	G. W. PALMER	P. WINCH
T. CREE	J. N. ROBERTSON	
R. H. DEASET	J. M. SIM	

J. R. Darling softened, broadened and enriched this pattern beyond expectation. Hobbies, for instance, were at risk in the boarding-houses in the absence of suitable space until, during second term in 1930, a room was provided for them in the Bracebridge Wilson Hall. Characteristically, boys rushed to build model aircraft and stormed the tower to see who could first fly a machine safely to earth.

If a measure were to be made of the difference between Corio then and thirty-one years later, few better indications are available than the lists of school office-bearers which head the *Corian*. In May 1930 they took up a single page, half of it occupied by the General Athletics Committee and its sub-committees. To organize the other out-of-school activities only five committees were needed: Corian; Out of School; Library; Literary, Debating and Musical, and Ionians. By contrast, the names of committees in 1961 occupied three pages: Corian; Library; Chapel; Pilgrims; Servers; Guild of the Sanctuary; Art School; Musical; School Press; Camera; Literary; *If Revived*; Yacht Squadron; Carpentry; Mechanics; Mathematical; Scientific; Natural History; Museum and Archives; Historical; Philosophical; Out of School. And whereas in 1930 Bull, Masterman and the headmaster, with some help from Nall, Hancock and the chaplain, carried most of the burden, in 1961 it was widely spread. There were strong contributions, besides those of the headmaster, from Ponder, Hutton, Mappin, Westcott, Persse, Brazier, Bechervaise, Dean, Tomkinson, Eyre-Walker, Maggs and Hollis.

Even so, when summing up the leisure activities of the Darling era, A. S. Marshall noted how they fluctuated in response to the enthusiasm of masters and boys or responded to changing fashions. He counted over forty different clubs and societies in thirty-two years and identified very few which had been strong, or had even existed, throughout. The same was true under Garnett and Fisher. At times idealists despaired because boys made so little use of their opportunities. In the large gap between rhetoric and performance, clubs wasted away for lack of enthusiastic members. Even when given school time every second Tuesday afternoon in the mid-1940s, few of the sixteen existing societies met regularly: the mass of boys took a half-holiday and aimlessly kicked footballs or played table-tennis. Although sarcastic to individuals he found mucking about in that way, Darling was philosophical about their shortcomings and generous with funds to support the activities they scorned. His successors have continued that approach.

SUMMONING THE MUSES, 1930–1961

Various places in Australia at various times have been dubbed 'Athens of the South'—Adelaide and Ballarat for instance—but few communities have been so Athenian in their approach to the arts as GGS under Darling. From Temple at Repton he had received the torch that set Corio alight. A residual muscular Christianity was enlivened by the ideal of the civilized (Christian) man, equally at home with physical, intellectual and cultural pursuits. That new cultural emphasis came chiefly through art, drama and music, each of them interpreted widely and geared to educational goals, and each of them reconstituted, if not actually brought into being, in a spirit that attached them not only organically to the classroom but also to the boys' leisure time and to the general life of the whole school community. It was an approach that filled out the curriculum like a giant Dalton plan.

Drama

Repeatedly in the 1930s Darling organized pageants that brought the whole school together to the service of all three muses at once. C. R. Bull, his chief support, claimed that the pageant-plays of the 1930s were an educational master-stroke, redeeming those who found school work dull and developing in all the incentive, interest and perspective to give learning more meaning by putting it in the wider setting of human action, thought and feeling. Rather than interrupting the regular work of the school, as his opponents contended, Darling was mostly reclaiming many out-of-school hours spent mindlessly filling a vacuum.

For the first time at Corio, by harnessing also the talents of masters' wives, indoor and outdoor staff, the school became a coherent community, valuing the potential of everyone within it. And not only the human potential—a feature of the pageants was the use they made of landscape and buildings.

So Aeneas came ashore in the lagoon on a golden October day in 1931, two thousand years after Virgil had been born. Blending the school's rowing and classical traditions, Masterman edited and arranged the text, Darling and a group of boys (including the future poets John Manifold and Michael Thwaites) wrote an English chronicle and the waters stirred to the oars of fishermen and warriors. Bull recalled three unforgettable sights: a small boat from which three colourfully-dressed fishermen threw and hauled their net, the arrival of the hero's barge, and a helmsman being thrown overboard for losing a hectic race. Thus Limeburners' Bay had been clothed in timelessness and the school had been lifted dramatically out of the mundane.

The recipe was repeated in front of the dining hall in 1933 with Hardy's *The Dynasts*, which began with a straggle of refugees fleeing inland from the English coast in fear of a Napoleonic invasion and culminated, after the Duchess of Richmond's Brussels ball (inside the dining hall), with the battle of Waterloo. Or did it? Another interpretation insisted that it began in first term with the selection of forty out of 130 of Hardy's scenes, which the sixth form gave as a very, very dull reading in the Bracebridge Wilson Hall. Cutting in second term reduced the play (which Hardy had intended for 'mental performance' only) to twenty-two scenes, which were further cut after the first rehearsal. Bull, the producer, Dicker, his assistant, and Pinner, the stage-manager, co-ordinated the efforts of a cast of 250 as well as the Napoleonic army of helpers needed to provide props and

SICILIANS

ACESTES	... ...	J. G. MANN
ENTELLUS	... ...	H. M. RUTTER

and

E. D. BEAUREPAIRE	K. O. B. GRANT	G. L. LINDON
S. G. BEGGS	C. HEATHCOTE	R. E. McDONALD
A. L. DAVIES	H. R. LATREILLE	K. V. ROBERTSON
D. E. FAIRBAIRN	P. B. LEFROY	G. TOPP
P. J. HANDBURY	S. C. McCULLOCH	A. E. DAKING-SMITH
W. G. A. LANDALE	K. F. PALMER	C. M. EADIE
J. N. LEARMONTH	D. RUTTER	F. S. LAMBLE
J. S. MANIFOLD	S. R. C. WOOD	D. J. G. MACMEIKAN
G. S. MOFFAT	J. H. CARR	W. R. MINELL
S. J. ROSS-EDWARDS	W. R. DEXTER	E. A. R. ROSS
K. WHITEHEAD	J. HADWEN	J. R. WETTENHALL
D. R. M. CAMERON	R. L. JOHNSON	
D. A. DEXTER	S. J. LEACH	

THE PROPHETESS	... ...	A. S. ELLIS

NUBIAN SLAVES

R. T. H. ANDERSON	G. A. FAIRBAIRN	P. D. WALLACE
J. H. BEAUMONT	D. O. HAY	W. O. WINTER-IRVING
J. G. CROSSLEY	J. TURNBULL	

THE CHOIR

Under the Direction of J. J. McKINNELL.

E. BAILLIEU, C. F. BELCHER, C. G. CLARKE, A. L. DAVIES. M. G. G. DUFFIELD, G. H. GUNNERSEN, R. K. LINTON. W. H. PATERSON.

A. H. BAIRD, J. E. JERMYN, R. B. LEFROY, G. E. NATHAN. G. F. BELLMAINE, G. M. BRAMMALL, R. H. CORDIA, M. EVERETT. R. A. EVERETT, C. B. MANIFOLD, A. G. C. MASON, A. M. MORRIS. W. M. DEMPSTER, R. B. PATERSON. R. S. ROWAN, H. M. SHAW.

O. J. WHITE, L. J. WOODS, E. G. BANKS, A. W. CORDIA. D. H. COLMAN, R. N. HAMILTON, C. C. KELLY, W. MURRAY. K. S. ROWAN, R. I. WINTER-IRVING.

costumes. The hats and uniforms were professionally made. Including parts of Beethoven's 'Eroica' symphony, the music was arranged by J. J. McKinnell, who composed songs specially for the play. From among the boys, S. J. Leach, I. D. Mackinnon, J. W. Merewether and M. R. Thwaites helped with script and production. One excited youth was allowed to bring his grey pony to school to herald the invasion, but despite his efforts the end result was not exciting.

In 1936 the north side of the chapel became the backdrop for 'Alpha and Omega', a linking of Old and New Testament characters and events. It culminated with the Hallelujah Chorus after a procession of heroes, martyrs and humble followers of Christ throughout history had filed into the chapel. Darling had been playing with the idea since 1934, when he told John Masefield (who said he would return for it) that he would like to attempt a pageant of St Paul. In June 1936 he wrote to T. S. Eliot requesting permission to adapt *The Rock* for Australian conditions, but the reply, on beautiful Faber and Faber writing-paper, came too late. In a great rush the narration for the tableaux was derived from the Bible. Once more the art school and the carpentry shop, the needles of masters' wives and the soldering irons of electrical enthusiasts were called in. With chisel and saw, the senior master, C. A. Cameron, blocked out, carved and gilded a life-sized wooden calf—a small task compared to his construction in 1931 of the great barge for Aeneas. To what extent boys were conscious of the link between this pageant and the curriculum is problematical, depending perhaps on their attitudes to religion.

:: PART TWO ::

Overture . . . . . . Good Friday Music

ACT IV.

A.D. 35.

SCENE 1 : "Brother Saul"

Damascus. The Conversion of Saul.

PAUL . . . . G. A. RICHARDSON
Ananias of Damascus . . . . H. A. L. MORAN
Judas of Damascus . . . . J. V. C. deCRESPIGNY
Barnabas . . . . T. M. STOKOE
Temple Guards . . . . G. R. PATTERSON
A. B. C. HARRISON

Jews of Damascus

J. G. M. BLACK, E. A. CALLANAN, G. H. COLMAN, W. A. FREEMAN,
E. J. P. JONES, G. L. MACLEOD, J. PITT,
D. R. SPOONER. C. STEPHEN.

Diana of the Ephesians.

After 1938, when a pleasantly humorous 'Pickwick' was given at the new music school, there was a break from pageants until the centenary year, 1957. Apart from the loss of Bull in 1939, the war brought different communal objectives and Darling, feeling anyway, perhaps, that the pageants had done their work, moved on to the subtler challenge of Shakespeare. In 1945 his production of *Julius Caesar* began a new tradition. It was not that Shakespeare had been ignored before. During first term 1936, the year of 'Alpha and Omega', a tentative beginning had been made with briefly rehearsed, scarcely audible, often clumsy and typically schoolboy performances of *Twelfth Night* (in modern dress), *Julius Caesar* and a shortened *A Midsummer Night's Dream*.

According to Ken Mappin, who worked on productions side by side and turn about with Darling for fourteen years, the 1945 *Caesar* was in a far different category, achieving a verve few people thought possible with schoolboys. Then in a great succession came *The Tempest* (1947), *Twelfth Night* (1949), *Henry IV part 1* (1950), *Macbeth* (1951), *A Midsummer Night's Dream* (1952), *The Merchant Of Venice* (1953), *Henry V* (1955) and *Julius Caesar*, *Macbeth* and *Henry V* again (1957, 1959 and 1961). At various times in between there were Anouilh, Barrie, Shaw and Wilde, a Brazier and Mappin *Marriage of Figaro* and a rollicking *1066 and All That*, complete with an additional scene about electronics in the home, written by Mappin and Persse. A. S. Marshall and S. P. Gebhardt also produced.

As always, Darling led by example and by daring, cajoling and dragooning others to become involved. He made it his business to commit footballers, rowers, cricketers and athletes to this more ancient and more delicate sport, thus extending the range of sympathy for those who excelled at it. The music and art departments were constantly involved. Indeed after Hirschfeld (see p. 202) came from prisoner-of-war camp in 1942, the horizon exploded. His brilliant sets enhanced every production. Without them *The Tempest* could scarcely have been attempted and without his Bauhaus ideas the transformation of the workshops, begun for Darling's National Service programme (see p. 199), would not have led to so much delight.

Strength of involvement increased at the same time as depth. Mappin spoke with wonder about 1956 when, only three years after annual house plays were introduced, and with no noticeable effect on academic results, six three-act plays of the calibre of *Ned Kelly*, *Saint Joan*, *Richard of Bordeaux*, *The Happiest Days of Our Lives*, *Charley's Aunt* and *The Miser* were performed at Corio. In December 1958 the *Corian* commented that *1066 and All That* was the seventh full-length production for the year—following five house plays and a Timbertop play.

In a special effort for the centenary in 1957, the school's theatrical talent was brought to bear on the history of the school. After a Brazier—Mappin *Figaro* in first term and a Mappin—Darling *Caesar* in second, the most ambitious of all Corio productions, *Their Succeeding Race*, took shape. Darling had the original inspiration to

SCENE 9

THE WILLOWS CAMP, 1888, AND THE TIMBERTOP COUNTRY, 1957

" . . . . to-day becomes to-morrow
In the body's resurrection
Into spirit, into mind."

Mr. JAMES LISTER CUTHBERTSON	G. N. RAYMOND
HARRY GILLETT	H. M. MORGAN
JOHN DAVISON	I. L. HORE-LACY
THOMAS PARKIN	G. H. SPRY
EDGAR BAGOT	J. G. HINDHAUGH
First Timbertop Boy	H. M. ROSS
Second Timbertop Boy	R. H. DUREAU
Third Timbertop Boy	P. C. J. FISHER
Fourth Timbertop Boy	J. R. E. LOCKHART

The Choir sings Easy All and two verses of What is the Bond that Binds Us (two of the old School Songs) and The Song of the Old and the New (a new School Song).

INTERVAL

OF FIFTEEN MINUTES

Chorus

SCENE 10

THE HEADMASTER'S STUDY, 1891

" At heart a school is deeply personal,
And what the persons at its heart are that
it is."

Mr. JOHN BRACEBRIDGE WILSON	R. L. HARDIMAN
WILLIAM HARWOOD PINCOTT	R. W. ANDERSON
Mrs. BRACEBRIDGE WILSON	W. D. A. MACINTYRE

Chorus

SCENE 11

CORIO, 1913 AND 1957

"That Heaven may break through on these mud-flats . . . ."

A. A. O. DAVENPORT	J. J. G. PRINGLE
CHARLES HAWKER	M. L. INGPEN
Dr. FRANCIS BROWN, Headmaster of the School	J. M. GRAY
K. McG. RONALD	J. R. HYDE
G. K. BURSTON	A. P. CHARLES

The four Boys of 1957 from Scene 7.
The Third Forms in the background.

Chorus

SCENE 12

GALLIPOLI, 1915, AND CORIO

" . . . . an age
That's bred in monstrous, cataclysmic war."

Sergeant WINTER COOKE .... S. N. STUART

The Anzac Day Guard:
Under Officer D. A. R. McLEAY, Sergeant B. R. KEDDIE. Corporal P. H. HEYSEN.
Corporal W. E. S. HASKER, Cadets G. H. BURSTON. P. McK. KEDDIE. R. J.
LEMMON, I. E. MACKAY, P. B. MARKHAM, D. S. MORTON. J. D. PICKETT-HEAPS.
G. L. RICHARDSON, J. D. W. ROBERTSON.

The Band
The Headmaster's voice is heard reading the Roll of Honour.

The Choir sings Sir Edward Elgar's They Are at Rest (from a poem by
Cardinal Newman) in the Chapel.

A scene from *Their Succeeding Race* depicts J. L. Cuthbertson with a Saturday Party at The Willows.

SCENE 9

The Willows, 1888, and the Timbertop Country, 1957.

A rowing-party, consisting of Mr. Cuthbertson and four boys, John Davison, Harry Gillett, Edgar Bagot, and Thomas Parkin, are arriving at the Willows in December 1888. They moor their racing four and come in and settle themselves during the singing of "Easy All," resting their oars vertically against the Cloisters. The boys carry some sandwiches, which they eat during the Scene, and Tom has some oranges in an orange string-bag.

Mr. Cuthbertson

> Shall we rest today a while?
> All this morning we worked hard,
> Rowing in Regatta style
> On the Barwon: nothing marred
> Unison of arm and oar.
> As the shadows fall we'll row
> Back to School: but here, on shore,
> Let us rest and watch the flow
> Of the river as it glides;
> Let us, like Ulysses, linger—
> Think like him of men and tides,
> Though with us there shall no finger
> Pointing at us say, "Don't linger
> Lest the lotus-bloom seduce you
> With its sweet and luscious fruit."

1 *Corian*, Aug. 1961, p. 125.
2 *Corian*, Aug. 1961, p. 125.

link the history of the school with that of the nation, and Michael Persse in the writing, Ken Mappin in the production, and Denny Evans with set and costumes, as well as the usual almost unlimited back-up of the whole community, proved groundless the fears of some of the Pageant Committee that the project would be much too difficult. The main action was on the chapel lawn, but in extensive scenes actors controlled by 'walkie-talkies' moved across the oval behind; Aborigines hunted, Captain Phillip landed, convicts, sheep and cattle were mustered. More intimately, suspending the rule of silence in the cloisters, Bracebridge Wilson gently admonished a boy, hallowed Cuthbertson hosted a rowing party at The Willows and Sergeant W. L. Winter Cooke, dazed from his wounds, dreamed at Gallipoli, near trees that later seeded, by his hand, the chapel oaks. Space and time dissolved.

It would be fitting for a future pageant on the life of the school to show Darling creating a pageant or producing a play. The *Corian* critique of Mappin's great *Henry V* in Darling's last term, staged magnificently in the dining hall, began with words directed towards this history:

> The future historian of the School, surveying the period 1930–1961, must very soon be struck by the sudden flowering of drama, in its early years, and the continuance of the tradition then established right through to the present day...the tradition has been astonishingly even and continuous, and hardly a year has gone by without at least one notable production, and probably other plays are presented at Corio and Timbertop each year.[1]

The writer went on to point out a similarity between the first and the last plays of Darling's era:

> Each had a unique and splendid setting; each used in its producing huge numbers of boys; and there was even at a deep level, a certain similarity of theme. Heroism and high adventure, the nobility of man's aspiring and the fragility of his achievements; the creative and attractive power of noble spirits...[2]

In turning that full circle the wheel of Darling's ambition had moved the school an immense distance.

Art

The same can be said about art. Darling came to the home of Philistines, where most masters and boys thought that artistic activity was dangerous and artists subversive. In the climate from which Russell Drysdale emerged, Mary Finnin, a magnificently alive young colourist and poet, struggled to make headway for creativity. A room in the south-west corner of the quad was furnished with uncomfortable desks and an unclosable cupboard. Equipped with a few battered T-squares, a cone, a cylinder and a cube, it was designed for careful reproduction to which generations of boys had responded by covering their 'appalling copy cards' with the 'high stomachs, bottle noses and runaway chins' of caricature masters. Darling groaned and found £25 for curtains, drapes, painting materials and plaster copies of Greek sculpture. Bare walls were treated with British Railway posters or Medici Society prints and art, as craft, became associated especially through the pageants with drama, music, literature and religion.

When the building programme of the early 1930s made two classrooms available in the quadrangle for a studio and workroom, Darling's policy of opening the school to the world brought in Merric Boyd (who kicked off the pottery wheel), Paul Montfort (the Shrine of Remembrance sculptor), Napier Waller (stained-glass artist) and exhibitions or the loans of paintings by a succession of notable artists including Jessie Traill, George Bell, Arnold Shore, William Frater and Rupert Bunny. The scale of Bunny's canvases demanded the use of the dining hall, and, this being the most comprehensive show of his work ever mounted in Australia, it drew not only parents but also art teachers and critics. When the Bunny exhibition was reviewed in the Paris press, GGS had moved at last into that international sphere which Mackinnon, especially, had hoped for with Darling's appointment. Victor Cobb brought his half-ton press (and many layers of clothes against the wind) and Mary Cecil Allen, a superb colourist and a major figure in the art battles of the 1930s, persuaded all and sundry, headmaster's guests included, to sketch the local landscape. This broad approach was reinforced in 1933 when Ola Cohn took over temporarily in the art room from Mary Finnin. 'She has been turning us all into sculptors' said the *Corian*, which also reported that a head by R. Cordia had won first prize at a show in Geelong.

Darling was opening up the same general territory as the famous Bauhaus in Germany. He asked Margaret Preston, in November 1934, whether she knew of 'an artist craftsman who would live here and work in the art rooms and encourage the young to do the same'. Far from 'art school quality' or formal teaching, he wanted an enthusiast with broad interests to match those of the boys. He was so sceptical that a normal art training would suit his purpose that, until he saw his work, he responded lukewarmly to an approach from J. S. Derrick, a young hopeful who, in 1935, became the first permanent appointment of the new era. Darling then enlisted the help of the wrought-iron worker C. R. Caslake, who took Derrick into his factory for a week and who spent a day at Corio showing boys how to use two newly-acquired forges. In this way, greatly assisted by the involvement of dozens of boys in preparing costumes, scenery and props for the pageants of the 1930s, ground was gradually won from the school's conservative tradition. Darling was so convinced that this was the proper way to fill a boy's time (and especially his kind of boy) that he made the provision of separate art and music schools the subject of a special appeal through the *Corian* in December 1936. Extras they might be, he admitted, and, unlike a boarding-house, would generate no revenue, but they were essential if the school was really to educate.

His prayers being answered (as usual, you might say, during those years) by late 1937, several cypress trees along Biddlecombe

Ken Mappin

Avenue had made way for a two-storey T-shaped building containing separate spaces for drawing, painting, metalwork, leatherwork, sculpture, pottery, etching, woodcutting, photography, printing and bookbinding. A forge was next door. Already Mr Derrick had inspired a group of boys to construct a large pool and garden on the east side. Through Keith Murdoch, the Melbourne *Herald* presented a press (whose dimensions—3 metres long, 1.2 metres wide and 1 metre high—greatly impressed the *Corian*). It spat out editions of the *Corio Courier*, as well as programmes, leaflets and so on to grace and illuminate the expanding activities of the school. It was symptomatic that the hand-printed curtains, the stair rail and the door furniture were to be made on the spot, anonymously, in that spirit, cultivated by the headmaster, of giving selflessly to the community.

So far, so good. But whereas what Darling had cultivated in drama Bull and Mappin had brought to fruition, the potential of the art school was not fully realized until during the war, when a chain of circumstances, dating back to Hitler's persecutions of the early 1930s, brought a man whose talents and beliefs matched the original vision and provided an enrichment that, because it was continental rather than British, encouraged a challenging universality. L. Hirschfeld-Mack brought a flood of ideas to enlarge life at Corio and to shake it, as Darling hoped, out of a too-cloistered world of its own. When he left sixteen years later the school knew that it was losing 'a great and lovable man' who had brought 'dignity and distinction' to the Corio community and whose influence on the school and on Australian art teaching was indelible. A painter of great talent, who was called just 'Hirschfeld' at GGS, he had been a colleague of Gropius at the Bauhaus, had fled to Britain with his chief in 1934, had been interned as an alien in 1939 and was sent to Australia among the richest cargo (of intellect) ever delivered to these shores. After his passage on the notorious *Dunera*, he was languishing at Tatura when Darling heard of him, realized that he was what the art school needed and set to work, with the help of the old-boy network, to get him out. It was only fair that the war, which had snatched away so many vital members of staff—including John Derrick and Mary Finnin from the art school—should be brought to account.

For Hirschfeld, Corio was both a refuge and an opportunity. It suited his philosophy that he came at a time when the school was thrown on its own resources and when art and craft were being brought to the service of the community. He triggered an outburst of fresh activity and in particular gave painting new life and constant renewal. Boys followed him into experimental techniques, whether montage in 1949 or scraping from a colour base in 1950 or using plaster of Paris to mount pieces of glass they had painted with oils in 1956. At an all-schools show in Geelong in 1946 the 'progressive painting' from Corio was outstanding and much of it stood way ahead of Geelong taste. After he gained an assistant and a utility truck in 1947, Hirschfeld was able to make regular visits to Bostock

284

and Glamorgan. In 1954 the fruits of his creative approach were seen in a pace-setting exhibition at the Peter Bray Gallery in Melbourne, where the year before Hirschfeld himself had shown 100 abstract paintings, and where the art of the junior forms attracted over 3000 people, who, with the help of Professor Joseph Burke, had their eyes opened to the significance of emotional development through art. Even so, in the land supposedly recaptured from the Philistines, although more boys were choosing art as a subject, the eight who included it in their Leaving Certificate course in 1953 were regarded as a remarkably large number. There were fifteen at Leaving and two at Matriculation level in 1954. Despite his general impact, Hirschfeld was rather reserved and only the really talented like David Foulkes-Taylor and Daniel Thomas, who were in his senior classes, came to know him well.

That thin edge of the wedge in the curriculum was only a fraction of Hirschfeld's influence. Whether torch of life or safety-valve, the hobbies and activities of the art school were a major aspect of Darling's educational effort. In pottery, leatherwork, metalwork and silversmithing, for instance, boys gained craft skills within an artistic atmosphere. And in building and painting sets for school plays, like the exciting *Tempest* designs of 1947, they learnt to channel their individuality. Hirschfeld also introduced them to model-making through the displays and relief maps that were a major element of the 'Today and Tomorrow' exhibition of 1942 and the Asian exhibition of 1952, when staff and boys responded to the headmaster's urging that the school should open itself to world issues. Darling commented after the event in 1942:

The idea was to set our minds thinking in an objective and constructive way about the social problems confronting us and to demonstrate how, by working together, much can be accomplished which at first sight seems impossible. Surely a practical understanding of the problems facing the world is one of the necessary objectives of education, as well as that of a mind trained to cope with the problems?[3]

As with the pageants, Darling was calling for experiential education, and for the development of attitudes and skills, not just command over information:

I cannot see why qualities of mind, accuracy, thoroughness and imagination, should not just as easily be trained by such studies as they are supposed to be by the present abstract subjects.[4]

He had a splendid ally in Hirschfeld, who was often able to respond to the latest interest displayed by his charges, as when boys caught the skiing bug at Timbertop and, when back at Corio, rushed to make sheepskin waistcoats, jackets and mittens. He helped them think through the designs and added much practical wisdom about the new sport. Through an ingenious colour-coding of the strings and keys of guitars and xylophones, he also extended many boys' experience of music. An art school garden band was formed in 1950. Before chapel on Sunday mornings they struck or strummed according

[3] *Corian*, Dec. 1942, p. 144.
[4] *Corian*, Dec. 1942, p. 145.

From the school's art collection; an etching of The War Memorial Cloister by Ludwig Hirschfeld Mack, artist and art master.

to the colour of discs displayed by the conductor. Later Manifold House had a 'colour band' and when Dr Stoller, Director of Mental Health, heard of the technique, several more xylophones were made in the art school for the use of the mentally retarded. Hirschy's love of music was also expressed through his own compositions played on a button accordion.

Through all this activity the art school became a powerful community resource. Few terms passed without potters baking for the stalls of charitable organizations. Many sheepskin coats were sent abroad for the destitute and homeless victims of World War II. A sculptured sundial was given to St Wilfrid's Church, Mt Duneed, which had been rebuilt by staff and boys after a bush fire in 1944 (see p. 201). Gates for the school swimming pool were designed and built in 1954. From work on its own fittings and garden in the late 1930s and on a Christian mural which led to the first life classes and paintings in oils of 1943, the art school and its surrounds became a gallery of boys' work.

During 1948 the most ambitious of Hirschfeld's projects, the new entrance to Corio, beside the art school, was planned by three boys. W. J. T. Honeybone and P. W. Titterton designed the gates and Rix Wright the figures of Study and Sport which surmounted them. Wright, who had developed great skill in figure pottery, devoted his spare time for two terms in 1948, and then two months after leaving, to a model of the school weight-putter, C. W. Maxwell. This balanced his earlier model of John Gubbins reading. Both emerged from clay figures, through plaster casts to the reinforced concrete of their final form. The days were never long enough for Wright; he had to sprint everywhere to avoid trouble. Honeybone and Titterton's iron gates were fabricated by senior boys of Manifold House, for whom the sport and study of the old tradition were unforgettably welded to artistic endeavour. Their efforts strengthened the hope expressed by Professor Joseph Burke at the opening on 11 July 1949:

May these gates stand for many years, and may the spirit that made them always remain with Geelong Grammar School.[5]

On the same day, a portrait of the reigning embodiment of that spirit, James Ralph Darling, given by the painter, Hilda Rix Nicholas, mother of Rix Wright, was hung inside the main entrance of the music school.

The art school was further embellished, beginning in second term 1950, with a tiled path made by the boys. In most terms thereafter, about sixty tiles were added, and a record 150 in first term 1955 after a reawakening of interest through tiles commemorating the Queen's visit to Australia in 1954. In the early 1950s the garden was also restored and extended. The removal of further cypresses not only gave more space and light but excellent wood, whose conservation for turners and carvers was a measure of their activity

[5] *Corian*, Aug. 1949, p. 96.

and in marked contrast to the great burn of 1937, when the site was cleared. For the centenary, emblematic of an enriched Corio, new entrance gates, 2.4 metres wide, were designed and largely constructed at the art school. On the eight pillars bronze motifs represented major activities at the school—music, sport, religion, art, science and an association with agriculture and the sea. The governor, Sir Dallas Brooks, opened the gates on speech day in 1957. It was Hirschfeld's final year.

Music

The clef that represented music on the centenary gates stood for a muse little known at GGS before Darling's time—little served, indeed, at any Australian school. Brown had economized through the use of the chaplain 'Joey' Allen as choirmaster and his wife as organist. Scotch was not to be reborn through John Bishop until 1938 and even in England relatively few schools had moved beyond exquisite chapel singing and a hearty rendering of their sporting songs to the broader and deeper thing Darling intended. Two which had were Rugby, whence he called J. J. McKinnell in 1931 and Clifton, where William McKie, McKinnell's successor from 1934 to 1938, had been director of music. Among his many priorities in 1930, egged on by Masterman, who had a great love of music, Darling put the appointment of a good director of music somewhere near the top. 'Nothing would make more difference to the place', he wrote to Archbishop Head, who was going to Lambeth and who would, he hoped, see whether McKinnell was the kind of man who cared about the service rather than just the music in chapel. He was, and more. Besides his music McKinnell was a man of immense

Tableau at the art school gates, beneath the concrete sculptures of Rix Wright, 1957. The gates themselves were fabricated by senior boys from Manifold House to designs by W. J. T. Honeybone and P. W. Titterton.

GEELONG CHURCH OF ENGLAND GRAMMAR SCHOOL, CORIO.

SCHOOL SONGS

DEDICATED BY KIND PERMISSION TO
The Rev. F. E. Brown, D.D.
HEADMASTER 1912 - 1929.

Edited by META S. MOORE.

For private circulation amongst present and past Geelong Grammarians.
3rd Edition, December 1930.

GEELONG CHURCH OF ENGLAND GRAMMAR SCHOOL

... CORIO ...

MUSICAL SOCIETY

OPEN REHEARSAL

of a Selection from

"MESSIAH"

By GEORGE FREDERICK HANDEL
(1685-1759)

SATURDAY, 22nd AUGUST, 1936
———— at 7.30 p.m. ————

strength and toughness, who put many in that hearty place to shame by going for long runs across neighbouring paddocks (some of them newly sown), much to the indignation of the farmer, Spitty, who levelled his shotgun at the tall intruder.

Darling later described McKinnell as the rock on which the school's music had been built—'or perhaps I should have said blasted'. He had the patience to conjure a band and an orchestra out of nothing but a few instrumentalists, the energy to fight Darling for the funds he needed and the enthusiasm to capture the school. As Darling told Donald Mackinnon, in March 1932, music was beginning to flourish exceedingly. Forty-one boys were studying the piano and twenty-four—learning 'various horrid instruments'—were practising all over the place for the orchestra. He cursed the lack of a hall and pointed to the need for a proper music school, which he foreshadowed in 1933 by getting the Geelong bandmaster and trumpeter Percy Jones to start a cadet band and by moving all the oom-pah-pah from the south-west corner of the quadrangle to a large new music and band room west of Perry House. McKinnell, always on the scrounge for space and instruments, was as excited by this as he had been in June 1931 when his prayers for a concert piano ('nothing would do more to foster music') were answered with a Steinway grand.

Fostering music became a passion, but converts were relatively few. Although the school seemed to have moved with astonishing speed from scorn and ignorance to interest and understanding, with a Music Society of 130 members (about a third of the enrolment in 1934), the true picture was tainted by the presence of a large number of 'ne'er-do-wells who wish only to get out of study on Friday nights'. On Sunday afternoons, when special concerts were arranged, there were only fifteen or twenty boys in an audience of thirty or forty. Those concerts, which Darling was prepared to fund generously, brought to Corio musicians like Dr A. E. Floyd, Bernard Heinze, Lorna Stirling, Isabel Carter, Richard Chugg, the Prockter trio and the Sydney String Quartet. Dr Floyd, by the way, was one of the allies Darling sought early in his crusade. Organist at the first service in the chapel, in 1915, he was the first adjudicator of a house music competition which was launched in 1932 and was successful in involving more and more boys. Every week the chapel choir, which McKie described as immensely keen, grew stronger and the whole school was exposed to the enlightenment of congregational practice when, if the singing dragged, Darling would clap to the time and prowl around calling for mouths to be opened, then suddenly shout, 'Do it again', and keep them all back. He was making steady progress but was frightened that a residual antipathy would surface.

There was nevertheless plenty of blood in the stone. To William McKie, an Australian who became famous as organist and choirmaster at Westminster Abbey (1941–63), the 1936 *Messiah*, with the junior school and chapel choirs, other volunteer singers, tyro instrumentalists and a few experts from Melbourne and Geelong, was unforgettable. Although technically 'aboriginal', he remembered it twenty-five years later as one of the most inspiring of his career. By 1938, when McKie left for Magdalen College, Oxford, a great salient had been gained. From 1935 music had been an optional subject in the timetable and there was an orchestra, a small string ensemble, a competent cadet band, a good gramophone, a growing record collection, excellent Sunday afternoon concerts and a spirit of give-it-a-go that was expressed most strongly in the members' concerts of the Music Society and hearty house music competitions. Through the houses a great river of song represented by such pieces as 'The Poacher', 'Trade Winds', 'Oh, no John!' and 'Where'er You Walk' flowed into the school. A sign of the times was an exchange of visits in 1938 by the choir, band and soloists with Scotch College, where John Bishop was reaping his first crop from similarly virgin soil.

All this, as the Scotch visit showed, was placed on a new plane by the construction of the music school, with its pleasant hall, in 1938. Now there was room, and containment in soundproof studios, for the Babel of musical voices, storage for instruments and scores, a library, gramophone room and director's study, with separate quarters for the band. Buchan, Laird and Buchan, pursued at every step by a headmaster anxious that this would be an emblem of his ideals, found the way to link beauty with robustness and, through McKie, with functional clarity. Completed in April and opened on 14 August 1938, by Dr Malcolm Sargent, the music school was the response of the Bell family,* to Darling's expressed desired to civilize through music and to William McKie's energetic pursuit of that aim. After a rush inside from the north terrace because of a shower of rain, John Manifold officially accepted the building 'as one of those things we have hoped for and dreamed about, but, waking, have been forced to put from our minds as utterly impossible and utterly unattainable—at least in our time'. Malcolm Sargent, never having heard of Geelong Grammar until his invitation, was surprised with what he found and, as reported, was English enough to feel for the fragility of Australian society, set between the traditions of Europe and the 'get-rich-quick' philosophy of another continent. He took home with him a model of a kangaroo, presented on behalf of the architects by the headmaster, whose philosophy he had underlined by depicting music as spiritual food balancing a diet that had traditionally nourished mainly the brain and the body.

Like the art school, the music school made possible things only dreamed of before and made easy what had previously required minor miracles of organization. Under Lance Hardy (1939 and 1946–49) and John Brazier (1940–45, 1950–65), assisted from time to time by John Dawson, Percy Jones, Len Barrett, Jock McKinnon and others of a tribe of visiting instrumental teachers, the building was a sounding-board for change and development. In big efforts

---

* W. Max Bell was a member of the council. He joined with his sister, brother and aunt Mrs J. Biddlecombe to remember his mother, Anne Carstairs Bell.

S. PAUL'S CHURCH, CAMPERDOWN

RECITAL

by

WILLIAM McKIE
City Organist, Melbourne

and

THE CHOIR
of
GEELONG CHURCH OF ENGLAND
GRAMMAR SCHOOL

Sunday, 2nd May, 1937
at 3 p.m.

Geelong Church of England
Grammar School

HOUSE MUSIC COMPETITIONS
SATURDAY, 29th JULY, 1944
at 7.15 p.m.
JUDGE: A. E. FLOYD, Esq., Mus.Doc., A.R.C.M.
(Organist, St. Paul's Cathedral, Melbourne)

The following song has been prepared by all Choirs:
"YARMOUTH FAIR" .. .. (Norfolk Song, arr. Peter Warlock)
Each House has two Reserve Items, which will be performed only in the event
of their being called upon by the Judge.
————PROGRAMMES————

GEELONG HOUSE:
CHOIR: "Linden Lea" .. .. (R. Vaughan Williams)
PIANO SOLO: Valse, Op. 64, No. 2 .. .. (Chopin)
D. C. SOWDEN
CHOIR: The Set Song.
PIANO TRIO: "The Wedding March" (from the "Midsummer
Night's Dream") .. .. (Mendelssohn)
PART SONG: "The Lass of Richmond Hill" .. .. .. (James Hook)

CUTHBERTSON HOUSE:
CHOIR: "Impatience" .. .. (Schubert)
ENSEMBLE ITEM: "Soeur Monique" .. .. (Couperin)
Violin: J. S. NALL: Cello: D. H. A. NALL: Flute: J. M. COURT:
CHOIR: The Set Song.
PIANO SOLO: Etude in G flat, Op. 10, No. 5 .. .. (Chopin)
R. W. BENN.
PART SONG: "Simple Simon" .. .. (J. C. Macy)

like those in drama, the 1936 *Messiah* was followed in 1941 and again in 1949 and 1958 by Haydn's *Creation* and in 1943 and 1944 by parts of Bach's *Mass in B Minor*, which was performed in its entirety in the centenary year, 1957. The 1941 *Creation* was notable for the singing of the famous Australian tenor, William Herbert, and for the first use of the whole school in the choruses. Across the years other performances included *The Marriage of Figaro*, *Trial by Jury*, *Samson*, *Christmas Oratorio*, *Blest Pair of Sirens*, and the *Faery Queen*. The counterpart of Virgil's bimillenary pageant of 1931 was the Bach bicentenary of 1950, which concluded in a darkened chapel with the composer's final work. Choral music was always stronger than instrumental, except perhaps for the band, which passed from Percy Jones to Len Barrett in 1948 and to Jack McKimm in 1955. It was usually placed first or second in competitions between school cadet bands.

The military band outside the music school in 1957, a year of pageant for the school's centenary.

Visiting artists continued to open many doors into the mansions of classical music and frequently left their stamp of approval on what was being done at Corio. During a visit with his renowned orchestra, Boyd Neel adjudicated the 1947 house music competition and said that he knew of no school that could provide such a concert produced entirely by the boys. He would have enjoyed the 1958 *Creation*, sung in the chapel on Sunday evening, 17 August. All the soloists were boys and the chapel had rarely contained such a thrilling sound as when the whole school joined the choir in the choruses. In the chapel in general and in the place found for music in pageants and plays, as well as in closer involvement through instrumental work, the emotional mainsprings of the new generation were being wound. Fixed near the heart of the school and extended through all its lateral involvements, music was its own fanfare for Darling's day. As early as 1938 it had been possible to mount a Sunday-afternoon concert entirely provided by recent old boys, some of whom, like Ivar Dorum, were making their way into professional ranks.

It is easy to see the headmaster's influence in the emphasis on oratorio rather than, say, Gilbert and Sullivan, as at Geelong College, although he had to be convinced that Haydn's *Creation* was a great work. Brazier believed that Darling's chief interest was the music for chapel services, which he helped to draw up, thinking carefully about the impact of tunes and words. On one occasion Darling, who had not been well, suggested the hymn 'Strong Son of God'. When it was pointed out to him that the last verse began, rather infelicitously for schoolboys, with 'Our little systems have their day', he retorted, 'Well, I don't know about yours but mine is having a hell of a spin at the moment'.

During 1958 and 1959 the system of the chapel organ was in more than a spin. Brazier had nagged the headmaster about it for years. It had not been adequate for the enlarged chapel all through Darling's period. At last, in March 1958, dismantling began and there was complete silence from September until January. It was not fully alive again until the May holidays of 1959, when Mr Goodey, the chief voicer of J. W. Walker and Son, arrived from England to complete the voicing of the pipes and their scaling to the size of the chapel. Lost in the process was the animal whine given by the old motor when starting up after periods of silence. Instead there was a long-awaited trumpet. The rebuilt organ gave a new dimension to sacred concerts, with stirring fanfares and swelling support for the great choruses. In gentler mood it was a delightful instrument for recitals like those frequently given for organ and flute by J. R. Brazier and the Reverend Howard and Mrs Margaret Hollis, whose arrival in 1959 from Westminster Abbey greatly enriched the school's musical life.

Play-reading
The presence of buildings and equipment at the Yacht Club, mechanics and carpentry shops and the art school ensured a permanence for their activities that had no parallel on the intellectual side of things. Some clubs, like Darling's Shakespeare Society, played the same role as the pageants in lifting life at Corio to a new plane. For five years, until Shakespeare was tackled on stage in 1936, Darling sent formal, gilt-edged invitations to a dozen senior boys every fortnight, asking them to gather after evening chapel to read a play. Later cartoonists might have had fun with J. G. Gorton as Malvolio and R. J. Hamer as Shylock. Darling included his many guests, two of whom, in July 1932, were allowed to take over: Dame Sybil Thorndike and her husband, Lewis Casson, acted the murder scene

from *Macbeth* and a lively part of *The Taming of the Shrew*. Then there were tea and buns.

A phenomenon of the 1930s was the appetite for modern plays, which were introduced through a Play Reading Circle in 1930 to supplement the activity of the Shakespeare Society. Soon four societies were needed to cater for the demand. In 1934 the Thorndike met with C. R. Bull, the Casson with N. H. Roff, the Wilkie with W. N. Jaffray and the Garrick with D. I. Cameron. On Sunday nights after chapel, attracted also by cosiness and good suppers in masters' houses, as many as fifty boys were engaged in reading from such collections as *Famous Plays of 1933* and *Fifteen Modern British Plays*. The secretaries had to be well organized to arrange the supply of texts. The importance of the suppers and the warmth is evident from the sporadic and not very successful meetings—in a cold class-room—of only one group in 1935. After that Bull took them back to his own house where Mrs Bull provided 'very fine suppers'. In 1937, when the school moved to more serious productions, play-reading was restricted and in 1938 was confined to the fifth forms.

After Bull left there was a gap, filled more and more after 1945 by productions of Shakespeare. And when another Dramatic Society emerged in 1949, with K. J. Mappin and P. M. C. Hare in charge, the emphasis was on performance, not reading. A one-acter, *The Playgoers*, was given on Boat Race Night and in the May holidays twelve boys went into camp at Mornington to prepare for *Twelfth Night*, the major event of the year. With the beginning of house plays in 1953 this emphasis on performance became the norm, as we have already seen.

If

MUCH VIRTUE IN IF
—AS YOU LIKE IT.

Geelong Grammar School,
Corio.   December, 1931

Literature was pursued out of school in an occasional literary society and through the *Corian*, *If* and *If Revived*. The original *If*, to which C. R. Bull was midwife, had emerged in 1929 and had survived Darling's 1930 decision that boys would write the *Corian*, which thus became an important part of the civilizing upon which he was engaged. *If* was more fragile than its big brother but, before it died in 1935, it had patches of brilliance in the poems of Michael Thwaites and John Manifold, who edited it in turn during 1931—32 and 1933.

Out of the ashes of *If* rose a more plebeian creature, the *Corio Courier*, during second term 1935. It was a gossipy broadsheet that had a circulation of five or six hundred, including 170 subscribers outside Corio, and appeared regularly until the paper shortages of World War II curtailed production. An advertising leaflet in the *Corian* of December 1935 announced that the paper was written and partially printed each fortnight by the boys of Geelong Grammar School. Rates (posted) to parents and old boys were 1/6d per term or 4d per copy. In December 1941 an 'extra special' one hundredth issue appeared, with a cover and three times the usual number of sheets. At the same time, indicating an integration not achieved by the media in the outside world, a *Corio Courier* newsreel was filmed by a special unit of the paper and screened in the last week of first and third terms.*

For a time, when shortages of paper closed the *Courier*, the newsreel stood alone, but by 1943 there was no more film. After the war the *Corio Courier* made desultory appearances and in 1949 the Camera Club promised a regular Corio newsreel in colour for Saturday night entertainments. The first edition featured the Scotch football match and the cadet camp. In the 1950s the *Corio News* was a short-lived successor to the *Courier* and in 1961 *Tempo* was born to fill the same slot.

The use of the movie camera for journalism was typical of the general linkage at Corio between art and craft, which was also expressed by the school press. Stimulated by Peter Westcott, who succeeded Bull as senior English master in 1940, with energy and zest no less than Bull's, the *Corio Scrapbook*, forty or fifty pages of original contributions 'tied with ornamental string' was produced in 1942. It lasted a number of years before being succeeded in 1949 by *If Revived*, the organ of a new literary society, whose first editor, Rupert Murdoch, hoped to achieve the standards set by the *If* of Michael Thwaites and John Manifold. Using the press donated by his father (see p. 284) he was able to include art (there was some now) as well as literature. To the surprise of the headmaster, who set aside a few lines in his annual report to congratulate the editor for his enterprise, efficiency and business acumen, the articles were of a high quality, though not as high as the advertising charges, which were forty times the ruling rate!

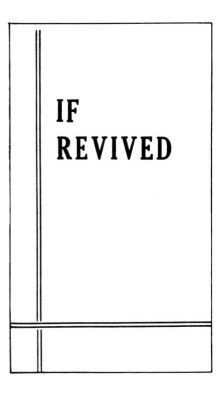

FURTHER STIMULATION, 1962–1980

Drama

Although the pattern set in the arts by Darling continued in the 1960s and 1970s there was growth, fluctuation and change. In drama, Ken Mappin left in 1967 after producing fourteen school and eleven house plays in twenty years. Having overlapped with Mappin since 1959, Tim Murray took over the main load of providing stage experience, usually as producer but occasionally as writer or actor and always as adviser and organizer. Dick Johnson mixed skilful acting—his Fagin of 1971 was unforgettable—with considerable production skills, and John H. Buckley, mostly to be found behind the scenes, produced from time to time.

Murray, Johnson and Buckley, as writers, with Murray as producer, helped by other masters, some wives and several boys in what was called 'The Group', put on sparkling reviews in 1965 and 1967. Mappin found the second instalment delicious, with writing of professional quality from Murray. Tommy Garnett was not as involved in drama as Darling had been, but he took the narrator's part, movingly, in *Lord of the Flies* at Easter 1971. Charles Fisher was

* An earlier attempt had been made in 1936.

Twelfth Night, 1964.

more adventurous, appearing (alternately with the bursar, Jim Winchester) as the bishop in *Salad Days*, a role he had had nearly a lifetime to understudy.

Theatre at Corio was more relaxed and perhaps more varied in this period. Shakespeare had almost gone and in his place came many recent works like Rattigan's *Ross*, Stoppard's *Rosencrantz and Guildenstern Are Dead*, *Salad Days*, *Oliver*, and *Oh, What a Lovely War!*. Comedy and satire predominated and, as always, musicals were deftly handled, the resources of the music school providing a range of sound.

As in the past, drama contributed to special occasions. When Easter was late and the school remained at Corio, or sometimes on Anzac Day, relevant plays were performed. One of the most memorable (for its crucifixion allegory) was the aforementioned *Lord of the Flies* in 1971. Anzac Day 1975 brought two plays—David Campton's *Us and Them*, and 'Anzac Scrapbook', devised by Tim Murray and two students, Clytie Prime and Hugh Crole, using wartime letters and diaries.

The history of drama, since its birth under Darling, could have been read from the paraphernalia of dozens of productions stashed in the Bracebridge Wilson Hall. Flies, backdrops, costumes, cardboard armour, wooden swords, papier-mâché props and all manner of things into which hours of work had gone, were jumbled together. They were fused in flames and scattered as ash when the hall burnt down just after midnight on Wednesday 6 October 1976. Fortunately Westcott's great fear that an audience might be trapped inside was not realized. The fire put an end to the torture of June and July nights when major productions were staged in the icy hall. The phoenix that rose from the ashes was a new beginning. Warm, carpeted and comfortable, with a spacious and flexible stage, it accepted small informal pieces as easily as large-scale productions.

294

Whereas drama had once been exotic, it was by then everyday. From 1972 there was a drama option in form five, with a broad syllabus. Besides group drama, resulting in lively activity, middle-school boys were strongly involved in *Lord of the Flies* and *Oliver* in 1971 and parties from all levels attended the performances of the Melbourne Theatre Company's seventh season. The Children's Arena Theatre actively involved their audiences during visits to Corio. House plays flourished, and while there was no ballet at the school, one of the notable changes of attitudes during the 1960s was related to men and dance. When Mappin persuaded Peggy van Praagh, art director of the Australian Ballet, to talk to the school in 1963, scepticism and resistance melted, especially when Karl Welander and Kathleen Geldard danced excerpts from *The Melbourne Cup*.

Music

In the 1960s instrumental music strengthened in many schools, but especially at GGS, where it had been neglected. Darling's appointments had been choirmasters and organists. His own preference was for sacred music. McKie, Hardy and Brazier (who, although trained as an architect, had studied music under Dr A. E. Floyd) had all favoured the choral tradition, which was further strengthened in 1959 by the appointment of a fine singer and organist, Howard Hollis, as chaplain. Garnett, on the other hand, moved quickly to recruit Arthur Tomalin, a string player, to lay the foundation of a proper orchestra.

When Tomalin arrived in 1962, after playing the violin in two London orchestras and teaching at several schools, there were few string players at GGS. For two years he had to fill out his timetable by taking extra pupils at Geelong College, The Hermitage and Morongo. When saying farewell to him in 1971, Mervyn Callaghan, who had taken over from Brazier as director of music in 1966, paid tribute to Tomalin's orchestral pioneering and hinted at the price he paid by describing him as too gentle to have been completely happy at Corio, where sensitivity had to be balanced with toughness. Among Tomalin's achievements was a combined orchestra with The Hermitage, which led to annual combined concerts, beginning in 1964, with The Hermitage, Morongo and Geelong College.

By 1969 there were three orchestras at Corio as well as various ensembles, including five string quartets, a woodwind and brass group of twenty-one and a chamber orchestra. Music was given status by the appointment of the first captain of music, Malcolm Garnett, in 1969. The numbers taking outside examinations had increased tremendously to 121; the piano (53), violin (34), flute (10) and clarinet (12) were the most popular instruments. An important foundation had been laid with the introduction of string classes at Bostock and Glamorgan in 1967, but cellos and basses remained scarce. Despite an increase in visiting teachers and greater depth of playing, instrumental music was relatively thin until the late 1970s, when girls added a gentler outlook on life. An idea of relative standards was given to Music Society members in 1969, when they attended a concert at Melbourne Grammar. They were amazed by the string playing achieved there under the baton of Harry Hutchins. In that year, after the resignation of Jack McKimm, the brass band was reconstituted. Woodwinds were added and the brass augmented to form a full military band, which, with the addition of strings, became the school orchestra. The first full-time bandmaster, M. A. Guzelian, was appointed in 1970. He taught the bulk of the wood-winds and brass at Corio and Bostock.

In a hard-hitting review of music in 1972, Mervyn Callaghan tried to persuade parents to start instrumental instruction early—the violin and piano before eight years, the bassoon and double bass by thirteen. 'Too old at fourteen' was his catch cry. Somewhat conserva-tive in taste, he was a perfectionist and scholar. Although strong in choral music after experience at Wells Cathedral, he was committed to a comprehensive policy and was grateful to Garnett for persuading Bostock, Glamorgan and Timbertop to co-operate. The construction (by boys) of practice rooms at Timbertop in 1970 helped many musicians to maintain their skills during their outdoor year. When Dr M. S. John succeeded Callaghan in 1975 there were six full-time members of the music staff and the music school at Corio was overcrowded. To simplify teaching, much more group work was introduced—even on the piano, which six students could play at once by using an electronic keyboard laboratory.

In a weekly musical interlude during Monday lunchtime at Corio, students and staff performed solo and ensemble. Regularly, usually on Friday afternoons, local and international celebrities gave concerts for the Music Society. Carl Dolmetch brought ancient instruments (in March 1965). Singers like Morris Williams, Brian Hansford, Elsa Haas, William Herbert and The Scholars (graduates of King's College, Cambridge) appeared and there were groups and solo players from the Melbourne Symphony Orchestra and visits from the Concert Band of the RAAF. The school's musicians gave many concerts in Geelong, often with other schools. In September 1975 fifty-seven students and nine staff toured the old GGS heartland of the Western District as orchestra, choir, ensembles and soloists. At the end of each year at Corio there was a full-scale concert, extending to two nights from 1971. However, for most boys, and later girls, their major musical experience was in the houses, during and leading up to the annual house festival of choral and instrumental music, usually run as a competition.

Despite the improvements in instrumental work, choral music re-mained central in the life of the school. The chapel choir was the most cohesive group and provided a reservoir of singers for other choral work. An Opera Society flourished briefly in the late 1960s under Alan Woodend, a veteran of Gilbert and Sullivan productions in Geelong, who also conducted the senior choir of about thirty voices. *H. M. S. Pinafore* in 1968 was the Opera Society's highlight, thanks to the superb soprano voice of Michael Fullerton and David G. Parsons' excellent tenor; but the day of boy sopranos singing female parts was nearing its end.

Girls added great depth to music and triggered a more positive response among boys. Even before the deluge of 1976, Elizabeth Hurley was captain of music and Robyn Edwards leader of the orchestra. A senior girls' chapel choir with thirty-eight voices was started by the organist, John Leggett, in 1977—when the boys' choir of about fifty, under David Wade, a fine tenor and French horn player, contained six middle-school girls. With this stimulus, rather than diminishing when chapel was for a time made voluntary, sacred music strengthened. A Gregorian Society was founded to perform plainsong. Finding rehearsal times for all these groups was a headache. In addition to pupils, members of staff could be seen hurrying off at lunchtime or assembling before the evening meal. In 1977, for instance, Messrs Pringle, Endean, Persse, Pope, Roberts-Wray, and Winchester were in the chapel choir, just as, apart from the professional musicians, Tassie Pappas and John Bedggood (violins), Ian Edwards (double bass) and John Pascoe (trombone) were in the school orchestra. Not many staff were interested in a short-lived Folk Society which was formed to sing and listen to singers in 1965.

Art

After Denny Evans' departure to Scotch College in 1962 the art school was lifeless at weekends, except for a time in 1963 during a craze for wall panels, coffee tables, drink coasters and pot stands, treated with mosaic tiles. Inspired by J. H. Buckley, a fine colourist, excellent work was produced in 1965 and 1966 by Bill Beasley, Fraser Fair and Mark Downing. When Buckley left in 1967 Brian Magson, a graduate in advertising art and an experienced teacher, came from Newington College, Sydney, where he returned in 1973. He was styled co-ordinator of the arts and technical departments. An organizational man, he absorbed boys studying pottery and general art into his regular Council of Adult Education classes and began a life class involving senior boys and their peers from Chanel College, Morongo and The Hermitage. In June 1968 GGS hosted a student and teacher art workshop run by the Art Teachers' Association of Victoria, with 180 participants in all kinds of media. A week later 1200 people visited Corio for an exhibition of student art from New South Wales and associated workshops.

Garnett's concern for the development of the individual was expressed in 1970 by a sixth-form course in design; students were encouraged to solve problems by experimenting with different materials and approaches. In 1971 and 1972 three Geelong craft workers came to teach part-time. They were Mary Gartlan, a potter, Ken Jenkin, a printer and Cliff Barclay, a photographer. Scouts were out looking for a sculptor, but he did not emerge locally. Ki Nimori came in 1974 from the American school in Tokyo, after studying in the United States and Germany. In 1972 David Dipnall, designer and draughtsman, was appointed art school assistant to control materials and stores. He also inspired hot wire polystyrene and fibreglass sculpture. Choices in the fifth-form art course were expanded to take in art history, painting, graphics, sculpture, pottery, stage design, advertising, silk-screen printing, photography, fabric printing and mural work. The base in middle school was a choice of art, sculpture, pottery, letterpress/graphics, woodwork and photography. All this was stronger in the classroom than out of school. A council of students to help run the art school was not mooted until 1972, despite the rhetoric of participation.

That was a long way behind the carpentry and mechanics shops, where student committees had operated almost continuously. Carpentry was the stronger. From 1966 to 1969 there was no Mechanics Club. Although metalwork had been in the curriculum for senior boys since 1963, the mechanics shop was mainly a hobbies area where they experimented with machinery. In 1963, for instance, Whitfield mounted a Ford Prefect motor on a large, self-propelled slasher. Lower down the school metalwork remained central during class hours. All members of form 2 and two groups of form 3 were given a general course of metal, bench and lathe work.

There was an interesting displacement in the late 1960s. With the fading of the Mechanics Club, the listing of J. L. P. Elmes as mechanics master changed to carpentry, cabinet-making and joining. Alongside him P. E. J. Jardine ('Jards' to generations), who was president of the Carpentry Club and responsible for the shop, changed from carpentry master to woodwork master. A wizard with wood, a great enthusiast and a good organizer, Jardine had come from experience in England in 1961, like a new edge on a chisel. An era of sculpture in cedar and Huon pine, and inlays with many woods, began. The trend was from saw and plane to lathe and carving tools. The twenty-fifth anniversary of the shop in 1965 produced new benches and tools and a healthy display of work. The *Corian* took note. From 1964 until 1966, when other art and craft began to appear, woodwork led a trend towards illustrating creative achievement. Jardine encouraged boys to enter outside competitions run by the Arts and Crafts Society of Victoria, and the Geelong and Melbourne Shows. Many first prizes were won. He wanted the school to know itself, so a glass case appeared in the quadrangle to hold a continuing exhibition. In an annual show, to which in 1966 Richard Weatherly contributed a superb buck antelope carved from cedar, the shop became a gallery.

Jardine took leave in England during 1973 and 1974 and worked for a time, fortuitously, with the great craftsman-sculptor, Cecil Thomas. He came back recharged, determined to push for a craft centre and for craft as an option at HSC. In the meantime, together with new lathes and jigsaws, the shop was refurbished so pleasantly that it was used for a barn dance and as a gallery restaurant. As in the old Big School in Geelong, during Speech Day weekend in 1976 gum branches were hung from the rafters. Pride in craftsmanship, long-standing loyalties, a recent association with the royal family and a new-born enthusiasm for Australian woods inspired silver-jubilee gifts for the Queen and Prince Charles in 1977. The Queen received a jewel case of Huon pine, inlaid in Queensland maple, with the arms of the school. Made by Jardine and five boys, it was rimmed inside with red bean and contained polished pendants of coolabah, sheoak, gidgie and banksia. For Prince Charles, George Chirnside had turned an orb-shaped stud box of Huon pine.

Mick Lodge painting, c. 1959

'What is going on? Is it art?' In 1977 Claire Hanley, head of the art department from 1974, answered her first question with a description of the multitude of activities available for boys and girls, from first to sixth form, in and out of school. At HSC students could submit folios in forty-seven different categories of art and craft, and GGS included most of them. Batik, spinning and weaving, enamel-work and macramé were more recent additions. The art school was open for 'activities' on four weekday afternoons and on Saturdays and Sundays. That question was easier to answer than 'Is it art?', which sparked a further series of questions about the relative importance of intuition and logic and about notions of beauty. In a time of rapid changes in fashion, she concluded that one had to keep an open mind. Ferment and uncertainty were even stronger than when Hirschfeld had urged boys to experiment in the 1940s and 1950s.

Festivals

In a trend towards a greater concentration of activities into blocks of time that was paralleled in Easters spent at school and in holding cadets on Fridays once a term rather than on scrambled afternoons each week, Corio held festivals of arts in 1972, 1975 and 1978, from Friday afternoon until Sunday night. They were a step up from open days, featuring music and art, which were often held in conjunction with the school play, Speech Day or Middle School Parents' Day. The 1972 festival was organized by Alan Woodend and opened by Barry Humphries. All the muses were active, through art and craft workshops, choral and instrumental music (including a jazz concert), plays, debates, poetry and essay competitions, experimental films and many exhibitions. Cocktails were served on Friday in the headmaster's garden and a buffet dinner on Saturday in the Darling Hall.

In 1975 Derek Nimmo and a fanfare of brass launched a larger festival, which included both Speech Day and the patronal festival of the Chapel of All Saints. The list of activities was much longer than in 1972. 'Big Games' were held for children in the Perry Quad. Young poets read their own work. An 'any questions' panel, gymnasts and sailors performed. Asian students prepared traditional food and the school looked at its own traditions through a words-and-music hour of the Darling era, featuring his speeches, McKie's music and poems by boys like John Manifold and Michael Thwaites. Films and

299

slides were shown of current outdoor activities involving Timbertop, the Explorers and the Camping Club. To the tidal wave of visitors 800 extra afternoon teas and 300 buffet dinners were served on Friday 31 October. On the Saturday, hundreds of parents and friends hived off to their children's boarding-houses for lunch. At the sung Eucharist on Sunday morning the former chaplain, Howard Hollis, preached about artists and saints. The festival was medieval in its mingling of secular and sacred, renaissance in its gusto, and very Geelong Grammar School.

The jubilee of the Corio campus in 1964 was echoed in those festivals. It began on All Saints' Day, 1 November, with a jubilee service and ended a week later (just over 400 years after Shakespeare's birth) with *Twelfth Night*. During an interval in the play a candle-light dinner for 450 was served at the baths, after which boys with lanterns quietly shepherded the crowd to points of vantage for a *son-et-lumière* display. The flavour of a Venetian fiesta or Elizabethan carnival was maintained with fireworks, and boats sliding like glow-worm gondolas across the lagoon. At a fanfare from the tower, the front of the school from Barwon House to the war memorial was successively illuminated. Later the band played in a square of light near Cuthbertson House, gymnasts performed on the main oval and small boys with sparklers snaked and whirled. At the main entrance beneath the tower the laying of the foundation-stone was re-enacted to a *feu de joie* from the cadets and the pompety-pom of the band. Then the guests filed through the quad for the second half of a brilliant *Twelfth Night*, in that ghost of earlier days, the Bracebridge Wilson Hall.

The success of such concentrations of time led to an experiment with 'extended activities' in September–October 1976. Organized by Elizabeth Britten, Jonathan Harvey and Roger More, the idea was to enlarge activities usually crammed into Tuesday and Friday afternoons, except that for the sixth form there were special seminars (Manning Clark came back) and the middle school was given two days for excursions. Forms 4 and 5 could choose between a ceramic dig and on-site firing near the lagoon, cadets, photography, drama, shooting, a four-day excursion to the Grampians, gliding and golf. Over five days in 1977, while the sixth form sat for mid-year exams, forms 1 and 2 had special subject days, form 4 was led by staff and visitors in creative and performing arts workshops and form 5 left Corio to give community assistance, gain work experience or undertake challenging recreation. Some went to the Civil Defence School at Mount Macedon; others made wine or dresses; some skied cross-country, some walked, some glided.

Literature

Just as the might of the sword declined in the early 1960s, so did the might of the pen. *If Revived* died in 1961 and it was five years before creative writing was published again—in the *Corian* when Michael Persse became master-in-charge. However, as a successor to the

300

Corio News of the 1950s, *Tempo* appeared in 1963, at first in the swaddling clothes of seven roughly-stapled, cyclostyled, foolscap pages. For three years it was set at school and usually printed there, but technical trouble with the school press in 1965 led an energetic schoolboy chairman, John Davies, and an American master, A. Saalfield, to arrange for the complete printing in Melbourne of a much more ambitious journal. Earlier losses were recouped as advertising revenue and circulation leapt. The only snag was censorship from the 'powers-that-be', which was, perhaps, a natural outcome of the policy of editors Christopher Wood and Ed Lewis to produce a newspaper rather than a literary magazine. In 1966, under joint editors Mick Forwood, Ted Mann and Rob Southey, *Tempo* grew to twelve and then sixteen pages. A special Head-of-the-River edition sold out at 1350 copies. Girls' schools were targets of an external sales drive, but *Tempo* lived hand to mouth.* The fourth of a pleasing six issues in 1967 was the first in a long time to make a profit. With an inherited debt of $400, the 1968 committee returned to in-house printing and tried to overcome problems of lack of continuity. None of the staff in 1969 had worked with *Tempo* before. They put a lot of work into an aborted edition about the history of the school. In 1970 the ailing magazine put out *Corio 1969*, containing sixty-eight informal photographs of the school and its surroundings, bound in (horror!) Melburnian blue, and expired.

It is worth commenting that the school press, which had been intimately associated with the *Corio Courier* and had set early *Tempos*, had been in crisis over the jubilee celebrations edition of *Tempo* in 1964, partly because the removal of third form from the senior school (with the fourth form at Timbertop) had cut off the flow of apprentices. From then until 1969, when Peter Westcott finished his thirty years as master-in-charge, the press concentrated on stationery and programmes. In 1971 under Ken Jenkin, a Geelong printer, the press was back at the art school, with much better facilities, and third-form students were learning the craft.

In balancing tradition and change, the *Corian* stepped unexpectedly out of line in 1966, when Michael Persse took over from John Ponder as master-in-charge. One of Darling's champions, Persse inadvertently added to Garnett's difficulties with old boys and with many present ones by including poetry and much more art. From one lonely page of woodwork photographs each year in 1964 and 1965, seven of woodwork, painting and drawing appeared in 1966 and a continuing level of about fifteen from 1967, with pottery and clay sculpture as well. From a sprinkling in 1966, poetry grew to a separate section of sixteen pages, on blue paper, in 1968. The format changed. The floppy overlap was guillotined from the cover, much larger main headings were used and—as they had in the 1930s—attractive illustrations headed major topics. Anonymity retreated; for

---

* Twenty years later a copy emerged from beneath floorboards at Braemar College (formerly Clyde). Lipstick was visible across Mick Forwood's face in a photograph.

Michael Persse

the first time since 1935 club and sports reports bore the initials of members of a large *Corian* team. From three boys it soon grew to seventeen, many of them scarcely noticed otherwise in school affairs. Andrew Lemon, boy editor in 1967 (there was another change of cover), remembers going along enthusiastically with Persse's policy and learning a great deal about the practicalities, yet being aware that the new (or was it reborn?) *Corian* was regarded as somewhat off-beat both at home (his father was a council member) and at school.

Michael Persse was surprised at the conservative forces lined up against him, but his team stuck to its guns in 1968 when, in a survey, senior-school and old-boy readers panned the poetry and artwork. The survey revealed that OGGs were much stronger readers than current boys of everything except sport. Only a quarter of the expensive publication was being read within the school. There was a bored response to requests for suggestions about additional topics. The new cover just scraped through against the old coat-of-arms and almost half the old boys would have preferred an informal digest and the full *Corian* only on subscription.

Funding was always a problem and the crunch came in 1968 when the council decided that it could support only two issues a year. First and second terms were thrown together. Explaining their plight, the editors pointed out that the school paid most of the cost of the *Corians* for an old boys' society increasing by over a hundred a year. In 1966, of 5000 copies printed, 3000 had gone to old boys, whose society paid only $400 of an annual cost of $5000. It was also impossible to compress the activities of three times as many boys and three extra sites into the same number of pages as in the 1930s. Inflation was at work on printing and postage costs. These difficulties led in 1973 to a subscription approach at $1 an issue. With more secure funding, and with an eye to a postal subsidy, the magazine moved back, for the first time since 1913, to quarterly editions.

Under Persse there was a more self-conscious tone. Greater space was given to the Geelong Grammar family in longer and more numerous appreciations and obituaries of teaching and general staff. Many personalities were reclaimed from the past. Masters and headmasters like Bracebridge Wilson, Cuthbertson, Morris, Lindon, Williams, Garrard, Brown, Darling and Cameron; council members like Harwood, Manifold and Mackinnon; old boys like Belcher, Hawker, Hudson Fysh, the Fairbairn tribe and the Jacksons lived again. Some covers carried four or five portraits, others showed line drawings of the school past and present—including, in 1976, views of The Hermitage and Clyde. Bill Beasley's return to sketch the quad was recorded in June 1973 and Jamie Grant, maturing as an Australian poet, was represented in 1971, as he had been copiously as a schoolboy in 1967. The school archives, another of Persse's babies, swept into print through reminiscence and illustration. With the mantle of Cuthbertson on his shoulders, the teacher of history was giving his version of the school's story. It was good.

Finances were not good, despite subscriptions. As another first

W. Beasley. 80.

in its history, in June 1974, during troublesome financial times in Australia, the *Corian* took advertisements. Geelong businesses scrambled in ten to a page in contrast to whole pages bought by national and Melbourne firms like Merchant Builders, rural enterprises and hi-fi and swimming-pool firms. Stockbrokers put in their bids and Gentry Hairdressing, 'by appointment only', announced that it was ready 'for the man on the move'. Further financial difficulties led to the binding of the last two quarters together in 1977, after which 'the quarterly' often appeared indiscriminately and double-banked. Michael Collins Persse apologized and promised to catch up. He had to contend with rapid changes at the school, its size and complexity, and his own perception of flux—'three headmasters and a lengthy interregnum, all within seven years'. The achievement, for him, was that the journal survived as a full and faithful record during a trend to extreme informality in school magazines.

Young potters at work, 1969.

CRAFTS

At the mechanics and carpentry shops and the art school, apart from their public contributions to the art school path, the art school and centenary gates, props and sets for plays and pageants, and toys and clothes for the poor and refugees, many boys invested long hours in boats, radios, leathergoods, pottery and all manner of things for themselves, their parents and their friends. Helped by family wealth, some moved close to the frontier of technology in leisure equipment. In 1930 after the plague of model aeroplanes had finished crashing from the tower, the craze was canoes for the lagoon. A canoe club was formed, whose main rule was that craft should be unsinkable. In 1936 the school erected a hut for a model-railway club, and soon there were a hundred metres of track. In 1949 a rash of boat-building began when Kelly, Little, Masters and Hollis-Bee produced a speedboat. By December twenty boats were under construction, five had been finished and a school launch was on the drawingboard. In 1952 Kelly, Landy and Chirnside made a hydroplane, whose launching in its black and white racing colours was one of the events of the year. With Hirschfeld's help, 1954 and 1955 were the years of skis, stocks and accessories for the newly formed Ski Society, and 1956 saw the first production of tents and rucksacks for the Camping Society. By then the aquatic spirits had made a surf boat, as well as many surf skis and water skis, and in 1960 Richardson attempted a polystyrene and fibreglass 'okinoie' which, being successful, led to another craze that got so out of hand that the process had to be banned from the carpentry shop. It undoubtedly counted against the craze that surfing could be linked to social deviance.

Later, in the 1960s and 1970s, much out-of-school activity, especially in woodwork and art, became an extension of creative work done during school. Every now and then a boy displayed a talent for maintenance and construction. In one term in 1961 Stephen Bailey rejuvenated the engine of *Redwing*, made a trailer for the Boat

Club and a saw bench for the woodworkers and kept the mechanics shop machinery in marvellous order. Cars and car engines were sometimes modified and overhauled. In 1960 there was a rush to make go-carts. The most common activity earlier in Darling's period was bicycle repairs—more and more bicycle repairs—for few at that time could bear life at Corio without wheels.

The presiding mechanical genius for eleven years from 1941 was Mr A. H. Grueber, who had retired after thirty years as chief engineer of the Geelong Harbour Trust's dredge. Instead of the huge buckets, chains and pistons of his old charge, he started the third forms, in options periods, on paperknives, dustpans and garden-trowels, or helped more advanced workers to construct wireless bodies, radiators, pen-holders and brass cannon. In 1948 some of the more expert were copying his model of a small steam-engine. The Mechanics Club faded out in the late 1960s, then reappeared in 1971 as a Motor Cycle and Car Club, fulfilling an accustomed role for those who liked to play with machinery. The Radio Club was given a room at the Bracebridge Wilson Hall in 1950. These yeomen of the soldering-iron not only built receivers but repaired them and other equipment like the Bostock House projector. When radio parts were taxed heavily in the 1950s they became almost as political as the school's embryo socialists. Spurred on by a room in the new science block in 1965, radio enthusiasts explored new fields. They experimented with an ex-Catalina flying-boat transmitter and made a radio-operated salinity-meter for the Science Society's lagoon project.

A similar association with technology is apparent in the history of the Camera Club, which was linked, like the art school in which its darkroom was placed, to many exhibitions and activities and especially to bird photography, which was a vital element of natural history in the school. Not only was the *Corian* embellished with members' prints but their skills and equipment made the *Corio Courier* newsreel possible in the early 1940s and led them to launch the 'Corio Newsreel' (in colour) in 1949. It was one of the oldest and most resilient of clubs, having been founded in June 1930 and functioned continuously, except when hit by a shortage of supplies between 1943 and 1946. In the 1960s the emphasis in photography became more artistic and the *Corian* frequently contained students' work, which improved in the 1970s when Cliff Barclay came to teach the medium.

Starting with the gift of a hand press in 1935, printing became one of the strongest activities at the school. The *Corian* reported in August 1935:

The printing press is now a veritable power in the land. 'Corio Couriers', Chapel Service sheets, and notices of all sorts are coming from it day and night, and its metallic clank will soon be reckoned as essential a sound as the proverbial shooting of hot water from the pipes on the tin roofs.[6]

Part of the Art Club at first, the press achieved independence in second term 1938 as a result of the completion of the art school (in

[6] *Corian*, Aug. 1935, p. 128.

which it was housed) and the acquisition of a power press, on which *Corio Couriers* and other material type-set in Geelong were run off. Both power and hand presses often worked flat out, producing programmes for plays, concerts, exhibitions and the athletic sports, hand-blocked Christmas cards, special menus, cards for the library and house libraries and official school stationery. It could be hectic. In third term 1942, apart from routine items and the *Courier*, there were 2000 sixteen-page exhibition programmes, 800 sports programmes and 400 thirty-page *Scrapbooks*. First term 1943 closed with an attempt to print 10 000 two-colour pamphlets in a few days. Through Peter Westcott's influence, the Press was notably effective in giving boys responsibility and creative challenges. Because it was a considerable industry, the Press was reorganized in 1954. Three printers were given keys and the rest, about thirteen, were enrolled as apprentices, forbidden to use the guillotine or to print by themselves. As part of the well-established consumer society, customers were offered eleven colours of house writing-paper, five styles of type and three sizes of paper. In a special effort for the fair in November 1958, 1500 two-colour envelopes were printed and sold from the downstairs windows of Cuthbertson House, ready stamped for postage in the Antarctic by John Béchervaise, who was taking a year's leave in charge of the Australian Antarctic base at Mawson. The Press usually made a profit, which was ploughed back into more and better equipment, but in the 1960s it found the production of *Tempo* beyond it. Timbertop had made recruitment difficult. The presses were getting old, but there was a significant injection of new life in 1971, with new presses and the appointment of a Geelong printer part-time to encourage art and letterpress work.

INTELLECTUAL SOCIETIES

For the blooding of intellect there were always several discussion groups at Geelong Grammar. In the 1930s, and again in the 1960s and 1970s, the greatest emphasis was on debating, in the 1940s and 1950s on history and philosophy; but all through, perhaps deriving through Darling from Gollancz (see p. 179), there was a focus on public questions and social issues. The club which spearheaded Corio's new openness to the world was the Public Affairs Society, founded in 1936 by J. C. Nield as an extension of the work he had begun with the public affairs form (see p. 211). To stimulate concern for a just society and to challenge boys to think and act on the plight of the poor in the slums of Melbourne, he asked reformers like Oswald Barnett, Padré Baldwin of Toc H and Dr Dale, the City of Melbourne Health Officer, to speak to them. This was followed up by a tour of Melbourne and an attempt at a survey of Geelong's slums by a group of day boys. Later in the 1930s the society discussed the situation and intentions of Germany and Japan and in 1940 whether Britain should bomb Germany and Australia send troops overseas. In the depth of the war they were wondering if democracy was doomed and in 1944 organized a symposium on the merits of 'yes' and 'no' at a Commonwealth referendum. Whatever the contemporary issue, like the treatment of Aborigines in 1946, the society took it up and exposed the school to it. More philosophical questions were tackled by the Philosophical and Historical Society, founded by Manning Clark in 1942 (p. 213). It attracted young academics to speak on a wide range of intellectual issues.

The demise of the Public Affairs Society in 1951 reflects a trend to more philosophical and historical discussion, but also expresses the popularity of a new approach to debate represented by the Areopagus, founded in 1947 under the wing of Mr J. B. Ponder and Mr P. N. Thwaites. Based on the Oxford Union, it provided greater participation and frivolity, although attracting much the same type of speaker as the Public Affairs Society. It unearthed schoolboys who would later speak even more forcefully on their chosen topics—as in December 1949 when R. H. Carnegie argued that atomic energy would bring great benefits to the world. Topical questions gave interesting results. The house predictably agreed in 1948 that the American way of life was a menace to civilization, but in 1955 surprisingly voted 32−7 against the abolition of exams. It was deadlocked on the subject of compulsory sport until the president cast his vote against it. In 1961 traditional sporting rivals, Geelong College, joined members of the Areopagus in the music school for a debate broadcast over 3GL on the likelihood that space exploration would increase the chances of world peace. It was perhaps apt that the last debate of Darling's final year should be a theological-scientific-philosophical questioning of the proposition that the Earth is flat. Flat indeed, concluded Mr M. D. C. Persse, the society's *eminence grise*, on the two counts that it had lost its original cosmic effervescence and was musically flat in the harmonies of heaven.

As well as making regular appearances in the 1960s on 3GL's Forum of Youth, the Areopagus took a plunge into television in 1964 on HSV 7's Parliament of Youth. Fifty schools competed. Great prestige was won in 1965 when the previous winners, Star of the Sea, were skilfully 'wrong-worded' in a semi-final by a GGS front bench of John Burnell, Barry Apsey and James Philp, who had the assistance of thirteen not so heavily made-up backbenchers. The winning idea for the topic 'Does slang corrupt the language?' was not merely to admit that it does but to add that out of the compost heap of that corruption the richest blooms appear. Having twisted that key word so neatly, the team laughed when they heard that the topic for the final was 'Does power corrupt?'. 'Yes', they said, and won.

Many hours of preparation for both rounds of the competition were distilled in Mr Persse's study into what Niall Brennan, speaker for the series, described as 'a degree of subtlety bordering on profound scholarship'. These were good words to take home as a counter to insinuations in the press, regarding the enrolment of Prince Charles, that the school was no place for civilization or intellect. Taken home, too, were £100 for the school library and an impressive plaque.

Though without such public exposure, the Areopagus continued into the 1970s as one of the oldest and strongest of the school's societies. Sometimes the tendency to hair-splitting and word-twisting generated concern, as in 1972 when a debate on the sensitive situation in Ireland was bawdy and trivial. As a result, the committee decided that all who attended debates must be prepared to speak.

In the ebb and flow of intellectual societies, a Social Order Club came into being in 1948, Rhetorical and Political clubs in 1949 and International and Historical societies in 1950. The last had dissolved its marriage with Philosophy, which later also functioned alone. The 1950s were the province of history to a tried formula of papers each term from a master, a visitor and a boy. Peter Moyes (1949–50), Barry Connell (1951–55) and Michael Persse (1956–72) were presidents. Among the guests were A. G. L. Shaw, P. L. Brown, J. A. C. Mackie and R. G. Tanner. Godfrey Tanner, a very amusing speaker, later professor of classics at Newcastle, came to GGS in some guise or other nearly every term in the late 1950s, when the Philosophical Society was strong and vitally concerned with the relationship between history and theology.

The Historical Society drew large audiences in the 1960s to numerous papers (ten in 1962, eleven in 1964) and in 1964 held its 100th meeting. However it seems to have folded after a quiet year in 1972. Similarly, in the 1970s there was apparently little life in the Philosophical Society, which had been revived in 1968 after a long lapse. A record attendance of eighty people, including Morongo and Hermitage girls, attended an address on existentialism by Peter Westcott in 1969.

Apart from the Areopagus, the intellectual flavour of the 1970s was found in chess, bridge and film. The Film Society, founded by Mr Eyre-Walker in 1964 to encourage an appreciation of the cinema and to view films of artistic merit, was still going strong in the late 1970s.

A Political Science Society had a burst of activity in the mid-1960s. In 1965 B. A. Santamaria, with a well-received message about the dangers to our region of Chinese communism, preceded R. J. Hawke, who was taken with a grain of salt on industrial arbitration and trades unionism. As a sad commentary on the school, it was considered daring to have asked Hawke—in much the same way as Russel Ward's action in asking the communist Ralph Gibson to address the Public Affairs Society had brought storms of protest in 1939. Although Arthur Calwell was received enthusiastically in 1964, the society was more at home with Liberals like Billy Snedden and the Country Party's Ian Sinclair, but it was ailing, and expired in 1967, the year before John Gorton became the first Old Geelong Grammarian prime minister of Australia. A regular in-school current-affairs session for the sixth form came to cater for appetites in this direction by covering a wider range of topics and attitudes. It reflected the school's ability to attract prominent and interesting people.

Science out of school was supported in 1930 by the Ionians, who

At the commencement of his address Mr. Calwell warned that if as a result of his visit 'the flag of revolution is raised over the Western Districts', then the Headmaster must be held responsible. It is unlikely that Mr. Calwell sowed the seeds of such a change. However he did make a profound impact upon all who heard him speak. Seldom has the School heard an address presented with such conviction and sincerity.

Mr. Calwell went on to speak of the philosophy of the Labor Party and its relevance for the present day. He recalled those forces which motivated the founders of the party and suggested that these very forces still provide the fundamental ethos of the labour movement. He pointed out that socialism is not something new or revolutionary, but is a political ideal which has always been associated with human suffering and the dignity of man. As such, it is just as relevant within the affluent society of the 1960's as it was at the beginning of this century, for just as poverty reduces the dignity of mankind so does capitalism and affluence.

Arthur Calwell, leader of the opposition, spoke to a packed meeting of the Political Science Society on 5 June 1964, about the aims and methods of the ALP. Afterwards he presented to the school a copy of his book, *Labour's Role in Modern Society*.

aimed to broaden the physics and chemistry of the curriculum with geology, botany and zoology, but who did not see out the year. At that time the strong natural history tradition of the old school was carried by the Corio Ornithologists' Society, with its more practical approach, linked to Saturday Parties and the museum. Details of nests and birds observed were reported to the society and written up for the *Corian*, which in 1935 made much of a nest curiously shared by a chestnut teal and a kookaburra, and reported D. Hawker's rescue of a week-old, black-cheeked falcon chick from the cliff of the Batesford quarry. He set out to train this 'excellent pet' for falconry. Swarms of bees were taken in 1936 and one hive was set up in the museum in such a way that the bees entered through a ventilator and were visible through a glass panel in the side of the hive. At that time Mr Ponder was busy reorganizing the museum as a centre of scientific activity. He had begun an aquarium of lagoon life in the quadrangle and hoped to encourage bird photography and butterfly collecting. To cover this new approach a Woodburn Society (naturalist, not just ornithologist) was founded in 1937 and took over the running of the museum. Years of neglect meant months of work classifying and rearranging exhibits. Special displays, changing every few weeks (ahead of much professional practice), were developed, some with a social focus: on Anzac Day, for instance, the museum's grab-bag of war souvenirs was supplemented by loans from the headmaster, Mr Bull and Mr Coulter.

After World War II, when John Ponder and Rolf Baldwin returned, the Natural History Society entered a brief golden age. Saturday Parties were challenged to go beyond traditional nesting to bird photography and beyond that again to a survey of all the animal life of the Corio district. Prominent in their activities was John Landy, as tireless and successful then in pursuit of butterflies as he was later chasing the world mile record and more butterflies. Members used their skills to organize the extinction of local mosquitoes. They also planned camps—in the Grampians, for instance, in September 1946. At Grub Lane, near Queenscliff, one weekend in 1948 four adults and seven boys covered about 65 kilometres searching for the nest of the swamp harrier. Much ingenuity, thanks to the carpentry and mechanics shops, was displayed in making hides, lofty camera stands and camera-release mechanisms as part of a healthy rivalry to take the best bird photograph of the year. A stray dog took a good shot of a swan's nest, when it triggered the mechanism on one occasion.

In 1949 the society went out regularly on weekend camps by bicycle, with blankets, tents, equipment and food strapped on behind, and in 1952 they were granted permission 'to stay the night among the birds' in order to photograph them by flashlight and to observe their early morning activity. Different members of Saturday Parties had special skills. In 1952 Falkiner was the tree climber, Traill the photographer and Dureau, Gubbins, Hinchley, Gittins, (Tony) Landy and Kelly the spotters:

A. F. AUSTIN NATURAL HISTORY SOCIETY
GEELONG GRAMMAR SCHOOL

GARRARD MEMORIAL RECORD
1948

JUNE. 1949

308

The highlight of the season was the discovery of the peregrine falcon's nest near Lascelles Dam containing four eggs, but was impossible to photograph, since it was about 60 feet from the ground and required all Falkiner's skill to reach.[7]

This activity was given an important fillip in 1948 when a Garrard Prize for natural history was given by Colonel Garrard's widow (Bracebridge Wilson's daughter), who also provided funds for the publication of an annual illustrated record of the society's activities. The first issue of this was greeted with delight in second term that year.

For the study of science, rather than just nature, a Scientific Society, limited to twelve members, was founded in 1937 to give sixth-form scientists a forum. It focussed on work like that of B. C. Sinclair-Smith (who demonstrated the embryology of the chicken), but did not survive the war. A more lasting format was devised by Mr Howard in 1952 when science was furthered by 'lectures' and the construction of 'scientific apparatus'. It flourished, especially as the vehicle for bringing to the school many celebrated speakers. In second term 1958 the society's secretary talked about the history of nuclear research. He was followed a term later by Bart Bok and in 1959 by Linus Pauling. Bok spoke to the whole school, 'with all the authority of a very great man', about the frontiers of astronomy. But the scientists were a little deflated at the end of his talk when his offer of 'a valuable monetary prize' for the first intelligent question was snapped up by a linguist.

From the Cinderella of the disciplines in Brown's period, science had become fashionable and exciting. It was at the frontiers of knowledge and gradually attracted many of the best scholars in the school and provided challenging avenues for individual activity. The idea of constructing scientific apparatus was taken up by the Science Teachers' Association of Victoria, who instituted a Science Talent Search, with generous prizes for experimental initiative. In 1959 the three GGS boys who entered each won a bursary: R. H. Crozier studied ants, S. M. West examined some little-known silicon compounds and an electronics whiz, M. J. Molesworth, built an oscilloscope. The emphasis on investigation was appropriate at GGS and each year thereafter the school's entrants to the Talent Search explained their work to the society before submitting it for judging.

The new science building of the mid-1960s provided for research of this kind. It indicated a greater emphasis on physics and chemistry. There was a crisis of confidence at the museum, which moved once again in 1964 (fatally, as it turned out) to the Bracebridge Wilson Hall. Largely through the efforts of R. D. Patterson, the collection was reorganized; but there were few visitors. Rather than arrays of rocks, butterflies and birds' eggs, modern science museums were concerned with life-histories. It also came as a shock that some Timbertop naturalists failed to transport their enthusiasm to Corio. For one of them—the indomitable Peterjohn Nicholson—it may just have been that there were no wombats, into whose holes he had crawled in the cause of science during 1960. Decades later the school

Bird List for Yan-Yangs

March 24 1947 (see P. 3)

Eastern Shrike Tit
Yellow Robin
Grey Fantail
Black and white Fantail
New Holland Honey eater
Orange-winged Sittella ?
White plumed Honey-eater
Grey Thrush
Dusky Wood Swallow
Rainbow Bird
Whistling Eagle
Fairy Martin
Eastern White face
Eastern Rosella
Spotted Pardalote
Restless Fly catcher
Bronze-wing Pigeon
Nankeen Kestrel
Black Swan
Grey Teal
Blue Wren
Yellow-tailed Thornbill
Red backed Grass Parrot
Red browed Finch
Spotted sided Finch
Stunning Plover
Black fronted Dotterel
Quail ? winted . (G.M.P)
Peregrine Falcon
Brown Hawk
Welcome Swallow
Magpie
Magpie Lark
Raven

[7] *Corian*, Aug. 1952, p. 105.

has received requests for his article on wombats from all parts of the world.

On a different plane, bringing to science the group activity Darling had instituted in drama, the Scientific Society conducted a major project in 1966–67 to investigate the Limeburners' Bay lagoon. Very little was known about such places. Physics, chemistry and biology were involved, and help was given by the Fisheries and Wildlife Department, CSIRO and the Shell company. Boys were soon unchallenged experts on the lagoon's salinity, temperature variations, plankton and plant types, crabs and other residents. The Radio Club provided a buoy with a transmitter to signal water and air temperatures and salinity, until it was run down by early-morning rowers. In a later enquiry, in 1973, the effects of sewage on seawater were measured at the lagoon, Breamlea, Torquay and Anglesea. In addition to this research the Science Society brought in visitors with interesting ideas, information and gadgets.

Closely related to science was an Astronomical Society, founded in 1945 as a result of the gift by the chaplain, the Reverend J. H. Allen, of an old 6½-inch reflecting telescope by which the moon, the planets and the brighter stars were studied. The history of the society reveals a Micawberish waiting for the completion of an equatorial mounting, which began with concrete foundations near the rifle range in 1947 and was completed to gear box and traversing wheels in 1952, after which there is silence. The speculum had been resilvered and the mirror reground and in the *Corian* almost every term's report from August 1948 included the refrain, 'next term we hope to have the telescope operating'. Fifteen years later, thanks to Mr and Mrs Richard Perkin, who gave new mirrors, a dome on top of the physics and chemistry block held an effective telescope. A group of boys spent a year helping Jimmy Goucher, the laboratory assistant, prepare the mounting for the 10-inch instrument, which Mr Perkin unveiled on 15 October 1967.

In another field related to science, a Mathematical Society, founded in 1956, drew audiences of fifteen or so to frequent talks on subjects outside the matriculation syllabus and forty or more to annual Mathematical Association lectures at Melbourne University. Conversant as they were with complex numbers, computers and Einstein's theories, the top mathematics form made their presence felt on the day of the Centenary Garden Party, in April 1957, by setting up an exhibition which Alice might have found appropriate on the other side of the looking-glass.

This included a centrifuge, a double cone that rolled uphill, linkages for drawing straight lines and describing other loci, conic envelopes and loci of conics, a demonstration that the cycloid is the brachistochrone, and a machine, McLeay's brainchild, for solving cubic equations hydraulically.[8]

In the intellectual ferment of science elbowing the humanities aside, it should be no surprise that 'The Society' was formed in 1953 to try to bridge C. P. Snow's divide. It flowered for two terms but failed to

[8] *Corian*, Aug. 1957, p. 157.

310

continue into 1954, perhaps because it was one of the few societies started and sustained by boys—even though they called in staff to help maintain order.

The only rural emphasis in such a country-based school was given by an Agricultural Society, founded in 1949 and having a very strong base in boys from the agricultural forms (see p. 206). Presided over by Mr J. S. Cook from 1949 to 1958 and then for three years by Mr I. A. Dean, it was probably the strongest GGS society, with 130 members in 1951 and over 200 in the late 1950s. For the first time since the heyday of Saturday Parties there was a natural outlet for the interests and energies of that rural core in the school, and a chance to brush off on others their belief in the land. For the first time in Darling's period the basic principle of civilizing through a general education was relaxed, although Darling had been tempted during the war, as Gordonstoun did, to use boys on the school farm.

Because of its size the Agricultural Society was frequently divided into four or more sub-groups, sometimes having their own group leaders and seconds. One of its strengths was its ability to tap, through the State Film Centre (thanks to the efficiency of Mr Eyre-Walker and his projectionists) a spate of films developed for agricultural extension work. With these, lectures by visitors and trips to the State Research Farm, the Sheep Show and nearby properties (Norman Gubbins at Birregurra was frequently their host), as well as with larger tours when Ivo Dean took over, the society kept in touch with the best of farm practice. There were always old boys ready to help. It tried also to be active, first with the fencing and planting of a 2.4-hectare wattle plantation between the golf course and the playing-fields, and later, when trace elements were in the news, with experimental soil plots to give the lead to local farmers. Senior boys from the land also helped to look after the school sheep, and a centenary good intention was the clearing of weeds and rubbish from the foreshore. In the 1960s the society reverted to a programme of films and talks, maintaining its popularity until the 1970s, when it faded away.

OPEN TO THE WORLD

The great panorama of out-of-school activities which Darling instituted was linked to his plan to open up the school to the world. Early in his headmastership Saturday nights were community nights, available for lectures, entertainments, plays, clubs and societies.* Although a boy was expected to be somewhere, there was a sense of relaxation about Saturdays, reflected in the unpopularity of community singing, introduced by William McKie in 1935. When there were no lectures, where at least one could sleep, clubs met early so that at 8.15 the whole school could go to the torture in the Bracebridge Wilson Hall. Two or three times a term, especially on the first Saturday, films,

---

* Later, clubs and societies usually met on Friday.

preferably British, would be shown. In the 1930s there was the miracle of sound, in the 1940s colour and in the 1960s the competition of television, when audiences shrank back into the houses. All through there was the winter chill of the breezy hall and scuffling interludes when reels were changed or when the projector broke down.

The visitors Darling regularly invited to speak to the school and open its mind and heart were a who's who of contemporary Australia. Because they excited him and he them, the young headmaster often gained their support for his wider vision of the school. This attitude brushed off on staff, who as a matter of course sought and gained as guest speakers for clubs and societies people who could draw large audiences and stimulate new thought. This was especially true of the Public Affairs Society and the Areopagus, though it is fascinating that for all their politicians, scientists and other public men (women were as rare as roosters' teeth) the largest audience ever to hear a Public Affairs speaker was drawn in 1948 by Ernie Old, a cyclist aged 72, who was covering long distances across Australia.

By 1932 most of the professors of the University of Melbourne had spoken to the school, as had Sir John Monash, Robert Bernays, H. S. Gullett, Napier Waller and many other artists and public men. A privileged group was conferring further privilege. Over the years local and international celebrities, thinkers and doers, came almost every week. There were radicals, dreamers, explorers, journalists, scientists and all other categories of people, among them Robert Speaight, the British actor; Dr Kagawa, the Japanese mystic; Walter Gropius, the German-American architect; Dame Sybil Thorndike, the actor and Roy Curthoys, editor of the *Argus*. Darling turned to Curthoys and English contacts like Archbishop Temple and Sir Frank Fletcher of Charterhouse in seeking further visitors for whom a day or two at the school, with the headmaster as host, came to be highly regarded. He also received a stream of priests and bishops who arrived for weekly chapel services and the annual confirmation. His house, in fact, was the threshold of an interesting adventure, the meeting-place of the real world and the semi-ideal society he was trying to construct. The school will probably never lose that influence. Although not as numerous, as varied or as exciting as those Darling attracted, the stream of visitors has continued.

Some visitors are held briefly in focus through the records of the school archives, an out-of-school activity that commenced after a room was set apart for it in 1949. In association at first with the museum, and under John Ponder's care, it burgeoned under Michael Persse in the 1960s. The meagre documents and photographs at its beginning did not build up rapidly, but a spectacular find in a school storehouse during 1952 of hundreds of photographs of the old school and early Corio was a great stimulus. This made possible a large display for Founders' Day 1953, when Pinner, who came from retirement to talk about the school's ninety-eight years and especially to reminisce about his own time, drew an audience of 300 who stayed on after the lecture for an epidiascope show of the pictures. A tradition of special displays also began in 1953 with a selection of material about building projects to honour the retirement of the bursar, Milton Thewlis. At the same time, to catch history on the hoof, a record book of fledgling Timbertop was commenced.

Little, though, did the people who called those materials the archives realize that as they slowly gathered such precious relics of the past Darling's energy was continuing to create a body of correspondence, and the school's operations were laying down a set of records that would delight and give years of employment to a professional archivist.

In the game of musical spaces at GGS, the archives were often on the move; from the quadrangle to the Bracebridge Wilson Hall in 1964, to part of the old forge in 1968, to a room above the kitchens in 1969, to the history centre in 1972 and (apparently with some permanence) to the Hawker Library in 1979. The rolling stone gathered a wealth of material. The commissioning of this history started an avalanche of gifts from old boys, staff and friends. With help from groups of boys on Tuesday and Friday afternoons, Michael Collins Persse organized the cataloguing of the collection and the indexing of the school magazine. He could feel satisfied that few schools in the world have the raw materials of their history preserved so well.

Drawn by Denny Evans, 1959.

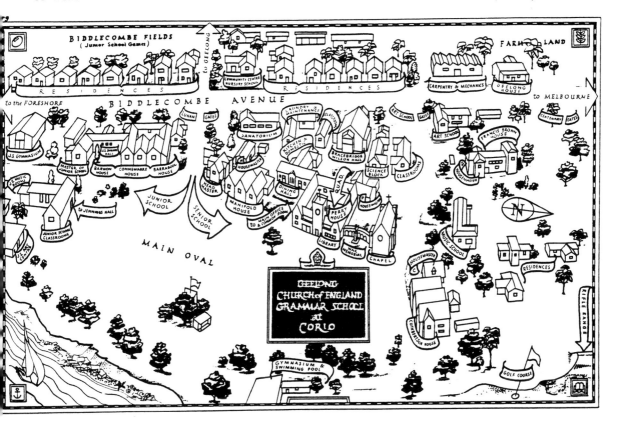

13

Toughened and tested

The same feet which trod the path to enlightenment at Corio were shod with boots to continue the school's hearty nineteenth-century tradition through the bush, cadets and games. Athletes and sailors wore special shoes but accepted the same challenges to stretch themselves and consummate a marriage of heart, mind and body that expressed another Athenian ideal with which English public schools, perhaps through their classical tradition, were imbued. The addition of the bush, as we saw in chapter 7, and then its extension to Timbertop as Darling's empire expanded, remained a unique contribution of Geelong Grammar to Australian education. It has been copied, although as a short-term experience, by many other schools. The aim has usually been to remove students from the consumer society, to throw them on their own resources and help them to learn to be humble in the presence of nature.

In charting the path to the mountains, in more detail now than was possible in chapter 9, and recording experiences there, it is important to notice the shrinking of our world, the loss of virgin environments and the multiplication of distractions and amusements as the concept and use of leisure time has permeated society.

OUT OF SCHOOL
The bush
The range of alternative activities discussed in chapter 12 may partly explain a decline of Saturday Parties. The editor of the *Corian* in 1931 lamented the fact that the increasing pressure of Saturday games against other schools was hindering 'one of the first things of which a stranger hears and the last thing an old boy forgets', and that golf, tennis and other attractions, 'easier to arrange, but not such good exercise', were leading many to waste the greater part of the day for a few hours' pleasure. For, although there was probably general agreement that the parties fostered a desirable independence and love of the bush and that more lasting friendships had been formed during Saturday Parties than in any other part of school life,

changing circumstances eroded their popularity. Except for rowers on training trips down the Barwon to The Willows, Cormorant and other favourite spots, it was left to an enthusiastic minority to keep the old spirit strongly alive. In the 1930s, for instance, Frank Kellaway loved to get up before 4 a.m. and wake the rest of his party, one of whom tied a string to his big toe and dangled it from the second-floor window of another house. They cycled into the bush to walk, swim, and climb trees to photograph nesting birds. A later editor, in May 1948, mourned the fact that only about 10 per cent instead of a former 80 per cent of boys were taking that traditional break from the discipline and restrictions of the rest of the week. He calculated that 40 per cent of the school were now playing organized sport, a further 10 per cent were at the music and art schools or in the carpentry and mechanics shops and 10 per cent huddled over wirelesses, listening to jazz or league football. The rest, not on Saturday Parties, were just sun-baking or aimlessly loafing about. He was not optimistic that the parties would revive if sport was abolished because he detected a laziness, selfishness and softness in his generation. Perhaps, though, the school was just a more pleasant place to be in. It certainly provided alternatives lacking before.

To attack softness with more extensive outdoor activity the ex-Royal Marine, Arthur Seels, founded an Outdoors Society in 1950, to organize hikes, weekend camps, cycle trips and interstate tours. It was succeeded in 1956 by the Camping Club, organized by Béchervaise and Stone. Fifth and sixth formers were allowed to spend weekends away, as long as they had a distinct purpose (ornithological, historical, etc.) and were prepared to submit a proper account of their activity. They made their own tents and rucksacks, planned their own scale of rations, opened a well-stocked store and, as well as local hikes, explored the Tasmanian wilderness. In January 1960, when Béchervaise was on leave in Antarctica, Stone emulated his absent colleague's 1949 Geelong College Exploration Society climb of Federation Peak with a party of seven boys supplied by air and flown out from Lake Pedder. In May 1960 three old boys and two present boys, hiking from Timbertop, spent several days half-lost in the mists and snows of the Great Dividing Range, plagued by wet sleeping bags, taking three hours to light a fire and subsisting on hard-tack biscuits designed for Antarctic use. These were said to be capable of sustaining working bullocks.

For the third forms an equivalent activity was The Explorers, a club through which John Béchervaise put their legs to work in the near country, with nature observation in mind. He always wanted something more than 'the freedom to eat his burnt chop when he likes, and to send rocks crashing down the hill into the river' of many Saturday Parties. In groups, sometimes of twenty or more, but often reduced by games commitments, they went by bus to such places as Steiglitz, with its old mines, the Lerderderg and Moorabool Gorges, Blackwood and the You Yangs.

315

In the shrinking world of the 1960s and 1970s the rhythms of life changed rapidly. Informal Saturday Parties lost all appeal. Timbertop made the Moorabool and Steiglitz seem tame. The You Yangs were infested with cars; the Barwon was civilized. Adventure prescribed greater challenges, found during the holidays through hiking in the mountains. More sophisticated pleasures represented by four-wheel drives, speed-boats, surfing and skiing swamped the ideal of the simple life.

That Timbertop was the bench-mark was indicated in 1960 by the decision to take the third form out of the cadets into a third-form training scheme, as 'a basic introduction to the challenge of Timbertop'. Despite a military hangover of house platoons drilling for Anzac Day, their corps afternoons were spent learning bushcraft, which was put into practice in the Otways for a week at the end of second term. In 1963, under Garnett's influence, a broader philosophy was evident. The pressure of Anzac Day was removed and, because the aim was to help boys live in harmony with the bush, an attempt was made to jettison the term 'Timbertop Training', by which the scheme was usually known, and to suggest a progression of experience from third form through Timbertop into later life. The title 'Bush Training' was used. There were ten groups of about ten, each with two sixth formers. The senior boys lectured on practical matters and, with slides of their own bush adventures, inducted the young into the mystery of the high country.

Coincidentally, third formers were used quite deliberately in The Explorers to keep the old Saturday spirit alive—especially during lulls in the sports programme. Parties were *organized* (and that is the difference) by John Béchervaise and Rolf Baldwin for outings by bus to the ancient Moorabool Gorge, where they found wedge-tailed eagles, falcons, orchids, koalas and an occasional platypus. Because parties of twenty were necessary economically, they had often to be made up with second-form boys. Perhaps never again, Baldwin lamented in 1967, would it be possible to get even third formers regularly into the bush; certainly not on bicycles, as they had on one of three excursions in first term that year. The goal was Stonehaven on the upper Barwon, 21 kilometres away, but many became lost, their bicycles broke down, and the escort car was involved in a collision. It seemed, after that, that their fathers had been he-men in the 1930s to make the 32 kilometres by bike to Steiglitz and back—even though that generation could not compare with the walkers and rowers of the nineteenth century.

The school's outdoor tradition was brought to an essence at Timbertop. Alarmed by the softness and inconsequence of many boys, and aware, like the *Corian* editor of 1948, that substantial challenges were missing from their lives, Darling exposed them to the wilderness. His philosophy and Montgomery's initial interpretation of it have already been discussed (p. 219ff). The effect on boys has not, except for the way Timbertop increased the irrelevance of Saturday Parties.

Mike Hanley briefs a group of boys setting out on a hike from Timbertop (in the background), 1965.

The Timbertop weekend hiking programme, building up through first term to a long journey and by the end of the year to five days in the bush, was seized upon by the strong and adventurous as an opportunity to perform epic feats. Whereas the Saturday Parties from the old school had well-trodden paths to follow, there was competition at Timbertop to plan more and more challenging hikes. Parties pored over the ordnance survey maps, talking about possible routes. Time was precious. It became a science to cut down the weight of packs, to set up and break camp quickly and read maps efficiently. As had been hoped, the majority emerged much more independent and resourceful.

But even Timbertop, remote in the 1950s, enjoyed little more than a decade of challenging solitude. By 1965 Forest Commission roads and tracks were turning the wilderness into a four-wheel-drive playground. Family cars could reach the Wonnongatta and Howitt Plains. Mt Buller was an all-weather intrusion. During trips over the Crosscut Saw in the 1970s unsympathetic chainsaws snarled continuously. Not only were challenges removed but dangers were added. In 1967 vandals burnt the Eight Mile hut and the school's hut on the Timbertop–Buller track. In dry summers the fire danger multiplied. Shooters were also an unpredictable menace. In November 1967 two boys, one terrified by indiscriminate shooting, were lost for hazardously long periods. It took several days of the combined efforts of staff, the Police Search and Rescue Squad, local police, the Mansfield Civil Defence Organization and other volunteers to find them. Pressures like this led to changed procedures in the 1970s. First term exploratory hikes were fully supervised. A staff member was in the lead, another brought up the rear. Walkie-talkies were introduced; everyone checked in and out. A little Timbertop army was on the move, putting extra pressures on the bush when numbers rose from 120 to 160 in 1977.

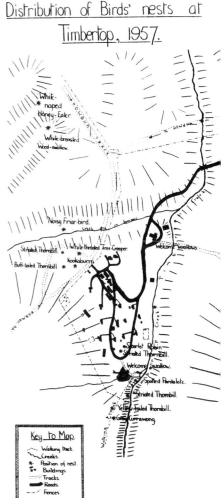

Distribution of Birds' nests at Timbertop, 1957.

317

Timbertop folklore, stemming from narrow escapes, feats of endurance, wild weather and wonderful views, might have needed reassessment when the wilderness retreated, if the bus had not been used to bring into range challenges formerly out of reach at weekends. As soon as the snow melted in third term 1967, parties were taken to the edge of virgin bush to achieve what had been an epic before, the crossing of the Razor to the Viking. Some even went to Terrible Hollow. Now that every other peak was no more than two hours from a track, the Razor had become the most inaccessible Victorian mountain. This gave it a new flavour. For some time boys talked about two waterfalls seen on The Cobbler:

so a party set out to visit them. After following a ridge from Mt. Despair for two hours, they found that the falls were only two large trees with white trunks. However, on their way back to Mt. Speculation they found a deep gorge in which the Catherine River goes over three waterfalls, separated by attractive pools and rapids, with interesting rock scrambling up the bottom of the gorge.[1]

Similarly, during one three-day weekend four boys managed to reach the ghost town of Talbotville from the bottom of Howitt Spur. On the four-day trip a party became the first from Timbertop to climb Snowy Bluff. Just when a generation of hikers had left little new to be achieved, the use of the bus extended the horizon. In 1975 a four-day hike to Mt Feathertop was thought to be a first for the school. Of course the untameable weather provided an extra dimension. February and March 1968 were so dry that the Timbertop Creek petered out. Swimming had to be abandoned and showers skimped. Dust flew everywhere. Cross-countries were shortened, fire-drill stepped up and cold rations stashed in weekend packs. A deluge followed in April and May. The four-day hike through mist, rain and snow was among the wettest on record.

The snow was brought into play for cross-country skiing and snow-camping with the completion of the school's hut on Mt Stirling in 1965. Before that, Saturdays had often been worked during the snow season so that Sundays and (quieter) Mondays could be enjoyed downhill at Mt Buller. The season seemed to go on forever in 1964.

White water from the snows was merely a spectacle until the 1970s when, from a Victorian Canoe Centre mould and drums of fibreglass, boys made twelve kayaks. They joined three school-owned two-man canoes in weekend activities on the Howqua and Delatite rivers. In 1974 seventeen paddlers used the five-day expedition to follow the Howqua downstream into the Goulburn. Most reached Yea and some Seymour. More moulds were purchased in 1975 when twenty-four boys, sometimes working late at night, made single kayaks for themselves and twelve extra for the school.

And girls! After much debate, the Corio infection spread to Timbertop in third term 1975. Fourteen girls arrived, and the change-over from fourth to third form also began (see p. 274). Then fourteen more at the beginning of 1976. Apart from chaperones on overnight hikes, little change was needed. Although some girls showed

(see p. 274).

[1] *Corian*, Third Term 1967, p. 351.

318

no interest at all, others were better in the bush than boys. Their presence, nevertheless, helped to firm up the safety organization, especially on long hikes, when vehicles went to prearranged rendezvous each night.

During Timbertop's twenty-fifth year in 1977, the co-ordinator of outdoor activities, Ian Stapleton, spelt out the routines and the reasons for them. Strict control of first-term training hikes had reduced initiative but had raised to 95 the percentage of those who completed them in every detail, thus ensuring a strong grounding in navigation, camping and emergency procedures. After the first free hike, lasting three and a half days at the end of first term, there was a lull until the main hikes of third term. Most second-term activity was on the slopes of Mt Buller each Wednesday, when tariffs were surprisingly low. Stirling was too far away and too dangerous for downhill, the only possible approach to a day's activity. Stapleton welcomed the safe skiing, but noticed the negation of Timbertop values in that trendy, monied world, which he hoped would be countered later by a three-day ski-touring programme centred on the school's hut at Mt Stirling. Units went by turn, just squeezing into the hut. The trek in and out, with heavy packs, was an adventure in itself, but that was increased when one student broke a leg and the rescue sled, stored at the hut, was brought into operation. The CB radio warned the school and the difficult rescue went without incident.

For a period after the snow, when Saturdays were again available and while the weather was uncertain, the school took on various science projects and voluntary service. Some groups worked on local farms, some at Timbertop itself and some cleaned up campers' rubbish (ten trailer loads in 1977) from sites along the Howqua River. Before free hiking resumed, subject teachers took their class-rooms to the bush, during a four- or five-day camp on the Howqua. In third-term hikes, parties of four planned their journeys, had them checked and were then under pressure to carry them out as planned. For safety, fifty-eight log books dotted the area. Land Rovers went to prearranged points at prearranged times in case of accident or illness, averting, by that precaution, any serious outcome from several close calls with appendicitis. Walkie-talkies were in constant use, even on the celebrated five-day hike to distant places, after which the high country was strongly printed on every mind.

There might have been interesting results if an electronic surveillance system had been possible. Within the mystique of long hikes there was, as timber tracks and vehicles increased, a counter tradition of clandestine lifts. In a piece he contributed to the *Corian*, entitled 'What I Have Learned From Timbertop', Hugh Deasey included a revealing paragraph:

I did training-hikes. When I was returning from Eagles' Peak, via Eight-Mile Gap, several groups got lifts in logging trucks. I went in a car for the last mile and a half, and was seen by Mr. Stapleton near Sheep Yard Flat. I tried hard to hide. Those who were in logging trucks said they sat down on the floor, covering themselves in army greatcoats and putting their packs among the logs because there was no room in the cabin.[2]

[2] *Corian*, Sept. 1975, p. 121.

319

Overall, it was hoped, a balance had been struck between appreciating and challenging the bush. Yet there were, as with the Saturday Parties on the Bellarine Peninsula in the nineteenth century, severe environmental pressures, in this case on the Timbertop site itself. Strong measures were called for during the twenty-third year of occupation. Soil studies in their environmental science course alerted boys to the problem of the multiple tracks they made and their disregard for vegetation. The consequent erosion was remedied by contour drains, terracing, the application of 35 tonnes of bark chip, and sowing grass seed. Also in 1975 a major dam, with an island breeding-ground for water birds, was added to the Noel Learmonth Wildlife Dams,* themselves part of an environmental reassessment begun in the 1960s through which a general plan was adopted for the sensitive development of the site and the control of vermin and noxious weeds. In 1971 lyrebirds were rediscovered just above the school. In the years that followed many recordings were made of their songs. To trace their movements, other birds and animals were fitted with tiny radio transmitters.

A minority of students came out of Timbertop delighted by the bush and its challenges. The Camping Club was their route back to the mountains. Every vacation its log book recorded parties tramping the high plains. Some camped in the snow, by using Antarctic tents or building igloos. During the long summer break parties (six of them totalling twenty-five boys in 1963) explored the Tasmanian highlands. The most ambitious planned six air-drops of supplies on its way to Lake Pedder via Federation Peak. Complex operations became routine. By 1963, instead of a secretary-quartermaster the society needed three specialist quartermasters and a secretary. Yet, of all the hundreds who passed through Timbertop in the 1960s, only a handful returned to the mountains:

And so you see—in all the violent activity of this most noble of clubs, the same names recur continuously.[3]

Andrew Hannah, Jonny Madin, Jamie Grant and Andrew Bowman were always in the forefront, with incredible journeys in the Victorian Alps. They walked from Mt Buffalo to Timbertop during Easter 1967, and at the end of that year made a summer jaunt up fifteen peaks between Ensay and Mt Twynam in the Snowy Mountains. The original prime-mover, John Béchervaise, was president of the club until 1964, then Rolf Baldwin, who handed over to Chris Roberts-Wray (fresh from a stint at Timbertop) in 1968. A few years later the name was changed to Mountaineering Club and in 1976 a formal constitution was adopted as a prelude to membership of the Victorian Federation of Walking Clubs. OGGs could remain members.

When skiing strengthened in the community at large as well as at Timbertop, the club fostered Nordic skiing as an extension of

---

[3] *Corian*, First Term, 1967, p. 51.   * Named after a remarkable OGG (1895–8) naturalist and historian.

both the mountain experience and Timbertop forays to Mt Stirling. It proved uncomfortably wet and tough. The first party of two girls and eight boys under Messrs Roberts-Wray and Ross planned a week at huts 8 kilometres from Falls Creek in August 1973, but found their provisions sled unmanageable. Ignominiously, after a wasted day, a snow-cat was hired. Days of cold and wet followed. Klister wax stuck to everything. Undeterred, a party of twenty-one repeated the experience in 1974. Just as feebly they struggled under heavy packs, then waited two days for mechanical help for which the snow was too soft. An eventual arrival was rewarded by several wonderful days. Learning was faster in 1975. The masters went to Nordic courses, an expert visited Corio to give instruction and the party of twenty included an outside expert. Pack-weight was much reduced and the huts were reached for lunch on the first day. Despite churlish weather some excellent snow-camping was done, as a prelude to 1976, when three girls, four boys and Roberts-Wray spent a week in the Snowy Mountains.

The Timbertop experience also extended down the rivers. Just after Christmas 1976 fourteen canoeists from GGS entered the five-day Red Cross Murray Marathon, a bruising, blistering, sun-struck 400 kilometres from Yarrawonga to Swan Hill. According to their organizer, Gordon Ross, who had assisted with Nordic skiing and had considered it the biggest test of a GGS student, this was much more demanding. Two girls were winners and a Canoe Club was formed to perpetuate the torture. At Christmas 1977 forty-one paddlers and five support crew assembled at Yarrawonga for another dose. Well prepared through training on the lagoon and the Barwon and with long outings on the Glenelg and Goulburn rivers, they won a first, a second and three third prizes, as well as raising $4127 for the Red Cross. Entries for the Marathon were regular thereafter.

Sailing

It seems strange that sailing was not taken seriously at Corio until first term 1941, when, with the headmaster as commodore and J. R. Brazier as vice-commodore, the Yacht Club was formed. A boy, W. A. Jaffray, was the moving spirit. By the end of that term Brazier's ancient *Avalon* had been joined by two Jubilees, two twelve-foot dinghies and three other craft and a shed, built almost in a day by eight school carpenters and forty boys (subsisting on pies and lemonade), had been erected beside the baths. Thirty novices had become fairly competent, and in second term the young club was courageous enough to cruise across Corio Bay. It settled down to a routine of Saturday sails and Sunday races in first and third terms with occasional cruises, usually overnight. In winter many hours were spent repairing and painting boats. *Avalon*, eighty years old in 1956, was usually slipped each year.

By 1945 there was an aura of tradition. With twelve boats, six belonging to the school, there could be a genuine sail-past for the opening of the season, when the commodore stood in the stern of

The yacht club sails past the governor, Sir Dallas Brooks, in *Curlew*, during first term, 1950.

Avalon to take the salute and the vice-commodore led the line in *Redwing*, looking very trim in the white paint that had replaced the wartime grey she had worn as the patrol boat of the school's navy class. The advent in 1949 of *Curlew*, a twenty-six-foot motor sailer on loan from Mr M. L. Baillieu, provided a much-needed rescue boat. Being capable of taking a crew of twelve, she was also ideal for cruising. For the annual sail-past of a record nineteen boats that December, the school band played on the cliffs all afternoon and the crews of *Avalon* and *Curlew* were dressed in white slacks, white shirts and naval caps, a turnout they repeated on 26 March 1950 for the vice-regal visit of Sir Dallas Brooks.

As time passed, faster boats such as Gwen 12s joined the fleet, which had also to cope with the increased popularity of boating. In 1955 the Victorian Speed Boat Club churned up the lagoon one weekend and in 1958 the Shell Yacht Club moved into permanent occupation. The hazards of yachting were brought home to the school when two men drowned in the lagoon during the Christmas holidays of 1957. Safety regulations were overhauled in accordance with those of the Royal Geelong Yacht Club, with which the Corio Club had long been affiliated and from which, in 1955, thirty yachts had gathered at the Spit for an annual picnic.

In the ebb and flow of life as well as water, the 1960s witnessed a low point and then a great recovery. When J. R. Brazier retired in 1965 with the gift, for life, of ancient *Avalon*, there was one serviceable sailing dinghy and little activity. W. E. Goldstraw took over and moved the club from the preserve of a small group of boys, using mainly their own boats, to a widely-based activity. The sale of *Redwing* financed the purchase of its namesake, a new Cadet dinghy, which, with a donated Penguin and a school-built Cherub became the nucleus of a fleet. Racing, however, was unsatisfactory until there were boats of the same class. Cadets were chosen, another being purchased and two built at the school in 1967. With these, a Gwen 12, an outboard launch *Crusader* and Brazier in *Avalon*, boats were out every day of the week in 1969, carrying four separate groups of boys. About a hundred took sailing as an activity or sport in 1970, using six school and nine private boats.

The fleet grew to twenty-six in 1971 and forty in 1972, when fourteen Cadet dinghies provided excellent racing. An annexe was added to the shed and a compound was fenced and landscaped to provide a picnic spot for the many parents who joined in at weekends. After his death in 1971, Brazier's memory lived on in annual Brazier Cup races with the Royal Geelong Yacht Club and in the presence of *Avalon*, whose hundredth birthday was celebrated in 1976. By then a girl was captain of sailing, competition was strong and an annual regatta was held with Sydney's Cranbrook School.

Cadets

Born anew, out of a high moral purpose to help restore national self-respect at a low point of Australian defence preparedness in 1930, when the Commonwealth Labor government abolished compulsory military training, the School Corps began as a volunteer body, modelled on the officer training corps of English public schools. The headmaster and council, thinking that the government was passing the buck almost entirely to the British navy, decided, with the blessing of the Defence Department, to replace the house drill units of preceding years with a more military organization. 'The abolition of compulsory military training has reacted with startling effect on the school', reported the *Corian*. A company of four platoons, one from each of the three houses and a composite recruit platoon, was formed under Lieutenant W. N. Jaffray, who, whatever his rank thereafter, and he rose to major, was always called 'The General'—at Corio, that is, for when he joined the Armoured Division in 1941, as a major, his rank was certainly not inflated. Cartwright (1941−45), then Baldwin (1946−56), then Cartwright again (1957−61), took over.

Although assisted by the army, the corps was entirely the school's responsibility and the cadets paraded proudly in their own made-to-measure khaki uniforms. They sported a light-blue rosette on the side of their slouch hats and wore breeches, puttees and jackets with light-blue facings and piping. The puttees were a problem; ridiculous according to one boy and a great art for another. A third remembered that his incompetence left great verandahs on his calves. At first school prefects, smart with canes and Sam Browne belts, were appointed second-lieutenants, but after two years Captain Jaffray had persuaded colleagues in Bull, McKinnell, Fletcher, Clayton and Gordon to be his lieutenants and only one boy, the school captain, H. M. Rutter, was commissioned. Rather than the monotonous old-style drill, the corps provided variety and greater purpose through rifle firing, machine-gun instruction and field craft. There was a 'definitely martial atmosphere about the school', and an alteration of its routine when lunch on parade day, Thursday, was moved to 1 p.m. to allow an NCO class to meet on the chapel lawn beforehand.

The corps occupied a no-man's-land between school and military regimes, carrying a flavour of both and giving staff and boys the opportunity to stiffen formal discipline or undermine it. Overall the soldiers were probably more frustrated than the pedagogues. As one soldier-teacher said in *Thirty-Two Years*, about the problem of satisfying both the headmaster and 3 Cadet Brigade:

However loudly the military watchdogs of efficiency might bark, it was tolerably certain that they would give no bite that might offend the school authorities.[4]

The two systems reflected on each other. There was always shock at the thought of a school prefect serving in the ranks, as many did when promotion depended on attendance at courses during the long vacation.

Among dozens of stories of civilian attitudes gleefully puncturing military pomp, is one of a domino switching of hats to provide cover

[4] *Thirty Two Years*, p. 112.

323

for three cadets who had lost theirs during camp just before a very formal Sunday parade, when 'The General' was on the prowl inspecting his troops and thinking that nothing would escape his eagle eye. Expecting some sort of military efficiency and getting the opposite could also be amusing. There was always joy for one boy in 1944 in the half-hour of 'complete disorganisation', 'as usual', at the beginning of parades when 'Captain Mont tried to work things out'. As his platoon commander, cadet-lieutenant N. G. Maxwell, was cynical and witty, he looked for amusing times ahead, but got more than he bargained for when Captain Montgomery detected a year's rust in his rifle barrel and set about him in his famous way: 'No, you've made no attempt to clean this. I mean to say, the whole corps is permeated with futile people like you.'

Darling indicated his concern that the cadets expressed his goals when he gently deflected Dr T. G. Leary from giving a cup for a military competition between the houses. We are 'rather moving away from that', he replied, and in typical manner, though he said he hardly liked mentioning it, suggested that help would be welcome with expensive outlays for signalling, field telephones and a miniature range. Although there was still a cup for drill that kept house competition alive, he was hoping to reorganize the corps on a non-house basis. When, during the war, the headmaster served as company commander of the recruits, military logic was sometimes confounded by civilian authority. A corporal and his section on Field Day at Mt Duneed were about to make the sublime capture, not just of the military Captain Darling, but of 'the boss', when the forbidding voice called out, 'You get back! I am the headmaster'. What a weapon that would have been for Napoleon to use against the games players of Eton on the field of Waterloo. Darling would also make use of the army's penchant for a 'narrative', or imaginary field situation, and turn to his cadet-lieutenant and say, 'I'm killed, you take over', and leave to deal with some urgent civilian matter. He was happy to make cadets compulsory but accepted conscientious objections like those of Don Baker, who in the later 1930s fed his friends pacifist books and pamphlets. Baker was excused cadets provided that during corps parades he broke bricks with a sledgehammer for school paths.

Soldierly tone was at risk immediately after World War II. Perhaps as a reaction to war, perhaps just because boys were fed up with discipline and restrictions, the corps went through several difficult years. Officers and NCOs were niggled by petty obstruction symbolized in the action of a house prefect who marched past on a formal parade at the war memorial with an armourer's cardboard label fluttering from his rifle barrel. The summary quality of school discipline was invoked at that time, as the following story reveals:

A truculent corporal was paraded by his Company Commander for insolence. Marched into the orderly room under armed guard he was awarded a reduction which was quite unconstitutional, had he but known it. That was not the only indignity, however. Just outside the door was waiting a grim-faced W. O. Bryceson who, on his own initiative and in full view of many gaping cadets, snipped off the offending chevrons with a big pair of scissors.[5]

To Bryceson (visiting quartermaster 1938–49), a warrant officer in the permanent army, such an action would have been unthinkable outside the school. It was not, anyway, his own idea. Apart from the CO, Major Baldwin, who had had extensive war experience, it was Bryceson and his successor, Lieutenant Arthur Seels,* ex Royal Marines who gave a true military flavour to proceedings. Seels was lucky. When he came in 1950 virtually every boy in the school was in uniform and the corps was working well. With the help of colleagues in Cartwright, Montgomery, Glover and Barber, Baldwin had pulled it around. He had not wanted to be a housemaster, so made a special contribution in this field. He agitated for a new self-contained head-quarters, very different from the earlier 'orderly room-cum-storeroom in the III Form block and the rats' castle of armouries and storerooms in the Bracebridge Wilson Hall', where any work at all was done only at 'the great expense of time and patience'. Talking of time and patience, in 1950 everyone gave them to the blackening of boots. The army sent out cans of raven oil and boys initially spent an afternoon effacing the age-old brown and giving more uniformity and a better shine to the articulation of 'atten-shun'! Much else was blackened in the process.

At no step in the movement of those boots, whether brown or black, whether forming fours before World War II or threes after it, was a cadet ever far from the mystique and nationalism of Anzac. The major focus of the corps, apart from annual camps, was its performance, and particularly the showing of the band and the guard on Anzac Day. There was always a panic in first term to get all ranks, and especially the recruits, up to scratch for 'the climax of the term's activities' on 25 April. The school was on public show and each new generation could feel its mettle and be judged on that one day of the year. They practised and practised

until they were considered capable of the march to the Main Oval, the elaborate ceremonial fall-in and inspection of the guard, the march past and the long stand during the service at the Memorial. A measure of the spirit of a year was the rhythm of the marching, the steadiness on parade and the facility with which the guard could 'rest on the arms reversed'.[6]

Linking the school to the nation and the corps to the AIF on Anzac Day, a senior army officer usually gave the oration and inspected the guard. As a rare exception, Charles Hawker, as famous as anyone at GGS, spoke not of the wonderful evacuation or the handling of the troops, 'for many of Australia's greatest generals had already spoken to the school of that', but stressed the part played by private soldiers. He gave examples of their stamina and audacity and

---

* Adjutant, quartermaster 1950–60, described in the school staff list as 'late Phys. Ed. Royal Marines'.

[5] *Thirty Two Years*, p. 111.
[6] *Thirty Two Years*, p. 112.

emphasized that through them Australia became a nation on 25 April 1915.

This rhetoric was sealed in blood during World War II. Anzac Day gained poignancy when, during the memorial ceremony, the headmaster added to the names on the Roll of Honour those of many old boys killed in the new conflict, 'and the realisation that personal friends and acquaintances had died in the service of their country, lent a particularly solemn air to the ceremony'. That immediacy was heightened in 1942 when the salute was taken, not by a general or outside celebrity but by one of the 'rats of Tobruk', a master on leave from the school, Major 'Vic' Tunbridge. In 1943, as the list of old boys in the forces lengthened, and as the navy and air force became stronger fields of service, the Anzac Day parade included the school's Navy Class and its flight of the Air Training Corps, who also marched in Geelong. For the first time in its history, that year the whole corps, accompanied by the Air Training Corps, marched through Melbourne during a Liberty Loan rally.

No keen eye was needed on Anzac Day 1943 to notice that preparation for war had led to specialization. No great intelligence was needed to conclude that in this different war the army had strong competition for public-school enlistments from the air force. Among the dead, by then, there were twenty-nine members of the RAAF and RAF, twenty-two from the British and Australian armies and three from the RAN and RN. Overall, of the total of 1242 named in the *Corian* as having enlisted by December 1945, just over half (632) served in the army, well over a quarter (354) in the air force and a tenth (123) in the navy. There were also six Red Cross officers, two merchant seamen and two war correspondents.*

The new order came in at the instigation of J. R. Brazier and with the support of the navy in 1942, when a Naval Class made its debut at the Anzac Day parade. It settled down to the study of knots, signals, navigation and elementary seamanship, which were put to the test on the Geelong Harbour Trust tug *Penguin*. In 1943 the school acquired its own patrol boat, a fishing vessel called *Redwing*, which, when repainted and overhauled, was able to join the Geelong division of the naval auxiliary on harbour patrol. It also carried the cadets in an amphibious operation, without seasickness, across the lagoon to 'attack' Avalon.

There were twenty-one members in 1943 and more in 1944, becoming skilled at taking soundings with a lead line at the baths and running aground on practice charts. They stayed at school to camp in 'HMAS Perry' in the August holidays and marched proudly on Trafalgar Day. From Chief Petty Officer Ford, their instructor, they felt they caught the spirit of the navy: his quips and yarns were quite as important as what he taught.

---

* The school's Book of Remembrance, delineated after the war by John Derrick (himself a master on active service), includes two names from the South African War, 88 from 1914−18 and 143 from 1939−45.

The first enrolment of Sea Cadets, 1950.

The Navy Class disbanded in December 1946 but was revived as Sea Cadets, again under Brazier, in 1950, when the RAN sought support from the school. Their first and most difficult task was to learn to get into and out of their uniforms and the second how to iron them. This time there was no auxiliary patrol, no pretending to be at sea in 'HMAS Perry'. Instead, for their camp they sailed, forty-seven strong, to Flinders Naval Depot in HMAS *Gladstone*, the first school to take up the navy's offer. Spit and polish was at a peak on 17 November 1954 when Vice-Admiral Sir John Collins, chief of the naval staff, inspected them and their work and talked about the Nelson tradition. The Sea Cadets were popular, with an enlistment of about eighty and with Brazier still in charge in the early 1960s.

A flight of the Air Training Corps was formed at Corio in first term 1942 from twenty-six senior boys who intended to join the RAAF in 1943, but air-force blue was not seen at Anzac Day until 1943. Flying Officer A. S. Marshall, helped by 'civilian' instructors, C. A. Cameron, R. Baldwin and F. N. B. Newman, taught them science, maths, morse, navigation and aircraft recognition for a proficiency certificate. This was not much different from schoolwork, but there were visits to RAAF stations and short flights in service aircraft. As prospects of aircrew enlistment diminished in 1945, the corps lost impetus and was disbanded.

The greater individualism and the glamour of the air force were brought home to the school on a number of occasions during the war when old boys stationed nearby beat up the school with hair-raising, low-level passes. No one in the army or navy could ever imagine stirring the place as two Wackett trainers did one morning in third term 1942. For half an hour, just after breakfast, they skipped over

Shooting team, 1965, with trophies.

roofs, dipped their wings along the avenue and touched down on the ovals, carrying away the string protecting the main wicket. Bill Panckridge remembered vividly seeing one pilot, his scarf blowing across his face, haul his machine up perilously over Cuthbertson House. 'The boss' was furious, and after an enquiry the high-spirited culprits were demoted and put in the cooler. After such a show the performance of two Spitfires, which roared in much faster, but safely, over the rifle range and stopped cricket for ten minutes as they circled and swooped, on 1 December 1944, seemed tame. It was certainly much tamer than the performance of another Spitfire, which buried its nose in the ground and was itself swooped upon by schoolboy souvenir hunters.

With Frank Covill as major then colonel in charge from 1963 to 1971, the cadet corps reached a high point, helped by the absence, after 1960, of third form on bush training. In 1964 it won the proficiency cup for the most efficient unit in camp during the year at Puckapunyal. Drill was good and shooting excellent. In 1964 and 1965 the shooting team won both the Earl Roberts Trophy and the Clowes Cup in competition with all Australian cadet units, and was the most successful of Victorian schools for seven years running, between 1964 and 1970. Out of this enthusiasm for shooting, and stemming perhaps from the abolition by the Whitlam government of the issue of free ammunition in 1972, small-bore rifle shooting gave way in 1976 to shot-guns firing at clay targets. After the school bought a trap in 1977, shooting was organized on Tuesday afternoons over the school rubbish tip.

Field days were elaborately organized in the 1960s to give tactical experience. On one occasion the attackers were taken 30 kilometres from school and challenged to return undetected to inflate a balloon at the rifle butts. Some were eliminated as far away as the streets and stores of Geelong, but one boy persuaded his mother to drive him, lying in the back of her car, to the rear of the range, whence he crawled to his objective. Another boy hid a canoe upstream from the lagoon the day before.

Great changes came to the cadets towards the end of the 1960s, partly in response to questioning of Australia's commitment to the Vietnam war but mainly as part of a new, participatory, educational philosophy. Because the fifth form were two years older than recruits at most schools, licking them into shape for the traditional Anzac Day parade was seen as counter-productive. After 1968 only the guard and band paraded. Because the Sea Cadets folded with 'Admiral' Brazier's retirement in 1965, an extra company of cadets had to be absorbed. New ideas were tried. From 1969, rather than the weekly scramble on Tuesday afternoons, one day a month was set aside. It gave greater continuity. At the same time the recruit fifth formers were given a crash course in basics before being allotted to specialist sections. In their second year, small sixth-form groups tackled un-military tasks like amateur radio, endurance hiking, underwater diving, canoeing, civil defence, small boats, engineering, police and lagoon evaluation, reflecting Garnett's view that the corps was not a piece of the school in the army but a piece of the army in the school. Jonathan Harvey, who served with the Hertfordshire Special Constabulary (1963—70), was able to organize a comprehensive programme of familiarization with police work, thanks to co-operation from the Victoria Police. Gliding (at Benalla) was added in the 1970s when the logic of extended activities (see p. 274) led to the allocation of one corps day (a Monday) each term, in association with a return to regular Friday afternoons, so that, sport permitting, the rare corps Monday could include the whole weekend. In 1974 there were ten girls in the endurance hiking section, tramping the Otways and skiing cross-country in the alps. The extent and intensity of this adventure training represented a spillover from Timbertop. Indeed Timbertop, as in other activities, forced a reassessment of previous policy.

By the end of the period, however, cadets were more military again. The fourth form, more suitable recruits, were back at the main school, the army was taking more interest and Charles Fisher was happy to see Captains N. J. Clark and P. E. J. Jardine place emphasis once more on Anzac Day and camp, with bush stalks, ambushes, contact drill and an all-night exercise.

THE GAME'S THE THING

Changing values

The move to Corio in 1914 had unexpected effects on games. From casual encounters after school, in which informality was often stronger than competition, the creation of houses gave sportsmen a stronger focus and an interesting self-sufficiency within the school. At the reconstructed boarding-school, houses were efficient instruments of coercion and sport was the perfect means of achieving *esprit de corps*. To Cuthbertson's ideal of loyalty to school was added a more

At the school sports in 1923, a venue well adapted to visits by parents in motor cars.

Watching cricket behind a traditional rope, 1927.

parochial loyalty to house. On the isolated site, where time was hard to fill, muscular Christianity, which was ebbing in England, in favour of more gentle and intellectual approaches, had a field day. With limited facilities and spacious grounds such controllable, outdoor activity was also economically determined. Sport and work were twin deities brought under the one God by regular reminders in chapel that in proper association with religion they could create a whole person.

The school used games to provide social meaning, and intense house rivalries were preparation for battles with outside rivals on which the mystique of the place depended. Although gymnastics, boxing, shooting, tennis, fives and swimming were available, most emphasis was given to the big four of cricket, football, rowing and athletics. The faint-hearted were expected to steel themselves for encounters with hard balls and charging shoulders or learn to endure blistered hands, aching backs, bursting lungs and jelly legs on the water. There was more time. The morning swim and the afternoon row, run, kick or hit were only a minute away. Sportsmen were able, as never before, to dominate the school.

Houses also gave teams their greatest chance of success. Already losing out in the early twentieth century to the greater growth of its metropolitan rivals (see p. 113), the senior school expanded from 156 in 1914 to only 360 in 1930. It was hopelessly outgunned by Scotch and Melbourne Grammar. From 350 in the senior school in the same period MGS reached 800 and Scotch grew from about 500 to 900. Wesley was smaller, with 504 on the roll in 1920, and stayed at about that level until the depression.

On this scene J. R. Darling's impact from 1930 was revolutionary.

330

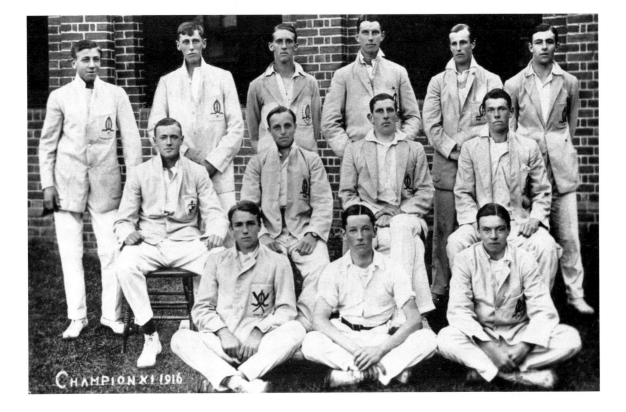

Champions in 1916, and well-dressed.

Not only did he shift the focus away from sport, but he tackled squarely the emphasis on winning. He was openly at odds with Australian society. He came from a tradition where largely rurally located schools played seasons of individual matches and where premierships like the Football Association Cup were frowned upon. They were more strongly linked to a professional—amateur division, with class overtones, than the widely popular competition of the Victorian Football League. There was also for him a gentlemanly participatory air about school games which he wanted to foster and a nasty lower-class spectatorism about the professional arena which he was determined to avoid. In this his gentlemanly side smothered his social awareness. Sportsmen were rarely among his heroes—too often they were not good sports.

More significant in Victoria than just premierships was media attention to a privileged group of schools, whose feelings of superiority were fed by press reports of all their encounters. The Head of the River and the Combined Sports, especially, were social as well as athletic news. The concentration of schools in the same city assisted the process and Melbourne's middle class liked to savour the prestige for which they were paying high fees. A journalist like Jim Blake, the *Herald*'s 'Mentor', could be employed more or less full time sniffing out the form and making schoolboy heroes into community figures, who were hard to bring back to earth in their own schools.

Darling's first Head of the River was an unpleasant baptism of fire. At that so public event on the Barwon, after a good win over Scotch in their heat, the GGS crew was disqualified in the final, following a clash of oars with Wesley. The outcome was taken so seriously that Clare Chomley wrote the next day from 'Corio Villa' to

331

offer sympathy. Knowing how 'bowled over' she felt herself, and how keen the school was to give the headmaster a victory in his first year, she put her finger on something it took the school community some time to unravel—that, although he hated the fuss that put unnecessary strain on boys and deplored the pursuit of victory for its own sake, Darling was delighted to see a good win. Had he not, Mrs Chomley enquired, despite 'slight stirrings of disapproval (isn't that so?)' waved his pipe and hat with the best of them? Of course he had.

His stirrings of disapproval were so obvious that they would have been well known around the school by the end of 1930, when he began a paragraph of his Speech Day report with:

You have probably heard that I am not interested in sport. This is said of most headmasters. The truth is that there is no need for me to encourage sport: the natural inclination of every British born man or boy is on its side. All I have to do is prevent it from occupying the whole time and attention of everyone. But let us for a moment examine it as an attribute to education. It was once the harmless recreation of men and boys; schoolmasters seized upon it to make of it part of their system of education, and from that it has become almost a business in itself.[7]

He particularly disliked the emphasis on the 'training of a single team to win laurels for a country or a school', and he joined, from the outset, the few voices in Australia which were raised against making a business and a spectacle of public-school games. As he said in his autobiography, the premierships and the publicity confirmed the privileged position of the Associated Public Schools. His radical social principles were neatly lined up with his inbuilt class prejudices against premierships.

To bring about change, he began with the prefects, his hot line to the school and the chief interpreters of his ideals among the boys. By feeding them with information about English practice and, like Cuthbertson before him, overwhelming them with his fervour, he started a current which flowed into the *Corian* of December 1930, through the editor, Alan Brock Brown, more forcefully than Darling might have thought diplomatic from his own pen. Only a few months before, he had slashed with blue pencil a passage in a letter from his mentor Donald Mackinnon, urging him to turn a promising football eighteen into a premier team. Brown's argument (so clearly Darling's) was that the schools had become captives of the premiership system and its inflexible rules, with points 'in the best professional manner' for cricket and football and cups for running and rowing:

and so much is done in public. Football matches are played on public grounds in all the professional atmosphere of those grounds; the Boat Race has become, next to the Melbourne Cup, the great 'sporting event' of the year; the Combined Sports attract more of the outside public at each meeting; cricket alone preserves some of its traditional friendly and informal nature.[8]

While the schools battled in the limelight, Brown thought that the spirit that should have animated them had fled. Typically, for GGS,

[7] *Corian*, Dec. 1930, p. 191.
[8] *Corian*, Dec. 1930, p. 191.

the true spirit was found at Winchester, where a recent cricket team, beaten for the first time in five years by Harrow, had arrived home in the early hours of the following morning to the reflection that 'there are better things than an unbeaten record, and one of them surely the sort of match we had just enjoyed'.

Few things in life stood out as clearly as the small, nicely-mannered groups of senior GGS boys marshalled behind the goals at Melbourne grounds, to cheer their eighteen, and exchanging ends between quarters in a gentlemanly way no other school could (or would want to) achieve. By comparison Scotch, Wesley, Xavier and MGS were somewhat unruly mobs herded by sheep-dog prefects. At the MCG and Olympic Park they crowded around the stoically cheerful 'peanuts, a'minties, a'chewing-gum, a'chocolates' and the ice-cream and toffee-apple men. Home at Corio, after Darling insisted that the games could be played on school grounds, the pressures were a little different, but they were strong enough to give a young Keith Dunstan the satisfaction of abstaining, by going off into the country on his bicycle, in protest at what he saw (and throughout his life has continued to see) as the stupid rites of football. An equivalent apostasy at Melbourne Grammar was Barry Humphries knitting behind the goals.

Throughout his headmastership Darling railed against premierships and campaigned to have the public spectacle of schoolboy games abolished. In 1932 Xavier and Scotch co-operated by having their football fixtures with GGS played on Saturdays on school grounds and in 1954, with a strong ally in Brian Hone at Melbourne Grammar, he persuaded the headmasters to make a public statement criticizing the premiership system on three grounds. The first was that it took up too much of the time of good gamesplayers,* the second that the importance attached to it threatened the true standard of values in the community and the third that it helped to make the six Associated Public Schools exclusive. From that Darlingite philosophical base two 'very modest reforms' were introduced, the one to reduce the time taken up by cricket and the other to reassert an existing rule (which continued to be breached more often than observed) that crews would not begin training until the first term of each year. In a momentous foreshadowing of the widening of the association in 1959, the statement concluded with the hope that the athletics and the rowing might be opened to other schools. GGS had already made a humble beginning with a quadrangular athletics meeting, beginning in 1947, with Melbourne High School, Geelong College and the local club, Geelong Guild. Football matches against Melbourne High had begun in August 1954, just before the headmasters' statement, but no matches are recorded with any of the lesser league of Associated Grammar Schools.

Darling took the scarcity of sporting victories in his era

---

* Darling had tried in 1935 to get the headmasters to start cricket matches at 3 p.m. on Fridays rather than in the morning.

philosophically. He wanted the school to be known for other things. Even so he was hard pressed by the value old boys placed on winning and by the public nature of the rowing and athletics competitions.

In Darling's thirty-two years GGS was five times Head of the River, won four times at the Combined Sports and only achieved a cricket premiership (the first since 1925) in his final year. The footballers drew a blank as they had since 1902. The expectation of defeat was always so strong that one boy was quite flummoxed by victory at the Combined Sports in 1946, when there was a stunned silence under the light-blue caps. 'It's so long since we won anything, I didn't know what to do', he said.

Lack of confidence, resulting from this pattern, helped to perpetuate it. The 1951 cricket team (and 1955 was similar) had good prospects but fell apart under pressure, causing its scribe to comment, 'we seem to lack the spirit of victory throughout the whole school'. Like many before them, he pointed out that under-age teams failed to 'pave the way to a cricket premiership':

At the moment too many just play the game for fun. In future they must play to win. If they do this, they will get more fun out of the game than ever before. It is up to the older members of the School to instil this attitude into the younger boys who are just beginning their cricketing careers at the School.[9]

In 1952, when an underrated side played brilliantly, the *Corian* came out with, 'We are sorry we are not able to reward them in the only way they can be repaid—by the winning of a premiership'.

Darling must have winced at the way he was undercut by community mores, for he trod a straight and narrow path concerning the morality of giving oneself to the game not the prize. Time and again he approved of the will to win and recognized what a difference winning made to the school. He wrote to Mrs Brougham in August 1931 about her son Ken, the captain of the football team which, for the first time in five years, had won more than a single match:

I am personally very much indebted to him for what he has done; he has broken the spell of defeats and helped to put a new spirit into the school.[10]

The fragile school was very vulnerable, despite his polemics, to external values which placed mere winning ahead of character building. As he said in his 1951 report, he did not believe that good results in games or exams indicated much about the essential quality of the school. Indeed it was dangerous to pay too much attention to them. 'We are, however, human', he added, 'and it is pleasant to win occasionally, as in the Combined Sports'. In that sense, others were more human than he was. Among older members of staff, like Cameron, the tough Australian way remained the best.

[9] *Corian*, May 1951, p. 37.
[10] Darling's official correspondence —boys left 1932.

The essential quality of the school was affected quite deeply in the 1950s by a move away from the big four sports of rowing, cricket, football and athletics. For many years there had been tennis, both inter-house and inter-school and rifle-shooting, swimming, cross-country and golf between the houses, but no serious attempt to cater for the unathletic, despite the fact that there had always been boys like Harold Barrow, whose mother wrote to the headmaster in 1930 out of concern that boys who were not in first teams were neglected. Harold's peers just acted the fool at cricket practice and his tennis was frustrated because the courts were always occupied. Darling agreed that there were problems but suggested that the main trouble was Harold's diffidence. Such diffidence was not taken seriously until 1944, when, as a let-out for those whose housemasters considered them incapable of profiting from the usual school games, a programme of alternative activities was organized. Eighteen boys, either physically handicapped or with little ball-sense, turned up. Despite a lack of equipment to extend the range of activities, they achieved enjoyment and physical challenges from deck tennis, swimming, walking, cycling, volleyball, badminton, cross-country and paper-chases. In a neat piece of diplomacy, to help assuage the scorn of their peers, it was stated that the activities were not to be regarded as a soft option but as more strenuous than the participants would 'enjoy' on the outskirts of football and cricket.

Whether that initiative was successful or not, no more was reported about alternatives until 1950 when Arthur Seels, the former Royal Marines PT instructor, brought in soccer, hockey, volleyball, badminton, basketball, bicycle paper-chases and water polo in a pro-gramme designed for forty boys who were not enjoying traditional games. From this base new possibilities unfolded. Hockey rapidly became a separate club, which from games in 1950 against The Hermitage, Scotch and the staff had a full fixture list on Saturdays by 1953, with forty-four players available for one under-16 and two open teams. They looked splendidly alternative in their quartered hockey shirts of light blue and gold, and the firsts had the rare experience for a Geelong Grammar team of being undefeated. In 1958 rugby, which had been an occasional foreign excursion for footballers in the 1930s and early 1950s, also became full-time although, as with hockey, fixtures were at first hard to arrange. Among the public schools only MGS and Scotch fielded sides. This development of winter alternatives pruned the open football list from six eighteens in 1957 to five in 1958, four in 1959 and three in 1961.

Lack of suitable competition had probably kept soccer at bay. Two of Darling's enthusiastic imports of the 1930s, Dicker and Gordon, had tried it out in 1934, persevering with an *ad hoc* internal competition using English club names to lend a gloss to clumsy efforts. The players found it an amusing way to fill the same rather flat period, when public school and house football matches were over, which rugby had occupied in 1932. The school is pictured as viewing these end-of-season efforts with tolerant amusement, and despite an initial success in forming a Rugby Union Club in July 1932 and playing a match against Scotch, who won 24–9, no permanent intrusion was achieved at the time. The headmaster, as chairman of the General Athletics Committee, put rugby under the wing of the Football Committee—whose conservative opposition probably frustrated expectations for 1933, 'when most of the present members will be returning'. If Darling had wanted it one suspects that rugby would have been introduced then as some antidote to what he told the Provost of Oriel was 'the comic game they play here'.

At various times in the 1950s other new games were introduced, sometimes beginning with house competition. Basketball became semi-respectable out of the alternative games programme when, in 1956, at least Manifold and Francis Brown fielded teams. Cross-country became an inter-school event in 1951 and swimming in 1956, the latter going back internally to J. B. Wilson's day but the former an innovation of 1935, when the runners swarmed madly at the start, crushed into a mêlée at the Lunan Gates and were banked up at the railway by a Neanderthal goods train which bisected the field. Overseas influences, usually English, were behind most of the innovations. For instance, Michael Charlesworth, on exchange from Shrewsbury in 1953–54, imported Eton fives. A club of fifty members, sustained by gloves and balls from England, had its heyday in 1956, when its popularity as an all-year alternative led to a house competition and a school championship. Locals soon mastered the technique of re-covering the hard little balls and made their own gloves, but within a year or two of Charlesworth's return to Shrewsbury the game was not much played. It must have stayed alive, however, at least formally, because in 1973 the London *Observer* noticed that of four overseas branches of the Eton Fives Association GGS was one. Give-it-a-go Australian attitudes found interesting challenges in these foreign sports and adapted them in a way that surprised true practitioners. In basketball, which at Corio was essentially a modified form of Australian rules football, the arrival of an American brought 'conflicts between American rules and our local adaptation':

When he became used to our quaint rule that unless a player is actually punched on the nose it is always 'play on', he showed us how the game should be played.[11]

The flowering of alternatives brought a new crop of sub-committees of the General Athletics Committee. From seven in 1930 and nine in 1950 they grew to fifteen in 1961. It was an extraordinary retreat from the purity of the old way, and yet it was, perversely, a reinforcement of athleticism. The tendency for every new game to become legitimized through house and school competitions led to further encroachments upon leisure and reflective time. Even in 1950 Darling was concerned about the pressure:

I have almost reached the conclusion that the tyranny under which we groan most grievously is that of taking seriously both school sport and house sport, that compulsory games—almost every day and on most Saturdays as well, are an unreasonable imposition in a school which provides alternative activities in such profusion, and

[11] *Corian*, Dec. 1956, p. 220.

that some relaxation there even over the littered corpses of Housemasters, Games Masters and Old Boys, will have to be part at least of the answer.[12]

Crushed under that institutional inertia, he was conscious of driving the best boys too hard, just as he had always been conscious that premierships heaped up undesirable public pressure and pandered to a crass materialism. The most powerful expression of that aspect of his position was also made during his report on Speech Day 1950:

It is customary in a vague way to condemn the materialism of the age. I believe that the condemnation is right and justified enough, but it may be well to analyse more exactly what we mean by it. It is useless to play a game which one does not want to win, and yet it is essential that the playing of the game should remain more important than the winning. You ought to be able to enjoy a good game lost as well as if it was won. I doubt whether most people in this country believe that; the failure to believe it is materialism.[13]

Interestingly, his strongest assault on materialism, Timbertop in the challenging bush, so interrupted the development of games-players by denying them a vital year's experience at fourteen and fifteen that it made winning by first teams much less likely. A materialist, premiership-loving headmaster would have had second thoughts. A sportsman would have been worried about the psychological danger to which GGS teams were exposed by their failures against very much larger Melbourne schools. This was evident in the tendency of *Corian* commentators to moralize about defeats by emphasizing the lack of a will to win rather than a shortage of talent.

The elevation of games like golf, fives and hockey to house competition extended the range of house rivalry which was often more important to participants than school games. Pressures could be focussed intensely, as in 1930, when cricketers in one house leapt from their beds at 6 a.m. for coaching by members of the eleven. The toughness of Brown's day did not disappear and in some houses under some housemasters and house captains, despite the headmaster's rhetoric, winning was the only goal. In their toughness they were unmerciful to boys who bucked the system. Hugh Luiggi (1937—40), a gentle-looking, fair-headed, non games-playing American, gave expression to his frustrations in pointed bravado and in winning divinity prizes.

Just as older boys in the houses organized the games of juniors, and the printers at the school press supervised their assistants, there were two areas, the gym and the baths, where designated 'seniors' were responsible for safety and sensible behaviour. No one was to swim and the gym apparatus was to remain quiet without a senior in control. Less formally, experienced rowers inducted juniors and in that close-knit fraternity were called upon to accept responsibility for the maintenance of their boats.

When the school geared up for games, most masters were expected to lend a hand and the young and athletic were prized. Gone were many of their afternoons, their Saturdays and odd hours in between to supervising, selecting and coaching teams. Gone but

[12] *Corian*, Dec. 1950, p. 177.
[13] *Corian*, Dec. 1950, p. 177.

337

not lost, for here the human face of a teacher might be exposed—and his frailty! For years afterwards, those who saw it savoured the moment in a masters-versus-boys football match when Mr Jaffray was unceremoniously flattened from behind. Darling's emphasis on coaching by masters was most noticeable at the boatshed. Old boys supplied most of the coaches in the early 1930s—the 1930 list included the former school oarsmen W. H. Pincott, A. C. Bell, C. O. Fairbairn, G. A. Fairbairn, J. H. Lindon and D. J. S. Mackinnon. However by 1937, when A. C. Bell could no longer continue, all the senior crews except the firsts were coached by masters. Then in 1944 W. H. Pincott gave up and J. E. L. Barber took the firsts to make it a clean sweep for the staff.

Apart from some innovation to accommodate the arrival of girls and with a further strengthening of previously minor sports, the pattern of games established under Darling has remained. Basketball, for instance, became an official winter sport in second term 1976, when open and under-15 boys' teams played on Saturday mornings in the Victorian Independent Schools' Basketball Association, and some girls played that traditionally male game. By 1980, in addition to the original seven or eight with which life at Corio began, there were twenty-four official games. To cricket, football, rowing, athletics, swimming, shooting, boxing, gymnastics and occasional tennis had been added sailing, life-saving, hockey, rugby, soccer, softball, netball, basketball, cross-country, gymnastics, karate, squash, badminton, dance and movement, cycling, fives and golf. Boxing had gone and more pupils were playing tennis and cricket. Participation had strengthened and greater satisfaction was achieved overall. A visiting researcher in 1977 was astonished at the speed with which the school moved from lessons to leisure. Compulsion was accepted easily: 'No one seems to be actively in charge of organizing this mass manoeuvre. It just happens; quickly, smoothly and without fuss or direction'. He contrasted Corio with the ragged starts, time-wasting and disruptions of many school sports programmes and observed that the motivation for so regular a positive response must have come from within the participants.

The strength and depth of participation were nevertheless at odds with feelings of failure suffered by first teams, especially at cricket and football. Cries of anguish from captains and coaches became seasonal in the *Corian*. Dick Johnson can speak for them all in his summary of the cricket in 1976:

The review of the 1975−76 cricket season contains both good and bad news. The good news is that The Tunbridge Club has continued to grow and flourish, enthusiasm has been high, most teams registered a handful of victories, and the weather was excellent. And now for the bad news...for the fifty-seventh time since World War I the first XI failed to win a premiership.

Of course there is a degree of facetiousness in this bold statement, and one would never pretend that winning premierships is the major reason for playing the game, or even that the results of the 1st XI are the only important ones. But over recent years victories have been very hard to come by and defeats have become very much the norm. This trend has not been restricted to cricket, but wherever it occurs it is to some degree non-educational, particularly when it breeds an attitude of accepting defeat as almost inevitable. It is, after all, a rather pleasant experience to play in a winning team. Strangely, enthusiasm does not seem unduly blighted by such a record and there is a touch of masochism in the manner with which teams depart, winter and summer, for the eighty mile round trip to Melbourne![14]

In looking for reasons for the trend, he arrived finally at the view that the school promoted non-competitive values:

I strongly believe that there is a psychological handicap affecting games played at Corio. During the past decade most of the successful cricketers have come into the school in forms IV and V, having received their sports grounding elsewhere. The competitive streak, the determination to make the most of one's ability and the desire to succeed have been noticeably absent in most of the school's sportsmen, regardless of their ability. Whatever the reasons for this state of affairs, and it may not be entirely unrelated to silver spoons, it does make the role of coaches a difficult one.[15]

The message was clear for Highton, Glamorgan and Middle School.

A coach who found the tendency even more frustrating was the old Geelong Collegian, Test cricketer and superb schoolboy footballer, Paul Sheahan, who coached the first eighteen from 1974 to 1983, except when he was at Winchester in 1978. There was a high point in 1976. 'We won five P.S. matches', was his eye-catching summary of that season, which he put in context by pointing out that no previous team from GGS had done such a thing—not even the champions of 1902, unbeaten in four matches. Indeed, he added, some boys would have been extremely happy to win five games in a school career. It *was* a good season. The losses, to Scotch and MGS, were by margins of only seven and fourteen points. But things were back to normal in 1977:

I am sure that too many of our boys lack the real competitive spirit. How you instil it or how it is acquired, I am not too sure. But I do know that, if you do not have it, you do not earn your fair measure of success and, if that does not happen, you develop a negative attitude to competition; and that runs against the principles of inter-school sport.[16]

Life was harder for the coaches than the boys. They were stuck with failure for years on end, while a few victories seemed enough to satisfy their charges. Conscious of being taken to task for attempting to rationalize continued defeat, Sheahan searched harder for an explanation for an unproductive season in 1979. The vigour was there, he observed, but not the 'crisis calm' other teams seemed to possess:

It never ceases to amaze me that Geelong Grammarians remain optimistic, if at times unrealistically so, through successive defeats; this undoubtedly says something about their outlook on life. If it does reflect their characters truly, then that is a very healthy sign.[17]

Notice the 'if'. Had he softened his 1977 diagnosis that a negative

[14] *Corian*, June 1976, p. 405.
[15] *Corian*, June 1976, p. 405.
[16] *Corian*, Sept. 1977, p. 54.
[17] *Corian*, Dec. 1981, p. 142.

attitude to competition ran against the principles of inter-school sport, and joined Dick Johnson in a sneaking admiration for the strange enthusiasm with which teams sacrificed themselves in Melbourne? He was clearly giving his charges the benefit of the doubt. Perhaps they were closer than he was to the Olympic (and Darling's) ideal of participation, the school having so rounded them that they did not need to win to prove themselves. Anyway, Paul Sheahan was cheerful again in 1980. Another five victories set him talking about an unusual level of desire. As the seconds had won six matches, it was a vintage year.

Sheahan had hit upon an answer to the motivation issue in 1977. He saw a 'compelling need for a pavilion'. Apart from rowing, school teams at Corio had little sense of belonging. The house emotion, he thought, was so strong that for the school a mere collection of individuals took the field. It is interesting that the houses, which had given games greater meaning at Corio, should have been credited with so much influence that lack of school spirit should have been seen as the price paid for being a predominantly boarding school, and one in which, through the houses, compulsory games were so easily organized and so comparatively friendly and relaxed. Dick Johnson's suggestion that being born with silver spoons in their mouths made boys less competitive does not stand up to examination against the achievements of Cuthbertson's day, when most of the spoons were not only solid silver but carried Western District crests or monograms.

The girls' hockey team, 1972.

Girls, and their coaches, were not subject to such pressure. After 1976, when Clyde and The Hermitage added the necessary numbers,

girls were to be found in every sport except cricket and football. In athletics and swimming they had been able to participate in their own events for the boys' houses in 1975. Thereafter a girls' house competition was possible in most games; members of the mixed-sex day houses of Allen and Fraser combined to compete against girls-only Clyde and Jennings.

In shooting they took on the boys' houses in 1977, without much success, but that did not matter; they were performing naturally in an area closed off before. Indeed, girls had the run of facilities no girls' school possessed and were committed to a level of participation no girls' school expected. Co-education freed them from generations of neglect.

Netball, 1973.

From two in 1975, there were five school hockey teams of girls in 1976. The first eleven was unbeaten against other schools and in a lightning premiership among Geelong schools GGS won all three trophies. Whereas one girl had played in the boys' tennis team in the early 1970s and there had been mixed doubles at school, girls now had separate teams and clamoured for extra courts. In athletics, the traditionally restricted boys' field-games programme was shown up by the inclusion of the triple jump, javelin and discus for the girls. Highlighting a different culture, a system of hiring spiked shoes to girls had to be introduced to help improve performances. Pinpointing its absence at Clyde and The Hermitage, only one girl took gymnastics as a sport in 1976. The most interesting situation was in sailing. Two of the committee of five students controlling the sport in 1975 were girls and in 1976 Susan Smith was captain of sailing.

The river, still supreme

Rowing has remained the glamour sport throughout the twentieth century. It is the Geelong Grammar specialty. The heavies of old sent their sons to replace them and the move to Corio coincided with the first light-blue victory in eights. Although the Barwon was more distant and was difficult to reach until the school bought a bus, the lagoon, quite deep in those early days, and with a separate boatshed, was a great resource.

Approaching the finish of the 1924 head of the river on the Barwon.

341

Legends gathered around W. H. Pincott, who was coach of the first eight from 1923 to 1944. He coached Geelong College for about twenty years until 1922, when, so we hear, the headmaster told him who was to be stroke. 'You are now the coach', responded Pincott, walking away, probably with an inevitable cigarette drooping from the corner of his mouth. It would have been thought broad-minded of him to have coached the College at all; not only was he from the Grammar himself (between 1884 and 1894) and senior prefect, but his father (foundation president of the OGGs) was one of its first pupils and both his grandfathers had been council members from the 1860s to the early twentieth century. Unlike Steve Fairbairn, probably because he was a day boy, he was not a noted rower at school, but at the same time as he played league football for Geelong, between 1898 and 1904, he rowed with the Barwon Club and joined Cuthbertson in linking it to the school. Apart from that his connection had been as coach of the football team from early in the new century until he took over the rowing. Strachan and Co., the woolbrokers, with whom he was an accountant for sixty years, gave him time off. A gruff, craggy man, he continued the Cuthbertson tradition. John Bell remembered:

Our Saturday outings to the Willows with him were a wonderful experience. He did most of his coaching from the boat in the earlier stages of training, and then, while down the river, he would take various boys out in a tub pair: and this was where he taught us most. Everyone enjoyed him: he knew everyone's family history and affairs, and gave all and sundry advice, encouragement, and if necessary sympathy.[18]

Pincott was not a winning coach, with only three victories in twenty-two years, but he won boys. His successor, John Barber, summed up his influence for good:

This was because of his absolute sincerity, his sportsmanship, and his simplicity of approach. It was Pinny who made permanent the traditions of the Rowing Club which were laid by J. L. Cuthbertson and others.[19]

This good influence, however, was described as having a streak of irreverence by a boy to whom he said, with daring for those days, 'Put your cap in your pocket, and Alan and I will show you Chloe at Young and Jackson's'. A young master, later a fine historian, Russel Ward, remembers that when coach of the thirds in 1939 he was asked to have his crew pace Pinny's firsts for the final quarter of their last row before the Head of the River. After the thirds had drawn away to finish a length or two ahead, their coach expected a compliment from the great Pincott:

Instead he trumpeted a volley of heartfelt but unimaginative insults at me, my ancestry and my crew...When reminded he had conjured me to squeeze the last pip out of the Firsts, he replied, 'Yes but I didn't tell you to shit all over them'. It was then that I decided to start looking for another job.[20]

Sunny days in training remained enchanting. Sam Wood remembered with delight Saturday picnics at The Willows in the 1930s, when the

A. F. Garrard, the first eight and the Fairbairn Cup, 1914.

[18] *Corian*, June 1975, p. 331.
[19] *Corian*, June 1975, p. 332.
[20] *Corian*, Dec. 1985, p. 12.

342

four competition eights were accompanied by several leisurely fours, laden with bread, butter, steak, chops and sausages. According to D. R. M. Cameron, a trip on such occasions in the 'executive four', with Pinny and distinguished guests, was 'as ritualistic as the Lord Mayor's show', and the row-past after lunch was 'as keen and well performed as the Trooping of the Colour'.

Pinny had also followed the Cuthbertson tradition in rowing style, favouring the neat body action of S. M. Bruce's *Notes on Rowing* over Steve Fairbairn's unorthodox emphasis on a powerful leg drive. But in the early 1930s Alan Bell, the seconds coach, gradually wore him down. Bell had followed the Fairbairn path through GGS (where he was Senior Prefect and Captain of Football in 1909 and 1910) into the Jesus College, Cambridge, eight, and had been excited by the development of Fairbairn's ideas in the late 1920s. Pinny grunted at first, but had the wit to listen and with Bell's help produced remarkable winning crews in 1934 and 1935. The latter was for long regarded as one of the best to become Head of the river. The legs were those of R. H. G. P. Cordia (bow), A. P. S. Wood, J. L. Pearson, C. D. Smith, L. W. Manning, J. Turnbull, H. W. Spry and A. E. Laycock (stroke). A. G. C. Mason was cox.

In a different drama in 1935, on a swollen river, one of the practice eights was broken in three pieces against the piles of the Barwon railway bridge. The crew had great difficulty in scrambling clear and wading across the breakwater through more than a metre of rushing water. At about this time there was some disenchantment with the river downstream. By 1937 the Willows had lost its sheltering lignum and the Break was deplorable, dangerous to both crews and

Cuthbertson would have been pleased with the activity of the rowing club, *c*. 1957.

W. H. Pincott

boats. Further down and across Lake Connewarre the old delights of tea-tree and clematis might have remained but, because for Pincott distance covered did not mean what it did to Fairbairn, long rows downriver were neglected. The traditional territory had to be re-discovered under Pinny's successor, J. E. L. Barber. The explorers were a senior four who, in 1949, although frustrated for a while looking for the outlet from Lake Connewarre, rowed from the sheds to Barwon Heads and back one Saturday. It was a taste of the keenness that preceded success in 1950, when three potential crews, selected in third term 1949, came back early for a rowing camp. When school began the first eight rose early two days a week to practise on the lagoon before they started going to Geelong every day. Into the racer early, they had 'covered three hundred measured miles in her by the day of the race'. After beating Geelong College by three-quarters of a length in their heat, the first eight came from behind and held on strongly to beat Scotch by a third of a length in the final. The seconds and thirds also won. Apart from the cheers and beers and throwing of caps and coxes that followed this record achievement by the three crews, a barrage of congratulations kept the coach and the captain of boats, C. H. Mylius, busy at their desks, answering ninety-four messages and telegrams. That was the year when, at Speech Day, J. R. Darling made his strongest statement ever about the tyranny of games.

John Barber went for size, strength and hard work. His 1953 winning crew, which averaged 12 stone 12 pounds (82 kilograms) and broke the Yarra record, was just as likely to break its boat. Three training eights had been sent back to the boatbuilder for new ribs or stretchers. Pincott had watched their initial antics with alarm, but, when the 1954 eight, coached by Roger Blomfield, was also victorious, there had in ten years been as many winning crews as under Pincott in twenty-two.

The rowing fraternity also worked hard behind the scenes, keeping their equipment efficient and up to date. A harbinger of the 1950 result was the winter activity of 1949, when all the boats and oars were overhauled and varnished and a colour coding applied to the stretchers, slides and oar blades so that the perennial confusion about what went where would not impede training. In a mystique sustained only in rowing, the captain of boats appealed to old-boy rowers to help keep up-to-date the honour boards on which the names were recorded of those who rowed in state crews or represented Australian and overseas universities. It was common knowledge that the majority of Australians who had won rowing blues since the inception of the Oxford–Cambridge boat race had been Old Geelong Grammarians. Sixteen of them had rowed in 21 races by 1950. Old boys and parents were fair game during appeals for new boats and oars. In 1935 the *Corian* lamented that, as well as *Avalon*, the practice eight broken at the Break, *Curnow* would have to be scrapped, sixteen-year-old *Orala* was falling apart and three junior boats were ancient wrecks.

In 1945, towards the end of World War II, the story was similar. Through the National Service scheme (see p. 200) boys had accepted most of the maintenance tasks, but materials were scarce and neither love nor money could produce a new boat like the four eights given by Mr and Mrs S. O. Wood, Mr E. B. Laycock, an anonymous old boy and a mystery donor in 1935, and the English oars with which Mr Turnbull replaced (as he had the year before) those won by the victorious crew. Not surprisingly, J. Turnbull and A. P. S. Wood were in both the 1934 and 1935 crews and A. E. Laycock was stroke in 1935. The Woods' new racer was soon out-of-date: in 1939 the first three eights were modified to take swivel rowlocks, the greatest technical change of the era. Throughout the 1930s and until his death in 1944 Alan Bell, the anonymous old boy of 1935, was rowing's most secret and generous benefactor. Long after his death it became generally known that each year he gave two crates of oars. At one stage he gave two practice eights, named ABC and DEF to retain anonymity.

One aspect of rowing needs special explanation. Although the move to Corio cut the school off from the river, the lagoon at the doorstep provided a marvellous nursery for junior rowers, as well as being adequate for the initial stages of senior training. In the 1930s and early 1940s, except for some vandalism at the sheds, the lagoon was a pleasant haven, especially if, as in 1934, the weather was good. By 1945, however, rowing was impeded by silting, which reduced the depth and area of water and made conditions rough, especially in the afternoon and at low tide. Coxes had to be more and more alert to avoid collisions as yachts and power-boats multiplied.

Paul Sheahan's plea for a pavilion, to strengthen the spirit of football teams, is given meaning by the rowers' story. Their Barwon shed was a shrine. After a drought from 1954 to 1971, they were head of the river again then and in 1974 and 1975 and were often in close contention. In each of the years from 1967 to 1970 they bettered the school record for the Barwon course, on which, by then, the head of the river regatta was always held. (The choice of venue was Cuthbertson's revenge, at last, for the insistence by Melbourne schools in the nineteenth century that the race should be held on the Yarra.)

Aware of a great school tradition, rowers, like individualist athletes, were less influenced than cricket and football teams by house loyalties, and the toughness of Timbertop was not the dis-advantage it seemed to be to others. Rowers went a step further, in March 1962, with the formation of a W. H. Pincott Club, which, by the end of 1963, had 200 life members at £5 each. Their aim was to provide equipment for rowing. Twenty-five subscriptions would buy an eight, fifteen a four. This direct route to old boys' hip pockets was so successful that similar clubs (the Tunbridge and the John Landy) sprang up in cricket and athletics. Neither could match the rowers, who floated on a permanent spring of sentiment and affluence dating back to 1874.

In its first year the Pincott Club supplied materials for two 'lagoon eights' and a unique twelve-seater training barge, the *Corio*, built by the school's boatman, Jimmy Goucher, and a group of boys. It replaced his clumsier invention, the sixteen-oar *Corian*, which was two old eights joined together by a central gangplank, on which the shouting coach shivered and swayed and the bowmen, in rough seas, were constantly drenched. The influx of funds from the club and other donors soon had the fleet in unparallelled condition. The racing shell *J. R. Darling* was added in 1964, the year the first crew grabbed a bucketful at the catch with their first shovel oars. The pace was kept up by a new boatman, Don Cameron, who came in 1965 when, for the first time in house competition, the senior eights rowed five abreast on the Barwon mile. By 1967 he had made five new training eights, five new fours and numerous tubs. Cameron then pointed the rowers in a new direction with four practice sculls, which opened the way for a sculling championship in third term. The riches of rowing were spread wider and wider. Almost every year there was a new racing eight and new equipment.

In 1968 a boat-trailer added flexibility. Vital in a programme that had grown stronger since 1964 and by then involved half-a-dozen regattas (at Ballarat as well as Melbourne) instead of the old all-embracing head of the river, it was also valuable for ferrying boats between the Barwon and the lagoon. When enlarged in 1972 it could carry six eights and all their equipment and could be loaded in an hour. A coaches' launch followed, then an intercom system for the first boat. Without shouting the cox had everyone's ear. In 1973, as a measure of the application of science to rowing, an ergometer was purchased. Crews were being significantly strengthened and tested in the gym as well as on the river.

Coming to terms with all that equipment in 1976 was a large array of coaches, 140 boys and 30 girls. From 1959 to 1965 Hubert Ward, an Englishman, who had rowed at Trinity College, Cambridge, was master in charge of rowing and coach of the first eight. Then Frank Covill took over the organization and Adrian Monger was principal coach until his stint among the top hats and tails of Eton in 1970, when both tasks became Covill's. Perhaps because of the Pincott Club, there was a return to old-boy coaches.

The rowers' Barwon 'pavilion' was replaced in 1971. Apart from anything else the rickety old shed was inadequate to display the gifts of oars emblazoned after victories on Barwon, Yarra, Isis, Cam, Thames and other British rivers across the world. Martin Clemens, chairman of the appeal which helped to fund the new building, opened the comfortable and efficient brick structure on 27 November 1971. With tribal ardour, his wife (a Turnbull) upstaged him by lending indefinitely fourteen oars used by members of her family between 1894 and 1940, four of them in GGS head of the river crews. A separate shelter could by then have been built with ceremonial oars. Even if they had had a pavilion, the cricketers,

346

footballers and athletes would have been unable to adorn it with comparable trophies and attach meaning to them like that held by S. F. Mann's 1883 oar, which had been half sawn through before the race. When it broke, he leapt from the boat. R. L. C. Hunt, who in 1914 had rowed in the school's first head of the river in eights, presented the 1974 crew with their oars, a hundred years after rowing began at GGS. He received a commemorative pewter and the president of the Pincott Club handed ties to those boys leaving who were joining the club.

The late 1960s and the 1970s were great years in rowing. Often all crews were strong, but special note was taken of a long string of successes by Adrian Monger's sixths. They were undefeated at the Junior Regatta from 1971 to 1975, when he left to teach at Scotch in Perth. These fifth formers, often called the Colts, fed into a succession of formidable first crews, the fruit of Frank Covill's coaching. He had learnt to row Fairbairn under Wally Ricketts at Melbourne Grammar and was committed more than any GGS coach before him to the Fairbairn dictum that mileage makes champions—and what

The first eight, 1970.

347

mileage! In 1971 the first eight sweated and swung a blistering 300 miles before their first regatta, and a total of 531 miles in 1974 was eclipsed by 581 in 1975. Metric calculations were slow to enter their cheerful slavery. Proud of the punishment, they logged their distances meticulously and knew that the effort paid. In 1970, after being narrowly beaten for the Fairbairn Cup by a record-breaking Wesley crew, they became the first schoolboys to win the Victorian Junior Eight Championship, and in wonderful April weather in 1971 GGS captured the Fairbairn Cup for the first time since 1954. Three years later they were at it again, and again in 1975. A hat-trick was possibly missed when in 1976, after a close victory in their heat, a crew member became sick. With Monger's support a ferociously quiet Covill had achieved more than any coach since Cuthbertson. As master-in-charge, he had greatly improved the depth of rowing. Woe to a colleague who held up the Barwon panting bus by delaying a rower after school; woe to a boy or girl who failed to contribute appropriately to preparations for the river; but woe also to the coach who sent the first eight out on 'the roughest day ever' in 1976. The head of the Yarra had been cancelled so, in pursuit of those precious miles, the crew took The Willows upstream on the Barwon against a strong west wind. They had to swim for it when she went down near the MacIntyre Bridge.

Rowing was an administrative headache. In 1976 coaches were needed for ten boys' eights, ten boys' fours and six girls' fours, split, at various stages, between lagoon and river. In 1977 the boys' list was formally divided into seniors (sixth form), juniors (fifth), novices (fourth) and beginners (second). The *Corian* tried a superfluous 'oarspeople' in speaking of the thirty rowers who were girls, but the sex difference was real, calling for separate changing rooms at the shed. The 'ladies' won first up at the Junior Regatta against a similar set of newcomers wearing the dark green of The Geelong College. They considered themselves tactful in confirming Mr I. F. Edwards' selections for the firsts, seconds and thirds, who finished in that order. The new experience brought mud, slime, backaches, blisters, jellyfish and, also on the lagoon, terrifying 60-centimetre waves. There was a brave moment when the first and second fours combined to take out an eight, and unexpected publicity when the *Sun* ran an article on Geelong Grammar and Geelong College girl rowers.

By the 1980s rowing was a mass enterprise; over three hundred participated in house regattas. Increased competition in school rowing prompted the construction of the Fairbairn Rowing Centre at Corio. Donated by the Fairbairn Trust and the W. H. Pincott Club and opened in October 1979, it gave dedicated oarsmen a home in the off-season and offered coaches the chance to teach and evaluate out of the rain, wind and dark. Lined with mirrors and enclosing a new rowing pond and the ergometer, it replaced the old open-air pool near Francis Brown and was close to the weight room and the lagoon shed. Notice the year-round claim upon rowers. Out-of-the-boat training in the winter was Covill's answer to the MGS combination of Tony Smith and David Bishop, who seemed to have a strong hold on the Fairbairn Cup. Perhaps the loss of Monger was critical.

In 1980 Don Cameron, who had completed fourteen years as boatman, and had designed and built, as well as repaired, numerous craft, produced during the Christmas holidays his first racing shell. She was christened *Anne* by the Honourable Mrs Charles Fisher, whose name she bore. Perhaps the enrolment of girls explains the use of a woman's name—one of the very few upon the bow of a Grammar boat since the *Alice* of over a hundred years before. 'Very fast, light and a pleasure to row in' was the crew's verdict, although they found that the round bottom made balance a problem. 'About half the retail price', said a satisfied master-in-charge, who paid a warm tribute to Cameron's equally important role as receiver of confidences and sounding board for coaches and crews.

Pages could also be written about house rowing, squeezed in after athletics at the end of third term, and divided until 1969 between lagoon and river. In 1965, for instance, the senior eights rowed five abreast on the Barwon, as they had since 1963, while senior fours, middle eights, middle fours and junior fours splashed across a newly-surveyed course of three-eighths of a mile on the lagoon. Through the Pincott Club Cameron had provided each house with two eights and a four. A departure was made in 1967 when, because the lagoon was troublesome late in the day, the junior events were held in the morning, the senior eights on the Barwon in the afternoon and a Boat Club–Pincott Club barbecue, with presentations and films, at Corio in the evening. Cuthbertson House (as in 1966) won the Fairbairn Cup (what wasn't Fairbairn?), while Manifold (as they often did) won the Robertson Cup for house rowing. The juniors, from the middle-school houses—Barwon, Otway, Barrabool and Connewarre—finished in that order and the Barwon 'A' crew was 'Head of the Lagoon'. In 1969 even the Head of the Lagoon was rowed on the Barwon, a departure that led to an 'overwhelming' attendance, yet signified the loss of another amenity at the once unpolluted, unsilted and unfrequented haunt of Limeburners' Bay.

Taking the field

Apart, at times, from rowing, as we have seen, the Olympic ideal of participation was easier to achieve in the major sports than victory in competition. Being used to defeats, however, teams were often thankful for small mercies, as with the 1949 eighteen which was beaten (quite narrowly) by only MGS and Scotch. The captain, D. McC. Lear, achieved the remarkable tally of thirty goals in five matches from strong marking and straight kicking at full-forward. The only comparable forward in Darling's period was A. G. Schofield, captain (as of cricket) in 1932, who kicked twenty goals from centre-half-forward. By those days, beating MGS, to whom Cuthbertson had been a god, had become like climbing Everest. When there were defeats by twenty-three goals, as in 1937, or by nineteen, as in 1941, getting within four points of MGS in 1939 (when a two-point loss to Scotch

Chris Mitchell

decided the premiership) was a great achievement.

Although depth of talent was a great weakness, there were always skilful players to admire, like Mick Dexter (1942), Graeme Cameron (1944), Bill Morrison (1944), Dick Woolcott (1945), Jim Perry (1945), John Jolley (1946), David Lee (1948), Geoff Dahlenburg (1950), Alby Twigg (1950), David Merkel (1952), Geoff Ainsworth (1964) and Chris Mitchell (1964), who made their way into a series of great teams at Melbourne University. Natural athletes were likely to play in the first eighteen while still young, except that between 1953 and 1975 fourth formers were out of consideration at Timbertop. The most famous footballer to emerge from Corio was W. H. Pincott's grandson, 'Nogger' Newman's boy, John (usually called Sam), who in 1962 and 1963, with some fine marking, showed the potential that made him outstanding in the ruck and at centre-half-forward for the Geelong Football Club. Chris Mitchell joined him there later, in the footsteps, also, of Ian Toyne (1948). Coaching football, as Paul Sheahan found, could be frustrating. W. H. Pincott was in charge until 1922, then C. A. Cameron, W. N. Jaffray, V. J. H. Tunbridge, W. H. Mason Cox, E. H. Montgomery, A. Hickinbotham, H. B. Connell, A. H. Cash, G. A. W. Renney, D. P. Happell, A. C. Monger and A. P. Sheahan.

The longest stint in any sport, except Pincott's in rowing and perhaps Newman's in tennis, was Vic Tunbridge's distinguished and philosophical coaching of the cricketers from 1937 to 1940 and from 1944 to 1959. His 1955 team almost won a premiership, but was thwarted on a wet wicket by Scotch. A few runs or a few minutes in 1942 and 1943 frustrated teams coached by that famous Australian, Manning Clark, who had been an elegant bat for Melbourne Grammar and Melbourne University. In both years the eleven finished in second place. The length of the drought in football and cricket draws attention to cricket premierships in 1961 and 1962, under Don Marles, whose ability to get all players to achieve their best and to play as a team was remarkable. The fielding was always exceptionally good. During his five years from 1960 to 1964, in twenty-five matches, the first eleven won eighteen and lost only five. His successor was Tim Murray, captain of Tunbridge's 1953 side.

The 1961 cricket team, well captained by M. A. S. Landale, had two accurate and aggressive new-ball bowlers in S. N. C. Murch and G. L. R. Teal, backed up by the swing of M. B. D. Fraser. Apart from St Kevin's, by whom they were defeated, no team scored more than 109 against them. Paul Sheahan, who had a prolific season for Geelong College, made only 1 and 22. Murch, who later played for St Kilda and Victoria, took twenty-five wickets at an average of 10.0, Fraser sixteen at 6.9 and Teal fifteen at 13.1. Murch and Teal both achieved hat-tricks. Highlights of the batting were centuries by P. M. A. Richardson against Haileybury and P. G. Laing against Carey. A. O. Hay and Fraser played a number of good innings but the tail usually collapsed, and never more frustratingly than in the final against Melbourne Grammar, when the last five batsmen made twenty between them. In that low-scoring match GGS sent in to bat on a tricky pitch, made 149 and MGS 109. A hard-hitting fifty-nine by Laing was decisive. The only other batsmen on either side to pass twenty were Hay and G. A. M. Robinson with twenty-three and Sandars of MGS with twenty-four. For once Murch was without a wicket. Teal with 5 for 30 and Fraser with 4 for 26 did the damage. Excitement was high as Melbourne Grammar struggled on the final day.

Notable individual performances in cricket included two centuries scored by the captain, C. G. W. Mitchell, in 1964. The 1971 side, unlucky to be defeated, had three outstanding bowlers. Jim Martin, a paceman, and Peter Josephson, a left-arm spinner, each took twenty-seven wickets. The captain, Charles Baillieu, with twenty-four wickets and a century, was the most successful all-rounder in the competition. He captained the Victorian schools' eleven which won the Australian carnival in December that year. When captain in 1972 Josephson took another nineteen wickets.

High points in athletics were victories at the Combined Sports in 1936, 1946, 1951 and 1954. On a wet track and a windy day in 1936, D. W. Deasey hung on to run second in the final event, the open 440 yards, edging out MGS by 1 1/6 points. The 1946 victory was convincing: N. C. Rundle won three under-16 events and P. J. Kennison had a first and two seconds in the open sprints. That was the year D. R. T. McMillan of Geelong College ran an Australian schoolboy record of 4.27 in the mile, an event in which athletes worldwide were pruning their times almost week by week. Just a junior then, J. M. Landy, who had a school time in 1948 of 4 minutes 41 seconds (well outside K. F. Mollard's 4 minutes 38.5 of 1932) achieved the world record of 3 minutes 58 seconds in 1954, the year before he came back to GGS to teach. The most famous of old boy athletes, he was ABC Sportsman of the Year and was awarded an MBE in 1955. Captain of the Australian team in 1956, at the Melbourne Olympics, he won a bronze medal in the 1500 metres despite a leg injury. A pathfinder for Landy was Gerald Backhouse (at Corio 1927–29), who won six consecutive Victorian one-mile championships in the 1930s and reached the final of the 800 metres at the Berlin Olympics in 1936. He raced for the joy of it. Another middle-distance Olympian was J. W. Ramsay, whose schoolboy time of 1 minute 59.2 seconds at the Combined Sports in 1945 was a school record for the 880 yards until D. G. Houseman, with the benefit of Landy's coaching in 1954, established a new public-school record of 1 minute 58 seconds in 1955. Also outstanding was the weight-putter C. W. Maxwell, who threw a public-school record of 48 feet 9¼ inches at the Combined Sports in 1948, adding a foot to the two feet by which he had broken the school record at the house sports. His style was captured by Rix Wright in one of the sculptures on the Art School gates. The 1951 Combined Sports win came from all-round strength, but was highlighted by wins from A. C. Monger in the high jump and hurdles, E. A. Cameron in the weight and R. M. Wilkins in the mile. Again in 1954, when the sports were decided by the last event, the open section was very strong. G. P. King equalled the record of 10 seconds in the 100 yards, won the 220 and was second in the 440. J. R. Joyce won the hurdles and high jump, D. L. A. Pym the long jump and A. F. Chirnside, in that strong GGS tradition, was first in the weight.

Since 1954 there have been many fine athletes at GGS but, except in 1956, little overall strength. In addition to his 880 record in 1955, after a thrilling duel with Olsson of Scotch, Houseman won the Combined Sports 440. At Corio he captured the school mile, 880 and 440, as well as a second in the 220 and a third in the cross-country. Especially versatile, R. R. Burgess claimed all events between 100 and 880 yards at the school sports in 1956, the year H. M. P. Rundle, with a put of 49 feet, broke the school weight-putting record. Other strong putters in a GGS tradition were A. R. Legoe in 1969 and P. R. J. J. Clarke in 1973.

Good sprinters like R. M. Russell in 1938, G. P. King in 1954 and E. O. Newcomen have been rare. Russell, the typical sprinter—long jumper, was successful at the 1938 Combined Sports in the 100, 440 and long jump. He set a school record of 51 seconds in the 440. In 1958 (soon after the age group was included) Newcomen carried off four under-17 events at the Combined Sports, breaking two records and running a 440 yards which was faster than the open record. The 440 was his great event. After running second by inches in both the 100 and 220 yards open in 1959 (he had a 10-second 100 at the school sports), he came from behind to win a magnificent race in the 440 with a record 49.6 seconds. Among high jumpers there were memorable performances from J. M. Haslope, with 6 feet 0¼ inches, using the old-fashioned scissors style in 1939; Robert Watt with 6′3″ in 1967; David McFarlane, who established new school records of 5′11″ under 16 and 6′3″ under 17 in 1973 and 1974; and Viktor Svarcs, who, with 6′4″ equalled the school record (defeating McFarlane) in 1975. By then jumpers had moved from Haslope's sand-pit landings, feet first, through the hands and feet of the roll to the elevated upside-down landings on foam cushions of first the straddle and then the revolutionary head-first, arched-back, leg-flipping Fosberry flop. A special high-jump area beside the main track, with a cinders apron, similar to a previously-installed cinders long-jump track, was laid in 1958 by masters and boys. Long jumpers of note were R. S. Morton in 1931, C. G. W. Mitchell (a sprinter and winner of the school championship) in 1964, D. N. Burnell in 1971, D. P. Raggatt in 1972 and Svarcs (the high jumper) in 1975. Good hurdlers were rare: D. McC. Lear broke the school open record with 15.5 seconds in 1949; W. R. Macarthur Onslow broke the Combined Sports under-17 record in 1961 and was followed in 1963 by John Newman, who ran second at the Combined Sports. Distance runners seemed to disappear after Houseman and Burgess in the middle 1950s, except for Ian Hopkins, who, after training with Percy Cerutty in the holidays, broke the school mile record with 4 minutes 31.6 seconds in 1963.

To focus on outstanding performances is to distort a picture of considerable social and athletic importance. There were interesting carry-overs from the nineteenth century in separate handicap and championship events at the school sports which did not drop the sack, three-legged and obstacle races until 1959 and the old boys' 100 yards handicap much later. Until 1967 the sports were as much an individual as a house competition. In the latter year special attempts were made to stimulate greater interest in athletics. Masters went back to school to improve their coaching. The running track was laid out on the Perry oval with the same configuration as that at Olympic Park. At the house sports, spread over two days, there were A and B divisions, as well as two competitors per house in each event. There was less attention to individual championships (decided on all events in each age-group) and more time and energy (exclusively in the first three days of the season) to 'qualifications', which enabled every member to support his (and later her) house by achieving points for personal performances against graded times and distances. Following a Scotch College model, qualifications had been introduced in 1942 when, because of wartime shortages, no under-15 boy was allowed to wear spikes. The war also swept away the glittering array of cups previously awarded to the winners of individual events. The money went to the school's war-effort ambulance fund.

Gone by the 1960s, incidentally, was the rule, favouring sprinters, which decided a tie in the school championships by a further race over 300 yards.

New-fangled metrics were in (leading to the scrapping of many old records), and so were more efficient styles in most events, as scientific coaching methods and knowledge of sports medicine filtered through to the schools. Field games at GGS were extended in the early 1970s by the addition of the javelin, discus and triple jump. Like the rowers, dedicated athletes fitted in techniques training during second term. From 1975 separate handicap sports were held before the school sports which, with 189 events, extended over two weekday afternoons and all day one Saturday early in October. Apart from anything else, this was a way of insuring against the weather, which at that time of the year was usually reported to be awful.

Beginning in the 1940s, a traditional focus on two meetings— the school sports and the combined public schools sports—was broken down. In 1945 triangular and in 1946 quadrangular meetings were added. The 1946 meeting included Geelong College, St Josephs's College and an Old Geelong Grammarians' team, the latter being replaced by Melbourne High School, who participated from 1947 to 1958. These and, from 1953, the Victorian Schoolboys' Championships, a week after the Combined Sports, enlarged the season for the most talented athletes, while a 'Little Combined', beginning in 1957, gave second-string performers an extra opportunity.

Apart from John Landy for a time in the 1950s, until specialist physical education teachers came more on the scene in the 1960s and 1970s athletics coaching was ardent but amateur. W. N. Jaffray had been in charge, except when in the army, from 1930 to 1951. It was also far from a one-man shop. In Jaffray's last year Cash looked after the under-age and Howard the open sprinters, Montgomery the long-distance runners, Hickinbotham the high jumpers, Newman the weight putters, Tunbridge the open hurdlers and long jumpers and Jaffray himself the under-age hurdlers and long jumpers. Alan Cash took over from Jaffray until 1966. His successor, Ian Weber came from Junior School to take charge of gymnastics and physical education. Under his supervision, from 1962 to 1978, as we have seen, the programme was expanded and training intensified, but not everyone agreed with his methods. Peter Jardine crossed swords with him and wrote a book, *Track Running for Schoolboys and School-masters*, to expound his own approach.

For girls there was a slow start. However, despite a paucity of athletes (and none in lower age-groups), the little band at GGS mustered a team for inter-school competition in 1975. House sports began in 1976, when Clyde, Jennings and the combined day houses competed. At a meeting with Toorak College, PLC, Morongo and Merton Hall, Rosemary Norton won the open 400 and 800 metres and was equal first in the high jump. Katharine Cordner won the hurdles. Geelong Grammar came last. The school was still hampered by low enrolments in junior forms, but was first at one quadrangular meeting and second at another. Helped by a system of hiring spikes in 1977, performances improved.

On October afternoons, with the training lists clustering in their specialist groups and with qualifications in full swing for the rest of the school, Corio was as busy as an ants' nest. On each occasion about ten staff would be rostered for duty on the windy plain as marshals, starters, timekeepers, measurers, interpreters and recorders for the also-rans, whose performances were written on a slip of paper, handed in for scaling and then presented for recording in a huge ledger. Each person's previous scores could be checked to indicate, typically, improvement over the weeks and totalled for house points. Some made stupendous efforts for marginal gains, others shrugged, all were involved. Informal contacts with staff were multiplied.

As part of the expansiveness of the vast Corio site, the royal and ancient game of golf came to the rifle-range paddock in 1930. There were plenty of golfers about, as almost half the field at the state junior championship that year came from GGS—an aspect of social class like the preponderance of Old Geelong Grammarians among Australian rowing blues at Oxford and Cambridge. Annual fees for the golf club were four shillings and four hours' work on the links. A rule unworkable in the supposedly harsher outside world protected members from interlopers who failed to pay the monstrous two shillings visitor's green fee, by providing for the confiscation of their clubs. There were nine holes, with bunkers, tee boxes and flags. The fairways were much like the rough and the greens much like the fairways until autumn 1931, when Mr Fraser and a new committee burnt the grass, mattocked the tussocks and levelled and top-dressed the greens. Score cards were a penny, but if you paid threepence and signed your score you were automatically included in a competition.

By 1933 a groundsman helped with greens and bunkers and there was an official opening of the season; Ned Austin, MLA, drove the first ball towards a scavenging mob intent on claiming ten shillings for retrieving it. Being a keen golfer and more relaxed than Dr Brown about Sunday sport, J. R. Darling ensured that the sabbath would be the popular day for golf. He revived the game after the war on a new course north of the school, where birdies took over from cows and greens were oiled sandscrapes. After three years' preparation, the headmaster drove the first ball on Sunday 14 June 1953, and parted with ten shillings to J. Tunbridge. Then, with the president, Mr H. D. L. Fraser, and the captain, A. R. Gilder, he led the large field through the seven holes to afternoon tea in well-placed tents. A month later at a parents' golf day, ninety players teed off for championship and handicap cups. In 1953 the course record of twenty-two was shared by A. R. Gilder and the Australian Open Champion, Norman von Nida, who paid a visit in third term. Because nearly a third of the senior school became members, the course was often very congested and house competition was keen.

In the late 1950s golf was a major part of school life. In 1956 there were 132 members and the course was being extended to nine holes and planted with hundreds of trees—wattles, gums and broom. Three pages of the *Corian* were needed to report the events. Voluntary maintenance was a problem, but in 1954 the head groundsman, Albert Moodie, took over the mowing of fairways on which a future national sponsor of professional cricket and golf, Kerry Packer, was practising the strokes which helped him win the scratch foursomes that year in partnership with Mr Webb, and in 1956 gave him a handicap of six and scores (for seven holes) of 29, 34, 32, 31 in the qualifying rounds of the school championship. He was beaten in a quarter-final.

Golf boomed in the 1960s and in 1969 the rostering of cadets on whole days left Tuesday and Friday afternoons free. Following a record influx of bags and buggies, the Friday group was limited to fifty. The course was described as magnificent, with new flags, well-mown fairways and extra sand on the scrapes. After the girls came, golf seemed to outgrow its local links and, with transport easier, the regular list went off to the luxury of greens at Eastern Beach.

The sea baths, which had seemed such an amenity in Brown's day, grew gradually shallower with the lagoon, and more dilapidated. The bottom became unpleasantly muddy. In the 1940s swimming was only enjoyable at high tide. Whereas, formerly, tidal almanacs had been consulted just to get the right day for the swimming sports,

On open day, 29 July 1961, 'Dr Darling drove a straight ball to open the newly extended golf course'. He looks pleased with the shot.

they were now needed if one wanted merely to be reasonably wet. The policy of appointing swimming seniors, one of whom had to be leg-roped before a plunge could be taken, also restricted activity. The school was emphatic that all new boys should learn to swim, which Darling viewed not just as a safety measure but as more intelligent than lying about on the beach. He liked to swim and was brave about it. Accepting the custom of swimming naked, he put sharply to the test a boy's sense of the ridiculous when confronted by his headmaster clothed in much less than a little brief authority.

As a return to privacy in the face of increasing public use of the lagoon and to get a decent depth of water, as well as avoiding major repairs to the dilapidated baths (which were so shaky by 1947 that spectators could not be admitted for the house sports), a 50-metre pool was dug in a corner of the golf-course paddock in 1954. In 1949 and 1950 the old structure was so unsound that the house swimming was held in the morning, without spectators, at Eastern Beach and from then until 1954 there was no swimming at all. The new pool was given by Mr and Mrs W. A. Kilpatrick of Great Western in memory of their son Bill (at school, 1933–39), who was shot down over France in 1943. They announced their intention in 1946, but the pool was not completed and filled until March 1954 and was not officially opened, in conjunction with a new gymnasium, until 26 March 1955. Swimmers were on their blocks for the first house sports in the new pool on 21 April 1954, when a list of new metric records was established. Every detail of the 50×14 metre pool was well known to swimmers within a few years, as they carried out the annual job of painting it.

In a new lease of life for swimming, the first-term programme in 1955 included a meeting (with both races and water polo) against Melbourne Grammar, and the third term, apart from the school championships, saw a large list of boys complete the tests for the life-savers' bronze medallion. Swimming became an alternative sport in 1956 and more fixtures were arranged with other schools. Activity increased all the time, despite the fact that the pump, which had replaced the tides in circulating the as yet scarcely polluted sea water, was always breaking down. It was abolished in 1967 when a filtered fresh-water system was installed. Daily at 7 a.m. the swimming seniors gave it a clean, a chore that was eased in 1968 by the removal of surrounding eucalypts that had, on the other hand, contributed much of its charm.

As an important part of the old order of things, though giving way to more recreational physical training in the 1950s and 1960s, gymnastics was a stronger feature of life at GGS than at other public schools, except perhaps at Wesley, with whose teams there was regular competition. The Webb brothers kept it going through the 1920s and Darling smiled on its rhythmic gyrations. The photographs of gym teams in the *Corian* have the look of a special art form. They were often shown draping their sleek, white bodies across the fountain in

the quad. In 1937 the outlook was very bright. Ninety boys were taking instruction on Monday evenings in a succession of hourly classes until 10 p.m. Whenever a gym senior was present, the apparatus in the Bracebridge Wilson Hall groaned under multitudes of boys practising. At school fairs and on other special occasions gymnasts formed complicated pyramids or bounced, balanced and tumbled on the cushioning mats and challenging apparatus, emulating the feats of Mr Lorbach, their instructor. Their bonanza was the construction of the new gymnasium during 1954, as a World War II memorial, which was opened at the same time as the Kilpatrick swimming pool on 26 March 1955. The new gym became host to new routines as the training of athletes became more scientific and as the use of weights and circuit exercises improved fitness and strengthened specific muscles. In third term 1960 the rowers adopted the new training and found it of great benefit, enabling them to work at higher pressure in the boat.

Prominent in discussions about the revolutionary approach that linked the gym as never before to rowing, football and athletics, was Arthur Seels, who came in 1950 as full-time physical education instructor and whose departure in 1960 was much lamented. Crisp and down-to-earth in the Royal Marines tradition, and at the forefront of a broadening of challenges and opportunities (as in alternative games), he took charge of boxing and swimming as well as the gymnasium.

In boxing, which had always been strong at GGS, he took over from Montgomery, who with Howard had organized the pugilists for most of Darling's headmastership. Special instructors like Len O'Brien, an Australian eleven cricketer, took boxing classes during gym sessions on Monday nights. Always a second-term activity in the corner of the Bracebridge Wilson Hall or gym, boxing moved

Gymnasts on the lawn in front of the Darling Hall.

357

from punch bags and sparring early in the term to preliminary bouts in late July. Eight boys in each of the four weight divisions were gradually pruned to two, who fought the finals over three rounds in August. In most houses every boy was expected to put up his fists and take his punishment like a man. Many could be recognized as Old Geelong Grammarians from the shape of noses broken during second term and not regarded as particularly needing medical attention. Manifold House under C. A. Cameron were expected to be particularly tough, just as their housemaster, when acting head in 1934, gave an 'England expects' speech to the whole school before the boat race. His son remembered something like this:

It has come to my notice that boys wearing light-blue caps have had their caps thrown into the river. This will stop forthwith. You will not provoke an incident, but if involved defend yourself. Mark your man and remember—the first blow counts two; make it a good one.[21]

Cameron would not have been pleased had he known that boxing would fade out in the early 1960s.

Striking appropriate blows for sport, the rowers' W. H. Pincott club (p. 345) was followed by similar clubs in cricket and athletics, though neither could imitate the rowers precisely. The needs and the ethos of their games were different and the injection of funds was less critical. Although a group of old boys had provided the cricketers with a bowling machine in 1965, the direct route to their hip-pockets was not established until the Tunbridge Club was founded in 1975, through the efforts of Tom Austin and Owen Moore. It was the focus for an old boys' eleven which played a dramatic tie with the school on its inaugural day, 15 February 1975. The game was followed by an annual general meeting and dinner for fifty-four of the 238 members. Arthur Liddicut, the most famous OGG cricketer, was present.

After Noel Rundle had chaired a steering committee earlier in the year, the John Landy Club, with John himself as patron, held a founding dinner on the night of the Combined Sports heats in 1976. Peter Jardine, who with his colleague Ian Weber had promoted the idea, emerged as secretary. Bill Ramsay, a great schoolboy half-miler and 1948 Olympian, was president. When asked to outline the aims of the club, Jardine made four points. It was to foster athletics, help purchase equipment, assist with coaching and perhaps form an OGG athletics team. John Landy spoke at the first annual meeting in 1977. Among other things he stressed the importance of technique by calling for specialist training in Middle School. It was an attitude that revealed the distance that approaches to games had run since the first playing-fields were constructed at Corio. Then, on the whole, athletes did what came naturally.

As well as influencing the school, these clubs were officially associated with the Old Geelong Grammarians, as were the Old Geelong Football Club (founded in 1954) the John Brazier Club for yachting (1972), and the Ski Club (1959).

[21] *Corian*, June 1976, pp. 379–80.

14

Figures in a landscape

HORIZONS

The whole school, swaying in Cobb and Co's four-in-hand drags across a flat and treeless landscape, made the journey from the confinement of the old Geelong buildings for the laying of the foundation stone of spacious Corio on 3 April 1913. Like a blank slate, the land was theirs to fill. Savouring a contrast that the eighty-seven new boys of 1914 would not know, the eighty-three who were returning to GGS were startled by the space, the wide horizon, the fresh air and the feeling of freedom. Their world was to be entirely their own. No unfamiliar face would be encountered on the early-morning dash to the baths or the walk to baths and boatshed after school.

And so it was. They owned the silence. Austin's Avalon was out of sight beyond the quiet lagoon where, on still mornings, the splashing feet of hundreds of black swans, bugling skywards, could be clearly heard. From the clock tower the school bell rang un-challenged. From the ovals the stone whetting the groundsman's scythe cut a crisp scar of sound. It was easy to hear the afternoon swish and creak of crews at work on the lagoon, except when the wind was westerly and carried the only outside noise, the hoot of passing trains. This private world was not inviolate but, apart from tradesmen's carts, few foreigners impinged upon it. Occasionally yachts sailed inquisitively across the bay to the lagoon, or workboats recovered logs floating free from the Oriental Timber Mills beside the freezing works at Cowie's Creek.

The empty slate was expensive to fill. No one else wanted even to doodle on it. The school could not find the capital to house married staff and gave to its (preferred) bachelor masters quarters almost as Spartan as the boys'. The view from the tower was mainly of paddocks, the crouching You Yangs and the bay. Away from the central red-brick complex of classrooms, offices and the temporary quarters of Perry House, there were Cuthbertson and Manifold houses, the headmaster's home, the first stages of the dining hall and

J. Beasley. 80.

Looking from the tower at the first stage of the chapel, the Cuthbertson housemaster's residence and Cuthbertson House.

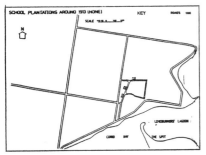

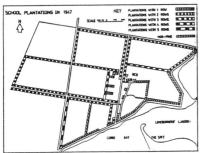

chapel and two staff residences. The place was as self-contained as one of the squatting stations from which Western District pioneers had sent their sons to GGS and, as with many of those properties, you entered from the back, an orientation that has remained disarmingly informal. The architects and council presented a bold semi-circle of buildings to the bay, looking across a broad close of ovals to a sweep of water and a distant shoreline. The gates were close to the bay. In practice, however, the straight line of the road from the station hit the imposing semi-circle from behind, near the centre of its perimeter, and struck an entry straight in. A formal approach from the front has never been successful, even though in the 1980s the reconstructed Lunan Gates* and the headmaster's house have been put in the east opposite the tower and convenient to the foreshore road along which hordes of outsiders, earlier undreamt of, gain access to the lagoon.

Like Topsy, the place has just grown, and because the formality of the front gave little scope for expansion, the informal tail has wagged the dog. At right-angles to the road from the station, a straight line drawn to give access to the service areas of the early school was too close for logical long-term development. Along it were built staff quarters, boiler, kitchen, laundry, hospital and across the road, starting in Brown's time, though very slowly, appeared a line of houses for married staff. Because six of these were given in the 1920s by Commander John Biddlecombe of Golf Hill, the street behind the school was named Biddlecombe Avenue. At first leading nowhere, it gradually became the school's workaday axis and in 1957, was opened to the north as a short cut to Melbourne. Similarly, in the 1950s it led south to an alternative (bumpy at first) route to Geelong past the Shell Refinery. Closed off to Melbourne after the opening of Shell Parade, further west, as the route to North Shore (Geelong), it is now defended by 'No Entry' signs at the foreshore end.

Keeping traffic down became a major objective once the school expanded across Biddlecombe Avenue with the removal of the Bracebridge Wilson Hall in 1963, the construction of Kennedy medical centre in 1969, Allen House in 1971 and the spread of staff housing. The fact that the school chose to develop Biddlecombe Avenue as a public road (saving it huge amounts) has provided the flavour of a shoreline, where waves from the outer world must beat. To deflect them a little, and to give a sweep for cars around the chapel to the front of the school, the art school gates, decorated by the sculptures of Rix Wright (see p. 286), were opened in 1949, 200 metres to the north of the original direct entry, which was barred in 1963 and closed off permanently by building in 1982. Melbourne traffic, es-

---

* Given by the Bell family who bought them when the Lunan House estate, North Geelong, was subdivided in 1911. They were re-erected near the foreshore as a grand entrance to Corio in 1913 but, not being used, were moved to Biddlecombe Avenue in 1926. Later they were closed as being dangerous and were considered to be beyond repair, even before some youths tore into the north post in a car.

360

pecially heavy on occasions involving parents, came down Biddlecombe Avenue from the north from 1957 until the 1970s. This new route may have inspired the idea of centenary gates further north again, from which a still wider entrance sweep was contemplated. They rust. The closing of that Melbourne entry and the construction of a cluster of staff houses as well as the advent of Clyde, the Fisher Library and finally a new Perry House beyond Cuthbertson, seem to have made them redundant.

It can now be seen clearly that the original layout was featurist and badly organized for traffic-flow. Gates a kilometre away, at the western entrance to the school property, might have stimulated a more flexible treatment of the rear of the original plan. Thus, the vision of 1914, although ambitious, failed to provide more than thirty years of coherence. The need for further building in surrounding paddocks had not been foreseen—master planning was a later art. By the time it came to Corio (if, indeed, it has) the place was anarchic, spilling over into a ribbon development tempered by self-contained precincts. The prosaic public roads at the rear act almost as powerfully as the poetic private drive around the front. What would have happened if William Guilfoyle had been able to provide a landscape plan as W. T. Manifold suggested for the Belmont site (see p. 132), can only be guessed. The basic rectangularity of Corio, expressed so forcibly by the cypress plantations, might have been avoided. Softer lines would have prevented that abruptness. Yet linear Australia fitted the council's approach. Because as much of the property as possible had to be leased for farming, to help balance the books, it was laid out almost in rectangles.

Financial pressures were thus written, like wrinkles of stress on a human face, across the Corio landscape. Constantly-recycled buildings and do-it-yourself structures reveal a school as poor as it is rich. In having to achieve all its own infrastructure it took on a capital burden scarcely understood during the original move and crippling to staff development in Brown's era (see p. 140). Once the truth hit home, houses for teaching staff increased from the two of 1914 to eight in 1930, fifty-eight in 1960 and seventy-eight in 1980. When cars changed everyone's world, the spread of Geelong and the development of Lara meant that workers 'out the back' wishing to commute had little distance to travel. The bachelor quarters, designed to hold thirty-seven workmen, could then be converted to Allen House. From a virtual term-time captivity, too, apart from theatre excursions in the school bus, the possession of cars released teachers and their families.

The isolation of Corio had its credit side. In a farewell tribute to Don Marles, Tommy Garnett generalized about the immense contribution made to the school by masters' families. Fay Marles, for instance, later Victoria's Commissioner for Equal Opportunity, contributed, formally, through research into this history, and informally in hundreds of ways as wives had done ever since Darling called them into action to help prepare the 1930s pageants. Thinkers many

The Lunan Gates in their original position at Corio, *c*. 1923. They provided a sweeping entrance from the shore of Corio Bay, but were little used because approach roads were poor.

The Timbertop chapel.

Tom Judd at the bell-rope, 1969.

DEDICATION OF KNEELERS

During the Timbertop information Service held in the afternoon of Saturday, 9th November, 1968, His Grace The Archbishop of Melbourne Dr. F. Woods dedicated all the kneelers in the Timbertop Chapel.

of them, and vigorous in extending the range of community activities, they were unpaid workers enriching the school. It could be viewed from their level as a village, servicing regular invasions of students, but having its own life, the quality of which was a measure of the success of the whole undertaking. Penelope Garnett turned the embroidery of chapel kneelers into a community activity. District Commissioner of Girl Guides, she also guided girls—as housemistress, so to speak, of the eight who stayed initially at the headmaster's house. Significantly, when she left, she was given a set of photographs of all the Corio children with their pets.

Much evidence exists of the effectiveness of Ada Brown as creator of a garden and hostess to boys, and Margaret Darling in involving her generation, Anne Fisher's thoughtfulness, the musical talents of Margaret Hollis, Margaret Masterman's taste and wit, the grace and hospitality of Marion Hutton, the intellect and energy of Betty Westcott, Nan Newman's warmth, Olive Cook's open house to old boys, Joan Fraser's commonsense, the charm of Marjorie Tunbridge and Gwyn Glover's understanding. The personalities of 'Bill' Mappin, Dulcie Spear, Janet Tomkinson, Barbara Parsons, Joyce Weber and Alison Hayward (the last always unruffled and hospitable) are strongly remembered, their roles as wives and mothers constricting them until the women's liberation of the 1960s and 1970s and finally the supportive climate of co-education made sex stereotypes less powerful at Corio. Penelope Garnett's team of embroiderers, making 500 colourful kneelers for the chapels at Corio and Timbertop in 1971, might be seen as one of the final acts in the recruitment of wives for specifically women's work.

As is well known, the school had other horizons—urban, suburban and country. In 1962 Bostock was moved from Geelong to the slopes of the Barrabool Hills, on farming land beyond Highton. It grew slowly, as we have seen (p. 258), but it grew free, with new buildings and playing-fields. Amalgamation confirmed the original site-sharing with The Hermitage, on either side of the main drive leading to Marcus Oldham.

Nothing in Geelong is like Melbourne's Toorak. No school in that wealthiest of suburbs could be spacious or easily reposed. To satisfy the aims of Isabel McComas, Glamorgan had room enough, but grown to 450 and with land prices too expensive for much expansion, it is the antithesis of Highton and Corio. It is compact and at the centre of suburban life. Along Jackson Street cars jostle for Toorak Village parking spaces. The noise of the world is always present. So are parents, readily recruited for help with open-plan teaching in the 1970s. From its different social horizon Glamorgan sends on to Corio children with attitudes and expectations quite different from those of the Highton stream, most of whom are anyway destined to be day pupils, not boarders. Like Highton, though, it has been mainly a day school subject to the flow and ebb of its human tide, both children and staff—a far cry from the self-contained communities at Corio and Timbertop. Like Highton, also, its value as a feeder has often been in doubt; only a handful of boys moved on each year to Corio during the 1960s.

Carved out of the bush, during the struggles and achievements of its first years, Timbertop looks up at the mountains, which were thought at that time to be its refuge and strength. Dedicated to the purpose of challenging adolescents to become resourceful and independent, it was a more focussed community than the others, and was most effective while under construction and while areas of virtually unexplored bush, like that 'country further out' of the early pastoral settlers, still cast their spell. Linked to the original Saturday Parties of the Geelong school and early Corio by legends of prodigious walks, it had to adapt more fundamentally than Corio to the shrinking of the world. Within a decade of its foundation, four-wheel-drive vehicles began to penetrate the seclusion: Later, forestry tracks fanned out along the Howqua River. Shooters, often firing indiscriminately, threatened peace and safety. Commercialized skiing turned some mountains into holiday pads. In much of this activity parents of pupils for whom the mountains were to be a spiritual challenge treated them as frantic playgrounds. The site itself was inviolate, except that its dams, residential units, classrooms, houses, flats, kitchen, dining hall and chapel presented an ecological problem. Because of mountain rain and feet compacting the soil, all who went there were obliged to learn the principles of conservation.

WALLS

To strangers approaching the senior school the point of focus has always been the tower, visible kilometres away. Near its eastern base are two foundation stones, one for the Corio venture and the other a portion of the stone laid in Geelong on 24 June 1857. A little higher, also on opposite sides of the doorway, are medallions commemorating William Manifold, chairman of the council who planned the move, and his son John, who presided over much of the expansion at Corio in the 1930s. Twenty-six metres from the ground, the four faces of the clock given by Mrs J. P. Chirnside semaphore the importance of routine. Every morning when he was in charge of the day boys' bus, 'Jarps' Morris dismounted near the jubilee oak, took out his pocket-watch and checked it for Corio time. Not long afterwards Tom Judd junior, the porter, would consult the face of the clock and grab the rope to ring Percy Chirnside's bell, calling the school to worship. That summons of 150 strokes would last for three minutes, during which Francis Brown, gown flapping, would stride from his house to take his seat in chapel precisely at 9.10 a.m. On rainy winter days, with a chill wind beating on his face and the drips from the bell-rope running up his arms, Judd suffered agony and kept suffering. He had already rung first to wake the school and then for breakfast and would reappear to give ten strokes at the end of periods and fifty to mark the resumption of school after morning recess and lunch.

Although the original cloistered quadrangle from which Judd rang the bell has been duplicated with a more open space—the

Place of encounter, the fountain in the quad.

Designs

NOS 131 - 180
by Ross + Bethley - This Ben.
students of Fine Arts, Gordon Institute
Nos 131 - 133 Draw with Clive Branch
  134 - 141 Based on Timbertop Chapel
  142 - 145 Galah - King Parrot
  146 - 152 Kangaroo
  153 - 159 Gum nut and leaves
  160 - 163 Bottlebrush
  164 - 170 Timbertop Activities
  171 - 176 St. Francis and Birds
  177 - 181 St. Francis and Fish
  182 - 186 Possum

363

Unheard-of comfort—the extension to the staff common room in 1965.

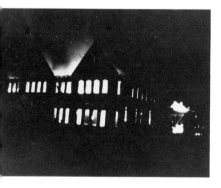

Everyone's nightmare. Cuthbertson House on fire, 10 March 1925.

Darling Quadrangle to the west—and although classrooms have spread far beyond it, 'the quad' has remained a centre of activity during teaching hours and the heart of the school's administration. Until Darling came it was a special precinct. Its entrances, apart from the main doors, were closed off after hours by folding metal grills. Cruciform paths of shell-grit, replaced in the 1930s by a herring-bone pattern of brick, led between squares of grass to a central fountain given in 1914 by the New South Wales pastoralist Sir Samuel McCaughey. It still stands above the original water supply, a 182 000-litre underground tank fed from surrounding roofs. Boys used to raise a drink with four hand-pumps located on the perimeter of the fountain, which had been dry for years when Charles Fisher arrived. He revived it.

Through growth, greater complexity and professionalism the administration has expanded from the headmaster's study just south of the tower and the bursar's office in the south wing to absorb half the ground floor of the quad, leap upstairs under the tower and spill into the housekeeper's flat around the back. The library, started in one classroom north of the tower, spread into three and was furnished with memorial bays to become the Hawker Library. When it was superseded by the Fisher Library in 1979 it was transformed into the school archives and specialist history library. The masters' common room at the south-east corner was originally little bigger than was necessary to hold its billiard table* which, in the more serious Darling days, was banished along the corridor westwards to a space beside the Morris Room. In 1965 what had been the sixth-form room, where Darling appeared from his office next door to civilize the top of the school, has become the Gladys Bell Room, the comfortable end of the common room. Furnished with armchairs, it opens by French windows onto the driveway and playing-fields.

The Bracebridge Wilson Hall was not the only major building outside the quad as it had been in Geelong. Houses, junior school, dining hall and chapel were there by the 1920s but, as at the old school, the first external teaching space was the science wing, erected near the hall in 1930. When the more distant art and music schools were completed in 1937—38 the rounds of the school porter, carrying stationery supplies or bringing 'the book' by which messages were sent around the school, were greatly extended. With further expansion into the old sanatorium and new classrooms beyond the chapel, beside the Fisher Library, teaching has been largely decentralized.

The sanatorium was a place of antiseptic smells, a sanctuary from crowded dorms, a step up from the simpler, routine treatment of house matrons. There was a sense of crisis during inevitable epidemics; and alarms, like the broken ankle of the boy who tried to escape from the fire at Cuthbertson House by leaping out of an

---

* As an appropriate link with the school's pastoral traditions it had come from Chirnside's Werribee Park. Given by George Chirnside in 1914, it was exchanged for another in 1975 so that it could return to a restored Werribee Park.

upper-storey window grasping a rope of knotted sheets he had forgotten to fasten to his bed.

Medical attention came daily but part-time, first from Dr T. J. M. Kennedy, later (1924–49) from Dr R. N. Scott Good, an old boy who earned Darling's praise for the admirable, vigilant, untiring and successful way he had carried 'perhaps the heaviest burden of responsibility of any of us'. A large man, with an angular face and strong chin, he had been an outstanding sportsman when at school.

As a link with earlier days, although otherwise completely different, a sophisticated medical centre, opened in 1969, was given the name Kennedy. The first Corio doctor had left money for it in his will. It cost $160 000 and provided care for the whole Corio community—up to 5000 visits by boys and 1500 by adults and children each year. There are sixteen beds in five wards, including a self-contained infectious diseases ward, a suite of outpatient rooms and two self-contained flats for the nursing sisters. Serious medical and surgical cases are transferred to the Geelong Hospital.

Professor R. R. Andrew (OGG), Dean of Medicine at Monash University, who opened it, remarked that without such facilities it was hard to do a good job, but without the right medico, impossible. Like an effective priest or schoolteacher, Andrew expected a good doctor to recognise the signals of people in distress and find opportunities to help them. That fitted Garnett's vision of the medical centre caring for the whole person and especially for adolescents during their years of adjustment—as did his and council's decision to appoint Dr D. B. Mackey full-time resident medical officer. David Mackey had been senior prefect in 1952.

From the north-east corner of the quad the war memorial cloister with its rule of silence leads to the chapel where, until the 1960s, every school day used formally to begin.

Strangely proportioned until the extension that delighted Francis Brown in his final year, the chapel was rather austere until fitted with the memorial windows that bathe it in splendour on cloudless days and the 350 embroidered kneelers—base colour blue—added in 1970. A year later, after 8000 hours of embroidery, three long kneeling cushions covered the sanctuary steps.

The hours spent by Joseph Hollins Allen, chaplain from 1917 to 1945, have not been computed. Under an unsentimental, almost harsh facade, according to J. R. D., the stocky, round-faced 'Joey' hid the warmest of hearts. He made the school his parish and in the day boys' Geelong House (later named after him) extended the range of his pastoral care. Of straightforward faith, punctual and conscientious, he venerated Francis Brown but adapted quickly to the different religious approach of his lay successor.

Mervyn Britten (1946–49), who came from the chaplaincy at Duntroon Military College, succeeded Allen for a year and then became associated with Stephen Jones, who had been at Junior School since 1937. 'Poppa' or 'Jonah', as he was called, came to GGS from experience in the AIF, a number of parishes, prisons and the

Clergy from Geelong assisted the headmaster during the ceremony on 3rd April, 1914, at which Mrs. F. S. Falkiner of Boonoke, New South Wales, laid the foundation stone for the Chapel of All Saints. She was the mother of the five old boys who gave the funds.

'Let us all praise famous men.' The Chapel of All Saints during the farewell ceremonies for J. R. Darling, whose eloquence and faith had stimulated and strengthened the stream of boys who had passed through it.

mission field. He was master of several languages and, like Allen, a man of immense sympathy and simple faith. Boys found him disarmingly innocent and were influenced especially by the directness and sincerity of his prayers. His wife, Marjorie, at one with him, began a Sunday School at Corio soon after their arrival, directed the Nursery School and in 1956 became head of the junior school at The Hermitage, where 'Poppa' joined her to teach Latin and mathematics after he retired in 1958. Both made a large contribution to Australian links with the peoples of Asia.

Howard Hollis (1959—64) studied music then theology. He stepped from the organ bench at Christ Church, South Yarra, to become curate there, then spent some years alongside William McKie (organist at Westminster Abbey) while chaplain at Westminster School. At the coronation of Queen Elizabeth in 1953, he intoned the litany, and was able to fill the chapel at Corio not just with his beautiful voice but frequently with sacred music in association with his wife Margaret (on the flute) and other artists. Peter Thomson, later chaplain then Master of Timbertop, found it exhilarating.

The change of mood that accompanied Garnett was clearly expressed in the appointment of John Davison (1964—71). An Englishman, educated at Marlborough, he was infuriating, enlivening and inspiring. According to one Roman Catholic headmaster, he had the keenest theological brain in Victoria. Noted at Corio for challenging sermons and talks, for an open chapel policy that has been described already (p. 247) and for cutting away pretence, he provided, like Peter Westcott, intellectual stimulus to the common room. To succeed him Ivan Turkington (1972—76) came down from the mountains. He had been at Timbertop in 1965—66. A shy man he was at his best one-to-one with boys and girls and in his thoughtful, almost conversational sermons, and most at home in the chapel sanctuary during communion. Anastasias (Tassie) Pappas (1977—   ) came directly from the hills at Mansfield, alongside Timbertop, where he had been vicar for seven years.

Beginning the day much less formally the boys had already been mustered in their house rooms to start them on the way to time-honoured rituals at the dining hall. As Judd rang the breakfast bell latecomers would be seen flying from the houses, pulling on their clothes, in fear of being locked out. Prefects on duty would turn them away for shoelaces untied or buttons undone. Until the austerity of World War II each maid set her table then changed into a waitress uniform. She wore a light-blue dress with long sleeves and starched cuffs, covered by a vast white apron and bib held in place by a stiffly-starched white calico belt. A large starched cap, its front turned back from the face, beige stockings and black shoes completed the uniform. Maids served tables of about twenty boys and some could carry ten plates of food at a time. Servings were adequate but not always appetizing. Boys remembered the inevitability for breakfast of cereals, porridge, toast and an occasional egg (watery and horrible when scrambled) or fearful fried bacon on fried bread. At

midday there might be stew, a grill, spiced meat loaf, 'boiled baby' (lamb in white sauce) and once a week a roast from which leftovers were later recycled as shepherds' pie. The best or worst remembered sweets were 'Yarra mud'—a chocolate blanc-mange covered with gloomy artificial cream—and a thick banana custard, as yellow as a paint advertisement. Glutinous steamed puddings and baked rice were other contenders. Bread, scones, jam and fruit were lined up for the evening meal. The boarders' view was, of course, a traditionally jaundiced one. The school and its catering staff went to great trouble to provide appetizing meals. They could be very good. Boys supplemented school food from private stocks of favourite cereals, jam, cocoa, etc., carted in from food lockers. Concentration on the better-looking maids—called 'Biddies' for their presumed Irishness—was occasionally shattered with sharp explosions from supposedly unbreakable glasses that sent dangerous fragments into nearby plates of food or bowls of jam and sugar.

Those days came to an end in 1940, when boys took over most of the tasks carried out in the handsome, panelled dining hall. The savings were large, and in the face of a wage explosion and problems of finding suitable staff, peace saw no return to the old order. In 1976, with the sudden increase in population from co-education, a self-service cafeteria system was adopted and automatic dishwashers were installed. Although its quality was sometimes a source of discontent (p. 244), food was low-key and the atmosphere of the dining room much less formal.

Each year, in a special panic, the hall was prepared for the Old Boys' Day dinner. Emma Gilpin, when housekeeper, would search for both blue iris and yellow broom to make table decorations in the school colours, the yellow given an unusual prominence for its effect against the oak panelling and red brickwork. Young old boys noticed most the unusual flow of beer and wine and the unexpected presence as drink waiters of male staff called in from their usual tasks out the back.

In close focus, until the 1930s, the life of the school centred on its red-brick boarding-houses, appropriately clothed in Virginia creeper in contrast to the ivy of the old gray school. Each house had a life of its own; each demanded a boy's primary allegiance, involved him in menial chores and called on him to play or support competitive games, to study at night and pray and sleep. There was little other focus for his social life.

Because they were designed with large dormitories and open study rooms—there was nowhere to go for quiet relaxation—the first three houses, Manifold, Perry and Cuthbertson, as well as Junior House from 1916, suited the hearty routines encouraged by Brown, who deliberately turned away sensitive boys. Solidarity was maintained by prefects, study-room leaders and the senior dorm, who ensured maximum participation in the house activities that distinguished the new school. There was less chance of escape than in the old where

368

Wilson, in his remarkable way, had subdivided the original dormitory cavern into bedrooms each holding four or five boys.

Leonard Fell, who had one year at the old school, thought that the architects had learnt nothing from its deficiencies. Perry not only lacked heating but was defenceless against howling gales, which broke the western face of the clock four times in as many years. An annual attack of colds was taken for granted. In summer shell-grit from the paths was whipped up by the wind to cause nasty facial abrasions which festered because of some toxicity at the lagoon. In winter the same material clogged centimetres thick on the soles of boots.

Because boys (and most masters) knew of no other way, there was general acceptance of the tough environment. It was regarded as character-building. In 1974 Sir Keith Angas, a prefect in 1918, said that his contemporaries seemed to thrive on conditions which today would be called brutal or inhumane and cause an outcry. Geoffrey Lemprière found his schooldays a perfect preparation for prisoner-of-war camp; they were his 'backbone and standby'. 'Our allies', he said, 'never have been taught to give or to obey orders and accept any sort of discipline or hardship'. Brian Jones thought that, because it was small, well-ordered and happy, the school of the 1920s was in certain ways 'outstandingly civilized'. The houses and the isolation welded it together. The boys were a nice lot who treated each other well; there was no brutal caning or dreadful bullying. He believed that no one questioned the numerous rules, automatic punishments, beatings and detentions. This view may be set against John Manifold's 'perfectly consistent' loathing of the place until he reached fifth form in 1932. Although others less in love with the school than Jones questioned its humanity, the experience of A. S. Ellis (Cuthbertson 1928−31), who says he liked the structured life, indicates tolerance. A Jew and 'a swot', he worked all the tricks he knew to avoid football and once his reputation was established—'Oh, Ellis, it's no use picking him!'—he was left alone. He was envied his freedom from chapel: 'half your luck', they said.

The friendliness increased under Darling, and punishment was more humane, as in Bracebridge Wilson's day, but the core of the Spartan tradition remained. Keith Dunstan (Francis Brown 1939−42) remembered fagging (although no one called it that) for house prefects by cleaning their studies, pots and pans and polishing their buttons and boots before cadet parade. There was a strict caste system; boys were numbered from the captain at one to the most junior at, say, sixty-eight. Your number appeared on your tuck-locker, clothes-peg, everything, and you were very conscious of your position as you mounted the ladder according to your seniority in the house, your class in school and your performance at games. The senior dorm bullied any presumptuous juniors early on Saturday mornings, calling them out in shorts and sandshoes for a mile run across paddocks to an icy mud-pond, where they were obliged to push themselves round and round on their stomachs. After that, as

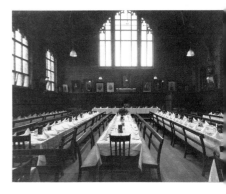

The dining hall in the 1920s, the day of waitresses and a high table.

369

Term I., 1947

PERRY HOUSE

House Master:

Mr. V. J. H. TUNBRIDGE.

House Tutors:

Mr. J. W. GLOVER,

Mr. P. N. THWAITES.

VIU1—**WINCHESTER, E. J.**
VIU1—**LEE, D. A.**
VIU1—HOWEY, R. I.
VIU1—**Backwell, L. E.**
5 VIU1—**Barber, D. D.**
VIU2—**Dawes, C. B.**
VIU1—**Foster, A. W.**
VIU2—**Kent, D. J.**
VIU1—Geroe, G. A.
10 VIU2—Bert, G. E.
Harrison, D. G.
Uglow, A. J.
VIU3—Cominos, T.
Granat, S. B.
15 Piper, J. A. D.
Ritchie, R. J.
VA—Foster, J. L.
Gordon, P. J.
Hall, M. A.
20 Happell, J. W.
Lear, D. McC.
Phillips, P. C.
Walker, H. H.
VB—Ashkanasy, A. S. N.
25 Johnstone, D. H.
Jones, B. M.
Morrell, E. G.
Mylius, C. H.
Nevett, J. G. K.
30 VC—Davis, J. T.
Hall, E. P.
Hall, J. C.
Lear, J. C.
Manton, G. O. V.
35 Sayers, M. C.
VD—Allison, G. H.   §
IVA—Hawkins, H. S.
Jones, C. W.   §
Kent, B. E.
40 Murray, M. F.
Ritchie, D. F.
Smith, H. F.
Welsh, D. I. B.
IVB—Granat, R. J.
45 Happell, D. P.
Korman, J. S.
McDonald, D. A.
Mirams, J. A.
Myer, B. J.
50 Titterton, A. W.
Vine, M. X.
IVC—Baldry, R. F.
Crooks, H. N. T.
Eadie, G. L.
55 Lees, A. J. L.

after football, getting the mud off under the cold showers was agony. Dunstan has described the morning cold shower as a gymnastic feat—sprint in, arms stiffly outstretched, take the shock on the wall and rebound out—time under water 1/50 second. House captains could cane. Hugh Luiggi (a founding member of Francis Brown 1937—40) remembered a boy caned for insulting the King by sticking his image upside down on a letter. Luiggi thought that caning, the preferred method of enforcing discipline at Corio, was weakened by its frequency and the lack of distinction in degree of punishment. Had he been in Manifold, he would have found life much tougher. There also, the language of the shearing shed was assembled for export to the rest of the school.

Houses were clearly more than walls. Into them Brown had drafted distinctive groups through whom separate attitudes and traditions developed and were maintained. Manifold received the original Western District families. Nearly everyone there seemed someone else's cousin and many looked forward to a comfortable pastoral life. In Brown's day many senior boys in Manifold were, in Fell's words, 'technically excluded from the school curriculum'; they gave their time to the eighteen, eleven and eight. Cuthbertson contained the sons of farmers and professional men in country towns. Luiggi thought it more cosmopolitan and wholesome than its rural rival. Perry harboured the sons of Melbourne's professional and business establishment. Less hearty and more studious, it was the right place for the Old Etonian G. C. T. Giles (p. 150), who was housemaster in 1922—23. His relaxed attitudes might have foundered in the other two houses, although his white socks were probably imitated more rapidly in Manifold than Perry. According to GGS folklore the latecomer, Francis Brown House, was systematically filled with misfits. Luiggi thought it had a spurious reputation for nonconformity but could fairly claim in 1940 to be the most cultured of the houses.

Darling improved the houses. He made sure that his contribution, Francis Brown, would be bright and airy, that each boy would have a place of his own in the study rooms, that the dormitories would be smaller and have pleasant bathrooms attached. Study rooms in the other houses were modified along the same lines, but his decision to overcrowd the houses with eighty-five rather than sixty-five boys* prevented more drastic changes. Under Garnett, when the pressure of numbers was reduced, some sixth-formers in Perry House were given study-bedrooms with face-high partitions along 'Cubi Passage'. The old study passage, decorated with 'Do Not Spit', 'No Smoking' and 'One Way Traffic' signs borrowed from the outside world, remained the preserve of the most senior boys. In the early 1970s Lindon's sixth-form boys and girls were given study-bedrooms. That this should be the norm was indicated by the construction of Clyde in Fisher's day with suites of sixteen study-bedrooms around a

---

* They had been designed for 44. In the early 1950s they grew towards and even topped 100.

central core. But philosophies change. Later, in the belief that students in shared studies worked better, separate studies and bedrooms returned. Affected perhaps by greater comfort in offices and public buildings, the gap between a student's environment at school and at home was no longer the huge distance it had been in the early years at Corio.

Although houses reflected the personalities of their housemasters, most routines were in the hands of senior boys who, like tribal elders, ensured that hallowed customs and conventions were passed on from year to year. Unlike tribal life, oral tradition and ritual behaviour were reinforced by written accounts. House captains kept records of how they had interpreted their tasks and the houses kept journals of each year's activities that grew over generations into volumes of lore.

The most admired housemasters were those who, like Pinner, Tunbridge, Parsons and Marles, kept their fingers on the pulse without seeming to spy and influenced behaviour without interfering. Their senior boys knew where they would draw the line and trusted their motives. Housemasters' work was never ending. They were the chief interface between parents and the school and for an effective knowledge of their charges they needed to be aware of everything that was going on.

A list of housemasters represents a chosen few in the school who were entrusted with its central task. Not to have become a housemaster was for some (and their wives) a measure of failure. An honour-board would read as listed.

As a general rule the tenure of housemasters was limited to fifteen years, but after his war service Tunbridge, whose excellence Darling admired and needed, was allowed to begin all over again. He finished with a record twenty-six years. In contrast to the early years at Corio, housemastering became an art, stimulated by exchange experience at English schools and the injection of ideas at regular housemasters' meetings. By their influence at that level men like Bechly, Covill, Happell, Hutton, Mappin, Marles, Parsons, Roberts-Wray and Spear, who held their boarding-house posts for five years or more, had a major influence on the life of the school.

There was a difference in the day-house to which Allen, Newman, Glover, Covill and Murray gave similar care and in which they fought for equal status against lack of numbers and a long-standing sense of inferiority. Amalgamation and the advent of Fraser as a second day-house in 1976 made 'day-boarders' less of a minority. The girls' houses were similarly outside the mainstream while the school adjusted to co-education. With its former headmistress, Alice Pringle, and then Jean Gupta in charge, Clyde (p. 271) retained a

---

* The Headmaster was nominally Housemaster of Manifold *passim* until 1962 (and until 1934 a bridge joined his residence to the House): he was also officially and effectively so at certain periods, though G. A. Hancock assisted Brown in 1919–20, C. W. R. Dart and W. G. L. Cartwright assisted Darling from 1940–44, and T. C. Murray assisted Garnett early in 1962.

CUTHBERTSON
1914–18	E. V. Butler
1919–26	J. W. Gardner
1927–34	E. L. Nall
1935–50	E. W. H. Pinner
1951–61	A. J. Spear
1962–67	K. J. Mappin
1968–71	I. B. Collier
1972–(80)	C. W. Roberts-Wray

MANIFOLD
1914–20	F. E. Brown*
1921–34	C. A. Cameron
1935–39	C. E. S. Gordon
1940–44	J. R. Darling*
1945–52	C. W. R. Dart
1953–55	W. J. Howard
1956–61	C. W. R. Dart
1962	T. R. Garnett*
1962–64	H. Ward
1965–78	C. E. R. Parsons
1979–(83)	A. P. Sheahan

PERRY
1914–22	E. T. Williams
1922–23	G. C. T. Giles
1924–28	L. de C. Berthon
1929–36	K. C. Masterman
1937–40	V. J. H. Tunbridge
1941–44	J. S. Cook
	(Acting while V. J. H. Tunbridge on active service)
1944–62	V. J. H. Tunbridge
1963–71	D. M. Marles
1972–(83)	F. C. Covill

GEELONG
1933–45	J. H. Allen
1946–53	F. N. B. Newman
1954–69	J. W. Glover
1970–71	F. C. Covill
Renamed ALLEN	
1972–76	T. C. Murray
1977–	J. F. C. Harvey

FRANCIS BROWN
1937–41	W. N. Jaffray
1941–44	F. N. B. Newman
	(Acting while W. N. Jaffray on active service)
1945–56	W. N. Jaffray
1957–71	H. B. Hutton
1972–76	D. P. Happell
1977	I. W. Good
1978–(87)	G. A. Bechly

LINDON
1972–75	I. F. Edwards
1976–(85)	R. G. C. Johnson

CLYDE
1976–77	Mrs A. Pringle
1978–(89)	Mrs J. Y. Gupta

JENNINGS
1978–(87)	G. A. Bechly
1978–(84)	Mrs C. M. Rimmer

FRASER
1976–78	N. J. Clark
1979–	D. A. Endean

family atmosphere, but had to adjust to being just a little bit of a large school. Whereas Jennings, the other girls' house, was new, Glen Bechly gave it for two years (quite apart from his personal magic) the fruits of his experience in charge of Connewarre and his established place in the school. Also, although Jennings and Clyde stood apart from the boys' sporting world, their coming together (with the girls of Allen and Fraser Houses) in competition helped them to share the spirit that had given the original boarding-houses much of their identity.

Before the girls came, boys thought themselves sex-starved. That is why some invested the maids with a special romantic glow, although one boy told Tom Judd that he was sure that Miss Bright and Miss Gilpin chose their maids for advanced age and ugliness. Judd did not agree; but he was sure that there was 'not a sophisticated one amongst them and should such a one manage to slip through, she was most certainly asked to leave'. On another level, however, there was a strong feminine influence from the proxy mothers and aunts who worked as boarding-house matrons. 'Matrons', not 'maids', expresses the difference. They were often well-connected and could be relied upon to reinforce standards of politeness and fair play. They identified with their charges and remembered them and their exploits with microscopic clarity.

By the 1930s, most matrons were qualified nurses, including veterans from the 1914—18 war. They were remarkable, according to one observer. He remembered particularly the tall sisters, Rose 'Perry' Walker and Lucy 'Cuthy' Walker, Ella Tubbs and Florence King of Manifold, Florence Mosey, first matron of Francis Brown and Frances White at the sanatorium. A few, like Claire Crocker (sister of historian Russel Ward) had had wide experience, in her case, through her husband, at diplomatic posts across the world.

Many were treasured for their long service and loved for their kindnesses; others had indelible quirks. White-haired, fair-skinned Miss Jessie Gemmell, at Perry in the 1920s, looked like a ghost in her white uniform and square muslin cap. Tall, formal and snobbish, she hated menial tasks. Because gloves were not enough protection when sorting unsavoury handkerchiefs and filthy football socks for the laundry, she used a pair of fire-tongs to count them into appropriate bins. In contrast, Miss Adèle Wade of Manifold was a true mother-figure, a keeper of confidences and fanatically devoted to *her* boys. She grew old in their service. At her farewell from the house 'Cac' Cameron paid her warm tributes and added that he had come to love her. 'Oh!' she responded, in a tone that indicated unmistakeably, 'so he ought to'. Later in Manifold Miss Jean Cox, who had been an army nurse, ordered boys about like a sergeant-major but defended them against all comers and fought vigorously to improve their environment. She toughed it out successfully in a man's world, whereas others, typified by Sister Jane Stoddart of Perry, used charm and tact. One of the most warmly remembered of all matrons,

Jane was a considerable figure in the wider Corio community for more than thirty years. Her farewell brought a great tribal gathering, made memorable also by the feat of a former house captain, John (the footballer) Newman, who called the roll of his day flawlessly from memory.

In the period after Darling's arrival women were less isolated. He not only involved them in pageants, plays and other activities but also changed the mood of the place by employing an attractive young woman secretary. A line of boys like a guard of honour waited to see Vi Moden enter the quad each morning. Margaret Darling, in her role, helped to break down barriers that had been precious to Mrs Brown, in whose broom-cupboard she found a meticulous set of rules and duties for the servants. That Margaret was Australian and very young made a big difference. Even so, there were male taboos; no woman dined in the hall until the Darlings' farewell.

OUT THE BACK

The third world of Corio, after those of staff and students and then wives and families,* developed its own mores and traditions. To begin with, in fact, until housing was provided for a sizeable group of masters and their families, there were only two worlds, each constrained by poor transport to official celibacy. Men on the general staff were housed in bachelor quarters across Biddlecombe Avenue, maids ('biddies' to the boys) in little rooms behind the kitchens. Although staff 'out the back' were not expected to know their place as rigorously as in England, a strong hierarchy descended from the bursar through the maintenance manager and the foreman on the outdoor side and the manageress indoors. The word of these three was law and it needed to be for the staff was a small army. In 1930 the outdoor team under Sergeant-Major Bill Batterham included two boilermen, a carpenter, a painter, a labourer, two groundsmen, two gardeners, a boy with a dray, a supply-truck driver and a bus driver. Indoors, under Miss Cecil Bright and the housekeeper, Emma Gilpin, were six laundresses, twelve kitchenmen, four housemen, thirty housemaid-waitresses and a girl to wait on the matrons. Tom Judd junior, the porter, was in a class of his own; he linked the world of the quad to that out the back. The bursar-secretary's office held an accountant and a boy, the forerunners of an administrative staff that grew substantially later and experienced a sex change.

Individuals stood out in special roles that took them into public view. Tom Judd senior, who as chief laundryman knew boys at first only through their clothes, became bus driver and sprinkled his cockney humour further afield. His son Tom, as porter, was Corio's encyclopedia and directory. Head groundsmen, like Jock Lennox, gained an aura from their role in sporting rites. Through attendance at particular house tables maids became personalities and the head

* Boarding-house matrons were in a sort of no-one's-land, though closer to the first world than the others.

waitress, with the jealously guarded privilege of waiting on the headmaster and prefects at lunch and (after its creation in 1931) the Morris Room bachelors at breakfast and dinner, became a minor celebrity. The Morris Room and the Matrons' Dining Room were the only personal arenas left when a cafeteria system was adopted in 1976 for serving meals in hall—and even they had a degree of self-service.

For most of the men 'out the back' contacts with the first world of the school were tangential, yet real enough for many to develop strong loyalties. Long service gave them an identity that was recognized with acclaim by staff and students, with whom countless and often strong friendships developed. Individual notices in the *Corian* bade them farewell when they retired and honoured them with obituaries when they died. Three men whose combined service totalled 130 years were paraded to meet Prince Charles during his first visit to Corio in 1966: Frank Meyrick as horse and then bus driver had notched fifty years; Tom Judd junior forty-four; and Stan Riddell, the chef, a mere thirty-four. Some families could boast a high score; the Judds—father, son and daughter—made a century.* There were chain migrations of three or four girls in succession from country families, particularly those in the Ballarat district.

Despite the hierarchy there was freedom for individual characters to flower and for critical currents of opinion to sum up their immediate bosses, the headmaster, boys, staff and their families. Cecil Bright, the long-term manageress, had immense discretion and very high standards. Shoddy floor-scrubbing during a vacation clean-up once brought her to her knees with bucket, brush and orders for rags and fresh water with which to demonstrate what clean boards looked like. She selected and trained her girls with care and encouraged them to develop their talents, just as she took young Judd aside when he was laundry boy and set him on the path of enlightenment by encouraging him to read. Emma Gilpin, the housekeeper ('Miss Gulps' behind her back), shared a sitting-room with the manageress. When she checked the staff coming on duty each morning she seemed to be as starchy as their uniforms, but she melted to kindness if they were ill or unhappy.

Among the men Sergeant-Major Batterham became a Corio veteran, although his loyalty to Colonel Garrard in 1915 had troubled Francis Brown (p. 154). He stood ramrod straight but shed dignity with the rattle of his loose false teeth. Tom Judd senior, who was disarmingly cockney as well as rich in experience and tattoos from service in the Royal Navy, was a 'character' and a tease. His son Tom (there was no inflated Thomas on either of their birth certificates) completed fifty years of service at Corio in 1971. A walking legend and repository of GGS folklore, he became the chronicler of 'out the back'. After writing *Fifty Years Will Be Long Enough* in 1971, he stayed until the end of 1972 and would have liked some more. An

---

* Quite apart from Mrs Judd's part-time help during crises in the laundry.

early caution from Miss Bright about the need for absolute discretion stayed with him all those years, but from his privileged position (note how the tables can be turned on privilege) he saw more of the GGS game than most other players. Inquisitive, intelligent, diplomatic, hard-working, he came to be a key member of staff, by accretion enlarging the porter's job with a range of tasks that matched his talents. He ran the bookroom, sorted mail and assisted in the library while still keeping a finger on the pulse by ringing the bell, taking around 'the book', serving morning tea to the headmaster and common room and ferreting out mislaid equipment. Judd acted in amateur theatre and wrote and produced several plays. During 1935 he tried an acting career in London—with so little success that the pull of home brought him back to the quadrangle to take the bell-rope in his hand for the beginning of 1936.

Judd's determination to be of meaning in the school was matched by that of another remarkable individual, Lily Hawkesford. 'Little Lil's' 132 centimetres, surmounted by rich red hair, contained immense energy. Peter Westcott was heard to say that her father had split the atom long before the scientists. She was born at Ballarat in 1891 and came to GGS in 1923, having failed because of her size to get employment as a waitress. Her stature also hampered her career at Corio. Out of fear that the boys might make fun of her, she was installed in the matrons' dining room from which, with a fierce resolve not to be put down, she fought to emerge. Already she had battled for a uniform of her own choice. All-white, it was appropriate when she was serving similarly clad matrons, but distinctive when she finally won the right to wait in hall. Being different suited her ambition, which she inevitably achieved, to serve the headmaster and prefects and to take charge of the Morris Room. For over twenty years she reigned among the bachelors for whose benefit in 1973 she donated her silver, including a tray presented to her by the school council on her retirement in 1964. They knew her well from their breakfast and dinner meetings in the Morris Room, where she can still be seen in a lively portrait by one of its artist members, Bruce Fletcher.

Unforgettable in the flesh, Lil left many memories. At a rather formal dinner at the Darling's one night she brought 'Monty' a cup of tea during the meat course. To Mrs Darling's protest that coffee would be served at the end of the meal she replied that Mr Montgomery always had tea with his meat and vegies. One dark night she almost failed to reach the Darlings'. She fell head-first into a rubbish bin that had been used as a wicket behind Manifold House. She was still kicking and screaming when some Manifold boys pulled her out by the legs. The afternoons of her days off in first term were spent at the river watching the rowers. Even in retirement she hardly missed a head of the river, and she proudly supported cricket and football teams at home and cheered them away to foreign grounds, vigorously waving her own school flag. At Corio fairs she badgered the throng to guess the number of jelly-beans in a bottle or the length of a

Lily, a portrait by Bruce Fletcher.

375

bundle of string. Her fame at the school has been eclipsed by few of the illustrious names she captured in her book on such occasions.

Apart from Tom Judd, no one served the school for as long, and few as conscientiously, as Frank Meyrick, who was employed as a groundsman in 1918. Soon he was to be seen driving a Corio institution, 'the cabbage cart'. While horse drawn, until 1922, it was used to transfer supplies from *Avalon* to the storeroom; when motorised, it made pick-ups daily in Geelong. Frank succeeded Tom Judd senior as bus-driver in 1940. Before the school woke each day, he would begin the first of eight trips to Geelong, to ferry workers, then boys. Kind and cheerful, yet correct and reserved, if not shy, he was warm to those who knew him well—and epitomised the family ethos that was precious to the school. He retired in 1968.

Megs Hogarth, a different kind of man, was indispensable at Timbertop from 1966 to 1981. A mountain cattleman, with vast experience of the bush, he was known for his dry humour, wonderful yarns, 'good healthy mischief' and an indestructible hat. In his company no task could be boring. Initiates watched with delight as he sent 'rent-a-poms' (he coined the term to describe young English assistants) climbing trees to search for the eggs of the bush-chook. Once, he kept some victims waiting at the sewer outlet with sledge-hammers to clobber an enormous snake he said was hiding there; eventually his pipe-cleaner appeared, pushed through from behind a building by a triumphant Megs. Everything he did, and often only he could do it, was done well. When Ian Stapleton was searching for fresh hiking challenges, he found the mountain man a godsend. Megs knew every spur and gully, every trick that would keep equipment working or maintain the Mt Stirling hut.

HIGHWAY

If anything changed Corio as much as J. R. Darling's arrival it was the internal-combustion engine. Between them the man and the motor-car brought depth and flexibility to connections with the outside world. Tom Judd senior began the revolution in 1926 when he bought a Chevrolet car, which gave the domestic staff an advantage over the teachers by breaking down their isolation. Until then it was not possible, for instance, to experience the excitement of the cinema, because the last train left Geelong about 9 p.m.. To go to the wrestling in Melbourne was quite unthinkable. So the 'Chevy' became an unofficial taxi, though only on Friday nights and Saturdays, to which Judd restricted his trips.

Childbirth was an exception to Judd's rule. R. R. P. Barbour and his wife were probably Judd's first passengers when they made a midnight dash to hospital for the birth of their son, Peter. Soon afterwards Barbour was the first of a growing number of masters to buy a car. It caused a mild sensation among the boys and led Francis Brown to ask if he really thought it necessary. But the school had already moved in the same direction. In 1922 Messervey, the boatman, became a landlubber when *Avalon* was replaced as the day-boy transport with a chartered bus. Through him the school provided a service for staff and their families, who could order provisions from shops in Geelong and have them collected and delivered to individual lockers near the kitchen. In 1928 when 'Old John', the cabman, while riding a bicycle, was killed by a truck on the Melbourne Road, a little motorbus replaced the cab and Tom Judd senior, with the Gilbertian title of Chief Motor Mechanic, left the laundry to drive and maintain it. A bigger bus, with Judd and later Frank Meyrick in charge, was purchased in the 1930s. It was needed for educational visits to theatres, factories and slums, for trips to other schools for sporting fixtures and to the Barwon for rowing training. That was the beginning of a trend to large vehicles which aided the closure of the Lunan Gates in 1963. They had been weakened by several encounters in which the sides of visiting buses were ripped open like sardine tins. The Art School (1949) and Centenary Gates (1957) had made the narrow entrance unnecessary.

Darling bought a Morris and drove it to freedom and to his many appointments. The hazards of the narrow highway overtook him in 1934 when he was sideswiped by a car in which a young woman was fatally injured. He was free of blame but carried an emotional bruise which his conscience helped to heal through membership of the Road Safety Council of Australia, of which he became chairman in 1961. Relief from constant driving up that boring road came when Judd senior was appointed his chauffeur. Others used the road less often but with similar meaning. Masters, especially young ones, found that even a night in Melbourne, only possible in a car, was a welcome escape, but those who joined Masterman for a theatre or concert were wise to make sure that he had enough fuel; the classicist was notoriously illiterate mechanically. Daring boys made for the highway to thumb lifts unless, as one boy managed in Brown's day, there was an elder brother to pick them up on the pillion of a motorbike. According to Tom Judd junior, Rupert Murdoch, who obeyed rules only if they suited him, kept his own motorcycle clandestinely at the garage on the highway. There was a phone at the garage which figured in 'escapes' by unhappy newcomers in junior school; they rang their gullible mothers to ask to be collected. Stephen Murray-Smith, an organizer of escapes, said that when any were missed masters would leap into sports cars and scour the countryside.

The garage was sustained at first by imported petrol in drums and tins, but eventually the appetite of cars and trucks brought bowsers to its door and, in 1952, a Shell refinery across the road. At that environmentally-ignorant time, slumbering tanks, a maze of pipes and a forest of steel were placed within a kilometre of the school, which had later to plead for special exemptions from more rigorous shire regulations that prevented the erection of houses within 2 kilometres of the site. Like the Boeing 747s that rumble overhead from Avalon airfield, it has been a symbol, except when magically lit at night, of the price we pay for the convenient shrinking of the world.

At Spencer Street station, Melbourne.

Parents were rarely seen at Corio until the 1930s. Then, three times a term, in a Sunday routine like an up-market Saturday Party, many would arrive after morning chapel to take their sons away for a day by the sea or in the bush. Some boys liked to show off their Saturday haunts; others concentrated on lunch, especially if it was at the Barwon Heads Golf Club. Just before tea, strings of cars, including the latest and the best, with which boys were immediately associated by their peers, came rolling back and out again, the flow of a tide that would have disconcerted Dr Brown, to whom Sundays were not for pleasure. Cars brought parents, as never before, to school functions to meet face to face people who would have been only names to an older generation. Increasingly, as roads and cars improved and more women drove, the exodus from school for exeats or at the end of term was by car. Even so, the prize departure remained that of Keith Hornabrook, who was flown away sensationally from the school grounds in his father's Sopwith Gnu on 1 July 1920.

So the world intrudes continually on what was once almost a monastery, but departs leaving little trace. Tower, quad, chapel, dining hall, classrooms, houses, homes, libraries, music school, art school, theatre and all the laboriously built environment remain self-contained, the result of a history that planted them at great expense beyond the influence of the mundane tides of life.

A note on sources

The material on which this history is based is held largely at the school. There is a distinct division between official and unofficial sources, the former being held in the office strongroom and at various storage locations. The latter are under the custody of a staff member designated archivist and are housed at the Hawker Library. In addition, the association's minutes and a comprehensive file on old boys is held at the Old Geelong Grammarians' office, while the various houses keep their own records and memorabilia. Portraits of headmasters hang in the dining hall.

The routinely generated records are voluminous, but the major elements are admission books (1868–   ); the minutes of the board of management/council (and those of The Hermitage and Clyde, which amalgamated with GGS in 1975); annual reports, letterbooks, correspondence files, ledgers, accounts books, and the minute books of numerous, sometimes short-lived, committees. Independently housed is a remarkable collection of J. R. Darling's correspondence, organized separately in general files and those concerning boys left in a particular year.

The archives contain a wealth of diaries, reminiscences, photographs, memorabilia and carefully organized annual files, covering events and personalities. Many individuals have been allotted separate collections and there are runs of the school magazine (*Annual, Quarterly, Corian*) and less consistent publications like *If, If Revived, Corio Courier* and *Tempo* as well as minute books and other records of school societies. Among the treasures in the archives are J. B. Wilson's letter books and mark books, the 'Hands Off!' file of those who resisted a change of name for GGS in the 1920s, and Francis Brown's correspondence.

Works published about the school are relatively few. The major works are: *Church of England Grammar School, Geelong: History and Register, Jubilee 1907*, Geelong, 1907; P. L. Brown, *Geelong Grammar School. The First Historical Phase*, Geelong, 1970; J. R. Darling and E. H. Montgomery, *Timbertop*, Melbourne, 1967; Tom Judd, *Fifty Years Will Be Long Enough*, Melbourne, 1971; and 'Thirty-Two Years', GGS, 1961, (the volume produced for Darling's retirement). A collection of Darling's writings, *The Education of a Civilized Man*, ed. Michael Persse, Melbourne, 1962, is also significant, as is Persse's pageant play, *Their Succeeding Race*, Melbourne, 1958.

There are unpublished theses at the University of Melbourne. Jane

Carolan, 'A History of Geelong Grammar School, 1912—1929', MA, 1974; Kevin Carolan, 'Geelong Grammar School, *c*. 1850—1914', a thesis for the subject History of Australian Architecture in 1971; Fay Marles, 'The Early Headmastership of J. B. Wilson at Geelong Grammar School, 1863—1875', MA, 1974, and 'The Premature Retirement of L. H. Lindon as Headmaster of Geelong Grammar School in 1911', MA Preliminary, 1971.

Some former students and teachers have written about the school: among them Keith Dunstan, *Sports*, Melbourne, 1973; Russel Ward, *A Radical Life*, Melbourne, 1988; and Rod Andrew in an introduction to the paintings of Russell Drysdale published in 1979 by Richmond Hill Press.

Outside the school there is important material in the La Trobe Collection at the State Library of Victoria, in the Diocesan archives in Melbourne and (for the young J. R. Darling) at Repton School.

Other works consulted include: *The Church of England Record*, *The Church of England Messenger*, *The Geelong Advertiser*, *The Scotch Collegian*, *The Melburnian*, C. E. W. Bean, *Here My Son*, Sydney, 1959; I. Hansen, *Nor Free, Nor Secular*, Melbourne, 1979; D. Newsome, *Godliness and Good Learning*, London, 1961; G. Blainey, J. Morrissey and S. E. K. Hulme, *Wesley College*, Melbourne, 1977; Greg Dening, *Xavier*, Melbourne, 1982 G. McC. Redmond, *The Geelong College History Records and Register 1911*, Melbourne, 1911; B. R. Keith, *The Geelong College 1861—1961*, Melbourne, 1961; Ian Wynd, *Geelong, the Pivot*, Melbourne, 1971; Margaret Kiddle, *Men of Yesterday*, Melbourne, 1961; Geoffrey Serle, *The Golden Age*, Melbourne, 1962.

While in the book reference is limited to identifying quotations, the manuscript lodged in the school archives carries full notes.

Index

Page numbers in **bold** type refer to illustrations.

375.9452

BAT   BATE

Light blue down under: